TRADE AND INVESTMENT RELATIONS AMONG THE UNITED STATES, CANADA, AND JAPAN

TRADE AND INVESTMENT RELATIONS AMONG THE UNITED STATES, CANADA, AND JAPAN

Edited by
ROBERT M. STERN

The University of Chicago Press
Chicago and London

ROBERT M. STERN is professor of economics at the University of Michigan at Ann Arbor.
Currently, he is visiting professor of economics at Brandeis University.

The University of Chicago Press, Chicago 60637
The University of Chicago Press, Ltd., London
© 1989 by the University of Chicago
All rights reserved. Published 1989
Printed in the United States of America

98 97 96 95 94 93 92 91 90 89   5 4 3 2 1

Library of Congress Cataloging-in-Publication Data

Trade and investment relations among the United States, Canada, and Japan / edited by Robert
M. Stern.
    p. cm.
Papers from a conference held at the University of Michigan. Apr. 2–3, 1987.
Includes indexes.
ISBN 0-226-77317-5 (alk. paper)
    1. United States—Foreign economic relations—Canada—Congresses. 2. Canada—Foreign
Economic relations—United States—Congresses. 3. United States—Foreign economic
relations—Japan—Congresses. 4. Japan—Foreign economic relations—United States—
Congresses. 5. Canada—Foreign economic relations—Japan—Congresses. 6. Japan—Foreign
economic relations—Canada—Congresses. I. Stern, Robert Mitchell
HF1456.5.C2T69   1989
337.73052—dc19   89-31248
                                                                                         CIP

⊗ The paper used in this publication meets the minimum requirements of the
American National Standard for Information Sciences—Permanence of Paper
for Printed Library Materials, ANSI Z39.48-1984

Contents

Preface

This book contains the papers and discussants' comments that were prepared in connection with a conference on U.S.-Canadian trade and investment relations with Japan that was held at The University of Michigan on April 2–3, 1987. The convening of this conference was motivated by the very close economic ties that characterize the relations among these three nations and the evident need to understand the structural determinants and policies that shape these relations. All too often, the public debate seems to focus primarily on short-term issues and policy solutions. Our objective at the conference was to bypass the preoccupation with events and policies of the moment and to concentrate instead on the underlying theoretical and empirical fundamentals involved. It is our hope, therefore, that the papers and comments that constitute this book will serve to inform the public debate on the important issues and provide the basis for a dispassionate evaluation of the current and prospective policies that are designed to affect the economic relations among the three nations.

The planning and organization of the conference represent the joint efforts of Robert M. Stern, Gary R. Saxonhouse, John Whalley, and the associated staff members of the Institute of Public Policy Studies (IPPS), the Japan Economy Program of The University of Michigan, and the Centre for the Study of International Economic Relations of the University of Western Ontario. We would especially like to thank Judith Brown and Judith Jackson of IPPS and Irita Grierson of the Japan Economy Program for their assistance in organizing the conference and taking care that everything ran smoothly. Judith Jackson is also to be thanked for her assistance in typing and revising the conference papers and comments and preparing the final manuscript. Finally, Filip Abraham is to be thanked for providing critical comments and editorial assistance on several of the papers.

Financial assistance for the conference was provided by several organizations, including the Foundation for Advanced Information and Research

(FAIR), Japan External Trade Organization (JETRO, Chicago), Ford Foundation, Donner Foundation, Canadian Embassy (Washington), Business Fund for Canadian Studies in the United States, Institute for Research on Public Policy (Ottawa), and Bank of Montreal. We are grateful to the officials of these organizations for their encouragement and support of our efforts.

1 Introduction

Robert M. Stern

The decade of the 1980s has been marked by unprecedented macroeconomic imbalances between the United States and the other major industrialized countries. The source of the imbalances seems to stem primarily from the U.S. macroeconomic policy mix that was implemented by the Reagan administration beginning in 1981 and involved highly expansionary fiscal policies together with relatively tight monetary policies. This combination of policies served to increase U.S. aggregate expenditure. The fiscal stimulus was provided by substantial reductions in personal and corporate income taxes, and given that it proved difficult to effect major reductions in government expenditures, it is not surprising that sizable budget deficits emerged.

In a closed economy, the effects of these policies would be to crowd out private spending and, if the fiscal expansion were to be financed in a noninflationary manner, domestic savings would need to rise to accommodate the increased budget deficit. In an open economy with internationally mobile capital, however, the policies may induce a capital inflow from abroad, so that foreign savings could in effect serve to finance some part of the government budget deficit. In these circumstances, the inflow of capital would create an excess demand for the country's currency and, under floating exchange rates, the currency would appreciate. The counterpart of the capital inflow and currency appreciation would be a deficit on current account as imports of goods and services increased and exports declined. The foregoing scenario seems broadly descriptive of what occurred in the U.S economy between 1981 and 1985. In particular, the expansionary fiscal policy appears to have crowded out the foreign sector since expenditure and output increased substantially elsewhere in the economy and, in the aggregate, the economy moved toward essentially full employment following the 1981–82 recession.

Japan's experience is the mirror image of what took place in the United States. That is, beginning in the early 1980s, especially in the wake of the financial liberalization that was occurring in Japan, there was a sizable capital

1

outflow as Japanese savings were increasingly directed to investment in various kinds of official and private assets in U.S. financial markets. The Japanese current account in turn moved into surplus to accommodate the capital outflow, and a very sizable proportion of the current account surplus had its counterpart in the U.S. current account deficit already mentioned.

As a result of the difficulties that U.S. import-competing and export firms were experiencing because of the dollar appreciation, considerable pressure was brought to bear on the Congress to take measures to improve the situation of different industries. It was inevitable in the circumstances that Japan was subjected to sharp criticism because of the substantial trade surpluses that it was experiencing vis-à-vis the United States. The Japanese were also criticized at times for saving too much. What is especially interesting is that there was little recognition and acknowledgment in all of this of the impact that U.S. macroeconomic policies were having domestically and abroad. A continuing air of tension and crisis has thus marked U.S.-Japanese economic relations during the 1980s.

When one considers U.S.-Canadian relations, there has been a remarkable calm in comparison to U.S. relations with Japan. This is the case even though Canada is the single largest trading partner of the United States and accounts for a substantial proportion of U.S. foreign direct investments. Further, even though Canada was also experiencing a sizable trade surplus vis-à-vis the United States, it was not singled out for criticism in the same way as Japan. It is of interest to note that Canada's macroeconomic situation has paralleled that in the United States, with sizable government budget deficits both in absolute terms and as a percentage of gross national product. In the United States, as was noted above, foreign savings were instrumental in helping to finance the U.S. budget deficit. In Canada, in contrast, domestic savings have increased substantially enough to finance the budget deficit. Thus, deficits and foreign capital inflows are not inevitable, so the U.S. experience appears to be unique.

While the United States accounts for a predominant share of Canada's exports and imports, Japan is an important trading partner for Canada as well. The Japanese market provides a major outlet for Canadian exports of agricultural foodstuffs and raw materials. Since Japanese import restrictions are severe for a number of primary products, Canada and the United States have a common interest in inducing the Japanese to reduce or remove these restrictions. Canada is a significant importer of a variety of manufactured goods, including vehicles, from Japan. Canada may, therefore, experience some of the same competitive pressures from Japanese imports as the United States. In the automobile industry in particular, Canada has followed the U.S. lead in negotiating a voluntary export restraint (VER) agreement limiting imports of automobiles from Japan.

In the winter of 1985, the appreciation of the U.S. dollar reached its peak and since then the dollar has depreciated substantially, especially against the Japanese yen and the German mark, and to a lesser extent against other major currencies. The reasons for the onset of dollar depreciation are not entirely clear. But it appears that the combined effects of the passing of the Gramm-Rudman-Hollings deficit reduction legislation and an easing of U.S. monetary policy may have altered expectations about future interest rates and the exchange rate, and thus reversed the appreciation that had occurred in the previous five years.

Under ordinary circumstances, it would be expected that dollar depreciation would bring about a reduction in the U.S. trade and current account deficit. While this has in fact occurred, many observers have been surprised with how long it has taken for the external deficit to decline. Here again, the explanations are by no means clear. It may be the case that the macroeconomic forces behind the budget and current account deficits are still sufficiently strong such that any sizable reduction in the current account deficit will be constrained. Also, it appears that the U.S. economy has continued to expand significantly in 1986–88 relative to its major trading partners, so that imports have not declined as much as might have been expected. Finally, some foreign exporters may have opted to absorb a substantial proportion of the exchange rate changes by reducing their profit margins in an effort to retain their market shares in the United States, while other foreign exporters in countries with currencies pegged to the U.S. dollar have been able to increase their exports to the United States.

Whatever the explanation may be, because the nominal U.S. external deficit has not been materially reduced, the pressures on the U.S. Congress to implement restrictive trade actions have not abated. Whether this state of affairs will continue is difficult to determine. It may be that the sudden decline in equity prices that occurred in the United States and other financial centers in October 1987 will provide the impetus to take more effective measures to reduce the existing macroeconomic imbalances among the major industrialized countries, and that the external imbalances will be correspondingly mitigated. Also, implementation of the U.S.-Canadian Free Trade Agreement and progress in the ongoing Uruguay Round of multilateral trade negotiations may serve to diffuse a variety of trade policy irritants between the United States and its two major trading partners. Only time will tell.

1.1 Pertinent Insights and Conclusions of the Conference Papers and Comments

The conference papers and comments that follow address many of the foregoing issues in depth. Each session in the conference involved authors and discussants from the United States, Canada, and Japan. While an effort was made to have the authors focus their papers on issues common to the three countries, this was not altogether feasible. The discussants' comments may thus provide a national perspective that supplements the individual papers.

In anticipation of what is to follow, some readers might find it useful to have an idea of some of the pertinent insights and conclusions that the authors and discussants offer in their respective contributions and that cut across a number of the contributions. These are:

1. While the simple life-cycle model is useful in understanding saving behavior, it cannot fully explain intercountry variations in private saving rates. It is necessary to take into account such factors as differences in the rates of economic growth, differences in institutions and cultural determinants of behavior, tax incentives, and demographic characteristics in trying to explain why private saving rates are higher in Canada and especially in Japan, compared to the United States.

2. In the coming decades, it is possible that Japan and Canada will continue to expand and converge on U.S. efficiency levels and per capita income. The same may be true for the newly industrializing East Asian economies. Private saving rates in Japan may be sustained at relatively high levels, although demographic changes may necessitate higher taxes to support an aging population.

3. The yen/U.S. dollar exchange rate has been considerably more volatile than the Canadian/U.S. dollar rate. The yen volatility may be explained in part by the deregulation and internationalization of financial markets and the resulting substantial increase in international capital mobility in Japan. The comparative stability of the Canadian dollar may reflect the close integration of the Canadian and U.S. economies and the exchange market intervention of the Bank of Canada. In designing an empirical framework to investigate the sources of exchange rate volatility, it is important to take into account the different types of shocks to which the exchange rate is subject, the problems of collinearity in the returns on domestic and foreign assets, the stability of the demand for money, central bank intervention in the exchange markets, the effects of innovations in financial markets, and the consequences of uncertainty in the design and implementation of macroeconomic policies.

4. Divergent fiscal policies have been the major sources of the macroeconomic imbalances between the United States and the other major industrialized countries in the 1980s. The empirical modeling of the determinants of these imbalances, future predictions, and recommendations for policy call for careful consideration of the underlying national policies and institutions, the global linkages, and the relevant parameters to describe the behavior of the important transactors and policymaking authorities.

5. The increases in Japan's exports of manufactures have been concentrated in automobiles, office machinery, telecommunications equipment, and

electric machinery. While Japan has been criticized for having relatively small imports of manufactured goods, there is evidence that this is changing dramatically, particularly in response to the appreciation of the yen. The use of VERs by the United States and Canada to limit imports of manufactures from Japan may be undermined by product upgrading, shifts to other sources of supply, and competition from Japanese firms that have expanded production by means of direct investment in importing countries.

6. Japan has very substantial barriers limiting the importation of agricultural foodstuffs and materials. Reductions in these barriers would be beneficial both to the United States and Canada, but attention must be given to policies that would ease the process of adjustment in the agricultural sector in Japan. U.S. domestic agricultural policies may be highly detrimental to Canada and other major agricultural exporters because they may result in lower world prices. U.S. export subsidies may displace competing suppliers and, furthermore, result in sizable income transfers to importing countries.

7. Industrial policies to aid declining manufacturing industries are often motivated more by political than economic considerations, and the policies differ noticeably among countries. Trade policies have been the most prevalent form of assistance to industries in the United States and to a lesser extent in Canada, whereas in Japan a wider range of policies has been used in apparent recognition of differences in industry characteristics and adjustment needs. Japan has outperformed both the United States and Canada in productivity improvements in declining sectors, but it is not obvious that Japan's experiences are readily transferable to other countries. In the United States and Canada, it may be necessary to take a much longer view of adjustment problems and policies, and to contemplate longer-term policy options that may be more costly than the shorter-term policies currently being used.

8. Existing taxes and proposed tax reforms have a variety of effects on international trade and investment flows. The most important effects stem from fiscal deficit imbalances and the overall impact of a nation's tax structure. The effects of indirect and trade taxes are of lesser importance in the aggregate, but may have sectoral importance.

9. Economic growth and development in the nations constituting the Pacific region have been marked by a dynamism resulting from the outward-looking and liberal policies adopted in the major countries there. The continuation of this dynamism will be assisted by intergovernmental cooperation to maintain open markets and expand international financial flows. In view of its very sizable current account surplus, Japan should be encouraged to assume a position of leadership in the region and to promote large-scale transfers of capital to developing countries, thus reducing some of Japan's financial flows to the United States.

10. Access to markets in importing countries may be affected by cultural factors that stem from the characteristics of a nation's social network,

social custom, and the reputation of domestic firms. Policies of administered protection and the strategic behavior of imperfectly competitive firms may also serve to limit market access. In the case of Japan, certain business practices that appear to be restrictive may in fact reflect rational behavior in designing long-term contracts and maintaining long-term relations between firms and consumers.

11. The empirical evidence relating to formal trade barriers suggests that Japan's tariffs and nontariff barriers are relatively low overall and comparable to those maintained by the United States and Canada. When both formal and informal barriers are taken into account, the empirical evidence also suggests that Japan's trade barriers are not distinctive in comparison to the United States, Canada, and other major trading countries. Japan's trade performance can thus be explained in terms of its national factor endowments and distance from markets, rather than by its trade policies.

1.2   Brief Summaries of Conference Papers and Comments

1.2.1   Helliwell: "Some Comparative Macroeconomics
of the United States, Japan, and Canada"

Helliwell begins by reviewing the alternative approaches to the modeling of the balance of payments and the macroeconomic linkages among nations in order to provide a framework in which to examine the behavior and possible future evolution of the important macroeconomic aggregates of the United States, Japan, and Canada. He shows that the private saving rate—which includes both household and corporate savings—is substantially higher in Japan than in the United States, and that the Canadian rate has risen since the 1970s nearly to the level of the Japanese rate. In order to explain saving behavior, one can rely on the simple life-cycle model. But, as Helliwell notes, although the model may identify the reasons for international differences in saving rates, its parameters may not be robust in forecasting the future evolution of saving rates for the three nations. Helliwell also notes that the model is limited insofar as it does not take into account such factors as liquidity constraints and the diversity of motives and circumstances characterizing the actual behavior of households. He mentions several additional factors that may explain intercountry differences in private saving rates, including: the tax treatment of consumer borrowing, availability of consumer credit, tax treatment of interest income and private savings for retirement, differential rates of inflation, increases in life expectancy, differences in the role and structure of the family, the work ethic, the Japanese bonus system, and differences in female labor force participation rates.

In presenting evidence on government saving rates, Helliwell notes that net government savings have become significantly negative in both Canada and the United States since 1980, but have remained positive and fairly stable in Japan since 1975. The growing fiscal deficits in Canada are largely attributable to rising transfer payments and falling revenues, while the U.S. fiscal deficits stem from growing current spending and falling taxes. The evidence on net foreign saving rates is that there has been a net outflow of capital from Japan amounting to over 3 percent of GNP by the mid-1980s. Canada has been a net capital importer for the most part. The United States had a relatively small rate of net capital outflow/inflow until the early 1980s, but net capital imports rose to 3 percent of GNP by the mid-1980s, mirroring the experience of Japan. While there are several different views of the forces determining net capital movements, a currently popular view stresses the importance of high international capital mobility combined with the absence of tightly integrated international markets for physical capital and lack of effective arbitrage between equity and debt markets within countries.

It is especially noteworthy, according to Helliwell, that Japan has had higher and more stable rates of growth of per capita output and income than either the United States or Canada. These higher rates of growth have facilitated or caused the much higher rate of Japanese private saving and may themselves be partially caused by the much higher Japanese rate of investment. To help understand the links between investment and the growth of output, Helliwell develops a factor-utilization model of production. In this model, technical progress is treated according to whether the rate of technical efficiency is constant or whether there is a process of catch-up or convergence among the countries. The constant-efficiency-growth model is nested within the general-convergence model. Helliwell's empirical results clearly favor the convergence model. It is thus suggested that Canadian and Japanese efficiency levels are approaching U.S. levels, and in time would even exceed U.S. levels if higher capital stock growth is maintained in the two countries. He also presents results for the behavior of output and employment in the three countries.

In reflecting on the empirical evidence presented, Helliwell stresses the need for a quantitative model that would capture the important macroeconomic linkages both within and between countries. While some models do exist, they do not adequately portray the supply-side structures of the national economies or capture longer-term trends. Nonetheless, these models suggest that fiscal contraction in the United States would have an important impact in reducing the U.S. current account deficit over a period of years. However, fiscal expansion abroad does not have symmetrical effects on the U.S. current account deficit because of offsetting changes in exchange rates.

In considering the likely future evolution of savings, investment, and external balances in the three countries, Helliwell offers the following tentative conclusions:

1. The rate of productivity growth and the saving rate in Japan will converge on the rates in the United States and Canada.
2. Changes in the tax treatment of interest expense and interest income
   will tend to raise saving rates in the United States and lower them in
   Japan.
3. It may well be that Japan's characteristically high rates of saving and
   investment will be emulated by other countries, but that Japan will
   continue to have saving rates well above the average of comparable
   high-income countries.
4. Public and private saving rates in Japan are likely to be sustained to
   provide for the retirement incomes of older persons in the first quarter
   of the new century.
5. Japanese capital markets will continue to be internationally integrated,
   resulting in greater equality in interest rates on similar types of assets.
   There may also possibly be greater equality in returns on equities because of the increasing internationalization of business.
6. The convergence of growth rates in the United States, Japan, and Canada may be below the world average as the locus of economic activity
   and international real capital shifts to the emerging industrializing
   countries.

In his comment on Helliwell's paper, McKinnon notes that the sudden
emergence of large U.S. trade deficits and Japanese surpluses in the mid-
1980s is attributable to the increase in the structural U.S. fiscal deficit rather
than to long-term trends in saving and investment behavior. It is interesting
that, in Canada, a large fiscal deficit did not result in a current account deficit
because there was a large increase in Canadian private savings. McKinnon
attributes this increase to the more generous treatment of individual retirement plans in Canada beginning in the mid-1970s. He also considers the
question of whether exchange rate changes are important in the process of
transferring capital between countries. He argues that international transfers
of capital are better expedited without nominal changes in exchange rates,
noting the experience of the U.S. dollar appreciation in the early 1980s and
the subsequent depreciation in 1986–87.

In his comment, Fukao stresses the aging of the Japanese population
and its interaction with the government sector via the pension system. He
notes that the percentage of the population in Japan over 65 years of age will
increase from 10 percent in 1985 to an estimated 22 percent by 2020. This in
turn may result in a significant increase in the tax rate on employee income
and a decline in savings. He also maintains that the surplus in the Japanese
government's social security fund will be substantially reduced in the future.
He is, therefore, much less sanguine than Helliwell about the continuation of

relatively high saving rates in Japan. Fukao calls further attention to the international crowding-out effects of high real interest rates, as investment is affected by changes in the real cost of capital and there is accompanying international movement of capital.

1.2.2 Sazanami: "Trade and Investment Patterns and Barriers in the United States, Canada, and Japan"

Sazanami notes that Japan's trade with the United States accounted for over two thirds of its $56 billion global trade surplus in 1985, and Japan's capital outflows have been increasingly directed toward the United States. Japan's trade with Canada was roughly in balance in 1985. Between 1980 and 1985, Japan's imports from the United States increased by only $1.5 billion, while Japanese exports to the United States rose by $34.4 billion. Thus, the U.S. share in Japan's total exports increased from 24 percent in 1980 to 38 percent in 1985. Japan's increased exports to the United States were concentrated in automobiles, office machinery, telecommunications equipment, and electrical machinery. This same pattern of change was evidenced as well in Japan's exports to Canada. On the import side, there was a shift in Japan away from resource intensive products, which adversely affected both the United States and Canada.

The increase in U.S. imports from Japan has led to increasing friction between the two nations, with the United States instituting restrictive import measures involving such products as color televisions, automobiles, and iron and steel products in the late 1970s and early 1980s. For its part, Japan has introduced a number of measures to improve foreign access to its markets in a number of sectors. They took these steps even though there is no clear evidence, except for agricultural and food products, that Japanese tariffs and nontariff barriers are unusually high relative to the other major industrialized countries. While it is difficult to assess the impact of Japan's market-opening measures, there has been a noticeable increase in recent years in the share of manufactured goods in total imports. Some of this increase may be attributable as well to the sharp appreciation of the yen since the winter of 1985. While the U.S. restrictions apparently reduced imports of color TVs from Japan, there is no indication that imports of other restricted goods, such as electronic products and automobiles, were seriously limited. The most noteworthy Canadian trade action was its decision to follow the United States in imposing a VER arrangement on imports of Japanese cars.

It is well known that Japan has emerged in the 1980s as a very significant exporter of capital. This has involved both financial capital and foreign direct investment. Japan had formerly concentrated its foreign direct investment in resource industries, but had switched to manufacturing toward the end of the 1960s. With the oil crises of the 1970s there was a renewed tendency toward foreign investment in resource industries, but this has changed once again as foreign investment in manufacturing and service industries has grown. Japan's direct investments in the United States have been concentrated in electric machinery, transport equipment, and metal products, all of which had been targets of U.S. import restrictions. Japan's direct investments in Canada have been primarily in resource-based industries. Foreign direct investment in Japan has also increased noticeably in the 1980s in a variety of manufacturing and service industries.

Sazanami cites evidence of product upgrading by Japanese exporters to the United States in response to the VERs on electronic products and automobiles. As mentioned, the U.S. restrictions also resulted in increased direct investment in the U.S. market. The Canadian restrictions may have had a similar effect, although some of the investment may also have been designed to take advantage of producing in Canada and exporting to the Untied States under the free trade provisions of the Auto Pact. Japanese automobile investments in North America will thus have an impact on both final products and parts, but it is possible that some Japanese investments may be directed towards certain newly industrializing countries (NICs) such as South Korea. The experience with U.S. restrictions on color TVs is interesting because it led to a shift in the development of other sources of supply in the American market. At the same time, Japanese producers increasingly shifted their production and exports to newer electronic products such as audio equipment and videotape recorders.

Sazanami notes that Japan's trade surplus reached a record high of $9.8 billion in September 1986, which was more than a year after the yen had started to appreciate. Most of the change was in the value of exports, especially automobiles and parts, semiconductors, other electronic products, and machinery. The differential effects on imports and exports may be due to the fact that a substantial proportion of export contracts are expressed in yen, so that export prices may not respond until new contracts have been concluded. This is especially the case for VCRs and other electronic and electrical products, as well for automobiles. Yen appreciation appears to have had an impact on Japan's imports of manufactured products. Since the prices of crude oil and other raw materials declined, there was some increase in the import demand for these products. Japan's foreign direct investment seems to have also responded to the yen appreciation, with increased outflows to the United States and to other Asian countries whose exchange rates are pegged to the dollar. Sazanami concludes that Japan's trade and foreign direct investment will continue to respond to the yen appreciation and that there will be further changes, particularly in the composition of Japanese imports.

Sazanami draws a number of inferences from her analysis and discussion, as follows:

1. Country-specific trade barriers do not significantly reduce competition from foreign firms when foreign direct investment can take place in the restricting country, as well as in third countries. The Asian NICs may thus benefit directly as a result of the U.S. restrictions aimed at Japan.
2. While the effects of the yen appreciation are somewhat difficult to assess especially on the import side because of the decline in the prices of crude oil and other raw materials, there is evidence that the volume of Japan's imports of manufactures has increased substantially.
3. The appreciation of the yen may give rise to increased foreign direct investment in the United States and in the Asian NICs.
4. Canada's close association with the United States may be a further factor motivating Japanese direct investment in Canada in order to serve the U.S. market.

In his comment on Sazanami's paper, Baldwin notes that the Asian NICs have become increasingly competitive in their own right and have enlarged their market shares substantially in the United States, Japan, and Canada. These developments have been reinforced by some of the changes in trade policies and exchange rates that Sazanami noted. Baldwin also calls attention to the ineffectiveness of selective protection, which is something that he has stressed in his own writings on trade policy. Finally, he notes the need for greater multilateral agreement on a variety of issues, including safeguard actions, antidumping measures, and subsidies and countervailing duties. He focuses on safeguards and the issue of selectivity and discrimination in designing an acceptable safeguards policy. He suggests that safeguard measures might be applied on a tariff line-item basis that would distinguish the products to be restricted from those available from other sources that are not responsible for any import disruption that may have occurred.

Wonnacott suggests that, in light of Japan's record-high trade surplus, it might consider a policy of massively increasing its imports. This would benefit economic welfare and, at the same time, it might defuse the restrictive pressures in the U.S. Congress aimed at Japan. He also notes that the substantial appreciation of the yen since 1985 has created a strong incentive for Japanese investors to buy large quantities of U.S. and Canadian financial and real assets. Wonnacott considers whether the negotiation of a free trade arrangement between Canada and the United States would be detrimental to Japanese trading interests. He concludes that trade diversion would be unlikely in view of Japan's comparative advantage, especially in electronic products. Wonnacott is less sanguine, however, about Japanese and other East Asian automotive investments in Canada that are designed to serve the U.S. market, especially if this investment has been encouraged by special incentives provided by the Canadian government. This could turn out to be troublesome in phasing out the current arrangements under the Canadian-U.S. Auto Pact as the free trade agreement between the two nations is implemented.

1.2.3   Schmitz: "Trade in Primary Products:
Canada, the United States, and Japan"

In his paper, Schmitz discusses the importance of trade in primary products among the three countries. He notes that Canada supplies about 7 percent of Japan's total farm imports, with canola, wheat, and barley together accounting for 70 percent of the value of Canada's exports to Japan. Canola in the form of raw seed is Canada's most important export, given that Japan's tariff on refined canola serves to discourage its import in processed form. Wheat and barley prices in Japan are several times higher than the world price. Japan's imports of wheat and barley are regulated by the purchases of the Japanese Food Agency. Canada supplies about 25 percent of Japan's imports of pork and pork products, and less than 2 percent of Japan's beef imports. The United States provides about 40 percent of Japan's total farm imports and is a major supplier to Japan of feedgrains (corn, especially), soybeans, meat, and wheat. Schmitz notes that Japan's agricultural trade barriers are substantial, with the methods of protection including quotas and special buying arrangements by Japanese domestic agencies. For many commodities, Japanese producer protection is more than four times greater than in Canada or the United States. Nonetheless, Japan's imports of agricultural products have risen substantially over the years, although of course these imports would be much greater if Japan were to remove its protection. In considering the competition between Canada and the United States in the Japanese market and in other markets, Schmitz calls attention to the 1985 U.S. farm bill that has resulted in lower loan rates and thus cheaper prices in importing countries. Both Canada and the United States use export subsidies to compete in the Japanese market and other markets, which results in a gain to these importing countries.

In examining Canadian-U.S. agricultural trade, Schmitz notes that Canada's main exports to the United States include live animals and meats, and its main imports are fruits and nuts. Canada uses marketing boards in an effort to stabilize producer incomes in the dairy, poultry, and egg sectors, and the policies of these boards vary by province. The greatest social cost to Canada arises from the dairy sector. Provincial stabilization schemes are also common for red meats in Canada, and in the case of live hogs this led to the imposition of a countervailing duty by the United States in order to offset alleged Canadian subsidies. Canada provides significant domestic subsidies to grain producers, although the subsidies in the European Community and the United States are considerably higher. Schmitz notes that the liberalization of agricultural trade as part of the U.S.-Canadian free trade arrangement would provide significant, but fairly small, benefits. In contrast, he estimates that the annual cost of the 1985 U.S. farm bill exceeded $1 billion for Canadian western wheat producers alone, which was at least five times greater than the potential net gain from free trade in farm products. Schmitz also discusses nonagricultural trade and notes the recent actions taken by the United States to limit imports from Canada, especially of softwood lumber, uranium, and potash. Canada thus has an important stake in trying to limit U.S. protective measures involving primary products, although it is much more unfavorably affected by the price-depressing effects and export subsidies arising from U.S. domestic farm policies.

In conclusion, Schmitz notes that Japanese agriculture is highly protected and that efforts at liberalization would benefit both Canada and the United States. The widespread resort to agricultural subsidies has unfortunate effects on exporting countries and results in transferring resources to large importers such as Japan. More cooperation among the major agricultural exporters would be desirable to remove the downward pressures on world prices that result from their attempts to maintain or expand their market shares. There is also much to be gained if the United States would agree to refrain from instituting countervailing duties against the imports of its major trading partners such as Canada.

In his comment, Honma notes that Schmitz did not discuss forest products and minerals, both of which are important in Japan's trade with Canada and the United States. He further notes that cooperation among the major agricultural exporting countries might well lead to the creation of cartel arrangements, and he prefers instead to seek multilateral negotiations to reduce agricultural distortions under GATT arrangements. While there is evidence of tariff escalation in Japan affecting the imports of processed primary products, Japan's imports of processed products have in fact increased substantially. In this regard, Canada and the United States may not have been taking full advantage of these developments in Japan's imports. Changes in exchange rates are also important in terms of their impact on agricultural trade and should be taken into account in conjunction with trade policies. Honma notes that Japan's overall level of agricultural protection was 102 percent in 1984. Based on the average exchange rate in 1986, the weighted average rate of protection more than doubled to a level of 210 percent, and presumably further changes will have occurred in response to subsequent changes in the yen/dollar exchange rate. Honma's final point is that more attention should be paid to issues of structural adjustment in Japanese agriculture since this is really what is at the heart of the agricultural trade frictions between Japan and its major trading partners.

In his comment, Carter notes that Japan is basically an importer of primary products and an exporter mainly of capital goods. This specialization has been favorable for Japan because the prices of primary products have, on the whole, been relatively low since World War II. He further notes that Canada's agricultural exports to Japan have been limited for noneconomic reasons. Carter takes exception to Schmitz's contention that Canadian agricultural subsidies are lower than those in the United States, arguing that Canadian subsidies are on a par with, and maybe even higher than, those in the United States. Carter also notes that Japan's policy on lumber is designed to encourage the import from Canada of raw logs, rather than plywood or lumber. Finally, Carter notes that reduction of the U.S. government budget and trade deficits is needed to restore macroeconomic balance between the two nations. But it is not clear whether and how this would affect the composition of U.S.-Japanese trade.

1.2.4   Lawrence: "A Depressed View of Policies for Depressed Industries"

In his paper, Lawrence distinguishes economic from political paradigms regarding the conduct of industrial policies. According to the economic paradigm, allocative policies may be required to complement market forces in the event of market failure. On theoretical grounds, it can be said that intervention may be inappropriate if it makes matters worse, the instruments of intervention should be used to achieve their objectives as directly as possible, and the policies should be long run in nature—not used to reverse underlying market forces—and applied at the margin to correct market failures wherever they may occur in an economy. In the actual practice of industrial policy (IP), the foregoing economic principles are, however, rarely applied. Rather, political objectives are sought, which means that IP is more commonly used to maintain productive capacity, preserve capital, enhance technological capabilities, increase national prestige, redistribute income, reinforce job property rights, and support employment. Further, policies are frequently sector or firm specific rather than designed to correct market failures, and there is a general faith that governments can achieve their objectives. Even though governments profess to follow market principles, the actual record indicates frequent departures from these principles, especially in the case of declining industries, which are the focus of the paper. Lawrence notes that there is a common theme in the employment experiences of the United States, Japan, and Canada, although the actual policies used have differed in interesting and important ways. In considering the policies adopted, Lawrence seeks to explain why different approaches have been used, how well they have worked, and whether the experiences can be applied to other countries.

Lawrence observes that in the United States the pluralistic system of government and the continuously evolving economy have served to limit the direct role of government in the economy. Except for antitrust and regulatory policies, IP in the United States has been largely concentrated on trade. Trade policy in the United States is a shared responsibility of the president, Congress, and the International Trade Commission (ITC). U.S. industries seeking government assistance have followed a two-track procedure, either through the mechanisms under the aegis of the ITC or by exerting political pressure directly on the president and Congress. The larger industries, such as textiles and apparel, steel, automobiles, meat, and sugar, have achieved the most noteworthy successes by following the political track to obtain aid, even if the ITC would have found little evidence of trade-related injury. It appears that protection administered by the ITC route has been credibly regarded as temporary and conducive to industry adjustment, whereas the politically motivated protection has tended to be quasi-permanent, with industry adjustment being forestalled rather than encouraged. In these latter cases, trade protection is an extremely imprecise method for either limiting the dislocation to existing workers or inducing modernization. Lawrence cites the examples of the U.S. textile and apparel industry, steel industry, and the Chrysler bailout to illustrate the risks involved with detailed government policy intervention and the excessive costs imposed on consumers due to the protection involved. Lawrence suggests a number of changes in the administration of the escape clause in trade investigations by the ITC and in the program of trade-adjustment assistance that are designed to improve the effectiveness of U.S. policies, without at the same time imposing unduly large costs on the nation.

Some observers argue that the Japanese experience with policies to aid declining industries demonstrates that government, business, and labor can act cooperatively to implement policies that both facilitate industrial adjustment and assist those adversely affected by the changes taking place. It appears that Japan's approach to IP does not single out trade as a source of structural change calling for intervention and does not use trade policy as such in devising policies for declining industries. Lawrence attributes this to Japan's distinctive political and economic institutions. The structure of Japanese firms and banks is such that they are subjected to strong pressures to adjust to change. Japanese policymakers also appear to provide considerable guidance to industries for which they are responsible. Yet, budgetary outlays for industry assistance are kept to a minimum and efforts are made to avoid the use of restrictive trade barriers. In resorting to the use of cartels to deal with overcapacity during times of recession, large firms are favored, in part because it is believed that they may be better able to promote adjustment and equity. Japan's policies have apparently been most effective in reducing capacity in the relatively more highly concentrated industries, although it could be argued that the changes might have been induced by market forces in any case. While some observers have argued that Japanese policy anticipates the need for adjustment, Lawrence notes that this may not be the case. It may also be that the use of cartel arrangements rather than explicit subsidies disguises the social costs involved. Further, despite the claim that Japanese intervention does not explicitly involve the use of trade policy, there are several noteworthy instances of trade intervention designed to assist particular industries. Lawrence concludes that the Japanese experience is less attractive than admirers or government spokesmen would suggest. Nonetheless, the Japanese experience offers some potentially useful lessons to other countries: (1) trade problems are only one aspect of IP; (2) industrial structure must be taken into account in designing policies; (3) government policies create vested bureaucratic interests that may be difficult to change; (4) costs of adjustment may be shifted to third parties by policies that are not immediately transparent; and (5) Japan's distinctive economic and social characteristics serve to shape its policy interventions and may not readily carry over to other countries.

Canada's IP involves a mixture of approaches, including both formal trade protection and explicit aid to depressed firms, regions, and sectors. As a relatively small country, Canada is subject to nationalistic pressures to develop a diversified manufacturing sector, and there are important regional influences as well, stemming from the power and influence of the provincial governments. While market forces operate pervasively in Canada, at times there has been more of a propensity to intervene. Policies have tended to vary, however, as responsibilities shifted among various government agencies. Nonetheless, as Lawrence notes, in industries such as textiles and apparel, and to some extent footwear, policies have been adopted that are not conducive to adjustment and that impose substantial costs on Canadian consumers.

In his comment, Okuno notes that the United States appears to have relied to a large extent on trade-related measures of policy intervention to protect declining industries, while Japan has used supply-oriented collusive policies to help promote adjustment in declining industries. Okuno takes issue with Lawrence and maintains that Japan's policies have been quite "open." Okuno shares some of Lawrence's doubts about the effectiveness and desirability of recession cartels in Japan, but notes that the evaluation of cartels must take into account whether the industry is competitive, as in the case of textiles, or composed of a small number of relatively large firms. In the latter case, strategic considerations become important, especially insofar as there is incomplete information about the financial and/or demand conditions among competitors. The evaluation of Japan's cartel policy should thus consider how the behavior of the firms is affected. While there may well be distortionary effects involved, Okuno notes that Japan's policy has prohibited the industries from expanding or building new capacity, something which is quite different from the U.S. experience. Okuno further points out that Japan's policies must be viewed in a broader context as promoting adjustment in local and regional labor markets, again something which is in contrast to the U.S. experience. Okuno maintains that the use of trade intervention by the United States has many undesirable features, resulting especially from the tacit collusion and rent-seeking activities that the intervention serves to foster.

Okuno recommends that multilateral discipline and the rules of GATT be utilized to deal with trade and related interventions as the most effective way of avoiding the distortions arising from unilateral and bilateral restrictions.

Although there is cause for concern about the policies adopted in the three countries, Trebilcock notes in his comment that a substantial amount of adjustment has occurred in the depressed industries despite the interventions that were implemented. Trebilcock also notes that it is necessary to examine the rates of adjustment both within and between individual sectors in each country. In this connection, he concludes that Japan has outperformed both the United States and Canada in productivity improvements in most of the declining sectors since 1955. He cites his own research on Canada and finds that there is little evidence of structural adjustment in textiles, clothing, shipbuilding, or coal mining. He stresses the importance of the political regime in Japan in understanding the effectiveness of Japan's policies. Trebilcock is skeptical of Lawrence's proposals for improving the effectiveness of policies on the grounds that they ignore the longer-run interests and concerns of the labor and capital employed in the affected sectors and the political influence that these vested interests may have in seeking permanent protection. A much longer view of the problems must be taken, therefore, and more costly measures for adjustment considered. Efforts must also be made to reduce existing trade barriers through forceful negotiations. All of these considerations raise difficult and important political questions that must be addressed beyond the strictly economic issues involved.

1.2.5 Whalley: "Taxes in Canada, Japan, and the United States: Influences on Trade and Investment Flows, and the Role of Tax-Based Trade Irritants"

Whalley notes that major changes in tax policy were introduced in the United States beginning in 1987, and similarly far-reaching changes have been proposed in both Japan and Canada. There are a number of issues arising from the impact that particular types of taxes may have on trade. After reviewing the main features of trade flows among the three countries, Whalley considers differences in their tax structures. It appears that indirect taxes are more important and payroll taxes less important in Canada than in the United States or Japan. Japan has a much heavier emphasis on corporate taxes. The tax structure in all three countries tends to be biased against traded goods and services, and individual sectors may also be differentially taxed which will have important implications for trade. The taxation of personal income in the three countries differs mainly in the way that capital income is taxed, with comparatively little taxation in Japan, and more generous treatment of capital income in Canada as compared to the United States. These differences may explain some of the intercountry differences in private savings. There are also substantial differences in sales and excise taxes among the three countries at both the federal and subnational levels.

In assessing the importance of tax differences for the pattern of trade and factor flows between countries, Whalley considers whether differences in tax levels between countries affect trade and how differences in tax structure may be significant. He shows under simplifying assumptions that differences in levels of taxes, in and of themselves, will not have any effect on trade between countries insofar as relative consumer prices and the terms of trade are invariant to the taxes. However, taxes may apply more heavily to traded goods and services, so that a country with higher tax rates will tend to restrict its trade. There may also be effects on labor supply and saving decisions that will in turn affect trade and international capital flows.

Differences in tax structure, for example, the tax treatment of savings and border tax adjustments, may influence the size and composition of trade and international factor flows. As already mentioned, Japan's tax system apparently works to stimulate saving in comparison to the United States. This may in turn generate an excess supply of savings and, depending on relative rates of return, result in substantial international movement of capital between the two countries. Tax-based investment incentives or disincentives and foreign tax credits may similarly affect international capital flows. Border tax adjustments depend on whether taxes are levied on an origin or destination basis. It is most common to levy indirect taxes on a destination basis so that imports are taxed and exports leave free of tax. Indirect taxes that are broadly based will not distort real economic activity and trade since domestic relative prices will not be altered. But, if the indirect taxes are not broadly based and fall more or less heavily on, say, manufactures or resource products, it may make a difference whether the country levies the indirect tax on an origin or destination basis given the structure of existing trade. In order to judge the effects of domestic taxes on trade flows, Whalley reports some results based on his computational general equilibrium model of global trade. It appears that the effects of taxes on global trade and welfare are important, especially as compared to conventional trade policies such as tariffs.

Whalley presents information on the changes in taxes that were introduced in the United States in 1987 and that had been proposed in Canada and Japan. What is involved in all three countries is a reduction in personal tax rates and some broadening of the personal tax base, a lowering of corporate tax rates, and termination of various investment incentives. In addition, Japan and Canada hoped to implement some type of value-added tax. It is possible that these changes in taxes may affect saving and investment in the United States and Japan in ways that will reduce capital movements between the two countries and thus reduce the U.S. trade deficit.

Whalley considers a number of tax issues that have been the focus of trade disputes involving the United States and other major trading countries. These issues include the deferral of corporate taxes on income, border tax adjustments for indirect taxes, and the use of countervailing duties to offset foreign tax rebates. While these issues have attracted a great deal of attention in trade policy relations, Whalley notes that they are only of minor significance compared to the wider influences of taxes on patterns of trade.

In his comment on Whalley's paper, Auerbach contends that Whalley may be exaggerating the impact of Japanese taxes in stimulating saving and that other societal factors may be more important. Auerbach also argues that origin and destination taxes may differ if intertemporal factors affecting factor supplies and production and consumption are taken into account. He reinforces Whalley's view that the four types of tax policies affecting trade—fiscal balance, overall direct tax structure, indirect taxes, and tariffs—decline in importance as they become more closely associated with specific markets and private economic decisions. On the subject of U.S. tax reform, Auerbach does not anticipate much of an impact on the U.S. trade balance nor does he see any significant change in the intensity of feelings associated with tax-based trade irritants.

In his comment, Ishi notes that the proposed tax changes in Japan are designed to be revenue neutral, and that they would not have much of an impact on GNP and the balance of trade. He is also doubtful that Japan's tax treatment of capital income has had any clear impact in increasing Japanese savings. Ishi further contends that a change in Japan's existing system of commodity taxes would not necessarily be detrimental to the United States, as Whalley had argued. Finally, Ishi is skeptical of the computational results reported by Whalley that purport to show that replacement of existing differential taxes by a uniform rate would be detrimental to Japan.

1.2.6 Okita: "The Current Economic Situation and Future Problems in the Asia-Pacific Region"

In the conference keynote paper, Okita calls attention to the increasingly important role that the Pacific region has come to play in the growth of the world economy. He attributes the dynamism of the Pacific region to several factors, including export-oriented development policies, high rates of domestic investment and saving, an aggressive and active private sector operating within what is basically a market economy system, improvements effected in agricultural production and productivity, and the success of domestic adjustment policies in response to the world recession of the 1970s and early 1980s. He further notes that there existed a climate of cooperation that helped to coordinate and reinforce the individual national efforts in the region. This fostered an intraregional division of labor that has been called the "flying geese" pattern in which the leader surplus country (the United States/Japan) develops new technologies, invests in countries that are at earlier stages of industrialization, and absorbs the exports of the low-cost producers.

In examining the recent trade and investment performance of the major nations in the Pacific region, Okita notes the need for the United States to take measures to reduce its very sizable budget and trade deficits. If such measures are adopted, the United States may no longer provide a rapidly expanding market for the products of the Asian countries as in the past. While there are signs that Japan's saving rate may diminish in the future because of demographic changes and increases in personal consumption, Okita nonetheless expects that Japan will continue to experience a net capital outflow for the next decade or so. He further expects that high rates of growth will be sustained in the rapidly industrializing countries of Asia, as well as in the member countries of the Association of Southeast Asian Nations and the People's Republic of China.

Okita stresses that Japan must assume a leadership position in the region, as well as globally, in view of its role as a major creditor nation. He argues in particular that Japan should increasingly direct its external capital flows to help finance the deficits of the developing countries. This would serve to enhance the import capacity of these countries and sustain Japan's exports at a time when the United States might be playing a less expansive role internationally. Okita envisions a "Marshall Plan for the developing countries" in which Japan would attempt to recycle some of its current account surplus by increased subscriptions to multilateral lending agencies and by extending risk insurance and interest rate subsidies to borrowing countries.

Okita emphasizes the need for economic cooperation in the future among the countries in the Pacific region. This should entail participation in the various governmental, private, and academic organizations and institutions that have been established in the region. There is also a need for the region's problems to be dealt with by all countries concerned rather than bilaterally, as has often been the case previously, and to provide new perspectives on global issues as they bear upon the interests and concerns of the region. Cooperation on a variety of noneconomic issues is also deemed vital for the region. In these ways, the essential dynamism of the Pacific region may become a catalyst for betterment in the global economy as a whole.

1.2.7   Harris: " 'Market Access' in International Trade"

In his paper, Harris notes that the term "market access" has several different meanings. One definition is that a foreign seller can capture a reasonable market share, relative to firm size and degree of competition in the foreign market, for goods that are comparable in terms of price and quality. A second definition is the security of the right to sell in a market without undue interference from government. A third definition relates to the practices of competing firms and/or their governments that lead to anticompetitive or entry-deterring results. The preservation of market access is important, Harris notes, as a means for preserving the efficiency and consumption gains from international trade.

Harris considers the first definition of market access in terms of cultural bias as a possible barrier to imports. He notes, for example, that foreign firms may face barriers in the Japanese market because the complexities of modern manufactured products make close customer-dealer relationships important. There may be a kind of social network that exists about which foreigners will have to learn and then undertake the requisite investments to make their operations profitable. There may also be certain aspects of reputation and social custom involved that lead firms and consumers to prefer domestically produced goods rather than imports. These factors may make market access more difficult to achieve for products in which brand names and durability are important. By the same token, the internationalization of assembly and production operations of international firms may blur the distinction between a domestically and foreign-produced good. Firms might, therefore, be advised to try to convince foreign consumers that their products are actually produced in the importing country itself.

The second definition involving the security of market access relates especially to the contingent or administered protection that foreign firms may encounter in import markets. The key considerations here involve the commitments that firms may make in production and distribution, and the degree of contestability that will determine entry or exit in the industry. In cases where there are substantial sunk costs in the capital equipment of exporters, contingent protection could potentially be very damaging. By the same token, contingent protection could be beneficial to import-competing firms. It is possible that firms may deal with contingent protection by setting up production and/or distribution facilities in the importing country, or by engaging in licensing arrangements that will facilitate market access. The presence of contingent protection may also lead to lobbying activities by both foreign and domestic firms that are trying to protect their interests. Harris considers the risk-shifting aspect of contingent protection, as this protection may compensate for incomplete markets that prevent firms from insuring against costly disruption from imports. He points out that contingent protection is not an efficient policy in these circumstances as compared to providing unemployment insurance and improving access to equity markets. Policy coordination may be necessary to make contingent protection effective, but this coordination may be difficult to achieve. Finally, small countries are not in a good position to shift risks by imposing contingent protection.

Harris's third definition of market access involves imperfect competition, scale economies, and strategies that are central to the "new" trade theory. He sees three lessons from his analysis: (1) fostering competition is an important way to curb the abuses of monopoly power and thus enhance welfare; (2) increasing market size may be beneficial in enhancing gains in real income; and (3) entry deterrence by incumbent firms or by governments may potentially be very damaging to competition and welfare. The issue is to assess the empirical importance of these lessons and at the same time urge governments to adopt measures that will foster greater competition rather than protectionism.

In his comment, Deardorff characterizes Harris's analysis of market access in terms of informal barriers arising from the behavior of demanders, governments, and competing suppliers. Deardorff asks whether consumer preference for domestic goods should be considered grounds for trade policy action. The issue is whether the preference is autonomous or policy induced. If the former, there are no grounds for a trade policy response since preferences for domestic goods are as legitimate as any other preferences. Deardorff also considers whether Harris's framework is helpful in understanding barriers to international direct investment. Deardorff argues that barriers to direct investment might be defended on grounds of national sovereignty and, accordingly, Harris's framework might be more applicable to questions of market access for goods than it is to direct investment.

Itoh calls attention in his comment to the importance of whether or not traded goods and services are standardized. Market access is not a serious issue if there is standardization, but otherwise, for trade in nonstandardized goods and services, the service content becomes a critical variable, especially in terms of providing for distribution and assuring a particular level of quality. This suggests that certain unusual business practices may arise in expediting efficient transactions between firms. Itoh offers two examples from Japan. The first relates to long-term transactions that are common in the paper and steel industries in Japan. Newspaper publishers in Japan are greatly concerned about the quality of the newsprint that they purchase and this creates incentives to undertake long-term contracts with firms supplying their paper. As a consequence, this may generate intense competition among the suppliers for these long-term contracts. Such arrangements may be common in other industries, such as auto parts, and may serve to explain why imports into Japan may be slow to respond to exchange rate movements. The second example relates to long-term relations in the Japanese distribution system. Itoh notes the differences between the United States and Japan in the purchase of used cars, with newspaper advertising being the main medium used in the United States and purchases from dealers being most common in Japan. This indirect dealing in Japan can be explained by the relatively more limited geographic mobility of the Japanese population, the importance of dealer reputation, and the multiple transactions that may occur over long periods of time as customer-dealer relations become firmly established. There is considerable saving in information costs to consumers in these circumstances, which serves to solidify long-term relations and create a barrier to entry to new firms (both domestic and foreign). Long-term transactions may thus play an important role in defining the conditions for market access. Itoh suggests that these considerations based on rational behavior may be more important than those Harris attributes to cultural factors. This same point applies to Harris's treatment of barriers to entry due to monopoly or oligopolistic behavior. That is, it makes a difference whether the barriers to entry are generated by some rational mechanism arising in long-term contracts, or whether the barriers are created intentionally by incumbent firms.

1.2.8 Saxonhouse and Stern: "An Analytical Survey of Formal and Informal Barriers to International Trade and Investment in the United States, Canada, and Japan"

In our paper, Saxonhouse and I seek to assess the role of formal and, especially, informal barriers in the trade and investment relations of the three nations. We are concerned in particular with whether Japan's barriers are unusual in restricting the access of imports into its domestic market.

Formal barriers include tariffs and nontariff measures that are stated explicitly in official legislation or government mandates, whereas informal barriers may arise from the conscious efforts of governments to favor domestic over foreign interests, or as byproducts of practices and policies that are rooted in domestic institutions. Informal barriers may be associated with administrative procedures and unpublished government regulations and policies, characteristics of market structure, and political, social, and cultural institutions. A list and brief description of the most important nontariff measures in current use provide examples of the chief formal and informal barriers that may exist in particular countries. It appears that there is some difficulty in distinguishing policies that are used to achieve particular domestic objectives from those designed to restrict trade and investment. Also, while it may be the case that social and cultural institutions influence consumer behavior and attitudes such that the purchase of domestic goods is favored, it is by no means clear that these institutions should be considered as informal barriers.

The evidence presented on formal tariff barriers for the three nations indicates that the weighted average tariffs on total imports are about 5 percent or less, although some of the sectoral rates are considerably higher. This is especially the case for Japanese imports of agricultural and food products and for certain labor-intensive imports in each of the countries. The evidence presented for nontariff barriers (NTBs) suggests that the percentage of trade covered by NTBs is roughly comparable between Japan and the United States once fuels are excluded from the coverage calculations. Formal NTBs are concentrated in particular sectors in each country, especially agricultural and food products in Japan, printing and publishing, food products, clothing, iron and steel, and transport equipment in the United States, and clothing, footwear, food products, and transport equipment in Canada. In terms of ad valorem equivalents, the formal NTBs appear relatively small when allowance is made for trade coverage. Information is provided on the main formal restrictions on inward foreign direct investment in the three countries, but it is not possible to assess the severity of these restrictions except in a qualitative manner.

There is unfortunately no unambiguous way to identify the informal barriers that exist. One approach is to list the complaints that have been lodged by exporters and foreign investing firms with a nation's trade authorities. Information of this kind has been collected for Japan and Canada by the Office of the U.S. Trade Representative and for the United States by the European Community. While the lists of barriers look imposing for all three countries, it is not possible on the basis of the lists to assess how valid the complaints about the barriers may be, nor to make comparisons between countries concerning the severity and impact of the barriers. What is needed is some type of empirical framework that can be used to gauge how the countries compare in their use of barriers.

In devising a framework to assess how important the existing barriers are in each country, some difficult conceptual issues arise. With respect to particular formal barriers, it would be best to consider the specific details of the implementation of that barrier. But it may be the case that there are formal barriers that the investigator does not recognize, and it may be difficult to compare and aggregate across different barriers, and to take into account the substitution and complementarities among barriers and possible general equilibrium effects involved in their use. In any event, informal barriers will be left out of consideration since they cannot be explicitly observed.

This suggests the use of more general approaches to assess the importance of barriers. These approaches include: (1) the construction of price-impact measures in terms of tariff equivalents or price relatives; or (2) the construction of quantity-impact measures based upon econometric estimates of models of trade flows. Price-impact measures involve serious information problems since they require knowledge about supply and demand conditions, market prices, product characteristics, and market structure. Quantity measures are in principle preferable insofar as they reveal the extent to which existing barriers may reduce trade. An estimate can be made of what trade would have been in the absence of existing barriers, and then this can be compared to the trade that actually occurs. In order to implement this approach, it is necessary to have a satisfactory model of the determinants of trade covering a variety of trading situations for individual countries. There are two models that suggest themselves for use. One is the Heckscher-Ohlin model in which differences in factor endowments are the primary determinants of trade, and the other is the Helpman-Krugman model in which product differentiation and scale economies are the motivating factors determining trade. Regardless of which model is chosen, there is a considerable burden placed on the model because barriers are presumed to account for all differences between the predicted values of trade based on the included explanatory variables and the actual values of trade that are observed. Also, the models are only capable of determining patterns of trade in an average sense and may not be able to accurately predict trade for particular countries and industries. Finally, the models cannot assess how far observed patterns of trade depart from free trade. While it is granted that these are important qualifications, the models may nonetheless be useful in identifying relative levels of nontariff protection across countries and sectors.

We call attention to several studies that have attempted to assess whether national trade barriers are distinctive in their limitations on market access. Since the studies differ in the time periods examined, countries sampled, level of aggregation, and empirical specification employed, care must be exercised in interpreting the findings reached. As an aid in evaluating the different studies, a formal statement of the Heckscher-Ohlin model is presented in which net exports of individual sectors are shown to be linear in factor endowments. Leamer has used this framework in a cross-national analysis of trade flows and concluded that few countries have distinctive trade policies that affect their sectoral trade patterns. Saxonhouse has used a similar framework, but with allowance for differences in factor quality, and reached essentially the same conclusion. Results of a more comprehensive empirical analysis are presented in our paper, based on a test of the influence of trade barriers on trade structure over all sectors in a given country. We concluded that there is no statistically significant evidence on the effects of trade policy in Japan, the United States, and Canada.

The Helpman-Krugman framework attempts to explain gross trade flows and intra-industry specialization in terms of product differentiation and scale economies. This framework has been used by Lawrence, but we note that his work does not make allowance for the simultaneous determination of import, exports, and production shares, and, furthermore, that his model is not appropriately identified. Lawrence's findings that Japan's trade policies are distinctive in comparison to other major industrialized countries are thus not convincing. We develop an estimating equation based on Helpman-

Krugman in which factor endowments are the main explanatory variables, and conclude as before that Japan's trade structure is not distinctive. The empirical findings are thus invariant to whether the Heckscher-Ohlin or Helpman-Krugman models are used to account for the effects of trade policies on the structure of trade in Japan and the other major countries.

We also review a number of studies that have focused on the total volume of trade rather than the structure of trade. Of these studies, the one by Balassa is the most noteworthy because of its conclusion that Japan's trade structure is highly distinctive. Aside from conceptual problems and possible specification error in his estimating framework, Balassa's results are highly dependent on his rather unusual treatment and measurement of distance and transport costs, which would appear to vitiate his findings. We conclude, therefore, on the basis of our review and assessment of empirical studies of trade structure and volume, that Japan cannot be singled out as having distinctive NTBs in comparison to other major trading countries once account is taken of cross-country differences in factor endowments and distance considerations. As for informal barriers affecting foreign direct investment, we note that there is not sufficient evidence available to reach any conclusion about the restrictiveness of the existing barriers for individual countries. Our overall conclusion is that if one wishes to understand the causes of the existing U.S.-Japanese trade imbalance, the focus should be on the macroeconomic structure and determinants of absorption and output in the two countries, rather than on national trade policies.

In his comment, Markusen objects that the methodology employed in the studies by Leamer and Saxonhouse does not distinguish differences in the level of protection among countries, and that the methodology is not very sensitive in accounting for existing protection. It would be useful, he notes, to determine how large or small the effects of protection might be on sectoral employment or profitability, which is something that the methodology used does not address. Markusen is also critical of the approach because important elements of the trade performance and national endowment vectors are endogenously determined, rather than exogenous as assumed. He notes that factor endowments may respond to changes in protection, as will the transfer of technology between countries. There may also be changes in per unit costs when protection enables an industry to capture scale economies. He suggests, therefore, that the methodology being used is not capable of reflecting cumulative influence, especially of Japanese trade barriers and the ways in which Japan's economic structure has adapted over time, resulting in its remarkable performance in international trade.

In his comment, Kreinin notes that the list of barriers we compiled does not in itself provide an indication of the restrictiveness of the barriers. He suggests that the classification of barriers might be organized according to how sensitive they are to changes in relative prices and their impact on the structure of protection. He also suggests that the list of barriers might be used as a check in interpreting the results of the studies of trade structure. He expresses some concern, moreover, that the methodology used may not fully account for all variables of importance, intercountry similarities in the structure of protection, and the influences associated with differentiated products. He notes, finally, that international general equilibrium effects must be taken into account in evaluating the impact of such nontariff measures as voluntary export restraints.

1.2.9 Henderson and Alexander: "Liberalization of Financial Markets and the Volatility of Exchange Rates"

Henderson notes that there has been a significant reduction in restrictions on financial transactions in several major industrialized countries, including Japan, since the mid-1970s. During this same period, most measures of exchange rate volatility have increased. It might appear, therefore, that financial liberalization has contributed to the increase in exchange rate volatility.

In order to investigate the effects of financial liberalization, Henderson develops a theoretical, two-country portfolio balance model. The thrust of the model is that financial liberalization affects exchange rate volatility by increasing the degree of substitution between assets denominated in different currencies. Two types of substitution are involved: currency substitution (CS) between different national moneys and bond substitution (BS) between bonds denominated in different currencies. Henderson considers how increases in CS and BS may exaggerate or dampen the exchange rate changes resulting from changes in three exogenous variables: the foreign interest rate, the home money supply, and the expected exchange rate. He concludes that increases in CS *dampen* the exchange rate changes resulting from changes in the foreign interest rate and the home money supply, whereas increases in CS *exaggerate* the exchange rate changes resulting from changes in the expected future exchange rate. As for increases in BS, exchange rate volatility is increased no matter which of the three exogenous variables is changing.

Henderson is careful to point out that, even though CS and BS may have increased, the observed increase in exchange rate volatility may be due mainly to increases in the variances of disturbances, rather than to increases in CS and BS given the same distribution of disturbances. He also notes that, even if exchange rate volatility has increased, this would have to be weighed against any efficiency gains resulting from financial liberalization.

Alexander concentrates on the question of why the Japanese yen appears more volatile than the Canadian dollar. He notes that, based on research conducted in the Bank of Canada, there is evidence of currency substitution, but this substitution has not increased since 1980 and is in any case very small in economic terms. Further, Alexander notes that there is an extremely high degree of asset substitutability in Canada and virtually perfect substitutability between U.S. and Canadian financial assets. He also stresses the high degree of integration between the U.S. and Canadian economies, and the fact that the Bank of Canada actively sought to smooth out exchange rate movements after 1982 when monetary targeting was abandoned. In these circumstances, the more limited volatility of the Canadian dollar compared to the yen does not appear to depend on changes in currency substitution. Alexander concludes by noting that innovations in national and international financial markets may have contributed importantly to exchange rate volatility, and that policy uncertainty has resulted in unstable expectations with regard to exchange rates. Factors such as these, rather than changes in currency substitution, may thus be what is behind exchange rate volatility or stability for individual currencies.

1.2.10   McKibbin, Roubini, and Sachs: "Correcting Global Imbalances: A Simulation Approach"

In their paper, McKibbin, Roubini, and Sachs call attention to the large swings in trade balances and exchange rates that have occurred in the world economy during the 1980s and that have led to growing economic tensions among the industrial countries. They attribute these swings in large measure to the divergent fiscal policies followed in the major countries. To study the macroeconomic linkages that exist in the world economy and the policy options available to deal with the current imbalances, they use a dynamic general equilibrium model of a six-region world economy that includes the United States, Japan, Canada, the rest of the OECD countries, non-oil developing countries, and OPEC. The model allows for a full intertemporal equilibrium in which agents have rational expectations of future variables. It has a mix of Keynesian and classical properties in its assumption of slow adjustment of nominal wages in the labor markets. The model is solved in a linearized form to permit policy optimization exercises and to use linear-quadratic dynamic game theory and dynamic programming solution techniques. The parameters of the model are based on econometric estimates obtained from the literature rather than estimated directly. All stock-flow relationships are carefully observed, asset markets are efficient and allow for intertemporal arbitrage conditions and rational expectations in order to analyze anticipated future policy changes, and the supply side is specified to allow for intertemporal profit maximization by firms, differing wage-price dynamics by country, and lags in the pass-through of exchange rate changes into prices.

The model is first used to analyze the effects of fiscal policy, taking into account that tax and spending policies are consistent with the intertemporal budget constraint of the public sector. The experiment involves a permanent increase in government spending equal to 1 percent of potential output, with the fiscal deficit assumed to be financed by the issuance of public debt, and the money supply constant. The results for the United States conform to what would be expected from the Mundell-Fleming model of policy transmission under flexible exchange rates. That is, there is an increase in domestic income, an appreciation of the exchange rate, a rise in short- and long-term interest rates, and a worsening of the trade balance. The effects abroad are ambiguous since there is an increase in world interest rates that tends to depress investment, coupled with an appreciation of the dollar that tends to increase foreign net exports. Canada is stimulated by the U.S. fiscal expansion, but the other major industrialized countries experience a contraction. Fiscal expansion in Japan has contractionary effects abroad, which suggests that this type of measure in itself would not be helpful in stabilizing world economic growth as some observers have argued. Fiscal expansion in Canada results in a larger and more sustained increase in output compared to the other countries, a much larger trade deficit in view of Canada's openness, but a relatively small impact abroad.

Monetary expansion is examined next. A permanent increase of 1 percent in the U.S. nominal money stock is considerably more inflationary in comparison to fiscal expansion because of the currency depreciation that occurs. But it is striking that there is little net impact on the U.S. trade balance or on the level of economic activity. The reason for this is the lower interest rates that occur in the United States and the higher rates abroad, with associated effects on investment and consumption. The results of monetary expansion in Japan and Canada are broadly similar to those obtained for the United States.

The model is then used to examine whether the overall changes in fiscal policies in the major countries between 1980 and 1985 can explain the overall shift in trade balances and exchange rates that occurred. The results reinforce the expected effects of own-country fiscal policy on the trade balance and the movement of the dollar-yen exchange rate, but the exchange rate effects for the other OECD countries are not well tracked because West Germany is not considered separately. The final question considered is the explanation of the dollar depreciation that has occurred since 1985. The modeling of the Gramm-Rudman-Hollings law on reducing the U.S. budget deficit suggests that the shift in public expectations that may have occurred explains only a part of the dollar depreciation. A number of other hypotheses are investigated, including a policy mix of fiscal contraction balanced by monetary expansion, an autonomous decline in private spending, collapse of a speculative bubble, a rising risk premium on dollar assets due to foreign portfolio shifts, monetary expansion by itself, and the start of a new speculative bubble in-

volving dollar depreciation, it is suggested that the main contributing factors
include the combination of the anticipated shift to tighter fiscal policy, a decline in private investment demand, and relatively expansionary U.S. monetary policies. There is reason to expect that these factors will serve to bring
about some improvement in the U.S. trade deficit, but not enough to restore
trade balance by the early 1990s.

In his comment, Truman questions the use of assumed coefficients since
then the model used by McKibbin, Roubini, and Sachs (MRS) does not have
to be consistent with the underlying data, and there is no way to determine
how the results compare to those of other models. He also notes that MRS
did not take into account the problems and policy failures of the 1970s that
led to the difficulties of the 1980s, and that their assumption of offsetting
monetary policy in the context of fiscal expansion is at variance with what
actually happened. Truman cites some alternative results based on the multi-
country model used by the Federal Reserve Board. He notes that the effects
of a U.S. fiscal expansion are larger and more persistently positive than MRS
report, and suggests that MRS's parameterization may be inappropriate.
Also, he notes that their results of a Japanese fiscal expansion are inexplicably
small and may not reflect some important feedback effects on other countries.
Further, he maintains that the apparently trivial results obtained by MRS for
their U.S. monetary policy simulation ignore the positive effect of the dollar
depreciation, particularly on investment income inflows, and that they may
underestimate the impact that lower real interest rates abroad may have on
aggregate demand. Finally, he questions the way in which the Gramm-
Rudman-Hollings legislation was modeled. On the whole, Truman is skeptical that MRS's model and its results can provide a convincing and useful
explanation of macroeconomic linkages and policy options since their results
may be model dependent and their policy characterizations incomplete.

While simulation models are useful in providing information on the
magnitude and direction of change resulting from changes in policies, Hamada notes that it is important to understand the crucial features of such
models and to exercise caution in basing policy decisions on the results. The
use of parameters based on the econometric literature is convenient, but there
may be some arbitrariness in what is selected and what ideally should be used
in terms of the theoretical structure of the model. It is also not clear how to
model the expectations of economic agents with regard to whether changes
in announced policies will be considered temporary or permanent. Furthermore, the handling of speculative bubbles poses difficulties in conducting
simulations across time periods. Another problem arises from the dynamic
modeling of consumption behavior in relation to changes in wealth and the
formation of expectations about changes in taxes. The specification of independent policy instruments raises difficult issues as well, and there might be

some merit in considering how real exogenous shocks affected the model results. Finally, Hamada notes that differences in country size should be taken into account in assessing the effects of alternative policy packages. Thus, MRS's model may embody a number of ad hoc features and contain some technical drawbacks which should be carefully considered before using the results in making policy predictions and prescriptions.

1 OVERVIEW

2 Some Comparative Macroeconomics of the United States, Japan, and Canada

John F. Helliwell

2.1 Introduction

To set the stage for any investigation of the economic relations among nations, it is useful to start with a comparative review of the key macroeconomic features of the countries in question. This is desirable when the countries are large enough to influence the whole world economy or closely enough linked by trade and capital movements that each is influenced by what happens in the others. It is especially important for Japan and the United States in the late 1980s, since they both have large and largely offsetting current account imbalances of such a size as to make the timing and nature of their reversal the major source of uncertainty in a world economy that does not lack uncertainties.

This paper attempts to set the stage by:

1. reviewing the alternative approaches to explaining current account imbalances;
2. presenting comparative data on the evolution of private, government, and foreign savings in the United States, Japan, and Canada;
3. analyzing the growth of investment, output, and productivity in the three countries; and
4. attempting a synthesis of the factors affecting the evolution of current and capital account imbalances in the three countries.

2.2 Alternative Approaches

Over the past several decades, there have been many alternative approaches to the modelling of the balance of payments, and hence of the macroeconomic

The author is grateful for the research collaboration of Alan Chung, Leslie Milton, and especially Esther Yeoh, and for the continued research support of the Social Sciences and Humanities Relinkages among nations. A brief attempt to summarize some of the more important alternatives may help to place some of the recent studies in a wider context and to introduce the evidence and synthesis to follow. Broadly speaking, the approaches can be separated into those which have a sectoral orientation and those that are fundamentally macroeconomic. Naturally, as will be seen, the different sectoral approaches may well be incorporated into one or more of the macroeconomic approaches, and the macroeconomic approaches differ considerably from one another in the range of variables they set out to explain.

2.2.1 Sectoral Approaches

1. *Elasticities Approach to the Current Account.* This approach concentrates on the effects of the real exchange rate on trade flows, with some version of the Marshall-Lerner condition being a necessary condition for the stability of the current account in response to an exchange rate shock.

2. *Elasticities Approach to the Capital Account.* This approach concentrates on the effects of interest rate differentials on the international movements of capital.

3. *Portfolio Approach to the Capital Account.* This approach (as developed for example by Branson 1979) extends the above in three key respects:

a. international interest rate differentials determine desired portfolio proportions rather than desired flows of capital (although this distinction becomes blurred when economies are growing and there are costs of realigning existing portfolios);
b. the rate of return on foreign assets includes the foreign interest rate plus the expected rate of increase in the price of foreign exchange; and
c. the foreign exchange rate is treated as a "jump" variable that moves immediately so as to restore temporary portfolio equilibrium when there is any change in the determinants of desired portfolio holdings.

4. *Partial Keynesian Approach.* If the elasticities approach to the current account is augmented by the positive effect of income on import demand, and if this model of the current account is combined with the elasticities approach to the capital account by inserting both into the balance of payments identity, the result can be described as a partial Keynesian approach (Gylfason and Helliwell 1983), and more commonly appears as the Balance of Payments or BP curve in macroeconomics texts, or as the FF curve in earlier

search Council of Canada. He is grateful for helpful advice and comments from Keizo Nagatani and Andre Plourde. In revising the paper for publication, the author has had the benefit of helpful comments from Mitshurio Fukao, Ron McKinnon, Don Daly, and other conference participants.

expositions by Mundell (1968, chaps. 16 and 17). In terms of changes and setting the change in foreign exchange reserves equal to zero, this can be written, using d to represent the differential operator, as:

$$0 = -mdY + \theta de + \beta di \tag{1}$$

where m is the marginal propensity to import, θ the effect of the exchange rate on the current account, and β the effect of the interest rate on capital inflows.

2.2.2 Macroeconomic Approaches

All of the macroeconomic approaches make use of the conventional national income identity:

$$Y = C + I + G + X - M \tag{2}$$

For the moment, we shall deal with nominal magnitudes, measured in terms of domestic currency, and shall consider aggregate investment to include changes in inventories as well as fixed capital expenditure. The alternative macroeconomic approaches include the following.

1. *Absorption Approach.* This approach starts by defining domestic spending or absorption:

$$A = C + I + G \tag{3}$$

and then substituting this definition in equation (2) and solving to show the current account surplus as the excess of income over domestic absorption:

$$X - M = Y - A \tag{4}$$

This approach either ignores the capital account or treats it as passive, and then interprets the current account as the result of independently derived changes in income or absorption.

2. *Mundell-Fleming Approach.* This model first fleshes out the absorption approach by introducing some behavior into the determination of absorption, making it a function of both income and interest rates. The income effect encompasses both a marginal propensity to consume and induced investment, while the assumed negative effect of the interest rate on absorption is the net effect of interest rates on consumption and investment. This gives the familiar IS curve, which can be shown in differential form as:

$$dY = dG + adY + \theta de - bdi \tag{5}$$

where a is the marginal propensity to spend (on either investment or consumption) and $-b$ is the effect of the interest rate on spending. The next step is to add the money market equation (the LM curve):

$$dH = kdY - hdi \tag{6}$$

where H is the stock of high-powered money, and k and $-h$ are the effects of income and the interest rate on the demand for high-powered money. Equations (5) and (6), when combined with the BP equation (1), constitute the flexible exchange rate version of the Mundell-Fleming model, which remains in one form or another the main workhorse of international macroeconomics. For example, it is used extensively by Turner (1986) in his recent analysis of savings, investment, and the current account in the major OECD countries. The three equations determine changes in income, the interest rate, and the exchange rate in response to changes in government spending or the money supply, or in response to changes in portfolio preferences, foreign interest rates, or foreign incomes, although these latter variables are not shown explicitly in the simple version illustrated here. Even in this simple version, however, changes in spending, whether private or government, can lead to capital inflows or outflows depending on the parameters of the system, and particularly on the relative slopes of the LM and BP curves.

   3. *The Mundell-Fleming-Phillips Approach.* This approach generalizes the basic Mundell-Fleming model by adding, at a minimum, a Phillips curve determining changes in the price of domestic output as a function of the level of output. To capture the effects of changes in exchange rate changes on relative prices and real incomes, it is necessary to go somewhat further, and to distinguish the price of domestic output (which may be determined by foreign prices as well as by capacity utilization) from the price of absorption, which is a weighted average of the price of domestic value-added and the landed price of imports.

   4. *Savings and Investment Approaches.* In recent years there have been a number of alternative approaches that have emphasized the fact that inflows of foreign capital can be interpreted as the excess of domestic investment over domestic savings. This can be illustrated by first rewriting the national accounts identity as an identity linking savings and investment:

$$Y - C - G - X + M = I \tag{7}$$

The left-hand side of this expression represents total savings, which can be decomposed into private, government, and foreign savings:

$$(Y - T - C) + (T - G) + (M - X) = I \tag{8}$$

where T is total taxes. In this general range of approaches, this identity is used to explain the capital account (i.e., foreign savings or FS, equal to the negative of the current account) as the amount by which domestic investment plus the government deficit exceeds private savings ($PS = Y - T - C$):

$$FS = M - X = I + (G - T) - PS \qquad (9)$$

Several versions of the savings/investment approach have been used to explain the evolution of the balance of payments:

a. *The intertemporal optimization approach.* In this approach (e.g., Sachs 1982), the country is assumed to face perfectly elastic supplies of world goods and capital at fixed prices, and hence to be fully employed. In these circumstances, the investment decisions of firms and the saving decisions of households are made optimally and independently, with the current account being the difference between these independently chosen values for domestic investment and national savings. To the extent the government runs a surplus or deficit, this is just another component of national savings, with no crowding-out effects on private spending. Within this approach, large capital inflows are neither a signal of trouble nor a symbol of national prestige, but simply a feature of optimal intertemporal exploitation of world markets for goods and capital.

b. *Capital inflows determined by the government deficit.* This approach, which was known as the "New Cambridge" approach in the United Kingdom in the early 1970s, assumes that domestic investment and private savings are either independently determined or else mutually determined by some process that keeps them in balance with one another. This approach has also been used to explain the U.S. current account deficit in recent years as a consequence of the increasing public sector deficit.

c. *Domestic investment determined by national savings.* This approach, which gained prominence chiefly through the Feldstein and Horioka (1980) results that showed a high international correlation between domestic investment and national saving rates, was used by them to argue that changes in national saving would lead to corresponding changes in domestic investment, and hence that there were greater costs to savings distortions than there would be under the perfect international capital markets assumed in the intertemporal optimization approach.

d. *Capital inflows determined by domestic investment.* This approach, which might be regarded as an empirical attempt to validate the perfect capital markets assumption of the intertemporal optimization approach, was based on a positive international correlation between investment expenditure and capital inflows (Sachs 1981, 1983).

Within a more complete macroeconomic system, one would not expect to find any unique match of sectoral savings rates with one another, or with investment, except as a fortuitous consequence of particular patterns of shocks that existed during a given period of a country's history. More generally, since investment and all of the sectoral saving rates are jointly endogenous variables, it would seem appropriate to analyze their comovements within the context of the more general system in which they are all determined, and not by simple correlations among the ratios.[1]

However, an inspection of the comparative behavior of sectoral saving and investment behavior may help to highlight some of the key differences among the United States, Japan, and Canada. These differences must then be capable of explanation by any model that claims to be general enough to capture the main elements of behavior in each of the countries.

2.3 Private Savings

Figure 2.1 shows the private saving rates in the United States, Japan, and Canada. These saving rates are based on the OECD standardized System of National Accounts (SNA), and should therefore be comparable among countries. Expenditure on consumer durables is treated as consumption rather than investment for all countries. Since expenditures on consumer durables are more cyclical than the flow of services from the stock of durables,[2] the saving rates shown here will be more cyclical than the alternative series with consumer durables treated as investment goods. This difference will be more marked for Canada than for the other countries, as consumer durables average about 15 percent of total consumer spending in Canada, compared to 11 percent in the United States and 6 percent in Japan, with these ratios showing no substantial trend over the sample period, as shown in figure 2.2. Boskin and Roberts (1986, table 2) conclude that treating consumer durables as an investment good would raise the U.S. net saving rate by 2.13 percent in 1984, and by 1.75 percent on average for 1970–79, while a similar adjustment for Japan would raise the net saving rate by 0.73 percent in 1984, or 0.92 percent on average for 1970–79. Thus the adjustment would bring the two private saving rates closer together by 1.4 percent in 1984 and 0.83 percent on average for 1970–79. Boskin and Roberts therefore conclude that comparable treatment for consumer durables in the two economies would not explain any material part of the difference between Japanese and U.S. net saving rates.

There is another measurement problem with private savings. For the United States, private savings do not include the retained earnings of United

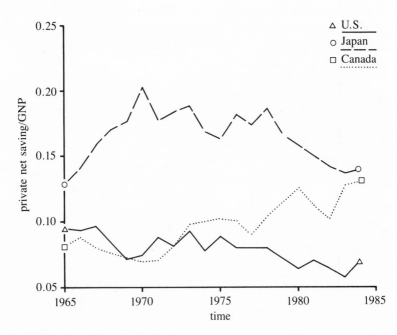

Fig. 2.1 Private Net Saving Rate in the U.S., Japan, and Canada. *Source:* OECD (1986, vol. 1).

States subsidiaries abroad. For Canada, private savings include the retained earnings of foreign corporations with direct investments in Canada. Adjusting these series appropriately would lower Canadian savings and raise those in the United States. Foreign direct investment has in the past been less important for Japan, so this adjustment is not likely to have much impact on the Japanese series.

Although there has perhaps been more analysis of household saving rates than of private saving rates (which include both household savings and corporate savings), it is more appropriate to concentrate on the broader concept in a comparative macroeconomic context. In any event, corporate savings should be included in the wealth of the household sector, either directly or indirectly. Because corporate dividends are generally smoother than corporate profits, the time series for private savings will be correspondingly more cyclically sensitive than the series for household savings.

In the search to find explanations for the large U.S. current account deficits of the mid-1980s, much attention has been focused on the low rate of private saving there; while explanations of the Japanese current account surplus have often focused on the high rate of Japanese private or household savings. Figure 2.1 shows a large and sustained difference between the private

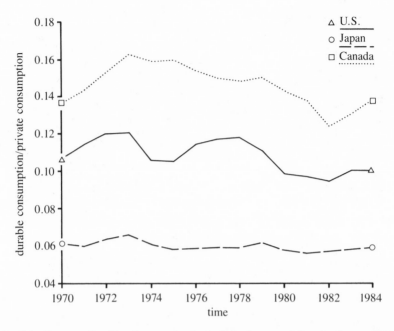

Fig. 2.2 Consumer Durables Consumption in the U.S., Japan, and Canada. *Source:* OECD (1986, vol. 1 and 2).

saving rates in the United States and Japan. Even more remarkable is the behavior of the Canadian series, which is roughly equal to the U.S. series in the early 1970s and rises progressively thereafter, until it almost equals the Japanese rate in 1983.

The Life Cycle–Permanent Income (LC-PI) hypothesis has been the basis for most systematic studies of saving behavior, whether cross sectional or time series.[3] Can it provide a basis for explaining the large and persistent international differences in private saving behavior? First it is necessary to recognize that much of the empirical evidence appears inconsistent with the simplest form of LC-PI models. The tests by Hall (1978) showed that consumption was too much affected by current income to be consistent with a simple LC-PI model. However, King (1985, 255–57) notes that the tests employed by Hall and others using time-series evidence to reject the LC-PI model may be invalid without their assumptions that the relevant interest rates are constant, and that preferences for consumption and leisure are separable.

Subsequent time-series analysis has attempted to distinguish whether the excess dependence of consumption on current income reflects liquidity constraints or myopic expectations. Flavin (1985) has argued that, if the unemployment rate can be taken as a proxy for liquidity constraints, its inclusion in an equation based on U.S. data removes the evidence of excess dependence of consumption on current income. Hayashi (1982) assumed that the excess effect of current income reflected liquidity constraints, and calculated 17.1 percent as the liquidity-constrained households' share of aggregate real disposable income in the United States. A subsequent study applying Hayashi's framework to Japanese data (Ogawa et al. 1986) estimated that liquidity-constrained households in Japan held 23 percent of aggregate real disposable income. The existence of strong liquidity constraints in Japan (for which there is independent evidence, based on the relative unavailability of consumer and mortgage credit) may interact with the relatively steep Japanese age-wage profile of earnings to force higher-than-otherwise-optimal saving rates on Japanese households, and hence contribute to the high Japanese saving rates.

A second general feature of the evidence is that households do not generally run down their wealth fast enough or early enough to permit their savings to be reconciled with simple LC models, even when social security wealth is calculated and included as part of total wealth. In Japan especially there appears to be little or no cross-sectional evidence of wealth being run down during retirement (Hayashi 1986). The Japanese data also show much evidence of inter-vivos gifts. The explanations offered for continued saving after retirement include bequest motives and uncertainty about the date of death. King and Dicks-Mireaux (1982) argue that some of the negative cross-sectional evidence may be based on failing to control for differences in permanent income when comparing saving rates at different ages. Using evidence from the 1977 Canadian family expenditure survey, they find that the age distribution of the ratios of wealth to permanent income shows the humped shape required by the theoretical LC model. They also note, however, that there are many families whose saving behavior is not consistent with the model, either through inadequate saving before retirement or excess saving thereafter, reflecting a variety of motives and circumstances. Granted that there will always be a dispersion of saving behavior in any economy, does the demographic or other evidence support the LC model as being equally applicable to the three countries, and hence able to explain the differences in private saving behavior?

Modigliani and Sterling (1983) report the results of cross-sectional tests applying the LC model to explain intercountry differences in private saving rates in twenty-one OECD countries. Their equations explain the average saving rates in the 1960s, and show that differences in average growth rates in per capita real disposable income have the biggest explanatory power, with other life-cycle variables (ratio of children, ratio of retired population, and the labor force participation rate of those over 65) having roughly the values predicted by a relatively simple life-cycle model. The importance of the growth rate variable is such that Modigliani and Sterling (p. 44) calculate that the higher Japanese growth rate (relative to the United States) is itself responsible for the Japanese saving rate being 13.8 percent higher than that in the United States. Over the 1960–70 period used for their analysis, the actual Japanese private saving rate was 13.8 percent higher than the U.S. rate, implying that the net effect of all other factors is zero. For the three countries, the actual average private saving rates in the 1960s were 10.3 percent for the United States, 24.1 percent for Japan, and 11.8 percent for Canada. In Modigliani and Sterling's preferred equation, the larger number of children in the United States makes the U.S. saving rate 2.6 percent lower than in Japan, the larger number of retirees makes the U.S. saving rate 3.9 percent lower, while the smaller labor force participation among the elderly raises the U.S. saving rate by 8.8 percent relative to the Japanese rate. These demographic and participation rate effects, whose net effect is to raise the U.S. saving rate by 3.3 percent relative to the Japanese rate, are offset to some extent (a saving rate effect of 1.7 percent) by the much lower coverage and size of the Japanese old age security payments in the 1960s.[4] Putting all the estimated effects together, the Modigliani and Sterling equation underestimates by 0.6 percent the actual 13.8 percent difference between the Japanese and U.S. private saving rates in the 1960s.

What do their results suggest about the Canadian saving rate? Overall, the Modigliani and Sterling equation suggests that the Canadian private saving rate should be 0.6 percent higher than the corresponding rate in the United States, while the actual rate was 1.5 percent higher in Canada. The factors making the Canadian rate higher are a smaller proportion of retired population (0.7 percent effect on the saving rate), higher average growth of per capita real income (0.9 percent effect on the saving rate), and lower labor force participation among the elderly (+0.4 percent effect on the saving rate). The factors pulling the predicted Canadian saving rate down relative to the U.S. rate are a higher share of children (−1.2 percent savings rate effect) and a wider coverage of the old age security system (−0.2 percent impact on the saving rate).

While the Modigliani and Sterling model explains quite well the differences among the saving rates in the United States, Japan, and Canada, and has estimated parameters that strongly coincide with the values predicted by a simple version of the LC model, it cannot be accepted as empirically robust unless it can also forecast reasonably well the evolution of saving rates in the 1970s and 1980s. Put another way, if the model has correctly identified the reasons for international differences in saving rates, then the parameters should not change materially if the equation is applied to the data from a subsequent decade. A point of particular concern is the large estimated effect of the growth rate of income in explaining differences in saving rates. One reason for this concern is that any factor causing international differences in saving rates is likely to lead to somewhat corresponding differences in investment rates (as evidenced by the Feldstein-Horioka regressions), which in turn show up as higher rates of growth of the capital stock, and hence of per capita output and income in the faster-saving countries. Even if the high-savings countries invest abroad rather than at home, there will still be faster growth of per capita disposable income in the countries with higher savings. Thus there is ample reason to fear that the large positive effect of the growth rate of income on the estimated saving rates is at least partly due to the causation running from the saving rate to the growth rate of income.[5] The best way of avoiding this problem would be to attempt to separate the rates of labor-embodied and disembodied productivity increase from the increases in per capita incomes that flow simply from higher rates of accumulation of capital and wealth.

In the absence of a complete set of data matching those used by Modigliani and Sterling, it may still be useful to see what their model is likely to predict about the relative saving rates of the three countries in the 1970s and 1980s. Figure 2.3 shows the key demographic ratios in 1965, 1975, and 1984 for each of the three countries. Between the mid-1960s and the mid-1980s, the proportion of the population aged less than 15 years has moved towards equality in the three countries, removing one of the important effects holding down the Modigliani and Sterling savings predictions for Canada and the United States. Treating the series in figure 2.3 as roughly equivalent to the Modigliani and Sterling series for young dependents, the aging of the baby boomers implies a 2.6 percent increase in the U.S. saving rate and a 3.8 percent increase in the Canadian saving rate between 1965 and 1984. For the population share aged 65 and above, there has so far been only a slight increase in each country, leading to a small fractional decrease in each country's saving rate, with no material change in the difference between the countries.

It might also be useful to list some of the other reasons that have been, or could be, advanced to explain why saving rates differ in the three countries:

1. *The tax treatment of consumer borrowing.* Throughout the sample period, although this is likely to change if U.S. tax reform goes ahead as planned, borrowing for purchases of consumer durables has been tax deductible in the United States, but not in the other two countries. This clearly lowers the net cost of consumer durables and decreases the incentive for U.S. residents to save for their purchases.

2. *Availability of consumer credit.* Until recently, consumer credit has been much more easily available in North America than in Japan. This makes consumer durables more likely to be financed by saving than by borrowing for Japanese, thus lowering purchases of durables and raising saving rates in Japan.

3. *Tax treatment of interest income.* Much of interest and other invest-

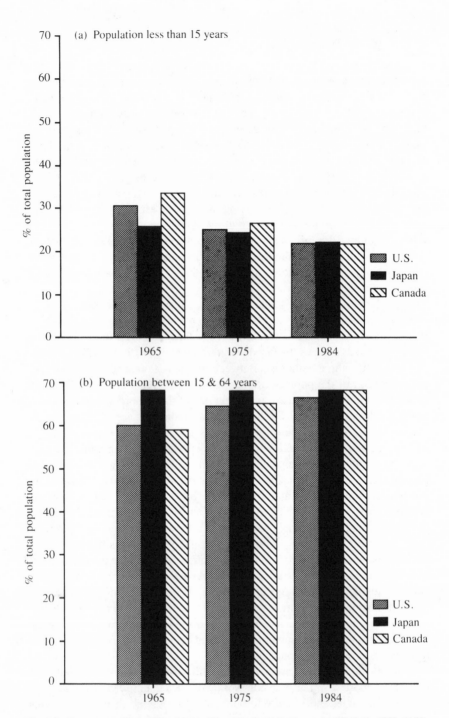

Fig. 2.3 Percentage of Population by Age Groups in the U.S., Japan, and Canada, 1965, 1975, and 1984. *Sources:* OECD, *Labour Force Statistics, 1963–1984;* 1984 data from country yearbooks for 1984.

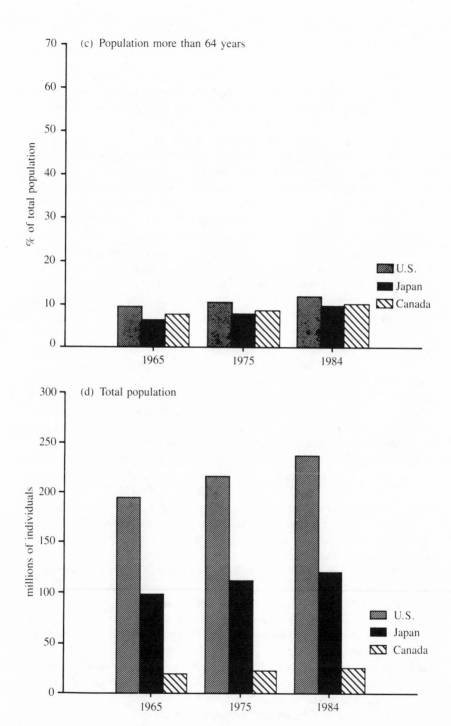

(c) Population more than 64 years

70
60
50
40
30
20
10
0

% of total population

1965   1975   1984

U.S.
Japan
Canada

(d) Total population

300
250
200
150
100
50
0

millions of individuals

1965   1975   1984

U.S.
Japan
Canada

ment income is not subject to tax in Japan because of large exemptions for interest income and low reporting of business and property income. This may encourage savings there relative to North America.[6]

4. *Tax treatment of private savings for retirement.* One of the reasons advanced (e.g., by Wirick 1985) for the sharp increase in the Canadian saving rate relative to the U.S. rate in the mid-1970s was the increase in the availability and flexibility of Registered Retirement Saving Plans (RRSPs), for which contributions are tax deductible, investment income nontaxable, and the entire proceeds subject to income tax when they are withdrawn. The rapid increase in the use of these plans may also have been encouraged by the joint run-up in inflation rates and nominal interest rates in the 1970s, which made the real after-tax rate of return of taxable interest income substantially negative. This suggests that a good part of the increase in the use of RRSPs may have been as a substitution for other forms of savings, since the latter became subject to very heavy effective tax rates.

5. *Inflation has been used to explain higher rate of savings in several countries.* Wirick's results suggest that the effect was bigger in Canada than in the United States. One reason for this may have been that the higher inflation increased the tax advantages of tax-deductible consumer borrowing in the United States. Mortgage interest is also tax deductible in the United States, even after the proposed tax reforms, while it is not deductible in Canada or Japan.

6. *Any increase in the expected number of postretirement years will lead to a higher rate of saving in the LC framework.* Between 1970 and 1983, life expectancy at birth grew from 72 to 77 years in Japan, while increasing from 73 to 75 in Canada and 71 to 75 in the United States (World Bank 1986). This would tend to raise saving rates in Japan by more than in North America, especially if, as seems likely, workers in early or mid-career do not know by how much more their life expectancy will have increased by the time their own old age approaches.

7. *The differing role and structure of the family.* The much greater prevalence of the extended family in Japan, and the much greater frequency of three-generation households, can have conflicting effects on total saving rates. On the one hand, the sharing that is central to the extended family is likely to increase the frequency and size of bequests and inter-vivos gifts. Hayashi (1986) argues that the different role of the family, with its lowering of time preference and increasing of bequests, provides the most parsimonious explanation for the apparent insensitivity of Japanese saving rates to demographics, age, and social security. On the other hand, the extended family provides a form of insurance against individuals outliving their accumulated wealth, thus reducing the precautionary motive for saving against the uncertainties of future health, income, and life expectancy. In addition, the

extended family, with its varied pattern of incomes and wealth, is likely to reduce the saving incentives that would otherwise be created by the steeply rising income structure coupled with the lack (until fairly recently) of easy access to consumer credit.[7]

8. *The work ethic.* In Japan there is a deep commitment to one's job and to one's colleagues, and great value is attached to loyalty and service to the enterprise. In such circumstances, the tradeoff between work and leisure is much more likely to favor work than it does in North America. This will produce more income but reduce the time available to spend it, thus increasing average saving rates. These implications for aggregate saving rates are well understood in official circles, and probably underlie recent efforts in Japan to popularize the idea of taking more holidays.

9. *The Japanese bonus system.* The correlation between bonus payments and household savings has been used as evidence that the large and lumpy bonuses may influence the average size, as well as the timing, of household saving. (e.g., Shinohara 1983). If I am right to aggregate household and corporate savings (as also advocated by Modigliani and Sterling (1983) on the grounds that shareholders look through the corporate veil), then the bonus payments should lead to increases in household savings that are exactly offset by decreases in corporate savings, with no implications for the long-run aggregate private saving rate. There may be a cyclical correlation, however, as quasi rents, bonuses, and savings will all be high at cyclical peaks.

10. *Increases in female labor force participation rates.* These increases have been marked in all three countries, but especially so for Canada. These increases have the effect (for given unemployment rates) of increasing family income and lowering spending time, and are therefore likely to raise average saving rates. Figure 2.4 shows the net labor force effects of the demographic changes and the increasing labor force participation of women, by graphing the labor force as a share of total population in 1965, 1975, and 1984. In 1965, the labor force, as a share of total population, was more than 10 percent higher in Japan than in Canada, with the United States falling in between, but rather closer to Canada. Over the next twenty years, the labor force in Canada grew from 37 percent to 50 percent of the total population, while that in Japan remained almost constant at 49 percent. By 1984, the labor force was almost the same share of total population in all three countries, with Canada being highest and the United States lowest, but only 1 percent lower than in Canada. The full implications of the rising female participation rate, especially for immediate and longer-run saving rates, remain to be worked out. It will be surprising if they do not have at least some role in explaining the rise in the Canadian saving rate relative to that in the United States. Whether one should expect a higher average saving rate to result in the longer

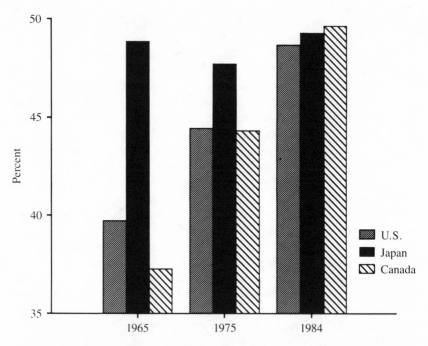

Fig. 2.4   Labor Force/Total Population Ratio in the U.S., Japan, and Canada. *Sources:* OECD, *Labour Force Statistics, 1963–1984;* 1984 data from country yearbooks for 1984.

run is less obvious, although Horiye (1985) reports cross-sectional Japanese evidence that two-earner families have higher average saving rates in all family income classes.

2.4   Government Savings

Figure 2.5 shows the net government saving rates in each of the three countries. In these OECD data, all government (nonmilitary) capital expenditures are treated as investment.[8] The cyclical sensitivity of government revenues in all three countries shows up clearly in the government net saving figures, especially in the post-OPEC recession of 1974–75. The Japanese net saving series is less cyclical than that in North America, and is positive throughout the data period. Prior to 1980, net government savings were generally positive for Canada, averaging about 3 percent of GNP, while being about zero on average for the United States. Since 1980, government net savings have gone sharply negative in both Canada and the United States, reaching about 4 percent of GNP in the mid-1980s. By contrast, in Japan net government savings have remained positive and fairly stable since 1975, fluctuating between 2 percent and 3 percent of GNP.

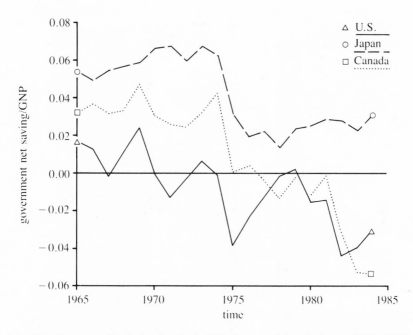

Fig. 2.5 Government Net Saving Rate in the U.S., Japan, and Canada. *Source:* OECD (1986, vol. 1).

In all three countries, the net government savings figures mask the fact that government current disbursements and receipts both grew, as they did in most OECD countries, much faster than GNP in the twenty years from 1960 to 1980. Table 2.1 shows the growth of government final consumption, transfer payments, and total government current spending in each of the three countries. By 1978–80, government current disbursements were highest in Canada, although still below the average for the OECD, while those in Japan were the lowest of any OECD country at about 60 percent of the average. In all three countries, as for the OECD as a whole, transfer payments have been the fastest growing part of government spending. Since 1980, the growing fiscal deficits in the North American economies have been based on growing current spending and falling taxes (as a share of GNP) in the United States, and rising transfer payments and falling revenues in Canada.

2.5 Foreign Savings

In contrast to the correlations evident among the government saving ratios in the three countries, the net foreign saving ratios shown in figure 2.6 have moved quite differently. Except for short periods following each of the upward shocks to crude oil prices, there has been a net outflow of capital from

Table 2.1   Government Spending/GNP Ratios in the United States, Japan, and Canada (1965–84)

Year	Government Final Consumption			Government Transfers			Total Government Current Spending		
				(% of GNP)					
	U.S.	Japan	Canada	U.S.	Japan	Canada	U.S.	Japan	Canada
1965	16.9	8.2	15.1	6.4	5.4	7.3	25.2	14.2	25.4
1970	19.1	7.5	19.5	8.8	5.9	9.4	30.0	14.0	32.7
1975	18.9	10.0	20.3	11.9	9.6	13.1	33.1	20.9	37.4
1980	18.0	9.8	20.1	11.7	12.0	13.2	33.0	25.0	38.9
1984	18.5	9.8	21.7	13.3*	12.8	15.9	36.4*	27.1	45.6

*Equals 1983 ratio.
Source: OECD National Accounts, vol. 1, main aggregates, and vol. 2, detailed tables.

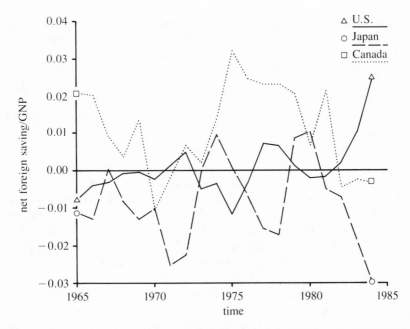

Fig. 2.6 Net Foreign Saving Rate in the U.S., Japan, and Canada. *Source:* OECD (1986, vol. 1).

Japan to the rest of the world, although not previously in excess of 3 percent of GNP, as it has come to be in the mid-1980s. Canada has, for most of the postwar period, been a net importer of capital, following a pattern closely aligned with changes in the ratio of gross fixed capital spending to GNP. The peak use of foreign savings was in 1975, when they exceeded 3 percent of Canadian GNP. The United States has until recently followed an intermediate path, with net capital imports or exports less than 1 percent of GNP until the mid-1980s, when net capital imports have risen to 3 percent of GNP, following a pattern very much the reverse of that in Japan. Since 1982, it has been Canada that has been in the intermediate position, with small net capital exports between 1982 and 1984, and net capital imports since then.

There are many different views about whether and how one should attempt to explain net capital movements between countries. At one extreme, the savings/investment view would advocate explanation of savings and investment in each of the countries, with foreign capital movements being the residual. At the other extreme, the view that changes in domestic saving and investment rates are highly correlated within each country, which is associated with the results of Feldstein and Horioka (1980), would lead one to treat capital movements as independently determined. This evidence has also been used to conclude that capital mobility between countries is limited, so that any shocks to national savings or domestic investment lead to matching changes in the other, rather than triggering capital movements. A third view has received much attention as an explanation of the recent U.S. experience. It argues that capital mobility is very high, at least in relation to the interest elasticity of the U.S. demand for money, so that the increase in the U.S. government deficit between 1980 and 1984 combined with a restrictive monetary policy to increase the value of the U.S. dollar. This in turn led to the rapid increase in the U.S. current account deficit with its matching inflows of foreign savings. According to Frankel (1985), this view can be made compatible with both high international capital mobility and the high correlations between national savings and domestic investment if one accepts that purchasing power parity (PPP) is not maintained, and that deviations from PPP are not readily forecast. In this view, the part of the savings/investment approach that is missing is not a tight linkage of financial markets but a tight-enough linkage of goods markets to maintain PPP. To understand this point readily, it is helpful to distinguish narrower from broader measures of capital mobility. The two most important narrow measures are:

1. *Covered interest parity,* which ensures, if it holds, that comparable assets in different currencies have interest rates that depart from the forward exchange differential by no more than the transactions costs involved in the currency exchange. Caramazza et al. (1986) report that departures from covered interest parity have frequently been larger than accountable for by transactions costs, which they calculate as being less than 6 basis points (0.055 percent per annum) for ninety-day arbitrage between the Canadian and U.S. dollars, and less than four basis points between the U.S. dollar and the Japanese yen (p. 21). Even where covered interest parity does hold reasonably well, the significance of this may be slight if, as Marris (1985) points out, it is achieved by changes in the forward differential without any implications for the future value of the spot exchange rate.

2. *Equality of interest rates among deposits or securities denominated in the same currency but issued or sold in different countries.* This definition of capital mobility is advocated and tested by Caramazza et al. (1986) for six major OECD countries. They find that for Germany, Japan, France, and the United Kingdom there have been periods when there were spreads of 3 percent or more between the returns on similar assets issued in terms of the home currency, but sold in domestic and foreign markets. For Germany, Japan, and France the divergences have reached and exceeded 9 percent per annum during periods when there were controls on capital movements. For the United States and Canada, where there have been no controls on short-term capital movements during the 1973–85 sample period, there were much closer linkages between domestic and offshore interest rates.

Neither of the narrower definitions of capital mobility implies the tight linkage among national interest rates that is assumed by the savings/investment approach to the balance of payments. For that it is necessary that interest rates on comparable assets in different currencies differ by the expected rate of change of the exchange rate or, equivalently under the maintained hypothesis of PPP, the difference between the inflation rates in the two countries. Since ex ante changes in price levels and exchange rates are not directly measured, any test of this broader definition of capital mobility must be a joint test of capital mobility and some hypothesis about the formation of expectations. Most studies assume rational expectations about future price levels and test for international differences in uncovered ex ante real interest rates. All studies find systematic and substantial departures from ex ante real interest rate parity, and the literature is divided between those who treat the differences as potentially explicable risk premia or discounts, and those who regard the evidence as showing substantial inelasticities in the supply of capital for uncovered international interest arbitrage. Attempts to explain the risk premia in terms of existing portfolio shares have generally proven unsatisfactory in that the coefficients estimated are seldom significant and change from sample to sample.

Overall, the studies show that flexible exchange rates have been sufficiently unpredictable to substantially limit the extent of capital mobility on an uncovered basis. Obstfeld (1986) and others have found that the correlations between changes in national saving rates and domestic investment rates are highest for the largest countries. Obstfeld (1986) interprets this as happening because the larger countries are big enough to influence world interest rates. However, it would be useful to distinguish size from openness, as the effects of the two might be different. A large country might appear to be closed because it was closed, and not because it influenced offshore financial conditions. Conversely, a small country is more likely to be an open economy, with a larger share of its output going directly or indirectly into foreign trade. Under these conditions, there are likely to be more firms that have reasonably predictable earnings of foreign exchange in the future, and hence be able to switch the currency mix of their borrowings without departing substantially from a reasonably balanced currency mix of future payments and receipts.

Among the three countries under review in this paper, Canada is the smallest as well as the most open, and also had, in Obstfeld's results (1986, 90), a lower correlation between quarterly changes in national saving and domestic investment ratios. None of this evidence denies the possibility that the current high foreign savings flowing into the United States may be due to the high dissaving by government (as argued in Feldstein 1986). However, it does mean that the result should flow from a more general system in which the private saving rate, the government saving rate, the domestic investment rate, and international capital movements are determined interdependently, but without the assumption that either goods or capital move so freely that PPP or uncovered interest rate parity can be assumed to hold.

Obstfeld (1986, table 2) finds that the correlations between changes in national savings and domestic investment are lower for most of the countries studied (including Japan, the United States, and Canada) after 1973 than they were before, and uses this as indirect evidence that capital mobility is increasing over time. There is ample evidence of more direct sorts that the increasing ease and decreasing cost of long-distance transactions have greatly increased the scale and scope of international financial arbitrage.[9] However, the continuing evidence (e.g., Caramazza et al. 1986) of substantial international differences in ex ante real interest rates shows that the continuing uncertainty about future changes in exchange rates is great enough that financial assets in different currencies are far from being perfect substitutes. But, Frankel, Dooley, and Mathieson (1986), using a large sample of countries, find that the correlations between savings and investment are lower after 1973 than before. They suggest that this result could be consistent with increasing financial arbitrage if the markets for physical capital are not tightly integrated internationally, and if there is not effective arbitrage between equity and debt markets within countries. Put in broader terms, the point they are making is that neither the rates of return on saving nor the real rates of return on investment may be equalized among countries even if international financial arbitrage is highly developed. Reasons for this include the difficulties and informational asymmetries involved in predicting real exchange rates and the return of business ventures, as well as the variety and uncertain effects of the tax treatment of international and domestic investment income.

2.6 Investment, Output, and Productivity Growth

Except for a statistical discrepancy, which has hardly ever reached 1 percent of GNP, the net domestic investment ratios shown in figure 2.7 are the sums of the private, government, and foreign net savings ratios described earlier. The Canadian and U.S. series have shared a certain amount of cyclical variance, although the Canadian series has tended to be about 2 percent of GNP higher than that in the United States, and moved upward after each of the upward surges in oil prices, while the U.S. ratio moved down. This reflects the greater relative importance of energy investment in Canada than in the United States. The Japanese investment ratio has followed a downward trend since about 1970, but has at all times been higher than the almost trendless series in North America.

Figure 2.8 shows the capital/output ratios for each of the three countries, revealing that the high Japanese net investment ratio has been rapidly increasing what had previously been a relatively low capital intensity of production. In 1965, the Japanese capital-output ratio was two-thirds that in the United States, while by 1984 it was almost equal. The capital stock includes business and housing, and the output measure is GDP. The rapid rise of the

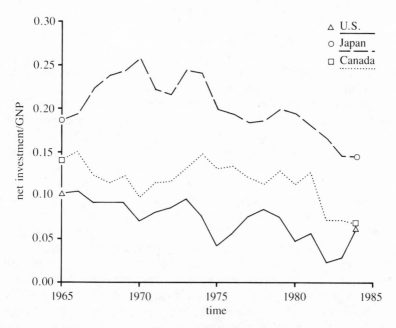

Fig. 2.7 Net Domestic Investment Rate in the U.S., Japan, and Canada. *Source:* OECD (1986, vol. 1).

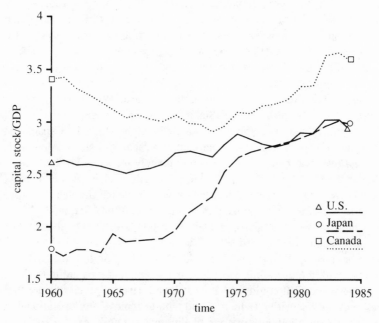

Fig. 2.8 Capital-Output Ratio in the U.S., Japan, and Canada. *Sources:* Adapted from Statistics Canada, OECD data tapes, and OECD (1986, vol. 1).

Japanese capital stock is made more apparent when it is shown in per capita terms, as in figure 2.9.[10] In the mid-1960s, the Japanese per capita stock of fixed capital was less than one-quarter that in North America, while by 1984 it was fast approaching the North American levels. Over the twenty-year period from 1965 to 1984, the Japanese capital stock per capita grew at an average annual rate of 7.8 percent, compared to 3.2 percent in Canada and 2.6 percent in the United States.

Perhaps the most arresting macroeconomic difference between the Japanese and North American economies lies in the higher and more stable Japanese rates of growth of per capita output and income. These higher rates of growth either facilitate or cause the much higher rate of private saving in Japan, and are themselves partially caused by the much higher Japanese rate of capital accumulation. Figure 2.10, which uses the OECD PPPs to put real per capita output in the three countries into a common currency, shows that the Japanese real per capita output was less than half that in North America in the mid-1960s, but has converged rapidly over the succeeding twenty years. To what extent has this been due to a faster rate of capital accumulation, and how much has been due to faster technical progress in Japan than in North America?

To give a first impression of the relative size and stability of capital expenditures in the three economies, figure 2.11 shows per capita private gross fixed capital formation in international dollars at PPP exchange rates. The Japanese series is the fastest growing, reflecting the faster growth of the Japanese economy. Until 1973, real investment per capita was very similar in Canada and the United States, having roughly common cyclical movements. Since 1973, however, the changes in investment have tended to be in opposite directions in the two economies, in particular since 1982 when investment has grown strongly in the United States but not in Canada, so that in 1984 U.S. investment per capita was substantially higher than in Canada. The growth rate of capital investment per capita in Japan has slowed down since 1973, and over that period has had approximately the same level and rate of growth as the U.S. series. As we shall see later, these changes are fairly well explained by a capital stock adjustment model in which the desired capital/labor ratio is chosen to minimize normal unit costs of production.

Comparative regressions of real per capita investment on time and a variable reflecting unexpected sales (SS, to be defined below), show investment to be most cyclically sensitive in Japan, and least so in Canada.[11] Is this consistent with the prevailing view that investment horizons are much longer for Japanese firms? It could be, either if longer-term expectations are themselves cyclically sensitive (which would tend to remove any operational distinction between planning horizons of different lengths), or if a substantial part of the unexpected changes in sales reflected structural changes requiring changes in the size and structure of the capital stock. The problem with this

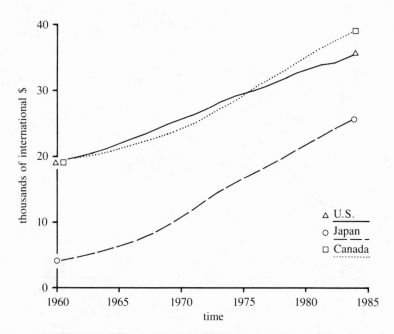

Fig. 2.9 Real Capital Per Capita in the U.S., Japan, and Canada. *Source:* OECD (1986, vol. 1).

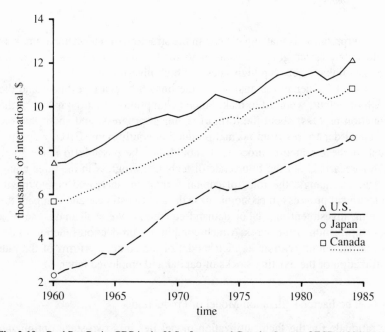

Fig. 2.10 Real Per Capita GDP in the U.S., Japan, and Canada. *Source:* OECD (1986, vol. 1).

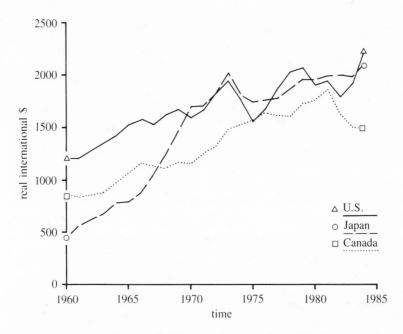

Fig. 2.11 Private Gross Fixed Capital Formation Per Capita for the U.S., Japan, and Canada. *Source:* OECD (1986, vol. 1).

latter interpretation is that any change in the structure of international markets should entail larger gross investment to realign the capital stock, with no necessary linkage between high sales and high investment.

To get further in the analysis of the links between investment and the growth of output, we need to make some assumptions about the nature of the production process, about the form of technical progress, and about the role of cyclical departures from normal production equilibrium. Given a specific model of the production process, it should then be possible to make some rough forecasts about the future rate of technical progress in the three countries, to disentangle the roles of capital formation, increased employment, and technical progress in economic growth, and to estimate and compare the matching investment and labor demand equations. We shall make use of a 'factor utilization' framework, which combines a production function to define normal output with an explicit model of the choice by firms of the rate of utilization of the existing stocks of capital and employed labor.

2.6.1   The Factor-Utilization Model of Production

The rationale for the factor-utilization model lies in a two-stage optimizing procedure by firms. The first stage models the forward-looking process whereby firms make sets of interrelated plans for the levels and prices of output and for the levels of factor inputs, to maximize the present value, in risk-adjusted terms, of future quasi rents. In doing this, they are assumed to face a less than perfectly elastic demand for output, to form expectations about the relative costs of factor inputs, and to choose factor input combinations to minimize the costs of producing the desired levels of output at normal intensities of factor use. An explicit production function is used to relate planned output to factor inputs. In such a context, the long-run production function can best be thought of as determining a synthetic measure of output: normal output, or the amount that would be produced if all employed factors were used at normal or average rates. In the example calculations reported in this paper, I use real GDP as the output concept and employ a two-factor CES function to determine normal output (QS):

$$QS = [\mu(\Pi N)^{(\tau-1)/\tau} + \nu K^{(\tau-1)/\tau}]^{\tau/(\tau-1)} \tag{10}$$

where μ and ν are scale/distribution parameters, τ is the constant elasticity of substitution between the two inputs, which are efficiency units of labor (ΠN) and the fixed capital stock (K).[12]

In the second stage of the optimizing process, firms choose their preferred short-term combinations of utilization rates, inventory changes, and prices to respond to final demand conditions, cost conditions, and inventory levels that differ from those anticipated at the time the commitments were made to build or hire the currently employed stocks of capital and labor. Under the most usual assumptions about the costs of abnormal utilization rates and abnormal inventories, the derived model of optimum factor utilization will depend on unexpected or abnormal final sales, profitability, and inventories. Each variable is measured relative to its normal or target value, with the utilization rate constrained to take its own normal value when sales, profitability and inventory stocks are all at their normal values. Normal output is scaled so that the normal value of the utilization rate is 1.0 by construction. The form for estimation is therefore:

$$Q/QS = SS^{\beta_1}KGP^{\beta_2}CQ^{\beta_3}\nu \tag{11}$$

where SS is the ratio of actual to normal final sales, with both terms expressed as proportions of normal output, KGP is the ratio of desired to lagged actual inventory stocks, with desired stocks expressed as a constant proportion of normal output, and CQ, an inverse measure of profitability, is defined as current unit costs relative to the output price. The theoretically expected values of the parameters are therefore: $\beta_1 > 0$, $\beta_2 > 0$, $\beta_3 < 0$.

In this paper I shall concentrate more on the underlying production function and the derived demand equations for capital and employment, since they are what is most important for analyzing the longer-term macroeconomics of investment and growth. To analyze consistently the cyclical and longer-term movements in productivity and growth, the longer-term production function and the factor-utilization or output equation are analyzed in tandem, as was done for the major OECD economies in Helliwell, Sturm, and Salou (1985).

The elasticity of substitution is estimated by a logarithmic regression of the actual capital/labor ratio on its lagged value and the rental price of capital relative to the wage rate.[13] The elasticity of substitution for the normal production function is then given by the equilibrium response of the capital intensity to changes in the relative price ratio. I find the elasticity of substitution to be close to 1.0 in all three countries, being slightly higher for Japan than for the United States and Canada.[14]

2.6.2 Estimating Technical Progress

In applying the framework to the three countries under study in this paper, I use two different ways of modelling Π, the index of labor-embodied technical efficiency. In the "constant" case, the rate of increase of technical efficiency is assumed to be constant at the rate which makes actual and normal output grow at the same average rate over the sample period. In the "catch-up" (or "convergence") case, technical progress in Japan and in Canada is modelled such that the index of labor efficiency starts at a level below that in the United States and then gradually approaches the U.S. level. The catch-up model, which was applied on a comparable basis to data for the seven largest OECD economies in Helliwell, Sturm, and Salou (1985), would serve to explain the higher Japanese growth rate (to the extent that it was not already explained by higher capital accumulation), since the Japanese productivity level, using the PPP exchange rates to convert national outputs to common units, is still below that in North America. Baumol (1986) has recently emphasized that the catch-up or convergence hypothesis appears to explain more than a century of comparative growth data collected by Maddison (1982) and others. The next twenty years will provide a strong test of the convergence hypothesis, since it will require either that the Japanese rate of productivity growth (adjusted for the different rate of capital accumulation) slow down to permit the Japanese productivity levels to fall into line with North American levels, or else that North American productivity growth accelerates with the adoption of new international best-practice standards determined in Japan and elsewhere in the world economy.[15] If either of these, or some combination of the two, should take place, there will be profound implications for savings, investment, and capital movements in all three countries. That the convergence hypothesis is not a sure thing is attested to by the postwar performance of the

United Kingdom, which has shown no tendency to close the productivity gap between itself and countries with higher levels of output per capita.[16]

In applying the convergence model, I wish to be able to test the assumption that the rate of technical progress converges to the same value for each country and, further, that the index of technical efficiency has the same long-term level in all three countries. If these two conditions are satisfied, and if the estimated elasticity of substitution between capital and labor is the same in all three countries, then the long-term production function will be the same in all three countries, with different levels of output per worker then depending only on the capital/labor ratio.

In order to test the catch-up model, I first estimate for each of the countries an index of technical progress implying constant efficiency growth, so that I can use the index for the United States in the convergence model. This is done by inverting the production function (10), using actual output instead of normal output[17] and the actual levels of capital and labor inputs to define a "measured" index of labor efficiency. The logarithm of this bundle can be regressed on time to estimate the rate of growth of Π, which is about 0.75 percent for the United States, 1.6 percent for Canada, and 4.6 percent for Japan. If common production-function parameters are assumed for each country, it is possible to convert the measures of capital and output in each country into international constant currency and compare the efficiency levels in the three countries. Using 0.97 as a common value for τ and 0.32 for γ, the efficiency measure is highest in the United States throughout the sample period, as one would expect to find from the output per capita and capital per capita series already examined. However, that situation changes as time passes, given the slower rate of growth of Π in the United States than in the other countries. By 1984, the efficiency levels in Japan and Canada are 75 percent and 86 percent, respectively, of that in the United States, while by 1990 the Japanese level is 93 percent, and the Canadian level 90 percent, of that in the United States. By 1993, Japan leaps ahead of North America, so that by 2000 its efficiency level is 31 percent higher than in the United States and 33 percent higher than in Canada. In these calculations, everything depends on the future constancy of each country's rate of technical progress, and on the lack of any links between countries in the achievable levels and rates of growth of technical progress.

The convergence model implies, in contrast to the results reported above, that at least the rates of growth, and possibly the levels, of technical progress should converge as time passes. Table 2.2 shows the results of fitting the catch-up model for Japan and Canada. This is done by regressing the "measured" efficiency variable described above on its lagged value and on the calculated efficiency index for the United States, which in logarithmic form is simply a linear function of time. The two equations are estimated as a

Table 2.2   Catch-up Model of Technical Progress (1961–84)

Country	Estimated Coefficients		Regression Statistics		
	lnLELF	lnUSHAT	R^2	s.e.e	D-H
Japan	0.91838	0.08162	0.9800	0.043	−0.9029
	(72.25)	(6.42)			
Canada	0.89821	0.10179	0.9650	0.023	0.7751
	(37.26)	(4.22)			

Notes: Dependent variable is lnELF. The two equations are estimated as a system, with output and capital stocks measured in billion 1980 international dollars, and using the iterative Zellner SURE method. F-test for constraints that the coefficients sum to one and the constant term equals zero: Japan, 0.80; Canada, 0.68.

  lnELF = logarithm of the "measured" efficiency level.
  lnLELF = lagged dependent variable.
lnUSHAT = logarithm of calculated U.S. efficiency level at a constant rate of efficiency growth.

Homogeneity Test	F-stat	d.f.	Fc*
lnLELF^J = lnLELF^C Const.^{J} = Const.^{C} = 0	0.54	3,24	3.01
lnUSHAT^J = lnUSHAT^C	0.92	1,24	4.26
Const.^{J} = Const.^{C} = 0	0.74	2,24	3.40
lnLELF^J = lnLELF^C = 1.0 lnUSHAT^J = lnUSHAT^C = 0	5.05	4,24	2.78

*Critical at 5 percent.
Note: For the restrictions to be accepted, the F-stat should be below the critical value.

system, so that it is possible to test whether the same catch-up process applies in both countries. If the equations are also estimated using common parameters for the production functions, and using capital and output data converted to common units, it is possible to test whether the efficiency measures in the three countries, or in any pair of countries, are converging to the same level.

The test results shown in table 2.2 show that the convergence rates for Japan and Canada are not significantly different from one another, with the point estimate of the coefficient on the U.S. efficiency index almost the same for both. In the equations shown in table 2.2, the coefficients on the calculated U.S. productivity index and on each country's lagged dependent variable are constrained to sum to 1.0, which implies eventual convergence to the U.S. rate of productivity growth. This constraint is tested and is accepted easily by the data. It is also possible to test the convergence model directly against the constant-efficiency-growth model, since the constant-efficiency-growth model is a nested case of the general convergence model[18] obtained by constraining the coefficient of the lagged dependent variable equal to 1.0.

This test strongly rejects the constant-growth model in favor of the convergence model.[19]

When the catch-up model is applied using common parameters for the production functions in all three countries, the insignificant constant terms in the productivity index equations for Canada and Japan show that convergence applies to levels as well as rates of growth.[20] The catch-up equations in table 2.2 can be used to calculate efficiency indices for Japan and Canada, using the 1960 'measured' value of the efficiency index as a starting value. Over the 1970s, 1980s, and 1990s, the Japanese efficiency index grows at annual rates of 1.3 percent, 2.4 percent, and 1.6 percent. For Canada, the corresponding growth rates are 1.7 percent, 1.2 percent, and 1.0 percent. As for efficiency levels, in 1970 the Japanese and Canadian efficiency levels are 49 percent and 76 percent, respectively, of the U.S. values. By 1980 they are 67 percent and 83 percent, and 78 percent and 86 percent by 1990, while by the end of the century the Japanese and Canadian efficiency levels are 84 percent and 88 percent of the U.S. levels. According to this evidence, which must certainly be treated as provisional and as requiring confirmation by other studies, labor efficiency levels in the three countries are converging to the same growth paths. Output per unit of labor would, however, continue to grow faster in Japan than in North America as long as capital stock growth continued to be faster there than in North America. Output per capita in Canada could remain above that in the United States given the higher capital stock per capita and the more rapid growth of labor force and labor efficiency in Canada.

2.6.3   Output, Investment, and Employment Equations

The output, investment, and employment equations shown in tables 2.3, 2.4, and 2.5 are based on constant efficiency growth for the United States and the catch-up model for Japan and Canada, with the production function parameters and speeds of convergence permitted to take different values for each country. The parameters and goodness of fit of these equations are very similar under the constant and catch-up models of technical progress, so that both sets of results need not be reported. However, this also means that the derived output and factor-demand equations cannot be used to help decide which of the alternative models of technical progress is most likely to represent the future growth prospects for Japan and Canada.[21]

In the output or factor-utilization equations shown in table 2.3, the results for each country easily accept the theoretical restrictions imposed to ensure that actual and normal output should be equal when sales, profitability, and inventories are at their normal levels. The equations for the three coun-

Table 2.3   Catch-up Model of Output Supply Equations (1961–84)

Coun-try	Estimated Coefficients				Regression Statistics		
	lnQS	lnCQ	lnSS	lnKGP	R^2	s.e.e	D-W
U.S.	1.000	−0.1963	0.9476	−0.0291	0.9990	0.0069	1.1634
		(8.40)	(21.65)	(0.94)			
Japan	1.000	−0.1509	0.5982	−0.0053	0.9986	0.0171	1.3500
		(3.69)	(5.50)	(0.09)			
Canada	1.000	−0.3117	0.5374	0.0657	0.9991	0.0091	1.0694
		(6.46)	(11.25)	(3.62)			

Notes: Dependent variable is lnQ. The three equations are estimated as a system using instrumental variables, iterative Zellner SURE method. F-test for constraints that coefficient on lnQS = 1.0 and constant term = 0: U.S., 0.17; Japan, 0.23; Canada, 1.25.

  lnQ = logarithm of real GDP at factor cost.

lnQS = logarithm of normal output.

lnCQ = logarithm of current unit costs relative to output price.

 lnSS = logarithm of the ratio of actual to normal final sales.

lnKGP = logarithm of the ratio of desired to lagged actual inventory stocks.

Homogeneity Test	F-stat	d.f.	Fc.*
$lnCQ^{US} = lnCQ^J = lnCQ^C$ $lnSS^{US} = lnSS^J = lnSS^C$ $lnKGP^{US} = lnKGP^J = lnKGP^C$	13.79	6,24	2.51
$lnCQ^{US} = lnCQ^J = lnCQ^C$	3.91	2,24	3,40
$lnSS^{US} = lnSS^J = lnSS^C$	33.15	2,24	3.40
$lnKGP^{US} = lnKGP^J = lnKGP^C$	6.19	2,24	3.40
$lnCQ^{US} = lnCQ^C$ $lnSS^{US} = lnSS^C$ $lnKGP^{US} = lnKGP^C$	26.48	3,24	3.01
$lnCQ^{US} = lnCQ^J$ $lnSS^{US} = lnSS^J$ $lnKGP^{US} = lnKGP^J$	3.00	3,24	3.01

*Critical at 5 percent.

Note: For the restrictions to be accepted, the F-stat should be below the critical value.

tries are estimated as a system, so that it is possible to test whether production behavior, for given production functions and factor supplies, differs significantly between countries. The sales effect is largest in the United States (implying a smaller buffering role for inventory stocks), while the profitability effect is greatest in Canada. This difference might be expected, as Canada is the most exposed of the three countries and is the most likely to be faced with exogenous changes in the terms of trade that alter the ratio of domestic costs to the output price. The inventory disequilibrium term is correctly signed and significant only for Canada. Tests of equality of sets of coefficients show that production behavior is significantly different in Canada than in the other two countries, but that the parameters for Japan and the United States are not significantly different at a 95 percent confidence level, although they are at a 90 percent level.

The gross private capital formation equations reported in table 2.4 are fitted as investment rates, with the actual investment rate determined by its lagged value, by the ratio of the desired to the lagged actual capital stock, and by the current profitability measure. The latter variable is intended to capture the possible effects of current quasi rents affecting either liquidity constraints or business confidence. In all three countries, the gap between actual and desired capital stocks is closed slowly, with adjustment significantly faster in Japan and slower in Canada. Investment behavior is most autocorrelated in Canada, and least so in the United States, with these differences also statistically significant. The profitability or liquidity effects are similar in Canada and the United States, and are significantly larger in Japan.

The real cost of capital is treated as a constant in all three countries[22] and no allowance is made for different tax treatment of investment expenditures at the corporate level or of investment income at the personal level. As pointed out by King and Fullerton (1984), Shoven (1985), and Daly et al. (1987), there are substantial international differences in the "tax wedges" between the pre-tax cost of capital to business and the post-tax return to savers. In all three countries, these wedges also differ materially by type of asset, by type of financial instrument, by industry, by the form of the business venture, and by the income and tax status of the holder of the debts and equities of the firms. Thus, the estimation of representative marginal tax rates is tricky enough using the closed economy assumptions usually employed for these

Table 2.4 Catch-up Model of Business Fixed Investment (1962–84)

Country	Estimated Coefficients				Regression Statistics		
	J1LIK	IKD	CQ	Constant	R^2	s.e.e	D-H
U.S.	0.1430	0.0379	−0.0118	0.0631	0.9015	0.0017	2.8108
	(2.31)	(10.34)	(2.53)	(8.88)			
Japan	0.4973	0.0415	−0.0883	0.1451	0.9826	0.0035	1.6510
	(9.82)	(8.02)	(6.49)	(8.02)			
Canada	0.8234	0.0169	−0.0124	0.0206	0.8467	0.0022	0.8861
	(9.12)	(4.49)	(2.62)	(3.22)			

Notes: Dependent variable is IK. The three equations are estimated as a system using instrumental variables, iterative Zellner SURE method.

IK = ratio of gross real private fixed investment to the mid-year capital stock.
J1LIK = lagged dependent variable.
IKD = (desired capital stock − mid-year stock)/mid-year stock.
CQ = ratio of average unit costs to the output price.

Table 2.5   Catch-up Model of Employment Equations (1963–84)

Country	Estimated Coefficients		Regression Statistics		
	lnNL	lnNSTAR	R^2	s.e.e	D-H
U.S.	0.78617	0.21383	0.9975	0.0067	1.4266
	(61.61)	(16.76)			
Japan	0.94913	0.05087	0.9830	0.0083	1.9055
	(106.28)	(5.70)			
Canada	0.78340	0.21660	0.9969	0.0094	2.1053
	(55.12)	(15.24)			

Notes: Dependent variable is lnN. The three equations are estimated as a system using instrumental variables, iterative Zellner SURE method. F-test for constraints that the coefficients sum to 1 and that the constant equals to zero: U.S., 2.08; Japan, 7.11; Canada, 12.53.

    lnN   = logarithm of employment level.
    lnNL   = lagged dependent variable.
lnNSTAR = logarithm of desired employment level.

calculations. As Arnold (1986) and others have shown, international investments pose even trickier problems because of the prevalence of tax havens, inducements to foreign investment, withholding taxes, and complicated arrangements for the crediting of foreign taxes paid. These difficulties have thus far prevented us from evaluating quantitatively the impact of taxes on capital mobility and investment spending.

The equations shown in table 2.5 show employment responses to be four times faster in North America than in Japan, and equally fast in Canada and the United States. This result confirms the long-established Japanese practice of stabilizing employment, at least in the larger enterprises, in the face of cyclical changes in output. Employment growth, but not output growth, is more stable in Japan than in North America, and this shows up as very damped responses of employment to changes in output.[23]

2.7   Toward a Macroeconomic Synthesis

The earlier sections have provided a review of the comparative behavior of private savings, government savings, foreign savings, investment, and output growth in the United States, Japan, and Canada. Throughout this review, the evidence has been mainly of a partial equilibrium nature, without the use of macroeconomic constraints to put the pieces in their proper context.

To provide a consistent quantitative synthesis of the relative importance of, for example, government spending, monetary policy, exchange rate developments, private saving behavior, taxation systems, and long-run productivity trends in the determination of the past and future evolution of income,

savings, and the balance of trade and payments in the three countries clearly
lies beyond the scope of this paper.

What would be required for each country, as well as for their key trading partners in the rest of the world, is quantitative models reflecting the main
structural factors that jointly determine the eventual level and distribution of
world savings and investment. The evidence and research surveyed in this
paper makes it clear, I think, that none of the assumptions necessary to reduce
the problem to a simple correspondence between, for example, government
deficits and current account deficits, or between national savings and domestic investment, is valid. Put in a more positive way, the evidence suggests that
exogenous changes in government spending, private consumption, investment, or trade are all likely to have implications for all three savings rates
(private, government, and foreign), and that the effects on the saving rates
will be different for each type of exogenous shock.

A minimal quantitative model sufficient for the task would require, in
my view, explicit supply modelling for each country, perhaps of the type used
in the previous section, combined with modelling of the final demands in
each country for consumption and investment, of the matrix of trade flows
among countries, of wage and price determination in each country, of the
main endogenous components of the government balance in each country, of
some rules for the determination of monetary policy, and of the portfolio
preferences and behavior of the private sectors and public sectors, especially
as it relates to the holding of foreign assets or the issuance of foreign liabilities. Exchange rates would also have to be determined, either fixed by some
constraints on the formation of monetary policy (possibly supplemented by
direct intervention in the form of either official purchases or sales of foreign
reserves, or by changing the currency mix of government debt issues), or
determined by the expectations and portfolio preferences of private market
participants, or perhaps by some combination of these mechanisms.

Some existing empirical models of international linkage have several of
these features, although not usually in a form that is sufficiently transparent
and comparable to permit the measurement and testing of the importance of
the various channels and factors that determine domestic and international
savings and investment. Where these models generally fall short is in their
supply-side structure and their ability to depict the longer-term trends in national output, investment, and savings. Nonetheless, they do have important
evidence to offer on some of the important questions of the day, such as, for
example, the extent to which there is a linkage between the Japanese and
U.S. current accounts, and how past and potential changes in exchange rates,
government spending, and taxation in the United States or Japan might affect
the structure and international distribution of savings and investment.

Most multinational models show that the U.S. current account will turn around relatively slowly even with further falls in the level of the U.S. dollar. It has already been suggested that national monetary authorities are likely to respond to the lower value of the dollar in part by lowering their own national interest rates, to some extent in direct response to their higher currencies, and to some extent in response to the lower prices and employment caused by the exchange rate changes.

What of the possibilities for fiscal policy to be used to accelerate the current account adjustment, or to ameliorate the depressive activity effects in the surplus countries? The model evidence is fairly unanimous that fiscal contraction in the United States has a material effect on the U.S. current account, acting partly through the exchange rate and partly through the in-duced effects on domestic spending, and hence on imports. For example, a sustained reduction of U.S. government spending equal to 1 percent of GNP would, in the third year, improve the U.S. annual current account by $US 14 billion, accompanied by a reduction of 2 percent in the real external value of the dollar.[24] A reduction of the U.S. dollar caused by fiscal contraction thus has much more impact on the current account[25] than is achieved by a "pure" or expectations-induced drop in the value of the dollar.[26] Whether there is any scope for faster reduction of the U.S. fiscal deficit probably depends more on internal politics in the United States than on anything decided or advised in international meetings. What these model results suggest clearly, however, is that no conceivable rate of reduction in the U.S. fiscal deficit will serve to eliminate the U.S. current account deficit before the end of the decade.[27]

What are the possibilities for and likely effects of fiscal expansion in the appreciating countries? Here the model evidence is again fairly unani-mous that fiscal expansion outside the United States does not have as big an impact on the U.S. and foreign current accounts as does fiscal change within the United States. The chief reason for this asymmetry is that fiscal expansion in other countries tends to lower the value of their currencies, or at any rate to raise their currencies by less than U.S. fiscal expansion raises the value of the U.S. dollar. This relative weakness of the domestic currency tends to reduce the current account effects of the change in domestic spending.[28] Thus fiscal expansion throughout the non-U.S. OECD[29] improves the U.S. current account by an average of $US 8 billion in the third year, accompanied by a reduction of 1.1 percent in the external value of the dollar.[30] These results suggest a fairly marked asymmetry, whereby U.S. fiscal contraction and for-eign fiscal expansion tend to decrease the value of the U.S. dollar by quite different amounts.[31] However, experiments with the latest version of the Eco-nomic Planning Agency's (EPA) world model (Yashiro 1987) show that mak-ing Japanese interest rates much more responsive to Japanese fiscal expansion by enough to cause the yen to appreciate rather than to depreciate, still does not cause a marked change in the Japanese bilateral current account with the United States. This is partly because the higher value of the yen lowers the size of the fiscal multiplier and hence cuts the income-induced demand for imports, and partly because the EPA model shows the income elasticity of demand for imports to be low in Japan and high in the United States.[32] In any event, the results suggest that fiscal expansion outside the United States has more effect on activity within the expanding countries and on their immediate neighbors,[33] than on either the current account or the activity level of the United States.

Putting the available evidence together, is it possible to draw some tentative conclusions about the likely future evolution of savings, investment, and external balances in the three countries? A preliminary list might include the following.

1. Even if the convergence hypothesis should not be borne out in a strict form, it is likely that the underlying rate of productivity growth in Japan will continue to approach North American rates. Under most models of comparative saving behavior, this will tend to cause the private saving rate in Japan to converge to that in North America.

2. Tax reforms planned or underway in the United States and Japan will change the tax treatment of interest expense in the United States and interest income in Japan in a way that will tend to raise saving rates in the United States and lower them in Japan. The Canadian tax system, in its treatment of private savings, is likely to remain intermediate between the other two.

3. Despite these factors favoring convergence of private saving rates, including efforts to build consensus in Japan that increased consumption spending may improve national welfare and the international trading environment, I suspect that the long planning horizons typically underlying Japanese savings and investment decisions will sustain high levels of government and private investment, coupled with private and government saving rates well above the international averages for countries with comparable levels of income. In these respects, convergence may involve some export of these attitudes from Japan to other countries rather than, or in addition to, Japanese adoption of international habits of spending and saving.

4. The long planning horizons used in Japan are likely to combine with changes in the demographic structure to keep Japanese saving rates, both public and private, high enough to provide for the retirement incomes of the very high proportion of older persons in the first quarter of the next century.[34]

5. Further development and internationalization of Japanese capital markets is likely to lead to fewer departures from equality among interest rates for the same type of asset, in the same currency, issued in different countries. Further movement toward international equality of ex ante real returns on equities and fixed interest securities with returns in different cur-

rencies is less certain, and is difficult to measure in any event. Some increased equality of returns on equities is likely to flow indirectly from the increasing internationalization of business ventures, with multinational locations for both production and sales becoming more typical for firms of all sizes.

6. The increasing ease with which production can be split among countries, which is part of the reason for the increased internationalization of business, is itself likely to contribute to the speed of the convergence process, especially for countries with incomes far below the world average. Since Japan has closer and more longstanding links with many of these countries, which include the "Little Dragons" of Southeast Asia as well as China, this may contribute to a drop in the Japanese domestic investment rate as Japanese-led ventures shift more of their production to lower-cost centers.

7. Convergence also implies that all three countries are likely to have less than world average growth rates of income, and especially of domestic output, as more countries establish themselves on paths of convergence. To the extent that real capital is internationally mobile, this is likely to lead to higher private savings and lower domestic investment than would otherwise be the case in each of the three countries. This possibility is contingent on the extent to which the emerging industrial economies generate high savings as counterparts to their high growth, and to the sensitivities of international bankers still burdened with nonperforming loans to developing countries.

Much of the above evidence has been derived from comparative analysis of the likely growth of output, savings, and investment in the three economies, supplemented by evidence from macroeconomic models of international linkage. Similar conclusions follow from direct analysis of the current account itself, as in Helkie and Hooper (1987) for the United States, under comparable assumptions about the growth of output and final spending. Of course, as I have emphasized throughout this paper, there is no conflict between the results flowing from alternative ways of viewing the current account. They are all equivalent and consistent when couched in a full macroeconomic framework that forces income, prices, and interest rates to take the values that satisfy the key structural relations that determine trade flows, capital flows, output, savings, and investment. In the absence of such a framework, it is important to compare the results from alternative partial approaches. If the results are mutually consistent, then they are probably making use of mutually consistent values for the key macroeconomic variables. If they are not, then there are strong grounds for proceeding directly to an explicit macroeconomic framework before accepting results from any of the apparently conflicting partial approaches. The intended contribution of this paper has been to provide some building blocks based on a comparative empirical review of some of the key structural relations determining savings, investment, and capital movements in each of the three countries.

Notes

1. A similar viewpoint is expressed by Feldstein (1983) and by Obstfeld (1986).

2. When saving rates are revised to include expenditure on consumer durables as investment rather than consumption, income is raised by an implicit rate of return on the stock, and consumption is changed by subtracting expenditures on consumer durables and adding in a rental charge equal to the replacement value of the stock multiplied by the sum of the depreciation rate and the rate of return. See, e.g., Boskin and Roberts (1986) or Ogawa, Takenaka, and Kuwana (1986).

3. Modigliani (1986) provides a retrospective survey of many of the key papers, and Blades and Sturm (1982) survey the results on comparative saving behavior.

4. To compute the net effect of social security on private savings, Modigliani and Sterling follow Feldstein's (1977) extended life-cycle model in also estimating the effect that more generous social security has on the labor force participation of those eligible for retirement benefits. Both studies find that retirement is influenced by social security and smaller labor force participation of the elderly increases savings, so that the net effect of social security on savings is smaller than the direct effect on savings. Feldstein (1977) estimates the net effect to be 20–30 percent smaller than the direct effect, while Modigliani and Sterling (1983) show a net effect that is very close to zero, although they are not confident of this result. The issue is important for current analysis, as Japan greatly increased the scale and coverage of its social security system during the 1970s.

5. Hayashi (1986, 172) notes that the theoretical presumption that high growth rates of income lead to increases in the saving rate may in fact be overturned if a country has, like Japan, a time profile of earnings that is skewed towards the higher age groups.

6. Implementing a recommendation in the Government Tax Commission's October 1986 review of the Japanese tax system, the availability of tax-free interest income was reduced in fiscal year 1987, especially for those with higher incomes.

7. Hayashi (1986, 197) suggests that the continuing importance of liquidity constraints can be consistent with the important role of the extended family if people do not realize the importance of the linear family until they reach middle age. I think it more likely that the young are aware of the importance of the family, but do not wish to draw personal benefits from it, and therefore save at high rates to accumulate resources to buy housing and consumer durables for their own use.

8. Boskin and Roberts (1986) calculate that affording the same treatment to military capital spending would make little difference to either the U.S. or the Japanese saving rates during the 1970s, but would raise the U.S. saving rate by 0.4 to 0.7 percentage points in the early 1980s.

9. These developments are surveyed by Bryant (1986) and Watson et al. (1986).

10. The capital stocks are converted to 1980 U.S. dollars using OECD (1987) PPP exchange rates for 1985. These new PPP figures are 225 yen/$US and 1.25 $C/ $US. The earlier data (Hill 1986) when updated to 1985 are 200 yen/$US and 1.13 $C/$US. Thus, U.S. real output per capita has risen by 10 percent relative to Canada and 16 percent relative to Japan because of the revision in the PPP numbers. This can

be seen by comparing figure 2.10 with figure 10 in Helliwell (1987). The units are called "international dollars" because PPP exchange rates rather than market exchange rates are used for conversion, and the PPPs are based on average OECD expenditure weights. The GDP and gross fixed capital formation data were obtained from OECD (1986).

11. The regressions are in logarithmic form; the coefficients on the unexpected sales variable are 2.0006, 4.4396, and 1.4113 for the United States, Japan, and Canada, respectively.

12. The parameters of the two-factor CES production structure are estimated by the procedures described for the estimation of the outer level of the two-level CES production structure (using a vintage bundle of capital and energy rather than, as here, the capital stock) described in more detail in Helliwell and Chung (1986).

13. The equation also includes the cyclical demand and profitability variables from the factor-utilization equation (11), because the factor-share ratio has, in addition to its responsiveness to relative prices, a cyclical variance caused by the fact that labor adjusts more quickly than the capital stock to changes in desired output. Except for the use of the cyclical variables and the distributed lag response to the relative price term (which tends to produce a higher estimated equilibrium elasticity of substitution), the estimation procedure follows that described by Helliwell et al. (1986, 125–27). Instrumental variables estimation is used.

14. In the case of constant efficiency growth, the elasticities of substitution are 0.99 for Japan, 0.97 for the United States, and 0.96 for Canada. In the catch-up case, the elasticities for Japan and Canada are 1.01 and 0.97, respectively.

15. In their examination of Japanese growth, Denison and Chung (1976) assumed that the Japanese rate of increase in output caused by advances in knowledge and other unmeasured factors would converge to that in the United States by 2002.

16. Among the seven countries studied in Helliwell, Sturm, and Salou (1985), the United Kingdom was the only one not to show some apparent evidence of convergence over the 1960 to 1982 period under study.

17. Normal output is not determined at this stage, of course, since the productivity index is not yet defined. The elasticity of substitution has been estimated as described above, and the scale and distribution parameters can be obtained from sample averages.

18. In the most general convergence model, both estimated coefficients and the constant term are free to take any values. This would permit each country to have an efficiency index that converged to its own specific growth path, with a growth rate different from that in other countries. As we have already seen, however, after these growth paths have crossed, the model of convergence turns into one of divergence.

19. This simple test is not completely satisfactory, since the cyclical departures from normal utilization rates, as modelled in the factor-utilization equation (11), are no doubt correlated with the "measured" efficiency bundle, thus biasing upward the coefficient on the lagged dependent variable and tilting the evidence in favor of the convergence model. Alternative tests regressing the "measured" efficiency bundle on catch-up and constant growth efficiency indexes also show the catch-up model to be much preferred by the data. Other evidence presenting a broader range of tests of the

convergence model, with specific allowance for cyclical elements, is reported in Helliwell, et al. (1986, 89–95).

20. Since the estimated constant terms (which were negative for both countries) were insignificant, they have been constrained to equal zero in the equations reported in table 2.2 and for the calculations reported in the text for the levels and rates of growth of efficiency levels in the catch-up model.

21. Other work, e.g., that reported in Fisher, Chung, and Helliwell (1986), applies the translog and other flexible functional forms that permit a more general modelling of technical progress, while simultaneously estimating the parameters of the utilization equation (11). This additional evidence tends in general to support convergence relative to a model of constant efficiency growth, although simple comparisons cannot be made because in the more general functional forms the rate of technical progress depends on the relative growth rates of the factors of production.

22. As reported in Helliwell, Sturm, and Salou (1985), the derived investment equations fit better when a constant, rather than a time-varying, series is used for the real supply price of capital. See also Fisher, Chung, and Helliwell (1986) for further tests of this sort. As Mitsuhiro Fukao rightly points out in his comment on my paper, the effect of interest rates on investment is likely to be an important part of the process whereby prices, exchange rates, and interest rates adjust so as to mutually determine savings, investment, and the current account in the macroeconomic context. He also presents some evidence from Fukao and Hanazaki (1987) showing the possible effects of the cost of capital on investment within the context of the OECD INTERLINK model of interdependent factor demands. However, the INTERLINK supply model is essentially the same as that presented in this paper, and the derived factor demands also fit better if the real rental price of capital is treated as a constant. For the purposes of model simulation, the INTERLINK factor demand equations have been estimated making use of a long moving average of real interest rates to provide better linkages between the financial and real sectors. I agree with this strategy, but the puzzle remains that the empirical evidence continues in general to show a preference for constant rather than variable measures for the real supply price of capital in the forward-looking choice of factor proportions.

23. Although there is a substantial incidence of lifetime employment in North America (e.g., Hall 1982), and the large majority of Japanese workers do not have lifetime jobs, comparative evidence shows that average job tenure in all age and education classes is longer in Japan than in the United States (Tachibanaki 1984). This does not mean that labor flexibility is less in Japan, however, as job rotation and acquisition of multiple skills within the enterprise are much more common in Japan than in the United States (Koike 1984).

24. These results are from a simulation with the U.S. and foreign money supplies held constant, and are summarized in table 16 of Helkie and Hooper (1987). There is a substantial range among the results averaged by Helkie and Hooper, as estimates of the current account effects range from $6 billion to $28 billion among the nine models.

25. About seven times as much, as a "pure" depreciation of the dollar improves the current account by about $US 1 billion for each percent change in the exchange

rate, while the fiscal contraction achieves a 14/2 = 7 billion improvement of the current account for each 1 percent change in the exchange rate.

26. These results, which have been added in the revised version of this paper, thus support the suggestion by Ron McKinnon in his comment on my paper that changes in the value of the dollar not brought about by changes in domestic absorption are unlikely to have substantial effects on the U.S. current account.

27. This evidence does not contradict the conclusions of Ueda (1985a, 1985b) that the differing stance of fiscal policy in Japan and the United States has been the main cause of their differing current account balances, but does suggest that reversal will take a considerable length of time.

28. As emphasized by the Japanese Economic Planning Agency World Economic Model Group (1986, 58–69), this result can be interpreted as one where the LM curve is flatter, relative to the BP curve, for other countries than it is in the United States. In the EPA model, the main reason for this is the difference between the LM curves.

29. In an amount equal to 1 percent of each country's GNP.

30. Over the same nine models whose results were averaged for U.S. fiscal policy, as recorded in Helkie and Hooper (1987, table 16).

31. It is suggested in Helliwell (1988) that at least some of this apparent difference may be due to modelling differences rather than differences in economic institutions, as many models of non-U.S. countries determine interest rates at least partly by reference to U.S. rates, while the reverse is not the case.

32. Bergsten and Cline (1987, appendix B) argue that there is a cyclical rather than a secular difference in income elasticities of import demand in the United States and Japan. They therefore do not share the view of the EPA modelling group (Yashiro 1987, 30) that there is a structural tendency for Japanese current account surplus and U.S. current account deficit that must be changed by structural policies. I have suggested earlier that the large and sustained Japanese current account surplus does make this a good time for structural policies designed to increase Japanese imports, assuming that the structural policies are justified in their own right.

33. This is especially important for the countries supplying materials to Japan and for all of the countries within the EEC.

34. Although the proportion of the population over 65 is now slightly higher in the United States than in Japan (as shown in figure 2.3), the Japanese Ministry of Finance (1986) forecasts that in 2020 the proportion of the population 65 and over will be 21.8 percent in Japan (more than twice the current ratio) compared to 15.4 percent in the United States. Mitsuhiro Fukao emphasizes, in his comment, the Japanese concerns about the scale of the medical and social security costs of this demographic bulge. The same issues face all three countries, although to a somewhat greater extent in Japan than in North America. The most striking difference among the three countries is in the extent to which these longer-term issues are highlighted in Japan while receiving much less attention in North America, where the planning horizons for both public and private decisions are much shorter. This difference is part of my reason for expecting that public and private saving rates in Japan will remain high until the end of the century and beyond, in anticipation of the costs of maintaining a large cohort of the aged in the first quarter of the next century.

References

Arnold, Brian J. 1986. *The taxation of foreign corporations: An international comparison.* Toronto: Canadian Tax Foundation.

Baumol, W. M. 1986. Productivity growth, convergence, and welfare: What the long-run data show. *American Economic Review* 76:1072–85.

Bergsten, C. F., and W. R. Cline. 1987. *The United States–Japan economic problem.* Policy Analyses in International Economics no. 13. Washington, D.C.: Institute for International Economics.

Blades, D. W., and P. H. Sturm. 1982. The concept and measurement of savings: The United States and other industrialized countries. Saving and Government Policy Conference Series no. 25, pp. 1–30. Boston: Federal Reserve Bank of Boston.

Boskin, M. J., and J. M. Roberts. 1986. A closer look at savings rates in the United States and Japan. Prepared for the Ministry of Finance, Japan/American Enterprise Conference, Washington, D.C., April 9–10, 1986.

Branson, W. H. 1979. Exchange rate dynamics and monetary policy. In *Inflation and employment in open economies,* ed. A. Lindbeck, 189–224. Amsterdam: North-Holland.

Bryant, R. C. 1986. The internationalization of financial intermediation: An empirical survey. *Brookings Discussion Papers in Economics* 51. Washington, D.C.: Brookings Institution.

Bryant, R., D. Henderson, et al., eds. 1988. *Empirical macroeconomics for interdependent economies.* Washington, D.C.: Brookings Institution.

Caramazza, F., K. Clinton, A. Cote, and D. Longworth. 1986. International capital mobility and asset substitutability: Some theory and evidence on recent structural changes. Bank of Canada Technical Reports 44, October.

Daly, M., J. Jung, P. Mercier, and T. Schweitzer. 1987. The taxation of capital income in Canada: An international comparison. *Canadian Tax Journal* 33:88–117.

Denison, E. F., and W. K. Chung. 1976. *How Japan's economy grew so fast.* Washington, D.C.: Brookings Institution.

Feldstein, M. S. 1977. Social security and private savings: International evidence in an extended life-cycle model. In *The economics of public services,* eds. M. S. Feldstein and R. Inman, 174–205. London: Macmillan.

———. 1983. Domestic saving and international capital movements in the long run and the short run. *European Economic Review* 21:129–51.

———. 1986. The budget deficit and the dollar. *NBER macroeconomics annual 1986,* ed. S. Fischer, 355–92. Cambridge, Mass.: National Bureau of Economic Research.

Feldstein, M. S., and C. Horioka. 1980. Domestic saving and international capital flows. *Economic Journal* 90:314–29.

Fisher, T. C. G., A. Chung, and J. F. Helliwell. 1986. A translog model of aggregate production and variable factor utilization. U.B.C. Department of Economics Discussion Paper no. 86–41. Vancouver: University of British Columbia.

Flavin, M. 1985. Excess sensitivity of consumption to current income: Liquidity constraints or myopia? *Canadian Journal of Economics* 18:117–36.

Frankel, J. A. 1985. International capital mobility and crowding out in the U.S. economy: Imperfect integration of financial markets or of goods markets? NBER Working Paper no. 1773. Cambridge, Mass.: National Bureau of Economic Research.

Frankel, J. A., M. Dooley, and D. Mathieson. 1986. International capital mobility in developing countries vs industrial countries: What do savings-investment correlations tell us? NBER Working Paper no. 2043. Cambridge, Mass.: National Bureau of Economic Research.

Fukao, M., and M. Hanazaki. 1987. Internationalisation of financial markets and the allocation of capital. *OECD Economic Studies* 8 (Spring).

Gylfason, T., and J. F. Helliwell. 1983. A synthesis of Keynesian, monetary and portfolio approaches to flexible exchange rates. *Economic Journal* 93:820–31.

Hall, R. E. 1978. Stochastic implications of the life cycle-permanent income hypothesis: Theory and evidence. *Journal of Political Economy* 86:971–87.

———. 1982. The importance of lifetime jobs in the U.S. economy. *American Economic Review* 72:716–24.

Hayashi, Fumio. 1982. Permanent income hypothesis: Estimation and testing by instrumental variables. *Journal of Political Economy* 90:895–918.

———. 1986. Why is Japan's saving rate so apparently high? *NBER macroeconomics annual 1986*, ed. S. Fischer, 147–210.

Helkie, W. L., and P. Hooper. 1987. The U.S. external deficit in the 1980s: An empirical analysis. *Brookings Discussion Papers in Economics* 58. Washington, D.C.: Brookings Institution.

Helliwell, J. F. 1987. Some comparative macroeconomics of the United States, Japan and Canada. U.B.C. Department of Economics Discussion Paper no. 87–04. Vancouver: University of British Columbia.

———. 1988. Macroeconomics for interdependent economies: What next? In *Empirical macroeconomics for interdependent economies,* eds. R. Bryant, D. Henderson, et al. Washington, D.C.: Brookings Institution.

Helliwell, J. F., and A. Chung. 1986. Aggregate output with variable rates of utilization of employed factors. *Journal of Econometrics* 33:285–310.

Helliwell, J. F., P. Sturm, P. Jarrett, and G. Salou. 1986. The supply side in the OECD's macroeconomic model. *OECD Economic Studies* 6 (Spring):75–131.

Helliwell, J. F., P. Sturm, and G. Salou. 1985. International comparison of the sources of productivity slowdown 1973–1982. *European Economic Review* 28:157–91.

Hill, Peter. 1986. International price levels and purchasing power parties. *OECD Economic Studies* 6:133–59.

Horiye, Y. 1985. Saving behaviour of the Japanese households. *Bank of Japan Monetary and Economic Studies* 3, no. 3 (December):47–128.

Japanese Ministry of Finance. 1986. *The budget in brief.* Tokyo: Budget Bureau, Ministry of Finance.

King, M. 1985. The economics of saving: A survey of recent contributions. In *Frontiers of economics,* eds. K. J. Arrow and S. Honkapojha, 227–94. Oxford: Blackwell.

King, M. A., and L. Dicks-Mireaux. 1982. Asset holding and the life cycle. *Economic Journal* 92:247–67.

King, M., and D. Fullerton, eds. 1984. *The taxation of income from capital: A comparative study of the United States, the United Kingdom, Sweden and West Germany.* Chicago: University of Chicago Press.

Koike, K. 1984. Skill formation systems in the U.S. and Japan: A comparative study. In *The economic analysis of the Japanese firm,* ed. M. Aoki, 47–75. Amsterdam: North-Holland.

Maddison, A. 1982. *Phases of capitalist development.* New York: Oxford University Press.

Marris, S. 1985. *Deficits and the dollar: The world economy at risk.* Washington, D.C.: Institute for International Economics.

Modigliani, F. 1986. Life cycles, individual thrift, and the wealth of nations. *American Economic Review* 76:297–313.

Modigliani, F., and A. Sterling. 1983. Determinants of private saving with special reference to the role of social security—Cross-country tests. In *The determinants of national saving and wealth,* eds. F. Modigliani and R. Hemming, 24–55. New York: St. Martin's Press.

Mundell, R. A. 1968. *International economics.* Chicago: University of Chicago Press.

Obstfeld, M. 1986. Capital mobility in the world economy: Theory and measurement. Carnegie-Rochester Series on Public Policy 24, pp. 55–104.

Ogawa, Kazuo, Heizo Takenaka, and Yasuo Kuwana. 1986. Recent patterns of consumption and savings behavior in Japan—Empirical results from a new series of consumption and income data. Discussion Paper no. 6. Institute of Fiscal and Monetary Policy, Ministry of Finance, Japan.

OECD. 1986. *National accounts.* Vol. 1, *Main aggregates.* Vol. 2, *Detailed tables.* Paris: OECD.

———. 1987. Purchasing power parities and international comparisons of price levels and real per capita GDP in OECD countries. OECD Press Release, February 10.

Sachs, J. D. 1981. The current account and macroeconomic adjustment in the 1980s. *Brookings Papers on Economic Activity* 12:201–68.

———. 1982. The current account in the macroeconomic adjustment process. *Scandinavian Journal of Economics* 84:147–59.

———. 1983. Aspects of the current account behaviour of OECD economies. In *Recent issues in the theory of flexible exchange rates.* eds. E. Classen and P. Salin. Amsterdam: North-Holland.

Shinohara, M. 1983. The determinants of post-war savings behaviour in Japan. In *The determinants of national savings and wealth,* eds. F. Modigliani and R. Hemming, 143–80. New York: St. Martin's Press.

Shoven, J. 1985. A comparison of the taxation of capital income in the United States and Japan. Mimeo. Palo Alto: Stanford University.

Tachibanaki, T. 1984. Labour mobility and job tenure. In *The economic analysis of the Japanese firm,* ed. M. Aoki, 77–102. Amsterdam: North-Holland.

Turner, Philip P. 1986. Savings, investment and the current account: An empirical study of seven major countries 1965–84. *Bank of Japan Monetary and Economic Studies* 4, no. 2 (October):1–58.

Ueda, Kazuo. 1985a. Investment-savings balance and the Japanese current account. Discussion Paper no. 1. Institute of Fiscal and Monetary Policy, Ministry of Finance, Japan.

———. 1985b. The Japanese current account surplus. Discussion Paper no. 2. Institute of Fiscal and Monetary Policy, Ministry of Finance, Japan.

Watson, M. et al. 1986. *International capital markets: Developments and prospects.* Washington, D.C.: International Monetary Fund.

Wirick, R. G. 1985. Canadian-American personal savings behaviour: Toward resolution of the paradoxes. Mimeo. London, Ontario: University of Western Ontario.

World Bank. 1986. The World Bank atlas 1986. Washington, D.C.: World Bank.

World Economic Model Group. 1986. The EPA world economic model: An overview. Discussion Paper no. 37. Economic Research Institute, Economic Planning Agency, Tokyo.

Yashiro, Naohiro. 1987. Exchange rate adjustment and macroeconomic policy coordination. Discussion Paper no. 41. Economic Planning Agency, Tokyo.

Comment

Ronald I. McKinnon

Helliwell is to be congratulated for his comprehensive coverage of an amazingly broad range of macroeconomic models which bear on what could determine the current accounts of international payments for Canada, Japan, and the United States.

First, he mentions the elasticities, absorption, Mundell-Fleming, and more general portfolio models of the balance of payments. Second, in longer-term perspective he considers comparative saving propensities of the three countries through the lens of the life-cycle model under alternative tax and demographic regimes. Third, he looks at the evolution of relative productivity growth through various convergence and catch-up models. In the course of this breathtaking survey of analytical constructs in different dimensions, he provides a wealth of comparative empirical data on the three countries' saving, investment, and outstanding demographic characteristics.

What does Helliwell's theoretical and empirical analysis tell us about the current huge imbalance in trade between Japan and the United States? He shows that Japan is naturally a high-saving country—"excessively" high insofar as the ordinary life-cycle model is concerned. And perhaps Japanese investment would naturally decline somewhat once technological catch-up, with labor productivity and compensation rising to American levels, had occurred. Obversely, net U.S. private saving remains very low by international standards, and in 1986 seems to have fallen even below the low level shown in Helliwell's figure 2.1 to only 3 or 4 percent of GNP.

However, these comparatively gradual long-term trends cannot explain the sudden emergence of large U.S. trade deficits and Japanese trade surpluses in the mid-1980s. Instead, the rapid rise in the structural U.S. fiscal deficit, for which Japanese investors are providing much of the finance, is the obvious explanation. In the mid-1980s, American private saving has not risen to offset the sharp increase in dissaving by the federal government. With the recovery of American private investment in 1985–87 back to a normal full-employment level, the dollar value of the American trade deficit increased to between 150 to 200 billion dollars per year—the same order of magnitude as the American fiscal deficit.

Differences in North American Saving Patterns

However, Helliwell's analysis of the fascinating Canadian data is a useful antidote to the idea that large fiscal deficits are inevitably associated with large trade deficits. In the 1980s, figure 2.5 shows that government dissaving rose even faster in Canada than in the United States. As a share of GNP, the Canadian fiscal deficit is even bigger than the American in 1987! Yet this was offset by a remarkable increase in Canadian private saving from the late 1970s to the mid-1980s, so as to give Canada a small current account surplus in the mid-1980s.

Which North American experience of a large fiscal deficit is more "typical" in its impact on the balance of trade? Does the Canadian or the U.S. case better represent how one should presume private and public net saving are related to one another?

At first glance, the Canadian experience seems to vindicate the Feldstein-Horioka hypothesis that capital markets are not well integrated internationally: national saving and investment—and the current account of international payments—are "forced" into a rough balance for each country. Because it cannot be financed internationally, a fiscal deficit would drive up "real" rates of interest within the country until there was a corresponding fall in private investment or an increase in private saving.

Although nominal interest rates in Canada have, at times, been one to two percentage points above their American counterparts, real interest rates have not moved markedly differently from those south of the border—given that price inflation has been a bit higher in Canada, and that Canadians are well known to have ready access to the New York capital markets. Thus differential interest rate movements in the two countries cannot explain their different responses to burgeoning fiscal deficits, as manifested in current account deficits in the United States and a rough balance in Canada.

The Feldstein-Horioka hypothesis of "insulated" national capital markets does not hold up. Instead, one must look at differing institutional circumstances in the two countries.

Helliwell mentions the much more generous tax treatment of individual retirement plans in Canada beginning in the mid-1970s. Being "defined contribution" plans, they are particularly attractive for savings when nominal interest rates are high—but take some time to accumulate to the point of inducing substantial increases in new net saving—as seems to have occurred by the early 1980s. (On the other hand, interest payments on household debt cannot be deducted from Canadians' tax liabilities.) Thus we get a once-and-for-all increase in the Canadian private propensity to save which (accidentally?) coincided with the rapid increase in the Canadian fiscal deficit.

In the United States, however, the experience with individual retirement accounts of the defined contribution type was very small scale and short lived from 1981 to 1986. Americans never succeeded in accumulating sufficient assets in this tax-sheltered form to include an increase in private net saving. Worse, most American private saving is institutionalized in the form of "defined benefit" plans managed by private corporations. Thus, when interest rates increase, companies actually *reduce* their contributions as my colleague John Shoven has analyzed. In effect, companies behave as target savers: higher interest rates allow them to meet their fixed future pension payments with lesser current contributions. In addition, interest payments on consumer (mortgage) debt can still be deducted from taxable income in the United States, with only slightly more difficulty under the new tax reform law. Hence, American private saving might well respond perversely to any (incipient) increase in nominal interest rates arising out of, say, a government budget deficit.

And, more than most countries, the United States has had virtually unique access to the international capital market. Because of its special status as reserve-currency country, the United States has—up to now—been able to sell massive amounts of Treasury bonds and private securities to foreign private trust funds and official institutions (such as central banks) denominated in dollars, thus avoiding foreign exchange risk. Hence, domestic interest rates in the United States have not had to be bid up much, and domestic investment has been well maintained despite the huge U.S. fiscal deficit.

In summary, the American economy exhibits negative or zero Ricardian equivalence on the saving side: private saving seems to have fallen a bit in response to the huge increase in government dissaving. In contrast, private saving has increased sharply (and investment fallen a little) in Canada in response to that government's equally pronounced fiscal profligacy. But different institutional circumstances, rather than the private sector's concern for future tax liabilities, seem sufficient to explain the differing responses of the two countries.

Generally, Helliwell's analysis indicates no natural tendency for the current account to remain invariant to fiscal deficits, unlike what either the Feldstein-Horioka model or Barro's Ricardian equivalence theorem suggest.

If a country's structural fiscal deficit (not financed by the inflation tax) suddenly increases, there is a strong presumption that a financially open economy will develop a corresponding deficit in its trade balance, as illustrated by the American experience of the 1980s.

The Role of the Exchange Rate in the Net Transfer of Capital

A more subtle question not treated in Helliwell's already extensive survey is whether or not exchange rate changes are a useful part of the process of transferring capital net from one country to another. Among advocates of exchange rate flexibility, there are "doves" and "hawks" in the current debate on whether or not exchange rate changes can systematically influence the net trade balance measured in foreign or domestic currency.

The dovish position is that, while exchange rate changes by themselves do not predictably affect an open economy's investment/saving balance, they facilitate net transfers of capital when a saving gap develops for other reasons. For example, given the emergence of the U.S. fiscal deficit in the early 1980s, exchange rate doves would suggest that the appreciation of the U.S. dollar speeded up and accentuated the subsequent development of a large (offsetting) American trade deficit.

The hawkish position is that exchange rate changes *by themselves* can systematically alter the balance of trade, and thus (implicitly) force some change in an open economy's saving/investment balance. For example, consider the great fall in the dollar from February 1985 to the present time (June 1987). Even though the U.S. fiscal deficit remains as large as ever, throughout 1986–87 many economists have actively advocated further dollar devaluation—below any reasonable measure of purchasing power parity—in order to reduce the dollar value of the U.S. trade deficit and net transfer of capital from abroad.

Let us consider both the hawkish and, seemingly more reasonable, dovish arguments for exchange rate flexibility.

The Exchange Rate and the Trade Balance Without Fiscal Correction: The Hawks

After the sharp appreciations of the mark and yen over the past two years, most economists expected that the German and Japanese loss of "international competitiveness," i.e., the relatively higher prices of their goods on world markets, would reduce their trade surpluses as conventionally measured in terms of dollars. Why weren't these direct price effects on the flow of imports and exports strong enough?

First, with sticky internal prices for domestically produced goods in each country, exchange appreciation improved the terms of trade of continental Europe and Japan against the United States. Hence Japanese and Europeans earned more dollars per unit of exports without paying any more per unit of imports.

Second, to keep their currencies appreciated(ing) to satisfy the American government, Japan and Germany have been forced to maintain relatively tight monetary policies. Indeed, in open economies the exchange rate itself is a manifestation of the relative tightness of national monetary policies. Moreover, currency appreciation directly forces (and signals) a decline in domestic prices, but with a considerable lag. Because of this expectation of domestic deflation to come, real rates of interest increase, thus putting the brake on domestic absorption.

In the continental European and Japanese economies from 1986 into 1987, therefore, internal deflations so depressed their demand generally for goods and services that their physical volumes of exports relative to imports did not fall sufficiently to offset their more favorable terms of trade. Consequently, both the Japanese and German net trade surpluses measured in dollars actually *increased* in 1986 and 1987.

That these terms of trade and domestic expenditure effects offset the direct price effects (loss of German and Japanese international competitiveness) was no accident. The huge U.S. trade deficit of about 150 to 200 billion dollars per year is rooted in the excessive American proclivity to spend for goods and services above what the U.S. economy can produce at close to full employment.

Given the still commanding reserve-currency status of the U.S. dollar in world finance, the American fiscal deficit acts as a huge vacuum cleaner that sucks up other countries' saving through the pre-emptive issue of U.S. Treasury bonds in world financial markets. Consequential macroeconomic adjustments then force them to generate dollar surpluses in their commodity trade, whether or not they have appreciated their exchange rates. Of course, forced deflation in Japan and Europe is not the only possible macroeconomic adjustment to secure the transfer of saving to America when foreign currencies are overvalued. An inflationary boom in the United States that sucked in imports, despite the undervalued dollar, would obviate the need for deflation abroad. In either case, however, the U.S. trade deficit would continue to be of the same order of magnitude as the U.S. fiscal deficit.

Because the great 1985–87 depreciation of the dollar has had, and will have, no substantial impact on the structural fiscal imbalance and consequent saving shortage in the American economy, it is incapable of correcting the U.S. trade deficit short of precipitating a major collapse of domestic investment within the United States.

The Exchange Rate and the Trade Balance With Fiscal Correction:
The Doves

But what about the ostensibly more reasonable position that a large devaluation of the dollar would be warranted if the United States were to dramatically reduce its fiscal deficit and thus make possible an improvement in the net trade balance? (Presumably, without any fiscal improvement in sight, a "true" dove would not argue for any devaluation of the dollar below purchasing power parity.)

Somewhat surprisingly, however, roughly the same arguments used against the exchange rate hawks also apply against the doves. A large dollar devaluation would set in motion inflationary pressure over a broad range of tradable goods industries in the United States. American real interest rates would fall, thereby inducing domestic absorption to increase and thus partially offsetting the impact of the reduced fiscal deficit. Conversely, in Japan and Europe, the deflationary pressure from currency overvaluation would impede the increase in their absorption necessary to rebalance foreign trade.

True, the position of the exchange rate doves is much more reasonable. There is less risk of an inflationary explosion in the devaluing country—or undue deflationary pressure in countries with appreciated currencies—if fiscal correction accompanies the exchange rate change.

Nevertheless, major exchange rate deviations away from purchasing power parity still cause aggregate absorption to move in the "wrong" direction for effecting transfer from the devaluing country to the one whose currency has appreciated. For example, the large appreciation of the U.S. dollar in the early 1980s reflected the Federal Reserve's switch from an easy to a tight monetary policy. This so deflated the American economy over 1981–83 as to delay the emergence of a trade deficit in response to the fiscal imbalance, which had developed at the same time.

Conclusion

Among highly open economies, there is a case to be made that international transfers of capital are better expedited without changes in nominal exchange rates. If mutual monetary policies are adjusted to keep the exchange rate close to purchasing power parity, direct adjustments in the investment/savings balance—by, say, correcting a fiscal deficit—will show up faster and more fully in a country's balance of trade.

In particular, the great rise in the U.S. dollar in the early 1980s did not expedite the development of the large U.S. trade deficit, which was (and is) a consequence of the large U.S. fiscal deficit. Similarly, the great fall of the dollar in 1986–87 will not itself have any predictable impact on the dollar value of the net U.S. trade deficit with the fiscal deficit remaining unchanged.

To be sure, such large exchange rate changes have major disruptive impacts on the macroeconomics of the United States and its trading partners, imposing unexpected inflations or deflations (McKinnon 1984). So too do actual, and the potential for future, exchange rate changes greatly increase uncertainty and reduce the efficiency of long-lived industrial investments (McKinnon 1988). But what exchange rate flexibility does not have is the oft alleged redeeming virtue of facilitating "proper" adjustment in the balance of trade.

References

McKinnon, Ronald I. 1984. *An international standard for monetary stabilization.* Washington, D.C.: Institute for International Economics.
————. 1988. Monetary and exchange rate policies for international financial stability: A proposal. *Journal of Economic Perspectives* Winter.

Comment
Mitsuhiro Fukao

Helliwell's paper deftly summarizes various analytical frameworks for the current account imbalances and shows the historic behavior of sectoral savings and total investment in the United States, Japan, and Canada. His summary of the theories of balance of payments emphasizes the investment/ saving (I-S) balance approach and the general equilibrium aspect of the determinants of saving and investment. Regarding sectoral saving behavior, he presents useful charts for international comparisons and surveys the empirical analyses of the private saving rates of the three countries, which are mainly conducted in the framework of the Life Cycle–Permanent Income hypothesis. With regard to the main cause of the high saving rate in Japan compared with the other two countries, Helliwell basically accepts the results of the Modigliani and Sterling model, which emphasizes the importance of the high income growth rate of Japan relative to Canada and the United States. After briefly discussing government saving, Helliwell analyzes the issue of foreign saving and international capital mobility. He takes an eclectic view; while financial assets in different currencies are far from being perfect substitutes, sectoral saving rates, investment, and capital movements are determined interdependently.

On the investment side, Helliwell analyzes the behavior of total domestic investment. With a sophisticated econometric technique, he analyzes the relationships among capital, labor, and output. His main working hypothesis is the "catch-up model." That is, the indices of labor efficiency in Japan and in Canada start at a level below that in the United States and then gradually approach the U.S. level. He shows that the empirical evidence is consistent with this hypothesis. Under this hypothesis, the Japanese growth rate will gradually fall in the future.

In his concluding section, he suggests that, as the productivity of Japan catches up with that of the United States, the productivity growth rate of Japan is likely to decline. The consequent fall in the growth rate of Japan will lower its private saving rate. However, the level of Japan's saving rate is likely to stay above rates in the other countries.

Some Observations

I read this paper with much interest because I have been studying the underlying determinants of current account balances in the major industrialized countries. Helliwell's analysis of the supply side of the economy was especially enlightening to me. On the other hand, I was rather disappointed that Helliwell did not provide his prognosis on the evolution of current balances of the three countries. It is true that the synthesis of all the factors affecting I-S balances of these countries is a very difficult task. He suggests using a large multicountry model for this synthesis like OECD's INTERLINK model, which incorporates the supply side of the economy. However, models cannot replace human judgments because any model forecast has to rely on the strategic scenario by forecasters. Therefore, the absence of Helliwell's judgment concerning the relative importance of I-S components on the current balances was disappointing.

I also have some reservations about the analyses in the paper. Firstly, I am concerned with the relative lack of attention given to the aging of a population and its interaction with the government sector via the pension system. Since personal saving depends importantly on the life cycle of the individual, demographic factors would affect the national saving rate. Secondly, the international aspect of the I-S balance did not receive enough attention. Since one country's current account surplus corresponds to the deficit of other countries, the ex ante I-S balance of one country cannot determine its current balance by itself. International linkage of national economies through the flow of capital and goods reconciles the ex ante I-S balances with the movements of real variables, as well as such financial variables as interest rates and exchange rates.

Aging of a Population and the Role of the Government

In addition to the recorded government saving discussed by Helliwell, the unfunded pension system can significantly affect the long-run behavior of the private saving rate. Japan is experiencing a very rapid aging of its population due to a highly skewed population pyramid. According to a recent estimate, the ratio of the old age population above 65 years old in the total population will increase from 10 percent in 1985 to 22 percent in 2020. This 22 percent is probably higher than the corresponding rates in the United States or in Canada. Since the financing of the Japanese pension system is close to the pay-as-you-go system, the social security tax rate for pensions is expected to increase from the current 10 percent of annual employee income to about 23 percent by 2020. Aging of population is also expected to raise the social security tax on medical care. According to an estimate by Japan's Economic Planning Agency, the demographic factor alone is likely to raise the social security tax rate on medical care from the current 6–7 percent of annual employee income to about 9 percent. Therefore, given the existing social security system, the total tax rate on employee income is likely to rise by 15–16 percentage points by 2020, which is thirty-three years from now.

Thirty-three years is not a very long time from the viewpoint of a person's life-cycle. If Japan's private saving rate declines as the total tax rate rises, it can greatly affect the I-S balance. Since this crowding out of saving by an increased tax rate has been observed in the data of the past ten years, this is a likely outcome.

Another important factor in the more immediate future is the prospect of a surplus in the social security fund of the Japanese government. Although the Japanese pension system is close to the pay-as-you-go system as mentioned earlier, it generates a significant surplus due to the skewed age structure. In recent years, it has been running a surplus of 2.5–3 percent of GNP. But, the surplus is likely to decline rapidly to about 1 percent of GNP in five years. Therefore, the rapidly aging population of Japan and its interaction with the social security system will play a very important role in determining the Japanese saving rate.

Although the population in the United States and in Canada is aging less quickly, this demographic development is an important determinant of the long-term trend of the saving rate in these countries. In the United States, private pension funds are a very important component of saving, with accumulated assets of about 1.7 trillion dollars in 1985. The U.S. social security system would also affect the behavior of the private sector in the long run.

To sum up, the aging process and its interaction with the social security system are very important determinants of the saving rate in the long run and thus deserve careful attention in their own right.

International Capital Mobility

Helliwell treats the investment of each country rather independently. His estimated investment function (table 2.4) does not include cost of capital variables. However, when one country has excess investment, it experiences a high real interest rate. This high real interest rate can be transmitted through various channels. Firstly, the currency of the country with the high real interest rate tends to appreciate against other currencies. Trading partners will have increased exports due to improved competitiveness, which will tend to increase income and push up the real interest rate. Secondly, international arbitrage in financial markets can directly transmit high real interest rates. Borrowers shift out of high interest markets to low interest markets. Investors also shift their funds from low interest to high interest markets. Finally, monetary policy can transmit high real interest rates. Since most countries are concerned with their exchange rate, monetary policy is often partially directed to the stabilization of exchange rates. When one country experiences a depreciating exchange rate due to high foreign real interest rates, monetary authorities tend to raise interest rates to sustain the external value of the currency. Thus, a high real interest rate in one country tends to spread to other countries, causing an international crowding-out process.

Since investment depends on the cost of capital, international financial linkage through interest rates and exchange rates plays a very important role in reconciling the ex ante international inconsistency of I-S balances. Even if one country's saving is expected to decline, it does not necessarily imply that its current account balance will deteriorate. If the other country's investment is very strong, it can even experience an improvement of its current account through the international crowding-out process. In view of this phenomenon and increasing international capital movements, the analysis of investment behavior has to take account of the cost of capital.

In Fukao and Hanazaki (1987), an estimate was made of the elasticity of business capital demand with respect to the real user of capital based on the supply block of OECD's INTERLINK model. In general, the elasticities of the seven major countries were about unity. According to these estimates, a one-percentage-point change in the real cost of capital changes the demand for business capital by about 10–20 percent of GNP in the long run. Obviously, these estimates overstate the likely outcome because they assume a classical equilibrium world with no frictions. However, they imply that a persistent difference in the cost of capital can eventually induce large international capital flows. Since corporate tax systems can easily create tax wedges of a few percentage points between the cost of capital and market real interest rates, the tax system can also affect the I-S balance among countries. Therefore, as international capital movements increase, the behavior of investment would become more difficult to analyze unless account were taken of the cost of capital.

Reference

Fukao, M., and M. Hanazaki. 1987. Internationalization of financial markets and the allocation of capital. *OECD Economic Studies* 8 (Spring).

3 Trade and Investment Patterns and Barriers in the United States, Canada, and Japan

Yoko Sazanami

3.1 Introduction

International trade flows between the United States, Canada, and Japan showed a substantial expansion in the early 1980s. The growth in trade between the United States and Japan was accompanied by a widening Japanese trade surplus. This trade imbalance rose from $9.9 billion in 1980 to $43 billion in 1985 (see table 3.1 below). Canada was one of the few developed countries whose bilateral trade with Japan showed a surplus at the beginning of the 1980s. However, by 1985, this surplus had turned into a small deficit.

The growing trade surplus of Japan vis-à-vis the United States has considerably strained the trade relations between the two countries. The disputes range from charges that Japan's exports are causing serious damage to U.S. manufactures (for instance, carbon and alloy steel products, color TVs, and automobiles) to criticism of the limited access to Japanese markets (oranges, beef, and some industrial products). The United States and Japan have coped differently with these trade frictions. The United States has relied increasingly on special import-restricting protectionist measures against Japan.[1] On the other hand, the Japanese government has announced an array of measures to liberalize imports, including the removal of disputed import quotas on leather and leather products.[2] These liberalization measures were adopted even though many studies have shown that current Japanese tariff and nontariff barriers are not particularly high in comparison to other industrialized countries.[3]

Despite the policy measures that were adopted on both sides of the Pacific, the bilateral trade imbalance did not change as much as expected even after the substantial appreciation of the yen following the G-5 agreement of September 1985. Japan's trade surplus reached a monthly record of $9.8 billion in September 1986. Part of the failure of both U.S. and Japanese trade policy to reduce the bilateral trade imbalance may be due to the fact that a current account deficit (or surplus) primarily reflects the balance between domestic investment and savings. Japan's savings surplus over its investment is especially clear in relation to the current account surplus with its largest trading partner, the United States, whose savings fall short of its investment needs. Nonetheless, changes in trade policies are important because they affect the commodity composition of trade flows as well as the investment behavior of firms.

Section 3.2 of this paper gives a more detailed empirical overview of the trade between the United States, Canada, and Japan. Changes in the commodity composition of trade are examined for the 1975–80 and 1980–85 periods. Microeconomic reasons are given for the steadily increasing Japanese trade surplus with the United States. The shrinking Canadian trade surplus with Japan is further interpreted in the light of a reduced Japanese dependence on industries that rely heavily on imported raw materials.

As mentioned earlier, the large Japanese trade surplus with the United States has worsened trade frictions between the two countries. Section 3.3 reviews the major trade issues raised between the United States, Canada, and Japan. Attention is also given to how the introduction (or removal) of trade barriers may have affected commodity trade and investment flows.

With a $56 billion trade surplus in 1985, Japan became an important supplier of capital to the world. Japan's direct investment reached a record high of $6.4 billion in the same year. Among the notable changes in Japan's direct investment in the early 1980s were the increased importance of investment in manufacturing industries, particularly in the United States, and the decline of investments in resource-related products. [The new direct investment in the United States was mostly situated in the electrical and electronics industries, automobiles, and iron and steel. It was primarily caused by the introduction of voluntary export restraints (VERs), which encouraged Japanese firms to move their production to the United States] Section 3.4 provides an overview of direct investment flows from Japan to the United States and to Canada.

Another important change in Japanese direct investment patterns in the early 1980s was the increase in investment in banking and insurance. Japanese institutions found promising investment opportunities in foreign financial markets for their ample financial resources supplied by excess domestic savings. As Japanese bankers accumulated managerial skills by operating in the less regulated foreign markets, they felt the burden of the regulations at home and supported a deregulation of the domestic market. Also, foreign demands for reciprocity in financial operations helped to liberalize Japanese financial markets. Those changes have increased foreign investment in Japan,[4] an issue which is also discussed in section 3.4.

The increase in direct investment from and into Japan reflects the internationalization of business activities in Japan. Japanese firms, which had largely concentrated their efforts on exports and on setting up subsidiaries and branch offices to supplement their sales abroad, started to build foreign plants. Typical examples involved color TVs and autos. Section 3.5 examines how the U.S. decision to impose VERs and Orderly Market Agreements (OMAs) on these products in 1977 and 1981 affected the trade and investment flows from Japan to the United States and to Canada.

Until the trend was reversed in September 1985, one of the major trade issues between the United States and Japan was the undervaluation of the yen and its impact on trade flows. Now that the yen has appreciated by nearly 40 percent between September 1985 and September 1986, the question arises whether this appreciation will reduce the bilateral trade imbalance. In section 3.6, the evolution of Japanese trade after September 1985 is examined. I will discuss whether the exchange rate appreciation has been passed through to export and import prices, to what extent trade flows have been affected by the exchange rate change, and assess the possible impact of exchange rate fluctuations on future investment flows. The final section addresses future policy issues in the trade and investment relations between the United States, Canada, and Japan.

3.2 Merchandise Trade Between the United States, Canada, and Japan

The importance of merchandise trade in multilateral and bilateral economic relations between the United States, Canada, and Japan is illustrated in table 3.1. For Japan, trade with the United States accounted for more than two-thirds of the $56 billion surplus in its merchandise account in 1985. Japan's deficits in the service and transfer accounts with the United States and with the rest of the world were rather modest. In 1985, the Japanese current account surplus with the United States, including investment income, amounted to $41.8 billion. The global Japanese current account showed a $49.1 billion surplus. Japan's share in the U.S. trade deficit declined between 1980 and 1985, but it still accounts for one-third of the total. One of the important changes that occurred in the early 1980s was that Japan's capital investments (both direct and indirect) were increasingly directed toward the United States. As a result, the Japanese surplus in investment income from the United States increased from $400 million in 1980 to $2.3 billion in 1985. If this trend continues, the bilateral current account imbalance will increase even further.

The overall importance of Japan in the Canadian balance of payments is rather small. The trade surplus with Japan was gradually reduced in the 1980s and was replaced by a small deficit in 1985.

Table 3.2 shows a sectoral disaggregation of the Japanese trade structure. The total import growth in manufactured (SITC 5, 6, 7) and food products (SITC 0) during the 1980–85 period was offset by a decline in imports of crude materials (SITC 2) and mineral fuels (SITC 3) due to a combination

Table 3.1 Japanese Balance of Payments 1975, 1980, 1985 (in billion $US)

	1975			1980			1985		
	Exports	Imports	Balance	Exports	Imports	Balance	Exports	Imports	Balance
Current account total									
U.S.	16.8	17.8	-1.0	42.2	35.9	6.3	81.3	39.5	41.8
Canada	1.2	2.3	-1.1	2.8	4.7	-1.9	5.4	4.7	0.7
World	68.4	69.2	-0.80	158.5	169.4	-10.9	219.9	170.8	49.1
Merchandise									
U.S.	10.9	9.9	1.0	32.4	21.5	9.9	65.6	22.6	43.0
Canada	1.1	2.1	-1.0	2.4	4.4	-2.0	4.4	4.2	0.2
World	54.7	49.7	5.0	128.7	124.6	2.1	174.0	118.0	56.0
Services									
U.S.	4.1	5.7	-1.8	7.3	11.1	-3.8	9.1	12.3	-3.2
Canada	0.1	0.2	-0.1	0.3	0.3	*	0.5	0.5	*
World	9.9	15.0	-5.1	20.3	32.6	-12.3	23.4	35.4	-12.0
Investment income									
U.S.	1.5	1.8	-0.3	3.3	2.9	0.4	6.4	4.1	2.3
Canada	*	*	*	0.1	*	0.1	0.5	*	0.5
World	3.6	3.9	-0.3	11.1	10.3	0.8	22.1	15.3	6.8
Transfer									
U.S.	0.1	0.2	-0.1	0.2	0.4	-0.2	0.2	0.5	-0.3
Canada	*	*	*	*	*	*	*	*	*
World	0.2	0.6	-0.4	0.4	1.9	-1.5	0.4	2.1	-1.7
Capital account (long-term capital only)									
Direct investment									
U.S.	-0.6	0.1	-0.5	-0.8	0.1	-0.7	-2.5	0.5	-2.0
Canada	*	*	*	*	*	*	0.1	*	-0.1
World	-1.8	0.2	-1.6	-2.4	0.3	-2.1	-6.4	0.6	-5.8
Securities									
U.S.	0.04	0.4	0.44	1.6	1.4	3.0	-31.6	1.7	-29.9
Canada	0.01	*	*	-2.5	*	-2.5	-1.7	-0.2	-1.9
World	-0.02	2.8	2.8	-3.8	13.2	9.4	-59.8	16.7	-43.1

*Negligible
Sources: Bank of Japan, *Balance of Payments Monthly*; Statistics Canada, Quarterly estimates of Canadian balance of international payments.

Table 3.2 Sectoral Disaggregation of Japan's Trade with the World, the United States, and Canada (in billion $US)

		Exports (fob)								
		1975			1980			1985		
Commodities	SITC	World	U.S.	Canada	World	U.S.	Canada	World	U.S.	Canada
Total	1–9	55.8	11.3	1.2	129.5	31.6	2.4	175.6	66.0	4.5
Food and live animal	0	0.7	0.2	*	1.4	0.2	*	1.2	0.4	*
Beverage and tobacco	1	*	*	*	*	*	*	*	*	*
Crude materials	2	0.8	0.04	*	1.5	*	*	1.3	0.1	*
Mineral fuels	3	*	*	*	0.5	*	*	0.6	0.1	*
Animal and vegetable oils	4	*	*	*	0.1	*	*	0.1	*	*
Chemicals	5	3.9	0.3	*	6.6	0.8	*	7.5	1.4	0.1
Manufactured goods	6	17.5	3.1	0.3	31.2	5.5	0.5	28.9	6.8	0.6
Machinery, transport equipment	7	27.4	6.0	0.6	75.8	22.0	1.5	119.2	50.8	3.8
Power machinery	71	0.9	0.1	*	3.5	0.6	*	5.0	1.4	*
Machinery for industries	72	2.0	0.2	*	5.1	0.7	0.1	7.4	2.1	0.2
Metalworking machinery	73	0.5	0.1	*	1.9	0.6	*	3.0	1.1	*
General industrial machinery	74	2.6	0.3	*	6.5	0.9	0.1	7.9	1.9	*
Office machine, data equipment	75	0.8	0.3	*	3.4	1.2	0.1	10.5	5.4	0.2
Telecommunication equipment	76	3.3	1.2	0.1	12.2	3.2	0.3	21.5	10.1	0.7
Electrical machinery	77	2.8	0.5	*	8.9	1.7	0.1	14.7	4.3	0.7
Road vehicles	78	8.2	3.1	0.3	29.4	12.6	0.8	42.9	23.9	1.6
Other transport equipment	79	6.3	0.1	*	5.0	0.5	*	6.3	0.7	*
Misc. manufacture	8	4.4	1.3	0.1	10.8	2.7	0.2	14.9	5.7	0.4
n.e.c.	9	0.7	0.3	*	1.3	0.3	*	1.7	0.7	*

Imports (cif)

Total	1–9	57.9	11.6	2.5	139.9	24.4	4.7	127.5	25.9	4.7
Food and live animal	0	8.4	2.3	0.7	14.0	4.9	0.8	14.8	4.7	0.9
Beverage and tobacco	1	0.4	0.2	*	0.7	0.3	*	0.8	0.4	*
Crude materials	2	11.5	3.1	1.1	24.5	6.8	2.4	18.2	4.7	1.9
Mineral fuels	3	25.7	1.9	0.6	70.6	2.1	0.7	55.9	1.9	1.2
Animal and vegetable oils	4	0.2	*	*	0.3	0.1	*	0.3	0.1	*
Chemicals	5	2.1	0.8	*	5.9	2.5	0.2	7.9	3.5	0.3
Manufactured goods	6	3.6	0.7	0.1	9.7	1.8	0.3	10.4	1.5	0.3
Machinery, transport equipment	7	3.8	2.0	*	8.4	4.3	0.1	10.6	6.5	0.1
Power machinery	71	0.3	0.2	*	0.6	0.4	*	1.1	0.8	*
Machinery for industries	72	0.3	0.1	*	0.9	0.3	*	0.9	0.3	*
Metalworking machinery	73	0.1	*	*	0.3	0.1	*	0.3	0.1	*
General industrial machinery	74	0.8	0.4	*	1.0	*	*	1.2	0.6	*
Office machine, data equipment	75	0.5	0.2	*	1.1	0.7	*	1.6	1.2	*
Telecommunication equipment	76	0.2	0.1	*	0.4	0.2	*	0.5	0.3	*
Electrical machinery	77	0.8	0.4	*	1.7	0.9	*	2.5	1.5	*
Road vehicles	78	0.3	0.1	*	0.6	0.2	*	0.8	0.1	*
Other transport equipment	79	0.5	0.4	*	1.6	0.9	*	1.8	1.6	*
Misc. manufacture	8	2.0	0.5	*	5.4	1.6	*	6.9	1.9	*
n.e.c.	9	0.2	*	*	0.9	0.1	*	1.7	0.7	*

*Negligible

Source: OECD, Statistics of foreign trade, series B.

of falling prices and declining demand. As a result, total imports were lower in 1985 than in 1980. While imports stagnated, exports continued to grow as a handful of industries, including automobiles, electric equipment, and electronics, successfully introduced new and improved products on the foreign market.

Japan's trade relations with the United States and Canada generally reflect the same trends as the world trade figures. Although Japanese imports from the United States increased markedly in chemicals and transport equipment in the early 1980s, most of this increase was offset by a decline of imports of foods (SITC 0) and manufactured goods (SITC 6). In those products, the United States lost some of its market share in Japan to imports from Southeast Asian countries. Between 1980 and 1985 the increase in Japanese imports from the United States was a mere $1.5 billion, while Japanese exports to the United States increased by $34.4 billion. Changes in Japan's composition of industrial output and the falling prices of crude materials and fuels reduced the Canadian trade surplus with Japan.

Japan's export dependence on the U.S. market showed a phenomenal increase in the early 1980s. The share of the United States in total Japanese exports increased from 20 percent in 1975 to 24 percent in 1980, and reached 38 percent in 1985 (see table 3.2). The major items that accounted for these increases in exports to the United States were road vehicles (SITC 78) in the 1975–80 period, and office machinery, telecommunications equipment, and electrical machinery (SITC 75, 76, 77) between 1980 and 1985. The proportion of iron and steel (SITC 67), which accounted for 16.5 percent of total exports to the United States, had declined to 4.3 percent by 1985. Thus, the Japanese export performance vis-à-vis the United States in the 1975–85 period was concentrated in a rather limited range of products whose combined share accounted for almost 70 percent of exports in 1985. Japan's export experience with Canada is very similar. Japanese exports of road vehicles nearly tripled between 1975 and 1980, and doubled again between 1980 and 1985. Exports of products from the electric and electronics (SITC 75, 76, 77) industry increased by a factor of 2.7 and 3.4, respectively, during the same periods. Thus, 71 percent of Japan's 1985 exports to Canada consisted of road vehicles or electric and electronics products.

The concentration of Japanese exports in autos and electric and electronic products reflect two factors. In response to the high energy costs of the 1970s, Japan was moving away from exporting resource-intensive products. Instead, firms produced final goods with a low resource content, especially machinery and equipment.[5] The strongest investment growth in Japan occurred in electric machinery and transport machinery. Only in these two industries did investment exceed one trillion yen for five consecutive years from 1980 to 1984 (MITI 1986, 298). It is not surprising that investment primarily takes place in industries with rapid output (value-added) growth. This was

Table 3.3 Japan's Export Dependence Ratio for Selected Commodities

Commodity	1981	1985
Electronic desk computers	79.1%	76.1%
Televisions	69.3	83.6
Semiconductors	16.6	18.7
Videotape recorders	77.4	89.3
Passenger cars	56.6	57.9
Trucks	30.1	32.9
Motorcycles	57.5	62.8
Iron and steel	31.7	33.4

Note: Measured as export production, in volume terms.
Source: MITI (1986, appendix table 20).

true for the iron and steel industry in the 1960s and early 1970s. The difference between the experience of iron and steel and the more recent export expansion of the electronic, electric, and transport equipment industries is the role of exports in output expansion. That is, a much larger proportion of output was sold abroad (in volume terms) in the 1980s (see table 3.3).

The output growth in the electric machinery and transport industries enabled the firms to enjoy scale economies and reduced costs. In addition, the introduction of automation and new quality control methods at the factory level helped to improve the quality standards and reduced the ratio of defective end-products. Also, these industries found that the introduction of new products or new designs played a crucial role in expanding domestic, as well as foreign, demand. Thus, not only were the ratios of research and development (R&D) expenditure to total sales higher in these industries, but the annual rate of increase in R&D exceeded 14 percent between 1975 and 1984 (MITI 1986, 299).

The shift in Japan's industrial structure away from resource-intensive products reduced the demand for imports of resources and thus changed the commodity composition of imports. The higher oil prices of the late 1970s more than offset this decline in volume, so that the share of mineral fuels (SITC 3) in total imports increased between 1975 and 1980. After 1981 this share started to decline as a consequence of falling oil prices. Imports of crude materials (SITC 2) followed the same pattern. In 1985, imports were $18.2 billion as compared to $24.5 billion in 1980. In 1975, about 44 percent of Japanese imports from Canada consisted of crude materials. Thus, Canada was severely hit by changes in the composition of Japan's industrial output. Also, the stagnant demand for housing in Japan depressed the import demand for wood and wood products, one of Japan's major imports from Canada. Crude material imports from Canada were $1.9 billion dollars in 1985, down from $2.4 billion in 1980. This decline was almost proportional to the fall in total Japanese crude material imports. Although imports of coal and coke (SITC 32) increased by 61 percent between 1980 and 1985, imports of these materials from Canada remained almost unchanged at $4.7 billion.

Crude materials accounted for about one-fourth of Japan's imports from the United States in 1975. Thus, the impact of changes in Japan's industrial output on imports from the United States was less than in the case of Canada. Nevertheless, Japanese imports of crude materials from the United States declined from $6.8 billion in 1980 to $4.7 billion in 1985. Japanese imports of food products (SITC 0) and manufactured goods (SITC 6) from the United States also declined between 1980 and 1985. As total imports of these items increased by $833 million and by $706 million, respectively, Japan replaced American products by imports from other regions, mainly from the Southeast Asian newly industrializing countries (NICs).

Most of the increase in Japan's imports of chemicals (SITC 5) and machinery and transport equipment (SITC 7) between 1980 and 1985 came from the United States. Imports of chemicals increased by $923 million, while total imports of chemicals went up by $2 billion. In machinery and transport equipment, imports from the United States increased by $2.2 billion, almost equal to the increase in imports from the world between 1980 and 1985.

I now proceed to a discussion of how the governments of the United States, Canada, and Japan responded to the overall and bilateral trade developments. Trade issues between the United States and Japan range from political issues, such as the introduction of import relief measures, to macroeconomic policy questions, such as the expansion of Japanese aggregate demand and the removal of Japanese nontariff barriers (NTBs). However, the following section will be limited mainly to industry-specific issues and the impact on trade barriers.

3.3 Trade Barriers in the United States, Canada, and Japan

Japan's current account surplus has led to heated trade disputes with its trading partners, particularly with the United States. The U.S. concerns cover a broad spectrum of macroeconomic and industry-specific policy issues. At the macroeconomic level, it has been argued that domestic U.S. savings have been insufficient in relation to aggregate spending,[6] and that insufficient liberalization of Japan's financial markets limits the use of the yen as an international currency, which keeps the yen/dollar exchange rate artificially low.[7] Industry-specific problems include unfair trade practices in tobacco, wine, and leather products. In 1977, U.S. industry complaints that the increases in imports of Japanese color TVs were causing serious injury to U.S. industry were settled by an OMA agreement. In 1981, the U.S. auto industry's similar complaint led to the introduction of VERs.

In the 1980s, bilateral trade disputes with the United States played a very important role in Japanese external policy. There were two important reasons for this. The first was the growing dependence of Japanese industries on the U.S. market. As Japanese firms expanded their business activities abroad, the U.S. market's strategic importance as an outlet for final products and for capital increased.[8] Thus, both Japanese business and government supported the aforementioned OMA agreement and VERs out of fear that the United States would resort to more general market restrictions. Also, for TV and auto producers, the introduction of the restrictions did not necessarily imply a loss of market share or lower profits because they could shift production sites to the United States.

Secondly, the Japanese government responded to the U.S. complaint that Japanese markets were still not sufficiently open by announcing a series of import liberalization measures.[9] In fact, the government occasionally used foreign demands for liberalization to promote deregulation. At times, domestic forces also supported deregulation, as in the case of financial and communication services.[10] Trade liberalization through tariff cuts eventually started to affect imported processed food prices. Cheaper imports squeezed the profit margins of the domestic food processing industry, while domestic agricultural prices remained high under various price support schemes. The difficulties of this industry, reinforced by the gradual shift of political power from the rural to the city electorate, led to an unprecedented open discussion of liberalization in agriculture inside Japan. Here again, demands by the United States—the major supplier of agriculture and foods to Japan—played an important role.

Let us turn now to consider Japan's policy response to the U.S. criticism that Japan's market was not sufficiently open to foreign products and foreign investment. The Report of the Japan-U.S. Economic Relations Group in Tokyo (January 1981) stated that ". . . in terms of average tariff levels and quotas on manufactured products, Japan's market at the end of the phasing in of current tariff reductions will be no more closed than that in the U.S.," and this probably serves as a convenient starting point for a discussion of Japan's trade barriers. Table 3.4 shows Japan's tariff rates after the tariff reductions mentioned in the Report. The Action Program for the Improvement of Market Access reduced the average tariff rate in Japan from 4.9 percent to 3.8 percent. The reductions of January 1986 covered 1,849 items, amounting to 8 billion yen. They included 69 special items (33 agricultural and fishery products, and 36 manufactured products) for which the reduction or abolition of tariffs was urgently requested by Japan's trading partners. The United States strongly pushed for tariff reductions in boneless chicken, walnuts, pistachio nuts, electric exchangers, wireless communications equipment, and aluminum plate for aircraft. In addition, a 20 percent across-the-board tariff reduction was implemented.[11]

Since 1983 average tariff rates—measured as the ratio of tariff revenues

Table 3.4   Japan's Tariff Rates Before and After 1 January 1986

	Before January 1986	After January 1986
(1) Agriculture and fishery products	21.7%	16.8%
(2) Manufactured products	4.1	3.2
(3) Average of (1) and (2)	4.9	3.8

Notes: (1) Tariff rates were reduced or abolished for 1,849 items (including GSP items) from 1 January 1986, and 4 items from 1 April 1986, based on the Action Program for the Improvement of Market Access announced 30 July 1985. (2) Tariff rates are weighted by value of imports in 1984.
Source: Ministry of Finance (1985).

to imports—were 3.5 percent for the United States and 4.2 percent for Canada,[12] it is fair to conclude that current Japanese tariff barriers are not higher and may even be lower than in those two countries. However, the fact remains that the average tariff rate on agriculture and fishery products still exceeds 16 percent, which is more than five times the tariff rate on manufactured products. With the lower tariffs on manufactured products, the discussion of Japanese trade barriers has shifted to: (1) NTBs and transparency issues in specific products, such as communications apparatus; (2) tariffs and NTBs in agriculture and food products; and (3) investment-related trade issues in services. This can be seen from table 3.5 which summarizes the industry-specific trade issues raised between the United States and Japan in 1985 and 1986. The table shows that current trade issues are concentrated in high technology, agriculture, and food products.

The removal of NTBs, such as the easing of technical standards on terminal equipment, the appointment of a representative from foreign companies to the Japanese Telecommunication Council,[13] the acceptance of foreign clinical test data, and the simplification of import clearance procedures for medical equipment, were among the major trade issues in manufactured products. These issues involve institutional barriers including standards and testing, the question of transparency in policy formation, and equal treatment of foreign and domestic companies.

It was not until the Tokyo Round negotiations of the late 1970s that the removal of NTBs became an important part of Japan's liberalization policy agenda.[14] The Task Force Report on U.S.-Japan Trade (U.S. Congress 1979, 29–33) viewed Japan's auto safety and emission standards as NTBs. A major remaining issue in the Tokyo Round negotiations was government procurement policy as typified by the Nippon Telephone and Telegraph Public Corporation. In 1980, Japan's foreign exchange law was revised to allow a freer use of foreign exchange for both trade and investment. The import inspection procedure was revised in the same year. The issues of transparency and equal treatment in standards and approvals were addressed the following year. The

Action Program for the Improvement of Market Access (July 1985) was aimed at improving market access and stimulating imports.[15]

It is very difficult to assess the global impact on trade flows of removing NTBs. This is especially true when the removal of NTBs is combined with tariff reductions, as occurred in Japan. In any event, the import-penetration ratio, defined as the ratio between imports and domestic demand, rose for most manufactured goods and, from 1978 on, contributed to an increase in imports.[16] The removal of trade barriers also made the domestic market more responsive to changes in the relative prices of imports and domestic goods, which, as table 3.6 illustrates, significantly increased the share of manufactured goods in total imports in recent years.

Opinions are divided on whether the small import share of manufactured products reflects Japan's factor endowments and location, or whether it results from the closed nature of the domestic market.[17] In the early 1980s, Japan's exports were rapidly growing in industries with lower resource content, and Japan was also discovering that nearby Asian countries could supply manufactured products relatively cheaply. These changes, together with improved market access, are probably the main reason for the higher import share of manufactured products. After the appreciation of the yen in September 1985, this share increased sharply if crude oil is excluded from the total. In other words, Japanese import demand started to respond to price changes, which is in part due to the opening up of the market for imported manufactured products.[18]

Although Japan's trade barriers for manufactured products have been substantially reduced, the agricultural and food industries continue to benefit from a complex system of protection. Seven products—including milk and cream, wheat, barley, and rice—are controlled by the government, and twenty-two items—including fresh beef, groundnuts, and fruit juice—are protected by import quotas. Also, as already mentioned, the average tariff rate on agriculture and fishery products exceeds 16 percent, while the rate on manufactured products is only 3.2 percent. These barriers are evidently keeping Japan's domestic prices far above the international price level. In particular, the price of rice is reported to be 8.3 times higher than the U.S. price when measured in terms of hourly wage costs.[19]

The United States, as the major supplier of imports of agricultural products and food to Japan, has been pressing hard for the reduction of trade barriers. In 1986, the United States requested GATT to investigate twelve agricultural products presently under import quota control because of alleged violations of Article 23 of GATT. Wine, tobacco, leather, and shoes are other sources of friction in U.S.-Japan trade relations.[20] Recently there has been some progress in reducing trade barriers for agricultural and food products. Yet, changes have been slow because of the negative impact of lower tariffs on the profit margins of food producers, who rely on high prices for domestic

Table 3.5 Major Industry-Specific Trade Issues between the United States and Japan, 1985 and 1986

Industries	Issues	Dates of Agreement
Market access to Japan		
Sectoral strategies*		
Telecommunications	Liberalization of telecommunication terminal equipment and network service	January 1986
Medical equipment and pharmaceuticals	Revising regulatory system to increase transparency of examination	January 1986
Forest products	Removing tariff and nontariff barriers	January 1986
Electronics and semiconductors	Liberalization of computer parts, improving the patent process, improving market access, monitoring cost and price of Japan's products	September 1986
Transport equipment (auto parts)	Increased market access of U.S. auto parts, relaxation of government regulations	Continued
Super computers	Increased transparency in government procurement, including public universities	Continued
Tariffs and import quotas		
Leather and leather shoes	Increase transparency, tariff quota scheme to replace import quota	Starting April 1986

Issue	Description	Date
Wine and alcoholic beverages	Tariff reduction on wine, tax revision to an ad valorem tax	Starting April 1986
Tobacco	Government monopoly in production, high tariff plus tax limiting market access	October 1986
12 Agricultural products under import quotas	Request for GATT panel based on Article 23	Continued
Service related issues		
Foreign attorneys (legal service)	Permitting legal service by foreign attorneys	March 1986
Kansai International Airport Project (construction service)	Requesting fair and transparent bidding on construction project	Continued
Special protection on imports from Japan		
Iron and steel	Keeping Japan's share in U.S. to 5.8% of consumption starting October 1984	May 1985
Auto	Continued voluntary export restraints limiting annual Japanese exports to 2.3 million units for fiscal year 1986	February 1986

*Issues taken up in MOSS (Market Oriented Sector Selective) approach.

Sources: Ministry of Finance, Bureau of Tariff; MITI (1985, 1986); U.S.I.S. Press office, *Background Bulletin* 10 January 1986; Nihon Kaizai Shimbun, 1 August 1986; Sazanami (1987); Ministry of Foreign Affairs, *Recent U.S.-Japan Trade Issues* 10 February 1987.

Table 3.6   Japan's Import Ratio of Manufactured Goods

	(1) Total Imports	(2) Imports excluding crude oil	(3) Imports from U.S.
1982	24.9	38.3	47.4
1983	27.2	39.8	50.2
1984	29.8	41.8	52.0
1985	31.0	42.3	55.2
1986	41.8	49.4	60.7
1985			
July	30.8	40.3	51.8
August	31.5	41.4	52.9
September	30.5	41.0	53.8
October	33.0	44.3	58.7
November	31.9	42.5	56.4
December	28.8	41.9	51.4
1986			
January	30.8	40.8	51.0
February	30.6	43.5	50.0
March	34.7	45.1	60.0
April	42.8	50.7	58.1
May	45.4	50.8	64.3
June	47.0	52.4	71.6
July	48.6	54.0	70.5
August	42.3	47.8	51.0
September	46.7	52.1	62.1
October	47.8	53.5	62.5
November	41.6	47.9	55.9
December	43.9	50.5	60.1

Source: MITI, *Boeki doko,* various issues.

agricultural products. Hopefully, the benefits of lower food prices for the increasingly powerful city electorate and the continued foreign pressure will promote changes in the present price-support schemes.

In the 1970s, the overvaluation of the dollar and the subsequent inflow of imports into the United States caused more and more U.S. industries to seek protection via escape clause actions, VERs, and OMAs. In other words, the importance of NTBs for restricting U.S. imports increased, while tariff-based protection was reduced (Baldwin 1984, 1985).

Imports from Japan were probably most affected by the increase in U.S. NTBs. For example, according to Hufbauer, Berliner, and Elliott (1986), twelve out of fourteen significant cases of special protectionist measures introduced after 1969 involved Japan.[21] Their study estimates the share of U.S. imports protected by these special measures at 21 percent in 1984 and the tariff equivalent of this protection at 20 percent. Since the list of protected industries covers such major imports from Japan as carbon steel, color TVs, cars, motorcycles, and semiconductors,[22] which will be subject to government surveillance under the U.S.-Japan agreement, the proportion of Japanese exports under U.S. government control will be substantially higher than the 21 percent average for all imports.

U.S. protection clearly reduced imports from Japan. The protection against color TVs was particularly damaging for Japanese exporters. However, the importance of the U.S. market for the Japanese electric and electronic industry was not affected by the introduction of the OMA. Likewise, the import of road vehicles continued to increase in spite of the 1981 VER which limited U.S. imports to 1.83 million units.

Aside from the general complaint that Japan is not buying enough manufactured products, there have been only two major trade issues between Canada and Japan. One concerned the issue of introducing the CANDU atomic reactor into Japan in the mid-1970s. The other was the Canadian request for VERs on Japanese autos. The share of auto imports from Japan in total Canadian sales increased from 8.7 percent in 1979 to 21.9 percent in 1980. A VER was introduced in 1981 limiting Japanese passenger car exports for that year to 174,000 units.

Finally, Japan responded to the higher trade barriers on automobiles and TVs by markedly increasing its direct investment in the United States and Canada. This evolution will be analyzed in the next section.

3.4 The Growth of Japanese Direct Investment in the United States and Canada

One of the notable changes in Japan's balance of payments in the early 1980s is the increase in capital outflows. Japan has emerged as an important capital exporter to the world and to the United States, with more than half of its net long-term capital outflow being directed toward the United States. Investment in securities accounted for about two-thirds of the capital outflows in the 1983–85 period. Net foreign direct investment in the United States doubled between 1980 and 1982 and again between 1982 and 1984 (see table 3.7).[23] In 1985, Japan's net direct investment in the United States of $2,043 million dollars represented one-third of Japan's total direct investment.

Japan's foreign investment and trade have always been closely linked. Even in the early 1960s, when capital outflows were severely restricted by foreign exchange regulations, the government sponsored projects for resource development. In order to build an industrial base around iron and steel and other heavy industries in a country poorly endowed with natural resources,

Table 3.7 Net Capital Outflow from Japan to the United States, 1978–85 (in million $US)

Net Capital Flows	1978	1979	1980	1981	1982	1983	1984	1985
Direct investment	851	745	729	1,871	1,423	1,041	3,180	2,043
Export credit	45*	27	15*	97	788	190	195	587
Loans	28	699	409	249	243	329	477	716
Securities	2,226	59*	3,001*	6	1,248*	3,943	10,591	29,874
Others	273	68	224	420	494	38	371	57*
Total long-term capital	3,333	1,480	1,654*	2,643	1,700	5,541	14,814	33,163

Note: *indicates inflow to Japan.
Source: Bank of Japan, *Balance of Payments Monthly,* April issues.

the government and the private sector engaged in resource development projects abroad that would assure the supply of raw materials.

The need to promote direct investment in manufacturing emerged toward the end of the 1960s. Nearby Southeast Asian countries, which previously imported Japan's light manufactured products, switched to a policy of import substitution behind high trade barriers. In the early 1970s, rising domestic wages and the relaxation of foreign exchange constraints, which accompanied the growing current account surplus, induced Japanese firms to invest more in these countries. As a result, Asian developing countries became a major recipient of Japanese capital. Japan's investments in industrial countries were primarily aimed at distributing export goods and providing after-sale service.

The precipitate rise in energy prices in the 1970s revived Japan's interest in resource development and processing. Among the major energy-related projects undertaken in the early 1970s were petroleum exploration and liquid natural gas in Indonesia and Peru. Because these development projects required a larger capital investment than other projects, the share of resource-related industries increased.[24]

Table 3.8 summarizes Japan's total foreign direct investment position for March 1973, 1981, and 1985.[25] It clearly shows that Japan's total direct investment has increased more than tenfold in the past decade. The industrial composition of these investments roughly followed the change in Japan's industrial structure. There was a continued decline in the proportion invested in primary industries. While the share of manufacturing expanded between 1973 and 1981, it declined slightly between 1981 and 1985 because of sharply growing investments in finance, insurance, and real estate. This change in Japan's direct investment pattern in the 1980s reflects the adjustment of Japanese industry to the decline in prices of primary products, particularly crude oil. It is also the consequence of intensified trade frictions with the United States and the European Economic Community (EEC) which resulted in higher trade barriers for Japan's major exports.

Japan's direct investment in the United States illustrates the general pattern. The share of the United States in Japan's direct investment increased from 19.1 percent in 1973 to 28 percent in 1985. With an annual growth rate of more than 37 percent between 1976 and 1984, Japan has become the third largest investor in U.S. manufacturing. Investment, especially in electric machinery, contributed to the growth rate of Japanese direct investment in the United States. In 1973, this industry attracted more than $27 million in direct investment, and by 1981, it amounted to $653 million, or almost one-third of Japanese direct investment in U.S. manufacturing. From 1981 to 1985, the transport equipment, iron and nonferrous metal products industries were the main targets of the Japanese investment effort. These industries accounted for 36 percent of Japanese direct investment in manufacturing during this period.

Table 3.8 Japan's Direct Investment Position with Respect to the World, the United States, and Canada, 1973–85 (in million $US)

	March 1973			March 1981			March 1985		
	World	U.S.	Canada	World	U.S.	Canada	World	U.S.	Canada
Total	6,773	1,273	275	36,497	8,878	920	71,431	19,894	1,575
Agriculture, fishery, & mining	2,406	112	98	7,981	550	282	12,325	738	498
Manufacturing	1,752	176	136	12,573	2,065	371	22,048	5,926	556
Food products	99	11	1	587	184	26	1,002	433	31
Textiles	416	7	3	1,637	124	57	2,055	185	57
Woods & pulp	296	90	128	758	138	195	1,106	290	307
Chemical	141	13	—	2,626	241	2	3,849	589	2
Iron products & nonferrous metals	240	1	1	2,619	304	68	4,805	811	102
General machinery	128	19	2	894	210	10	1,619	520	13
Electric machinery	171	27	1	1,579	653	9	3,234	1,725	26
Transport equipment	142	—	—	979	87	2	2,746	967	8
Other	117	7	—	894	116	2	1,633	405	10
Services	1,297	746	23	7,835	4,256	188	18,182	9,002	371
Commerce & trade	756	547	22	5,409	3,325	168	11,128	6,407	238
Finance & insurance	541	199	1	2,426	931	20	7,054	2,595	133
n.e.c.*	1,317	238	18	8,108	2,016	78	18,877	4,227	149

*Includes construction, transportation, and real estate
Source: Ministry of Finance, *Zaisei Kinyu Tokei Geppo*, various issues.

As mentioned before, these three industries faced protectionist trade measures by the United States in the mid-1970s and in the early 1980s which encouraged Japanese firms to establish U.S. subsidiaries.[26]

Another important change in the 1981–85 period was the increased direct investment in finance and insurance. As was shown in table 3.7, a large proportion of the net capital outflow from Japan to the United States between 1982 and 1985 was invested in securities and generated a greater demand for financial services of banks and financial institutions. Hence, an increasing number of Japanese companies opened branch offices and subsidiaries to carry out financial operations in the United States.

Japan's direct investment in Canada accounted for about 1 percent of total investment in Canada at the beginning of the 1980s. As British Columbia and Alberta are highly concentrated in resource and resource-based industries, they have been the major recipients of this investment. The goal of investments in other regions is to keep close contacts with Canadian firms, to facilitate market access for Japan's exports, and to acquire market information.

Although foreign direct investment into Japan expanded in the early 1980s, it was equal to less than one-tenth of Japan's total investments abroad. Even after the capital liberalization in the 1970s, investment was mainly limited to petroleum refining, chemicals, and machinery. It is quite possible that government intervention in services such as finance, communications, and distribution limited the penetration of foreign business. Indeed, U.S. service firms consider government policies to be the major impediment to entering the Japanese market.[27] Since branch offices or subsidiaries are more important for service-exporting firms, the U.S. request for trade liberalization in services was one of the prime forces that led to the deregulation of such Japanese service industries as finance and telecommunications. This deregulation of the Japanese market has benefited U.S. direct investment in information technology industries.

As seen in table 3.9, there was a marked expansion of U.S. direct investment in Japan in 1982 and 1983. Direct investment from the United States accounted for about one-third of direct investment into Japan at the beginning of the 1980s. Due to the aforementioned expansion of U.S. investment in electronics and computer services, the U.S. share increased to 52.7 percent in 1985. Active participation of U.S. firms in new satellite communication and information services may further increase U.S. investment in Japan. In manufacturing, closer business ties between U.S. and Asian companies may have the same effect. More than 65 percent of the foreign firms in Japan mentioned that they invested in Japan to establish a production base in the Asian region and to use high quality labor with high technical standards of production.[28]

Table 3.9   Direct Investment into Japan, 1980–85 (fiscal year, April–March; in million $US)

Fiscal Year	U.S.	Canada	World
1980	103.9	13.1	299.5
	(34.7)	(4.3)	(100)
1981	149.0	2.2	432.4
	(34.5)	(0.5)	(100)
1982	448.6	0.3	1,006.4
	(44.5)	(0.02)	(100)
1983	771.6	31.1	1,152.0
	(67.0)	(2.6)	(100)
1984	214.4	0.2	493.5
	(43.4)	(0.04)	(100)
1985	404.0*	12.9*	766.0*
	(52.7)	(1.7)	(100)

Note: Figures in parentheses are percentage shares in total direct investment into Japan.
*April–December
Source: Ministry of Finance (1986).

3.5   The Effects of Trade Barriers on Trade and Investment Flows

This section analyzes how U.S. and Canadian trade barriers in automobiles and in the electric and electronic industry have affected Japan's trade and investment flows. Products from these two Japanese industries combined accounted for almost two-thirds of the trade with the United States and Canada. Both industries have faced trade restrictions. Car imports were restricted by a VER in 1981, while the electric and electronics industry was subjected to a variety of protectionist measures, including the OMA for color TVs in 1977, increased tariffs on CB radios in 1978, and strict government surveillance of costs and prices of semiconductors in 1986. However, in spite of such trade barriers, exports from Japan to the United States continued to grow at substantial rates.

At first, Japanese auto makers responded to the VER in the U.S. market by upgrading their products. Feenstra (1984) estimates that two-thirds of the increase in imports of Japanese cars after the introduction of the VER was due to quality improvement.[29] The average price of Japanese autos in the U.S. rose from $6,709 in 1980 to $8,317 in 1984.[30] As it became increasingly clear that the VER was limiting the share of Japanese cars in the United States, both in volume and in value terms,[31] Japanese auto makers opened subsidiary production plants in the United States. They also invested in Canada, which had eliminated tariff barriers for U.S. automobiles in 1965 under the Auto Pact.[32]

According to a survey by MITI,[33] 66 percent of the firms interviewed pointed to trade restrictions as the primary motivation for Japanese direct investment in autos in developed countries. Adding the 24 percent of the firms that also emphasized market share as a motivation for direct investment, 90 percent of the firms were motivated by market-related factors. This result contrasts sharply with the results for Japanese firms investing in developing countries before 1979. The same survey found that their primary motivation was the cost advantage of producing consumer electronics, chemicals, textiles, and iron and steel in developing countries.

In 1978, Honda was the first among Japan's major auto makers to open subsidiary plants in the United States. In 1982 these plants operated at a yearly production capacity of 360,000 units. Honda was followed by other automakers: Nissan Motor Mfg. Corp. U.S.A. started production of passenger cars in March 1985; Toyota and General Motors jointly established New United Motor Mfg. Inc. in 1984, starting production in the following year. By 1985, all the major Japanese auto makers had set up subsidiaries or joint ventures to produce cars in the United States. Japanese auto investment in Canada followed a similar trend. Honda of Canada Mfg. Inc. was established in 1984 and started production at the end of 1986. Toyota Motor Mfg. Canada, established in 1986, produced its first cars in the fall of 1988. In addition, a joint venture of Matsuda Motors and General Motors Canada intends to start production by 1989.

The growth of Japanese auto investment in the United States and Canada will eventually affect the trade flow of autos and auto parts. Its impact is already evident in trade of auto parts between Japan and the United States. As seen in table 3.10, the U.S. net trade position in auto parts, excluding trade with Canada, deteriorated in the early 1980s. The surplus was reduced from $1,335 million in 1981 to $557 million in 1982, and turned to a $1,852 million deficit in 1983. The deficit increased in the following year to $3,212 million. This change partially reflects changing trade patterns with Latin America which, in 1983, became a net exporter of auto parts to the U.S. However, Japanese direct investment also led to growing imports of auto parts.

One important outcome of the introduction of the VER was the rationalization of the U.S. auto industry. The industry closed assembly plants, modernized production facilities, and increased component outsourcing (Hufbauer, Berliner, and Elliott 1986, 252). In fact, component outsourcing by U.S. auto makers is one of the important factors contributing to the increase in imports from Latin America. Yet, the United States not only imported more auto parts from Latin America, but also from Asia. Those imports, of which over 80 percent were supplied by Japan, increased markedly after 1983.

American-built Japanese cars contained about 50 percent of Japanese auto parts in the mid-1980s (Nissan Motors 1986). Japanese auto part manufacturers are increasingly shifting their production sites to the United States to prepare for the larger U.S. car production by Japanese auto makers. More-

Table 3.10 U.S. Net Trade in Auto Parts, 1976–85 (in million $US)

	1976	1977	1978	1979	1980	1981	1982	1983	1984	1984P	1985P
Total U.S.	1,259	1,102	2,202	1,353	2,747	3,724	2,737	-314	-1,507	74	-1,391
with Canada	1,374	1,309	1,429	1,487	1,933	2,365	2,180	1,538	1,705	1,985	1,534
Total U.S. excluding Canada	-115	-207	345	-134	901	1,335	557	-1,852	-3,212	-2,112	-2,925
with Europe	-24	-79	-363	-726	-461	-158	-37	-351	-866		
with Latin America	479	436	865	941	1,520	1,950	950	-426	-481		
with Asia	-1,106	-1,066	-912	-1,033	-994	-1,385	-1,337	-1,707	-2,663		
with Japan only	-1,087	-1,014	-860	-1,016	-1,006	-1,340	-1,286	-1,506	-2,248	-2,085	-2,577
with Middle East	179	200	268	233	269	337	410	351	297		
with Africa	122	93	95	101	163	200	183	104	47		
with Australia	152	134	146	196	184	214	199	110	170		

Notes: Exports (FAS) minus imports (CIF). 1976–84 data are based on U.S. Department of Commerce, *The U.S. Automobile Industry, 1984.* 1984P and 1985P are estimates made by Nissan Motors published in *Kaigi Jidosha Doko No. 80,* 5 July 1986. Excludes tire and tubes.

over, the appreciation of the yen should accelerate this reallocation. But, for the time being, the demand for auto parts by U.S.-based Japanese car producers has been absorbed by a significant import growth of 49 percent in 1984 and 24 percent in 1985. This growth undoubtedly contributed to the increase in U.S. imports of road vehicles inclusive of auto parts (SITC 77) from Japan between 1980 and 1985, despite the introduction of the VER in 1981.

The long-run effects of trade barriers on trade flows between the United States, Canada, and Japan will depend on the behavior of Japanese, as well as U.S., auto and auto part manufacturers. Japanese producers of auto parts are likely to invest more in the United States because export profits are declining as a result of the current rise in the yen.[34] On the other hand, Japanese auto makers are strengthening their relations with auto makers in nearby NICs. As the currencies of these countries are more or less pegged to the dollar, Japanese companies benefit from partially moving their production there because they avoid the risk of a currency appreciation and are not subject to the VER. Such an advantage is not limited to auto makers but extends to auto part manufacturers. There are reports that a group of parts producers in Hiroshima is planning to assign the production of the Matsuda Motors compact car Festiva to a Korean company (Nissan Jidosha Shimbunsha 1986, 179). These developments imply that U.S. trade barriers for imports from Japan may affect U.S. trade with Korea and other NICs via increased Japanese investment in these countries and a subsequent rise in exports to the United States.

Trade and investment between Japan and Canada are not only influenced by trade barriers in Canada but also by those in the United States. In fact, the influence of the latter may be even larger. For example, Toyota Motor Mfg. Canada plans to export 60–70 percent of its compact cars produced in Canada to the United States in the fall of 1988. Also, Suzuki Motors and GM Canada will reportedly export their jointly produced cars to the United States from 1989 onwards (Nihon Keizai Shimbun, 31 August 1986). In order to stimulate investment in Canada, the Canadian government gave preferential treatment to Japanese auto makers with plants in Canada when determining the allocation of the VER in 1986 (Nihon Keizai Shimbun, 14 August 1986). Since the Canadian market is too small to absorb both imports and cars produced in Canada by Japanese auto makers, a substantial portion of these cars may well be shipped to the United States under the U.S.-Canadian Auto Pact. If so, Canada will become the production base of Japanese auto makers for the U.S. market.

The experience of the introduction of a VER on cars in 1981 illustrates the complexity of trade barriers in a world with international capital mobility. Not only the final products such as cars are affected, but also production components like auto parts. In addition, bilateral VER agreements affect the trade and investment flows of third parties, as shown by the experience of

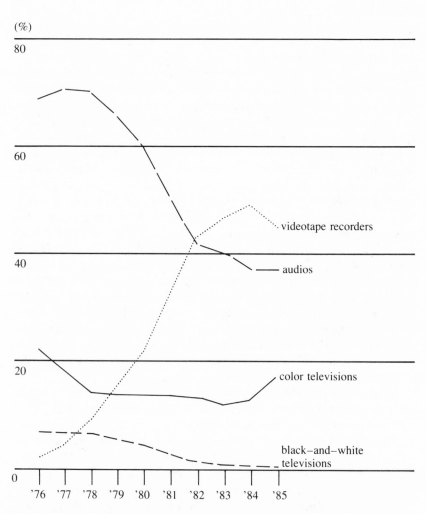

Fig. 3.1 Percentage Composition of Japan's Exports of Principal Consumer Electronics Equipment, 1976–85. *Source:* Electronic Industries Association of Japan (1986).

Japan and the NICs. Selective trade liberalization between the United States and Canada adds further complications because Canada gives preferential treatment to car manufacturers who invest in Canada.

The Japanese response to the OMA on color TVs appears similar to the response of auto makers to the VER. However, because the electric and electronics industry produces a wider variety of products, and because technological innovation was occurring more rapidly, the electronics industry was able to overcome trade barriers in the United States and maintain export growth, mainly by shifting away from color TVs and CB radios to new products.

Hufbauer, Berliner, and Elliott (1986) note that 1979 U.S. imports of complete Japanese color TV sets were at one-quarter of their 1976 level. However, country-specific trade barriers caused imports from Taiwan and Korea to increase fourfold in the 1977–78 period. There was also a substantial increase in imports of incomplete sets and subassemblies not included in the OMA. By the time the OMA ended, the major producers of electric appliances had shifted their plants to the United States and continued to expand their production. In the meantime, U.S. companies started to import incomplete sets from subassembly plants located in Latin America and Asia. Outsourcing by U.S. firms added to the increase in U.S. imports of subassembled parts. For Japanese electronics firms, the U.S. market for color TVs lost its importance after 1977. At the same time, color TVs were losing their importance in Japan's total exports of consumer electronics (see figure 3.1). Instead, audio equipment and videotape recorders became far more important in the 1976–78 period. Within the electronics product category,[35] electronic components and devices showed the largest export growth. I note finally that Japanese electric and electronics plants in the U.S. relied more on imports of parts from Japan than other industries such as food, paper, and pulp (JETRO 1985).

Although all the major Japanese electrical producers—Sony, Matsushita, Toshiba, Sharp, and Hitachi—either started or expanded their production of color TVs in the United States after the OMA, total U.S. production of consumer electronics did not expand significantly. The U.S. companies shifted their production from consumer electronics and electronic components and devices to industrial electronic equipment in the early 1980s.

The experience of the OMA on Japanese color TVs shows that, although higher trade barriers for Japanese products reduced imports of finished products from Japan, this reduction was offset by increased imports from other countries and by increased imports of parts by Japanese plants in the United States. Moreover, Japanese production in the electric and electronic industry moved away from protected products to new products. As a result, Japanese exports of electronic products as a whole continued to grow in the 1980s. As in the case of the car industry, serious trade conflicts and the introduction of the OMA prompted Japanese electronic firms to build plants in the United States.

3.6   The Effects of the Appreciation of the Yen on Trade and Investment Flows

Japan's merchandise trade account reached a record surplus of $9.8 billion in September 1986, just one year after the G-5 agreement and the subsequent appreciation of the yen. While the value of imports declined by 0.9 percent, the value of exports was 28.8 percent above the level in September of the previous year. Among the items that contributed to this increase were exports of cars, auto parts, semiconductors, and electronic parts to the United States, exports of cars and industrial machinery to the EEC, and exports of general machinery to the NICs.

This large surplus may partially reflect the rapid rise of the yen, which by raising the export price in dollar terms, more than offsets the decline in export volume (the well-known J-curve phenomenon). Even so, Japan's recent export performance seems to indicate that the short-run effect of the appreciation of the yen on the volume of exports has been very limited. For example, passenger car exports in the first half of 1986 amounted to 2.77 million units, 3 percent above the level of the first half of the previous year. The export volume of VCRs and office machinery also continued to grow and, as a result, the value of exports rose by 23 percent and 53 percent, respectively, during this period. On the other hand, imports in the first half of 1986 were $61.6 billion, as compared to $63.3 billion in the first half of 1985. The long-term impact of the exchange rate appreciation on trade flows depends on the adjustment of export (and import) prices and on the response of foreign (domestic) firms that produce close substitutes for exports (imports).

Robinson, Webb, and Townsend (1979) found that the extent to which exchange rate changes are passed on to domestic prices depends on the size of the country. Typically, the total adjustment for large countries such as the United States and Japan is about 60 percent and usually takes one year. When the yen rose by 29.7 percent between September 1977 and October 1978, about 70 percent of the appreciation was reflected in Japanese export prices.[36]

In Japan, import prices usually respond faster than export prices to a currency revaluation because import contracts are generally expressed in dollars, while one-third of the export contracts are expressed in yen.[37] Thus, the response of Japanese export prices in dollar terms to the yen appreciation takes place only after new contracts have been concluded. In 1985, the proportion of export contracts in yen was generally higher for electric machinery (51 percent) and cars (49 percent), than for metal products (21 percent) and textiles (27 percent). Japanese export items such as VCRs, TVs, and heavy electric appliances tend to be contracted in yen, because of Japan's strong competitive position in these products (Ministry of Finance 1986, 49). Forty-five percent of the yen appreciation between September 1985 and September 1986 was passed on to export prices. The figure for imports, excluding raw materials and mineral fuel, was about 70 percent.[38] Export prices of machinery and equipment adjusted by 52 percent of the total change in the exchange rate, as compared to 29 percent and 20 percent for textiles and metal products. In other words, the machinery and equipment industries raised their export prices significantly to avoid a decline in yen receipts.

**Table 3.11   Changes in Export and Import Volume Index September 1985–September
1986**

	Export Volume	Import Volume
	Total (% changes from previous year)	
1985		
September	1.9	5.8
October	2.1	6.9
November	2.1	0.6
December	1.4	2.3
1986		
January	2.2	2.8
February	0.2	6.1
March	−2.2	2.1
April	−0.2	7.2
May	−0.2	13.6
June	−2.2	32.3
July	−0.9	21.3
August	−3.5	13.7
September	3.7	21.3
	By Commodities (% changes from September 1985–September 1986)	
Food products	−8.4	18.6
Textiles	−3.0	29.9
Chemicals	15.8	23.3
Nonferrous metals	−12.2	
Metal products	−5.9	
Metallic materials		−10.9
Mineral fuels		9.4
Machinery & equipment	4.5	33.8
Raw materials		4.2
Miscellaneous	1.4	41.4

Source: Nihon Kanzei Kyokai, "Gaikoku Boeki Gaikyo."

In spite of these price increases for machinery and equipment, the export volume index rose by only 4.5 percent between September 1985 and
September 1986. As noted earlier, exports of such major items as VCRs,
general machinery, and cars to the United States, Europe, and the NICs continued to expand. Table 3.11 shows that, while the yen appreciated by nearly
30–40 percent between March 1985 and March 1986, the decline in the volume index of exports was only 2–3 percent.

A number of factors may explain this relatively small decline in Japan's
export volume. First, the electric and electronics industries could afford to
raise their export prices without affecting export sales because their products,
such as VCRs and other consumer electronics, were not produced in the
United States. Second, it is frequently argued that U.S. car price increases

are triggered by Japanese price changes (Kreinin 1984). The U.S. consumer price index for new cars, which was 214 in early 1985, reached 216 in October 1985, and had gone up even further to 221 by April 1986. Third, the Japanese export volume of nonelectric machinery hardly declined after the appreciation of the yen. Japanese exports of these products benefited from growing demand from nearby NICs, whose export-led economies were booming. Indeed, in spite of the appreciation, the value of Japanese exports to Korea and Taiwan increased by 38 percent and 26 percent, respectively, from 1985 to 1986. Japan mainly exported engines and parts, electric appliances, and general machinery to these countries.

Part of the decline in Japan's unit value of imports reflects the rapid fall in the prices of crude oil and raw materials toward the end of 1985. Moreover, the unit values of imports of manufactures and food products declined by 26 percent and 31 percent, respectively, between September 1985 and September 1986. Not surprisingly, the decline in import prices stimulated import demand. The volume index of imports increased by more than 10 percent after May 1986 (see table 3.11). This increase roughly coincided with a rise in the import share of manufactured goods (see table 3.6). Between September 1985 and September 1986, the imported quantities of chemicals, machinery and equipment, and miscellaneous manufactures rose by 23 percent, 34 percent, and 41.1 percent, respectively. Although the import data primarily reflect the sharp price cuts of crude oil and raw materials, the currency appreciation has also increased the volume of imports and, particularly, the quantity of manufactured imports.

We thus conclude that one year after the G-5 agreement, the currency appreciation has not curbed the volume of Japan's major export product group, machinery and equipment, but has effectively increased the volume of manufactured imports. Because the export share of manufactured goods is substantially higher than the import share, the short-term impact of the currency appreciation on Japan's total trade flows has been relatively small.

The long-term effect depends on the response of Japanese firms to the higher domestic costs. As noted in section 3.4, Japan's direct investment continued to expand in 1985. According to balance of payments data, its direct investment reached $14.4 billion in 1986, more than double the 1985 total of $6.4 billion. This figure partially reflects enhanced direct investment in the United States, concentrated in the car, electric, and electronics industries, aimed at easing trade conflicts and avoiding trade barriers. In addition, the currency appreciation is promoting Japanese direct investment in Asian countries, where labor costs have been reduced because the currencies of most of these countries are pegged to the dollar (Nihon Keizai Shimbun, 12 October 1986).

Earlier, direct investment by Japanese firms had already built close economic ties with those Asian countries, and the appreciation of the yen will strengthen this interdependence. Japanese subsidiaries in Asia are selling 61 percent of their products in the domestic markets of the respective countries. Twelve percent is shipped to Japan and the rest is sold in other countries. The ratio of domestic sales to total production is much lower than the 97 percent figure for Japanese producers of machinery in North America (EPA 1986, 206). The appreciation of the yen against the dollar will stimulate competition in the Japanese and U.S. markets between products from Japanese subsidiaries in Asia and Japanese exports. As noted earlier, such direct investment expands Japanese import demand for machinery and parts.

The experience of the currency adjustment since September 1985 suggests that a change in the yen/dollar rate not only affects trade and investment flows between the United States and Japan, but also has an impact on other countries. Although the sharp decline in crude oil and raw material prices has dominated the evolution of Japanese imports, manufactured goods imports have responded to the appreciation of the yen with a time lag of six months. If this trend continues, it may eventually significantly alter the commodity composition of Japanese imports. The short-run effect of the currency appreciation on the volume of Japan's main exports seems to be limited. This is partially due to the role of nonprice factors in determining exports and to oligopolistic price behavior abroad. One can expect that, with a more internationally oriented business attitude, Japanese firms will choose an optimal industrial location for selling to the home market and for exporting to the United States and Canada. The value of the exchange rate will be an important factor in considering their location.

3.7 Conclusion

The expansion in bilateral trade flows between the United States, Canada, and Japan in the past decade far exceeded the growth in total trade of these three countries. In particular, a strong expansion of exports from Japan to the United States resulted in a large bilateral trade imbalance between the two countries. The increase in Japan's exports to the United States and to Canada was concentrated in only a few product categories, including cars, electric equipment, and electronics products. A number of trade barriers such as VERs and OMAs were imposed on Japanese products. Yet, their effectiveness in correcting bilateral trade imbalances was reduced by product upgrading in cars, the emergence of new products in consumer electronics, and growing imports of subassembled parts.

An important effect of the U.S. trade barriers was to increase direct investment from Japan. More Japanese subsidiaries opened plants in North America to overcome the trade restrictions on imports of finished products. This expanded the import of subassembled parts. Also, U.S. firms relied more on ouutsourcing in an effort to rationalize production. Due to its location near Asian NICs, Japan provided an important production base for U.S. outsourcing. In other words, the strategic importance of Japan as a major trading partner for U.S. and Canadian firms was reinforced by the emergence in the early 1980s of several Southeast Asian countries as suppliers of more sophisticated products.[39]

According to the Bank of Japan's balance of payment statistics, U.S. direct investment in Japan increased fivefold between 1980 and 1985. U.S. firms not only invested in Japan to build closer ties with Japanese manufac- turing firms, but also to benefit from deregulation in the areas of finance, telecommunications, and information services. Indeed, their strong pressure to remove the remaining institutional barriers for trade and investment has been quite effective. In addition, several Japanese groups, such as the authors of the Maekawa Report (1986), supported improved access to the Japanese domestic market and greater imports of manufactured goods.[40] The reduction of Japan's trade barriers and the appreciation of the yen in September 1985 contributed to a substantial increase in imports of manufactured goods.

The analysis of the impact of trade barriers and exchange rates on trade and investment suggests a number of policy implications. First, country- specific trade barriers do not significantly reduce imports when there is active direct investment between countries. Faced with higher trade barriers in the North American market, Japanese firms can sell their exports to countries without such barriers. Another option is to set up assembly plants in the countries with trade restrictions, which amounts to substituting exports of finished products for subassembled parts. Moreover, when subassembled parts are cheaper abroad, domestic U.S. firms will not significantly expand their market share. In fact, product outsourcing by U.S. firms took place for automobiles and electronics, which are precisely the industries on whose fin- ished products additional trade barriers were imposed.

Second, the exchange rate may be an important factor in deciding where to buy imports and where to produce at low cost. As mentioned before, the overall effects of the recent appreciation of the yen on Japanese imports are difficult to assess because of the decline in the prices of crude oil and raw materials. Nevertheless, it is a fact that about six months after the rise of the yen, the growth rate of the volume of manufactured imports jumped into the double digits. If the "harmonious industrial structure" of the Japanese econ- omy stressed in the Maekawa Report implies that the Japanese economy is able to absorb more manufactured imports, policy measures to improve mar- ket access and to keep the yen at the present appreciated level are the way to go.

Third, policies aimed at altering the bilateral trade flows between the United States and Japan should take into account the trade consequences for Asian countries that are rapidly acquiring industrial skills. For instance, the OMA on color TVs from Japan resulted in a fourfold increase in U.S. imports from Korea and Taiwan in 1977–78, and the recent slowdown in the export growth of Japanese consumer electronics, arising from the yen appreciation, is causing a rapid expansion in color TVs and VCRs exported from Korea to the United States.

Fourth, at the current exchange rate between the dollar and the yen, Japanese foreign direct manufacturing investment is likely to increase. For example, Japanese auto part manufacturers, who face increased domestic costs as a result of the appreciation of the yen, may shift their plants to the United States or to some Asian countries with whom they have already built close business ties.

Finally, insofar as the U.S.-Canadian Auto Pact can be considered as an example of selective trade liberalization aimed at exploiting scale economies for manufacturing industries in small economies, Canada's association with the large U.S. market provides an additional incentive for Japanese direct investment. However, since efficiency in production usually benefits from the pressure of competition, selective liberalization in North America which shelters producers from worldwide competition could result, as well, in more expensive U.S. and Canadian finished products and subassembled parts. Here again, exchange rates play an important role in determining the cost advantages (or disadvantages) of North American firms and their competitors elsewhere.[41]

Notes

1. According to Hufbauer, Berliner, and Elliott (1986), in the postwar period there have been twenty-three cases in which the United States imposed protectionist measures—high tariffs, quotas, or other unusual limitations. Sixteen of these cases involved Japan.

2. Leather and leather products were shifted from the import quota list to the tariff quota scheme beginning in April 1986, and there was also an effort to improve transparency in market access. See Nihon Kanzei Kyokai (1986).

3. See Saxonhouse (1983), Cline (1985), and Bergsten and Cline (1985). Even the Report on the Trade Mission to the Far East (U.S. Congress 1981, 9) pointed out that: "In terms of formal tariff or nontariff barriers on industrial goods, Japan is a much more open economy than most Americans realize."

4. See Sazanami (1986a) for details.

5. The process of resource saving and its impact on Japan's commodity composition of imports is analyzed in the White paper on Trade (MITI 1986, 300–306) using input-output tables for 1970, 1975, 1980, and 1983. According to the white paper, resource imports were reduced after 1975 through three channels: (1) decline in the relative importance of resource-intensive industries in total production; (2) resource-saving devices reducing the resources input per unit of output; and (3) a shift in imports of resources to resource-processed intermediate products. The contribution

of the first channel was the most important in reducing the ratio of imports of raw materials to GNP between 1970 and 1984.

6. Bergsten and Cline (1985) stress the macro imbalance in the United States and Japan as a major cause of the bilateral imbalance.

7. A report by the Joint Japan-U.S. Ad Hoc Group on Yen/Dollar Exchange Rate (1984, 6) states that: ". . . among other factors that appreciated the yen from 278 yen per dollar in November 1982 to 233 yen by March 1984, in the Treasury Department's view, were market perceptions of Japan's commitment to internationalize the yen and liberalize its capital market."

8. The increase in the importance of the United States in Japanese capital outflows will be discussed in section 3.4.

9. Prime Minister Nakasone's 30 July 1985 message, at the time of the announcement of the Action Program for the Improvement of Market Access, ended by pointing out that: "Trade cannot be carried out by a single country. We hope that surplus countries and deficit countries will cooperate to overcome the present difficulties."

10. Domestic, as well as foreign, pressure resulted in the liberalization of finance, information, and communication services as noted in Sazanami (1986a). This is also true for the current discussion aimed at liberalizing agriculture and food products.

11. Based on Ministry of Finance (1985).

12. The same measure yields a 2.5 percent average tariff rate for Japan in 1983. But this ratio underestimates the actual barriers because of the high proportion of mineral fuel and crude material imports without tariffs. See Nihon Kanzei Kyokai (1986).

13. Liberalization issues in telecommunication equipment are discussed in Sazanami (1987).

14. Liberalization policies from 1971 to 1983 are reviewed in Sazanami (1983).

15. Four areas were stressed in the Action Program: (1) tariff reduction; (2) improvement of the standard approval system in the import process; (3) increasing government procurement of imports; and (4) liberalization of services and import promotion. See *Trade and Industry,* September 1985.

16. See Sazanami (1983, table 2).

17. See Saxonhouse (1983) for a discussion.

18. The response of Japanese imports to the recent changes in the exchange rate is analyzed in section 3.6.

19. According to estimates for major food products by the Ministry of Agriculture and Fishery, the price of agricultural products in Japan, measured relative to the hourly wage, was 7.8 times higher for wheat when compared to the United States. Japanese prices were also higher for sugar ($\times$ 2.9), beef ($\times$ 2.6), milk and cream ($\times$ 1.9), and pork ($\times$ 2.4). See Nihon Keizai Shimbun, 4 October 1986.

20. Leather and leather shoes disputes were settled in 1986 by changing the system from import quotas to one of tariff quotas. The tobacco issue was resolved by removing tariffs in 1987.

21. Hufbauer, Berliner, and Elliott (1986) define special protection to include: high tariffs, escape clause action, executive use of inherent constitutional power, discretionary protection, and statutes explicitly limiting imports.

22. U.S.-Japan trade negotiations on semiconductors continued for almost a year until a final agreement was reached in September 1986. For a discussion of trade-related issues in the semiconductor industry, see OECD (1985).

23. There are three sources of information on Japanese direct investment, each using different definitions. The Ministry of Finance data on direct investment are based on reports and are usually much larger than the Bank of Japan's balance of payment statistics which are based on annual transactions. MITI publishes information on foreign affiliates of Japanese companies, including their reinvestment activities, in *Kaigai Toshi Tokei Soran*.

24. See Sazanami (1986b) for a discussion of Japan's investment in the 1970s. The Japan Export-Import Bank (1986) gives an excellent summary of Japan's direct investment and of recent trends in Japan's investment in the United States.

25. Data in table 3.8 are based on reports to the Ministry of Finance and do not coincide with the data in tables 3.1 and 3.7 which are based on balance of payment statistics.

26. Details of the influence of trade barriers on trade and investment in the automobile industry and the electric and electronic industry are discussed in section 3.5.

27. For a discussion of Japan's entry barriers in services, see Alexander and Tan (1984).

28. See MITI (1986, 235).

29. Kreinin, in his comment on Feenstra (1984), suggests that the product up-grading took place after the VER because quantitative limitations are equivalent to a specific tariff and raise the price of cheap brands proportionately more than the price of expensive brands.

30. See Japan Export-Import Bank (1986, 42).

31. According to Hufbauer, Berliner, and Elliott (1986), between 1981 and 1984 the share of imports from Japan in U.S. consumption went down from 22.4 percent to 18.9 percent in volume terms, and from 16.2 percent to 14.5 percent in value terms.

32. See Fuss (1986).

33. From MITI, "Wagakuni kigyo no kaigai genchi seisan ni kansuru anketo chosa," quoted in *White paper on Trade* (MITI 1986, 182).

34. See Asahi Shimbun, 9 October 1986, for example.

35. Major items in consumer electronics include: TVs, videotape recorders, and audio equipment. Industrial electronics includes communication equipment, radio communication systems, electronic application equipment, electric measuring instruments, and electronic business machines. Electronic components and devices consist of electronic components, electronic tubes, discrete semiconductor devices, and liquid crystal devices.

36. EPA (1986, 25). Here and in the *White paper on Trade* the degree of export price adjustment is calculated as: [(changes in the exchange rate minus changes in the unit value of exports in yen)/the change in the exchange rate × 100.

37. See Miyamoto (1979).

38. The declining import unit values (in yen) of raw materials and mineral fuels reflect price cuts on international markets.

39. It may be worthwhile to quote the Royal Commission on the Economic

Union and Development Prospects for Canada (1985, 254). "Canada's trade relations
with the Asia-Pacific region are still dominated by our two-way trade with Japan;
commodity-based exports, on the one hand, and increasingly sophisticated manufactured imports, on the other. However, without exaggerating their absolute importance
in terms of size, our most dynamic two-way Pacific trade is with the fast-growing
NICs. . . ."

40. The recommendations in the Maekawa Report included: (1) expanding domestic demand; (2) transformation to an internationally harmonious industrial structure; (3) further improving market access and encouraging import of manufactured
goods; (5)promotion of international cooperation and Japan's contribution to the world
economy, commensurate with its international status; and (6) fiscal and monetary policy management.

41. See Fuss and Waverman (1985) for the impact of exchange rates on car
prices in the United States, Canada, and Japan.

References

Alexander, A., and H. W. Tan. 1984. Barriers to U.S. service trade in Japan. Santa
    Monica: Rand Corporation.
Baldwin, Robert E. 1984. The changing nature of U.S. trade policy since World War
    II. In *The structure and evolution of recent U.S. trade policy,* eds. R. E. Bald-
    win and A. O. Krueger. Chicago: University of Chicago Press.
———. 1985. *The political economy of U.S. import policy.* Cambridge, Mass.: MIT
    Press.
Baldwin, Robert E., and Anne O. Krueger, eds. 1984. *The structure and evolution of
    U.S. trade policy. Chicago: University of Chicago Press.*
Bergsten, C. Fred, and William R. Cline. 1985. *The United States–Japan economic
    problem.* Washington, D.C.: Institute for International Economics.
Cline, William R. 1985. *Exports of manufactures from developing countries.* Wash-
    ington, D.C.: Brookings Institution.
EPA (Economic Planning Agency). 1986. *Economic white paper 1986.*
Feenstra, Robert C. 1984. Voluntary export restraint in U.S. autos, 1980–81: Quality,
    employment and welfare effects. In *The structure and evolution of U.S. trade
    policy,* eds. Robert E. Baldwin and Anne O. Krueger. Chicago: University of
    Chicago Press.
Fuss, Melvyn. 1986. The Canada-U.S. Auto Pact of 1965: An experiment in selective
    trade liberalization. National Bureau of Economic Research Working Paper no.
    1953. Cambridge, Mass.: NBER.
Fuss, Melvyn, and Leonard Waverman. 1985. Productivity growth in the automobile
    industry, 1970–1980: A comparison of Canada, Japan and the United States.
    National Bureau of Economic Research Working Paper no. 1735. Cambridge,
    Mass.: NBER.
Hayami, Yujiro. 1985. *Nogyo keizai ron* (Agricultural economics). Tokyo: Iwanami
    Shoten.

Hufbauer, Gary C., Diane T. Berliner, and Kimberly A. Elliott. 1986. *Trade protection in the United States: 31 case studies*. Washington, D.C.: Institute for International Economics.

Japan Economic Research Institute. 1984. *Analysis of the degree of openness of the Japanese market*. Tokyo.

Japan Export-Import Bank. 1986. *Kaigai Toshi Kenkyu Joho* (Institute for Foreign Investment Monthly) 12(10). Tokyo.

JETRO (Japan External Trade Organization). 1985. Zaibei nikkei seizogyo keiei no jittai.

Kamiya, Mitsugu, and T. Korenaga, eds. 1985. *Nogyo hogo to nosambutsu boeki mondai* (Agricultural protection and agricultural trade problems). Tokyo: Nogyo Sogo Kenyu.

Kreinin, M. E. 1984. Comment on Feenstra. In *The structure and evolution of recent U.S. trade policy*, ed. R. E. Baldwin and A. O. Krueger, 61–65. Chicago: University of Chicago Press.

Maekawa Report (Report of the Advisory Group on Economic Structural Adjustment for International Harmony). 1986. Tokyo.

Minister of State for International Trade. 1983. A review of Canadian trade policy—Canadian trade policy for the 1980s. Ottawa.

Ministry of Finance. Bureau of Tariff. 1985. Summary of action program on tariff reduction. December 20.

Ministry of Finance. 1986. Bureau of international finance yearbook.

MITI. 1985, 1986. *White paper on Trade*. Various issues. Tokyo.

Miyamoto, Kazumi. 1979. Kawase reito henka to boeki shushi (Change in exchange rate and balance of trade). *Zaisei Kinyu Tokei Geppo* June. Tokyo: Ministry of Finance.

Nihon Kanzei Kyokai. 1986 and various issues. *Kanzei Kaisei no Subete* (All About Tariff Changes). Tokyo.

Nissan Jidosha Shimbunsha. 1986. Jidosha nenkan 1986.

Nissan Motors. 1986. Kokunai jidosha doko.

OECD. 1985. *The semi conductor industry trade: Related issues*. Paris: OECD.

Report of the Japan-U.S. Economic Relations Group. 1981. Tokyo.

Report of the Joint Japan-U.S. Ad Hoc Group on Yen/Dollar Exchange Rate. Working Group. 1984. Financial and capital market issues. Prepared for the Japanese Minister of Finance and the U.S. Secretary of Treasury. Tokyo.

Robinson, W., T. R. Webb, and M. A. Townsend. 1979. The influence of exchange rate changes on prices: A study of 18 industrial countries. *Economica* 46, no. 1 (February): 27–50.

Royal Commission on the Economic Union and Development Prospects for Canada. 1985. Donald S. MacDonald, chairman. Ottawa, Canada.

Saxonhouse, Gary R. 1983. The micro- and macro-economics of foreign sales to Japan. In *Trade policy for the 1980s*, ed. William R. Cline. Cambridge, Mass.: MIT Press.

Sazanami, Yoko. 1983. Nihon no boeki seisaku (Japanese trade policy in the 1970s). *Gendai Keizai* Autumn. Tokyo.

———. 1986a. Japan's trade and investment in finance, information and communica-

tion, and business services. Paper presented at the Workshop on Trade and Investment in Services in the Asia-Pacific Region, East-West Center, Honolulu.
————. 1986b. Japanese trade in the Pacific Rim—Relationship between trade and investment. In *The Pacific Rim: Investment, development, and trade,* ed. P. N. Nemetz. Vancouver: Univ. of British Columbia Press.
————. 1987. Information and communication services—Japan's recent experience. Paper presented at 16th Pacific Trade and Development Conference on Trade and Investment in Services in the Pacific, Wellington, New Zealand.
U.S. Congress-House. Subcommittee on Trade, Committee on Ways and Means. 1979. Task force report on U.S.-Japan trade. Washington, D.C.: GPO.
————. 1981. Report on trade mission to Far East. Washington, D.C.: GPO.
Wright, Richard W. 1984. *Japanese business in Canada.* Montreal: The Institute for Research on Public Policy.

Comment
Robert E. Baldwin

This is a very fine paper. Sazanami sets forth very clearly the main trends in trade and investment patterns among Canada, Japan, and the United States, and indicates the relationship between trade and investment flows in a highly perceptive manner. Her findings on recent changes in Japanese export and import volumes are particularly interesting. What I shall do is expand upon some of the relationships she points out and then discuss one of the trilateral trade policy issues that has arisen in the context of the multilateral negotiations getting under way in the Uruguay Round.

The Increased Competitiveness of the NICs

One of the interesting trade developments noted by Sazanami is the increase in exports from the newly industrializing countries (NICs) to the United States, Canada, and Japan. As she points out, part of this is due to increased Japanese investment for export purposes in these countries in response to the United States and Canada introducing selective quantitative restrictions against Japan. She also mentions the U.S. and Canadian outsourcing of industrial inputs to the NICs in response to increased competitive pressures from Japan. The recent appreciation of the yen is another reason for the increase in exports, but clearly the improving competitiveness of the NICs over the last twenty-five years or so is the major factor behind this trend. Whatever the reason, it needs to be emphasized that the major export competitors of Japan, the United States, Canada, and the European Community (EC) are not just each other but, to an increasing extent, a growing group of developing countries.[1]

The Asian NICs (the Republic of Korea, Taiwan, Hong Kong, and Singapore) and the Philippines, Malaysia, Thailand, and Indonesia—the so-called resource rich countries (RRCs) in the Pacific Rim—have increased their market shares in the United States, Canada, and Japan over the last twenty-five years to a remarkable extent. Their share in the imports of the United States rose from 7.6 percent in 1963 to 13.4 percent in 1984. Their share in the imports of Canada rose from 1.0 percent to 3.0 percent between these years, and the comparable figures for Japan are 18.3 percent and 27.9 percent. The People's Republic of China also became a significant supplier of Japan's imports, rising from nothing in 1963 to a 7.6 percent market share in 1984. (In 1984, China supplied only 1 percent and 0.4 percent of imports into the United States and Canada.)

In the case of the United States, the rise in the import share attributable to the NICs and the RRCs was at the expense of the EC and Canada, since Japan's share of imports into the United States rose even more sharply between 1963 and 1984, from 14.1 percent to 29.7 percent. Similarly, in Canada the share of imports from the EC and the United States fell as Japan's share rose from 2.4 percent in 1963 to 7.4 percent in 1984. In Japan, the import shares of the United States, the EC, and Canada all fell over this period, although the decline in the Canadian share was quite small. The rapid growth in the market shares of Japan, the Asian NICs, and the RRCs vividly demonstrates the growing importance of the Asian Pacific Rim in world trade.

This improved competitive ability of the developing countries of the Asian Pacific Rim is also evident in their own markets. The Asian NICs moved from an 8 percent share of their own market to a 12 percent share between 1963 and 1984, and from a 23 percent to 35 percent share of imports into the RRCs over this period. The shares of both Canada and the United States increased marginally between these years, while Japan's share of this market rose appreciably. The major loser was the EC.

The Ineffectiveness of Protection

Sazanami's analysis of the effects of selective protection against Japan supports a favorite theme of mine, that protection, particularly if it is discriminatory, often does not provide much assistance to the injured workers in the domestic sector. As she notes, in the case of quotas on color television sets, production merely shifted from Japan to Korea and Taiwan, with total imports into the United States declining only slightly. Japanese producers also invested in assembling operations in the United States. In the case of autos, Japan has responded by upgrading and also by investing in assembly operations in the United States. She points out that the U.S. trade balance in auto parts, excluding Canada, moved—in just two years—from a surplus of $1.5 billion in 1981 to a $3.2 billion deficit in 1983.

The effect of such investments on the trade balance of an industry, including its parts manufacturers, is an interesting issue. Empirical studies of the relation between trade and foreign direct investment have generally found a positive relation between investment and exports. Consequently, one might expect that direct investment by foreign firms in the import-protecting country would not improve the country's trade balance. A recent study by Blomström, Lipsey, and Kulchycky (1988) suggests, however, that this may not be the case. These authors found on the basis of U.S. data that net sales of foreign affiliates are positively correlated with exports from the home country. But if net sales of the affiliate are divided into net local sales and net export sales, there is some evidence of a negative relationship between U.S. exports and net local sales, while there is a strong positive relationship between U.S. exports and exports of the affiliate. Since Japanese automobile investment in the United States is motivated by the protectionist action of the United States, as the survey cited by Sazanami indicates, it seems likely that here one will find a negative relationship between investment and exports. It would be an interesting case to study.

Multilateral Issues

The bilateral disputes that have recently arisen among the United States, Canada, and Japan, and resulted in such arrangements as the Japanese voluntary export restraint (VER) on autos, the agreement between the United States and Japan to control the prices of computer chips, and the 15 percent Canadian export tax on softwood lumber, forcefully demonstrate the need for greater agreement at the multilateral level on such matters as safeguard actions, antidumping measures, and subsidies and countervailing actions. Indeed, one might expect that the recent dispute settlement experience of the three nations would lead their negotiators to give priority to improving GATT rules dealing with these matters. But such matters as trade in services and agriculture are likely to receive greater attention in the negotiations, and there is a danger that little progress will be made in the safeguards and subsidies areas, for example. Progress in these areas may also be disappointing because of the absence of past efforts to explore alternative approaches in intergovernmental forums, such as the OECD, that tend to reduce the areas of disagreement.

Let me briefly consider from a multilateral viewpoint one of the issues that has arisen: safeguards to deal with injurious (but fair) import competition. The Ministerial Declaration on the Uruguay Round states: "A comprehensive agreement on safeguards is of particular importance to the strengthening of the GATT system and to progress in the MTNs [multilateral trade negotiations]."

Safeguards

The key issue that prevented agreement on a safeguards code in the Tokyo Round negotiations was the selectivity issue, that is, whether country selectivity should be allowed when temporary import barriers are introduced as a consequence of serious injury to a domestic industry. The EC, in particular, pressed for the right to restrict imports of a product only from the countries whose imports were the main cause of the domestic injury. The developing countries vigorously opposed this modification in the basic most-favored-nation (MFN) rule of the GATT, maintaining that the change would result in unfair discrimination against them. The views of both these major participants do not appear to have changed since the Tokyo Round.

The selectivity issue involves ethics, international political relations, and economics. It is widely regarded as "unfair" to treat a product exported from one country less favorably at the border than the identical product exported from another country, unless there are special circumstances, such as the latter country is at a significant economic disadvantage or that it is a fellow member of an economic arrangement that increases the freedom of trade within the group. Tariff preferences for developing countries, and customs unions and free trade areas are regarded as ethically acceptable under these conditions.

Whether it is "fair" to impose higher import barriers against a country whose export success has been achieved without resort to so-called "unfair" trade practices condemned in the GATT, e.g., export subsidies and patent infringements, but whose exports are causing serious injury to an import-competing industry in another country, is a matter of dispute. Clearly, many people in the advanced industrial nations believe it is unfair for countries like Japan, Korea, and Taiwan to increase their exports so rapidly that they cause serious injury to workers and capital owners engaged in the same industry in other industrial countries. Many people in the advanced industrial countries also think it is unfair for exports from countries whose market shares have not been rising to be restricted as part of the effort to control imports from those nations whose exports are the cause of serious injury to a domestic industry. Most people in successfully competing countries like Japan and the NICs disagree, believing that economic success achieved in a "fair" manner should not be penalized, especially when the countries that wish to discriminate are enjoying significantly higher living standards.

At the time the GATT was established, it was widely believed that discriminatory treatment among foreign suppliers tended to worsen international political relations. It was thought that countries being discriminated against are likely not only to retaliate against the discriminators, but to reduce their economic, political, and social relations with these latter countries and seek closer economic, political, and perhaps military ties with other nations. Cordell Hull, the prime mover in the U.S. Trade Agreements Program and the formation of the GATT, reasoned that, "If we could get a freer flow of trade—freer in the sense of fewer discriminations and obstructions—so that one country would not be deadly jealous of another and the living standards of all countries might rise, thereby eliminating the economic dissatisfaction that breeds war, we might have a reasonable chance for lasting peace" (Hull 1948, 81).

The fears of Hull and his colleagues seem exaggerated in the world of today, in which there has been a long period of peace among the major nations. Yet there can be little doubt about the developing countries' and Japan's resentment over the discriminatory treatment they have received from the United States and the members of the EC. Perhaps these latter countries have the confidence of the self-made millionaire character, Daddy Warbucks, in the stage play "Annie," who stated that "he didn't have to be nice to anyone on the way up to the top, because he didn't expect to ever go back down," but the world's recent economic performance would suggest some reason for caution on this score. It may not be many years before those who are being discriminated against in international trade and do not now have the power to retaliate effectively, gain the power to injure other countries by discriminating themselves.

The economic efficiency implications of selectivity are more straightforward. Imports tend to be shifted from the country being discriminated against to suppliers of the product whose costs are higher. Compared to an increase in protection that applies to all foreign suppliers of the good and that thus reduces imports from all suppliers, this trade diversion worsens the allocation of world resources and lowers world real income. The country introducing the selective protection, and especially the domestic industry being protected, is less concerned with changes in world welfare than whether the protective measures actually remedy the injury to the domestic industry. Government policymakers who have imposed selective protection have invariably assumed that it would be effective in this regard. But, as Sazanami notes in her paper, this has not always been the case. In the color television and non-rubber footwear cases in the United States, there is general agreement that selective protection was almost completely ineffective in helping these injured industries. Shifts in supply from other country sources, quality upgrading, and consumer shifts to substitute products meant that domestic output and employment increased very little. Thus, one important conclusion about country selectivity is that it simply will not work if the product can be produced easily by other actual or potential suppliers and/or consumers can shift to close substitutes that are not protected. The imposition of U.S. quotas on textiles and apparel products against one country after another, while the domestic industry continued to complain it was being injured, also suggests the ineffectiveness of selectivity in some circumstances.

The Japanese auto case is somewhat different. While, as Sazanami notes, imports into the United States from non-Japanese suppliers have increased at the same time that Japanese imports have been fixed in quantitative terms, the shift to alternative sources and the upgrading by Japan has not yet been sufficient to seriously undermine the purpose of the import controls. The reason is the lower degree of substitutability between Japanese automobiles and those from other countries, and the greater difficulty of establishing production facilities for Japanese-type cars in other countries. The degree of substitutability between Japanese and other foreign cars is not negligible, however, as Levinsohn (1988) has recently found. According to his estimates, a 1 percent increase in the price of Japanese cars only (brought about, for example, by selective protection) will increase U.S. auto production by 0.219 percent, whereas a 1 percent price increase in all foreign cars (brought about by MFN protection) will increase U.S. car production by 0.436 percent. This is an appreciable price for the U.S. auto industry to pay for selectivity, but the degree of substitution between Japanese and other foreign cars is not so high as to completely undermine the restraint program.

What Levinsohn's estimates and the experience with the Japanese VER show is that Japanese-made cars and other foreign cars are not the same product. Consequently, one might x-out Japanese autos from the general tariff line item for automobiles and, after imposing quotas or tariffs against these cars, claim that the MFN principle was still being followed. But most would argue that this action was still discriminatory, since it singled out a country and not a product.

More relevant from an economic viewpoint is the likelihood that Japanese companies will gradually transfer production activities to other countries (Sazanami discusses the plans of Japanese firms to expand production in Canada and then send cars to the United States under the U.S.-Canadian free trade agreement in autos and auto parts) and into the United States itself (as they are doing to an increasing extent), and that other countries will learn to make the same kind of autos as those made in Japan. (The Koreans and Yugoslavians are capturing an increasing share of the small-car market.) The result of this shift in production is that sales of Japanese cars to American consumers do not fall nearly as much as expected, and injured workers and capital-owners in U.S. auto companies do not benefit as much as expected from the protection.

The charge of discrimination can be avoided and the likelihood increased that the protection will be effective in serving its intended purpose by defining the tariff line item in terms of the physical characteristics of Japanese cars or perhaps of all small cars. (This was what was done with respect to German-made small cars as part of the U.S. retaliatory action in the so-called Chicken War in the early 1960s.) That would eliminate the country discrimination and the threat of an import surge from other actual or potential sources of small-car production. Of course, the possibility still exists that U.S.-produced Japanese cars will capture the market formerly held by U.S. companies. This is one of the reasons economists often recommend direct subsidies to injured domestic firms.

Other problems remain with regard to the effectiveness of a safeguards action, even after x'ing out cars with physical characteristics similar to those produced by the Japanese. One is the shift toward more expensive, higher quality varieties of the product that often occurs when quantitative restrictions are imposed. This tends to reduce the increase in domestic employment and the value of domestic output that would take place without this upgrading. This problem can be handled, of course, by restricting imports by ad valorem tariffs rather than quotas. Yet, under pressures from the domestic industry, government officials are often reluctant to use tariffs due to their lack of knowledge of demand and supply elasticities, and thus their inability to make good predictions on the quantitative effects on imports. (Of course, as noted, the ability to fix imports does not mean that one can successfully predict the quantitative effects on domestic output.) One way to reduce the adverse domestic effects of quantitative import restrictions would be to use a compound protective measure consisting of a quantitative import limit coupled with an ad valorem tariff.[2]

Another problem is that there would still be some increase in the imports of other foreign varieties of the product, as has occurred under the Japanese VER on autos. This weakens the output-increasing impact of protection on the domestic industry. One way to handle this would be to impose a lower ad valorem tariff on these other forms of the product than on the form that is the main source of the import injury, or to set a quota at pre-protection import levels for these countries.

The conclusion from this discussion seems to be that the question of whether selectivity or the MFN principle should apply with regard to safeguard actions will be settled more by the realities of the marketplace than by arguments over ethics and economic efficiency. If the intention of safeguard actions is really to assist the injured workers and capital-owners in domestic firms, protection must be extended to all countries. Under the worst circumstance, the application of protection selectively by country is completely ineffective in providing assistance to the injured parties, while in the best circumstance, with poor substitution possibilities and a significant period of time required to shift production to other countries, protection is only temporarily effective.

Yet the need for protection to be applied on an MFN basis to be effective does not mean that existing tariff line classifications need be used in undertaking safeguard actions. In many cases, the products classified under the same tariff line are not close substitutes. Levinsohn found, for example, that the cross-price elasticity between Swedish and Japanese cars was quite low. Consequently, assuming that U.S. imports of Swedish cars had not been increasing at a significant rate, it would be neither ethically appropriate nor economically necessary to include Swedish cars in an MFN safeguard action against small, inexpensive cars. By following this x'ing out practice when economically appropriate and applying the MFN principle in protecting products in the new import category, both the arguments of those favoring selectivity and those opposing discrimination seem to be met.

Notes

1. For a further elaboration of this point, see Baldwin (1988).
2. In the simple competitive case with infinitely elastic import supply curves and import demand curves for the different varieties with the same elasticity, a tariff above the rate that itself would lead to just the fixed import quantity would be binding and result in no change in quality mix. A tariff set below this level would cause some upgrading but less than the quantitative restriction by itself.

References

Baldwin, Robert E. 1988. U.S. and foreign competition in the developing countries of the Asian Pacific Rim. In *The United States in the world economy,* ed. Martin Feldstein. Chicago: University of Chicago Press.
Blomström, Magnus, Robert E. Lipsey, and Ksenia Kulchycky. 1988. U.S. and Swedish direct investment and exports. In *Trade policy issues and empirical analysis,* ed. Robert E. Baldwin. Chicago: University of Chicago Press.
Hull, Cordell. 1948. *The memoirs of Cordell Hull.* New York: The Macmillan Company.
Levinsohn, James. 1988. Empirics of taxes on differentiated products: The case of tariffs in the U.S. automobile industry. In *Trade policy issues and empirical analysis,* ed. Robert E. Baldwin. Chicago: University of Chicago Press.

Comment
Ronald J. Wonnacott

The paper by Sazanami provides a great deal of interesting detail on Japan's changing economic relationship with Canada and the United States. It is all very well to observe that macroeconomic pressure in the United States has meant that the U.S. would be running a very large trade deficit; and roughly mirror-image macroeconomic pressure in Japan means that Japan will be running a trade surplus, with it being no surprise that these two pressures would result in a large bilateral U.S. trade deficit with Japan. It is still interesting to put the microeconomic flesh on this story. For example, Sazanami's paper shows how depressed resource prices and the drift in Japanese specialization away from resource-using industries explain the disappointing increase in the value of North American resource exports to Japan. This, in conjunction with the rapid growth in North American purchases of Japanese auto, electronic, and other products, provides the more detailed configuration of the rapid increase in the U.S. trade deficit with Japan and the Canadian switch from a trade surplus with Japan to a deficit.

At the same time, it seems to me, a number of questions are raised by this paper. Why don't the Japanese introduce, as a number one priority, policies to massively stimulate imports? These policies could include not only a reduction in tariffs and highly visible NTBs in response to U.S. pressure, but also, in response to their own interests, a vigorous and unrelenting attack on the less visible NTBs that restrict the increase in their imports? Their own interest in doing this should follow not just from a recognition that welfare depends on goods consumed, not produced. It should also follow from a recognition that, without such import-liberalizing measures, they can expect to be under continued threat from protectionists in the U.S. Congress seeking to "cure" Japan's bilateral surplus with the United States. Furthermore, Japanese import liberalization should also come from a recognition that, even in the absence of U.S. threats, increased imports are necessary to "support" the spectacular Japanese export performance. Specifically, increased imports can, by moderating the rise in the yen, prevent it from damaging some of the export industries on which Japan now places such a high value. In short, why aren't the Japanese authorities begging Sears, Wards, and Marks and Spencers to enter Japan with all the retailing force they can muster?

When I look at Japan these days—and this must also be true for the Japanese when they look at the rest of the world—I never cease to be surprised. Consider two phenomena:

1. Auto wages are now higher in Japan than in Canada; and, by the time this goes to press, perhaps higher than in the United States as well.
2. The value of Japanese assets is now very high relative to the value of assets elsewhere. For example, the value of Japanese real estate now greatly exceeds the value of U.S. real estate.

Very high values in Japan (for assets, auto wages, and everything else) are, of course, in large part just a reflection of the 75 percent rise in the value of the yen relative to the U.S. dollar—from 260–65 yen per U.S. dollar in early 1985 to substantially less than 150 today. (Canadians who note the recent rise of less than 10 percent in the value of the Canadian dollar from about U.S. 71 cents to just over 76 cents may have difficulty fully appreciating the magnitude of the yen's rise. It is as though the Canadian dollar went to over $1.30 U.S.) In addition, Japanese asset prices may well now be heavily speculative. Be that as it may, the current price of the yen and Japanese assets determine the rate at which Japanese assets can now be exchanged for bargain North American assets. And as long as this rate does not change greatly, the Japanese have both a strong incentive and capacity to buy large quantities of North American assets. The impact need not be trivial.

Let me turn now to the question of how a Canada/U.S. free trade area that is currently under negotiation may affect Japanese trade and foreign investment.

Possible Effects of a Canada-U.S. Bilateral Trade Agreement on Japan: Trade Diversion

Which Japanese sales in North America might be damaged as, say, Canadians divert some of their purchases from Japan to the United States? Sazanami's paper implies that the potentially most important area is electronic equipment; diversion in autos has already occurred, dating back to the Canada/U.S. Auto Pact in 1965. But given the growth of Japanese auto exports to the United States and Canada since, one can only wonder: did the Japanese even notice? Will Japanese electronics producers even notice? Certainly not in VCRs, which, at last report, were not being produced in North America. Moreover, in products where the Japanese or North Americans are now imposing voluntary export restraints or any other kind of quantity restriction on Japanese sales in North America, there will be good reason for expecting little trade diversion at Japanese expense. Although Canada/U.S. free trade may reduce the sales that the Japanese would make in North America *in the absence of quantity restrictions,* it would not reduce their *actual* sales in these products as long as the quantity restrictions still bind. Incidentally, this sort of argument may provide a partial explanation of the puzzle posed by McKinnon in his comment on Helliwell's paper: why hasn't the increase in the yen had a greater effect on Japanese exports? One answer is this: in products subject to quantity restrictions such as autos—where Japanese export restraints may have recently become more "voluntary," but nonetheless are apparently still imposed—the change in relative prices does not take effect until quantity restrictions cease to bind.

I have argued elsewhere that preferences granted Canadian producers in the U.S. market may be important for Canada in the development of new firms and the specialization of existing ones. While these preferences may or may not damage other third countries, it is difficult to see them having much effect on the Japanese, at least in the short run.

However, a Canada/U.S. free trade area may have more important effects on Japanese investment, especially in Canada.

Further Effects on Japan: Investment Flows

With bilateral free trade, inefficient foreign investment to satisfy the small Canadian market at high cost will, to a large degree, be replaced by investment aimed at servicing the entire North American market at much lower cost due to economies of scale. This has already taken place in the auto industry under the Auto Pact. What does this tell us about changing investment patterns in other industries?

In the auto industry, rationalization of investment occurred within each of the U.S.-owned auto companies as a result of the Auto Pact. But, as Sazanami points out, the Auto Pact has also provided an incentive for Japanese and other third-country firms to invest in Canada, to service the whole North American market under the free trade provisions of the Auto Pact. Recent commitments by Japanese auto companies to invest in Canada may seem to suggest that the same may occur in other industries, and I would be hopeful this would occur. But before arriving at this conclusion, some troubling complications in the auto industry should be considered.

Until very recently, there was in fact very little Japanese investment in Canada. Sazanami's paper indicates that as late as 1985 less than 1 percent of Japanese direct investment in autos in North America was in Canada ($8 million vs. $967 million in the United States). However, according to Wonnacott (1987), in the last few years, Japanese firms have made heavy commitments to produce in Canada: by 1990, East Asian (i.e., mostly Japanese) producers will have an estimated capacity of 630,000 units in Canada, and 1,700,000 in the United States (including joint ventures). This implies a substantial U.S. trade deficit with Canada in East Asian autos, a potentially much more sensitive issue for the United States than the deficit with Canada in North American automotive equipment that now exists. This raises several questions.

To what degree has Canada's recent relative success in attracting Japanese investment been due to the attractions of Canada as a place to produce and sell cars across North America? (As already noted, auto wages are now lower in Canada than in the United States or Japan.) And to what degree has it been due to financial incentives in the form of duty remissions granted by the Canadian government to some Japanese companies? If such incentives have played an important role, then the Canadian industry as it has now developed may face serious difficulties. Predictions are that, by early in the next decade, the North American auto industry will suffer from substantial overcapacity, at about the same time that the United States will be facing a substantial deficit with Canada in Japanese cars. If it is perceived that this situation has been caused by Canadian financial incentives that have drawn Japanese investment into Canada in order to use the Auto Pact for free entry into the United States, then there may be severe strains on the Auto Pact.

Canada's problem is this: If special incentives are not granted to the Japanese to invest in Canada, past history indicates that they will do very little. While the Auto Pact gives them secure access to the U.S. market if they invest in Canada, this access is still not quite as guaranteed as the access they will get if they build a plant in the United States instead. On the other hand, if Canada does provide special investment incentives to the Japanese, then this puts strains on the Auto Pact. The question for Canada is how to attract foreign investment through the locational advantages of Canada, rather than through government financial incentives which raise potential problems with the United States.

There is considerable pressure in Canada to keep the Auto Pact off the table in the current Canada/U.S. negotiations. To some extent I agree: it works, so don't fix it. On the other hand, it is important to ensure that it continues to work. Impending strains should be dealt with by a clear, negotiated understanding of what is a subsidy and what is not. This is unfinished business that must be cleaned up, with or without the current negotiations, with or without a broader bilateral free trade area. These auto issues will be surfacing on some table, the only question being: which one? The current negotiating table seems to offer a relatively promising way for reducing these strains.*

Concluding Observations

I have been critical so far of Japanese and Canadian policies. Let me now turn to U.S. policies—in particular, U.S. trade remedy laws. It is true that these laws have their bright side, since they restrict trade-distorting subsidy and dumping practices by trade partners. But on the dark side, they can be used as protectionist devices. And we are seeing more and more of the dark side. These laws provide a way for U.S. producers to acquire protection, if they can "get over" a quasi-judicial hurdle. If that hurdle erodes, it will become easier and easier for U.S. firms to acquire protection, i.e., to "tax the consuming public" in their own interest. While it may appear to Congress that it is exercising more power over trade policy, it may in effect be shifting that power in a very dangerous way to U.S. producing interests. Moreover, such a development is as serious for U.S. trading partners like Canada, who face damage in their export markets, as for the United States itself. That

---

*Author's note at time of press: The most serious strains in auto trade were in fact dealt with in the actual Canada-U.S. free trade agreement.

quasi-judicial hurdle is now eroding: it has eroded with the redefinition of subsidy that took place earlier between the judgment in favor of Canada and the 1986 judgment against Canada in softwood lumber.

The softwood lumber case raises other problems as well. "Leveling the playing field" makes sense when it comes to government subsidies. But it does not make sense if it is used to remove the natural cost advantage of foreign resource suppliers. Doing this is to apply the old discredited scientific tariff not to labor, but to resources; by offsetting comparative advantage, this destroys the gains from trade. That is damaging enough to the national interest of the United States. But also consider this: the eventual outcome of that softwood lumber action is that the United States has forced Canada to improve its terms of trade at U.S. expense. (The assessment that Canadians have been forced to impose on their softwood lumber has—in addition to creating domestic transfers in each country—resulted in an international transfer to Canada from U.S. buyers who have to pay a higher price for Canadian lumber.) The analogy that leaps to mind brings me back to Japanese trade: the Japanese voluntary export restraints in autos negotiated by Canada and the United States essentially forced the Japanese to cartelize their export sales in North America, earning them a profit here (at the expense of North American consumers) that did not exist in the more competitive Japanese market. The resulting transfer of income west across the Pacific provides a further example of how the attempt to protect often leads countries (in this case, the United States and Canada) to force a terms of trade benefit on their trading partners at their own expense.

Reference

Wonnacott, Paul. 1987. *U.S. and Canadian auto policies in a changing world environment*. Ottawa and Washington: Canadian-American Committee.

2 INTERNATIONAL TRADE AND STRUCTURAL ADJUSTMENT

4   Trade in Primary Products: Canada, the United States, and Japan

Andrew Schmitz

Trade in primary products is of vital importance for Canada, the United States, and Japan. As examples, the prairie region of Canada depends heavily on exports to the United States of uranium, potash, and red meats. On the other hand, Japan relies heavily on imports to satisfy its food needs. In fact, Japan is the largest food importer, while Canada and the United States are among its major suppliers.

This paper discusses the importance of primary trade among the United States, Canada, and Japan, and some of the tariff and nontariff barriers (NTBs) which are present. Some estimates are given of the gains from freer trade, along with a discussion of export markets where both the United States and Canada compete which includes, but is not limited to, Japan.

4.1 Canada's Trade with Japan

Canola, wheat, and barley together account for roughly 70 percent of the value of Canada's agricultural exports to Japan, with canola being the most important. Pork and pork products are also important. In terms of total primary products, Canada also exports sizable amounts of wood and paper products. On the other hand, Canada imports very little from Japan in the way of primary products (less than 10 percent of the value of exports).

4.1.1 Canola Trade

Canada is the largest producer and the world's largest exporter of canola. It competes with U.S. soybean exports where the United States dominates. Japan is a major importer of both of these products, but imports are in the form of raw seed rather than oil products. Japan removed its tariffs and quotas on both canola and soybeans in the early 1970s, but maintained import tariffs on both crude and refined canola and on soybean oil of roughly $70 US/ton (Carter and Schmitz 1986). Duties on processed products have both discouraged processing in the United States and Canada and stimulated activities with high value-added in Japan.

Carter and Johnson (1986) estimated the impact of Japanese tariff protection on Canada using a quadratic programming model of the Canadian, U.S., European, and Japanese oilseed trade. Demand, supply, and price linkage equations formed the basis of the model. They estimated that complete removal of the canola and soybean oil tariffs would increase the net revenue of Canadian crushers by 6.3 percent per annum.

4.1.2   Wheat and Barley

With roughly 20 percent of its imports from Canadian sources, Japan has been a traditional customer of Canadian wheat. The farm price of wheat in Japan is four to five times the world price, while barley prices for producers exceed world prices by five to six times (Australian Bureau of Agricultural Economics 1981). However, the prices paid by Japanese consumers are normally lower than farm-gate prices. For example, in 1983 the average producer return on wheat was four times the average cost of imported wheat and almost three times the price at which the government-owned Japanese Food Agency (JFA), which regulates imports and sales, sold wheat to consumers (Carter 1984). On 7 February 1987, the Canadian Wheat Board f.o.b. price for wheat was $146.90 U.S./ton, while the resale value (i.e., the price that the JFA charged to the millers) was $559.00 U.S./ton. In this case, the average producer price was roughly six times the cost of imported wheat.

There are no explicit tariffs and/or quotes on Japanese imports of wheat and barley. They are regulated by the amount purchased by the JFA. The barley market is not as distorted as the wheat market. The JFA buys the barley and auctions it to users at "anticipated retail prices." These prices are generally above the JFA import buying price.

In terms of Canada's export shares of barley and wheat, Japanese imports of feed barley increased from 866,000 tons in 1970 to 1,418,000 tons in 1980, an increase of 64 percent, while Canada's exports only increased by 22 percent. Thus Canada's market share declined. Also, Canada has not increased its sales of wheat to Japan in the past twenty years, even though Japanese imports more than doubled. Much of the total import growth has been in medium-quality wheats.

4.1.3   Pork Trade

As with canola, Canada is Japan's most important supplier of pork and pork products. They represent roughly 25 percent of Japanese imports. These imports are generally of high quality (Chadee and Carter 1986). Japan manages a price stabilization system which maintains a price band for pork. To do this, a set of import tariffs is used. Chadee and Carter estimated the importance of the tariff to Canadian producers using a spatial price model which incorporates econometric estimates of pork supply and demand equations (1970–84 quarterly data). They estimated that if the current tariff of 5.5 percent on Canadian pork were removed, Japanese prices would decline by 9.5 percent, Canadian prices would increase by 4 percent, and the volume of trade would increase by roughly 8 percent.

4.1.4   Beef Trade

In terms of Canadian beef exports, Canada supplies less than 2 percent of the Japanese import market even though the Japanese recently liberalized beef quotas to allow additional imports of 27,600 tons of high-quality beef over the four-year period from 1984–87. The beef trade is highly regulated by means of quotas. The Livestock Industry Promotion Corporation (LIPC) is the main regulatory agency. The entire LIPC share of the general beef import quota can, in theory, be imported from any country satisfying Japanese import requirements. Thus competitive factors alone cannot explain the small market share of Canadian beef exports to Japan relative to exports, for example, from Australia; politics also plays a role in allocating quotas among exporting countries.

4.2   U.S. Trade with Japan

4.2.1   Traded Items

The United States is the largest food exporter to Japan, followed by Australia and then Canada. For example, in 1983 the United States, Australia, and Canada supplied approximately 40 percent, 10 percent, and 7 percent, respectively, of Japan's total farm imports.

The United States is a major supplier of feed grains to Japan, primarily corn. As figure 4.1 shows, Japanese coarse grain imports more than doubled between 1970 and 1985. Also, U.S. exports to Japan increased significantly, comprising roughly 70 percent of Japanese import needs.

The United States supplies roughly 90 percent of Japanese soybean imports. U.S. exports have increased significantly as have Japanese imports, with both having increased by more than 50 percent since the early 1970s (figure 4.2).

Figure 4.3 shows total Japanese meat imports and the U.S. share in this total. Total meat imports have virtually quadrupled since the early 1970s, while U.S. exports to Japan roughly doubled. The United States provides 25–30 percent of Japan's meat import needs.

Japanese wheat imports have increased along with the market share

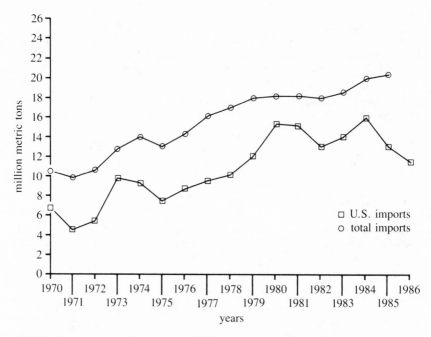

Fig. 4.1 Japanese Coarse Grain Imports, 1970–86. *Source:* Sanderson (1986).

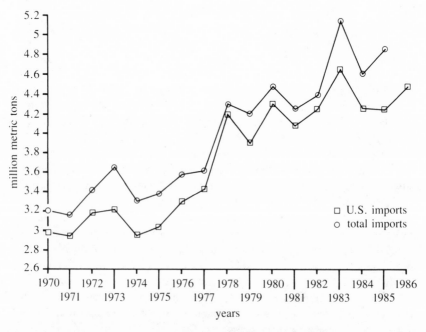

Fig. 4.2 Japanese Soybean Imports, 1970–86. *Source:* Sanderson (1986).

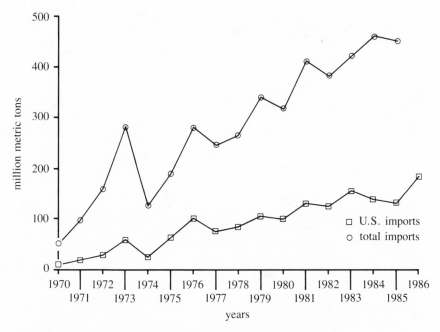

Fig. 4.3   Japanese Meat Imports, 1970–86. *Source:* Sanderson (1986).

occupied by the United States (table 4.1). Japanese imports more than doubled between 1960 and 1980, while U.S. exports to Japan more than tripled over the same period.

The United States exports commodities to Japan which are not exported by Canada. Two such commodities, soybeans and corn, have been mentioned above. Other commodities include rice and oranges, although these are of minor importance. The top six major Japanese agricultural imports in order of importance are: corn, soybeans, wheat, pork, coffee beans, and beef.

4.2.2   Trade Barriers

Japanese agricultural trade barriers are substantial. Tariff protection against soybeans consists primarily of a tariff on soybean oil of roughly 17,000 yen/ton. Japanese corn imports are free of duties and border restrictions. However, even though prices may fall as a result of a drop in world prices, only a partial pass-through of the reduced import costs to farmers results. For example, the yen prices of imported corn and soybeans dropped by 60 percent between July 1985 and December 1986, yet the feed compound prices in Japan decreased by only 23 percent (Sanderson 1986). One reason is that the Japanese cooperatives enjoy a virtual monopoly on feed imports. In addition, Japan maintains a quota on corn imports for industrial uses to protect Japa-

Table 4.1   Volume of Wheat Imported by Japan, by Source, 1959–60 through
            1980–81 Crop Years (in thousand metric tons)

Crop Year[a]	Argentina	Australia	Canada	France	U.S.A.	All Countries
1959–60	—	379	1,255	—	909	2,566
1960–61	—	358	1,539	—	916	2,834
1961–62	1	427	1,331	—	1,036	2,795
1962–63	—	345	1,262	—	1,005	2,663
1963–64	—	512	1,309	—	2,041	3,919
1964–65	2	443	1,433	27	1,678	3,584
1965–66	—	364	1,285	—	1,943	3,592
1966–67	—	431	1,620	—	2,136	4,260
1967–68	—	613	1,097	3	2,228	4,028
1968–69	18	1,147	1,247	16	1,839	4,267
1969–70	—	1,018	1,068	34	2,382	4,502
1970–71	—	821	1,000	1	2,878	4,834
1971–72	—	1,495	1,395	1	2,216	5,106
1972–73	81	752	1,364	—	3,373	5,569
1973–74	33	428	1,692	—	3,067	5,353
1974–75	33	1,009	1,187	—	3,073	5,404
1975–76	—	1,063	1,062	—	3,344	6,009
1976–77	—	1,076	1,320	—	3,152	5,548
1977–78	—	1,158	1,352	—	3,269	5,779
1978–79	—	969	1,236	—[b]	3,232	5,744
1979–80	—	985	1,290	—[b]	3,148	5,606
1980–81	—	756	1,463	—[b]	3,162	5,381

[a]July 1 to June 30.
[b]Exports of EEC, excluding intra-EEC trade.
Source: Carter (1984, 71).

nese potato farmers. Also, under Japanese law, a certain amount of domestically produced feed ingredients, such as fishmeal, must be used in mixed-
feed formulas, thus distorting the level of imports.

For wheat, the JFA essentially applies the same procedures for American exports as it does to Canadian exports discussed earlier. Japanese producer prices far exceed Chicago wheat prices, and Japanese millers' prices
for American wheat far exceed the Chicago price.

For rice, the Japanese producer price has been between three to four
times the world price. However, as a result of the 1985 Farm Bill, the Japanese producer price went up to approximately ten times the world price.

The LIPC, as mentioned, has a virtual monopoly on beef imports and
has protected Japanese producers from imports, especially of high-grade
beef, by limiting tenders to lower grades. American beef that is of "high
quality" is largely confined to the small hotel and private quotas. Despite the
beef quotas, not only have Japanese beef imports increased, but the U.S.
share of the Japanese market has also increased (table 4.2), while Australia's
share has declined somewhat. However, Australia still has the largest mar-

Table 4.2 Sources by Quantity and Value of Japanese Beef Imports, 1976–82

Quantity

Year	Australia tons	Australia % of total	United States tons	United States % of total	New Zealand tons	New Zealand % of total	Others[a] tons	Others[a] % of total	Total tons
1976	77,025	81.7	11,864	12.6	4,639	4.9	706	0.8	94,234
1977	72,055	85.2	7,330	8.7	3,903	4.6	1,257	1.5	84,545
1978	78,173	77.5	13,026	12.9	7,800	7.7	1,864	1.9	100,863
1979	101,268	76.8	24,672	18.7	3,510	2.7	2,342	1.8	131,792
1980	93,614	75.5	23,674	19.1	3,991	3.2	2,674	2.2	123,953
1981	87,071	70.4	27,543	22.3	6,148	5.0	2,884	2.3	123,646
1982	85,997	70.4	31,570	25.9	3,641	3.0	871	0.7	122,079

Value

Year	Australia million yen	Australia % of total	United States million yen	United States % of total	New Zealand million yen	New Zealand % of total	Others[a] million yen	Others[a] % of total	Total million yen
1976	34,931	69.8	12,026	24.0	2,645	5.3	450	0.9	50,052
1977	27,860	75.6	5,854	15.9	2,403	6.5	737	2.0	36,854
1978	32,189	69.1	9,922	21.3	3,500	7.5	951	2.1	46,562
1979	63,976	71.0	21,838	24.2	2,566	2.8	1,759	2.0	90,139
1980	69,867	69.5	24,927	24.8	3,804	3.8	1,890	1.9	100,488
1981	56,878	63.9	25,155	28.3	5,016	5.6	1,972	2.2	89,021
1982	59,703	61.4	33,540	34.5	3,205	3.3	706	0.7	97,155

[a]Other supplying countries include Austria, Canada, Costa Rica, Greenland, Iceland, Ireland, Madagascar, Mexico, Papua New Guinea, Sweden, Taiwan, United Kingdom, and Vanuatu.

Source: Carter (1984, 68).

Table 4.3   International Comparison of Wholesale Beef (Carcass) Prices (unit: yen/kg)

	U.S.	Australia	EC	Japan
1978	376 (32.5)	177 (15.3)	563 (48.6)	1,158 (100)
1979	494 (37.2)	367 (27.7)	774 (58.3)	1,327 (100)
1980	528 (43.9)	397 (33.0)	846 (70.4)	1,202 (100)
1981	488 (42.8)	331 (29.1)	715 (62.8)	1,139 (100)
1982	559 (46.5)	298 (24.8)	783 (65.1)	1,202 (100)
1983	514 (43.4)	345 (27.2)	773 (62.0)	1,183 (100)

Note: Figures in parentheses are relative prices assuming Japanese prices equal 100.
Source: Gustafson (1987, 69).

ket share of roughly 60 percent. As illustrated earlier, Canada's market share is less than 2 percent. Australia ships mostly grass-fed beef to Japan, unlike the United States.

Selective international wholesale beef prices are given in table 4.3. Japanese prices are well above those of other major producing areas and the ratios have more or less remained stable since 1981. In 1983, U.S. prices were 43 percent of the Japanese level.

Japan regulates its beef imports with a general quota and four major special quotas. Quotas are not allocated to specific countries—each country must compete for its share. Most of the imports fall under the general quota (e.g., 80 percent while special quotas take up the remainder (table 4.4). The majority of the general quota is allocated to the LIPC. Because of quality differences, Australia has the lion's share of the general quota but the United States has 90 percent of the hotel quota (Gustafson 1987). Beef import allocations by country are given in table 4.5. Exports to Japan must meet the specifications attached to the quotas allocated.

4.2.3 Trade Liberalization

Japan has one of the highest levels of agricultural protection in the world as measured by producer subsidy equivalents (table 4.6). For many commodities, Japanese producer protection is more than four times greater than in Canada or the United states. As examples, Japan has a producer subsidy equivalent of 107.1 for feed grains compared to 13.1 in the U.S., while for beef and veal the numbers are 54.9 and 9.5. Rice tops the list at 68.8 in Japan, compared to 5.4 in the U.S.

Japanese imports have risen despite a sharp increase in the level of agricultural protection. In 1955, the overall level of protection (tariff equivalent) was about 18 percent. By 1980–82, it had increased to around 150 percent at the producer level and around 100 percent at the consumer level. In 1955, the protection of rice, wheat, beef, and milk was 24 percent, 31 percent, 39 percent, and 4 percent, respectively. By 1980–82, the producer

Table 4.4 Japanese Beef Import Quotas, 1974–84 (in metric tons)

| Japanese Fiscal Year | General Quotas | | | Special Quotas | | | | | Total |
	LIPC	Private	Subtotal	Hotel	Okinawa	School Lunch	Boiled	Subtotal	
1974	n.a.	n.a.	n.a.	n.a.	5,650	n.a.	n.a.	5,650	5,650
1975	69,900	5,100	75,000	1,000	5,500	1,000	2,500	10,000	85,000
1976	71,000	9,000	80,000	1,000	5,500	3,000	7,000	16,500	96,500
1977	73,000	7,000	80,000	2,000	5,200	2,200	3,100	12,500	92,500
1978	86,500	8,500	95,000	3,000	5,600	3,000	5,400	17,000	112,000
1979	105,600	10,900	116,500	3,000	5,800	2,500	6,700	18,000	134,500
1980	106,800	12,200	119,000	3,000	5,850	2,250	4,700	15,800	134,800
1981	99,900	11,100	110,000	3,000	5,850	2,250	4,700	15,800	126,800
1982	107,280	11,920	119,200	3,000	5,850	2,250	4,700	15,800	135,000
1983	112,680	12,520	125,200	3,000	5,850	2,250	4,700	15,800	141,000
1984	119,880	13,320	133,200	4,000	5,850	2,250	4,700	16,800	150,000

Source: Gustafson (1987, 45)

n.a. = not available.

Table 4.5   Estimated Beef Import Quota Allocations for Recent Representative Period[a]
(in metric tons)

Quotas	Quota Allocation	Supply Sources[b]				Total Imports
		U.S.	Australia	New Zealand	Others	
General						
To LIPC	109,080	27,500	79,000	2,500	80	109,080
To Zennikuren	8,484	6,500	1,500	400	84	8,484
To Processors	3,636	0	3,300	336	0	3,636
Subtotal	121,200	34,000	83,300	33,236	164	121,200
Special						
Hotel	3,000	2,700	150	150	0	3,000
School lunch	2,250	0	2,250	0	0	2,250
Okinawa	5,850	1,000	1,900	2,950	0	5,850
(Time Lag & Quota Adm.)		13	2,852	1,388	875	5,128
Total Fresh/Frozen	132,300	37,713	90,952	7,724	1,039	137,428
Boiled Beef	4,700	0	4,292	89	1	4,382
Total	137,000	37,713	95,244	7,813	1,040	141,810

[a]Quota allocation for second half of Japanese fiscal year (JFY) 1982 (October 1982–March 1983) and the first half of JFY 1983 (April 1983–October 1983).
[b]Quotas are not allocated by country, but on a global basis.
Source: Gustafson (1987, 46).

protection rates had risen to 230 percent for rice, 280 percent for wheat, 300 percent for beef, and 200 percent for dairy products (Sanderson 1987).

There are some estimates of the gains from freer agricultural trade with Japan. In 1986 the American Rice Millers' Association filed a Section 301 petition with the U.S. Trade Representative to investigate restrictive Japanese rice policies. It argued that Japanese rice policies cost American rice growers $1.7 billion in lost sales annually.

Tyers and Anderson (1986) suggest potential additional Japanese imports under full trade liberalization of 6.3 million tons of rice, 3.0 million tons of ruminant meat, 14.3 million tons of dairy products, and 470,000 tons of sugar. The Japanese import bill in 1986 measured in world prices would rise from $20 billion to $32 billion. Beef would account for the largest increase. World prices would rise. For example, the prices of rice and beef would increase by 4 percent and dairy products by 3 percent.

No detailed estimates are available on the impact of removing the duty on oil derived from soybeans. As discussed earlier, Carter and Johnson (1986) estimated the effects of removing the tariff on Canadian canola oil exports. In regard to Japanese duties on processed agricultural imports, it should be emphasized that Canada and the United States have by far the lowest value-added components of agricultural exports of all the high income countries (Schmitz 1986). The Japanese tariff system is certainly a major factor in this regard.

Table 4.6   **Producer Subsidy Equivalents**[a] **by Commodity and Selected Countries**
(Average 1979–81)

Commodity	USA	Canada	EEC	Australia	Japan	New Zealand
Dairy	48.2	66.5	68.8	20.8	83.3	18.0
Wheat	17.2	17.6	28.1	3.4	95.8	−8.2
Coarse grains	13.1	13.3	27.9	2.9	107.1	5.3
Beef and veal	9.5	13.1	52.7	4.0	54.9	12.5
Pig meat	6.2	14.5	21.7	2.7	14.0	7.4
Poultry meat	6.3	25.7	16.4	2.5	20.5	4.7
Sugar	17.1	12.5	25.0	−5.0	48.4	—
Rice	5.4	—	13.6	14.4	68.8	—
Sheep meat	—	—	45.0	3.1	—	18.2
Wool	—	—	—	3.9	—	16.3
Soybeans	6.9	—	36.2	—	108.1	—
Average, all above commodities	16.0	23.9	42.8	4.7	59.4	15.5

[a]A producer subsidy equivalent attempts to measure the payment or subsidy that would be necessary to compensate producers for the removal of agricultural producer support policies. In this table it is expressed as a percentage of the value of output plus direct payments minus any producer levies or taxes. A minus sign indicates a tax on producers.
Source: OECD (1987).

4.3   Canada-U.S. Competition for Japanese and Other Markets

4.3.1   Feed Grain, Wheat, and Red Meats

Canada and the United States both compete in the Japanese markets in feed grains—largely corn from the United States and barley from Canada. Japan accounts for about one-third of world imports of corn. The United States accounts for roughly 60 percent of world exports. In terms of total coarse grains, Japan imports around one-fourth of the world total, while the U.S. exports between 40–45 percent of the world total. Canada's exports are less than 10 percent. As a result, an expanding feed-grain market in Japan would likely increase exports from both the United States and Canada, but the value of U.S. exports would increase substantially more.

In wheat, the U.S. exports about one-third of the world's total, while Canada has roughly 20 percent of the world export market. World exports in 1984–85 were 106.6 million metric tons. Japan imported only 5.6 million metric tons, which was about 5 percent of the world's exports in that year. At most, Japan imports 10 percent of total wheat exports from Canada and the United States. As a result, trade liberalization in wheat is not likely to increase wheat prices substantially because of Japan's small market share and the existing market distortions.

In red meats, Canada would benefit more from trade liberalization in pork than the United States, since Canadian exports far exceed those of the

United States. However, in beef the opposite would be the case. In addition, questions still remain as to whether Canada could, or would be willing to, compete in the Japanese market even if trade liberalization occurred. As the above data show, Canada's current exports of beef to Japan are insignificant even though quotas are largely allocated on a competitive rather than on a political basis. Perhaps it is clear why Canada cannot compete with Australia for the grass-fed beef quota, but it is difficult to see why Canada cannot compete with the U.S. for the grain-fed beef quotas. The type of institutions in the beef trade must be a major determinant in determining the observed outcomes.

It should be noted that the expansion of red meat exports to Japan through liberalized trade may not necessarily result in a simultaneous increase in exports of feed grains to Japan. The opposite would happen if domestic production of red meats in Japan were to decrease. However, expanded beef exports would increase feed use in the United States and Canada, and would benefit the producers of intermediate inputs for the export industry. Products containing domestic feed grains would be exported rather than feed grains in raw product form.

4.3.2   The 1985 U.S. Farm Bill

The 1985 Farm Bill established target prices and loan rates for corn, wheat, and certain other crops grown in the United States. A major feature of the bill is the substantial reduction in loan rates. Prior to 1985, the loan rate for wheat was $3.40 U.S./bushel and the target price was $4.43 U.S./bushel. Under the bill the loan rate for wheat was lowered to $2.40. For corn, the target price is $3.03 U.S./bushel and the loan rate is $1.86 U.S./bushel. The United States lowered the loan rates in response to lost export markets and large increases in inventories. In 1985, the United States held over 80 percent of the world corn stocks and roughly 40 percent of the wheat stocks. During the first half of the 1980s the U.S. market share for both wheat and corn declined substantially.

A drop in the loan rate allows buyers such as Japan to import grain more cheaply. In essence, a drop in the loan rate by $1.00 U.S./bushel caused import prices to drop by approximately the same amount. To compete, Canada also had to drop its export price. Partly because of the response by Canada and other major grain exporters such as Australia and Argentina, U.S. exports have not increased significantly even though export prices have been lowered as a result of the 1985 Farm Bill. Among the beneficiaries of lower loan rates are importers. These include not only Japan, but of course other importers of North American grain.

For a given exchange rate, it is clear that, given the fixed level of producer prices in Japan, a lower loan rate drives a wider wedge between world export prices and domestic producer prices. This is why, for example, the wedge betwen Japanese producer rice prices and export prices has been widening recently.

Japan is a market in which both Canada and the United States compete, and export subsidies from both countries are used extensively. For example, in 1985–86, the Canadian Wheat Board barley pool ran a deficit of roughly $200 million (Canadian) because the export price of barley to Japan was set well below the Canadian initial producer price. World agricultural trade is becoming more distorted. One of the beneficiaries from export subsidies in grains is Japan. Currently, grain is being shipped to Japan below its cost of production. To illustrate the effect of subsidies, consider the following example. The JFA collects approximately $225 million U.S. in additional revenue from a $1/bushel U.S. wheat export price reduction. The drop in the export price does not alter the resale or the producer price in Japan. The amounts received by other importers are also substantial. In the Japanese case, trade is in part a transfer of money directly from the U.S. and Canadian treasury to the Japanese government.

4.4 Canada-U.S. Trade

4.4.1 Agricultural Trade

Table 4.7 presents data on Canadian-U.S. agricultural exports and imports. The largest component of Canadian exports to the United States is live animals, while the major imports from the United States are fruits and nuts. The United States has a balance-of-trade surplus, with U.S. exports being roughly double Canadian exports. Canadian exports to the United States are far less than wheat exports from Canada to non-U.S. markets, where wheat is still the leading Canadian agricultural export. For example, in 1983–84, wheat export sales were more than three times the 1980–84 $1.59 billion average for Canadian agricultural exports to the United States. As stressed earlier, in the grain trade, Canada and the United States compete for third-country markets.

A large part of the trade in agricultural products between Canada and the United States is in red meats, followed by fresh fruits and vegetables. Very little trade occurs in eggs, broilers, and dairy products, which are the Canadian supply-managed industries where import quotas play a major role. There is some trade in wheat and in malt barley. Corn and oilseeds are imported into Canada from the United States. In the red meat trade, quotas exist on Canadian shipments of beef products but in 1986, for example, the quotas were not filled. In pork, a duty exists on the U.S. import of live hogs.

Table 4.7   Canadian Trade in Agricultural Products With the United States, 1975–84
(annual averages, in million $Canadian)

	Exports to U.S.		Imports from U.S.	
Commodity	1975–79	1980–84	1975–79	1980–84
Grains	38.6	57.4	115.0	185.2
Grain products	49.8	108.7	45.1	105.7
Animal Feeds	48.9	88.6	37.8	76.2
Oilseeds	22.1	51.6	143.4	174.8
Oilseed products	5.1	21.4	180.6	230.2
Live animals	128.4	268.9	52.4	99.7
Beef and veal	54.5	138.1	25.5	60.1
Pork	34.1	220.2	108.7	32.4
Other animal products	69.2	92.6	135.1	206.0
Dairy products	6.8	10.5	8.0	11.2
Poultry and eggs	6.8	15.9	54.3	76.6
Fruits and nuts	32.4	57.4	437.3	748.2
Vegetables (excl. potatoes)	22.6	61.8	266.4	453.9
Potatoes and products	7.1	38.0	28.0	40.4
Seeds for sowing	15.8	22.6	33.2	51.0
Maple products	8.5	16.7	—	—
Sugar	27.4	21.2	20.7	29.7
Raw tobacco	8.6	24.1	5.7	15.2
Vegetable fibers	5.8	15.0	70.2	108.7
Plantation crops	11.6	22.1	140.1	186.2
Other agric. products	79.9	190.5	163.0	291.8
Total	703.1	1,590.3	2,090.5	3,193.5

Source: Schmitz and Carter (1986).

4.4.2   Supply-Managed Agricultural Industries

As a consequence of attempts to stabilize incomes in the dairy, poultry, and egg sectors, the Canadian government established the Dominion Marketing Board in 1934. Subsequently, the Farm Products Marketing Agencies Act was passed in 1972, and it is this legislation that underlies the current supply-managed marketing boards. Regional patterns of trade have been adversely affected. Although a number of economic features are listed as guides to the allocation of quota among the provinces, the quotas do not gravitate to low-cost producers or regions with comparative advantage in producing particular commodities. As Veeman (1983, 66) notes:

> The tendency for political pressure towards self-sufficiency on a provincial level may be expected to lead to higher cost levels of the producing sector with consequent loss of the benefits of regional specialization in trade. The result has been a tendency for supply deficient provinces to become more self-sufficient since the supply controlling programs . . . have been introduced. There is evident pressure also for reallocation of quota to provinces where there

has been more rapid population and income growth and consequently more rapid increase in consumption levels. These pressures are in the interest of local producers but are not necessarily consistent with comparative advantage.

A considerable amount of research has been done on the economic costs of marketing boards. Veeman (1982), Schmitz (1983), Borcherding and Dorosh (1981), Barichello (1981), Cairns (1980), and Lermer and Stanbury (1985) have investigated the social costs of supply-restricting marketing boards. It is interesting to note parenthetically that this research effort is substantially greater than that devoted to the study of other agricultural sectors, and particularly to the issue of a Canada-U.S. free trade area (FTA). The consumer cost from these policy distortions for the egg, broiler, and dairy industries are $74 million, $73 million, and $980 million, respectively. However, in many cases, the gains to producers almost offset the consumer cost. As a result, the net cost to society, especially for broilers and eggs, is small. By far the greatest cost is for the dairy sector.

The regional nature of Canadian farm policy, as exemplified by the supply-managed marketing boards, presents a constraint on the establishment of a Canada-U.S. FTA. However, in the supply-managed sectors, dairy is likely to receive special consideration since supply-management schemes are in effect on both sides of the border (see Cullen and Kerr 1986). In the egg and poultry sectors, a FTA would result in the elimination of interprovincial friction, as well as in a reduction in the number of producers, as only the most efficient producers will survive. In order to survive, Canadian producers must achieve economies of scale by increasing the size of their operations. As Barichello and Warley (1984) point out, rationalization of the industry may occur without a subsequent reduction in output. However, there will be a reduction in the number of producers and a loss in quota value rents. Under free trade in poultry products and eggs, Canadian producers will be price takers, and hence Canadian producers will have little market power.

As will be discussed later, the cost of the 1985 Farm Bill in the United States to Canadian prairie producers exceeds $1 billion annually. Since the dairy sector will be excluded from the free trade talks, the net cost from supply-management programs in Canada is less than a $100 million annually. Thus, the cost of the Farm Bill to Canada is at least 10 times as great as the cost to Canadian society from supply-managed boards when diarying is excluded.

4.4.3 Red Meat Sector

Trade barriers among provinces, as well as between Canada and the United States, also exist in the red meat sector. Provincial stabilization schemes are common, although it is not clear that every provincial scheme provides subsidies to producers. While some provincial hog-stabilization programs do include a subsidy element, others do not, and some provinces do not have any form of stabilization. In the case of hogs, the United States levied countervailing duties on live hog imports from Canada in 1985. The countervailing duty came about as a result of a complaint by U.S. hog producers and a subsequent ruling by the U.S. Commerce Department that there were significant production subsidies in Canada. The duty was upheld by the International Trade Commission which ruled that the injury amounted to five cents per pound on live hogs (Schmitz and Sigurdson 1985). Alberta hog producers were outraged at the U.S. duty because Alberta has no stabilization program in hogs.

As a result of the countervailing duties on hogs, Canadian cattlemen are reviewing beef-stabilization programs, since some feel that these programs may also be subject to American retaliatory measures. However, the United States also subsidizes its beef even though those subsidies are not relevant in a countervailing duty action instituted by the United States. Subsidies do exist and include the fact that much of the ranching is on public grazing lands where the fees are low and, in addition, feed grain is subsidized under the 1985 Farm Bill. Currently there are no U.S. tariffs on imports of live beef from Canada. However, there are NTBs on live beef and quotas on processed beef, although the quotas have not been binding (Schmitz 1984).

4.4.4   Grains

The Canadian grain sector is characterized by: (1) the existence of the Canadian Wheat Board (CWB), which governs international trade in grains and is the sole exporter of wheat and feed grains; (2) a variety of subsidies ranging from the Crow benefit to crop insurance and stabilization schemes; and (3) an open market for non-Board grains, primarily canola and feed grains.

There is little trade in grains between Canada and the United States, and both countries limit imports of grain. There is a sizable export trade of malt barley from Canada to the United States. Corn is allowed into Canada under an historically small tariff, and most of this is imported into eastern Canada under the dual market system for feed grains. However, in February 1987, the Canadian Import Tribunal heard the countervailing duty case on corn imports from the United States (Ontario Corn Growers vs U.S.). This was the first countervailing duty action brought against U.S. agriculture. The ruling was not favorable for the U.S., as a sizable duty was placed on U.S. corn exports into Canada.

The free movement of grain between Canada and the United States would have an impact on the ability of the CWB to market grain and could, thereby, jeopardize the entire grain-marketing system in Canada, including the two-price wheat system where internal prices, at times, are held above export prices. Under a FTA, the CWB could have difficulties in using a system of producer quotas to market grain. In addition, a FTA in grains might result in the export of grain through U.S. ports on the Gulf, thereby lowering grain traffic in the Canadian railway system and the St. Lawrence Seaway. If transportation subsidies are permitted under such an agreement, they may offset this impact and, if subsidies are sufficiently high, cause an increase in traffic as U.S. producers ship grain through the Canadian system.

Both the United States and Canada provide subsidies to grain producers, although the institutions used to provide such subsidies differ. Canada employs a marketing-board system, namely the CWB, with transportation subsidies and subsidized insurance and stabilization schemes. A major subsidy is the Crow gap payment—an annual transportation payment of approximately $650 million. The United States provides a transportation subsidy to producers who move grain along inland waters, such as the Snake and Columbia rivers, since no user charges are levied. Crop insurance payments and payments made through the Western Grain Stabilization Act also constitute a form of subsidy to Canadian prairie grain producers.

In comparison to Canadian subsidies to grain producers, the level of U.S. and European Economic Community (EEC) subsidies is much larger, as indicated in table 4.8. One stumbling block to a Canada-U.S. FTA is the size of the U.S. government outlays to grain producers. U.S. support of grain producers is two to three times the level provided to Canadian producers. In addition, the U.S. grain-export enhancement program where wheat is sold at prices below the loan rate, will provide at least $1–$1.5 billion in the form of export subsidies for grain sales over the years 1985–88. These programs give the U.S. farmer a sizable advantage over his Canadian counterpart.

It would appear, therefore, that massive structural changes would be required on both sides of the border if a FTA in grains becomes a reality. U.S. subsidies will need to be reduced and/or Canadian subsidies will need to be

Table 4.8 Subsidies to Grain Producers by Country, 1985/86 and 1986/87 (in $Canadian/bushel)

| Commodity | Exporter | Government Outlays | |
		1985/86	1986/87
Wheat	EEC	2.60	3.13
	USA	1.49	2.63
	Canada	0.75	0.85
Barley	EEC	2.41	3.11
	USA	0.41	1.06
	Canada	0.36	0.33

Source: Schmitz, Carter, and Van Kooten (1986, 37).

increased. However, the gains from free trade in grains between Canada and the United States, if they are positive, would not be nearly as great as the cost currently imposed on Canada by the 1985 U.S. Farm Bill. In addition, it is not clear how the CWB could function under a free trade arrangement.

4.4.5   Gains From Liberalization of U.S.-Canadian Agricultural Trade

Using numerical general equilibrium models, researchers (e.g., Magun 1986) find that the benefits of trade liberalization to agriculture are small but, nonetheless, significant. However, the large models do not have a sufficient level of disaggregation to identify which agricultural sectors are likely to benefit and which ones are likely to lose.

Deloitte, Haskins, Sells, and Associates (1985) have estimated the direction of effect, and various implications of, freer liberalized agricultural trade between the United States and Canada. This information is provided in table 4.9. The data in the table indicate that: (1) the beef sector in Canada will gain; (2) the pork and sheep industries will not be affected; (3) the poultry industry will be negatively impacted; (4) there will be no effect on the wheat industry; (5) the feed grain sector will lose; and (6) canola, flax, and rye

Table 4.9   Estimated Effects of Free Trade Between Canada and the U.S.A. in 1995, Selected Agricultural Commodities, Prairie Provinces[a]

Commodity	Direction of Effect	% Change in Production in 1995	1983 Prairie Farm Cash Receipts[b]	Change in Farm Cash Receipts[c]
Beef[d]	+	12	$1,690 million	$200 million
Pork[d]	+	2	433	9
Sheep	0	0	9	0
Chicken and turkey	−	− 80	150	− 120
Wheat	0	0	4,118	0
Feed grains	−	− 6	906	− 53
Canola[d]	+	3	712	21
Flax	+	1	151	1
Rye	+	1	60	1
Mustard, pulses and specialty crops	+	1	99	1
Total	+	1	8,328	60

[a]Excludes impact on input and value-added (processing and distribution) industries.
[b]From Canada Grains Council, *Statistical Handbook 84*, and Alberta Agriculture.
[c]Impact after an adjustment period (1995), values are constant (1983) dollars. See commodity sections for details.
[d]Includes anticipated increase in sales in the current trade environment (Option B, Status Quo) of 5 percent for beef, 2 percent for pork, and 2 percent for canola. The incremental impact of free trade is, therefore, 7 percent for beef, no change for pork, and 1 percent for canola.
Source: Deloitte, Haskins, Sells, and Associates (1985).

producers, along with those growing mustard, pulses, and specialty crops, will gain. The net gain from the trade liberalization approximates $60 million per annum. However, these figures include anticipated increases in sales in the current trade environment, plus the incremental impact of free trade. In any case, the $60 million figure underestimates the true gains to Canada since consumer benefits, which are likely to be substantial, are not included in the calculations by Deloitte, Haskins, Sells, and Associates.

A number of questions remain, however. For example, it is still not clear that the poultry industry would be negatively affected. It certainly would be in the short run, but in the long run, economies of scale in production may be realized and the Canadian industry may well become rationalized to the point where producers in Canada could compete with those in the United States. This would require increased concentration and regional specialization within Canada.

The effect of lower loan rates under the 1985 U.S. Farm Bill can also be highlighted via table 4.9. Schmitz and Carter (1986) estimate the yearly cost of the 1985 bill to western Canadian wheat producers alone to exceed $1 billion. This cost is at least *five times greater* than the potential net gain from free trade in farm products between the United States and Canada. Canada and the United States appear to compete in international markets both with each other and with other nations. Competitive strategies involve such trade instruments as export subsidies, used, for example, by the United States.

A case study done by Bredahl, Schmitz, and Hillman (1987) on U.S.-Mexican agricultural trade shows that cooperative strategies have a much greater payoff and involve such policy measures as acreage set asides and soil conservation. These may be much less costly than the traditional competitive strategies.

4.4.6   Nonagricultural Industries

Rising U.S. protectionism characterizes U.S. imports of nonagricultural products from Canada (*The Financial Post,* 19 July 1986, p. 7). Recently, the United States either has brought, or contemplates bringing, countervailing and dumping actions against several nonagricultural industries.

Many of the manufactured exports from the prairie region of Canada enter the United States free of tariff and nontariff barriers. For example, farm machinery manufactured in Saskatchewan can be shipped into the United States essentially free of duties and quotas. Measures to inhibit the free flow of steel products into the U.S. market have been taken recently. In 1985, the U.S. Department of Commerce announced, in a preliminary ruling, that there would be a countervailing duty of 0.72 percent on IPSCO's oil tubular goods. This action was supported by the International Trade Commission and, currently, this duty is in place. In response, IPSCO filed a complaint with the

Canadian government protesting the dumping of U.S. oil and gas well casings into the Canadian market. The Canadian Import Tribunal supported IPSCO's claim and ruled that imports of oil tubular goods would be subject to duties in order to offset dumping margins ranging from 9.1 to 40.1 percent.

A part of the Canadian oil production is exported into the United States for refining and re-exported back into Canada. The barriers to trade in oil are insignificant. In forestry, the U.S. has levied duties on cedar shakes from British Columbia and on softwood lumber imports from all regions of Canada. In the softwood lumber case, an agreement was reached in which the U.S. duty was to be replaced by an export tax on Canadian lumber exports to the United States.

Potash is a major Canadian industry and its major market is the United States. Potash moves into the U.S. market duty free and there are few, if any, NTBs in place. The depressed nature of the potash industry is a result of the depressed nature of U.S. and world agriculture. In spite of this, the United States brought countervailing duty action against the Saskatchewan potash industry in early 1987.

The United States is also a large market for Canadian exports of uranium. The U.S. market has long been subject to trade disruptions. In 1965, the United States imposed a ban on the domestic enrichment of foreign uranium in order to supply domestically produced and enriched fuel for a burgeoning nuclear industry. Since the Department of Energy (DOE) had a virtual world monopoly on enrichment, this ban amounted to an embargo. The "embargo" level was reduced over the years so that by 1984, U.S. utilities were once again free to enrich as much foreign uranium as they wished.

However, a recent ruling by a Denver court has the potential of taking the United States back into the realm of the protectionism that characterized the 1960s and most of the 1970s. The court ruling, if upheld, will ban utilities from enriching foreign-sourced material at DOE facilities. If a utility has an enrichment contract with a foreign enrichment plant, however, it will be able to import foreign-sourced material. Currently, only about 10 percent of the uranium consumed in the United States is enriched abroad. The court ruling resulted from legal action brought by U.S. uranium producers alleging that the DOE had violated a thirty-year-old law requiring import bans whenever the domestic industry is considered to be nonviable. In 1984, the industry was deemed to be nonviable, largely because production from U.S. mines had been falling sharply. By 1985, U.S. uranium production had fallen to nearly one quarter of the 1980 level. The primary reason for this drop in production has been the low price of uranium combined with the fact the U.S. ore is of a much lower grade than that associated with some of the new discoveries in Saskatchewan and Australia. For example, the average ore grade in the United States is less than 0.12 percent. This compares with grades of 0.50 percent (Cluff Lake), 2.45 percent (Key Lake) and 0.45 percent (Collins Bay) in Saskatchewan. An interesting feature of the court ruling is that it was initiated by producers as a legal action. It did not go through the U.S. Commerce Department as a complaint (such as the case with the potash antidumping trade action) nor did it appear as legislation in Congress. This effectively puts trade policy, at least in the case of uranium, outside the jurisdiction of both the administration and Congress, a feature found in few other commodities.

All this activity is a sign of increasing protectionism which does not portend well for a FTA. Therefore, it is important that such protectionism be stopped.

As an overview, Canada exports primary commodities such as potash to the United States, but little to Japan except for forest products. In fact, Canada exports sizable amounts of forest products to both countries. On the other hand, Canada imports relatively few of these commodities from either the United States or Japan (table 4.10). Thus Canada's stake in free trade in minerals and forest products is sizable. These industries can only survive through export trade. For example, the Canadian potash industry is dependent on exports and sells virtually nothing on the domestic market since Canadian soils are not deficient in potassium.

4.4.7   Conclusions

The following issues should be of major concern in the Canada-U.S. free trade talks.

1. There appears to be growing protectionism in the United States in primary products. This is manifested by the imposition of countervailing duties on exports of Canadian hogs to the U.S. market and on Canadian corn imports from the United States, proposals to bring countervailing actions against the potash industry, countervailing duty action brought against IPSCO, and the quota threat on uranium shipments to the U.S. market.

2. Countervailing duty action merely requires that the United States determines the extent to which the Canadian industry is being subsidized. U.S. subsidies do not enter into the deliberations. However, as stressed in this paper, many U.S. industries are subsidized to a greater extent than their Canadian counterparts.

3. Canada is also seeking protection from U.S. exports, as evidenced by the Ontario Corn Growers countervailing duty case against the U.S. In this case, there is a parallel to the aforementioned U.S. procedure in that the extent of subsidization in Canada is not at issue.

4. In agriculture, U.S. subsidies far exceed those in Canada. As a result, the distortions that exist in U.S. agriculture are far greater than those that exist in Canada, despite the existence of supply-managed marketing boards which influence interprovincial and international trade.

Table 4.10   Canadian Trade with the U.S. and Japan, Primary Products, 1981 and 1985
(in thousand $ Canadian)

	U.S.		Japan	
	Exports	Imports	Exports	Imports
Live animals				
1981	179,437	196,336	5,069	35
1985	420,547	105,437	2,056	46
Food, feed, beverages, and tobacco				
1981	2,091,780	2,651,661	1,058,339	47,171
1985	3,308,700	2,996,491	1,017,836	66,207
Crude materials, inedible				
1981	9,237,037	4,415,122	1,943,072	46,857
1985	11,762,770	3,387,128	2,880,674	63,439
Fabricated materials, inedible				
1981	21,410,199	10,278,194	1,392,355	630,292
1985	28,881,325	12,770,821	1,654,598	692,052
End products, inedible				
1981	20,395,056	36,299,752	112,234	3,304,239
1985	45,661,982	53,875,883	190,002	5,221,499
Special transactions, trade				
1981	586,267	696,434	49	28,102
1985	309,091	1,241,198	163	70,180
Crude petroleum				
1981	2,504,948	1,173,054	—	0
1985	5,916,516	290,036	—	0
Iron and steel				
1981	1,955,323	277,771	19,017	0
1985	2,127,410	414,000	22,058	0
Wood and paper				
1981	8,281,071	793,081	815,608	9,700
1985	12,186,032	—	893,922	—
Radioactive ores and concentrates				
1981	152,473	15,484	—	1
1985	98,086	27,737	104,123	51
Fertilizers and fertilizer materials				
1981	940,738	150,554	611,571	26
1985	820,065	—	49,042	—

Note: Blanks indicate data not available or zero.
Source: FAO, *Trade Yearbook*, various issues.

5. Currently, as a result of the 1985 Farm Bill, the U.S. grain sector receives substantially greater subsidies than does the grain sector in Canada. Canada has to compete in the world market against countries such as the United States, and since the United States lowered the loan rate in 1986 as part of the Farm Bill, Canadian wheat prices have dropped substantially. These subsidies clearly have to be kept in mind when discussing a U.S.-Canadian FTA.

6. The cost to Canadian prairie wheat producers alone of lowering the loan rate in the 1985 Farm Bill exceeds $1 billion annually. Excluding dairying, this is at least ten times greater than the net cost to Canadians of supply-managed boards in Canada.

7. The net cost of the 1985 Farm Bill to prairie producers appears to be at least five times greater than the estimated potential gains from freer U.S.-Canada trade in agriculture.

8. Canada wants guaranteed access to the U.S. market for commodities such as red meat. However, to achieve this, the countervailing duty laws of the United States must be changed to include U.S. subsidies. This also applies to Canadian law and to Canada's actions against imports. In this regard, a U.S.-Canada arbitration board is badly needed.

9. The role of GATT is to promote freer international trade. Agriculture has not fared well under GATT and perhaps this is why there is considerable interest in Canada and the United States for direct bilateral trade liberalization. However, a substantial effort should be made in the upcoming GATT negotiations to deal with trade distortions in agriculture. Many of the problems facing Canadian farmers are also a result of EEC subsidies and other distortions worldwide. These were already stressed with reference to Japan.

10. It is important not to lose sight of the potential gains of cooperation in international markets where the United States and Canada are in competition. Perhaps the greatest payoff from freer trade talks between Canada and the United States lies in an attempt to harmonize policies and increase cooperation in export markets in which they compete. The 1985 U.S. Farm Bill, however, takes a different direction and threatens the profitability of Canadian sales in world markets. In this way, it has magnified the problem of policy harmonization.

11. The long-run survival of Canadian industries such as potash, steel, and uranium will require an open border policy by the United States. These industries are highly dependent on the U.S. market for survival.

4.5 Conclusions

This paper has focused primarily on agricultural trade among Canada, the United States, and Japan. The latter is the largest food importer in the world, and Canada and the United States are large suppliers. Japan exports very few primary products to either Canada or the United States.

Japanese agriculture is highly protected and its tariff and quota policies do not encourage the exportation of processed products from Canada and the United States to Japan. Under GATT, an effort should be made, for example, to lower import tariffs on Canadian shipments of canola oil and products and on soybean oil.

Japan is not the only country distorting agriculture through tariffs and NTBs. Others include the EEC, especially. In response, the U.S. 1985 Farm Bill attempted to increase exports through lower loan rates. An all-out trade war has in effect resulted, where Canada is one of the important exporters adversely affected by the lower world grain prices. Wheat is still Canada's major agricultural export good. The negative effect of the Farm Bill on Canada is greater than the potential gains from freer trade in agriculture between the U.S. and Canada, unless free trade talks would achieve cooperative export strategies in the world grain trade. Among the beneficiaries of the current export subsidy war are the Japanese, because of lower import prices. The effect of a decrease in protectionism by Japan would likely not be as great for Canada or the United States as would export cooperation by Canada, the United States, Argentina, and Australia aimed at raising rather than lowering export prices.

Policy action has to take into account the fact that the export demand for farm products is highly price inelastic. This is in part due to agricultural policies which isolate producer prices from world prices. What would happen, for example, if the United States and Canada decided to raise the export price of wheat to the Japanese "resale" price? With agricultural subsidies now rampant in the United States, Canada and other exporters are transferring resources from exporting to importing nations, and these transfers appear to be substantial.

In conclusion, even though freer trade is being sought between the United States and Canada, a large number of countervailing duty actions have appeared. It appears, therefore, that there is a conflict between the realization of the traditional gains from trade and the special interests of producers that threaten to undermine these gains.

References

Anderson, Kym. 1983. The peculiar rationality of beef import quotas in Japan. *American Journal of Agricultural Economics* 65 (February): 108–12.

Anderson, Kym, and Ujiro Hayami. 1986. *The political economy of agricultural protection: East Asia in international perspective*. London and Sydney: Allen and Unwin.

Anderson, W. J., and J. A. Gellner. 1985. Canadian agricultural policy in the export sector. *Canadian Journal of Agricultural Economics* 32 (August): 170–85 (proceedings issue).

Arcus, Peter L. 1981. *Broilers and eggs*. Technical Report no. E/13 prepared for the Economic Council of Canada and Institute for Research on Public Policy. Ottawa: Minister of Supply and Services, Canada.

Australian Bureau of Agricultural Economics (ABAE). 1981. *Japanese agricultural policies: Their origins, nature and effects on production and trade.* Policy Monograph no. 1. Canberra: Australian Government Publishing Service.

Barichello, Richard R. 1981. *The economics of Canadian dairy industry regulation.* Ottawa: Economic Council of Canada and the Institute for Research on Public Policy.

Barichello, R. R. 1984. Recent Canadian agricultural policy and its relevance for the United States. Working Paper prepared for the AEI Agricultural Studies Project, Washington, D.C., December.

Barichello, R. R., and T. K. Warley. 1984. Agriculture and negotiation of free-trade area: Issues in policy harmonization. Montreal: C. D. Howe Institute. Mimeo, December.

Borcherding, Thomas, and Gary Dorosh. 1981. *The egg marketing board: A case study of monopoly and its social costs.* Vancouver: The Fraser Institute.

Bredahl, Maury, A. Schmitz, and J. Hillman. 1987. Rent seeking in international trade: The great tomato war. *American Journal of Agricultural Economics* 69 (February): 1–10.

Bunch, Karen L. 1986. Consumption trends favor fresh, lowfat and sweet. *National Food Review* (USDA) Winter.

Cairns, Robert D. 1980. *Rationales for regulation.* Technical Report no. 2. Ottawa: Economic Council of Canada.

Canadian Wheat Board. 1986. Government outlays for grain producers. Unpublished paper prepared by the Planning Directorate, Winnipeg, May.

Carter, C. A. 1984. Japanese agricultural policies and trade: Current developments and prospects. In *World agricultural policies and trade,* ed. G. Lee. Saskatoon: University of Saskatchewan.

Carter, C., R. Chambers, A. McCalla, and G. Storey. 1984. Canadian-U.S. trade relations: Issues and policy options. Paper presented to the International Agriculture Trade Research Consortium, Asilomar, California, December.

Carter, C. A., and C. Johnson. 1986. The impact of vegetable oil tariffs in Japan. Unpublished paper, Department of Agricultural Economics, University of Manitoba.

Carter, C. A., and A. Schmitz. 1986. International implications of national policy developments: Canada. Paper presented at the Conference on Pacific Export Corporation, New Zealand, June 30–July 2.

Chadee, D., and C. A. Carter. 1986. Exchange rate effects on the Canadian pork sector. Unpublished paper, Department of Agricultural Economics, University of Manitoba.

Coyle, William T. 1983. *Japan's feed-livestock economy: Prospects for the 1980's.* Foreign Agricultural Economic Report no. 177. Washington, D.C.: Economic Research Service, USDA, February.

———. 1986. *The 1984 U.S.-Japan Beef and Citrus Accord: An Evaluation.* Washington, D.C.: Economic Research Service, USDA.

Cullen, Susan E., and William A. Kerr. 1986. Free trade: The implications for Canadian agriculture. *Earthkeeping* 1st Qtr: 8–11.

Dawson, Dau, and Associates. 1982. An overview of beef market opportunities in California, Washington, Oregon and Idaho. Calgary. Mimeo, March.

Deloitte, Haskins, Sells, and Associates. 1985. *Canadian agricultural trade issues:*

Free trade with the U.S.A. Report prepared for the Prairie Pools Inc., August.

Economist. 1986. Economic and financial indicators. May 24, p. 105.

F.A.O. *Trade Yearbook.* Various issues.

Forbes, J. D., D. R. Hughes, and T. K. Warley. 1982. *Economic intervention and regulation in Canadian agriculture.* A study prepared for the Economic Council of Canada and the Institute of Research on Public Policy. Ottawa: Minister of Supply and Services, Canada.

Gustafson, M. 1987. Understanding the structure and operating procedures of Japanese beef import quotas. U.S. Meat Export Federation, Denver, Colorado.

Harling, Kenneth F., and Robert L. Thompson. 1985. Government intervention in poultry industries: A cross-country comparison. *American Journal of Agricultural Economics* 67 (May) 243–50.

Hayami, Yujiro. 1979. Trade benefits to all: A design of the beef import liberalization in Japan. *American Journal of Agricultural Economics* 61:342–47.

Hedley, D. D., and J. Groenewegen. 1984. Canadian agricultural policy and trade. In *World Agricultural Policies and Trade,* ed. G. Lee. Saskatoon: University of Saskatchewan.

Japan International Agricultural Council. 1986. *Japan Agrinfo Newsletter* (Tokyo) November.

Josling, T. 1981. *Intervention and regulation in Canadian agriculture: A comparison of costs and benefits among sectors.* Ottawa: Economic Council and the Institute for Research on Public Policy.

Lermer, George, and W. T. Stanbury. 1985. Measuring the cost of redistributing income by the means of direct regulation. *Canadian Journal of Economics* 18 (February): 190–207.

Longworth, John W. 1983. *Beef in Japan: Politics, production, marketing and trade.* St. Lucia, Queensland: University of Queensland Press.

Magun, G. 1986. The effects of Canada-USA free trade on Canadian labour markets. Paper presented at the annual meetings of the Canadian Economic Association, Winnipeg, May 30.

O.E.C.D. 1987. *Working Party #1 of the Economic Policy Committee: Effects of agricultural policies in OECD countries.* Paris, February 19.

Sanderson, Fred H. 1982. Irritants in U.S.-Japanese agricultural relations. Talk before the Japan Society, New York City, April 2.

———. 1986. Agricultural issues in the forthcoming round of multilateral trade negotiations. Testimony before the Subcommittee on International Trade of the Senate Committee on Agriculture, July 5.

———. 1987. U.S.-Japan negotiating issues and opportunities in GATT. In *Agricultural reform efforts in the U.S. and Japan,* ed. D. Gale Johnson, chap. 3. New York: New York University Press.

Schmitz, A. 1983. Supply management in Canadian agriculture: An assessment of the economic effects. *Canadian Journal of Agricultural Economics* 31 (July): 135–52.

———. 1984. Prospects for change in livestock production and trade. In *World agricultural policies and trade,* ed. George E. Lee. Saskatoon: University of Saskatchewan.

————. 1986. Wheat trade and trade policy. In *Wheat: Production in Canada,* eds. A. E. Slinkard and D. B. Folwer, 580–96. Saskatoon: University of Saskatchewan.

Schmitz, A., and C. Carter. 1986. *Sectoral issues in a U.S.-Canadian trade agreement: Agriculture.* Washington, D.C.: Brookings Institution.

Schmitz, A., C. Carter, and G. C. Van Kooten. 1986. Problems and prospects of a U.S.-Canadian trade agreement. *Policy Research Notes* (USDA, GRS) 22 (November): 31–43.

Schmitz, A., and Dale Sigurdson. 1985. Stabilization programs and countervailing duties: Canadian hog exports to the U.S. Mimeo.

Schmitz, A., D. Sigurdson, and O. Doering. 1986. Domestic farm policy and gains from trade. *American Journal of Agricultural Economics* 86 (November): 820–27.

Schmitz, A., and G. C. Van Kooten. 1986. U.S.-Canada trade agreement. Brief submitted to Saskatchewan Committee on Canada-U.S. Trade Talks, July.

Simpson, James, Tadashi Yoshida, Akira Miyazaki, and Ryohei Kada. 1985. *Technological change in Japan's beef industry.* Westview Press: Boulder, Colorado.

Spriggs, John. 1985. Economic analysis of the Western Grain Stabilization Program. *Canadian Journal of Agricultural Economics* 33 (March): 209–29.

Thompson, R. L. 1977. Structural relationships for agricultural trade policy. *Proceedings of 1977 Annual Meeting of American Statistical Association.* Business and Economics and Statistics Section, Chicago, August.

Tyers, Rodney, and Kym Anderson. 1986. Distortions in world food markets: A quantitative assessment. Background paper for the World Bank's *World Development Report,* January 1986.

Van Kooten, G. C., and Douglas L. Young. 1986. Flexible cropping patterns to increase profits and save soil in the Palouse region of eastern Washington. Paper presented at the Annual Meetings of the American Agricultural Economics Association, Reno.

Veeman, M. 1982. Social costs of supply-restricting marketing boards. *Canadian Journal of Agricultural Economics* 30(March):21–36.

————. 1983. The regulation of interprovincial trade in agricultural products. In *Transforming western Canada's food industry in the 80s and 90s,* ed. B. Sadler, 55–70. Banff: Banff Centre.

Vogt, Donna U. 1986. *Japanese import barriers to U.S. agricultural exports.* Washington, D.C.: Congressional Research Service, October.

Wall Street Journal. 1986. Canadian farmers plan duty action against U.S. corn. Monday, 12 May, p. 43.

Warley, T. K. 1986. What would free trade mean to agriculture. Paper presented at Ridgetown College of Agricultural Technology, 17 January.

Warley, T. K., and R. R. Barichello. 1986. Agricultural issues in a comprehensive Canada-U.S.A. trade agreement: A Canadian perspective. *Policy Research Notes* (USDA, GRS) November:17–31.

World Bank. 1986. *World Development Report, 1986.* Washington, D.C.: World Bank.

Comment

Masayoshi Honma

Schmitz's paper provides a good summary assessment of present trade frictions in primary products among the United States, Canada, and Japan. While
his description is clear and well organized, it seems to me that he discusses
the trade problems mainly from the exporter's viewpoint. To balance the discussion, I shall look at the trade situation from the standpoint of an importer
of primary products such as Japan.

I would like first to comment on the coverage of Schmitz's paper. In
the first part of his paper, Schmitz discusses Japan's imports from the United
States and Canada, focusing on several agricultural commodities. But it
should be emphasized that Japan's imports of primary products from the
United States and Canada include not only agricultural products, but also
forest products and minerals such as coal. Thus, Japan's imports of wood,
pulp, and coal together, for example, amounted to $2.5 billion and $2.1 billion dollars in 1986 from the United States and Canada, respectively. Although Schmitz mentions just briefly the importance of trade in forest products, nonagricultural primary products should have been given much more
attention since these products may also cause trade frictions in Japan's market
due to high tariff rates and nontariff barriers.

A second point concerns his policy recommendations. Among his conclusions, Schmitz places the greatest emphasis on the fact that the 1985 U.S.
Farm Bill has resulted in a negative effect on Canada that is greater than the
potential gains from freer trade between the United States and Canada. To
remedy this situation, he recommends cooperation to raise export prices by
the United States, Canada, and other exporting countries. I agree with this
idea insofar as it implies that the distortions in world agricultural trade should
be corrected, whether on the import or export side. It is also understandable
that agricultural exporters have been disappointed by the failure of previous
multilateral trade negotiations to achieve freer agricultural trade. Nonetheless, we should keep in mind the possibility that export cooperation might
lead to an export cartel, which would jeopardize the orientation toward freer
agricultural trade. I expect the exporting countries to look for a constructive
path for trade negotiations that will include importing countries. The current
GATT negotiations are designed to deal with trade distortions in agriculture.
Agricultural subsidies are addressed as an important issue in these negotiations, and we should use this opportunity to strengthen the rules against subsidies. In such a case, not only export subsidies but also subsidies supporting
farmers in importing countries should be examined together.

My third comment concerns tariffs. Schmitz refers to tariff escalation
in Japan in the cases of canola and soybean. That is, tariffs are imposed on
their processed products but not on their raw form. Such tariff escalation is

also found in Japan's imports of forest products. The criticism of tariff escalation by the United States and Canada seems to have the same root as the demand for trade liberalization of beef and citrus. What exporters are seeking is market access for their high-value and high value-added commodities. But in fact, world agricultural trade has changed in structure and increased the value-added components. However, the United States and Canada have not fully accommodated the structure of their exports to increase their value-added components in such markets as Japan. While tariffs are still major obstacles for agricultural exporters, it should also be recognized that significant movements in exchange rates make the role of tariffs less important, as for example in the case of the substantial appreciation of the Japanese yen in 1985–86. Thus, trade studies should include an analysis of the role of exchange rates so that policy evaluation may be more comprehensive.

My fourth point concerns the levels of agricultural protection. Schmitz discusses trade distortions mainly in terms of individual commodities. In order to evaluate agricultural trade policy as a whole, we should consider overall agricultural protection levels by country. Schmitz briefly refers to the level of Japan's agricultural protection in the context of trade liberalization. To supplement his discussion, my table C4.1 shows the comparative development of Japan's level of agricultural protection based on nominal rates of protection (NRP) for a weighted average of twelve agricultural commodities for selected industrial countries. As Schmitz mentions, Japan's level of agricultural protection has been among the world's highest in recent years. Thus, in 1984, Japan's overall agricultural protection level was 102 percent. If we evaluate this level based on the average exchange rate in 1986, the weighted average more than doubles to a level of 210 percent. This may help, in part, to explain the strong external pressures on Japan for agricultural trade liberalization in recent years. The figures in table C4.1 thus reinforce the importance of taking exchange rate changes into account in evaluating trade policies.

The high level of agricultural protection in Japan is, however, a relatively recent phenomenon. Japan's NRP in 1955 was just 18 percent, about half of the EC level. But it rose rapidly as Japan began experiencing rapid economic growth, reaching the EC level in 1960 and the Swiss level in 1965. It was a reflection of Japan's rapid loss of comparative advantage in agriculture. Thus, the sharp increase in Japan's agricultural protection level during this period might be interpreted as the cost of intersectoral adjustment designed to avoid such drastic social and economic changes as rural depopulation and rural/urban income disparity, which might have been socially intolerable without protection. In this light, the problem of agricultural protectionism should, therefore, be considered in the framework of the dynamic process of industrial adjustment.

This leads me to my fifth point which is that studies assessing trade

Table C4.1 Nominal Rates of Agricultural Protection in Selected Industrial Countries[a]

	1955	1960	1965	1970	1975	1980	1984	(1986)[b]
Japan	18	41	69	74	76	85	102	210
European Community								
France	33	26	30	47	29	30	12	46
Germany, FR	35	48	55	50	39	44	25	75
Italy	47	50	66	69	38	57	49	86
Netherlands	14	21	35	41	32	27	20	67
EC average	35	37	45	52	29	38	22	63
Sweden	34	44	50	65	43	59	36	63
Switzerland	60	64	73	96	96	126	153	260
Canada	0	4	2	5	7	−3	−3	−9
United States	2	1	9	11	4	0	6	6

[a]Defined as the percentage by which the producer price exceeds the border price. The estimates shown are the weighted averages for twelve commodities (rice, wheat, barley, corn, oats, rye, beef, pork, chicken, eggs, milk, and sugar beets) using production valued at border prices as weights.
[b]Nominal rates using the exchange rates of September 1986 to evaluate the producer prices in 1984.
Source: Honma, M., and Y. Hayami, "Structure of Agricultural Protection in Industrial Counties," *Journal of International Economics* 20 (1986):118; and Hayami, Y., and M. Honma, *Reconsideration of Agricultural Policy* (Tokyo: The Forum for Policy Innovation, February 1987, p. 22).

liberalization tend to stress potential gains in a static framework. However, trade liberalization is essentially accompanied by a dynamic process of structural change in which domestic agriculture bears the costs of adjustment. In discussing Japan's trade policy, Schmitz does not touch on this point at all, perhaps because the question of agricultural adjustment is viewed primarily as a domestic issue. Yet structural adjustment in Japanese agriculture is at the heart of the agricultural trade frictions between Japan and its major trading partners. Thus, the analysis of current policies should assess their costs and benefits in a dynamic framework. If we can learn more about the processes of industrial adjustment, this might serve to enhance progress in agricultural negotiations in the current GATT round.

Comment
Colin Carter

Japan is highly dependent on the United States and Canada for primary product shipments. In 1985 Japan imported $45.5 billion in petroleum, $16 billion in foodstuffs, $4.1 billion in fish and shellfish, $5.3 billion in coal, and $4 billion in wood. Petroleum, agricultural products (including wood), and minerals account for about 75 percent of Japan's merchandise imports (see table C4.2). These commodities represent approximately 42 percent of Canada's exports and 29 percent of merchandise exports from the United States.

Schmitz chose to focus most of his discussion on agricultural trade. While I agree that current protectionist problems in this trade triangle apply primarily to agricultural products, the problems are not limited to agriculture. I will first comment on Schmitz's assessment of the issues in agricultural trade and then briefly raise a few points pertaining to other primary products.

There is a significant difference between the primary product self-sufficiency ratios in Japan and North America. Japan is basically an importer of primary products and an exporter of manufactures, especially capital goods. This situation has worked well for Japan since World War II because there has been a "buyer's market" in primary products, except for the short-lived 1973–74 commodity boom and the formation of OPEC. It is especially noteworthy that the IMF commodity price index for 1986 was 27 percent below the 1980 peak level. Prices for many agricultural commodities are at levels in real terms not seen since the Great Depression in the 1930s.

Schmitz argues that the Japanese have helped create the buyer's market situation in agricultural product through import barriers. He discusses Canada's trade with Japan in agricultural products and identifies the most critical trade issues. In discussing the beef trade, he suggests that Canada is unable to penetrate the Japanese market because of the "type of institutions." I would take this point further and argue that Canada is denied market access for noneconomic reasons. Canada has historically had a trade surplus with Japan (although a small deficit was recorded in 1985), and the United States has a large trade deficit with Japan. Thus, the Japanese government chooses to import grain-fed beef from the United States rather than from Canada. I believe this factor is also important in explaining why Canada's share of Japan's cereal grain imports has been declining and that of the United States has been increasing.

Schmitz devotes considerable attention to Canadian-U.S. agricultural trade. He discusses the impact of the passage of the 1985 Food Security Act

Table C4.2   Importance of Primary Commodities (agriculture, minerals, and energy), 1984

Country	% of GNP	% of Exports	% of Imports
Canada	16	42	18
Japan	6	3	75
US	10	29	32

Source: U.N., *Handbook of International and Development Statistics;* IMF, *International Financial Statistics.*

by the United States Congress. I agree that this was policymaking at its worst and a poor attempt to shift the burden of adjustment in agriculture onto U.S. taxpayers and onto other exporting nations. However, when Schmitz refers to Canadian subsidies, he argues they are only about one-third as high as those in the United States. This may be true for the two years he discussed (1985–86), but over a longer time frame Canadian subsidies are just as high if not higher than those in the United States (see Carter and Glenn 1988). Government transfers average out to about 15 percent of wheat farmer receipts in both countries. In March 1987, the Canadian government imposed a countervailing duty of 85 cents (U.S.) per bushel on U.S. corn imports, which was approximately equal to 55 percent of the price at the time. The U.S. Congress, in turn, began the process of investigating Canadian agricultural subsidies. These policy initiatives may be diminishing the prospects for a meaningful Canadian-U.S. free trade agreement. On the other hand, they appear to be politically driven and are so extreme that they may serve to force a more rational free trade agreement.

Schmitz mentions the lumber dispute between Canada and the United States and the eventual agreement whereby Canada imposed a 15 percent tax on softwood lumber shipped to the United States. However, he did not discuss the importance of Japanese trade barriers in lumber and lumber products. These are primarily designed to encourage the importation of raw logs rather than plywood or lumber. The United States is Japan's main source of wood (primarily softwood logs) and, as in the case of wheat and beef, the Canadian market share is very small. As a result of Canada's inability to market lumber in Japan, it may divert excess supplies into the United States, thus creating trade frictions.

Japan is a major importer of fish, given the importance of fish in the Japanese diet. While barriers to trade in fish are not as severe as those in agricultural products, nonetheless, barriers in the fish trade are not trivial (PECC 1986). For instance, the United States recently filed a complaint with GATT, charging that a Canadian law prohibiting export of unprocessed herring and salmon was discriminatory.

Japan enjoys a large trade surplus ($58 billion in 1986) with the United States, and this has resulted in the United States retaliating with steep tariffs on selected consumer electronics products. Protectionist discussions surrounding the 1987 U.S. Congressional Trade Bill do not adequately recognize the fact that the U.S. trade imbalance may well be due more to macroeconomic factors, than to trade barriers. For example, the Japanese Ministry of International Trade and Industry estimates that 40 percent of the 1984 trade surplus was due to the overvalued dollar and 10 percent of the trade surplus was due to the drop in oil prices (Mizoguchi 1986). Complete elimination of Japanese barriers to imports of U.S. products may only result in a $5–$6 billion reduction of the U.S. trade deficit according to Bergsten and Cline

(1985). While primary products would figure importantly here, there are many manufactured goods that would be important as well. What is less clear, however, is whether and how the composition of U.S.-Japanese trade would be affected by a major reduction in the existing macroeconomic imbalance between the two nations.

References

Bergsten, C. F., and W. R. Cline. 1985. *The United States-Japan economic problems.* Washington, D.C.: Institute for International Economics.

Carter, C. A., and M. E. Glenn. 1988. Government transfers to North American grain products. *Agribusiness* 4(3): 285–97.

Mizoguchi, M. 1986. Japan, the Pacific and the new round. In *Pacific trade policy cooperation.* Seoul: The Korea Development Institute.

Pacific Economic Cooperation Conference (PECC). 1986. Report of the Task Force on Fisheries Development and Co-operation. Fifth Pacific Economic Cooperation Conference, Vancouver, November.

Thomson, G. A. 1986. Trade issues for the Pacific Basin: Resource endowed exporter perspectives. In *Pacific trade policy cooperation.* Seoul: The Korea Development Institute.

5 A Depressed View of Policies for Depressed Industries

Robert Z. Lawrence

5.1 Introduction

Two paradigms, the economic and the political, provide strikingly different perspectives on the conduct of industrial policies. In the economic paradigm, allocative policies may be required to complement market forces when market failure results from monopolies, externalities, public goods, and the absence of established market institutions. Economic theory also lays out a set of principles about when and how such intervention should take place. First, even if markets fail, government policy may be inappropriate if it is likely to make matters worse. Second, when intervention does take place, the instruments chosen should achieve their objectives in the most precise fashion possible. For example, employment subsidies which maintain employment levels in a particular sector are more efficient than tariffs which distort both consumer and producer choice.[1] Third, structural policies are long-run policies. For the most part, they should not be used to maintain aggregate demand and employment. To attain their objectives, programs must be sustained over considerable periods of time. Fourth, these policies should not be used to reverse fundamental market forces. If, for example, a developed country loses its comparative advantage in labor-intensive and standardized commodities, it is unlikely to regain it. Government policies should facilitate, not resist, adjustment to such developments. Finally, intervention should be aimed at the margin and designed to compensate for market failures wherever they occur in the economy.

However, these principles, are scarcely recognizable in the actual practice of industrial policy (IP). Although the rhetoric may refer to facilitating adjustment, actual IP deviates from the economic paradigm in its objectives, instruments, time horizon, and assumptions about how markets function. Most IPs do not aim to complement market adjustment in order to maximize aggregate output. Rather, policies constitute a response to the conflict between the market's allocation of resources and the values and objectives desired by the political system. Instead of simply maximizing aggregate economic welfare, the political paradigm dictates that IPs be used to maintain productive capacity as an end in itself, to preserve capital, to enhance technological capabilities, to increase national prestige, to redistribute income, to reinforce job property rights, and to support regional employment. The instruments chosen are frequently not those which are, in principle, appropriate for achieving stated objectives, but rather those available and convenient for historical and institutional reasons. Policymakers often ignore the distinction between macroeconomic and structural policies, and use structural policies to maintain employment. Policies frequently focus on particular sectors or firms rather than on particular market failures. And finally, policymakers place great faith in the capacity of government policies to reverse market processes, believing that market failure is common while government failure is rare. As epitomized by the French socialist slogan, "there are no dying industries only outmoded technologies," interpretations of industry problems usually designate unfortunate and avoidable blunders as the source of industry problems, and point to modernization and modest government support as the solution to those problems.

No matter how fervent their attachment to free market principles, governments in the major developed economies inevitably succumb to political pressures to intervene and do so by means which often violate "positive adjustment" principles. Thus, despite its liberal rhetoric, the Reagan administration participated in the Chrysler rescue plan, used quotas when tariffs would have accorded with market principles in offsetting foreign subsidies on steel, sanctioned tighter restrictions in the Multifiber Agreement (MFA) for textiles, reintroduced quotas on sugar, concluded a cartel arrangement for semiconductors, and obtained voluntary export quotas on Japanese automobiles.[2] Similarly, the Japanese government, despite its strong reluctance to aid individual firms, bailed out the Sasebo shipbuilding company, and despite its abhorrence of formal trade barriers, protected its aluminum industry with tariffs. And the Canadian government, despite its commitment to the operation of market forces, has also requested voluntary export restraints (VERs) in automobiles and provided numerous large-scale subsidies to rescue individual firms.

These observations suggest that no positive analysis of industrial policies can ignore political considerations. Indeed, industrial policies fall within the scope of political science as much as economics. Moreover, the economist's role is not to question the desirability of noneconomic social objectives, but to accept those objectives. It is, however, within the economist's domain to identify the costs of achieving these objectives, to explore whether they are mutually compatible, and to evaluate the efficiency of the policies directed toward achieving them.

It would take many studies to analyze the full array of policies toward declining industries, labor markets, and communities in the U.S., Canada, and Japan. Inevitably, the present treatment must be impressionistic and partial, for to describe all of the policies would extend beyond the scope of this paper. I will focus primarily on policies toward declining industries.

The question of how to deal with declining industries is extremely topical in each of these three countries. The U.S. Congress is currently planning new trade legislation because it believes that trade has had such an adverse impact on U.S. industry that new approaches to industrial decline are imperative. In Japan, the strong yen has given rise to fears that the country will experience a serious "hollowing" of its industry that will have permanently damaging effects on its economic performance. In Canada, the proposal for the formation of a free trade area with the United States is being hotly debated, partly because of the fear that it will require massive structural adjustments for Canadian industry.

The three economies have much in common. Their democratic political systems have a wide array of interest groups which can affect policy outcomes. They have completed the phase of industrial development, characterized by the rapid growth of heavy industry and infrastructure, and they are involved in the transition toward services and knowledge-based industries. In each, the list of industries experiencing particular difficulties is virtually identical: clothing, textiles, footwear, steel, coal mining, and shipbuilding.[3] Rising unemployment has vastly increased the adjustment costs of dislocation, while slow growth and declining productivity have made the burdens of financing that adjustment more difficult. The adversely affected capital-intensive industries tend to have large plants, relatively high wages, and large numbers of employees. The difficulties of their employees stand out because the industries have assumed primary importance in regional economies and have been associated with industrial prowess. The workers' plight entails considerable loss of specific human capital for workers and profits for capitalists.

In tables 5.1 and 5.2, I report data on changes in employment shares in various industries collected by the United Nations. Unfortunately, the latest numbers are for 1983 (and 1982 in the case of Canada). They indicate a remarkable similarity in the nature and degree of changes, regardless of the differences in policies in each of the countries. The decline in employment in all three countries in labor-intensive sectors (such as textiles, footwear, and furniture) have been very similar in order of magnitude. The shifts out of capital-intensive sectors in Japan and the United States have also been remarkably similar, as has the growth in employment in high-tech sectors. The key difference appears to be the relatively smaller fall in Canadian employment in capital-intensive sectors.

Given the common nature of these experiences, it is no wonder that the debate in the three countries frequently cites one another's experiences. In

Table 5.1   Changes in Employment[a] Shares in Various Industry Types within the
United States, Japan, and Canada, 1973 and 1983 (Percentages)

Industry and Year	United States	Japan	Canada
Selected high-growth industries[b]			
1973	30.4	31.0	19.6
1983	34.5	34.5	21.8*
Change in share	13.5	11.3	11.2
Absolute change	5.2	5.3	8.4
Low-growth industries[c,d]			
1973	34.0	37.5	38.3
1983	29.9	32.2	35.2*
Changes in share	− 12.1	− 14.1	− 8.1
Absolute change	− 18.5	− 18.6	− 10.3
Labor-intensive industries[c]			
1973	19.2	21.6	22.9
1983	17.1	18.3	19.9*
Change in share	− 10.8	− 15.3	− 13.1
Absolute change	− 17.4	− 19.8	− 15.2
Capital-intensive industries[d]			
1973	14.8	15.9	15.4
1983	12.8	13.9	15.3*
Change in share	− 13.5	− 12.6	− 0.6
Absolute change	− 19.9	− 17.0	− 3.0

*Data refer to 1982.
[a]Employment: average number of employees for the United States and average number of persons engaged for Japan and Canada.
[b]Industrial chemicals, other chemical products, plastic products, machinery, electrical machinery, and professional goods.
[c]Textiles, apparel, leather, footwear, wood products, and furniture.
[d]Iron and steel, nonferrous metals, metal products, and shipbuilding.
Source: United Nations, Yearbook of Industrial Statistics (New York: UN, 1978, 1984).

particular, the Japanese approach to declining industries is viewed as a model for those who advocate a more interventionist program for positive adjustment in Canada and the United States, even though there are those in Japan who believe this approach has either not been particularly effective or is inappropriate for an economy at Japan's current stage of development and with its current trade frictions. And, others in the United States and Canada believe that their political systems are too different from Japan to apply its approach.

Accordingly, rather than provide an extensive, in-depth analysis of policies in the three countries, my emphasis will be on (1) explaining why countries have adopted differing approaches, (2) considering how well the approaches have worked, and (3) evaluating whether they could be adopted elsewhere. Because of space limitations, most of the paper will focus on the United States and Japan, but I will make some observations on the Canadian experience in the conclusion.

Table 5.2 Percentage Changes in Employment within Declining Industries in the United States, Japan, and Canada, 1970–85

Industry	United States			Japan			Canada		
	1970–75	1975–80	1980–85	1970–75	1975–80	1980–85	1970–75	1975–80	1980–84[a]
Manufacturing	−6	12	−8	−3	−3	5	6	6	−2
Textiles	−11	−1	−18	−21	−17	−9	2	−7	−14
Iron and steel	−9	−4	−37	−8	−15	−11	9	9	−22
Shipbuilding	23	8	−20	24	−50	−21	25	5	−14
Coal mining	47	16	−26	−49	−19	−17[a]	0	38	n.a.

[a]Data for 1985 not included.

Sources: United Nations, *Yearbook of Industrial Statistics*; BLS, *Employment and Earnings*; and OECD, *Indicators of Industrial Activity*.

5.2   The United States

The great strength of the U.S. economy lies in its flexibility as judged by virtually every indicator: rates of firm births and deaths; worker mobility between jobs, industries, and regions; relative and absolute wage flexibility; and highly developed capital markets and entrepreneurial traditions. The weaknesses are the mirror image of the strengths: difficulties in pursuing centralized and coordinated policies, in providing economic security, and in assisting the poor.

The pluralistic system of government in the United States has determined the nature and form of government intervention, with the process of government highly fragmented. The U.S. Constitution deliberately created a system of checks and balances in which a wide variety of groups, operating through diverse channels, may affect outcomes. This system leads to great difficulty in implementing policies which fail to reflect a broad national consensus. And, even where such a consensus does exist, opposition groups have a considerable capacity to use the legal process to inhibit major change.

A second impediment to sustained structural intervention is the lack of continuity in leadership. Eisenhower is the only postwar president to have completed eight years in office. Congressional elections every two years keep the time horizon of policy short. And, unlike other major industrial economies, where governments may come and go but the civil servants remain, each new U.S. president appoints a new group of managers to operate his executive branch.

While citizens are granted a variety of civil rights, the system of economic rights is considerably less extensive than in Europe. The government strives to achieve full employment, but does not guarantee individuals the right to be employed in their current jobs regardless of their economic value. For the most part, employers may freely dismiss their workers and close their plants without government sanction.

Unless they fulfill a self-evident public purpose (e.g., the railways or financial institutions or defense contractors), industries or firms which fail because of purely domestic competition have little recourse to federal assistance. Responses to decline (such as nationalization, subsidies, and cartels), quite common in other nations, remain unusual in the United States. Government-sponsored technological development has emphasized defense and space. While this research has yielded several important breakthrough of commercial value in electronics and aerospace, these breakthroughs occurred incidentally to the programs' goals.[4]

The United States has been a frontier economy for the postwar period, thereby making future patterns of development extremely difficult to forecast and promote. Accordingly, the government has had a virtually nonexistent role in overall structural planning. Similarly, the pluralistic nature of the system makes strategic and even coordinated strategies extremely difficult to pursue. Rather than direct leadership and mobilization of policy, the United States relies on general systems of rules and indirect price signals.

Political pressures make selective programs with specific goals difficult to implement. As Schultze (1983) has pointed out, the Model Cities program, which was to concentrate large amounts of resources in a few key urban regions, was successively diluted until it provided thin, but widely scattered, support to 150 cities. Likewise, the qualifications for the Economic Development Administration program, which aids depressed regions, were continuously broadened until about 80 percent of the counties in the United States qualified.

With the exception of antitrust and regulatory policy, industrial policies in the United States have largely concentrated on trade. The conduct of trade policy in turn reflects the U.S. system of government. The president, the Congress, and a quasi-judicial body, the International Trade Commission (ITC), share the responsibility of conducting trade policy. The First Article to the Constitution gives Congress the power to regulate commerce with foreign nations, and Congress jealously guards this power by limiting the president's ability to negotiate tariff reductions. By successfully petitioning the ITC to prevent injury from imports or unfair trade practices, firms, trade associations, unions, and groups of workers can induce presidential action that contradicts the overall thrust of his policies.

Throughout the postwar period, as foreign nations have begun to match U.S. production capabilities, American producers have felt growing pressure from international competition. Reflecting these pressures, the U.S. industries seeking assistance have gradually moved up the technological spectrum—first agriculture, then textiles, then steel and automobiles and, increasingly, high-technology products such as semiconductors.

U.S. industries seeking assistance have followed a two-track procedure. Some, typically smaller industries, have obtained protection by petitioning the ITC. They have successfully argued that imports constitute a serious source of injury, and in accordance with Section 201 of the Trade Act of 1974, they have received temporary protection. Other industries have argued their cases on the basis of unfair trade (e.g., foreign dumping or subsidies).[5] As Baldwin (1984) has noted, the ITC process does not simply rubber-stamp applications for protection. Of fifty-three petitions received by the ITC since 1975, only thirteen have resulted in higher tariffs or quotas.[6] Nor is the protection provided by the ITC permanent. The ITC requires industries to return after a three- or four-year period to request extensions of protection. Frequently these requests have been denied. Only fourteen of the fifty-seven petitions filed under section 201 since 1975 have actually resulted in import relief. Of approximately thirty industries that have received protection via the safeguard route since 1954, only three continue to be protected today. Indeed, the ITC has shown a remarkable resistance to political and industry pressure (witness its negative decision on automobiles, and recommendation and denial of protection to the same industries when circumstances changed). In a recent econometric study, Baldwin (1985, 103–14) tested the factors influencing the ITC's affirmative injury findings between 1974 and 1983, discovering that economic variables can better explain these decisions than political variables.

On the other hand, larger industries have generally tried the ITC route, but if unsuccessful, have obtained protection by exerting political pressure directly on the president and Congress. While only five industries (textiles and apparel, steel, automobiles, meat, and sugar) succeeded at this level, they represent about 25 percent of all U.S. imports according to Baldwin (1985, 693–94). Thus, despite the ITC rejection of the automobile industry's petition for import relief, the VERs on Japanese automobiles were implemented. The bilateral system of quotas negotiated with European steelmakers effectively rejected remedies suggested by the ITC, as well as the entire arrangement to protect the textile industry, first through the Long-Term Cotton Arrangement, and later the MFA.

Advocates of a new industrial policy for the United States have argued that this system of conferring trade protection is highly deficient. They suggest that new, more comprehensive approaches are needed. They argue that U.S. policymakers, blinded by an ideological commitment to free markets, have granted protection as an exceptional and temporary response to unusual circumstances. This free market perspective has resulted in protection which was not conditioned on the implementation of specific programs designed to restore competitiveness. Inevitably, according to this view, industries fail to pursue the appropriate actions for revitalization, and therefore trade protection becomes permanently necessary for the industry's survival. A coherent industrial policy, these observers argue, would provide easier access to government assistance, but toughen the conditions for which it is granted. The current debate in the United States, therefore, focuses on this issue of conditionality.

In fact, just the opposite trade strategy has worked effectively in the United States. By not embroiling itself in the detailed negotiations of programs for declining industries, U.S. policy has operated relatively successfully in facilitating adjustment in cases where protection has been administered via the ITC route. The key to adjustment has been that such protection has been credibly regarded as temporary.

The difficulties of implementing detailed conditional programs for entire industries stem from the complex nature of the required adjustment process. In the introduction to this paper, I contrasted the economic paradigm, which suggests that once competitiveness is lost, it is rarely—if ever—regained, to the political paradigm, which implies that government policies can restore almost any industry to competitiveness. In a recent study by Lawrence and DeMasi (forthcoming), the adjustment process was examined in sixteen U.S. industries which have successfully petitioned the ITC under Article 19 of the GATT.[7] This examination of the actual adjustment process suggests neither of these versions is generally applicable.

In the Lawrence-DeMasi sample, the economic paradigm occasionally proved appropriate. The problems confronting certain industries, such as those producing sheet glass or Wilton and velvet carpets, stemmed primarily from competition from a cost-effective, domestically available substitute. Exit, rather than modernization, was the appropriate strategy in these cases. Similarly, for trade-impacted industries making undifferentiated products in which costs alone determine sales, major declines inevitably resulted when the industries lost competitiveness (e.g., in the cases of high carbon ferro-chromium and nuts, bolts, and screws). Even where revitalization is feasible, however, it may require changing ownership (as was found with TVs), changing plant location (as in the case of bicycles), or narrowing the market focus (as in the case of ball bearings, footwear, and stainless steel flatware). Rarely will simply adopting the latest technology suffice, particularly for standardized products.

Foreign firms with lower labor costs will invariably emulate whatever innovations domestic producers can adopt. Instead, U.S. producers should exploit or develop advantages conferred by proximity to the market, superior servicing, marketing design, etc., or they should retreat to producing specialized, low-volume orders. Firms in numerous industries have pursued such strategies, either by remaining in the particular industry but moving out of labor-intensive activities (as in the case of flatware), or by shifting to alternative activities which require similar know-how (as in the case of producers of float rather than sheet glass). This avenue, however, will only rarely be open to all firms in the industry. Jose de la Torre (1978) studied adjustment in the apparel industry and, on the basis of an extensive set of case studies, concluded in a similar vein that efforts aimed at increasing or maintaining high productivity, while essential, were not sufficient conditions for successful operations. At the core of the growth companies' strategies was a dedication of time and resources to their external environment, that is, their marketing and their product policies.

It thus appears that the ITC process has facilitated adjustment relatively successfully. Many of the industries repeatedly attempted to secure trade protection once their relief expired. However, this should not be interpreted as a failure to adjust. On the contrary, the majority of ITC investigations for these repeat cases provided little evidence to support a case for protection. Indeed, adjustment had occurred, leaving a group of viable and competitive firms in the industry.

It should be stressed that the successful adjustment of these industries did not result from detailed government aid, but rather from credibly temporary protection, so that firms had no choice but to yield to market pressures. Among twelve of the sixteen industries that were examined by Lawrence and DeMasi, only one, bicycles, matched the political paradigm of an industry able to restore its competitiveness by expanding employment and output and reducing import shares.[8] Firms more typically responded by severely reducing (or eliminating) productive capacity to a few firms with appropriate survival strategies.

Ironically, adjustment has been considerable under these programs because they have been poorly designed and their objectives have been kept vague. Protection for industries adversely affected by international competition in the United States has been justified on two grounds. First, proponents argued that protection is required to prevent the "injury" resulting from free trade. Second, they maintained that protection would facilitate restoring competitiveness in the future. The political pressures for providing assistance to industries stem mainly from workers in individual plants. Naturally, policymakers expect aid to maintain specific jobs and plants,[9] but while "saving jobs" frequently provides the political motivation behind such actions, it is not necessarily the result.[10] Unlike the European policies, which explicitly subsidize particular firms and workers, the U.S. policies rely upon the relatively blunt instrument of trade protection and, consequently, often fail to achieve desired results.

The theory of economic policy recognizes that, in most cases, achieving a given number of objectives requires at least that number of policy instruments. Theory suggests, therefore, that only in unusual circumstances can a single policy achieve two goals. Yet in the United States, in most of the safeguard cases, only a single instrument, e.g., a tariff, quota, or orderly marketing agreement (OMA), has been used. Protection may be intended to prevent injury to current participants and to provide time to restore competitiveness. But, if long-run modernization requires displacement, protection which successfully induces adjustment may actually raise the amount of injury to some existing members of the industry. On the other hand, if protection retains or attracts resources incompatible with the long-run viability of the industry, it will preclude competitiveness. Trade protection thus constitutes an extremely imprecise method either for limiting the dislocation to existing workers and firms or for inducing modernization.

Moreover, while trade may produce dislocation in the industry, it is frequently not the only source. Dislocation may occur in any case, even with trade protection. Protection can actively increase competitive pressures for existing firms. For example, in the TV industry, protection attracted new competitors for U.S. firms by encouraging foreign direct investment. Protection can also increase the dislocation of existing workers. For example, in the bicycle industry, protection induced modernization, resulting in dislocation when plants moved.

The escape clause route has allowed adjustment, but it has also been extremely costly to consumers. Hufbauer, Berliner, and Elliot (1986) examined consumer costs of seven recent escape clause actions, finding that on average such actions cost consumers $340,000 for each job saved. Actually, costs may be greater because these estimates assume all industries to be perfectly competitive. To the degree that quota protection induces domestic oligopolists to raise prices, costs per job saved could be much higher. In fact, there has been a disturbing trend toward the increased use of quotas in recent years. Since 1975, OMAs have restricted imports of specialty steel, color televisions, and nonrubber footwear.

5.2.1 Trade Adjustment Assistance

The unique role that trade policy plays for declining industries in the United States is reflected by the special trade adjustment assistance (TAA) program for workers who lose their jobs in industries experiencing difficulties in trade competition. The program aids in training and relocating workers, but it has focused primarily on supplementing unemployment benefits. Originally implemented to persuade organized labor to agree to the Kennedy Round tariff cuts, the program has a mixed record of success.[11] From one viewpoint, a weak rationale supports this program: Why should workers displaced as a result of one particular source of change—trade—be treated better than those displaced because of demand shifts or technical change? However, it has been justified in a political context as compensation for removing protection or as an instrument allowing the political process to voice concern without providing protection. Indeed, one-third of the positive ITC findings resulted in trade adjustment assistance rather than protection.

A major problem with the program has been its impact on incentives. Providing assistance as a supplement to unemployment compensation actually rewards only workers who fail to adjust. Indeed, most of the program recipients eventually return to their original jobs. A superior system would provide workers with lump-sum grants or payments equal to a fixed percentage of the erosion in their earnings for a particular period of time—in essence, compensation for the erosion in their specific human capital.[12]

While temporary trade protection has generally facilitated adjustment, the United States has also yielded to the political pressures of several industries. This has resulted in the United States deviating from the conventional legal method of providing trade relief to a troubled industry. The following examples—the textile and apparel industry, the steel industry, and the Chrysler bailout—exemplify the risks involved with detailed government policy intervention.

5.2.2   U.S. Failure to Adjust: Textiles and Apparel

The political power of the American apparel and textiles industries enabled them to circumvent the route of the ITC to obtain trade protection, which has thus far proved to be permanent. Because of its permanence, the system epitomizes the pitfalls of protection for declining industries. Even when judged according to their own objectives of limiting dislocation and facilitating modernization and competitiveness, the policies have failed. They have also proved extremely costly to U.S. consumers.

First, aiding the declining New England region constituted a major motivation behind imposing the original protective measures. Yet the Long-Term Cotton Arrangement stimulated the development of the synthetics industry as a major new domestic competitor. Between 1961 and 1973, overall employment in U.S. textiles increased by 13 percent, and investment was strong, increasing at 2.3 percent per year. But the aggregate data masked a massive relocation occurring within the United States, as firms reduced their labor costs by moving from New England to especially the South. Whereas the United States began the 1960s with one group of textile workers needing protection because they worked in the Northeast, it ended the decade with another group of textile workers requiring protection because they worked in the South and West. Had these new entrants not been enticed into the industry, it could have accommodated significantly greater import penetration with no additional dislocation.

Thus, the real problem stems from the permanence of the MFA. A high turnover of firms and workers characterizes the textile industry. In principle, if new entry could be discouraged (as it has been in sectors such as footwear which have received credibly temporary protection), the industry is capable of significant shrinkage without dislocation. But the voluntary exit of some firms resulting from the MFA, raises product prices and creates incentives for new entry. This problem is generic in industries with relatively low entry barriers. In these cases, the "positive adjustment" principles of subsidies for capacity reduction will probably not succeed. As I argue below, even Japan's relatively unsuccessful experience in preventing new entry into this sector (through the subsidized retirement of looms) points to the imperative of a credible declining tariff mechanism as the principal tool of adjustment.[13]

5.2.3   U.S. Steel Industry: Failure or Success?

The poor state of the U.S. steel industry has tempted policymakers to pursue an explicit revitalization program. Thus far, no such policy has been implemented. Proponents of an industrial policy for steel perceive myopic management's failure to invest or to modernize the large integrated U.S. steel mills as a major reason for the industry's decline. This popular political explanation for the U.S. steel industry's decline rests on an argument of market failure: inappropriate behavior on the part of management in failing to invest and on the part of labor in demanding (and obtaining) wages that were too high. The solution, according to some, entails a government-led, tripartite program in which protection would be conditioned on wage concessions by the unions and major investments by existing firms.

This view represents a classic example of the degree to which political failure may exceed (alleged) market failure. The fundamental nature of the problems facing the integrated U.S. steel industry actually makes the modernization strategy highly questionable. In fact, those U.S. firms in big steel which followed the modernization strategy in the 1970s are those on the verge of bankruptcy today. Three factors make this approach questionable. First, as a result of lower construction and raw materials costs abroad, U.S. international competitiveness has eroded. Second, the demand growth for steel remains sluggish. Third, the availability of a superior and cheaper technology for making steel—the mini mill—has begun to replace the integrated steel mill.

In a paper by Lawrence and Lawrence (1985), it is argued that the dramatic increase in relative steel wages over the 1970s was actually a response to these developments. As early as 1970, long before U.S. steel investment declined and relative wages soared, U.S. capital markets signaled the poor prospects for the U.S. steel industry by pricing their stock at only one-third of replacement costs. Ignoring this market warning, government policies have insisted on chaneling more resources into the industry in the form of tax incentives and loan guarantees, and providing trade relief, all in the hope of improving the competitiveness of steel. And, despite the many policies over the 1970s, the U.S. steel industry has continued to decline steadily. Yet as late as 1984, the Congress passed, and the president signed, a bill mandating new investments by integrated steel as a condition for trade relief. It is the height of folly to channel resources toward sectors in which they will not earn a normal rate of return. Indeed, a similar conclusion is reached in the study by the Congressional Budget Office (1986, 57), where they argue that neither the voluntary restraint agreements nor the trigger price system provided the steel industry with the resources to increase its international competitiveness: "But even if protection had been more successful, it is doubtful whether a massive modernization program would provide adequate returns. Bethlehem Steel, for example, undertook a major modernization program in the early 1980s that has not proved profitable."

5.2.4 The Chrysler Lesson

The U.S. government under both Presidents Carter and Reagan strayed considerably from its free market principles by conferring loan guarantees on the Chrysler Corporation, thereby rescuing it from bankruptcy. Some suggest that this experience supports the view that, to perform such bailouts on a regular basis, a new banking institution should be part of U.S. industrial policy.

On the other hand, others argue that the very harsh nature of the concessions exacted from the Chrysler creditors and workers in order to qualify for aid were possible only because the threat of bankruptcy was credible and the process was extremely unusual. The company had no legal claim for government aid. It was forced to convince the government that it was prepared to undertake the necessary adjustments. Eads (1981, 467) correctly argues that: "A far different—and more ominous—signal would be given by the creation of a special 'revitalization' authority with general powers to receive petitions for aid and work out rescue packages . . . The current process certainly has been 'messy' but its very messiness helps assure that it will not be used very often."

5.2.5 Policy Suggestions

A major reason why even an administration as philosophically committed to free trade as the Reagan administration has found it necessary to cave in to pressures for protection is that the two "safety valves" in the U.S. system for absorbing protectionist pressures are imperfect.

The first, the escape clause, allows domestic industries to receive temporary protection from imports when they can prove to the ITC that imports threaten or cause them serious economic injury. Although this provision of U.S. law has been reasonably effective in screening out the most unworthy domestic industries—roughly 40 percent of all applicants since the law was last revised in 1974 have been denied relief by the ITC—it nevertheless has a fatal flaw. An industry can "win" its case before the ITC but still be denied relief by the president, thus encouraging it to turn to Congress for permanent protection (as the domestic shoe and copper industries have done in the last two years). In addition, the law has allowed the president to provide temporary relief in the form of quotas as well as tariffs; the latter are less distorting of trade flows and also raise revenue for the government (unlike quotas).

The second safety valve, the TAA program for firms, workers, and communities adversely affected by significant import competition, has been rendered increasingly ineffective because its funding has been severely cut back over the past five years. Moreover, even in its heyday, TAA delayed adjustment, particularly by displaced workers who were merely given extended unemployment compensation payments without being positively encouraged to find alternative employment.

In Lawrence and Litan (1986) we recommend several modest changes in both the escape clause and the TAA program that would make them more useful. First, the provisions of the U.S. escape clause would be more cost effective if declining tariffs were the sole form of temporary import relief for industries seriously damaged by import competition. In addition, all existing quotas and other quantitative restrictions should be converted to their tariff equivalents by auction; that is, all rights to import products within the quota ceiling should be sold off to the highest bidders. Tariff rates should then be scheduled to decline over time. The revenue raised by these tariffs should be earmarked for assisting workers adversely affected by imports.

Second, we recommend that an affirmative injury finding by the ITC *automatically* trigger two different types of relief. Mergers of firms in beleaguered industries (not protected by quotas) would be assessed under liberalized standards, as recently recommended by the Reagan administration. If an industry is judged by the ITC to be seriously damaged by imports, then there is little worry that mergers will lead to imperfect competition.

We also recommend that TAA be automatically extended to displaced workers, but only in such a way that the benefits provided encourage rather than delay adjustment. Specifically, we propose that the primary component of TAA benefits consist of insurance against loss of wages. That is, workers displaced by import competition would be compensated for some proportion of any reduction in wages they may experience in obtaining new jobs, thereby encouraging those workers to find and accept new employment quickly. The proportion of the loss compensated could vary with the age of the worker and seniority in his or her previous job. A second component would provide extended unemployment compensation to workers residing in regions where the unemployment rate significantly exceeds the national average. The remaining elements in our proposed program would provide relocation allowances and assistance for retraining. Federal loans for retraining would carry repayment obligations tied to future earnings and be collected automatically through the income tax system.

Even under highly conservative assumptions, our proposed TAA program could be readily financed for at least a decade by converting existing quotas into declining tariffs. As a result, there would be no financial pressures to impose new tariffs to fund the assistance program, although the president would still be authorized to grant tariff remedies in the future to domestic industries proving to the ITC that they merit relief.

Finally, we propose a new mechanism to ease the pain of economic dislocation for communities—a voluntary system of insurance by which municipalities, counties, and states can protect themselves against sudden losses in their tax bases that are not the result of reductions in tax rates. Under such a program, governmental entities choosing to participate would pay an insurance premium, much like the premiums firms currently pay for unemployment compensation, for a policy that would compensate for losses in the tax base caused by plant closures or significant layoffs.

5.2.6 Summary

In summary, transitory trade protection in the United States, while far from cost effective, has in numerous cases proved to be not permanent and has thus been associated with significant adjustment. The success of the program has stemmed from the trade relief mechanism allowing the political system to voice concern for the victims of change without becoming embroiled in detailed sectoral programs with specific and precisely defined objectives. Paradoxically, the very impotence of U.S. IP instruments has made the system relatively adaptable. In the introductory section of this paper, I noted that employment shifts in the United States have matched those in Japan. The relatively superior performance of the U.S. system is, however, not attributable to the superior capabilities of U.S. political leadership. It is more directly the result of the system limiting the ability of politicians to intervene "effectively."

5.3 Japan

In the United States and Canada, those who reject the call for new industrial policies for declining industries claim that these industries would inevitably be dominated by political interests which would seek to preserve the status quo. If applied in North America, they argue, such programs would delay adjustment, increase inefficiency, and raise the levels of trade protection.

Japanese policies are frequently singled out by IP proponents as evidence that these objections are incorrect. The Japanese experience, they contend, proves that government, business, and labor can act within a framework based on consensus to implement a policy which facilitates industrial adjustment while simultaneously aiding and compensating those adversely affected. According to the Japanese government, their experience proves that such policies can be implemented in keeping with the principles for positive adjustment enunciated by the OECD, in that they are: temporary, transparent, linked to the phasing out of obsolete capacity, and free of protectionist measures against imports. Another attribute claimed by scholars such as Trebilcock (1986, 241) is that they have been anticipatory rather than reactive: "Open and institutionalized communication among the key players permits anticipatory planning (using economic forecasts which reveal changes in market patterns) rather than reactive policy responses, to deal with sunset industries."

In this analysis of Japanese policies for declining industries, I will try to evaluate the validity of these claims. I will pay particular attention to the links between these programs and protection. Respected Japanese authors claim that trade barriers are absent in these programs. Uekusa and Ide (1986) and Sekiguchi and Horiuchi (1985) emphasize that they have taken place in an open economy.[14] The Japanese government is currently planning its IP response to the difficulties presented by the strengthening of the Japanese yen. Its policies are likely to be similar to those it has implemented in the recent past. If the favorable appraisals of Japanese policies are accurate, the policies will serve as a helpful complement to Japanese structural adjustment in response to the strong yen. However, if these programs actually entail import protection, albeit in a covert form, they will thwart the market-opening process which is the key to alleviating the trade tensions between Japan and its trading partners.

5.3.1 The Policies

Prior to 1978, Japanese policies toward declining industries were introduced on a separate, ad hoc basis in the agricultural, coal mining, sulphur mining, and textile industries. Tresize and Suzuki (1976) argue that, in these programs, efforts to delay adjustment have been the major focus of policy. In agriculture, the strength of protection is widely acknowledged. In coal, the central approach was to delay the decline by requiring both the electric power and steel industries to use quotas of subsidized coal. Nor was rapid adjustment the focus of programs for the textile industry.[15] The Ministry of International Trade and Industry (MITI) prescription was a cartel supported by a government program which sought (quite unsuccessfully) to retire surplus spindles.[16] While it is sometimes argued that the MITI encouragement of Japanese overseas investment was a major part of the approach in textiles, Tresize and Suzuki emphasize that such investment was largely devoted to production for export and local markets, not for reimportation into Japan.

The focus of this discussion, however, will be the programs that Japan has carried out for depressed industries (typically capital-intensive) since 1978. The broad, comprehensive, legislative framework for programs for declining industries in Japan was first laid out in the Law on Temporary Measures for the Stabilization of Specified Depressed Industries enacted in 1978. This law identified four sectors—shipbuilding, aluminum refining, synthetic fiber manufacturing, and open-hearth steel—as depressed. It allowed MITI to specify other industries as eligible for support, based on four provisions: (1) they had severe overcapacity; (2) more than half the firms were in dire financial condition; (3) firms representing two-thirds of the industry signed a petition seeking designation; and (4) there was broad agreement that scrapping of facilities was required to overcome the situation. In consultation with industry representatives, MITI then draws up a plan for restructuring. The plan is to be implemented by participant firms aided by government measures such as antitrust immunity and loan guarantees to compensate firms for scrapping facilities. When it is judged that firms cannot scrap capacity by themselves, MITI can ask the firms to form a cartel—an indicative or designated cartel—to coordinate reductions. Firm participation in these programs is voluntary. However, the law allows the ministry in charge of a particular industry to prohibit construction of new facilities once an industry has been designated as depressed.[17]

The Japanese approach does not single out trade as a source of structural change deserving particular policy approaches. In principle, it also does not entail any use of trade protection in the program's operation.

Fourteen industries participated in the programs under the 1978 law. Eleven of these owed their difficulties primarily to the increase in oil prices, either because they were energy intensive (linerboard, electric furnace steel, aluminum, and ferrosilicon) or because they used petroleum products as raw materials (synthetic fiber industries such as nylon filament, polyacrylonitril, polyester filament, and polyester staple and fertilizers such as ammonium, phosphoric acid, and urea). Only three industries had problems which were not specifically related to oil prices: cotton and wool textiles whose difficulties reflected slow demand and LDC competition, and shipbuilding which was globally depressed. Indicative cartels designed to reduce capacity were formed in eight of the fourteen industries, and at different times, seven were authorized to form more temporary recession cartels to control output.[18]

The 1978 law was part of a broader package of legislation to deal with the problems of industrial restucturing. In addition to the Law for Depressed Industries, other programs for assisting workers and regions were established. In particular, subsidies were provided to reimburse firms that relocated and trained workers for alternative employment and to finance early retirement grants. Workers in districts with high unemployment were also extended special assistance.[19]

Why these policies? Japanese industrial adjustment policies, like those in the United States and Canada, are the natural result of the particular features of their political and economic institutions, rather than the application of the normative principles enunciated by economic theory (or, for that matter, the OECD).

In Japan, firms and banks feel unusually strong pressures when confronted with excess capacity. The system of lifetime employment (or the need to provide large retirement benefits) implies that large firms have particularly high ratios of fixed to variable cost. The system of finance, which entails a much higher proportion of debt to equity than is found in the United States, implies greater financial pressures on firms and their banks during periods of low profitability.[20] In particular, since loans are usually secured by fixed plant, the retirement of capacity often requires repayment of loans or default. The greater reliance on banks, rather than on more anonymous stockholders, makes the organization of pressures from creditors considerably easier. Thus both firms and banks have strong incentives to seek aid in boosting corporate profits during times of stress.

Other features of the Japanese system ensure that these corporations will receive a sympathetic hearing. The Japanese system of government is highly centralized, with considerable power resting in the hands of the government bureaucracy. This bureaucracy is highly regarded and given much discretion in a system which emphasizes the achievement of consensus rather than a legalistic interpretation of the law. The bureaucrats have long followed a system of providing a great deal of guidance to industries over which they are responsible. The political system, which has resulted in the long-lived tenure of the governing Liberal Democratic party, is particularly sensitive to the interests of big business (and agriculture). Komiya and Itoh (1985) suggest that Japanese consumers have little political power. They argue that most Japanese believe that having a job in an organization which exerts influence is much more important than small reductions in the prices of some of the goods they buy. Similarly, labor is not strongly represented in Japanese industrial policy discussions.[21] Japanese notions of the nature of the firm and of the relative unimportance of antitrust principles also lead to the techniques used. Japan, of course, does have an antitrust law, written along American lines, but adherence to it has not been rigid.[22] Japan has a Fair Trade Commission which opposed the original draft legislation of the Depressed Industries Law and succeeded in reducing some of the power that MITI had sought. Nonetheless, measures under the 1978 law are exempt from antitrust laws. The view of firms as almost permanent social institutions leads to a preference for deviating from efficient capacity retirement when it would entail the elimination of particular firms.

All these features lead MITI to respond to depressed demand conditions by organizing cartels to mitigate "excessive" competition. In the strong growth environment of the 1950s and 1960s, such policies allowed Japanese firms to take a long-run view, secure in the knowledge that profitability would be protected during periods of excess supply. In principle, such policies induced excessive investment, since they distorted the true social risk faced by producers (by passing it on to consumers), but such efficiency losses were probably small relative to the dynamic gains from scale economies and reduced investment risk. And in any case, the costs of such policies were quickly disguised when excess capacity was fully utilized as growth was resumed. As Yamamura (1982) has argued, this legacy means that firms naturally look for government aid during periods of slump, creating a political expectation that was hard to resist during the slower growth period of the 1970s and 1980s.[23] In addition, according to Yamamura, MITI is inevitably drawn into policies to aid these designated industries because their difficulties were related to investments that they had originally made under MITI guidance.[24]

At the same time as they have been naturally drawn toward cartel arrangements, Japanese policymakers have studiously avoided the approaches dominant in most European governments—large subsidies—or in the United States—formal trade protection. In Japan, industrial policymakers have managed to keep budgetary outlays to a minimum, preferring to pass on the costs of their programs, either explicitly (as in the case of shipbuilding) to other industry participants or implicitly to consumers and those in smaller supplying industries. Similarly, industrial policymakers have sought to avoid explicit trade barriers. In part this was because some of the problem industries were not suffering from international competition, and some were export industries which already had a virtual monopoly in the home market. But, in addition, the frictions between Japan and its trading partners make formal trade barriers a last resort.

5.3.2   Principles

In what respect does a government-managed system for capacity retirement deviate from the outcome that would occur if market forces were allowed to operate? Let us analyze a simple case, illustrated in figure 5.1. First, assume that there are six plants in an industry, each with similar capacity but with different levels of average cost (AC). Assume further that marginal costs are zero, so that all costs are fixed for operating any given plant. The demand curve is initially D_0 at which all can operate profitably, with the sixth and least efficient plant simply covering its average costs. Q_0 is the quantity produced. Assume now that the demand curve shifts permanently inward to D_1. Over the long run, plant 6 can no longer operate profitably. If the market is allowed to operate freely, in the short run the price will decline to P_s and firms 5 and 6 will make losses. The formation of a recession cartel, with the mothballing of some capacity, could allow all firms to improve their profitability. The cartel could price its product at the profit-maximizing price P_m, where marginal revenue equals zero marginal cost, and allocate Q_m across its members. Under these circumstances, plant 6 will be able to survive for a longer time. But note that this arrangement entails a tradeoff. Firms may be more profitable, but consumers pay higher prices. In addition, since total output declines (from Q_0 to Q_m), the effect on workers who do have permanent employment arrangements and on firms which supply the industry will be aggravated. That is, short-run quantity volatility will be increased by temporary cartels.

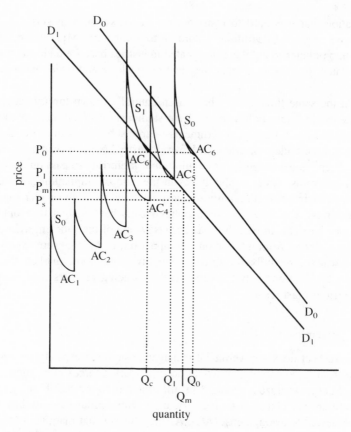

Fig. 5.1 Capacity responses to demand shifts

If the demand shift were permanent, under free market conditions the price would eventually stabilize at P_1—a price at which plants 1 through 5 could cover their costs. Plant 6 would be forced to close down. Imagine, however, in this instance, that a designated cartel is formed and its solution deviates from the market outcome. Assume plants 4 and 5 are retired. In that case, the industry supply curve will shift S_0S_1 and in the long run the price will be P_0—the price necessary for plant 6 to break even. Such a solution may be preferred by the political system, but it is important to stress that it involves a greater reduction in industry capacity, a higher price for consumers, and a permanently smaller demand for the products of the industry's suppliers. Thus, while the traditional literature has emphasized the ability of such programs to meet their capacity-reduction targets, their impact might well have been to exacerbate rather than alleviate the industry's adjustment difficulties. On the other hand, the cartel could agree to scrap plant 6, in which case the arrangement would simply duplicate the market solution in the long run. But if plant 6 were scrapped prematurely, the plan would again entail inefficiency since its social marginal cost is zero.

What if this program were carried out in the context of an open economy in which an infinitely elastic supply of imports was available at the price P_s. In that case, consumers would refuse to pay more than P_s at home. In the short run, the cartel would not improve the profitability of the industry since the product price would be given. In the long run, only plants able to produce profitably at that price could survive. If the cartel forced the closure of viable plants, it would make no improvement on the ultimate fate of those that were uneconomical. Nor for that matter would it help their short-run profitability.

Let us turn now to an appraisal of these Japanese programs.

5.3.3 Efficient?

It is difficult, a priori, to determine the efficiency of Japanese programs. Much depends on the degree to which they deviate from an outcome that would result from the operation of market forces. In principle, a designated cartel could choose to retire plants in an optimal manner. Cartels that are simply symbolic, and thus yield the same outcome as the market, might aid management in implementing the painful adjustment required in depressed industries. In a management system which rests on consensus, it may be easier to be forced to take steps in the name of the fatherland or of official government policy, than in the name of complying with market forces.

It is unlikely, however, that the market-based pattern is actually followed. In particular, the plans place more of the burden on large firms to reduce capacity since they are viewed as more able to pay. According to Anderson (1986, 24), "A number of Japanese academic economists, whose views were solicited by the JFTC (Japanese Fair Trade Commission) expressed doubt that the DIL (Depressed Industries Law) had in fact encouraged in all instances the least efficient producers to leave the market." In his analysis of the shipbuilding program, Anderson concluded that these decision rules resulted in an industry that protected pockets of inefficiency.[25] He also described how the shipbuilding cartel hindered the ability of Japanese shipyards to compete with those in South Korea. Such deviations from the market solution probably increased the dislocation in the shipbuilding industry.

A common rationalization used in Japan and elsewhere for policies which raise prices and profits for existing firms is that they induce investment and thus offer future benefits to consumers in the form of higher productivity. However, since bygones are bygones, there is in principle no need to preserve company profits because these are simply rents. Bankruptcy should not be confused with the shutdown of operations. An efficient system does not force viable plants or firms to cease operation when bankruptcy occurs. Instead it allows them to write down their assets to reflect current market conditions and to continue with forward-looking investment.

Similarly, Peck, Levin, and Goto (1987) point out that, in Japan, large firms do much of what governments do in Europe and the United States. By preserving these firms' profitability, the government can then leave them to administer schemes for the relocation and retirement of workers and the repayment of banks. In principle, however, as Peck, Levin, and Goto acknowledge, this is very much a second-best argument. The more direct, and thus more efficient, method would be to directly subsidize the aid given to workers and communities. Indeed, such subsidies are actually part of Japanese labor market policies under the 1978 act. Moreover, the role of job transfers within company groups can be exaggerated. Shimada (1986) found that, in general, such transfers remain of marginal significance in depressed industries. Firms appeared to be able to avoid dismissals principally by shifting the burden of adjustment to their smaller subcontractors.

5.3.4   Effective in Reducing Capacity?

How successful have the programs been in achieving their targets for scrapping? According to Peck, Levin, and Goto (1987), official government reports claim that twelve of the fourteen industries achieved at least 90 percent of their capacity-reduction targets. (The electric furnace industry is a notable exception in the data since it actually increased its capacity over the 1978–83 period by 15 percent.) They note, however, that these reductions tended to be greatest in concentrated industries, with MITI being much more conservative with industries in which it had less control: "Only one of the less concentrated industries, shipbuilding, set a target in excess of 70 percent of unutilized capacity in 1977. Indeed, only three of the eight sought to eliminate as much as one half of initial excess capacity" (p. 93).

Were the programs actually binding in the sense that they accelerated scrapping or were they simply fortunate forecasts about what would have taken place anyway? According to Sekiguchi and Horiuchi (1985, 382), the effectiveness of the 1978 act tends to be overvalued. They point out that there seems to be no difference in the adjustment behavior of firms who participate in designated cartels and those that do not.[26] They also point out that the actual use of money available for retirement subsidies was rather small and much less than was budgeted.[27] Peck, Levin, and Goto (1987) also note that in unconcentrated industries most capacity reduction came from exit, whereas in concentrated industries reductions were more widely distributed. This suggests that the programs were more effective in concentrated industries. Anderson (1986, 39) recounts the story of the aluminum industry, noting that, while the industry formed a capacity-reduction cartel with a goal of 32 percent retirement by 1981, in fact 61.5 percent of the industry's capacity was shut down. By the end of 1982, a second round of capacity reductions took place that again exceeded the MITI target. Indeed, Anderson comments, "MITI seemed not so much to be leading an orderly retreat as following behind in the medic's van, bandaging the wounded and burying the dead" (p. 37).

In sum, therefore, the programs have been more effective when applied to concentrated industries. But even in these cases, it seems that they resulted in an outcome which deviated only mildly from market forces in terms of total capacity.

5.3.5 Anticipatory?

Japanese programs have the virtue that they entail an explicit plan with forecasts and targets. However, the targets have been relatively conservative and, as I have indicated, in less concentrated industries constitute forecasts rather than implementable directives. But government officials are not prepared to stick their necks out and identify industries which are likely to run into trouble in the future. Nor are they willing to argue that major parts of an industry are no longer viable. The depressed industry measures are triggered on the basis of a prior consensus by the firms themselves that scrapping is required. In that sense, government programs are reactive rather than anticipatory. There is also considerable evidence that the approaches err on the side of preservationism. According to Tresize and Suzuki (1976, 800): "Few things could be less accurate, in fact, than the proposition that Tokyo was ever prepared to have its older or weaker industries run down as a matter of deliberate planning." The report of the U.S. General Accounting Office (1982, 57) comes to a similar conclusion in the case of textiles: "Government officials acknowledge that it is politically difficult to declare that an industry or segments of an industry should be phased out. Even though MITI may want to phase out the cotton spinning or textile mill products industries, it cannot present such a recommendation to the industry."

5.3.6 Transparent?

The Japanese programs for depressed industries are transparent, in the limited sense that their existence is made public and explicit in legislation, but the incidence and extent of their social costs are certainly not easily determined. Peck, Levin, and Goto (1987, 122) suggest that cartelization is to be preferred to subsidies since ". . . there is only so much that consumers can be made to pay to support the continued existence of a declining industry. Taxpayers however have deeper pockets." This argument of course could also be applied to trade protection but would be equally unconvincing. In fact, subsidies have the virtue that they make costs transparent. They force governments to come to terms with the costs of thwarting market forces. Cartels, like trade protection with quotas, shift the costs in a covert fashion. They impose costs on outsiders such as consumers, suppliers, and foreign competitors. Such programs also disguise the true social cost of institutions, such as lifetime employment and heavy debt financing, by shifting their burdens.

5.3.7 In an Open Economy?

In several cases, depressed industries owe their difficulties to the collapse of export markets or domestic demand. But some industries have faced severe import competition. Domestic plants cannot survive if their average costs exceed those of imports, unless they receive protection. Accordingly, it is difficult to understand how a structural cartel arrangement aids a sector facing import competition unless it is accompanied by trade protection. The literature on this question is divided. Some authors tend to emphasize the absence of import barriers. Accordingly, their conclusion is, essentially, that the policy has been relatively ineffective. According to Sekiguchi and Horiuchi (1985, 395): "While recession cartels might have been effective when imports were restricted, their effectiveness was eroded in import-competing industries after liberalization." On the other hand, other scholars have pointed to the important role that informal barriers, reinforced by administrative guidance, have played in bolstering the cartel arrangement.

It is hard to support the blanket judgment that protection has been absent. In the case of aluminum, an explicit tariff was used with an ingenious rebate allowing firms to import tariff-free the amount of capacity they had shut down. Thus, while the act did encourage adjustment, it entailed explicit protection for aluminum producers as suppliers and importers. Hence, it is no wonder that most of the aluminum imports into Japan came from fully or partially owned Japanese subsidiaries abroad.[28] Hidden protection is a major issue in the chemical fertilizer industries such as ammonia and urea. When oil prices increased in the late 1970s, the Japanese producers of these fertilizers made from naphtha found that their products were not competitive in global markets. According to Rapp (1986), imported urea, landed and bagged, was quoted at $192 per ton compared with the Japanese ex-factory price of $230–40. However, as Peck, Levin, and Goto (1987) note, there has been no rise in import penetration in ammonia, despite a substantial increase in domestic prices since the mid-1970s, and sales of imported urea remain a small share of the domestic market. Rapp argues, "there is apparently a consensus among Japanese government officials, urea manufacturers, and distributors to keep price-competitive imports out of Japan and several U.S. firms have received suggestions that they not attempt to export more to Japan" (p.

30). Sales of all chemical fertilizers in Japan are controlled by a legal monopoly created by the Chemical Price Stabilization Act. All sales to Japanese farmers must be made through the National Federation of Agricultural Cooperative Associations (Zennon). Once a year the price is negotiated and approved by the Japanese Cabinet. Zennon could in principle buy all its supplies from imports, but there are reports that it has been pressured into limiting its import purchases despite their lower cost. Peck, Levin, and Goto point out that this buying arrangement has existed for a long time and that it is not the result of the depressed-industry arrangement for urea. Nonetheless, the arrangement was clearly an important element in making the program a more effective aid to the industry than it would have been had trade been open.

The MITI policy toward cotton and mixed cotton and synthetic yarn industries is also not free of government intervention in trade.[29] In the spring of 1981, a recession cartel was arranged for the cotton yarn industries. Firms were required to reduce production and to set production capacity at a fixed level by sealing the gear boxes of spindles. A letter from the head of the Basic Consumer Industries bureau of MITI was sent out to some seventy trading firms, and a copy was also sent to the Japanese Textile Importers Association. All importing firms were required to complete forms reporting their import activities and asked to exercise "the utmost restraint." Then, twenty of the major importers were summoned to MITI at the rate of four a day for hearings. Finally, MITI sent officials to China and South Korea to request cooperation. A voluntary export restraint arrangement was concluded with South Korea.

In sum, therefore, it is hard to justify the contention made by Uekusa and Ide (1986) that Japanese policies toward declining industries have been implemented "in an open economy." Protection in a variety of forms, from overt use of tariffs to VERs, and less transparent use of buying cartels and guidance, has accompanied these policies. It still may be true that such protection is less extensive than elsewhere, but that requires a more detailed quantitative investigation that is beyond the scope of this paper.

5.3.8 Temporary?

In 1983, the program was amended and extended for another five years. The Law for Depressed Industries was renamed Temporary Measures for Restructuring Industries. Dropping the adjective "depressed" reflects the shift in MITI's objectives to broaden the program to cover restructuring, regardless of whether the industry is depressed. Significantly, all fourteen industries designated under the 1978 act remained covered by the law (or other special programs). Eleven new industries were added. The judgment made by

Uekusa and Ide (1986) that these programs "have been phased out when no longer necessary" may ultimately be correct, but thus far there is little evidence that the programs are temporary.

These programs have, in fact, been considerably expanded in scope. The new law allows MITI to go further than simply scrapping facilities, allowing it to play a role in forming business tie-ups between firms to cover production, transportation, and marketing arrangements, and even to form mergers. It should be stressed that, in contrast to the indicative and recession cartels, these tie-ups are permanent arrangements. The shift from "adjustment out" toward "modernization" is also evident in provisions in the 1983 act for subsidies for modernizing equipment and for research and development. These measures are viewed with some alarm by Sekiguchi and Horiuchi (1985), who fear that efforts to actively promote mergers and restrain competition among producers by such means as establishing "joint sales companies" will make import penetration more difficult. In addition, the employment measures accompanying the 1983 legislation put their emphasis on preventing unemployment rather than assisting displaced workers. Workers whom firms in depressed regions and industries are planning to displace are to be subsidized at two-thirds of the wage bill for six months, on the condition that firms extend their employment and retraining. Firms hiring displaced workers receive a subsidy of a quarter of the wage bill for the first year. These subsidies could apply to workers who find reemployment in the same industry, and therefore actually represent subsidies to the firms. Clearly, in both industry and labor market policies, the shift has been from exit to modernization.

5.3.9 Conclusions

The Japanese have adopted an ingenious approach to depressed industries which stems from the unique institutional character of the Japanese economy. A tolerance for cartels is its essential ingredient. The approach meets the political needs of a society highly responsive to the interests of large firms and banks, which experience particular pressures given the Japanese institutions of lifetime employment and highly leveraged finance. The policy has affected the timing and pattern of capacity withdrawal in which cartels generally may be expected to work, that is, where new entry can be effectively prevented and compliance effectively monitored. But even under such circumstances, as in the case of the aluminum industry, it has been overtaken by market forces. The approach is much less effective in competitive industries. In the Japanese textile industry, for example, success has not been noteworthy.

To be sure, by providing Japanese officials with mechanisms to show their concerns for distressed industries, the programs have helped avoid some of the market-thwarting forces that have been applied in other countries. Nonetheless, the Japanese example is less attractive than admirers or government spokesmen would suggest.

The process may be public, but its costs and some of its procedures are certainly not transparent. Effective recession cartels may be temporary, but they shift the costs in a hidden fashion to suppliers, consumers, and trading partners. Indicative cartels that retire capacity in a negotiated framework, may likewise increase dislocation by hindering competitiveness and by eliminating relatively more productive capacity.

Japanese programs are certainly tied to the elimination of capacity. Indeed, their greatest virtue is the signal they send to industry participants of the need for adjustment. But the plans as actually formulated are biased toward conservative estimates of the adjustment required. Officials have such a bias because they do not want their programs to fail to meet their objectives and because they are subject to political pressures from the industry. Industry participants have that bias because capacity reduction is painful.

The Japanese programs have not been temporary. All of the industries covered by the programs under the 1978 act remained in special programs after 1983. This experience suggests that, rather than allowing the government to withdraw more readily by participating in such programs, intervention begets further intervention by making the government increasingly responsible for the fate of the industry. Indeed, MITI officials have extended and increased their mandate from the relatively narrow focus of aiding exit in the 1978 law to the broader objective of rationalizing and modernizing the industries under the 1983 program.

The programs have the virtue that they view industry problems in their entirety rather than distinguishing the problems due to trade. This holistic and comprehensive approach has led to an emphasis on the use of cartels rather than trade protection to moderate adjustment problems. However, the philosophy behind this view is more appropriate to an economy which is, on the whole, growing rapidly in a market relatively closed to import competition, than it is to an economy with slower growth which is seeking to alleviate frictions with its trading partners. In a rapidly growing economy, static efficiency costs will be outweighed and disguised by dynamic growth. These costs will become more important, however, in the less forgiving environment of slow growth. Similarly, Japan cannot pretend to its domestic constituents that it has effective policies which aid them by raising prices through capacity retirement and, at the same time, pretend to its trading partners that it has no barriers. To the degree that domestic participants find their own capacity retirement unhelpful for raising their prices, they will, as they did in the case of aluminum, seek trade protection. On the other hand, to the degree that MITI continues to follow its practice of using guidance to inhibit imports, as it did in the case of textiles and urea, trade frictions will persist. The contradictions in MITI policy have thus far not been fully exposed because few of the troubled Japanese industries between 1978 and 1985 owed their problems to import competition. However, in the current phase of the strong yen these contradictions will be more apparent. To the degree that these policies entail restructuring through tie-ups and officially sanctioned permanent arrangements for production and distribution, they will further inhibit the ability of foreigners to enter the Japanese market.

What lessons should other countries draw from the Japanese experience? First, industrial policy is not just trade policy. If plans for restoring an industry to health are to be adopted, they cannot deal simply with trade problems. They have to deal with the industry as a whole. As such, the commitment to industrial restructuring would vastly increase the scope of government intervention in countries such as the United States or Canada. In particular, it would require a major shift in antitrust practices from trust busting to trust building.

Second, industrial structure matters. Even in Japan, programs that deal with large industries with low entry barriers are relatively ineffective in accelerating adjustment. Programs that are conditional on painful industry commitments inevitably have free-rider problems. Even in Japan, there have been numerous mavericks who have refused to comply with depressed industry programs. In other nations, in which bureaucrats have less credibility and clout, noncompliance would present a major problem. Either governments must be prepared to make new entry illegal or their programs will fail.

Third, even where the industry comes up with a self-initiated program of adjustment, there is no reason to believe that it will actually prove to be temporary. Once programs are created, there develop bureaucratic interests which seek to transform their mandate in order to perpetuate them. Thus, what began as a program in Japan mainly to retire capacity, has become a much broader based pretext for extensive intervention to promote industrial revitalization, with detailed government planning of mergers and distribution.

Fourth, when industry and government representatives get together, they will concoct a program which shifts the costs of adjustment onto the absent parties in the form of nontransparent costs.

Fifth, the Japanese approach works better in Japan than it would in either Canada or the United State. MITI officials have more credibility than their foreign counterparts, so that an official plan can aid management in forcing adjustment. In the United States or Canada, unpopular programs will have much less legitimacy. Japanese firms have extensive obligations to their workers which ensures that some of their increased profits will accrue to labor. In the United States and Canada, this is less likely to be the case.

5.4 Concluding Comments

The United States and Japan have diametrically opposed strategies for dealing with declining industries. In the United States, formal trade protection is the primary tool of industrial policy. Detailed programs for eliminating capacity and raising domestic prices through cartels are avoided, and trade is the only source of structural change that gives rise to government intervention. In Japan, formal trade protection is avoided, detailed programs for eliminating capacity and raising domestic profitability through cartels are the key instrument of policy, and industries are treated as depressed regardless of the source of their difficulties. Canadian policy entails a greater mixture of approaches, combining both formal trade protection and detailed government aid to depressed firms, regions, and sectors. Canadian policymakers find it more difficult than their American or Japanese counterparts to buffer themselves from pressures to provide financial support to declining industries.[30] Political pressures in Canada are harder to resist than in either the United States or Japan. As large economies, Japan and the United States may seek to aid particular victims of change, but they are rarely driven by the motive of having a broad and diversified industrial base. The Canadian dilemma is more typical of the difficulties for medium-sized economies of accepting economic specialization. Allowed to operate freely, economic forces would result in an economy even more strongly specialized than Canada is today. Nationalist pressures, however, seek a diversified manufacturing sector with firms which view their Canadian subsidiaries as more than simply a branch to service the Canadian market. These conflicts are compounded by geography, with the manufacturing industries concentrated primarily in Ontario and Quebec, while many of the resource-intensive sectors are in the West.

Canada's policies, therefore, reflect a broad adherence to market forces with a wide range of ad hoc approaches dealing with exceptions at the industry, regional, and firm level. Comprehensive industrial strategies are thwarted in a system with fragmented private sector interest groups, banks which mainly lend short term, and a decentralized federal system.[31] The one constant feature of Canadian programs is that they are continuously changing. The Department of Trade oscillates between the Ministries of Industry and Foreign Affairs. Control over textiles has gone through a bewildering number of agencies and programs.

In all three countries, the textiles industry has presented a major protectionist problem. None has been able to acknowledge as a policy goal the need to adjust, with reasonable speed, to global market forces. In addition to granting its sector tariff and quota protection, Canada has had an extensive set of programs aiming at textile modernization.

Canada supported the U.S. initiative to establish Long Term Arrangement for Cotton Textiles in 1962. In the 1960s it also relied on protection as the major aid for its industry. In 1970, however, the approach became more activist. According to Pestieau (1976, 14–15), "the import restraint measures were to be just part of the supportive package not the essence of the policy."[32] But she acknowledges that, despite this intention, there was a failure to stem the imposition of global import quotas for Canadian textiles under Article 19 of the GATT in 1976, and notes that "the clothing industry and the more fragmented parts of the textiles industry remain largely unaffected."

In 1981, dissatisfied with textile restructuring efforts, the Canadian government concluded that more generous incentives were required to permit smaller firms to design effective adjustment programs. It established the Industrial Renewal Board, which expanded the drive to modernize and restructure the textile, footwear, and tanning industries. The board's strategy was to select the most competitive firms on the basis of a a three- to five-year business plan and to support only those firms committed to restructuring—the test being an undertaking by firms to leave at least 75 percent of their after-tax profits in the company during a control period lasting three to five years.

Although Mahon and Mytelka (1983) argue that the federal government was able to implement the policy because it could promise the western resource-exporting provinces that protection would only be temporary, this promise has not been fulfilled. Appraisals of the program, however, suggest that little in the way of aggregate restructuring of the industry has taken place. According to Trebilcock (1986, 98), ". . . with respect to the adjustment problem faced [by the textile, clothing, and footwear sectors] little progress has been made during the past two decades. Indeed the problems of adjustment are now more acute than ever . . . As a result the government faces the invidious choice of attempting to maintain indefinitely high levels of trade protection or of facing an extremely rapid and socially disruptive contraction of these sectors if trade protection or equivalent subsidies are withdrawn."

In sum, while programs implemented in Japan and Canada for declining competitive sectors such as textiles and clothing may help individual firms and workers by providing them with resources, and may help governments in obtaining political support, it is not clear that they have succeeded in facilitating the type of adjustment which would ensure protection to be temporary.

Notes

1. For a more complete exposition, see, for example, Meier (1980, 93–101).
2. See Reich (1983, 3–19).
3. Shipbuilding, which has been heavily supported by defense spending in the United States, is conspicuously absent from the American list. Similarly, Canadian steel has been more healthy than its U.S. counterpart. See Lawrence (1985, 51–53)

for an empirical investigation of the amount of structural change across U.S. industries and regions.

4. Foreigners have frequently alleged that U.S. defense policies have represented a covert but powerful industrial policy. There may be some merit to this with respect to certain early products, such as the first semiconductors and jet aircraft. However, empirical investigations of the role of defense R&D in general industrial productivity growth suggest very little beneficial effect. Given the post-Vietnam reduction in defense spending in the early 1970s, the current competitiveness of U.S. electronics and computer industries owe very little to the defense efforts. In the 1990s this may change, given the renewed emphasis on defense R&D through the Defense Advanced Research Projects Agency (DARPA).

5. If the ITC makes a decision in favor of an industry, section 201 of the Trade Act of 1974 provides industries with a remedy, chosen by the president, which is best suited to "preventing serious injury or threat thereof to the industry . . . and to facilitate the orderly adjustment to new competitive conditions."

6. The president granted higher tariffs or quotas in thirteen cases, while recommending trade adjustment assistance for workers in six. See Baldwin (1984).

7. See also Congressional Budget Office (1986) for case studies of autos, textiles, steel, and footwear.

8. Of the sixteen industries examined, it was found that twelve had adjusted successfully, in the sense that upon the removal of protection, the industry could pay factors of production their opportunity cost without government assistance. In the remaining four, it was too early to tell.

9. Indeed, the weight that political decisionmakers place on preventing dislocation is indicated in the regulations under which the U.S. Commerce Department provides assistance for domestic industries.

10. The issue of whose interests industry protection is designed to protect (workers, capitalists, regions) is probably kept deliberately vague to permit maximum political use.

11. See Aho and Bayard (1980).

12. For more details, see Lawrence (1984, 131–32).

13. See Denzau (1983).

14. Uekusa and Ide (p. 16) also stress that they have been phased out when no longer necessary. As I will note below, Sekuguchi and Horiuchi voice misgivings that some features of the 1983 law could prevent foreign access to Japanese markets.

15. According to Ike (1980, 523) ". . . the actual pattern of government assistance to the [textile] industry during the postwar period can be described as nothing other than protective." Similar conclusions are reached by Ramseyer (1981).

16. The U.S. General Accounting Office (1982, 50) cites a study by Yonezawa which found that between 1968 and 1974, instead of achieving a target reduction of 2.62 million spindles, the number actually increased by 204,000. Similarly, while the government planned to dispose of 116,000 weaving machines for cotton, spun rayon, silk, and rayon, only 26,000 were scrapped.

17. For a more detailed description and analysis see Wheeler, Janow, and Pepper (1982).

18. See Peck, Levin, and Goto (1987) for a more detailed analysis. They also

mention the Smaller Business Switchover Act which helps small- and medium-sized firms to move to a different industry.

19. For a detailed analysis, see Shimada (1986).

20. For a discussion of the precarious financial situation of Japanese firms in declining industries, see Saxonhouse (1979).

21. For a revealing description of the negotiations to formulate policies over the objections of the labor unions and Socialists who wanted more emphasis on retaining employment, see Bower (1986, 197).

22. See Caves and Uekusa (1976).

23. Indeed, this is another example, borne out by the European experience, of the manner in which government commitments during periods of strong growth which are not particularly costly, may assume much heavier burdens when growth becomes less favorable. For a similar argument applied to European economies, see Lawrence (1985).

24. Yamamura (1982, 92) notes: "The 14 industries designated under the 1978 Act . . . were the industries allowed to form cartels repeatedly in the past. . . ."

25. Shipbuilding firms were given capacity-reduction quotas, but they retained discretion over which yards each would close. Thus, *within firm* reductions were probably efficient.

26. Peck, Levin, and Goto (1987) report similar findings.

27. On the other hand, they find more aid was spent on smaller firms (contractors) in depressed regions and on employment assistance.

28. See Balassa (1986).

29. This draws heavily on the account by Dore (1986).

30. In both the United States and Japan, governments have by and large avoided policies to aid specific firms. Chrysler and Sasebo are important exceptions. In Canada, government corporate bailouts have been much more common. For a description of Canadian bailouts, see Trebilcock (1986).

31. For a more extensive discussion, see Trebilcock (1986).

32. The Textile and Clothing Board conducts inquiries to determine injury and requires domestic producers to submit plans, offering proof of their intention to restructure. But, the goal of such restructuring is limited. Instead of accepting the need for the sector to eventually become viable in a free trade context, the board's programs were premised on the notion that the textile industry would not be allowed to disappear. Viability was therefore defined as "protected only by tariffs." The efficacy of the program in achieving its objectives is in some dispute. Mahon and Mytelka (1983) view its achievements as favorable in the case of some large textiles firms.

References

Aho, Michael C., and Thomas O. Bayard. 1980. American trade adjustment assistance after five years. *The World Economy* 3 (November): 359–76.

Anderson, Douglas D. 1986. Managing retreat: Disinvestment policy in the United States and Japan. Harvard Business School, Division of Research Working Paper 1-785-060, February.

Balassa, Bela. 1986. Japan's trade policies. Paper prepared for the Conference on Free Trade in the World Economy, Kiel, June 24–26.

Baldwin, Robert E. 1984. Rent-seeking and trade policy: An industry approach. *Weltwirtschaftliches Archiv* 4:662–77.

———. 1985. *The political economy of U.S. import policy.* Cambridge, Mass.: MIT Press, 103–14.

Bower, Joseph. 1986. *When markets quake: The management challenge of restructuring industry.* Boston: Harvard Business School Press.

Caves, Richard C., in collaboration with Masu Uekusa. 1976. Industrial organization. In *Asia's new giant: How the Japanese economy works,* eds. Hugh Patrick and Henry Rosovsky. Washington, D.C.: Brookings Institution.

Congressional Budget Office. 1986. Has trade protection revitalized domestic industries? Washington, D.C.: CBO, November.

de la Torre, Jose. 1978. *Corporate responses to import competition in the U.S. apparel industry.* Atlanta: Publishing Services Division, College of Business Administration, Georgia State University.

Denzau, Arthur T. 1983. Will an industrial policy work for the United States? St. Louis, Mo.: Washington University, Center for the Study of American Business, September.

Dore, Ronald. 1986. *Structural adjustment in Japan, 1970–82.* Geneva: International Labor Office.

Eads, George C. 1981. The political experience in allocating investment: Lessons for the United States and elsewhere. In *Toward a new industrial policy?*, eds. Michael L. Wachter and Susan M. Wachter. Philadelphia: University of Pennsylvania Press.

Hufbauer, Gary Clyde, Diane T. Berliner, and Kimberly Ann Elliot. 1986. *Trade protection in the United States: Thirty-one case studies.* Washington, D.C.: Institute for International Economics.

Ike, Brian. 1980. The Japanese textile industry: Structural adjustment and government policy. *Asian Survey* 20 (May):532–51.

Komiya, Ryutaro, and Motoshige Itoh. 1985. International trade and trade policy of Japan 1955–1984. Paper presented at a Japan Political Economy Research Conference, Tokyo, July 23–28.

Lawrence, Colin, and Robert Z. Lawrence. 1985. The dispersion in manufacturing wages: An end game interpretation. *Brookings Papers on Economic Activity* 1:47–116.

Lawrence, Robert Z. 1984. *Can America compete?* Washington, D.C.: Brookings Institution.

———. 1985. Industrial policy in the United States and Europe: Economic principles and political practices. *Brookings Discussion Papers in International Economics* 41 (November).

Lawrence, Robert Z., and Paula R. DeMasi. Forthcoming. Do industries with a self-identified loss of comparative advantage ever adjust? In *Dealing with decline: Trade policy for troubled industries,* eds. Gary C. Hufbauer and Howard F. Rosen. Washington, D.C.: Institute for International Economics.

Lawrence, Robert Z., and Robert E. Litan. 1986. *Saving free trade: A pragmatic approach.* Washington, D.C.: Brookings Institution.

Mahon, Rianne, and Lynn Krieger Mytelka. 1983. Industry, the state, and the new protectionism: Textiles in Canada and France. *International Organization* 37 (Autumn):551–71.

Meier, Gerald M. 1980. *International economics: The theory of policy.* New York: Oxford University Press.

Peck, Merton J., Richard C. Levin, and Akira Goto. 1987. Picking losers: Public policy toward declining industries in Japan. *Journal of Japanese Studies* 13 (Winter):79–123.

Pestieau, Caroline. 1976. *The Canadian textile policy: A sectoral trade adjustment strategy?* Montreal: C. D. Howe Research Institute.

Ramseyer, Mark J. 1981. Letting obsolete firms die: Trade adjustment assistance in the United States and Japan. *Harvard International Law Journal* Fall:595–619.

Rapp, William V. 1986. Japan's invisible barriers to trade. In *Fragile interdependence: Economic issues in U.S.-Japanese trade and investment,* eds. Thomas A. Pugel and Robert G. Hawkins. Lexington, Mass.: D. C. Heath and Co.

Reich, Robert. 1983. An industrial policy of the right. *The Public Interest* 73 (Fall):3–17.

Saxonhouse, Gary R. 1979. Industrial restructuring in Japan. *Journal of Japanese Studies* 6 (Summer):273–320.

Schultze, Charles L. 1983. Industrial policy: A dissent. *The Brookings Review* 2 (Fall): 3–12.

Sekiguchi, Sueo, and Toshihiro Horiuchi. 1985. Myth and reality of Japan's industrial policies. *The World Economy* 8 (December):373–91.

Shimada, Haruo. 1986. Employment adjustment and employment policies: The Japanese experience. Paper presented at conference on Domestic Adjustment and International Trade, Institute for International Economics, Washington, D.C., July.

Trebilcock, Michael. 1986. *The political economy of economic adjustment.* Toronto: University of Toronto Press.

Tresize, Philip H., and Yukio Suzuki. 1976. Politics, government and economic growth in Japan. In *Asia's new giant,* eds. Hugh Patrick and Henry Rosovsky. Washington, D.C.: Brookings Institution.

Uekusa, Masu, and Hideki Ide. 1986. Industrial policy in Japan. *Pacific Economic Papers* 135, Australia-Japan Research Centre, May.

United States General Accounting Office. 1982. *Industrial policy: Case studies in the Japanese experience.* Report to the Chairman, Joint Economic Committee, U.S. Congress, October 20.

Wheeler, Jimmy W., Merit E. Janow, and Thomas Pepper. 1982. *Japanese industrial development policies in the 1980s: Implications for U.S. trade and investment.* Croton-on-Hudson: Hudson Institute, October.

Williams, Douglas. 1987. Canadian adjustment policy: Beyond the Canadian industrial renewal board. Ottawa: The North-South Institute, January.

Yamamura, Kozo. 1982. Success that soured: Administrative guidance and cartels in Japan. In *Policy and trade issues of the Japanese economy,* ed. Seattle, Kozo Yamamura. WA: University of Washington Press.

Comment

Masahiro Okuno-Fujiwara

Lawrence's paper gives a comprehensive picture of the adjustment policies used for "depressed" industries in the United States, Japan, and Canada. He discusses the various policy measures, why they have been used in each country, and how successful or distorting each measure has been. He also ascertains whether certain measures, extensively used in one country, can be used "successfully" in other countries. In most parts, his analysis is extensive and well conceived, and his appraisal well balanced and fair. I agree with most of his points and appraisals. My discussion will, therefore, be mainly complementary to his paper.

His paper is very illuminating in that the policy measures taken by two of the countries are diametrically opposed. The United States has used trade-oriented and primarily protective measures, such as tariffs, quotas, orderly market arrangements (OMAs), and voluntary export restraints (VERs), while Japan has used supply-oriented collusive policies in order to facilitate contraction of troubled industries. There are many reasons why this has happened and most of them are listed in his paper. Especially important is the fact that the problems of most of the troubled industries in the United States were perceived to be trade related, while this was only the case for a few of the industries in Japan. However, there is another obvious reason which should be emphasized.

Japan is heavily dependent on, and benefits greatly from, trade and, especially in the last decade or so, it has become a strong proponent of the free trade system. Therefore, employing trade barriers even for declining industries would be inconsistent with its declared position. The government must avoid the use of any policy which looks outright protective. This political stance has become especially significant since the early or mid-1970s. Prior to this time, the ideology behind Japanese industrial policies had been basically interventionist. The goal was to protect domestic industries from imports and to promote export industries by means of legal, regulatory, and collusive measures. More recently, however, the declared main goal of the policies has shifted to complementing and facilitating the market mechanism as well as to assisting private incentives for growth and structural change. This shift is reflected in the fact that in the mid-1970s, Japan became one of the countries with the lowest (visible) tariff barriers in the world as noted, for example, in Komiya and Itoh (1988) or Komiya, Okuno, and Suzumura (1988, ch. 2–4). Thus, the difference between the United States and Japan in the choice of policy instruments to assist troubled industries should be, in large part, ascribed to the historical and political environment of this period.

I want to comment on Lawrence's view that Japanese policies have not been "open." To support this view, he cites several instances of alleged Japanese restrictions. The first is the VER on Korean cotton exports to Japan. But to my knowledge, this is the only VER arrangement for any foreign product to be imported into Japan. The other instances that he cites are mainly anecdotal and/or related to institutional arrangements in Japan. Contrary to his view, one could easily list some Japanese policies which have been open, at least compared to, say, U.S. policies. In order to evaluate whether or not Japanese adjustment policies have been "open," we must at the very least come up with a more precise definition and gather more conclusive evidence than Lawrence has done.

My second comment is concerned with Lawrence's analysis of the capacity-reduction cartel. Cartel arrangements have, as argued in his paper, many drawbacks, both economically as well as politically. In Japan, the evaluation of these cartels is, at best, mixed. Some argue that these arrangements simply delayed capacity reduction that would have occurred even if there had been no intervention. I, too, share serious doubts on whether such arrangements have been worthwhile. It is undeniable that they reduce economic welfare. But, in a final evaluation, we must compare these negative aspects with possible advantages of collusive arrangements. In this respect, I would like to make a few remarks on Lawrence's analysis.

When a cartel arrangement is considered, two forces work in opposite directions. Before a cartel is formed, there is an anticipated benefit for its participants, which creates an incentive to form and join the cartel. After the cartel is formed, however, there is always an incentive to deviate from the agreement. For example, if the price of a commodity is raised by a collusive reduction in the production level, any unilateral increase of production by an individual participant will bring in a larger profit. The cartel is formed and survives only when the incentive to join is larger than the potential gains of defection.

As the number of participants becomes larger, the benefits from a collusive cartel arrangement are reduced and rewards for cheating become relatively larger. This suggests that any cartelization policy is bound to fail if the industry consists of many small firms. In order to evaluate a cartelization policy, therefore, we should not look into cases such as the textile industry in Japan, which is very close to being perfectly competitive and where it is impossible for any cartel to work. Instead, we should consider industries with competition among a few large firms.

In such industries, strategic effects are important and these effects are surprisingly ignored by Lawrence. One strategic effect that may unnecessarily delay the scrapping of excess capacities is the "war of attrition," a phenomenon that may arise under incomplete information. Suppose that firms in the industry know their own costs and their own financial and/or demand conditions, but do not know the conditions of their competitors very well. In such a situation, they may postpone their exit because they hope that the situation in other firms is even worse, so that other firms might exit sooner than themselves. Then, in order to make sure that the conditions in other firms are not worse than their own, they would wait longer than they would have if they had known the true conditions of the industry. Arguments for capacity-reduction cartels in Japan, which are put forward by government officials as well as by cartel participants, seem to rely implicitly upon this theory. This argument is theoretically sound, but it does not necessarily justify policy intervention, especially in the form of capacity-reduction cartels.

From the policy viewpoint, there are at least two problems. First, would the government participation and cartel formation lead to better information sharing among the cartel participants and, hence, to early exit of the right firm? Second, even if early exit of the right firm occurs, would the resulting benefit exceed the potential cost of more collusive behavior in the production as well as in the pricing decisions of participants? In these respects, Lawrence's paper seems to be incomplete in fully assessing the welfare effects of the Japanese experience.

Before concluding my arguments on capacity-reduction cartels, I should also mention that Japanese law prohibits any member of the designated industry from expanding or building new capacity. Thus, though the law may have created some distortionary effects, at least it succeeded in containing the expansion or relocation of the industries that might have occurred otherwise. This experience seems to differ from that in the U.S. cited by Lawrence.

Let me now turn to the U.S. experience. There appears to be some confusion among four major policy options that have been adopted in the two countries. In the United States, temporary protective tariffs sanctioned by the ITC represent one instrument or means of policy, while OMA and VER arrangements won through political routes are another. In contrast, Japan's cartelization policy can be viewed as a way of assisting labor relocation and/or supporting depressed regions. By focusing on ITC policies in the United States and on cartelization policies in Japan, it is not clear whether the ITC rulings in the U.S. and the careful labor/regional relocation policies in Japan can be judged commensurably. That is, when an industry is in trouble, it may need assistance, albeit according to a clear set of rules and on the condition that the relief is temporary. The ITC route was successful because most of the recent troubles of U.S. industries may have been rooted in international trade. Furthermore, the ITC rules are explicit and clear and its protection is temporary. But even with a reasonably good system like the ITC, workers may have to be laid off. Thus to complement such a system, we need a carefully designed and multifaceted labor/regional policy. The Japanese experience thus seems to provide a more comprehensive framework in which the broader objectives of policies can be pursued.

While Lawrence forcefully argues that the Japanese cartelization policy does not appear to be a clear success and perhaps can be judged a failure, much of his argument can be applied as well to the use of OMAs, VERS, and similar trade interventions. In one sense, these latter arrangements may be worse than capacity-reduction cartels since they may create and support tacit collusion among producers in different countries. Consumers in the importing country are sure to lose because of the higher domestic prices, and the level of world efficiency is likely to be reduced as well. Moreover, these arrangements are political and hence discretionary, decided upon behind closed doors. Few rational arguments enter into the process of decision making. Furthermore, once these types of arrangements become prevalent, they lead to more rent-seeking activities, thus causing possibly even greater distortions. The Japanese have yielded to trade intervention in many industries, starting with textiles in the 1960s. In the VER arrangement for the automobile industry, nobody around the bargaining table was to lose from the arrangement: both American and Japanese automobile manufacturers and workers benefited in the form of higher prices, higher profits, and higher wages. Even governments might be seen as benefiting as well, especially the Japanese government, which obtained more leverage power in the Japanese automobile industry. However, once it was known that such arrangements were possible and could be achieved through political routes, many U.S. industries, with or without good reason, would be motivated to seek their own rents. This tendency is, in my view, the worst consequence of the recent experience with helping depressed or troubled industries.

There may be reason to believe that free trade is not necessarily optimal, as the "new trade theory" has made clear. Technology in many industries exhibits scale economies, externalities are an important factor in many new high-technology industries, and strategic protection of a home industry may shift rents from foreign competitors to domestic firms if the industry is oligopolistic. All of these and other factors indicate that there are market failures even in international trade. Thus, some types of protection, for example market arrangements or voluntary restraints, may be better than free trade, either in terms of domestic or world welfare.

However, just as Lawrence forcefully argued in the case of ITC policies, such nonmarket arrangements should be temporary and subject to a clear set of rules to succeed both economically and politically. In this respect, it seems very alarming to me that the agreements are negotiated bilaterally, without any input from other interested parties such as the NICs. In addition, the outcome of the negotiations depends heavily upon political power rather than economic arguments. It seems clear, therefore, that we should design some set of rules, preferably in the form of an international arrangement, by which all these negotiations must be carried out.

What can we do then? I think there are two possibilities. If one believes in the benefits of free trade and international specialization, GATT should be the answer. Any arrangements that have already been made should be reviewed by GATT and all future arrangements should be implemented if and only if they are allowed by GATT.

Even for those who do not believe in the benefits of free trade, but instead adhere to the new trade theory or believe that some countries are engaging in "unfair" trade practices, it should be realized that the creation of more OMAs and VERs does not solve the problem. It would only subject an increasing proportion of world trade to a system of arbitrary rent-seeking activities and would, therefore, reduce the level of world welfare. We need some established system, preferably an international institution such as the GATT, with enough enforcement power to settle international disputes objectively under a clear set of rules.

References

Komiya, R., and M. Itoh. 1988. International trade and trade policy of Japan: 1955–84. In *The political economy of Japan*. Vol. 2, *The changing international context*, eds. T. Inoguchi and D. I. Okimoto. Stanford, Calif.: Stanford University Press.

Komiya, R., M. Okuno, and K. Suzumura. 1988. *Industrial policy of Japan*. New York: Academic Press.

Comment

Michael J. Trebilcock

I am both less depressed at one level and more depressed at another than Lawrence with respect to adjustment processes in depressed industries in the three countries under review.

I am less depressed in that, as the figures in his tables 5.1 and 5.2 show, and as confirmed in his more extensive empirical findings in Lawrence (1984) for the United States, a substantial amount of adjustment has taken place in depressed industries in these countries irrespective of and usually despite the government's adjustment policies. The story of agriculture in both the United States and Canada further exemplifies how resistant market forces are to adjustment-retarding policies. About one-third of the labor force in Canada just prior to World War II was employed in agriculture, compared to 3 or 4 percent today, despite almost every conceivable effort by government to deflect efficient adjustment processes in this sector.

While the generalization that significant adjustment has occurred in all three countries in their depressed sectors seems warranted, I am concerned that the tone of Lawrence's paper suggests that there are few differences in the rates of adjustment in depressed sectors in the individual countries. I am skeptical that this is in fact so. Even the numbers in Lawrence's table 5.2 suggest that Japan began to adjust earlier in its depressed sectors than the United States and Canada. Indeed, many of the so-called adjustment effects showing up in the 1980–85 period in Canada and the United States may be little more than the cyclical effects of the recession, rather than the product of underlying major structural changes. In addition to looking merely at intersectoral shifts in resources as evidence of efficient adjustment, it would also seem important to examine productivity trends *within* depressed sectors on a comparative basis. In other words, one should focus on both *intersectoral* and *intrasectoral* adjustment processes. Put more colloquially, it is possible to adjust by shaping up as well as shipping out. In research in which I am currently engaged, preliminary data on productivity trends since 1955 in coal mining, steel, automobiles, shipbuilding, textiles, footwear, leather products, and wearing apparel, suggest that Japan has fairly consistently outperformed both the United States and Canada in productivity improvements in most of these sectors over this period.

While Lawrence may well be right that the Japanese Structurally Depressed Industries Law has perhaps done little more than ratify the operation of market forces in some sectors, it bears noting that 44,000 jobs were eliminated in shipbuilding between 1977 and 1979, that capacity in the aluminum industry was cut by over 50 percent between 1978 and 1981, and that for ten of the designated industries for which Peck, Levin, and Goto (1987) were able to obtain data (excluding shipbuilding), 15.3 percent of the workforce (48,000 workers) left these industries between 1977 and 1983. In the case of coal mining, while not directly affected by the Structurally Depressed Industries Law, employment fell, with government support and encouragement, from 294,000 in 1958 to 40,000 in 1971 (Trebilcock 1986, 41). Even if the Structurally Depressed Industries Law and similar industry rationalization plans are largely smoke and mirrors, as Lawrence implies, the fact of the matter is that the scale and rapidity of the adjustments (especially the shedding of labor) in industries such as the Japanese shipbuilding and coal mining industries would not be remotely conceivable in a Canadian political context. Indeed we can point to *no* examples of any transformations remotely as dramatic in any sector (other than agriculture). My own work on Canadian adjustment experience in depressed sectors shows almost no significant structural change in sectors such as textiles, clothing, shipbuilding, and coal mining over three decades.

My table C5.1, as noted in Trebilcock (1986, 77) shows trends in the Canadian textile, knitting, clothing, and leather goods industries in Canada

Table C5.1   Trends in Canada's Textile, Clothing, and Leather Goods Industries

Industries	1955	1965	1975	1980	1982
Textiles					
Number of employees	69,144	76,676	71,050	68,241	59,416
Value of shipments ($000)	734,515	1,276,657	2,439,005	4,423,248	4,507,573
Number of establishments	977	960	923	948	989
Knitting mills					
Number of employees	21,658	24,070	24,682	21,220	18,318
Value of shipments ($000)	155,187	308,890	624,490	944,704	947,795
Number of establishments	296	361	306	281	255
Clothing					
Number of employees	89,686	98,659	100,528	96,120	91,306
Value of shipments ($000)	684,362	1,063,401	2,306,619	3,867,140	3,962,352
Number of establishments	2,648	2,315	2,094	2,143	2,107
Leather products					
Number of employees	30,575	32,585	26,834	24,922	22,957
Value of shipments ($000)	218,043	343,055	619,191	1,083,793	1,105,960
Number of establishments	646	544	415	431	419

Source: Statistics Canada, *Industrial Organization and Concentration in the Manufacturing, Mining, and Logging Industries, 1980* (Ottawa: Minister of Supply and Services Canada, 1983), 9.

Table C5.2   Trends in Canada's Shipbuilding Industry

Shipbuilding & Repair	1955	1965	1975	1980	1982
Number of employees	16,829	18,586	16,344	17,185	16,128
Value of shipments ($000)	133,837	274,601	571,668	1,142,224	1,112,533
Number of establishments	70	71	58	69	69

Sources: Dominion Bureau of Statistics, *The Manufacturing Industries of Canada, 1955,* Section A (Ottawa: Queen's Printer, 1957), 20–21. Dominion Bureau of Statistics, *Manufacturing Industries of Canada, 1965,* Section A (Ottawa: Queen's Printer, 1968), 30–31. Statistics Canada, *Manufacturing Industries of Canada, 1980* (Ottawa: Minister of Supply and Services Canada, 1982), 8–9. Statistics Canada, *Manufacturing Industries of Canada, 1982* (Ottawa: Minister of Supply and Services Canada, 1984), 8–9.

over the past three decades. Only the leather products sector (the least protected) shows evidence of substantial downsize adjustment. Table C5.2 (Trebilcock 1986, 99) shows trends in Canada's shipbuilding industry over the past three decades.

As noted in Trebilcock (1986, 115–28), in the case of the East Coast (Cape Breton) coal mining industry, despite a government takeover of the industry in 1967—predicated on an orderly contraction of the industry over time and diversification of the local economy—and despite ongoing government subsidies since that time that now amount to about one billion dollars, output and employment in the industry are almost as high today as they were twenty years ago, and the economy of the region is still largely dependent on the industry.

What is most intriguing to me about the Japanese adjustment experience is not so much the economics of the policies employed (which may well be debatable), but the politics that allowed these market-driven adjustments to go forward. The politics need as much scholarly attention as the economics.

I am more depressed than Lawrence about our collective ability, at least in Canada, to fashion more effective adjustment-promoting policies in the future. In Lawrence and Litan (1986), it is proposed to re-tariff quotas, VERs, and OMAs that protect depressed industries, impose temporary and digressive five-year tariff protection under a reformed safeguard clause (Article 19) of the GATT, and use the tariff revenues to underwrite exit costs faced by labor through extended unemployment benefits, income insurance against lower earnings in alternative employment, and loans to finance retraining.

In evaluating such proposals, we must be careful to identify the currency of debate. It is not economic—"Economic Darwinism" is the most effective recipe for promoting the rapid adjustment of capital and labor. In the second-best (pragmatic) economic world in which Lawrence and Litan are dealing, the currency at issue is purely political, and the question posed is: will the proposed policies sufficiently assuage both capital and labor and other dependent interests that political demands for continuing protection can be met by policies that are less economically damaging than protectionism? I entertain a measure of skepticism. First, temporary protection (particularly tariff protection, given fluctuating exchange rates) and for that matter time-limited labor adjustment benefits are much less attractive to both capital and labor than semipermanent arrangements like the MFA or VERs that guarantee market share. Substantial capital losses will be entailed when the temporary protection expires. Substantial wage losses may be sustained by labor once extended unemployment insurance benefits and income insurance expire. And loans for institutional retraining seem unlikely to ameliorate the potential employment losses for large segments of displaced labor (e.g., older workers). Moreover, many of the *private* costs of adjustment faced by labor (which economists mostly tend to ignore) are not sufficiently taken account of in Lawrence and Litan's proposals. Programs designed to render displaced workers, their families, and affected communities *entirely indifferent* to the social and private costs of adjustment are likely to be extremely expensive. And investors are likely to view five-year digressive tariffs as a very poor substitute for the kinds of protection they presently enjoy in many depressed sectors. Is there any real reason for optimism that proposals of the kind advanced by Lawrence and Litan will buy off political resistance to trade liberalization from affected capital and labor in highly import-sensitive sectors?

My political judgment, for what it is worth, is that in order to effectively buy off political demands for trade protection in highly import-sensitive sectors, we may have to contemplate substantially longer phase-out periods for trade protection, generous compensation payments to labor for the *private* costs of trade-induced adjustment (such as loss of resale value on homes in dependent communities), and subsidies to firms to scrap physical capacity as envisaged in many of the Japanese rationalization plans. We may also have to play hardball with our major trading partners in demanding deep cuts in tariffs, NTBs, and so-called "invisible" trade barriers, including those applicable to the agricultural and service sectors, in return for more disciplined safeguard procedures so that our export-oriented industries can be enlisted as major, domestic political allies for a policy of liberalizing trade policy for our depressed sectors. Treating the negotiation of a new safeguards code as an independent bargaining exercise (as was the abortive strategy in the Tokyo Round) is unlikely to yield these concessions. The proposal to substitute tariff protection for quantitative restrictions is creative in that it eliminates the scarcity rents that foreign firms now often capture from the latter and would generate a new revenue source out of which to finance adjustment programs.[1] However, apart from probably needing to be of much longer duration in some sectors than Lawrence and Litan envisage, tariffs would also need to be adjustable to reflect exchange rate movements. It is also far from clear that either ethically or politically it is likely to prove defensible, as Lawrence and Litan argue, to confine the benefits of the proposed labor-adjustment programs to workers in trade-impacted sectors, when similar job-displacement effects frequently occur in other sectors as a result of changes in productivity, technology, and demand. Indeed, in general, the latter factors dominate trade effects as sources of labor displacement.[2]

Whether my political judgment call is superior to Lawrence and Litan's or not, in dealing in this political currency we have to pose the painful question to ourselves, as academic economists (and lawyers): are we likely to have called the political margins more shrewdly than the political entrepreneurs whose survival depends on maximizing economic and political benefits net of economic and political costs?

This is not to suggest that there is no room for better ideas in the policymaking process, nor to endorse the paralyzing Chicago theorem that the policies we presently have are probably the best we can hope for because if better policies were attainable, they would already have been identified and adopted by political entrepreneurs (a theorem that apparently does not apply to product and service markets). However, it is to suggest that, whatever the difficulties of identifying when political constraints become binding, we bring the same rigor and realism to bear in our analysis of the politically feasible policy set as we do in our analysis of the welfare effects of alternative economic policies.

Notes

1. This proposal was made earlier by, inter alia, Hufbauer and Schott (1985).
2. See, e.g., Krueger (1978).

References

Hufbauer, Gary Clyde, and Jeffrey J. Schott. 1985. *Trading for growth*. Washington, D.C.: Institute for International Economics.

Krueger, Anne. 1978. Impact of L.D.C. Exports on Employment in American Industry. Paper presented at the International Economic Study Group's Annual Conference, White House, Sussex, England, September.

Lawrence, Robert Z. 1984. *Can America compete?* Washington, D.C.: Brookings Institution.

Lawrence, Robert Z., and Robert E. Litan. 1986. *Saving free trade: A pragmatic approach*. Washington, D.C.: Brookings Institution.

Peck, Merton J., Richard C. Levin, and Akira Goto. 1987. Picking losers: Public policy toward declining industries in Japan. *Journal of Japanese Studies* 13 (Winter):79–123.

Trebilcock, Michael J. 1986. *The political economy of economic adjustment*. Toronto: University of Toronto Press.

6 Taxes in Canada, Japan, and the United States: Influences on Trade and Investment Flows, and the Role of Tax-Based Trade Irritants

John Whalley

6.1 Introduction

The fall of 1986 saw a spectacular turnaround in the tax reform process in the U.S. Congress. In a period of three months, deadlock, inactivity, and resigned acceptance of the status quo were transformed into frenzied discussion and action resulting in some of the most wide-ranging tax changes in U.S. history. Simultaneously, but with less public fanfare, tax reform efforts have also been taking shape in Japan and Canada. A government tax reform commission reporting in late 1986 has recommended major changes in the Japanese tax system, and in Canada ongoing consideration of sales and corporate tax changes has been elevated into a major reform exercise, the results of which were unveiled in June 1987. What all of this may mean for Canada-Japan-U.S. goods and investment flows is the focus of this paper.

Taxes play a curious role in discussions of trade policy. They are little discussed by trade policy practitioners, except where tax policies come into conflict with established international trading rules through so-called "tax-based trade irritants." Simultaneously, the current view in the United States, at least, seems to be that fiscal policies are crucial to an understanding of the size and scope of the current U.S.-Japan and U.S.-Canadian trade imbalances. How the influence of taxes on trade may be affected by these tax reforms, and what old and new tax-based trade irritants may surface as a result are discussed in what follows.

6.2 Trade and Investment Flows and Tax Structure in Canada, the United States, and Japan

Canada, the United States, and Japan have significantly different trade patterns and tax systems. Canada, being the smallest of the three, has the largest ratio of trade to GNP. The United States has the smallest ratio of trade to GNP and the largest trade deficit. Japan has the largest trade surplus, but despite

220

the perception in North America that Japan is a large trading nation, the ratio of trade to GNP in Japan has been approximately constant over the postwar period, with only a moderate increase between 1970 and 1975.

Although many people believe that trade and factor flows are influenced by intercountry differences in the structure of taxes, there is surprisingly little theoretical or empirical work that analyzes the role of taxes. Melvin (1970) shows how taxes can cause trade flows, where in the absence of taxes trade does not occur, and Whalley (1985) includes domestic taxes in his global general equilibrium trade model, allowing for some of the influences of taxes to be assessed. Nowhere, to the present author's knowledge, however, is there a piece that clearly lays out how taxes influence trade in such major trading areas as the United States, Japan, Canada, or the European Economic Community.

Table 6.1 shows some of the main features of trade flows among Canada, Japan, and the U.S. using the latest GATT (General Agreement on Tariffs and Trade) data available for 1984. Both Canada and Japan have large trade surpluses with the United States, which, in turn, are the source of major current trade frictions. Canada is the largest trading partner for the United States; but for Canada, the United States is the dominant trading partner, accounting for around 75 percent of both imports and exports. Japan, on the other hand, has a larger fraction of trade with both Europe and the Asian countries. In terms of the commodity composition of trade, Japan is a major exporter of appliances, autos, and electronics products, while the United States is a substantial exporter of agricultural products and machinery. Canada is a major exporter of forest and mineral products.

Table 6.2 presents information on taxes by country. The first row provides data on the level of taxes. It is evident in the second row that Canada has a larger ratio of taxes to GDP than either the United States or Japan. There are much smaller defense expenditures in both Canada and Japan, but, especially in Canada, much larger social welfare programs than in the U.S. The fraction of GDP collected in taxes in Japan has grown rapidly in recent years, especially under the social security tax, and is now comparable to that in the United States, having been significantly lower for many years. Because deficits today imply taxes in the future, table 6.2 also presents data on current deficits as a fraction of GDP. The largest ratio is in Canada, with the U.S. deficit also large.

Table 6.2 also presents data showing the relative importance of different taxes in each country. In all three countries, personal income taxes (progressive taxes on annual income of households or individuals) include a number of exemptions and deviations from a broadly-based tax. These include non-taxation of imputed income from housing, special arrangements for capital gains, and other specially treated components of income. Corporate taxes

Table 6.1   Trade Flows between Japan, the United States, and Canada, 1984

	Imports* by			
Exports by	Japan	U.S.	Canada	Others
Japan	—	60.37	4.41	105.17
U.S.	26.97	—	52.34	143.39
Canada	4.83	65.34	—	16.78
Others	91.11	212.48	16.48	—

	Surplus(+)/Deficit(−)* of			
Surplus/Deficit with	Japan	U.S.	Canada	Others
Japan	—	—	—	
U.S.	+ 33.61	—	—	
Canada	− 0.53	− 21.61	—	
Others	+ 2.70	− 69.09	+ 0.30	—

	Major Exports by		
Major Exports to	Japan	U.S.	Canada
Japan	—	1) food; 2) chemicals; 3) other machinery and transport equipment	1) food; 2) raw materials; 3) fuels
U.S.	1) household appliances; 2) transport vehicles; 3) office and telecommunications equipment	—	1) fuels; 2) other semimanufactures; 3) transport vehicles
Canada	1) household appliances; 2) transport vehicles; 3) office and telecommunications equipment	1) machinery for specialized industries; 2)transport vehicles; 3) other machinery and transport equipment	—

*In billion US $
Source: GATT, International Trade 1984/85 (Geneva: GATT, 1985).

(taxes on the return on equity to corporations which allow deductibility of interest) also differ among the three countries, especially as far as the degree of integration with personal taxes is concerned.

Sales and excise taxes include both broadly-based consumption taxes, such as retail sales or value-added taxes, and more restricted wholesale level taxes collected earlier in the production process, such as the manufacturers sales tax in Canada and the multirate commodity tax in Japan. Excise taxes are concentrated on "traditional" excisables (gasoline, tobacco, liquor) in all three countries. Property taxes in all three countries are used to fund locally

Table 6.2   Size and Relative Importance of Taxes by Country

	Japan	U.S.	Canada
1984 Taxes collected ($US billion)	347.9	1030.9	115.3
1984 Tax/GDP ratio	27.38	28.99	33.72
1984 Central government finance deficit or surplus ($ billion in national currency & % of GDP)	n.r.[1] 1.7	178.26 4.78	29.60 6.79
Taxes collected (% of total)			
Personal income taxes	24.46	35.26	33.90
Corporate taxes	21.12	7.14	8.80
Sales and excise taxes	12.97	15.81	26.48
Property taxes	9.41	10.27	9.75
Social Security taxes	29.66	29.10	12.77
Miscellaneous, including resource taxes	2.38	2.41	7.62
Collector of taxes (% collected)			
National government	74.05	68.89	54.52
Subnational government	25.95	31.11	45.48

[1]Not reported in IMF Statistics.
Sources: OECD, *Revenue Statistics of OECD Member Countries 1965–1985* (OECD, 1986). IMF, *Government Finance Statistics Yearbook* (IMF, 1985). IMF, *International Financial Statistics Yearbook* (IMF, 1986).

provided public services. Social security taxes also operate in all three countries as employer and employee payroll contributions which finance old age security and unemployment insurance programs.

The relative importance of these taxes across countries differs substantially. In Canada, indirect taxes are more important than in either the United States or Japan, and payroll taxes are less important. In Japan, there is much heavier emphasis on corporate taxes. Generally speaking, the tax structure in all these countries tends to favor activities involving nontraded goods and services over traded goods and services and hence, on average, restricts trade. Differences in tax structure also have important trade implications, especially where the relative costs of different activities depend on taxes.

Table 6.2 also reports the relative importance of national to subnational taxes in each country. The federal-provincial structure in Canada is such that a larger fraction of public expenditures occurs at the lower level, while the federal (national) government collects the majority of taxes. Subnational governments (provinces) thus receive large intergovernmental transfers. In the United States, intergovernmental transfers are smaller as are expenditures by state governments. Among the three countries, the national government is the most important on both the expenditure and the tax side in Japan.

Table 6.3 summarizes some of the main features of taxes in the three countries. In the case of personal taxes, both brackets and rates are scheduled

Table 6.3   Major Features of Pre-Reform Tax Structures by Country

	Japan[1]	U.S.[2]	Canada[3]
Personal income taxes			
Number of tax brackets	15	14	10
Top marginal rate (and income level)	70% (over $336,000)	50% ($84,510 for married individuals filing separate returns)	Ontario: 56% (over $47,863)
Corporate taxes			
Tax rate	Retained profits, 43.3%/distributed profits, 33.3%	46%	46%
Degree of integration	Dividend tax credit	None	Dividend tax credit
Acceleration of depreciation	Significant	Significant	Significant
Other features	Investment tax credit	Investment tax credit	Investment tax credit
Sales and excise taxes			
National taxes: sales	Commodity tax	None	Manufacturers' sales
Tax rate	1. class 1 commodities (including jewelry & precious metal products) 10–15% 2. class 2 commodities (including TV sets, autos, cameras) 5–30%		1. alcohol, tobacco & wine, 15% 2. certain construction materials, 8% 3. all other goods, 12%
Degree of coverage	Retail sales of class 1 commodities & manufacturers' sales of class 2, suspension of tax for shipment to other manufacturers or for export		Goods manufactured or produced in Canada. Exemptions for clothing, footwear, & foodstuffs

[1]Based on information provided by Yuichiro Nagatoni, Institute of Fiscal and Monetary Policy, Ministry of Finance, Japan.
[2]See Deloitte, Haskins, and Sells (1986).
[3]See Canadian Tax Foundation (1986) and Drache (1986).

to change substantially in the United States and Japan as a result of both recent and announced tax reforms.[1] Pre-reform marginal rates on labor income in Japan are higher than in Canada and the United States, but capital income is lightly taxed. Exemptions are much the same across the countries, covering imputed income on housing and private pension contributions. Capital gains represent a more complex situation. As a result of the recent changes, the United States is moving to tax such gains fully, but at the lowered marginal rates introduced. In contrast, Canada introduced a C$500,000 lifetime exemption on capital gains in the 1984 budget.[2]

The biggest differences at the personal level among these countries occur in the way capital income is taxed. In Japan, there is currently little taxation of capital income under the personal income tax, although this is scheduled to change as result of the reforms announced recently. In Canada, ignoring rate differences, there is more generous treatment compared to the United States, but not as generous as in Japan. Importantly, these differences are one of several factors explaining why savings rates are so much higher in both Japan and Canada than in the United States.

At the corporate level, tax rates in the three countries are similar, but the degree of integration differs. Pre-reform, there is little difference in the degree of acceleration in depreciation allowances across the countries, but this will change as the reforms are implemented. Among the features of corporate taxes that differ are dividend tax credits across countries.[3]

It is, however, in the sales and excise tax area that the largest tax differences between countries occur. In the United States, there is no national sales tax. In Canada, there is a manufacturers sales tax, which may well be replaced by a broadly based (either credit or subtraction) value-added tax as a result of tax changes that the government has proposed. This, in large part, reflects the many problems of the existing tax, such as the bias in favor of imports, unequal treatment across similar firms within industries leading to widespread use of administered values in tax assessment, and cascading of the tax. Finally, there is the Japanese commodity tax, effectively a multirate sales tax on a limited portion of consumption. A government proposal made in December 1986 was to replace this by a credit invoice VAT, with food, housing, and financial services exempt, but in June 1987 the government announced that the VAT would not be introduced.

At the subnational level, there are a large number of states in the U.S. with a sales tax, which in some cases combines with statewide or even citywide income taxes. In Canada the situation is somewhat different, with provincial surcharges on personal and corporate taxes, combined with provincial retail sales taxes. In Japan, there are prefecture-level taxes which apply to income, sales, and profits.

6.3 Trade and Factor Flows and the Role of Taxes

A number of issues arise in assessing the importance of tax differences for the pattern of trade and factor flows between countries. One is whether differences in the tax levels between countries affect trade. Another is how differences in tax structure come into play. It is often argued in the popular press that lower taxes abroad imply low costs, giving foreigners a competitive edge in world markets. If this is true, differences in tax structures can be important in determining trade patterns and need to be factored into a discussion of taxes and trade.

In analyzing this issue, the central proposition from existing academic literature is that, provided one is talking about balanced-budget situations and broadly based taxes, low taxes in and of themselves have no direct implications for trade flows.[4] In the simple case where all commodities are taxed at a uniform rate, if one economy has lower tax rates than another (providing the taxes which both economies use are of the broadly based type), there are no impacts on trade flows.

This can be seen using a simple, two-country example. Suppose country A exports good 1 and imports good 2, and country B vice versa. Suppose also that country A initially has a commodity tax on both goods at rate tA and country B has a tax at rate tB. If producer prices in each country are $P1$ and $P2$, the international terms of trade are $P1/P2$. Relative consumer prices in country A are

$$P1(1 + tA)/P2(1 + tA) = P1/P2, \tag{1}$$

while relative consumer prices in country B are

$$P1(1 + tB)/P2(1 + tB) = P1/P2. \tag{2}$$

If tax revenues are redistributed in lump sum form to consumers in each country, and if income distribution effects do not change demands (for instance, if consumers have identical homothetic preferences in each country), then changes in tax rates in either country will leave relative consumer prices and the international terms of trade unchanged. Trade flows will thus be invariant to the level of taxes in either country. Under these assumptions, differences in levels of taxes in and of themselves will not have any effect on trade between countries.

There are, however, a number of obvious departures from these simple assumptions which apply in each of the three countries under discussion, and these introduce a potentially significant role for taxes in determining trade flow. Government expenditures are labor intensive, and economies in which high taxes finance large nontransfer public sector expenditures will have smaller trade shares. Generally speaking, the taxes at issue in all three countries apply more heavily to traded goods (or activities producing traded goods) than to nontraded goods. As a result, the higher the tax rate, the heavier the substitution effect against the traded goods sector. Thus, taxes tend to be less trade restrictive in countries where taxes are lower.

Also, taxes distort labor supply and saving decisions, and heavier taxes more severely so. Since leisure is a nontraded commodity, higher taxes are also more antitrade biased than lower taxes on this score. Taxes can also influence capital inflows or outflows through their effects on savings and investment, and result in current account deficits or surpluses. These, in turn, have mirror-image effects on trade volumes, an issue discussed by Summers (1986) and also taken up more fully below.

In addition to differences in the level of taxes across countries, differences in tax structure can also influence the size and composition of trade and factor flows between countries. These differences in structure operate in an number of ways. Two which have been discussed in the literature are differences in the tax treatment of savings and differences in border-tax adjustments.

In Japan, it is widely agreed that the tax system stimulates saving and, partly due to this, there is a high saving rate in Japan.[5] In the United States, tax effects, if anything, tend to operate in the other direction, certainly as far as saving incentives are concerned at the personal level. Since capital is internationally mobile, there are large differences between savings and investment across economies, with Japan being a significant capital exporter and the United States a large capital importer. Along with these capital flows, which are in part tax induced, a large current account trade deficit in the United States and trade surplus in Japan (and Canada) occur. If taxes stimulate investment through investment incentives and penalize saving, the effect is therefore a capital inflow and a corresponding trade deficit.

The current trade imbalance with Canada and Japan is, of course, the major focus of the U.S. trade policy debate at the present time, and the growth in trade protectionist sentiment in the U.S. Congress in recent years is in part a reflection of this. The differential tax treatment of savings between countries contributes to the trade imbalances through its effects on savings and investment, and hence capital flows across countries. Taxes are, therefore, integral to current debates on trade policy.

Differences in tax treatment of savings, however, are not the only tax feature to influence trade flows. Large public sector deficits in the United States tend to absorb whatever savings are generated, further amplifying the situation involving capital inflows. Other features operate through investment incentives. The introduction of the accelerated cost recovery system (ACRS) in 1981 in the United States clearly stimulated investment, but had smaller (or no) direct effects on savings given the international mobility of capital. As a result, further large increases in inward capital flows occurred, again having a direct impact on the size of the U.S. trade deficit.

Another influence of the tax structure on trade and factor flows is the system of foreign tax credits used by all three countries.[6] Under a foreign tax credit system, if foreign taxes are fully creditable it is equally attractive for investors to invest at home or abroad, independent of the foreign tax rate. It has long been argued by Musgrave (1969) and others that in terms of national interest, source countries would be best served by allowing neither credit nor deduction for foreign taxes, since the social rates of return on investments at home and abroad would then be equalized. This tax feature affects capital flows by neither penalizing investment abroad, nor encouraging repatriation of foreign earnings, and hence affects goods trade imbalances.

A further set of tax-structure-trade issues concerns indirect taxes and their influence on trade. This set of questions attracted a lot of attention in the late 1960s and early 1970s, and is still an area of major potential trade conflict between Japan, the United States, and Canada because of the sharp differences in indirect tax structures among the three countries. The United States currently has no broadly based national indirect tax, whereas Canada and Japan both do. Both are administered on a destination basis, which involves taxes being collected on imports, with any taxes charged on production for export rebated at the border.

For many years, there has been a widespread perception in the United States that this provides an unfair trade advantage to foreign producers. The way the argument is usually put is that for U.S. producers exporting to either Japanese or Canadian markets, a tax barrier must be crossed, since commodities are taxed as they enter these markets, whereas commodities which leave these markets do so on a tax-free basis. In addition, heavier direct taxes become part of production costs and thus impede trade. In the late 1960s and early 1970s, this resulted in the United States arguing for the inclusion of the border-tax adjustment issue in GATT trade negotiations, with pressure on trading partners of the United States to administer their taxes on an origin basis. This would involve taxing at point of production so that imports would enter tax free and exports would leave on a tax-paid basis, in contrast to the arrangements under the existing destination basis. This issue has been less prominent in recent trade policy debates compared to former years, but remains a central question. It has also arisen in unfair trade practice cases in the United States, involving petitions for countervailing duties.

When faced with the border tax issue in the late 1960s, most academic economists argued that the level of indirect taxes is not important for trade flows. They argued this on the basis of so-called neutrality propositions which show that for any broadly based tax, a move between an origin and destination basis is neutral in terms of its impacts on the trade flows. Put simply, the argument is as follows.[7] A broadly based tax on an origin basis taxes all production. A broadly based tax on a destination basis taxes all consumption. In either case, there is no distortion of real economic activity, since under a flexible exchange rate regime a move from an origin to a destination basis will simply result in a change in exchange rates. Domestic relative consumer and producer prices remain unchanged. Alternatively, under a fixed exchange rate regime there would be a change in the domestic price level, which, in turn, would imply accommodating changes in domestic monetary policy for the outcome to be compatible with fixed exchange rates. Either way, no real impacts on trade flows result.

However, indirect taxes in Canada and Japan are not of the broadly based variety, and their influence on trade flows requires more discussion. Their possible significance has, for instance, been investigated in a recent paper by Hamilton and Whalley (1986). In this paper, Hamilton and Whalley use a numerical general equilibrium model of world trade to analyze the effects of possible changes in indirect tax arrangements in U.S. trading partners. Their results clearly indicate that were Canada to move to an origin basis from the existing destination basis in their indirect tax, this would be advantageous for the United States, but were Japan to do the same, this would be disadvantageous for the United States. The implication of their results is that whether or not it is advantageous for the United States to pressure its major trading partners to move to an origin basis depends upon the balance of trade in taxed commodities.

Both the manufacturers sales tax in Canada and the commodity tax in Japan are taxes which are heavier on manufactured than on nonmanufactured commodities. In its trade with Canada, the United States is a net exporter of manufactures and a net importer of resource and other nonmanufacturing items. In the case of trade with Japan, the United States is a net importer of manufactures and a net exporter of agricultural and other nonmanufactured products. Because manufacturing is more heavily taxed under both taxes, for a manufacturing net exporter country a tax on an origin basis operates in a similar manner to an export tax. For a manufacturing net importer a tax on a destination basis operates in a similar manner to a tariff. As a result, there is an asymmetry in Canada and Japan switching to an origin basis as far as the United States is concerned, given the commodity structure of their existing trade.

Thus, whether or not it is advantageous for the United States to encourage trading partners to move to an origin basis cannot be answered on any a priori basis in the nonbroadly based tax case. One needs to examine the bilateral balance of trade in taxed commodities. Equally, for the United States to negotiate some form of code on border-tax adjustments in the GATT, possibly restricting countries to the use of an origin basis, could be disadvantageous for the United States.

Even though the debate on indirect taxes used by U.S. trade partners has died down compared to what took place in the 1960s and 1970s, the issue remains and could resurface again in the future. Where this might arise is in connection with possible changes in sales taxes in Canada, in which the existing manufacturers sales tax might be replaced by a business transfer tax. The business transfer tax is a subtraction-method, value-added tax, administered using a destination basis. Under the destination basis, taxes would be collected on imports and taxes rebated on exports. If such a tax were ruled

Table 6.4   Effects of Removing Domestic Tax Distortions in the United States, Canada, and Japan

Country	Welfare and Terms of Trade Effects	
	Welfare Gain or Loss as % of GNP[1]	% Change in Terms of Trade[2]
EEC	0.0	+0.04
U.S.	1.0	+0.41
Japan	−0.3	−3.04
Canada	−0.1	−1.04

	% Changes in Trade Flows by Region[3]			
	Imports by			
Exports from	EEC	U.S.	Japan	Canada
EEC	0.0	−3.1	4.7	0.7
U.S.	0.2	0.0	0.7	7.4
Japan	4.5	2.1	0.0	6.9
Canada	3.1	6.2	2.1	0.0

Note: Calculations were made using Whalley's general equilibrium model of global trade (Whalley 1985).

[1]See the discussion in the text, which emphasizes how this model variant excludes effects of taxes on labor supply and savings and hence produces small estimates of the welfare costs of tax distortions compared to other numerical general equilibrium models (such as Ballard, Fullerton, Shoven, and Whalley 1985 or Piggott and Whalley 1985).

[2]Plus sign indicates improvement.

[3]1977 data.

by a GATT panel to be a direct rather than an indirect tax, such border adjustments could prove to be a violation of Article III of the GATT. Whether tax rebates on exports could also be construed as an export subsidy, and hence subject to countervailing petitions, would be a further issue.

Evaluating the impacts of all of the major trade-distorting features of domestic taxes on trade flows between the United States, Japan, and Canada is clearly difficult, and no single model is able to capture all of the effects involved. An indication of some of the effects is given in table 6.4 which presents some calculations from the general equilibrium model of global trade developed by the present author (Whalley 1985). Whalley's published work reports on a seven-region model of global trade which excludes Canada as a separate region, but in more recent work this has been extended to an eight-region model which also incorporates Canada. Whalley's model, which is a system of Constant Elasticity of Substitution (CES) demand and production functions, is calibrated to data on production and trade in each of the major trading regions identified in the model, and permits counterfactual equilibrium analyses. The model incorporates the influences of domestic taxes, modelled in ad valorem equivalent form as taxes on factors inputs by industry, industry outputs, commodity demands, and household incomes. Calculations can thus be made of the trade impacts of removing all existing domestic taxes as modelled, and replacing them by a yield-preserving, uniform-rate sales tax on all commodities.

It is important to emphasize that in the simple static version of this model, no effects of taxes on labor supply or saving decisions are captured and, therefore, the distorting effects of domestic tax policies are relatively small. Also, a number of key elasticity values need to be specified for the model, and results change as parameter values change. However, what emerges from these calculations is a sense that relative to conventional trade policies, such as tariffs, tax effects on global trade and welfare are important.

In the results reported in table 6.4, major gains occur for the United States after an elimination of the main distorting features of domestic taxes in all regions included in the model. These exceed those which would accrue to the United States in the model with an elimination of all tariffs by developed OECD countries. Indeed, the terms of trade effects associated with these changes are pronounced. There is a negative terms of trade effect against Japan of 3 percent and a change against Canada of 1 percent. Associated with these effects are significant changes in trade volumes, as reported in table 6.4. These show particularly large effects on trade volumes, on both the import and export side, in the Canadian and Japanese cases, reflecting the bias against nontraded good sectors implicit in the tax systems of all three countries.

These results clearly indicate the importance of tax features for trade, especially when compared to the modelling evaluations reported by Whalley for the effects of the elimination of existing tariffs on global trade, and suggest the need for further and more detailed quantification of the effects involved.

6.4 Tax Reform in Canada, Japan, and the United States, and Implications for Trade Flows

In addition to the impact of taxes on trade flows, a further set of issues is raised by the ongoing tax reforms in the United States, Japan, and Canada. The U.S. tax reform has been enacted in the 1986 U.S. tax bill, reforms in Japan were announced at the end of 1986 with implementation beginning in 1987,[8] and reform in Canada is at the discussion stage. The broad directions of reform are summarized in table 6.5 for the United States, in table 6.6 for Japan, and in table 6.7 for Canada.

Broadly speaking, what is involved in all three countries is a reduction in personal tax rates, some broadening of the personal tax base, a lowering of corporate tax rates, and termination (or reduction) of accelerated depreciation at the corporate level. Japan, in addition, hoped to replace their existing commodity tax with a credit invoice VAT, and Canada will likely similarly

Table 6.5   Main Features of Recent Tax Reform in the United States[1]
(Tax Reform Act of 1986)

Personal taxes
Previous 14-bracket federal rate structure (11–50%) replaced with a 2-rate structure (15%, 28%)
by 1988
Increases in and indexation of personal exemptions beginning 1990
Full taxation of capital gains
Modifications of exclusions and deductions, including itemized state and local taxes
Phase out deduction of retirement savings plan (IRA) contributions by moderate and high income earners
Limits on interest deductions through new passive loss rules
Corporate taxes
Top rate reduced from 46% to 34%
Investment tax credit repealed
Depreciation schedule largely reverts to pre-1981 system with sharply less acceleration
Intercorporate dividend deduction lowered
New limits on net operating loss carry forward
Alternative minimum personal and corporate taxes
New parallel systems of personal and corporate tax under which maximum of two tax assessments paid
Rates at corporate level 20%; at personal level, 21%
Bases differ from regular taxes; allowable depreciation is lower; tax-exempt interest on state and local bonds becomes taxable; special limits apply to interest deductibility; accounting rules differ

[1]See Deloitte, Haskins, and Sells (1986).

try to replace the manufacturers sales tax with a comparably broadly based tax (a credit invoice or a subtraction-method VAT).

However, these reforms differ with the kind of tax affected. The changes in the United States are planned to be revenue neutral, and involve a personal tax reduction and a corporate tax increase. In Japan, it seems that heavier taxation of capital income at the personal level may more than offset the effects of the personal rate reductions, resulting in a possible net revenue increase. At the corporate level, a net decrease in revenues should occur due to the rate reduction. In Canada what currently seems most likely is a personal level rate cut and reduction in revenues, financed by an indirect tax increase as the manufacturers sales tax is replaced by either a subtraction- or credit-method value-added tax.

In both Canada and Japan it is widely perceived that the pressures to follow the U.S. tax changes with similar reforms of their own are very strong. The belief seems to be that it is necessary to match reductions in U.S. corporate tax rates since otherwise, significant increases in debt financing by large multinationals in their own countries would occur, eroding their tax base. Canadian debate has also focussed on the incentives for outmigration of skilled labor unless rate reductions comparable to those in the United States also occur at the personal level.

Table 6.6 Planned Tax Reforms in Japan[1] (Announced December 1986)

Personal taxes
Previous 15-rate structure replaced by 6-rate structure. Top marginal rate reduced from 70% to 50%, with a 15% local income surtax
Changes in deductions for employment income, special exemptions for spouses, and tax treatments of pension benefits
New limits placed on nontaxation of investment income (low income and disabled); other investment income taxed at higher flat rate of 20%
Interest on postal savings and bank deposits and all other financial instruments to be fully taxed
Some capital gains on securities to be taxed, along with capital gains on land held for less than 2 years
Corporate taxes
Rate reduced from 50% to 37.5% over 3 years
Tax Free Reserved to be abolished
Asset lives for depreciation to be reviewed
Foreign tax credit limited to effective tax rate in Japan, and ceilings introduced on share of total income on which credits to be taken
Portion of intercorporate dividends taxable
Sales tax
Credit invoice VAT to be introduced
Small-scale enterprises removed from tax system
Financial transactions, food, education, excisables (e.g., gasoline) exempt
Tax rate of 5%
Existing commodity tax to be eliminated

[1]Based on information provided by Yuichiro Nagatoni, Institute of Fiscal and Monetary Policy, Ministry of Finance, Japan. These tax reform proposals have generated a lot of debate in Japan. As a result, Prime Minister Nakasone announced in April 1987 that he would introduce new proposals. In June, he announced his proposals would be released in August 1987. He further announced that the VAT would not be in these proposals, but he nonetheless reaffirmed his commitment to a new indirect tax system.

Table 6.7 Tax Reform in Canada (Changes Announced 18 June 1987)

1. *Personal taxes*
Reduction in number of federal rate brackets to 3 (19%, 26%, 29%)
Conversion of exemptions (including the standard deduction) into credits
Reduction in lifetime capital gains exemption from C$500,000 to C$100,000
2. *Corporate taxes*
Lowered corporate tax rate, as in 1985 government discussion paper, from (approximately) combined federal/provincial rate of 46%, eventually to around 33%
Investment tax credit to be eliminated
Lengthening of asset lines for depreciation
Approximately revenue-neutral change at corporate level (unlike the U.S.)
3. *Sales tax*
Existing federal manufacturers sales tax to eventually be abolished
Replacement to be either VAT or goods and services tax (subtraction method value-added tax)
Base likely to be comprehensive (possibly including food, clothing, financial transactions)
Increased transfers to lower income households could accompany the change
Sales tax change may well not be revenue neutral, but could be used to finance personal-level rate reductions
Involvement of provinces in sales tax change invited, but unclear how it might work

Source: Department of Finance, Government of Canada, 1987. 1. *Tax Reform, 1987.* 2. *Tax Reform, 1987: Sales Tax Reform.* 3. *Tax Reform, 1987: Income Tax Reform.*

If the major change in the United States is one in the structure of taxation which changes marginal but not average rates, the tax reform in the United States may not fundamentally alter the migration incentives to leave Canada, given that migration decisions involve an all-or-nothing choice. Also, the reduction in corporate rates in all three countries has the net effect of lowering taxes on old investments, as well as on new ones. From an efficiency point of view, this does not seem to have as much to commend it as leaving old tax rates in place and using investment incentives to offset the effects of higher tax rates.

A central issue, however, is what the tax reforms in the United States may mean for trade and factor flows in light of the discussion earlier in the paper. If the current U.S. trade deficit is indeed largely a reflection of fiscal policy, which generates large public sector deficits, and tax policies, which both penalize savings and stimulate investment, the effects may be substantial. The net effect of changes in the tax and budgetary policy mix in the United States between 1981 and 1986 has been a large capital inflow and large trade deficits, much of which is affecting trade with Japan. The tax changes will significantly weaken the incentives for investment introduced as part of the 1981 ACRS, and the reduction in personal tax rates may further weaken tax disincentives to saving, although this will be partially offset by the changes in the treatment of capital gains. It may well be, therefore, that net capital flows into the United States will be sharply reduced. This, in turn, has the implication that the United States trade deficit could be significantly reduced by these tax changes.

There are, however, other effects. The trade share of consumption in the United States is higher than the trade share of investment. Thus, a series of tax changes which lower investment through withdrawal of investment incentives and, as a result, stimulate consumption will cause an effect offsetting that on the trade deficit through impacts on capital flows. Also, the tax changes in Japan may well act to lower the Japanese saving rate, which will reduce capital outflows from Japan, raising interest rates in the United States and thus impact on existing current account imbalances.

6.5 Tax-Based Trade Irritants

Besides the direct influence of taxes on the size and composition of Canadian-U.S.-Japanese trade, tax issues also arise in trade disputes in the form of tax-based trade irritants. Such irritants arise where tax systems are either in open conflict with established international trade rules, or where the trading rules themselves are ambiguous in the way they treat particular taxes. As a result, pressures build for rule changes.

In the postwar years, most of these irritants have involved EEC-U.S. conflicts rather than disputes directly involving Canada and Japan. But most of the EEC-U.S. conflicts have had implications for other trading partners. Examples are the United States Domestic International Sales Corporation (DISC) being referred to a GATT panel on the grounds that it represented an export subsidy; petitions for both countervailing and antidumping duties in the United States, based either on tax rebates associated with cascading effects of turnover taxes in exporting countries, or on domestic taxes being administered on a destination basis (as with color TV exports from Japan in the late 1970s); border-tax adjustments under value-added taxes; and termination of domestic deductibility for certain expenditures made abroad (such as advertising broadcast costs and convention expenses in neighboring countries).

The rules of the postwar trading system, at least as they have governed trade between developed countries, are largely embodied in the GATT and the multilateral rounds of tariff reductions and codes which have been negotiated under GATT auspices. The GATT has also dealt with a number of other related issues, including domestic taxes. It was acknowledged early on that domestic taxes can provide an equivalent protective effect to a tariff. An attempt by Greece, for instance, to use an import duty relabelled as a "contribution", and hence outside negotiated limits on tariffs, was referred to a GATT panel.[9]

It is Article III of the GATT that places limits on domestic taxes and thus tries to deal with tax-based trade irritants. It draws a distinction between internal taxes and tariffs, and states that domestic taxes should not discriminate between imports and comparable domestic products. It does not exclude the protective use of taxes for a particular product which is heavily imported, but such taxes may not discriminate between domestically produced and imported products. What constitutes discrimination under Article III is not clearly defined, however. Whether and to what degree border-tax adjustments were or are allowable has never been adequately resolved, since the border-tax issue has yet to be ruled on by a GATT panel. Tax rebate schemes, such as occur under destination-based turnover or cascade taxes, have invited countervailing petitions by firms affected by foreign competition in domestic markets.

As far as Canada-U.S.-Japanese trade is concerned, the role which tax policies in these countries play in determining both the size and pattern of trade dwarfs the significance of any tax-based trade irritants. This applies equally to those which have been the subject of dispute over the last few decades, and those which seem likely to surface in the years ahead. But it is these tax-based trade irritants which have attracted the attention of the trade policy community.

To gain a sense of how tax-based trade irritants arise, and how they are typically dealt with within the existing institutional structure of global rule making, a few examples may help.

6.5.1 The Domestic International Sales Corporation (DISC)

The DISC was a feature of the U.S. tax system introduced in 1971 which allowed U.S. firms to defer corporate taxes due on a portion of income from export sales.[10] The DISC arose at a time when, unlike today, the concern in the United States was with the large size of U.S. net capital outflows. The DISC was advocated on the grounds that it would give U.S. firms an incentive to produce for export from the United States, rather than to locate abroad in order to service foreign markets. This provision clearly represented a tax incentive to engage in exporting, and brought the U.S. tax system into conflict with GATT rules on export subsidies.

In July 1972, shortly after the DISC was introduced, the EEC filed a complaint with the GATT under Article XVI which prohibits export subsidies, pointing out that exemption of direct taxes on export income was specifically included in a list of prohibited export subsidies agreed to by the GATT contracting parties in 1960. The United States in turn filed complaints against three EEC countries (France, Belgium, and the Netherlands) on the grounds that their practice of only taxing foreign-source income on receipt in the origin country also constituted an export subsidy.

A GATT panel was convened and concluded in a 1976 finding that both the DISC and tax practices in the three EEC countries constituted export subsidies, and hence violated Article XVI of the GATT. It was not until 1981, however, that the GATT Council accepted this report, and then with three important qualifications. The most important was that export income originating abroad need not be taxed by exporting countries (in effect making the EEC practices GATT compatible). The United States agreed to the adoption of the report because it interpreted the qualifications as effectively supporting the U.S. position on DISC. In 1983 the United States was therefore able to relabel the DISC as the Foreign Sales Corporation (FSC) with relatively little change in its form, and to terminate the source of the irritant, while keeping its policy largely unchanged.

6.5.2 The Border-Tax Adjustment Issue

Another major tax-based trade irritant, frequently debated over the last twenty years, is the question of border-tax adjustments, already discussed above. The issue is how domestic taxes are to be rebated on exports and compensatory taxes applied to imports. Like the DISC, the border-tax issue has primarily been an EEC-U.S. issue, rather than one directly involving Canada and Japan. But, because of the border adjustments used in these countries, similar issues arise.

The need for border adjustments arises from indirect sales tax systems such as cascading turnover taxes, or value-added taxes administered on a destination basis. It has long been the practice in Europe, even before the widespread use of the VAT, to apply taxes on imports equivalent to those deemed to be borne by comparable domestic products under domestic indirect taxes, and to rebate taxes on exports. The major source of the tax-based trade irritant in this area was the widespread adoption of the VAT in Europe in the late 1960s and early 1970s. There is nothing in Article III of the GATT which prohibits such border adjustments, but the introduction of the VAT sharply elevated this as a trade issue in the late 1960s for a number of reasons.[11]

Firstly, making the calculation of what the appropriate border adjustment should be under the previously widely used cascading turnover tax involved rough and ready calculations. Thus when West Germany introduced a VAT in 1968 in place of its previous turnover tax and its border adjustments doubled, great consternation in the United States was the result. Secondly, such border adjustments are only permitted under GATT for indirect taxes (value-added, sales, excise), not for direct taxes (income, corporate, payroll). U.S. business at the time widely viewed such adjustments as advantageous to Europe since imports are taxed and exports leave tax free. It was also noted then (and is still true) that the United States relied more heavily on direct rather then indirect taxes compared to most European countries. Thus, pressure arose in the United States either to clarify the legality of border-tax adjustments under the GATT, extending them for direct as well as indirect taxes, or to change the United States tax system by introducing a VAT or retail sales tax so as to allow such adjustments to be made.

At the conclusion of the Kennedy Round (1967), the border-tax issue was one of the central trade issues on the agenda for international negotiation. The issue is much broader in scope than just EEC-U.S. trade, since both Canada and Japan also have nationally operated indirect taxes which are administered on a destination basis and involve comparable border adjustments. These are the manufacturers sales tax in Canada and the commodity tax in Japan. Pressure thus seemed to be building for a substantive international negotiation on the border-tax issue to be included in the then emerging Tokyo Round.

In fact, little action has taken place on the border-tax question. Domestic business groups in the United States still frequently raise the issue, and arguments in favor of the United States adopting a value-added tax are often heard. But at the official level, the issue is no longer high on the U.S. agenda of trade irritants to be resolved, nor is it an item on the agenda for current GATT negotiations. No substantive discussion of the issue took place during the Tokyo Round, and no major initiative has been attempted since.

In part, this situation reflects a process within the international trade policy community of moving on to other issues after an initial flurry of discussions and pressure for change; a process which may be repeated in other areas of current trade policy attention, such as intellectual property and services. Also, the academic argument that for broadly based taxes, border adjustments have no real effects on trade flows[12] (since in equilibrium a move between original and destination bases results only in changes in exchange rates under a flexible rate regime) has undoubtedly contributed to a general weakening of policy interest in this issue.

6.5.3 Domestic Tax Rebates and Countervailing Duties

A further example of a tax-based trade irritant which for a while assumed center stage is the issue of border adjustments arising from domestic taxes and implications for countervailing duties.

This issue reached its peak with the case brought by the Zenith Corporation in the U.S. customs court against Japanese color TV manufacturers in April 1976.[13] The allegation was that Japanese color TVs sold for higher prices in Japan than in the United States, and countervailing duties were merited since Japanese producers had taxes rebated on exports. Zenith had earlier sought such duties from the U.S. Treasury Department, and went to court to test the legality of various interpretations of an 1897 Tariff Act.

Zenith was successful in the customs court in April 1979, and a wave of similar petitions followed. These included one by U.S. steel producers against rebates of VAT on European steel exports. But in higher courts, and eventually the Supreme Court, the Zenith petition was unsuccessful. The threat of countervailing duties based on rebating of taxes paid is no longer a major tax-based trade irritant. Such cases nowadays involve allegations of "over-rebating", such as the recent actions in the United States against India.[14]

Overall, tax-based trade irritants are probably of only relatively minor importance compared to the wider influences of taxes on trade patterns. Yet this has not prevented their attracting substantial amounts of attention over the years in trade policy circles. Currently, the level of tax-based trade irritants seems to be small but this situation could change, especially with major changes unfolding in all three countries. Their relative insignificance compared to the wider influences of taxes on trade should, however, be kept firmly in mind.

6.6 Some Concluding Remarks

Modern tax systems are structurally complex in all countries, and that does not exclude the three economies discussed in this paper. In the contemporary world economy, it is also clear that the linkages between economies involve both trade and factor flows, and the contribution of tax policies to these interactions is clearly worthy of more study than has been done in the past. Because of its breadth, this paper is inevitably unable to deal with all issues involved in assessing the importance of tax effects on trade flows between the United States, Canada, and Japan. I have, however, tried to raise what seem to be some of the more central issues for wider discussion.

It seems clear at the present time that the major trade irritant between Japan and the United States is the size of the trade deficit, and this is to some extent accounted for by the combination of tax and budgetary policy currently pursued in the United States. To the extent that this is true, the interaction between taxes and trade is central to a full understanding of the Japanese-U.S. trade relationship.

In addition, changes in tax policies in the years ahead, especially if the planned reforms in all three countries are implemented, may also have implications for trade and factor flows. But the tax-based trade irritants which often seize the attention of the trade policy community, including any new ones which may result from the new reforms, seem to be less important than the effects directly attributable to differences in tax structure.

Notes

1. See the discussion below in section 6.4.

2. This has been changed to a C$100,000 lifetime limit in the tax reform package announced on 18 June 1987. Seventy-five percent of capital gains above the limit will be taxed, in contrast to the 50 percent rule which previously applied.

3. These and other differences also lead to different effective marginal tax rates across countries. See Shoven and Tachibanaki (1986) for calculations of effective marginal tax rates in Japan, and comparisons with calculations for the United States by King and Fullerton (1984). Calculations for Canada are reported in Broadway, Bruce, and Mintz (1984).

4. See Shibata (1967) and Whalley (1979).

5. It also seems widely agreed, however, that the dramatically higher saving rates in Japan compared to the United States cannot be explained only by tax differences. Simple life-cycle theory predicts that high-growth economies will generate high saving rates, especially where technical change raises wage rates differentially across young and old workers. In addition, the common practice in Japan is for retirement at age 55 and movement into considerably lower paying jobs, thus also greatly amplifying life-cycle savings.

6. See the discussion of the Canada-U.S. situation in Bird and Brean (1985), including the current tax treaty covering withholding tax rates on interest, dividends, and royalties.

7. See Shibata (1967), Johnson and Krauss (1970), and Whalley (1979).

8. There has, however, been substantial debate on the tax reform proposals in Japan. In June 1987 Prime Minister Nakasone announced that he would present a new tax reform package in August, and this would not include the proposed VAT which was in the planned package in December.

9. See Dam (1970, 116).

10. This discussion is based in part on material presented in Mutti and Grubert (1984). See also Hobson (1977).
11. See Dam (1970, ch. 13).
12. See Shibata (1967) and Johnson and Krauss (1970).
13. See the discussion in Meltzer (1979, 431–32).
14. See Certain Iron Metal Castings from India, 48 Federal Register 38267, 38268, 56092, 56093, 56094 (1983); 49 Federal Register 32779, 32780, 40943 (1984).

References

Ballard, C., D. Fullerton, J. Shoven, and J. Whalley. 1985. *A general equilibrium model for tax policy evaluation.* Chicago: University of Chicago Press.
Bird, R. M., and Donald J. S. Brean. 1985. Canada/U.S. tax relations: Issues and perspectives. In *Canada/United States trade and investment issues,* eds. D. Fretz, R. Stern, and J. Whalley. Ontario: Ontario Economic Council.
Boadway, R., N. Bruce, and J. Mintz, 1984. Taxation, inflation, and the effective marginal tax rate on capital in Canada. *Canadian Journal of Economics* 17 (February): 62–79.
Canadian Tax Foundation. 1986. *The national finances, 1985–86.* Toronto: Canadian Tax Foundation.
Dam, K. W. 1970. *The GATT: Law and international economic organization.* Chicago: University of Chicago Press.
Deloitte, Haskins, and Sells. 1986. *The tax revolution.*
Drache, Arthur B. C., ed. 1986. *Canada tax planning service.* Vol. 1, *Principles of taxation.* Don Mills, Ontario: De Boo.
Government of Japan. 1986. *Tax commission report on the annual review of the tax system for fiscal year 1987.* Tokyo: Government of Japan.
Hamilton, R. W., and J. Whalley. 1986. Border tax adjustments and U.S. trade. *Journal of International Economics* 20 (May): 377–83.
Hobson, J. 1977. The GATT panel reports on tax practices in Belgium, France, the Netherlands, and the United States. *European taxation.* Amsterdam: International Bureau of Fiscal Documentation, 154–68.
Ishi, H. 1983. An overview of postwar tax policies in Japan. *Hitotsubashi Journal of Economics* 23 (February): 21–39.
Johnson, H. G., and M. Krauss. 1970. Border taxes, border tax adjustments, comparative advantage, and the balance of payments. *Canadian Journal of Economics* 3 (November): 595–602.
King, M. A., and D. Fullerton. 1984. *The taxation of income from capital: A comparative study of the United States, the United Kingdom, Sweden, and West Germany.* Chicago: University of Chicago Press.
Meltzer, R. I. 1979. Color-TV sets and U.S.-Japanese relations: Problems of trade adjustment policy making. *Orbis* Summer: 421–46.

Melvin, J. 1970. Commodity taxation as a determinant of trade. *Canadian Journal of Economics* 3 (February): 62–78.

Musgrave, P. B. 1969. *United States taxation of foreign investment income.* Cambridge, Mass.: Harvard University Law School.

Mutti, J., and H. Grubert. 1984. The Domestic International Sales Corporation and its effects. In *The structure and evolution of recent U.S. trade policy,* eds. R. E. Baldwin and A. O. Krueger. Chicago: University of Chicago Press.

Piggott, J., and J. Whalley. 1985. *Applied general equilibrium analysis of UK tax policy.* Cambridge: Cambridge University Press.

Shibata, H. 1967. The theory of economic unions: A comparative analysis of customs unions, free trade areas, and tax unions. In *Fiscal harmonization in common markets,* vol. 1, *Theory,* ed. C. S. Shoup. New York: Columbia University Press.

Shoven, J. B., and T. Tachibanaki. 1986. The taxation of income from capital in Japan. Revised version of a paper presented at an NBER conference on U.S.-Japan productivity, Cambridge, Mass.

Summers, L. H. 1986. Tax policy and international competitiveness. National Bureau of Economic Research Working Paper no. 2007. Cambridge, Mass.: NBER.

U.S. Department of Commerce. *Federal Register.* Various issues.

Whalley, J. 1979. Uniform domestic tax rates, trade distortions, and economic integration. *Journal of Public Economics* 11 (May): 213–21.

———. 1985. *Trade liberalization among major world trading areas.* Cambridge, Mass.: MIT Press.

Comment
Alan J. Auerbach

As one would expect, Whalley has produced an intelligent and reasoned analysis of the relationship between tax policy and trade problems among the United States, Canada, and Japan. I find myself in general agreement with his arguments, and would like to offer my own interpretation of them and what their message is.

Let me begin by summarizing the main arguments. One may distinguish four sources of tax-related trade problems. Starting from the most macro level, there are differences in government saving rates associated with the balance, or lack thereof, between taxes and expenditures. Though table 6.2 of the paper does not report the Japanese central government deficit, we all know that it has been substantially lower as a fraction of GNP than in the United States and Canada. The deficit leads to trade problems through its impact on the balance between national savings and investment. Through the national income identity relating the current and capital accounts, we know that a large increase in a country's fiscal deficit must raise domestic private savings, lower private domestic investment, or worsen the trade balance. Recent experience in the United States suggests that increasing private saving is not an easy task. Indeed, by some measures, it has actually decreased in recent years. Increasing net imports seems to have been more easily accomplished.

Second on the list of fiscal effects on trade are elements of tax structure that affect the overall incentives for private domestic investment and savings. These affect trade through the same channel as government deficits, through the relation of national saving and investment. There is a general view that, at least until the Tax Reform Act of 1986, the U.S. tax structure was more anti-saving and pro-investment than the tax structure in Japan. This may very well be true.

In fact, I think Whalley understates the case by his very similar characterizations of U.S., Canadian, and Japanese corporate tax systems in table 6.3. If one turns back to table 6.2, it is quite clear that Japan raises a lot more of its tax revenue from corporate taxes than does the United States or Canada. Since my own research (conducted with my colleague Albert Ando) confirms the view of others that Japanese firms have higher debt-equity ratios (and hence a smaller taxable equity base) and a somewhat lower rate of return to capital than American firms, the higher share of corporate taxes in Japan suggests a much higher average rate of tax on corporate profits than in the United States. At the same time, I believe that Whalley has overstated the tax inducements to save in Japan. The tax-free saving vehicles that have existed in Japan and are scheduled for repeal, the *maruyu,* have certainly led to tax reductions, but whether they have increased saving is at least as uncertain as whether the recently scaled back Individual Retirement Accounts did so in the United States. My own view is that such vehicles are extremely inefficient ways of using tax revenues to stimulate saving. For many taxpayers, they introduce nothing more than the income effect of lower taxes. That the Japanese saving rate is high is beyond question, but I think that the tax explanation belongs in a footnote, and the societal factors which are presently relegated to a footnote, as well as others we have not really considered, provide the bulk of the explanation.

The third type of tax factor influencing trade is the domestic tax policies affecting specific markets. Here, Whalley discusses indirect taxes and the distinction between origin- and destination-based taxes of the broad-based varieties, as well as taxes on narrower bases. There is a general view among the business community in the United States that a destination-based value-added tax would improve our trade balance. Since Whalley rejects the general idea that this is so, it is useful to consider the possible reasons for this discrepancy.

First, the proponents of such taxes may not be thinking of broad-based taxes, but rather taxes on certain commodities that they would like to see have a stronger export market. Taxing U.S. purchases of semiconductors clearly would have a different impact than taxing U.S. production of semiconductors. Though having little impact on the overall U.S. trade balance, the choice between these two policies would have a large impact on the U.S. semiconductor industry. It is therefore easy to understand why what Whalley calls "tax-based trade irritants," that is, tax policies that relate to specific commodities or narrow types of activity, are focal points for political lobbying efforts.

Further, some people may suffer from what is essentially "money illusion" in relating direct to indirect taxes, seeing, for example, an origin-based value-added tax on net output as being different from a proportional direct tax on personal income. Those who would dismiss this explanation should read the section of Whalley's paper which discusses the different treatment by GATT of direct and indirect taxes.

Finally, however, I think there may be some merit in the view that origin- and destination-based taxes are different. As Whalley points out, in a simple enough model, the taxes are equivalent. To me, the easiest way to see this is to start with a one-period model with a representative consumer. Here, an origin-based value-added tax reduces the factor incomes on one side of the consumer's budget constraint, while a destination-based tax raises prices on the other side. The impact on relative factor and goods prices is the same and so, therefore, should be the consumer's factor supply and consumption behavior. Suppose, however, that there were more than one period in the model. Then, a temporary tax on factor incomes would discourage current factor supply and production, while a temporary tax on consumption would discourage current consumption. The second policy would lead to more first-period exports than the first, consistent with the views I mentioned at the outset. I do not know if this model is the right one, but I do not think a one-period model with balanced trade is right, either.

On this subject of indirect taxes, Whalley quite correctly notes that indirect taxes are not of the broad-based variety, and reports the results of simulations showing that Canada would help the United States by moving from a destination basis to an origin basis, but Japan would not. The primary reason, in each case, is a terms-of-trade effect. The United States would gain by Canada's raising the price of its manufacturing goods competing with U.S. exports, while Japanese manufacturing exports to the United States would become more expensive.

Lastly, the fourth tax policy affecting trade is the one we all might have thought of after completing our first course in international trade, tariff policy. Whalley reports simulation results suggesting that this has smaller welfare effects than the indirect tax policies I just discussed.

In summary, then, there are four types of tax policy affecting trade: fiscal balance, overall direct tax structure, indirect taxes, and tariffs. These seem to decline in importance just as they become more closely associated with specific markets and private economic decisions.

Let me finally turn to the subject of tax reform. This continues to provide public finance economists with some measure of entertainment. While visiting different countries in recent months, I frequently encountered the notion that it would be important to follow the lead of the United States, whatever the benefits of doing so unilaterally. Whalley does identify some reasons why this makes sense, that borrowing and migration decisions may be very sensitive to differences in tax rates. I also think worth reporting the comment I heard, from a source I will not disclose, that since the U.S. tax policy was aimed at helping to solve the U.S.-Japan trade problem, Japan should adopt a similar tax reform to help achieve this objective.

Overall, my own analysis of the U.S. tax reform is that it is mildly anti-investment, with a less certain impact on saving. This suggests that the policy will encourage U.S. exports by weakening capital inflows. However, many have questioned whether the tax reform is really revenue neutral, suggesting that behavioral shifts away from more highly taxed activities will exceed those anticipated by government revenue estimators. If this is so, the increased budget deficit may have a more important impact on the trade balance than the change in tax structure itself. All in all, it is hard to foresee a large change in the trade balance being caused by the tax reform; nor do I see any reason why the change in tax structure should lead to changes in the intensity of irritation induced by tax-based trade irritants. Such irritants are visible because of their effects on specific industries. Their importance is overemphasized in the United States because of a poor understanding of the issues of tax incidence and because they are incorrectly perceived to be the source of the aggregate trade imbalance. Revenue-neutral reform of the tax structure both in the United States and abroad attacks neither the direct source of these irritants nor the ignorance and fiscal conditions that make them seem important.

Comment

Hiromitsu Ishi

Whalley has done a commendable job of describing the current state of taxes on trade and investment flows among the three countries. Overall I agree with his diagnoses of the problems. Surprisingly enough, there has been almost no work in Japan that has studied theoretically or empirically the relation between the tax system and international trade. In spite of the importance of the problem, neither tax experts nor international trade specialists have so far begun to investigate it systematically on a full scale.

In my comments I want to discuss four aspects of Whalley's paper, with particular reference to the Japanese experience.

The first issue is how we should understand the effects of the ongoing tax reform in Japan. Japan's proposed tax reform in 1986 follows the U.S. reform idea based on the assumption of revenue neutrality. The Japanese government is proposing both a $30 billion reduction in personal and corporate income taxes and a $30 billion increase in VAT and interest-income taxation. Based upon the combination of such tax changes, many empirical studies have already been made to analyze the effects on the Japanese economy. It is widely believed that the proposed tax reform would have a more or less neutral effect on the macroeconomic variables. This can be seen in the calculations presented in table C6.1. The neutral effect is particularly evident in terms of real GNP. It is also estimated that real exports and the surplus on current account would tend to increase slightly. Overall, there is not much argument that the tax changes would be of great help in reducing the substantial bilateral trade imbalance between Japan and the United States, although it should be emphasized that the Japanese government has no intention to solve the existing trade imbalance from the outset by changing the tax system.

Second, Whalley argues that special tax treatment of capital income plays an important role in explaining why saving rates have been much higher in Japan and Canada than in the United States. At first sight his argument seems acceptable, but as far as the Japanese experience is concerned, it is perhaps too simple. There are still controversies about the relation between the high saving rate and special tax treatment of small-size savings in Japan. In particular, from an overseas point of view, it is often pointed out that the higher saving rate in Japan is primarily due to the type of tax concessions it has, which is based on the tax-exempt savings account system (i.e., the *maruyu* system). In Japan, opinion on this matter is divided among academics, bankers, and bureaucrats. Some believe that it has contributed to the high rate of saving, while others believe it has contributed little or nothing. Neither view is supported by the available econometric evidence, however. My own view is that special tax treatment of small-size savings accounts has played no significant role in encouraging more saving. More importance might be placed on other factors such as high income growth, or demographic, social, or cultural forces, etc. It would be interesting to know how these other factors have affected saving behavior in the United States and Canada.

Under the present proposals for tax reform, the tax-exempt savings system is to be replaced by a flat rate of 20 percent on interest income. This tax change has already been proposed in the Maekawa Report (i.e., Report on Structural Adjustment for International Harmony by the Prime Minister's Advisory Group, chaired by the former governor of the Bank of Japan, Mr. Maekawa) in the context of stimulating domestic demand. But it would be problematic to regard such a tax policy as an expansionary fiscal device designed to resolve bilateral trade imbalances.

The third point is the issue of indirect taxes and international trade.

Table C6.1. Tax Reform and the Japanese Economy (fiscal year 1988, billion yen)

	Total	Tax Increase		Tax Cut	
		VAT	Taxes on Interest Income	Personal Income Taxes	Corporate Income Taxes
Real GNP	182.4	−1,021.2	−288.4	1,118.3	518.5
	(0.1)	(−0.3)	(−0.1)	(0.4)	(0.2)
Real personal consumption	−1,282.2	−2,117.2	−372.0	1,294.3	17.1
	(−0.7)	(−1.2)	(−0.2)	(0.7)	(0.0)
Real private fixed investment	586.8	−145.5	−43.3	186.4	604.8
	(1.0)	(−0.2)	(−0.1)	(0.3)	(1.0)
Real exports	95.2	286.6	32.5	−172.5	−46.6
	(0.2)	(0.5)	(0.1)	(−0.3)	(−0.1)
Corporate current profits	216.1	−79.3	−19.1	58.9	275.0
	(0.9)	(−0.3)	(−0.1)	(0.2)	(1.1)

Notes: Figures are computed in comparison with the case without any tax change. Figures in parentheses refer to percentages of the base values. On the basis of the calculations, the consumer price index is estimated to increase by 1.4 percent and the surplus on current account by $2.9 billion.

Source: Nihon Keizai Shimbun, Data Bank Bureau.

Japan currently has no broad-based indirect tax, like the VAT, at either the national or local government levels. The relative share of indirect taxes was about 27 percent of national taxes in 1986, and the four largest items were the liquor taxes, gasoline taxes, commodity taxes, and stamp duties. They are considered to be levied on much narrower tax bases than a VAT would be. On this point, Whalley's argument on the effect of a move from the existing destination basis to an origin one is worth noting. He argues that this move in Japan would be "disadvantageous" for the U.S. But, as he points out, this operates in a manner similar to an export tax on Japan's manufacturing goods, which would increase export prices and in turn reduce Japan's competitiveness vis-à-vis the United States. Thus, I am not clear why this would be disadvantageous for the United States.

Japan is considering the introduction of a credit invoice VAT like that in the EEC countries, although the current political situation may make it difficult to do so. In connection with this, it is interesting to consider the argument that the broader-based VAT might encourage more exports than the current indirect taxes. Since both are administered on a destination basis, it is unlikely to be important for exports. But it is still controversial and would be an issue worth further investigation.

Lastly, related to the third point, I am especially interested in Whalley's discussion of the tax-distorting features of present domestic taxes, the results of which are summarized in his table 6.4. After replacing domestic taxes by a uniform rate tax on all commodities, the United States has both a welfare gain and improvement in its terms of trade, while Canada and Japan have opposite results. What are the main factors which explain these differences? I believe intuitively that the broadening of the indirect tax base would contribute substantially to an increase in welfare gains by removing tax distortion or deadweight loss. If so, Japan should also have welfare gains rather than losses after introducing a broader-based sales tax. Proponents of the VAT in Japan, including myself, are always placing great emphasis on the potential increase in welfare that a VAT would bring as compared to the present selective commodity tax system. Whalley's argument does not favor this view.

In addition, I wonder why Canada is trying to introduce a business transfer tax, a subtraction-method VAT, which is likely to be out of fashion. In fact, the Japanese government attempted to introduce this type of VAT in 1979 and completely failed, mainly for political reasons. Why then would the Canadian government choose a subtraction-method VAT rather than other alternatives?

7   The Current Economic Situation and Future Problems in the Asia-Pacific Region

Saburo Okita

7.1   Introduction

World economic growth centered on the industrialized nations in the period between the end of the Second World War and the 1960s. The EEC's intra- and extraregional trade was at its peak, and the growth in the United States was reflected in the Atlantic region which acted as the support for worldwide economic growth, trade expansion, and regional development. With the turn of the decade, however, the economic growth of the industrialized nations in this part of the world slowed down drastically. The world economy's center of gravity shifted to the oil-producing nations and the developing and newly industrializing countries (NICs) of Latin America and Asia, as trade expansion and economic growth in these countries made remarkable strides.

The second oil crisis forced another shifting of roles. The world cut back on its oil consumption, disrupting the international balances of payments of many of the oil-producing countries. Several Latin American nations found themselves saddled with the heavy cumulative debts that plague them even today. Remarkably enough, the Western Pacific nations survived the second oil crisis better and have maintained relatively high growth rates. As a result, the Pacific region has become increasingly important for the growth of the world economy. For this reason, it is important to understand the past, current, and future economic developments in this region. This is the purpose of this paper.

The paper is structured as follows. Section 7.2 analyzes the factors which contributed to the success of the Pacific countries in the recent past. Such study is worthwhile because it highlights the conditions that have to be satisfied to make a regionally coordinated export-led expansion possible. It also offers a valuable perspective on the possibilities and limits of extending this pattern of economic expansion into the future.

This paper is based on the author's keynote address delivered at the conference and on his paper, "The Role of the Pacific Region in the World Economy of the Future" (November 1986).

The current opportunities and challenges for sustained growth in the region are discussed in section 7.3. It is argued that economic growth in the Asian NICs, the Association of Southeast Asian Nations (ASEAN),[1] and China may provide a new stimulus for intraregional and world trade provided that the surge of protectionist sentiments in the United States can be controlled and the expected decline in U.S. demand is absorbed by a strong economic expansion in Japan and Europe.

In all respects, Japan plays a crucial role in the adjustment process. Not only should it maintain a sufficient growth rate, it should also recycle its current account surplus to finance development projects in the Third World. Section 7.4 discusses Japan's contribution to global and regional economic development in greater detail.

The growing interdependence and the structural adjustments in the next several years will require close cooperation among the countries in the Pacific Basin. In section 7.5 some of the key issues for achieving such cooperation are explored.

7.2   The Dynamism of the Pacific Region

What factors explain the Pacific region's recent development? First are the export-oriented development policies. Whether a nation chooses import substitution or export promotion in its industrial development depends on the size of the economy, its access to natural resources, and its stage of development. The Asian NICs, which include South Korea, Taiwan, Hong Kong, and Singapore, and the ASEAN nations have consistently emphasized export promotion. There are several things to be said for concentrating on exports. For one, the process of tighter integration with the rest of the world economy exposes the domestic industry to world-class competition and thus both fosters industries which are globally competitive and imposes cost consciousness on economic planning and policy choices. Another advantage is that it draws on market mechanisms to encourage private-sector vitality. And yet another is that exports earn foreign currency and thus mitigate foreign exchange reserve limitations on development.

A second point of similarity is a high rate of investment, specifically investment backed by dramatically high domestic saving rates. In general, a country whose savings and investment exceed 20 percent of GNP can be said to have attained self-sustaining development. In 1960, Taiwan was the only nation among the Asian NICs and the ASEAN countries to have an investment rate exceeding 20 percent of gross domestic product (GDP). In recent years, however, most of these countries have exceeded the 20 percent figure. With their saving rates increasing faster than their GNP growth, and with additional financing from abroad, the Asian NICs and ASEAN countries have been able to invest heavily.

The result has been steady and rapid increases in the ratio of investment to GDP in the years between 1965 and 1984. In the Republic of Korea, for example, this ratio grew from 15 percent in 1965 to 29 percent in 1984. Malaysia experienced an increase from 18 percent to 31 percent in the same period, while the figure for Indonesia tripled from 7 percent to 21 percent. Likewise, the ratio jumped from 22 percent to 47 percent in Singapore and from 20 percent to 23 percent in Thailand. As a result of this strong pace of investment, the industrial sector has grown to a full 30 percent of GDP for most of the Asian NICs and ASEAN countries.

The third similarity common to this region is that of an aggressive and active private sector operating within what is basically a market economy system. Because price mechanisms do not function effectively within a rigidly planned economy, this often leads to uneconomical investment and inefficient management. In both the developing and the industrialized countries alike, there is a need for privatization and deregulation to promote more efficient operations. Care must be taken, however, that private ownership does not create or perpetuate social inequities. In mainland China, the trend of late is to retain public ownership and achieve efficiency and growth through allowing management greater latitude and, at the same, adopting market mechanisms to govern the flow of goods. Although the Japanese economy is basically one of private ownership, there has been a division of ownership and management, and ownership displays some features of a public trust.

The fourth reason for the success of the Western Pacific economies must be the improvements made in agriculture. As president of the Japanese government's Overseas Economic Cooperation Fund (OECF) in 1976, I jointly published with OECF's Dr. Kunio Takase a document entitled "Doubling Rice Production in Asia." In this paper, we argued that the Asian countries should seek to double rice production in fifteen years by developing better irrigation systems to enable them to use high-yield strains and fertilizer more effectively. I am pleased to see that the results of Asian efforts have been largely in line with that idea. According to the World Bank's 1986 *World Development Report,* the average annual growth rates of cereal production between 1971 and 1984 were 5.2 percent, 5 percent, and 4.5 percent in Indonesia, the Republic of Korea, and the Philippines, respectively. China and India, with their massive populations, also increased production by 3.2 percent and 4 percent which exceeded the growth rate of their population. These figures provide a striking contrast to the situation in Africa, where per-capita food production has declined by 1.1 percent per annum, which amounts to more than a 10 percent decline over the decade of the 1970s. The fact that agriculture has developed hand in hand with industrialization has been a major factor contributing to economic growth in the East and Southeast Asian countries.

A fifth contributing factor is the success of the various countries' economic adjustment policies in response to the worldwide recession of the 1970s and early 1980s. The countries of East and Southeast Asia adopted economic policies which enabled them to stem inflation and to adjust to the external dislocations. With only one or two exceptions, they weathered the world economic storm without incurring the kind of massive cumulative indebtedness seen in Latin America. Moreover, they achieved 3–4 percent growth, even as the OECD countries overall were showing zero growth, and hence were poised for nearly double-digit growth once the world economy got back on its feet.

The same mix of determined growth and successful policies applies to China as well. From 1979 through 1981, China checked inflationary pressures by postponing large-scale projects and tightening up on government spending to restore fiscal balance. The introduction of private incentives for agricultural production, the expansion of the autonomy of management at the enterprise level, the adoption of market mechanisms, the establishment of special economic zones to attract foreign investment, and other moves to bring the Chinese economy into closer contact with the outside world have enabled it to revitalize its economy and rapidly expand its agricultural and industrial production. The gross value of output increased by 8.8 percent in 1982, 10.2 percent in 1983, 15.2 percent in 1984, and 16.8 percent in 1985. China has thus become one of the main sources of economic dynamism in the Western Pacific. However, inflationary pressure built up once again in China during 1987–88, and the government has introduced tight monetary policies.

In summary, economic growth in the Pacific region has been market- and often export-oriented, has been fueled by a significant investment and savings effort, and has occurred both in manufacturing and agriculture. Moreover, there existed in the Pacific a climate of international cooperation that coordinated and reinforced the individual national efforts. This cooperation took the form of an intraregional division of labor which has aptly been called the "flying geese" pattern of development.[2] The leader surplus country develops new technologies, invests in countries that are at the earlier stages of industrialization, and absorbs the exports of these low-cost producers. The other countries in the region develop by following the lead countries. Once they expand their domestic markets, and open themselves to imports, all countries benefit from growing intraregional trade. In the Pacific region, for example, the United States developed first as the lead country. Beginning in the late nineteenth century, Japan began to develop its nondurable consumer goods, durable consumer goods, and capital goods sectors in that order. With Japan emerging as a new leader, the Asian NICs and the ASEAN countries are following Japan's development pattern and are rapidly expanding their production capacity.

7.3 Recent External Trade and Investment Performance in the Pacific Basin Region

So far, the Pacific region has successfully adopted a flying-geese pattern of diversified international division of labor led by the United States and Japan. The crucial question is whether and under what conditions such a development pattern can be continued in the future. To answer this question, this section analyzes the current situation and expected future trends in the most important countries of the Pacific region.

First consider the United States. In 1986, the U.S. total trade deficit reached $169.8 billion. Japan's share of the American trade deficit is about one-third. The United States has, furthermore, experienced trade deficits with the NICs every year since 1980. In 1986, it ran a $30.3 billion deficit in its trade with the NICs, which was nearly 20 percent of the total U.S. deficit.

The U.S. global trade imbalance reflects the large U.S. budget deficits that have been experienced since the early 1980s. The excess of consumer demand over the supply potential of the U.S. economy has been largely financed by savings from Japan, Europe, and the rest of the world. As a result, the United States, formerly a major source of development capital, is now the world's largest debtor nation.

It is clear that the United States cannot sustain a $170 billion deficit forever, and adjustments to reduce this deficit will inevitably be needed. To quote Professor Martin Feldstein at a National Bureau of Economic Research conference held in Palm Beach, Florida, on March 5–8, 1987: "The United States cannot continue to have annual trade deficits of more than $100 billion financed by an ever increasing inflow of foreign capital. The U.S. trade deficit will, therefore, soon shrink and, as it does, the other countries of the world will experience a corresponding reduction in their trade surpluses. Indeed, within the next decade, the United States will shift from a trade deficit to a trade surplus."

There are a number of changes evident in U.S. policy which will tend to correct the payments imbalance in the way predicted by Feldstein. One, for example, is the passage in December 1985 of the Gramm-Rudman-Hollings amendment requiring that the United States reduce its budget deficit from $200 billion to zero in five years. Another is the decision at the September 1986 Group of Five (G-5) meeting of finance ministers and central bankers from Japan, France, the United Kingdom, the United States, and West Germany to cooperate to correct the dollar's overvalued position in world currency markets. Since then, the dollar has depreciated sharply against the Japanese yen and the main Western European currencies. However, the value of the Canadian dollar, the Korean won, the Taiwanese dollar, and others have held steady or even depreciated against the dollar, which has limited the trade-weighted depreciation of the dollar. Moreover, the trade balance has been very slow in adjusting to the exchange rate changes.

For these reasons, increasingly protectionist pressures have built up in the United States, primarily directed against Japan and the Asian NICs. More and more the question is being asked whether the U.S. effort to turn its trade deficit around should depend solely on exchange rate adjustments, or whether more direct quantitative controls on imports, such as voluntary export restraints or import quotas, for example, should be used alongside these exchange rate adjustments.

In view of these developments, it is clear that in the coming years, the United States will no longer be a rapidly expanding market for the products of Asian and other countries. Depending on the degree of protectionism, the Asian Pacific region will be hurt more or less severely by America's reduction of imports.

In contrast to the United States, the Japanese economy has consistently recorded a substantial balance of payments surplus in the 1980s. There are a number of reasons for this. First is the fact that the economy has evolved from a resource-intensive, heavy-industry economy to a technology-intensive economy fueled by technological innovation. Second, Japanese automobiles, electronics, and other products are highly competitive in terms of both price and quality. And third, even though growth is slowing down and the appreciated yen is threatening to cause a severe recession, Japan's saving rate remains close to 20 percent of household income. This savings availability has enabled Japan to become a capital exporter and to achieve a structural surplus in its current account. However, there is a good chance that the rapid graying of the population, the expanded disbursements for social security entitlements, and increased personal consumption may erode the saving rate. Also, Japan may soon by exporting less and importing more as the rest of Asia industrializes and as higher Japanese wages make Japanese products less competitive in world markets. Nevertheless, it is expected that trade will continue to show a surplus and that Japan will continue to have a net outflow in its capital account for the transitional next decade or so.

The Asian NICs share a very strong export orientation and aggressive corporate management, as seen in their ambitious investment plans. Looking ahead, there is a need for these countries to stabilize their economies by expanding their domestic markets and reining in their export dependence, as well as to contribute to the growth of intraregional trade by opening their markets to imports. It is most encouraging that they have begun to contribute to intraregional economic growth and trade by offering cooperation, technology transfer, and other forms of assistance to the later-developing countries.

While development in the Asian NICs has already taken off, the

ASEAN countries are currently on the runway preparing for takeoff. Although their development will have to be based upon industrialization, taking advantage of their abundant labor and plentiful resources, the industrialized countries can do much to speed up this process with their capital and technology. And as wage levels rise in the Asian NICs, the ASEAN countries' labor-intensive products will become increasingly competitive. It is significant that these countries are shifting from import substitution to export promotion. As industrialization and urbanization progress, it will be increasingly important to improve the social infrastructure, including transportation, communication, and utilities. At the same time, the process of industrialization must be accompanied by enhanced productivity and broader diversity in agriculture.

Canada, Australia, and New Zealand will continue to be important suppliers of food products, energy, and other products for the region, and even greater market expansion can be expected as industrialization raises the standards of living in the nations of East Asia and ASEAN. These three countries also have an important role to play as industrialized countries providing assistance and technology transfer.

China has been promoting more open economic policies in recent years in light of the need to modernize its economy and technology. However, the country is bound to place primary emphasis on its domestic market in order to provide for its one billion citizens. Nevertheless, it is virtually inevitable that manufactured exports from China will, to some extent, come into competition with exports from the Asian NICs and the ASEAN countries. Given their different stages of development and China's resource reserves, the economic relations between China and the Pacific industrialized countries are complementary. The smooth development of the Chinese economy will contribute significantly to the expansion of trade and the promotion of economic growth in the Pacific region.

Given these trends, both an optimistic and a pessimistic scenario can be written for the Pacific region. In the optimistic view, the United States is able to reduce its budget and current account deficit. Japan and the countries in Europe push up their own growth rates enough to offset the deflationary impact of the adjustment in the United States and hence avert a contraction in world trade. Exports from the Asian NICs and the ASEAN countries continue to increase, and China further opens up its economy. The net capital outflow from Japan is directed towards financing investment projects in the ASEAN countries and China.

In the pessimistic scenario, Japan does not open its markets, while protectionism becomes even more virulent in the United States. Exports are stymied in the Asian NICs and ASEAN countries, the Chinese economy returns to its isolation, and economic disputes run rife. Given the fact that many countries of the Pacific region emphasize export-oriented policies, such a protectionist scenario could have a very adverse impact on the region's growth.

Japan's policy response is crucial for avoiding the pessimistic scenario. As a major creditor nation, the country should assume a leadership position. The next section discusses in greater detail what Japan can do and is doing to promote global economic development.

7.4 Japan's Contribution to Global Economic Development

In this section, I argue that the Japanese surplus should be directed toward financing the deficits of the developing countries. This would enhance the import capacity of these countries and sustain Japan's export-led growth. A growing Japanese economy would offset the decline in the growth momentum of the United States and counter any tendency toward world deflation. This is the basic idea of the April 1986 report by the World Institute for Development Economics Research (WIDER) entitled "The Potential of the Japanese Surplus for World Economic Development," which was written by WIDER Director Lal Jayawardena, WIDER Advisor on International Economic Issues and IMF Executive Director Arjun Sengupta, and myself as chairman of the WIDER governing board.

It is often argued that Japan needs to restructure its economy from growth dependent upon external demand to growth dependent on domestic demand.[3] However, while a part of the required policies most certainly involves stepping up Japanese investment geared to its domestic market, there are real difficulties in absorbing domestically a rate of saving as high as 27 percent of GNP. Likewise, exchange rate adjustments are important, but it should be recognized that there is a limit, economically and politically, to what they can achieve. Thus, even with all the best efforts that can be made to promote imports and to spur domestic demand, Japan will continue to record substantial current account surpluses for some years to come. As a consequence, Japan's net overseas assets could reach $730 billion by 1993, according to recent estimates based on the Economic Planning Agency's (EPA) world economic model.

The Japanese trade surplus is the consequence of an export-led expansion which has been the main source of growth in Japan. In the next several years, a high growth rate in Japan is necessary to offset the expected decline in U.S. growth. This implies sustaining the momentum of export growth in Japan. Even if this appears temporarily as a market loss for some countries like the United States, in the long run a growing world economy would allow for expansion of their markets. This would be the more so if Japanese export growth is attended by a recycling of her export surplus to finance the import surplus of the developing countries for products from industrial countries.

To achieve such recycling, it may be necessary for Japan to take a leadership role in formulating a "Marshall Plan" for the developing countries. One problem here is that the surpluses are entirely in the hands of the private sector. If the flow of capital is left to purely market mechanisms, the bulk of the capital will be drawn to the United States in search of investment security and high interest rates. Conscious policy measures, including risk insurance and interest subsidies to offset the low-interest and long-term nature of the return, are needed to divert at least some of this capital flow to the developing countries.

For its part, the government of Japan is moving to recycle its current account surplus to the developing countries with subscriptions to the Asian Development Bank, the IMF, the World Bank, and the International Development Agency (IDA). Following the extension of $1.3 billion of low-interest capital to the Asian Development Bank in 1985, Japanese Minister of Finance Kiichi Miyazawa stated at the 41st Joint Meetings of the IMF and the World Bank in September 1986, that Japan was prepared to make a special contribution of 3 billion SDRs (approximately $3.6 billion) to the IMF. In November 1986, Japan followed up by deciding on a $2.6 billion contribution to the IDA. Before 1986 was over, Japan had also agreed to assist the World Bank in raising an additional Y300 billion on the Tokyo capital market and to provide the World Bank with grant capital in the amount of Y30 billion in the three years starting in 1987. With this last set of agreements, it will be possible for the World Bank to channel an additional Y330 billion (approximately $2 billion) in development capital to the developing countries. Also in September 1986, the government of Japan announced a seven-year program to double its official development assistance by 1992.

These are among the positive steps taken so far by the Japanese government to recycle surplus savings to the developing countries. Yet substantial though they are, I believe that these efforts should be strengthened by adding further facilities for promoting the flow of capital. For example, an additional $10 billion a year of aid for a five-year period is not an impossible target. As Japan's military expenditure is about 1 percent of GNP, another 1 percent could be spent for global development assistance. An amount of $10 billion on top of the present overseas development assistance of 0.3 percent of GNP would eventually increase such assistance to the 1 percent target.

Combining government financial assistance with Japanese private direct investment, it would not be impossible for Japan alone to supply all of the foreign exchange capital that Asia needs for its development. China's seventh five-year plan (1986–90) calls for an expected $40 billion in foreign exchange. Likewise, India's seventh five-year plan for the same period will need $18 billion in foreign exchange. Indonesian development is expected to cost $2.5 billion in foreign exchange every year. All told, it is estimated that the

Asian countries' total foreign exchange requirements are somewhat under $20 billion a year. This is well below Japan's net long-term capital outflow of $65 billion in 1985.

7.5   The Future of Pacific Cooperation

In view of the increasing interdependence among the countries of the Pacific Basin and the challenges for economic development in the years ahead, there is a real need for cooperation between the countries in the region. The idea of economic cooperation has been a subject of active discussion among scholars, industrialists, and government officials. The following issues are of particular importance.

First, economic cooperation requires the participation of all countries concerned in institutions established for this specific purpose. In recent years, several platforms for discussing aspects of intraregional integration have emerged. In addition to the academically oriented Pacific Trade and Development Conference (PAFTAD) and the business-oriented Pacific Basin Economic Council (PBEC), the Pacific Economic Cooperation Conference (PECC) was established in September 1980. PECC has adopted a tripartite structure of scholars, businessmen, and government officials which enables it to take a pragmatic and flexible approach.

The PECC held its fifth general meeting in Vancouver in November 1986. Perhaps the highlight of this meeting was that Beijing and Taipei were both accepted as full members. Given the one-China policy pursued by both Beijing and Taipei, this question of Chinese representation is a very delicate issue, as has been shown, for example, in the dispute over membership in the Asian Development Bank. The Chinese participation not only presents a new facet for trade and economic relations within the Asia-Pacific region, but is very important for the political future of the region. It is imperative that a climate is created in which China can play a positive role in the interdependent systems of the Asia-Pacific region.

The Soviet Union is another major player that must be taken into account in discussing the outlook for the Asia-Pacific region. Having recognized the urgent imperative of revitalizing its economy under General Secretary Mikhail Gorbachev, the Soviet Union has become increasingly interested in the fast-growing Asia-Pacific region. Thus, General Secretary Gorbachev's speech in Vladivostok in July 1986 stated that the Soviet Union intends to take an active part in the future development of the region. Further indicative of the new Soviet interest in the Pacific was the application of the Soviet Union for membership in PECC.

While the organizational structure of the PECC serves well enough under the present circumstances, the establishment of a small-scale secretariat, somewhat after the model of the OECD, should be considered in the longer term. This would probably be something along the lines of the OPTAD (Organization for Pacific Trade and Development), as discussed within the PAFTAD several years ago. At the same time, the PECC should strengthen its ties with the other organizations mentioned above. Even so, given the diversity of countries within the Pacific region, it seems unlikely that an EEC-type of community structure can be achieved anytime soon.

Second, bilateral trade relations and problems, which affect the whole region, should be discussed by all countries concerned. As exchanges within the region expand, bilateral contacts are increasingly becoming multilateral contacts. For instance, Australian iron ore used to be supplied mainly to Japanese steel works. Now, however, it is also supplied to steel mills in Korea, Taiwan, and China. Likewise, the trade and economic relations between the United States and Japan have a major impact on the region's other trading countries. For example, the increase in U.S. beef exports to Japan has had an undeniable impact on Australian beef exports. Japan's efforts to lower tariff levels on plywood and chicken will not only benefit the United States but also the countries of Southeast Asia. At the same time, the liberalization of the yen, as agreed between Japan and the United States, will have a major impact upon financial markets in the other Pacific countries. It is clear that these issues need to be discussed, not simply as bilateral concerns, but as issues of interest to all the countries of the region.

Third, the Pacific countries should widen their cooperation to noneconomic issues. They should enhance their cultural, scientific, technological, educational, and other exchanges which will demand consciously planned efforts by governments, universities, and other parties involved.

Fourth, the Pacific region offers an excellent opportunity to address global issues on a regional basis. In particular, the presence of both industrialized and developing countries allows a regional approach to north-south issues. The search for global solutions by the United Nations and other forums has been hampered by the the diversity of the economies in the south and the conflicting interests in the north. Hopefully, promoting a discussion at the Pacific-regional basis will open new perspectives for the global dialogue. In this context, it is significant that the ASEAN countries, Australia, Japan, Canada, New Zealand, and the United States included human resources development in the agenda of their July 1985 meeting in Jakarta.

Finally, Pacific cooperation should, in principle, look beyond the region itself. It is hoped that the countries outside the region, for example the European countries, will be able to participate positively in the Pacific region's development. Pacific integration must be an outward-looking rather than an inward-looking regionalism. For example, while it would be well to state a common position for the pacific region in the new (Uruguay) round of GATT talks, institutionalizing discriminatory regional preferences should be avoided. At the same time, of course, it is only right that regional cooperation in such areas as financing, development assistance, personnel exchanges, and a regional scheme for compensatory financing to stabilize commodity earnings should be promoted.

7.6 Conclusion

In the last decade or so, the Pacific has emerged as the fastest growing region in the world economy. The challenge for the next years is to maintain these high growth rates in spite of the profound structural adjustments which are needed to correct the current imbalances in world trade.

Among the main problems facing the world economy today are the major current account surpluses in Japan and West Germany, the twin fiscal and trade deficits in the United States, and the developing countries' external indebtedness. These imbalances generate frictions, and there is an inherent fear that the European and North American countries could increasingly turn to protectionism. Accordingly, it is imperative that the necessary structural adjustments are made and that an effort be made to expand intraregional trade in the Pacific. This would strengthen economic and trade relations and help to fend off the protectionist threat to the free-trading system that has sustained the export-oriented economies of the Pacific. It is crucial, furthermore, that policies can be devised to make the Japanese savings surplus available to the world economy at large and to encourage greater Japanese imports in keeping with the yen's appreciation. By directing a part of the massive capital outflow from Japan to the developing countries, it should be possible for Japan to contribute to the growth both of the world economy and the Asia-Pacific region.

All of this will require an active cooperation among the countries in the region. The birth of regional cooperation cannot be entirely left to the midwife of market mechanisms. Rather, we need a steady and pragmatic approach, with all the countries of the region working step-by-step to promote mutual understanding, to conduct studies on the Pacific economy, to draw up specific action programs, and to otherwise encourage cooperation in full awareness of the mandate of history. In short, we should seek to maximize this Pacific dynamism so that it may become the driving force for dynamism throughout the world economy.

Notes

1. The ASEAN countries include Brunei, Indonesia, Malaysia, The Philippines, Thailand, and Singapore.
2. This term was coined in the 1930s by the Japanese economist, Kaname

Akamatsu, who also originated the concept of dynamic change in the international division of labor. See Akamatsu (1987).

3. See, for instance, the Maekawa Report (formally, the Report of the Advisory Group on Economic Structural Adjustment for International Harmony) of April 1986.

Reference

Akamatsu, K. 1987. A theory of unbalanced growth in the world economy. *Weltwirtschaftliches Archiv* 86:196–214.

3 MARKET STRUCTURE AND THE STRUCTURE OF INTERNATIONAL TRADE AND INVESTMENT

8 "Market Access" in International Trade

Richard Harris

8.1 Introduction

My task in this paper was to review the literature on "market access," principally the theoretical work, although with suitable reference to the relevant empirical literature or stylized facts. In addition, it was desirable that the theory could be related to the current situation in Japan-U.S.-Canada trade. When I first accepted the invitation to write such a paper, it seemed a fairly straightforward task. After all, we have a large body of literature on the "new trade theory" and "strategic trade policy" which could use summarizing, and there is certainly no lack of policy discussion or reports in the daily business press as to particular problems concerning market access. But what I started out to write is not what I finished, for a couple of reasons.

My first reason is that there is a problem in attempting to understand the proper use of the term "market access." As widely used in everyday language concerning international commerce, it does not have a corresponding technical term in the professional language of international trade specialists, In the theory of commercial policy, we often make reference to a variety of domestic policies which affect trade, and the ultimate effect of a number of these is either to raise the price of foreign goods and/or to reduce the quantity of foreign goods in the home market. Import substitution is the generic term we might use to refer to this whole set of policies. On the other hand, the term "market access" is much too vague for many purposes, but it is nevertheless widely used. Of particular note is the frequency with which this term is used in discussing the problems of Japan-U.S. trade. The apparent perception by a large segment of the American public that U.S. and other foreign firms do not have market access to the Japanese economy obviously does not refer to tariffs or quotas since, as so many observers have noted, these are virtually nonexistent.[1] The lack of market access in this case often refers to a

The author is grateful to the discussants for helpful comments. They are not, of course, responsible for the views expressed or any errors in the paper.

set of implicit guidelines and procedures followed by Japanese firms and the government, which effectively deny foreign firms the ability to sell their goods in the Japanese market when offered at, what seems to an outsider to be, a comparable price-quality package. The assertion that these implicit but ill-specified barriers exist remains thus far just that, an assertion. Nevertheless, it is one which is widely believed.

In terms of generating a useful taxonomy then, these observations suggest one definition of market access as: a foreign seller has market access if that firm can capture a reasonable market share relative to firm size and degree of competition in the market, provided the product is offered at favorable price-quality terms relative to the home-produced competing product. This definition is hardly precise enough, but it explicitly excludes those instruments of government policy directly focused on imports. It also, unfortunately, suggests a test for lack of market access, the failure to sell, which is of little practical use.

Another use of the term "market access" is commonly heard in Canada and other smaller countries which sell a large proportion of their total exports to a single market. In the case of Canada, the market in question is the United States, and Canadian newspapers are full of either complaints or worries by various exporters that they will be denied access to the U.S. market, or that they will be offered access but on terms not nearly as favorable as they felt once existed. Separating the substance from the rhetoric in these stories, as in the case of U.S.-Japan trade, is extremely difficult. Given the low level of tariff barriers now existing between Canada and the United States, what these comments often refer to are the exporters' worries about the application of U.S. trade law, either dumping or countervail, to their particular product. The increasing use of "contingent-protection" devices by a number of countries has worried many individuals in the trade policy community.[2] But the exporter from a small country has a particular worry, because in many cases the existence of the firm is crucially dependent upon this access. In this case it is the risk of losing that access which creates intense concern. This offers us yet another definition of market access as the *security* of the right to sell in a market without undue interference from government.

There is yet a third, but even more subtle, use of the term "market access" which is common to discussions of U.S.-Japan trade and Canada-U.S. trade. This use of the term surfaces most commonly in the strategic trade policy literature. Market access is often said to be restricted when the practices of competing firms (and sometimes their governments) lead to anticompetitive or entry-deterring results. A U.S. firm might complain about the nature of vertical integration in the Japanese market which makes it difficult for the firm to distribute in that market.[3] Canadian firms are often attempting to get enough volume for the economies of scale necessary to compete, not only for export, but with imports in the home market as well. If the

Canadian firms encounter predatory or entry-deterring practices by incumbent U.S. oligopolists, who are usually firms of considerably larger size, the Canadian firms will complain about market access.[4] In both these instances the lack of market access is rooted in the competitive practices of existing firms. This type of market access problem is hardly new, and is indeed the basis for a great deal of domestic industrial organization theory and antitrust policy. The global integration of markets has merely made common what was once a principal concern only in domestic economic policy.

This last definition or motivation for market access problems is, on theoretical grounds, fairly straightforward to address using what is known from oligopoly theory, and will be taken up in section 8.4 below. The strategic trade policy literature asks what incentives governments face in respect of policies affecting international oligopolistic industries. It is not my intention to survey this literature here. Concern with government intervention in these circumstances obviously bears on the *equality* of access to a national market and the potential for "beggar-thy-neighbor" outcomes. But this is one problem about which a great deal has been written, and we probably understand fairly well what the theory has to tell us.

Is there a theme then to the topic "market access" or are these alternative definitions just a loose collection of problems motivated by new and old trade disputes? My answer is a qualified yes. The theme is grounded in the well known "gains from trade theorem" that neoclassical economists are so fond of propagating to undergraduates and policymakers. That theorem loosely says that gains from trade are maximized, and hence exhausted, by the "free and uninhibited" exchange between nations. Free and uninhibited exchange is identified with the equilibrium of the neoclassical model of competitive markets. The new trade theory emphasizing imperfect competition casts considerable doubt on the generality of gains from trade since it starts with the assumption that competition is not perfect because structural characteristics of industries exist, such as scale economies or product differentiation, which make the competitive model inappropriate as either a positive or normative model of international trade. In a narrow theoretical and empirical sense I think this is true, but at a broader level economists tend to believe in a more general gains from trade theorem.

The quest for preservation of market access, in any of the three senses defined, can be thought of as a desirable, if not necessarily achievable, prerequisite for preserving the broader gains from trade. Economic competition is an important means to structure incentives so as to achieve these gains. Beyond these generalities, however, market access is probably an issue-specific topic. One of the conclusions of this paper is that it is quite important not to confuse alternative notions of market access.

The rest of the paper proceeds as follows. In section 8.2 the first definition of market access is taken up, and some attempt is made to sketch out a theory of "cultural entry barriers," for lack of a better term. In section 8.3 the basic issue of security of market access is examined. The perspective offered by a global industrial organization view is taken up in section 8.4.

8.2 Cultural Bias as an Import Barrier

To build a theory of import barriers around the idea of cultural bias is not an easy task using conventional economics, which suggests why many economists are perhaps justifiably skeptical of the whole idea. But let us see how far some simple theory can take us.

One starting point is the basic idea that ingrained habits are hard to change because sunk costs are sunk, and a change to an uncertain mode of organization and supply brings with it a host of contingent uncertainties that cannot be insured against. Williamson's (1975) writing on exchange is a good place to start here. Foreign firms may face barriers to selling in the Japanese market simply because most economic activity is a lot more complex than the simple exchange of a Ford for yen. The complex nature of modern products makes close customer-dealer relationships important. Foreign firms simply cannot make it in the Japanese market place in this model because they have not invested sufficiently in establishing the necessary exchange and customer-specific capital. This would involve extensive training of personnel in Japan, heavy investment in distribution networks within Japan, and a demonstrated long-term commitment to the Japanese market. For lack of a better term, let me refer to this as the "social networking theory of barriers to selling." A simple test of the theory would be that it ought to be a lot harder for foreigners to sell software in Japan than toasters or raw materials.

The social networking theory has a couple of obvious implications and one serious deficiency. First, a firm attempting to sell a complex product in the foreign market in which these network externalities are important may well prefer to do it via licensing the technology or via joint ventures, rather than through either export or foreign direct investment (the latter involving fairly direct control of the subsidiary by the home parent firm). Second, the success of entry for a given product will be greater, the longer the experience in the particular network. This is a version of the old "success breeds success" story. The deficiency of the theory is that it does not adequately explain why firms do not invest in breaking into the network if the returns are as high as claimed. Under a strict economic rationality hypothesis, all firms should be able to do these calculations, and if the returns are there, the appropriate investment should be observed. One possible defense against this criticism is rooted in the nonappropriability of the interfirm benefits of the network. Reference is often made in the case of Japan to the role of the *keiretsu* as preserving control and denying access to a particular market.[5] After the liberalization which occurred in Japan, foreign firms could not appropriate the spillovers from these organizations because of the overwhelming importance of reputation in these circumstances. Thus it was a case of barriers to entry against all outsiders, including potential domestic Japanese competitors as well as foreign firms. Some weak corroborating evidence of this is the low rate of entry and the persistence of the initial postwar firms within Japanese industrial structure.[6]

A more elaborate theory of "cultural entry barriers" can be erected out of a version of Akerlof's (1980) "theory of social custom," used by him to provide an explanation of unemployment, which in turn is an elaboration of Arrow's (1972) theory of discrimination in labor markets. In the context of international trade in goods, the discrimination is by domestic entrepreneurs and consumers against foreign products, when ostensibly there are economic benefits to not engaging in discrimination against these products. If the benefits exist, why does discrimination persist? In Akerlof's answer to this puzzle he introduces the idea that individual utility depends upon reputation in the community, and reputation in turn depends upon adherence to a code of behavior. The crucial element in the story, however, is that the importance of the code in contributing to reputation is related positively to the fraction of the population that believes in the code. If a large fraction of the population believes in it, then adherence to the code is much more important than when only a small fraction believes. The model is closed by slow adjustment of those who actually believe in the code, as a function of the discrepancy between the number who believe in and the number who actually adhere to it. For example, the number who believe in the code increases if the number currently believing it is greater than the number adhering to the code.

The interesting thing about these models is that they typically exhibit multiple equilibria. I claim, but will not show here, that this type of social behavior model can be applied to develop a model of discrimination against foreign goods. In this case the "code of behavior" is the belief that consuming domestically produced goods is important for the community and an act of patriotism. There are then two (or more) equilibria in the model. One equilibrium involves a high level of belief in and adherence to the code, and another involves a relatively low level of belief in and adherence to the code. In the former equilibrium, potential pecuniary benefits from breaking the code are foregone because of the severe loss of reputation in the community from breaking the code.

Now the interesting question in this model is: why might a country settle at one equilibrium versus the other? As Akerlof points out in his model, an important determinant of the equilibrium is the strength of utility loss from breaking the code. The greater the utility loss, the more stable any equilibrium is, and the faster an out-of-equilibrium situation will converge. It is worth noting that social custom can persist even if the utility costs of not following the custom are small to some individuals. Individual incentives to break with custom in this case can be weak because individual pecuniary incentives depend upon arranging mutual exchanges which benefit from simultaneous and mutual violation of the custom. In any case, the model gives a fairly simple explanation of why we occasionally see residents of particular countries exhibit what seem to be "unwarranted" preference for home goods. In the description of the Japanese postwar economy, this does not seem to be an implausible explanation given the homogeneity of belief in the population of the necessity to rebuild the Japanese economy.

The implications for trade of this model are quite interesting. The usual gains from trade are foregone, but replaced with reputation-enhancing consumption of the domestic good by all home consumers. The alternative equilibrium is one in which the "code" remains a belief in the virtues of buying domestic, but there is consumption of foreign goods by a large fraction of the population. A slightly different way of saying this is that the equilibrium in which all consume the cheap imports is welfare superior, because the reputation loss from buying foreign is small, given that everyone else is doing it. Note that as long as reputation per se is important in utility and not the code itself, the "free trade" equilibrium will be welfare superior to the "buy home" equilibrium.

Imagine now a foreign firm trying to sell their product into a market which is firmly entrenched in the "buy domestic" equilibrium. Their best hope is that, by offering a sufficiently superior price-quality package, they can attract some buyers for whom the reputation utility loss effect is small. However, if fixed costs for entering a foreign market are sufficiently large, then the returns from a relatively small market would not justify the necessary investment required. On the other hand, if fixed costs for entry are low and, in addition, the domestic-foreign difference in price-quality large, then there is a chance that entry will take place, albeit on a small scale. The dynamics of the process might ultimately lead to more and more consumers breaking the code and, over time, a lessening of the reputation losses from buying an import. Ultimately a new equilibrium would be established without discrimination against imports. From the anthropological point of view, the code in question is possibly malleable. A different set of dynamics might emerge if society could be convinced of the possible superiority of an alternative "free trade code." As in the racial discrimination problem, this is not easy to accomplish, although economic incentives play an important role in determining the ultimate status and stability of the codes that society adopts.

Returning to the question of market access, it seems clear that in the social custom model there is little that foreign firms can do. The potential importing country as a whole has an equilibrium-induced bias against foreign products which must appear as a form of "discrimination" to outsiders who do not appreciate the custom.[7] Is there a case for an "equal opportunity trade act?" Perhaps, although it seems difficult to imagine how such a law might be written. In traditional trade law, the concept of "national treatment" by governments deals with this to a considerable degree, but to apply it to millions of uncoordinated and uncoerced consumers seems fanciful. Subsidization of exports by the country discriminated against or subsidization of imports by the discriminating country might tip the scales in the long run toward the nonbiased equilibrium. However, whether the cost is warranted seems doubtful.

It seems important to recognize that the ability of a social custom or code to sustain itself strongly depends on the ability of all to recognize when they and others are breaking or following the custom. In the case of discrimination against imports, the custom is viable if the consumption of the import is recognized and visible. Durable goods with brand names are obvious candidates. Alternatively, consumption of simple goods or unidentified raw materials does not detract much from one's reputation as a nationalist if no one knows whether the good is domestic or foreign. There are two lessons to be learned from this. First, market access is going to be most problematic in those products where brand names and durability are most important. Second, the globalization of assembly and production operations by firms is making life tough for die-hard national consumers. "Made in the U.S.A." is little guarantee that much of any real economic activity related to the labeled good occurred within the United States. This generic false advertising provides an obvious solution to firms faced with product discrimination based on nationality of origin: invest in trying to convince domestic consumers that it is actually a home good. This policy has been practiced for years by foreign firms in North America, and is probably well worth U.S. firms trying abroad.

An interesting feature of equilibrium in this model is that country size and the initial pattern of specialization in production can be important in determining the viability of the "buy domestic" equilibrium. A small country which would otherwise be greatly specialized bears a very heavy cost if it settles in the "buy domestic" equilibrium. As a result, it is most susceptible to shocks in the absence of intervention. A deterioration in real income from goods consumption, for example, raises the relative importance of reputation as a source of individual utility. This can actually enhance the viability of the buy domestic equilibrium should it settle there. Secondly, because imports as a share of GNP are inevitably larger for small countries, terms-of-trade shocks carry proportionately greater real-goods-income impact than in large countries. When the terms of trade improve, on the other hand, while reputation becomes less important as a share of total utility, the *marginal* economic cost of satisfying the code becomes less. The net impact on the equilibrium is not clear. In the case of Canada it has been observed that periods of nationalism are most intense when times are good, and discrimination against foreign supply sources coincides with these periods.[8] This suggests that reputation in the utility function of individuals yields a higher marginal utility when goods income is high. Notice, however, that this model suffers from hysteresis, that is, the outcome is not initial-condition independent. In large countries the utility cost of obeying the code is going to be relatively less than in small countries, given that imports are a smaller share of total consumption in large countries. Thus the incentives to deviate significantly from the code are smaller. This suggests that an autarkic equilibrium in a large country will be more robust than in the small country.

8.3 Security of Market Access

A common feature of modern industrial societies is that governments of all levels intervene in markets for a variety of objectives and no less than in the area of trade. Many observers have noted that the system of tariffs traditionally used for protection within the GATT has come to be replaced with a variety of administrative trade interferences.[9] Some have labeled the current practices of governments in the trade area as "contingent protection," the contingencies usually being motivated by some considerations of injury to the domestic industry. For my purposes, the two important characteristics of contingent protection are that: (a) the contingencies which trigger the protection are essentially random events caused by unanticipated changes in technology, factor endowments, and the phase of the business cycle across different countries; and (b) the mechanism for triggering the administrative procedures, through which contingent protection is offered, is a process which to some degree is controlled by those seeking the protection and also by those against which the protection is directed. In order to focus the discussion, I shall first treat the simpler case where contingent protection is entirely random, and then turn to the more difficult problem where the participants affect the probabilities of protection being implemented.

It is unfortunate that, while the trade policy literature has had a fair amount to say about trade under a system of contingent protection, the theoretical trade literature has relatively little to offer.[10] Nevertheless, there is a reasonably large literature on market structures under uncertainty, and the basic lessons of that literature are fairly straightforwardly applicable.

We start by focusing on a single country with imports and domestic firms competing in a single market. The contingency protection can be thought of as either a quantitative restriction, say on market share, or a temporary duty such as might be levied under the U.S. countervail system. The crucial distinction with respect to market structure is the costs of entry and exit relative to the time frame of investment. One extreme case, referred to as "perfect contestability," is characterized by entry and exit that is without cost and instantaneous. At the other extreme, referred to as "permanent commitment," exit is completely infeasible short of shutting down all economic operations, and the cost of doing so is a complete write-off on all investment associated with the market.[11] In the latter situation we say that sunk costs (as distinct from fixed costs) occupy a large share of total costs. In the context of internationally traded goods and services, it is worthwhile making the distinction between distribution activities located in the country of final sale, and production, management, R&D, etc., activities which are assumed to be located in the exporting country. The degree of contestability versus commitment can vary depending upon whether one is referring to distribution or production. For example, a fairly standardized good with large-scale economies of production may involve a substantial degree of commitment in production, but distribution can be carried out in small retail outlets with no sunk costs and hence be contestable at that end of the market. On the other hand, in numerous activities involving services or complex products, the important commitment is in the distribution end of the market. Obviously, some products involve both. Old style trade theory is perhaps best suited to characterize trade in commodities where both production and distribution are perfectly contestable. Agricultural products and raw materials come to mind, although even this is not strictly true if distribution networks are product specific and subject to large-scale economies.

If both distribution and production of imports are perfectly contestable, then analysis of contingent protection is exactly analogous to the traditional analysis of protection. Anticipation effects are unimportant and the costs and benefits of protection are much as given in the textbooks. Suppose, however, that production is an activity with a high degree of commitment, say, due to large indivisibilities in capital equipment required for manufacturing. The ex post effect of contingent protection on the exporting firm can be quite significant, depending upon the share of the firm's sales in the foreign market. If all sales are in the foreign market, then the cost can be extremely dramatic, causing bankruptcy, layoffs, and other forms of economic distress. From the perspective of the country imposing the protection, the short-run impact on investment is likely to be small, given the significance of historical sunk costs in the industry. Rather, the main impact will be a restoration of profitability relative to the variable costs in the industry. This, however, is not the end of the story. In a world in which contingent protection is random but statistically anticipated to occur with some known frequency, ex ante investment decisions by both exporters and import-competing firms will be significantly affected. Exporters' expected returns on irreversible production investment will be lower as a result of the existence of contingent protection, and import-competing firms' expected returns will be higher on sunk investment. However, in a multimarket world, the extent to which the exporters cut back on investment would depend on their ability to shift sales from one market into another and on the size of their commitment to the protecting market relative to the total sales of the firm. There are implications of this model. First, the ability of contingent protection to affect exporters' long-term market penetration of a given country will be directly related to the size of the country importing relative to total sales. Thus, large countries using contingent protection against firms who sell only in the large country's market clearly will have the biggest impact. Second, small countries or countries which use contingent protection against products for which sales are a small fraction of total sales will obviously have little long-run impact on the total share of imports in the market.

Suppose now that we complicate matters by allowing that distribution as well as production is an activity with a high degree of commitment. In this situation, the difference is that even large diversified firms selling in the global market are subject to "hostage effects." The protection on the imported good is likely to induce losses to importing firms on the investment in distribution. If the distribution network is product specific, then it is possible that the domestic competitors will be able to buy up the distribution assets at firesale prices. The long-term impact in this case, however, is likely to involve shifting production activity from the exporting country to the country imposing the contingent protection. This shift in activity will be more significant the greater the size of investment in distribution activities relative to production activities, and the lesser the cost-competitive differences between production in the two locations. In this case, the probability of contingent protection can have an important effect on the location of economic activity.

If distribution is perfectly contestable, say through a short-term, arm's-length licensing arrangement with a foreign distributor which is without cost to negotiate, then the impact of contingent protection on location of production facilities is not likely to be as significant. In fact, if large-scale economies are present as well as large sunk costs in production, then there are certain advantages to not moving production to the country imposing the contingency protection. The benefits of large-scale production located at a single source may well overcome temporary losses in sales due to the imposition of the protection in a single country. If a firm is selling in several foreign countries, provided protection incidents are not highly positively correlated across countries, then scale plus diversification will outweigh the losses in any single country.

Let us now turn to a different aspect of the problem where the granting of contingency protection, under whatever administrative procedure is used, involves activities by both parties affected. First, there will be investment on the part of those seeking protection to bring their problem to the attention of the appropriate authorities. The costs of this administrative procedure may not be trivial and, of course, involve an investment which is highly uncertain in its return. Second, firms exporting into this market can affect the ex ante probabilities by modifying their behavior. Ex post, they may also have to invest in the administrative procedures attempting to deflect potential protection. Assume that the granting of contingent protection is dependent upon meeting some objectively measurable criterion. Of course, if the whole process is entirely subject to political manipulation, this last characteristic may not be true. But let us assume this is not the case, and protection is granted only if some objective evidence can be presented that a certain criterion is satisfied. A test of "injury" for example might be that the market share of imports reaches a certain level, or that employment falls below a certain specified minimum. Obviously, the particular form of the test will affect the results. For our purposes, what is important is that the form of the test be known by all. Random exogenous circumstances raise or lower the probability that the test might or might not be met.

Suppose now that trade between countries is essentially "free" of government interference, except that all countries use administrative trade laws that work as described. In this case the interesting feature of the process is the way that individual and collective incentives differ on the part of import-competing versus exporting firms. The import-competing firms in any country face a curious incentive structure, assuming the market is subject to a high degree of commitment. A large discontinuity appears in the payoff function of these firms if they can invest sufficiently and demonstrate that the test of injury is satisfied. The discontinuity occurs at the point on the scale where injury is found. From the importer's perspective it is a zero-one situation with either "relief" being granted or not, ex post. If relief is granted under the procedure to all industry members, which is typically the case, then there is little in the way of free-rider problems given: (i) individual payoffs are approximately equal to the firm's market share times the domestic industry's payoff; and (ii) the discontinuity in industry payoff function occurs at some critical level of investment in lobbying. Any single firm behaving Nash with respect to the other firms actually puts itself in the position of being the pivotal firm. That is, each individual firm views itself as determining at the margin whether relief will be granted or not to all in the industry. Thus a curious conjunction of private and industry incentives coincide. The industry will invest sufficiently to raise the expected return from relief to exceed the necessary cost of investment.

Full knowledge by the exporting firms of the test for granting contingent protection usually means that they have some degree of collective control over the probabilities of the test being satisfied and, hence, of contingent protection being granted or market access denied. If the industry is highly collusive, then rational decision making would take the existence of the contingent protection mechanism into account, and result in a reduction in exports to the country in question below the quantity that would prevail in the absence of the protection mechanism. However, if the industry is not collusive, being either a noncooperative oligopoly or a competitive industry, the free-rider problem looms large in the background, depending upon how the contingency protection mechanism works. Market share rules involve a restriction of the exports of a particular firm, depending upon its historical market share. They can actually induce the firm to attempt to increase its market share at the expense of the other exporting rivals, anticipating that the most probable outcome will be protection, and wanting as large a share of the protected, and possibly high profit, market that it can get.[12]

If duties are the mechanism by which contingency protection works, then clearly all firms have an incentive to avoid duties being levied on their sales in the foreign market. However, if this avoidance involves a collective reduction in total output, then we have a classic game of timing, a "war of attrition," in which the first firm to reduce sales in the importing country loses the most and leaves the biggest gains to those remaining. But refusal by all to decrease sales, increases the probability of damage to all as time goes on. Equilibrium in such games is quite sensitive to some assumptions, but usually ends up with opponents playing mixed strategies, thus giving a probabilistic outcome as to what will happen, which is that one firm eventually gives up and the winner takes all. Note that for this story to make sense the market must involve a fairly high degree of commitment on the production side. The theory is not terribly robust in situations like these, but it is clear that individual and collective incentives differ on the part of firms exporting to markets with contingent protection mechanisms. On balance it seems that equilibrium is going to involve a significant amount of investment by import-competing firms (and workers) in triggering administrative protection. On the side of those firms against whom the protection is directed, individual incentives are not as clear. It is certainly not the case that they will necessarily take actions which insure them against the protection contingency. This can either be because the protection itself is beneficial to the exporting firms, or because of a conflict between the incentives facing individual firms and those facing exporting firms collectively.

As a final comment in this section, I would like to remark on the risk-shifting aspect of contingent protection. Much of what has been said thus far is true independent of whether or not firms are risk averse. For many industries with large sunk costs, there are associated sunk costs in public infrastructure, human capital, and individual attachment to community and location. In short, risk aversion on the part of all the specific factors in the industry is a quite plausible assumption. We know that a great deal of domestic and international policy is an attempt to reduce the risk to immobile factors of production. Procedures of contingent protection by their very nature introduce an additional random variable into the resource allocation process, beyond the usual uncertainty associated with shifts in technology, comparative advantage, and state of the business cycle. At the same time, the contingent protection is often administered with the intent of reducing the income risk of industry-specific domestic factors of production. An old argument for the tariff was that it reduced the exposure of the economy to foreign shocks, thus stabilizing domestic income. Basically the same issue arises here. In the absence of complete insurance markets, one can ask whether contingent protection serves as some second-best policy for dealing with risk shifting at a global level. I think that in particular models you could probably come to this conclusion. For example, Newberry and Stiglitz (1981), in a class of very simple models that dealt with international risk shifting under incomplete markets, came to the conclusion that quotas near a free trade equilibrium could be welfare improving. In their analysis, quotas were permanent and independent of the state of the world. Their model can be generalized to deal with state-dependent quotas and tariffs, and the logic remains the same. An appropriate system of contingent protection could improve the global allocation of risk given rational expectations and incomplete insurance markets. The idea, then, is that in granting relief to industry X in the home country via contingent protection, the cost is borne by industry X in the foreign country and consumers in the home country. The loss in expected aggregate world real income is more than offset by the reduction in total risk faced by all industries in all countries. A suitable contingent protection policy for each industry in each country might be Pareto superior to free trade, using expected utility as the appropriate criterion.

It strikes me, however, that there are three problems with taking this argument seriously. First, there are probably much better instruments to deal with the risk-shifting problem domestically, such as unemployment insurance and equity markets. Second, the optimal second-best policy involves policy coordination on the part of all countries practicing contingent protection—a desirable objective, but one which has proved elusive. Third, the risk problem is, for practical purposes, insurmountable for small countries with export industries which involve a high degree of commitment either in capital or labor. Contingent protection by one country attempting to shift the risk of some given shock to other countries will impose costs which are far less diversifiable in small countries, where any given industry is both more dependent on exports and relatively larger in the economy. Small countries inevitably have to face the normal risks that international trade and possible loss of competitive advantage entail, and they are the inevitable recipients of large countries' attempts to shift these risks abroad. In situations of large asymmetry in country size, I would argue that Pareto-improving contingent protection mechanisms are unlikely to be viable as long-term institutional mechanisms for dealing with international risk sharing.

This leaves the interesting but unanswered question of what are the desirable tools for the international sharing of sector-specific risks? Market access, or temporary lack thereof, due to contingent protection mechanisms, is for many the major "market access" problem of the global trading system. It is a subject deserving greater attention from the theorists.

8.4 Barriers to Entry and the "New" International Trade Theory

In this last section I wish to take a different tack than in the previous sections and review briefly some old "new" ground on the relationship between international trade and industrial organization, and then offer a perspective on the role that endogenous market access plays as a determinant of international market structure and trade patterns. The theme of this section centers around the idea that conditions of market access in an industry can lead to equilibrium in the absence of government intervention in which resources are allocated differently than true comparative advantage would indicate. I shall first comment on the relationship between the new trade theory and the market access problem, and then return to the task of how conventional barriers to entry in concentrated industries affect international trade.

The new trade theory, and its bastard child—strategic trade policy— have been the focus of considerable attention in the journals for the last few years, and have been surveyed by a number of authors including Dixit (1986) and Richardson (1986). The explicit adoption of assumptions regarding imperfect competition, scale economies, and the role for strategic precommitment have generated a class of models in which a number of traditional conclusions have been upset. This is not surprising since departures from the basic assumptions of competitive models raise all those problems dealing with second best, nonconvexities, incomplete markets, and other assorted neoclassical nightmares. The new trade theory, however, has not concentrated a great deal on market access as defined thus far in the paper, other than by consideration of traditional instruments of trade policy, tariffs, quotas, and subsidies.

Beyond the theoretical points made, the reason that this literature has struck such a sympathetic cord in the trade policy and business community is the belief that imperfect competition and scale economies actually are important in explaining real world markets. To give a personal example, within Canada where trade theory is standard fare for any undergraduate and a necessity for any professional economist, the arguments as to the costs and benefits of trade liberalization which were most persuasive and documented most convincingly came from the field of industrial organization and not from international trade theory. A whole generation of economists studied the impact of domestic protection on fostering collusive oligopolistic behavior and inefficient scale and product specialization within the firm. As the productivity gap between Canadian industry and its competitors grew during the period of high protection, the plausibility of the arguments of this group increased and, furthermore, were understood by those involved in industry and government.

In the current international trade environment, the U.S. trade deficit, rightly or wrongly, has sparked a search for new explanations of why American industry has fallen behind. The imperfect competition story has fallen on sympathetic ears in the United States, where a large cross section of American industries find that their toughest competition is a few large firms based in Japan, but increasingly also in smaller countries of the Pacific Rim or other newly industrializing countries (NICs).

What can we learn from the simple models that have been used by international trade theorists to explain oligopolistic competition in the international arena? One thing that is easily learned is that a variety of simple models can lead to different policy conclusions, as Eaton and Grossman (1983) and Dixit and Kyle (1985) have pointed out. Beyond that, however, I think that there are three important lessons from this literature. The first is that an increase in actual, as distinct from potential, competition will generally reduce the causes of monopoly power and yield welfare gains. With international trade, an important mechanism for fostering competition is the maintenance of an open economic border across which entrepreneurs can arbitrage profitable opportunities. The second lesson is that, in the presence of scale economies, product differentiation, learning economies, or R&D costs, there are significant benefits to a larger market size. Unlike the neoclassical theory of trade, country size per se is not neutral in its effects, and increasing market size through trade is an important vehicle by which real income gains are enhanced. Finally, potential, as distinct from actual, competition in dynamic models of imperfect competition raises the possibility that incumbent firms may undertake actions to reduce market access to new entrants. This is an issue which has been studied intensively in the field of industrial organization, but has yet to be really given serious consideration in international trade. The significance of this issue will be taken up below.

The first two lessons noted, while not directly about market access, certainly cast light on the issue in a number of ways. Relative to the traditional theory, the first lesson is really quite new. In the traditional model, all firms were perfect competitors operating at assumed full technical efficiency and price equal to private marginal cost. Obviously, open market access might be used as a generic term to describe circumstances when the procompetitive benefits of trade liberalization are most likely to obtain. The second lesson, while new, is closely related to the spirit of the Ricardian model of comparative advantage in which achieving world production efficiency involves specialization of production across countries. The points raised in lesson two are simply put by the observation that world production efficiency requires locationally concentrated large-scale production and specialization. Whether markets themselves approximate such efficient allocations is an open question.

The basic problem is that the new theory does not have a "gains from trade" result of the same generality or status of the gains-from-trade theorem in neoclassical theory. In the traditional theory every country benefits from free trade relative to autarky. Unfortunately no such theorem exists for the class of models with imperfect competition and scale economies. The strongest result we have in this case is due originally to Markusen and Melvin (1981), who demonstrate in a particular model that a country gains from trade if the increasing-returns sector expands relative to autarky. This is a sufficient and not a necessary condition. The problem of course is that from the world point of view, it is unlikely that all countries can have increasing-returns sectors that will expand. Some country has to have that sector contract or, as is more likely, disappear altogether. In short, the world distribution of gains from trade is far from clear in models that underlie the "new" trade theory. If it were to turn out that one could demonstrate that under certain structural conditions a country would clearly lose from trade, this would substantially undermine the free trade position held by neoclassical economists. The subject requires a great deal more research, but it may well be that no general "clean" results are going to be forthcoming.

In the context of the spirit of the new trade theory, important determinants of market structure are conditions of entry and exit within the industry.[13] In looking at the global structure of a particular industry at a moment in time, an important aspect of that market structure will be relative conditions of entry across countries as well as relative cost structures across countries. The market structure of the industry will reflect not only traditional market structure variables such as scale and product differentiation, but also the extent to which national submarkets are effectively segmented, either by barriers to trade and investment created by governments, or by the extent to which incumbent firms in those markets can erect entry barriers to hinder potential competition from becoming actual competition. It is conceivable that competition might be hindered by the anticompetitive practices of these firms.

The problem is most acute when changes in external circumstances, such as a shift in factor endowments, changes in exchange rates reflecting macroeconomic trends, development of new technology, or the reduction of trade barriers, leads fairly quickly to a new set of potential entrants in a given industry. The industry thus consists of the old firms and the potential new firms reflecting "potential comparative advantage," with the old firms located in one country and the new firms in another country. Under conditions of perfect competition, the behavior of the old and new firms is not really of any concern. What typically is of policy concern is the displaced factors of production in the country losing competitive advantage. In industries where entry barriers are significant, however, another set of factors emerges centered around the behavior of the old firms.

It is in the interests of the old firms to prevent the entry of new firms, if it is possible to preserve profits and market share, by taking some appropriate entry-preventing action. Such an action might be lowering price, raising capacity, increasing advertising, or any of a variety of firm policies which threaten potential entrants with a plausible post-entry threat of high output and low profits. A crucial assumption in the theory of entry prevention as developed by Dixit (1982), Eaton and Lipsey (1979), and others is that the incumbent be given the advantage of the first move, that is, he must be allowed to take an investment action prior to the act of investment by the potential entrant. This is in the closed economy version of the theory. In the international context, if the incumbent is located in one country and the potential entrant in another, the time lags necessary for an entrant to set up a distribution network to service the foreign market may give the home market incumbent sufficient lead time to undertake entry-deterring investment. The interesting aspect of this theory is that just when an industry is losing its comparative advantage, it undertakes a burst of investment in the hopes of keeping out the new competition appearing on the horizon.

Entry-deterring activity will usually be wasteful in a world efficiency sense, although it may be in the national interest of the country in which it occurs. History suggests that incumbent firms meet with varied success in keeping out new entrants. But if incumbents are large, economies of scale significant, and investment largely product or firm specific, then entry deterrence is quite conceivably going to be successful for a long period of time. Note that this is true even though the basic assumption is that the new entrants would have costs which are lower than the costs of the incumbent firms if they could successfully enter. Furthermore, the point is valid both with respect to exporting and importing industries, although the natural case to think about is when an industry, previously export oriented, is on the verge of becoming an import-competing industry.

If the entry deterrence is successful, then the firms who could potentially enter the industry, but did not due to deterring activity of incumbents, will claim that they did not have "fair" market access. There are some simple general equilibrium repercussions. The country which was originally exporting and has lost competitive advantage may still export if entry is successfully blockaded in its export markets. However, if entry succeeds in the export market but is deterred in the home market, then the fall in exports must be matched under trade balance by a reduction in imports, or a deterioration in the trade balance as in a Keynesian model. If the initial shock is a reduction in trade barriers between two countries, the story is similar but with a different twist. Suppose the home country has a comparative disadvantage in the widget industry. With the reduction in trade barriers, home firms in the widget industry anticipating entry by foreign firms will raise entry barriers prior to the reduction in trade barriers. Upon removal of the trade barriers, if entry deterrence is successful, foreign firms do not succeed in penetrating the home countries' widget market, and the volume of trade is less than might be expected after the removal of trade barriers.

There is a strong intertemporal dimension to this problem. Clearly, if the cost disadvantage of the incumbent firms is strong enough, their actions will only slow down the process of losing world market share. Thus, the pattern of revealed comparative advantage will be slow to change.

An interesting application of this type of theory of restricted market access is to those industries where comparative advantage effects are minimal. In this case the initial competitive advantage of industry location is nonexistent. Nevertheless, history matters in the sense that investment creates location-specific preferences and advantages. Thus an industry once located in a particular country with substantial sunk costs may be invulnerable against new entrants from other locations for a considerable period of time.

The major unresolved issue in the new trade theory is the empirical relevance of lessons one through three. While the arguments seem compelling and appeal to those of "real world" persuasion, there are some who would claim that the traditional economic models of neoclassical trade theory and the associated view of market access within that theory are adequate for the analysis of the problems at hand. The only way one can answer that type of criticism is to demonstrate in a number of empirical applications that the theory actually improves our understanding of the world and confirms the significance of the basic assumptions used in the new theory. There are many empirical questions to be addressed, but let me stress two which bear directly on the importance of market access as defined in this section. First is the basic question alluded to earlier about the gains from trade, or the benefits of trade liberalization with scale economies and imperfect competition. As noted, this may turn out to be an essentially empirical and not a theoretical issue. Second is the extent to which preemptive investment strategies by new or incumbent firms affect the evolution of "revealed comparative advantage."

On the second point, our state of knowledge is quite primitive except for the weak confirming evidence on technological theories of trade.[14] Subsidiary evidence that I find compelling is that from closed economy industrial organization. In that literature, entry barriers are well-documented determinants of industry structure and dynamics.[15] If this is true for a closed economy the size of the United States, then trade between states within the U.S. must be explained in part by industrial organization features. Therefore, it seems highly probable that it is true for trade between nations like Japan and the United States. The really exciting problem in international trade is the testing of these theories in plausible ways.

The problem of identifying the gains from trade within a world of scale economies and imperfect competition is a less demanding one, either because one starts with a theoretical structure that is not "tested" (see Baldwin and Krugman 1989, for example), or one appeals to economic history and to what data exist to suggest the plausibility of a country losing or gaining from liberalizing its markets in the presence of significant scale economies. One important example that we have is the European Economic Community, at least in its early years, where significant gains were said to have accrued even though scale economies were thought to be quite important in many industries. In the case of Canada, Cox and Harris (1985, 1986) have used general equilibrium methods to do counterfactual computations on the costs of protection to the Canadian economy. The results bear out the proposition that the costs of protection are high relative to those calculated for traditional competitive constant-cost models of trade and that reduced trade barriers are welfare improving. The sources of these gains are closely related to lessons one and two noted above—procompetitive effects of enhanced international competition and the realization of economies of scale, accompanied by greater specialization within firms and across industries.

The point is often made that results like these are only relevant for small economies, and that large countries such as Japan and the United States are not likely to bear the same costs of small market size if market access is limited. I suppose that with respect to traditional economies of scale in production for standardized goods this is true, but we may be underestimating the benefits to an integrated Japan–North American market on a number of fronts. First, there are some industries, such as commercial aircraft, where the economies of scale are so great that even in the world market we do not expect more than two to four firms to survive. If market access to North America were denied to Airbus, for example, it is possible that Boeing could end up as a monopolist supplier. More realistic are industries where economies of scale in production and distribution are likely to lead to a small number of oligopolies. There are numerous examples—in fact, it is hard to think of a major industry where this does not seem to be occurring—autos, airlines, mainframe computers, chemicals, pharmaceuticals, consumer electronics, fast foods, banking, retailing, etc. In industries such as these, absolute firm size is apparently increasing, and in many cases industry concentration at the domestic level is rising. Governments have been encouraging this trend, using the argument that big firms are necessary to compete internationally. If there are these real economies to large firm size, then the important policy issue is how to preserve the benefits of size without suffering the potential abuses of tightly knit oligopolies. Freer trade might well be the most sensible way to preserve competition and achieve the benefits of large firm size.

8.5 Conclusion

In conclusion, I have examined three sets of related problems dealing with market access. One pertained to the perceptions of sellers in a market with cultural entry barriers and the other two to the actions of governments and firms in markets where large sunk costs and scale economies are important. In general the conclusion is that "market access" ought to be preserved if it can be defined to most parties' satisfaction. Thus, visible, objectifiably measurable barriers to market access which created asymmetries were usually distortions worth attacking or trying to measure. Yet, the examples also pointed to other asymmetries in apparent market access which were not so readily dealt with, yet may nevertheless be real. One barrier discussed was the cultural barrier which can exist in any society against certain products of foreign origin. The other barrier was the entry barrier created by firms suffering a decline in competitive advantage, but attempting to preserve their market position by engaging in activities which limit market access to new entrants. Our knowledge is too limited to make definite recommendations as to what is sensible or desirable in these contexts. What can be said is that we do not have to take the naive view that such barriers do not exist. To treat all these problems as equivalent in the conduct of trade policy would be a serious mistake. Certainly, not all market access problems are either due to government interference in the market or are cause for compensating government remedies.

Notes

1. Two excellent discussions of the U.S. perception of the Japanese trade problem are contained in McCulloch (1988) and Saxonhouse (1985).

2. For three alternative, but quite representative views on administered or contingent protection, see Baldwin (1985), Finger et al. (1982), and Grey (1981).

3. Yamamura (1986) contains a good discussion of Japanese postwar industrial policy. His discussion on pp. 180–82 covers vertical integration and its effects on entry. In the discussion of the television industry, he notes that there was virtually no entry after 1960 and the seven diversified major firms in this industry have coexisted since 1947.

4. For a discussion of the literature on entry barriers encountered by Canadian exporters, see Harris (1985b, ch. 5).

5. Yamamura (1986) discusses the role of the *keiretsu* in controlling entry, and the relevant literature.

6. See Yamamura (1986).

7. An interesting question in this model is whether this type of cultural bias affects trade patterns to the extent that the observed equilibrium could be distinguished from one without cultural bias against imports.

8. This is an old "folk theorem" of Canadian political economy.

9. See the references in note 2.

10. One exception is the paper by Ethier (1982) which is a model in the spirit of that described here.

11. The literature on contestability and commitment is quite large. Contestable

markets theory is presented in Baumol, Panzar, and Willig (1982). An early paper on commitment is Eaton and Lipsey (1979).

12. Brander and Harris (1983) develop a model with these characteristics.

13. Surprisingly, the formal models in the new trade theory are either models with a fixed number of firms or free-entry models. Entry-deterrence models have not been integrated into a theory of international trade. Harris (1985a) looks at one particular problem involving trade and deterrence.

14. Deardorff (1984) summarizes empirical tests of "technology-based" theories of trade. Those studies, mostly done in the 1960s, are now quite dated.

15. The voluminous empirical literature on entry barriers as a determinant of market structure is summarized in Scherer (1980, ch. 2 and 3). For particular references to the open economy, see Harris (1985b, ch. 5 and 6).

References

Akerlof, G. 1980. A theory of social custom, of which unemployment may be one consequence. *Quarterly Journal of Economics* 94 (June): 749–76.

Arrow, K. J. 1972. Models of job discrimination. In *Racial discrimination in economic life,* ed. A. H. Pascal. Lexington: D. C. Heath.

Baldwin, R., and P. Krugman. 1988. Industrial policy and international competition in wide-bodied jet aircraft. In *Trade policy issues and empirical analysis,* ed. Robert E. Baldwin. Chicago: University of Chicago Press.

Baldwin, R. E. 1985. *The political economy of U.S. import policy.* Cambridge, Mass.: MIT Press.

Baumol, W. J., J. Panzar, and R. D. Willig. 1982. *Contestable markets and the theory of industry structure.* New York: Harcourt Brace Jovanovich.

Brander, J., and R. Harris. 1983. Anticipated collusion and excess capacity. Mimeo, Queen's University.

Cox, D., and R. Harris. 1985. Trade liberalization and industrial organization: Some estimates for Canada. *Journal of Political Economy* 93 (February): 115–45.

———. 1986. A quantitative assessment of the economic impact on Canada of sectoral free trade with the United States. *Canadian Journal of Economics* 19 (August): 377–94.

Deardorff, A. 1984. Testing trade theories and predicting trade flows. P. Kenen (eds.), In *Handbook of international economics,* vol. 1, eds. R. W. Jones and P. Kenen. Amsterdam: North-Holland.

Dixit, A. 1982. Recent developments in oligopoly theory. *American Economic Review Proceedings* 72 (May): 12–17.

———. 1986. Trade policy: An agenda for research. In *Strategic trade policy and the new international economics,* ed. P. Krugman. Cambridge, Mass.: MIT Press.

Dixit, A. K., and A. S. Kyle. 1985. The use of protection and subsidies for entry promotion and deterrence. *American Economic Review* 75 (March): 139–52.

Eaton, J., and G. Grossman. 1983. Optimal trade and industrial policy under oligopoly. National Bureau of Economic Research Working Paper no. 1236. Cambridge, Mass.: NBER.

Eaton, C., and R. G. Lipsey. 1979. The theory of market pre-emption: The persistence of excess capacity and monopoly in growing spatial markets. *Economica* 46 (May): 148–58.

Ethier, W. 1982. Dumping. *Journal of Political Economy* 90 (June): 487–506.

Finger, J. M., H. Keith Hall, and D. R. Nelson. 1982. The political economy of administered protection. *American Economic Review* 72 (June): 452–66.

Grey, R. de C. 1981. *Trade policy in the 1980s: An agenda for Canadian-U.S. relations.* Toronto: C. D. Howe Institute.

Harris, R. 1985a. Export promotion in the presence of entry barriers. Mimeo, Queen's University.

―――. 1985b. *Trade, industrial policy and international competition.* Vol. 13, research series prepared for the Royal Commission on the Economic Union and Development Prospects for Canada. Toronto: University of Toronto Press.

Helpman, E., and P. Krugman. 1985. *Market structure and foreign trade.* Cambridge, Mass.: MIT Press.

Krugman, P., ed. 1986. *Strategic trade policy and the new international economics.* Cambridge, Mass.: MIT Press.

McCulloch, R. 1988. United States–Japan economic relations. In *Trade policy issues and empirical analysis,* ed. Robert E. Baldwin. Chicago: University of Chicago Press.

Markusen, J. R., and J. R. Melvin. 1981. Trade, factor prices and the gains from trade with increasing returns to scale. *Canadian Journal of Economics* 14 (November): 450–69.

Newberry, D. M. G., and J. Stiglitz. 1981. *The theory of commodity price stabilization.* Oxford: Oxford University Press.

Richardson, J. D. 1986. Strategic behavior and trade policy. In *Strategic trade policy and the new international economics,* ed. P. Krugman. Cambridge, Mass.: MIT Press.

Saxonhouse, G. R. 1985. What's wrong with Japanese trade structure. Discussion Paper no. 166, Research Seminar in International Economics, University of Michigan.

Scherer, F. M. 1980. *Industrial market structure and economic performance.* Boston: Houghton Mifflin.

Williamson, O. E. 1975. *Markets and hierarchies: Analysis and anti-trust implications.* New York: Free Press.

Yamamura, K. 1986. Caveat emptor: The industrial policy of Japan. *Strategic trade policy and the new international economics,* ed. P. Krugman. Cambridge, Mass.: MIT Press.

Comment

Alan V. Deardorff

I would like to say first that I found Harris's paper very stimulating. The issue of market access has received practically no attention in the literature on international trade, and it is very useful to have him interpret it from a theoretical perspective. He has broken the topic down in a way that helps a great deal in thinking about it. The distinction that he makes in the three parts of the paper may, I believe, be appropriately characterized as concerning informal barriers to imports that arise from three sources: behavior of demanders, behavior of governments, and behavior of competing suppliers.

In the first category of barriers on the demand side, Harris considers the possibility that demanders might show a preference for domestically produced goods. That such a preference would limit "market access" is clear. He devotes most of his remarks on this topic to trying to explain why such a preference might arise.

In the second category of barriers on the part of governments, he considers, not the formal trade barriers such as tariffs and quotas (or even VERs) that we usually discuss, but rather the phenomenon of so-called contingent protection. The reason that this is an informal barrier limiting market access is not that acts of contingent protection are themselves informal, for they are not, but rather the fact that a system of contingent protection creates an atmosphere of uncertainty about whether market access, once gained, will be preserved.

Finally, in the third category of barriers on the part of competing producers, Harris considers barriers to entry that participants in an imperfectly competitive market may be able to erect that, when the excluded potential entrants are foreign, constitute a barrier to market access.

My first question in commenting on this paper is to ask if Harris's categorization is complete. That is, are there significant ways that market access might be impeded that would not fall into one of these three categories? Try as I might, I have not been able to think of any such ways, as perhaps my own interpretation of the categorization in terms of demanders, suppliers, and government may make less surprising. Who else, after all, is there? I should say that within each category it would not surprise me to find other particular mechanisms than the ones he considers, whereby barriers to market access might arise. But by and large my own conclusion is that Harris has done a fine job, hitting the major general modes that should concern us in a discussion of market access.

That being the case, the rest of my remarks will focus on just two issues that should be regarded as extensions of Harris's paper. The first is to ask whether demanders' preference for domestic goods really constitutes a valid grounds for policy intervention. The second is to ask whether this same threefold classification can illuminate a discussion of another issue: that of market access in the context of international direct investment.

The Preference for Domestic Goods

Harris gives theoretical motivation to his discussion of barriers on the demand side by explaining and applying Akerlof's "social custom" model. He uses this to explain why demanders in a country may persist in a seemingly irrational preference for domestically produced goods over foreign goods that are objectively identical. His discussion of this model in connection with trade focuses primarily on the interesting dynamics that may cause such a preference to disappear, and this is of obvious importance in the context of trade policy.

I would like to devote a few of my remarks, however, to the much simpler question of whether such a preference, however it originates, should be properly considered grounds for trade policy action.

Suppose, much more simply than in the social custom model discussed by Harris, that consumers have a preference for domestically produced goods. It is clear that this preference, in comparison to a situation without it, will cause the country to trade less and, again in comparison to the situation without the preference, will improve its terms of trade exactly as if it had imposed a tariff. Does this make the importing country better off and the exporting country worse off? So long as the importing country is indeed large enough to influence the terms of trade by its behavior, the foreign country must lose unambiguously.

Is this grounds for a policy response? Not necessarily. Since the effects are so similar, the case for a policy response here can surely be no better than the case for a policy response to an effort to impose an "optimal tariff." And there the response makes sense only if the threat of the response may reasonably be expected to prevent the action in the first place. In the case of a preference for a domestic good, unless that preference is the result of a deliberate policy of, say, advertising that buyers should "buy domestic," it is quite likely that the preference would not be amenable to a policy change anyway. For without a government action to have caused it, the preference is not itself a deliberate action taken in cognizance of expected reactions. It is only a state of mind and is likely to be independent of foreign policies taken in response to it. If a protectionist response does not succeed in undoing the preference, it is only making matters worse.

This distinction between an autonomous preference for domestic goods and one that is somehow policy induced is also important, I believe, at another more philosophical level. My own view is that there is nothing wrong with a preference for domestic goods, even though such a preference does indeed restrict market access and thus trade, and even though it can be argued to be harmful to a country's trading partners, so long as that preference arises "naturally" and not as the result of a deliberate government policy.

To put it another way, suppose that there are domestic and imported goods that are in every way objectively identical except that it is somehow known where each of the goods was produced, and suppose that domestic demanders (consumers or producers, either one) have nonetheless a preference for the domestic goods. Presumably this means that buying the domestic good makes them "feel better" (or that buying the foreign good makes them "feel worse"). I believe such preferences to be as legitimate as any others, and they should not be taken as proper grounds for a policy response by other countries. One might argue that the country itself could be better off if it were not, in this way, so irrational, and perhaps an educational campaign should be undertaken to rid the public of the misperception, but that is a domestic issue. Given the preference itself, then, the economics of trade and its effects are just the same as if the preference did not exist, and I cannot see that the case for a foreign tariff is improved by it.

Direct Investment

I now consider whether Harris's framework may be helpful in understanding barriers to international direct investment as well as barriers to trade. Let me say first, though, that I am not convinced that barriers to direct investment should necessarily be viewed as undesirable, in the same manner as barriers to trade. To me, international factor movements impinge on national sovereignty in a way that trade does not. Perhaps foreign factors should be invited in and not presumed to be welcome guests.

On the demand side, it is clear that a subsidiary of a foreign corporation can be viewed just as skeptically when it tries to sell its products, as can a foreign exporter, and thus that a preference for domestic goods may interfere with the success of a direct investment. However, one advantage of direct investment is precisely that it allows the foreign producer to take on certain characteristics of a domestic producer and thus to avoid such adverse preferences. In that sense, if one accepts such preferences as being legitimate, as I do, then one may object to foreign direct investment itself as being a means of misleading people about their true preferences—a kind of false advertising, if you will.

Next consider market access for investment as it may be impeded by government intervention. Here again it seems that investment serves the purpose of getting behind a wall, even of contingent protection, and thus provides greater security of market access. In some countries this appearance of security is misleading, however, since by locating within a country the foreign firm exposes itself to the even more serious possibility of expropriation. In some countries I would think the possibility that a firm might be nationalized or expropriated would be a prohibitive barrier to market access for direct investment.

Finally, consider barriers on the side of the competing producers. Presumably, whatever competing sellers can do to exclude a seller of exports they can also do to exclude sales by a foreign-owned domestic producer. However, an additional possibility also exists, involving the many other economic transactions that a foreign firm must enter into within a country if it engages in production there. For example, competing firms may put pressure on domestic labor not to work for the foreign firm, or not to work on the same terms as they do for the domestic producers. Or they may use their connections with local banks to make it difficult for the foreign firm to obtain local financing. Indeed, for every transaction that a local producer must undertake, there is the potential for domestic producers to interfere in some way with the conduct of that transaction and thus make successful operation more difficult. Thus I would think that the scope for this kind of interference would be much greater for direct investment than for trade.

These considerations lead me, as a last point, to observe that the threefold classification that I have been pursuing here is not sufficient for the area of direct investment. Instead, there is a fourth category that should be considered. Since a producer must necessarily make a number of purchases in domestic markets, market access can also be impeded by preferential behavior on the part of domestic sellers—not competing ones, such as Harris considers in his discussion of barriers to entry, but sellers of all of the many inputs, including labor, that a producing firm would have to buy, or prefer to buy, on the local market. As just one example, if labor is reluctant to work for a foreign firm, then direct investment will be seriously impeded. Again, however, I would not be inclined to view such a preference as grounds for policy action, but would rather insist that we respect that preference as legitimate, even though we may not approve of it.

Comment

Motoshige Itoh

Harris discusses a variety of theoretical issues related to market access in international trade. Considering that market access has been neglected in the trade theory literature, this survey is quite valuable. Since the paper covers many topics, I would like to restrict my comment to the first and third issues of the paper.

Standardized Goods Assumption

There is a reason why the market access issue has been neglected in the trade theory literature in spite of the fact that the issue is so heated in practical discussions. Most trade models are based on the assumption that internationally traded goods are standardized. By standardized goods I mean goods whose quality is well known to both sellers and buyers and which do not contain any essential elements specific to a small number of people (customized goods).

The Ricardian theory of comparative costs is a good example here. Since the goods in the theory are standardized, all that matters is production costs. Neither the service content of the goods traded nor the marketing activities of suppliers have any essential role. If the majority of goods traded are standardized, market access is not an important matter. However, a large portion of goods and services traded internationally are far from being standardized.

When nonstandardized goods are traded, service content becomes a critical endogenous variable, and economists should explain how its level is determined. Service content may take a variety of forms such as various distribution services and guarantee of a certain quality level. According to the economics literature on transactions costs (see Williamson 1985) arm's-length market transactions are not necessarily appropriate for the efficient transacting of nonstandardized goods. Many unusual business practices are generated to expedite efficient transactions in nonstandardized goods. In fact, many business practices observed in Japan, which are referred to in Itoh and Matsui (1987) as Japanese-style repeated and long-term transactions, can be explained by this theory.

I would like to discuss two examples which may be useful in understanding Williamson-type long-term transactions.

Japanese Imports of Paper and Steel

The amount of Japanese imports of such commodities as paper and steel increased only gradually in the face of an appreciating Japanese yen. A story I heard from a paper production technician points to an important problem regarding long-term transactions. For newspaper publishers, who are under great time pressure as they try to get their newspaper printed, the cost of having paper tear in the midst of printing is extremely high. Therefore, finding newsprint paper which is highly resistant to tearing is extremely important. For this reason, newspaper publishers purchase newsprint from a limited number of paper companies and these relationships are long term. At fixed intervals, such as once a month, the newspaper publishers calculate the tear ratio for the newsprint from each paper company. This system has a number of interesting characteristics.

First, competition has a face-to-face character. Each producer of paper knows with whom they are competing. Face-to-face competition under this long-term contract may actually be more intense than anonymous market competition. According to interviews with paper production technicians, declines in their companies' ratings put intense pressure on them and provided an important motivation behind product improvement. It is quite possible for competition with rivals with whom one is very familiar to be more heated than highly anonymous, profit-driven competition. Though this is an area in which the point has not yet been sufficiently illuminated by theory, there are many other examples of the intensity of face-to-face competition. Perhaps, the theory of rank-order tournament will explain some competitive features of face-to-face competition.

Second, by carrying out its transaction on a long-term, face-to-face basis, it is easier for the newspaper publishing company to shift the focus of competition in a direction which is useful to it. In the competition over selling newsprint, there are a number of different aspects, such as price, tear resistance, thickness, weight, flexibility of delivery (just-in-time system), as well as others. If the newspaper publisher were to make clear its evaluation of these various other factors in its periodic report, then competition among the paper companies would probably come to reflect these other factors. It is not clear whether highly anonymous market competition would reproduce the results of "directed competition" or not, especially when quality improvement in the above factors need long-term and complicated coordination between publishers and paper producers. Some publishers in the United States vertically integrate the paper production sector in order to make this type of coordination possible. However, vertical integration may reduce competition among paper producers.

It is easy to imagine that face-to-face competition is observed in various transactions of intermediate products. An important example is subcontracting relations in the automobile industry.

If one notes that the long-term transactional relationship (organizational transaction) plays an important role, it is natural that imports of such products as paper and steel would not increase rapidly in the face of an appreciating yen exchange rate. It thus appears that price is only one factor determining demand.

Customer Relations in the Japanese Distribution System

The long-term relations mentioned above can also be observed in the Japanese distribution system.

The United States and Japan seem to have somewhat different ways of transacting for such items as used cars and real estate. For instance, in the case of used cars, direct dealing through newspapers is common in the U.S., but in Japan this is rare. Instead, in Japan it is much more common to buy a used car through a dealer, that is, through indirect dealing.

One merit of direct dealing is that it brings a large part of the supply and demand into a single, large arena such as newspaper advertising, which makes it possible to bring economies of scale to market information. On the other hand, when there are uncertainties regarding the quality of goods and services, there arises the problem of adverse selection. In the case of used cars, for instance, informing people of the quality of individual used cars is not so simple that it can be done through newspaper advertisements, and even if it were possible, the seller might not actually provide accurate information. If one tries to get a good used car through direct dealing, unless one knows a lot about cars or can use the services of someone who does, one may get stuck with a lemon.

But when one buys a car from a dealer who specializes in used cars, as long as the dealer is trustworthy, there is no danger of ending up with a lemon. In Japan the following mechanism works to make indirect dealings function effectively:

1. In regions where there is limited long-distance movement of population, the pool of people who are available to buy from a certain dealer is also limited. Therefore, as long as the dealer is going to do business in that particular region, he will have to deal with the same people again and again (long-term transactions).
2. Since in a relatively closed society there are many opportunities for the dealer's customers and potential customers to meet, it is easy for the dealer's reputation to change, either positively or negatively.
3. A dealer will tend to have a number of different kinds of dealings with a customer. For instance, when there is a fairly good relationship between a dealer and customers, the dealer does not merely sell used cars to the customer, but also continues to provide him with information about the car, does repair and periodic service on the car, and arranges for insurance. As the transaction expands to cover more things, that is, as the transaction becomes multiple, the long-run nature of the transaction gets stronger in the sense that transactions become more frequent.

If the customer trusts the dealer, then he will not have to collect any information about goods, but will leave this in the hands of the dealer. For goods like used cars for which the cost of collecting information about individual goods is quite high, the savings from leaving information collection up to the dealer are significant.

This example has many features of customer relations which can often be observed in the Japanese distribution system. Commodities with considerable service content have the same characteristics as used cars in our example. Sellers and buyers are involved in agency relations. Long-term relations existing between manufacturers and wholesalers, between wholesalers and retailers, and between consumers and retailers tend to be long term.

These long-term relations become barriers to entry for newcomers to the market, whether they be foreigners or natives.

Market Access and International Trade

The two examples raised above indicate the importance of long-term transactions. Although these types of transactions are observed in the United States and Canada as well, they are perhaps much more prevalent in Japan. This prevalence may be explained by various factors such as relatively cheap prices of services, until recently, in Japan, less rigid antitrust regulation, geographic immobility of population, and rapid growth of the economy, with the third and fourth factors facilitating the working of the reputation mechanism.

The above points have some implications for Harris's first and third arguments. I do not deny that there exist some cultural factors behind the market access issue. However, I think rational behavior in the context of long-term transactions is far more important than cultural factors. In fact, American brands such as McDonald's and Seven-Eleven have been more successful than other foreign brands in spite of the fact that the American element in these brands is far more visible. This would seem to contradict the cultural explanation.

Harris discusses monopolistic or oligopolistic behavior in terms of the issue of market access. While I agree with most of his arguments, nonetheless the economic efficiency of long-term transactions seems important here as well. Thus, it is essential to make clear whether entry barriers, if they exist, are created intentionally by incumbent firms for the purpose of entry deterrence or whether they are generated by some rational mechanism. My discussion of long-term transactions suggests the latter possibility. If so, the policy implication of the market access issue might be different from the case in which entry barriers are created intentionally by incumbent firms.

References

Itoh, M., and A. Matsui. 1987. Organizational transactions: One aspect of Japanese-style business relations. Paper presented at the Hitotsubashi-Stanford conference on perspectives on the nature of corporations.
Williamson, O. E. 1985. *The economic institutions of capitalism.* New York: The Free Press.

9 An Analytical Survey of Formal and Informal Barriers to International Trade and Investment in the United States, Canada, and Japan

Gary R. Saxonhouse and Robert M. Stern

9.1 Introduction

The purpose of our paper is to assess the role of formal and, especially, informal barriers in the trade and investment relations of the United States, Canada, and Japan. There has been heightened interest in this issue lately as the result of the very substantial merchandise trade deficit that the United States has been experiencing both overall and with respect to its major trading partners. Japan has been singled out for maintaining a variety of practices and policies that limit the access of foreign goods to, and direct investment in, its markets and confer special benefits to its export industries. Similar, although somewhat muted, allegations have at times been directed against certain Canadian policies and administrative procedures deemed detrimental to U.S. interests. For its part, the United States has not been immune from criticism by its major trading partners who have felt aggrieved, especially by the increase in administered protection in the guise of antidumping and countervailing actions and the constant pressures to reduce their exports to the United States on a "voluntary" basis.

In order to place formal and informal barriers in perspective, we provide in section 9.2 a list of the major categories of nontariff measures and related policies of governments that are widely observed. We then attempt to draw distinctions between formal and informal barriers and discuss the underlying rationale and possible consequences of differences in informal barriers among countries. Next we provide a brief account of the evidence pertaining to formal barriers for the United States, Canada, and Japan, including post–Tokyo Round (1987) tariffs, coverage indexes and ad valorem equivalents of nontariff barriers (NTBs), and restrictions affecting foreign direct investment.

We are indebted to Alan V. Deardorff, Bernard M. Hoekman, members of the Research Seminar in International Economics at the University of Michigan, and the conference discussants and participants for their many helpful comments on earlier versions of this paper. We would also like to thank the Ford Foundation and the Donner Foundation for their financial support.

Finally, we consider evidence relating to the major informal barriers that have been identified for the three nations.

In section 9.3, we discuss the important conceptual issues involved in measuring the effects of formal and informal barriers. A distinction is drawn between effects that are specific to particular kinds of NTBs and the general effects of an entire complex of NTBs. Informal barriers fit into this latter category. We then address the question of what is the appropriate analytical framework to use in estimating the effects of barriers to trade. Thereafter, we review and assess the major empirical efforts that have been undertaken to estimate the extent to which Japan's formal and informal trade barriers set it apart from the United States, Canada, and other major countries, and we offer some new results as well. Lastly, we comment briefly on the effects of restrictions on foreign direct investment. Our conclusions and implications for research and policy are contained in section 9.4.

9.2 Formal and Informal Barriers to International Trade and Investment

It is useful to begin by considering what is meant by formal and informal barriers. Formal barriers can be defined as tariffs and nontariff measures that are explicitly stated in official legislation or government mandates. Informal barriers refer to impediments arising from: (1) administrative procedures and unpublished government regulations and policies; (2) market structure; and (3) political, social, and cultural institutions. The impediments associated with informal barriers may be the result of a conscious effort by government to favor domestic over foreign interests or the byproduct of practices and policies that are rooted in domestic institutions.

Administrative procedures and government regulations and policies. A list and brief description of the most important nontariff measures in current use are given in table 9.1.[1] While many of the measures listed can be considered to represent formal barriers, the procedures employed to administer the barriers could in themselves constitute an additional impediment. Thus, for example, discretionary licensing could be used in implementing import quotas or export restraints. Customs procedures may rely on specially constructed measures of price for valuation purposes and involve costly administrative methods in order to favor domestic producers. Standards, testing, and certification requirements may also be designed and administered for the benefit of domestic producers. A final example is that antidumping, countervailing duty, and other types of investigation of alleged unfair trade actions may be used to foster a climate of uncertainty for foreign suppliers and as a method of harassment designed to bring about changes in foreign trading practices and policies.

Government regulations and policies may result in a variety of impedi-

Table 9.1   Major Categories of Nontariff Measures and Related Policies

I. Quantitative restrictions and similar specific limitations

1. Import quotas	Restrictions on quantity and/or value of imports of specific commodities for some given time period; administered globally, selectively, or bilaterally.
2. Export limitations	Same as above but with reference to exports.
3. Licensing	Some system of licensing is required to administer the foregoing restrictions. Licensing may be discretionary and also used for statistical purposes.
4. Voluntary export restraints	Restrictions imposed by importing country but administered by exporting country; administered multilaterally and bilaterally; requires system of licensing; essentially similar to an orderly marketing arrangement.
5. Exchange and other financial controls	Restrictions on receipts and/or payments of foreign exchange designed to control international trade and/or capital movements; will generally require some system of licensing; may involve multiple exchange rates for different kinds of transactions.
6. Prohibitions	May be selective with respect to commodities and countries of origin/destination; includes embargoes; may carry legal sanctions.
7. Domestic content and mixing requirements	Requires that an industry use a certain proportion of domestically produced components and/or materials and labor in producing final products.
8. Discriminatory bilateral agreements	Preferential trading arrangements that may be selective by commodity and country; includes preferential sourcing arrangements.
9. Countertrade	Arrangements involving barter, counterpurchases of goods, and payments in kind.

II. Nontariff charges and related policies affecting imports

1. Variable levies	Based on a target domestic price of imports, a levy is imposed so that the price of imports reaches the target price whatever the cost of imports.
2. Advance deposit requirement	Some proportion of the value of imports must be deposited in advance of the payment, with no allowance for any interest accrued on the deposit.
3. Antidumping duties	Imposition of a special import duty when the price of imports is alleged to lie below some measure of the costs of production of foreign firms; minimum foreign prices may be established to "trigger" antidumping investigations and actions.
4. Countervailing duties	Imposition of a special import duty to counteract an alleged foreign government subsidy to exports; normally required that domestic injury be shown.
5. Border tax adjustments	When indirect (e.g., sales or value added) taxes are levied on the destination principle, imports will be subject to such taxes but exports will be exempt; the effects on trade will be neutral except in cases in which the adjustments more than compensate for the taxes imposed or exempted, or when the size of the tax differs across commodities.

III. Government participation in trade, restrictive practices, and more general government policies

1. Subsidies and other aids	Direct and indirect subsidies to export and import-competing industries, including tax benefits, credit concessions, and bilateral tied aid programs.
2. Government procurement policies	Preferences given to domestic over foreign firms in bidding on public-procurement contracts, including explicit cost differentials and informal procedures favoring procurement from domestic firms.

Table 9.1 (continued)

3. State trading, government monopolies, and exclusive franchises   Government actions which may result in trade distortions, including government-sanctioned, discriminatory international transport agreements.

4. Government industrial policy and regional development measures   Government actions designed to aid particular firms, industrial sectors, and regions in adjusting to changes in market conditions.

5. Government financed research and development and other technology policies   Government actions designed to correct market distortions and aid private firms; includes policies relating to intellectual property (patents, copyrights, and trademarks) and technological spillovers from government programs, such as defense and public health.

6. National systems of taxation and social insurance   Personal and corporate income taxation, unemployment insurance, social security, and related policies which may have an impact on trade.

7. Macroeconomic policies   Monetary/fiscal, balance-of-payments, and exchange rate actions which have an impact on national output, foreign trade, and capital movements.

8. Competition policies   Antitrust and related policies (e.g., intellectual property regulations) designed to foster or restrict competition and which may have an impact on foreign trade and investment.

9. Foreign investment policies   Screening and monitoring of inward and/or outward foreign direct investment, including performance requirements affecting production and trade.

10. Foreign corruption policies   Policies designed to prohibit or restrict bribes and related practices in connection with foreign trade and investment.

11. Immigration policies   General or selective policies designed to limit or encourage international movement of labor and which have an impact on foreign trade and investment.

IV. Customs procedures and administrative practices

1. Customs valuation procedures   Use of specially constructed measures of price rather than the invoice or transactions price for the purpose of levying tariffs.

2. Customs classification procedures   Use of national methods of customs classification rather than an internationally harmonized method for the purpose of levying tariffs.

3. Customs clearance procedures   Documentation, inspection, and related practices which may impede trade.

V. Technical barriers to trade

1. Health and sanitary regulations and quality standards   Technical regulations designed for domestic objectives but which may discriminate against imports.

2. Safety and industrial standards and regulations   See above.

3. Packaging and labeling regulations, including trademarks   See above.

4. Advertising and media regulations   See above.

Source: Adapted from Deardorff and Stern (1985, 13–14).

ments to trade and investment, depending upon their intent and the structural changes and behavioral responses that are induced. The pervasive role of government in economic activity in many countries suggests that it will often be possible to find examples of impediments that may be associated with each of the government policies listed in part III of table 9.1. As already mentioned, governments may actively institute measures explicitly designed to benefit domestic producing interests, and there may also be significant external consequences of measures that are ostensibly intended to achieve domestic objectives.

These kinds of policies can and have been addressed in multilateral forums. Thus, it is noteworthy in this connection that, in the course of the Tokyo Round negotiations that were concluded in 1979, a number of the most important nontariff interventions were addressed. Agreement was reached to establish codes dealing with antidumping, subsidies and countervailing duties, government procurement, standards, customs valuation, and import licensing. These GATT codes were intended to increase the transparency and international harmonization of nontariff measures and to reduce the distortionary effects involved.

In their assessment of the GATT codes, Stern, Jackson, and Hoekman (1988) concluded that there have been: (1) noteworthy improvements in the transparency and functioning of antidumping procedures in the signatory countries; (2) some progress in improving the information and bidding procedures relating to government procurement; (3) improvements in the exchange of information, harmonization, and limitations on the discriminatory use of standards; and (4) substantial progress in curbing the use of arbitrary customs valuation methods. There has been less satisfaction with the code relating to subsidies and countervailing duties, but, as Stern et al. note, this reflects disagreements over the wording and interpretation of the code and problems in resolving disputes over agricultural subsidies. It also appears that the government procurement code has had less commercial impact than anticipated.

While there have been important benefits from the GATT codes, there are numerous issues that have yet to be resolved, including: (1) limited membership of developing countries in most of the codes; (2) ambiguities in design and interpretation, especially of the subsidies code; (3) somewhat restricted entity coverage of the procurement code; and (4) difficulties at times in detecting code violations and initiating ameliorative actions. It should also be noted that no agreement on an acceptable safeguards code could be reached in the Tokyo Round negotiations. The experiences with the Tokyo Round codes and current interest in issues such as intellectual property, investment requirements, and restrictions on international transactions in services suggest that both formal and informal barriers arising from government regulations and policies will continue to be of concern.

Market structure. Differences in market structure among nations are often perceived as resulting in impediments to trade and investment. While there may be grounds for such perceptions, it is important to understand what are the determinants of market structure in given circumstances. Again, government policies may be important. Thus, for example, nations may differ in the extent to which they rely on public ownership, monopolization, and the regulation of economic activity. Given these differences, there are bound to be difficulties when national policies impinge on the interests of foreign producers. The issue here is closely tied in with national sovereignty and the domestic objectives that governments believe they have the right to pursue. Many government policies no doubt result in substantial social costs domestically, and there may be significant potential for an improvement in welfare if existing policies can be liberalized or eliminated altogether. The recent experiences with deregulation in a number of countries suggest that governments have become increasingly cognizant of the significant benefits to be obtained by reducing or removing their intervention. At the same time, these changes may be beneficial to foreign producing interests. Granting all of this, it nonetheless remains the case that governments will continue to pursue (sometimes costly) domestic policies that are believed to be in the national interest. At the same time, other countries may view these policies as detrimental to the initiating country as well as to themselves. The question then is how to address these difficult issues that are so closely tied to national sovereignty. The GATT codes mentioned above are an important beginning, and perhaps more can be accomplished in future negotiations under GATT auspices and possibly in deliberations in the OECD as well.

In addition to the points just stressed relating to how market structure may be shaped by different types of government policy, we should note the important role that may be played by competition or antitrust policies designed to affect the organization and behavior of private business firms. Governments obviously may differ in the extent to which they actively pursue policies to promote competition or condone collusive market structures. Restrictive business practices have been a matter of international concern for a long period of time. Beginning in 1948 with the Havana Charter proposal for an International Trade Organization, and more recently with the adoption of OECD antitrust guidelines in the late 1970s and United Nations principles and rules in 1980, efforts have been made to devise codes of conduct designed to minimize the detrimental effects of restrictive business practices. But in contrast to the aforementioned GATT codes, the codes relating to restrictive business practices are advisory rather than binding, and as Davidow (1984, 119) has noted, "major controversies remain . . . and implementation procedures are still in their infancy."

Since the monitoring and regulation of restrictive business practices are therefore matters of national policy, differences in competition policies might constitute an important informal barrier to trade and investment. As with other government policies, there may be substantial benefits from more active pursuit of policies to foster competition. Both the domestic economy and other countries may benefit if market access is improved. It may be important accordingly to seek international cooperation in developing guidelines and procedures to deal with the trade-distorting effects of restrictive business practices.

Institutional factors. A final consideration has to do with whether differences in political, social, and cultural institutions should be viewed as constituting informal barriers to trade and investment. In a federal system, for example, the locus of economic policies may vary considerably among the central government, states or provinces, and local government. In the United States, state governments are generally not permitted to institute policies that are at variance with those of the federal government. However, conformity may not always be achieved, as witnessed by the preferential procurement policies that some states have attempted to follow and the current dispute over the unitary taxation of multinational corporations. Similarly, in Canada, the provinces have their own procurement policies and there is the unusual practice that permits provincial ownership of natural resources.[2]

Nations may differ markedly in their social and cultural institutions and in the policies that governments believe to be in the national interest. Thus, for example, countries may have different policies affecting the availability of residential housing and land, which could in turn have a significant impact on private saving behavior and on a nation's current account. Because such effects are operative to a certain extent between the United States and Japan, some U.S. government officials have urged the Japanese to adopt policies designed to reduce Japanese savings and increase consumption, thereby hopefully reducing pressure on the U.S. current account. Nations may also institute policies designed to enhance their cultural identity and values. Cases in point would be Canadian policies intended to promote the domestic media and film industries. A further issue is that consumer tastes and spending habits will be conditioned by the domestic social and cultural enviroment, and there may well be a reluctance to purchase foreign products that are considered inferior to their domestic counterparts. The question here is whether national differences in consumer behavior should be considered as an informal barrier to trade. Finally, it should be noted that many nations restrict foreign investment in certain sensitive industries on national defense or cultural grounds, or to maintain macroeconomic control over their economy. To the extent that these issues are of legitimate national concern, it is not evident that they should be considered as informal barriers.

It seems clear from our discussion that administrative procedures could be designed and implemented for protectionist purposes. The same is true for a variety of government regulations and policies, except that in these circumstances domestic objectives could be overriding. Impediments to trade and investment may arise from national differences in market structure, which in turn are often conditioned by government policies. Sovereignty considerations thus enter again, but the domestic costs of intervention measures may provide an incentive to reduce or eliminate the intervention altogether. Finally, while social and cultural institutions condition consumer behavior, and there may well be some hesitancy in purchasing foreign goods, it is far from obvious that the institutions constitute an informal barrier to trade and investment. This may be the case as well for certain investment restrictions.

Up to this point, our discussion has been rather general. Let us now consider the available information on formal and informal barriers for the United States, Japan, and Canada in order to put the discussion in perspective.

9.2.1 Evidence on Formal Barriers

We can look first at the evidence on post–Tokyo Round nominal tariffs indicated in table 9.2. These are the tariff rates that were negotiated in the Tokyo Round, which was concluded in 1979. The reductions in the pre–Tokyo Round tariffs were phased in beginning in 1980, and the rates in table 9.2 became fully effective as of 1 January 1987.[3] It can be seen in table 9.2 that Japan's overall weighted-average tariff rate is 6.2 percent, while the rates for the United States and Canada are 3.3 percent and 4.6 percent, respectively.[4] The sectoral breakdown in the table is based on the International Standard Industrial Classification (ISIC). The highest tariff rates for the United States are in wearing apparel (22.7 percent), textiles (9.2 percent), footwear (8.8 percent), and glass and glass products (6.2 percent). The highest rates for Canada are in wearing apparel (24.2 percent), footwear (21.9 percent), textiles (16.7 percent), and furniture and fixtures (14.3 percent). For Japan, the highest rates are in food and kindred products (28.5 percent), agricultural products (21.8 percent), footwear (15.7 percent), and wearing apparel (13.9 percent). Aside from Japan's relatively high tariffs on food and agricultural products, the three countries share relatively high tariff rates on labor-intensive consumer goods, while their tariffs on semimanufactures and durable manufactures are relatively low.

Evidence on existing NTBs is unfortunately more difficult to obtain. The United Nations Conference on Trade and Development (UNCTAD) has compiled an inventory of NTBs for the major industrialized countries which can be used to calculate indexes of the trade coverage of NTBs. These indexes reflect the degree to which imports are subject to nontariff restrictions, with a value of 100 percent indicating that all trade in a given sector/country was covered by NTBs and 0 percent denoting that no NTBs were present. The extent of NTB coverage for sixteen major industrialized countries is given in table 9.3, using 1983 own-country imports for weighting purposes.[5] For all products, Japan was clearly at the low end of the spectrum in terms of formal NTBs, while the United States was among the highest of the countries shown. But when fuels are excluded, Japan and the United States appear roughly comparable. If we consider the individual sectors, Japan has a higher degree of NTB coverage than the United States in agricultural products and footwear, while the opposite is the case in textiles, iron and steel, electric machinery, and vehicles. Canada is not included in the industrialized countries listed in table 9.3 so that it is not clear how it would rank in terms of its NTB coverage.

The NTB-coverage indexes have the important drawback that they do not measure how restrictive the barriers are in terms of their effect on trade. For this purpose, what is needed are the price-increasing or quantity-reducing effects of the NTBs. Some estimates of the former type, measured in terms of the NTB ad valorem equivalents by sector, are given in Deardorff and Stern (1987) for the major industrialized countries and are summarized in table 9.4.[6] The largest ad valorem equivalents for Japan are in agricultural products, food and kindred products, textiles and wearing apparel, and footwear. For the United States, they apply to printing and publishing, food and kindred products, textiles and wearing apparel, iron and steel, and transport equipment. For Canada, they are in wearing apparel and textiles, footwear, food and kindred products, and transport equipment. The fact that Japan's overall weighted average ad valorem equivalent is 8.2 percent reflects the concentration of its formal NTBs in agricultural and food products.

It is of interest, finally, to consider the existing formal restrictions that apply to inward foreign investment in each of our three countries. For the United States, there are federal and state regulations that prohibit or limit foreign investment in certain specified industries. Some details on these regulations are given in appendix table A9.1. It is evident that a number of the federal restrictions are in sectors or activities that involve U.S. concerns with national security, while there are some state regulations affecting foreign investment in banking, real estate, and insurance. It is admittedly difficult to determine the impact of these various regulations, but experience suggests that the effects are limited and that the United States appears on the whole to be quite liberal as far as inward foreign investment is concerned.[7] However, some observers have argued that U.S. securities regulations, antitrust policies, and the extraterritorial interpretation of U.S. laws possibly constitute important informal barriers to foreign investment.

Throughout most of the postwar period, Japan maintained numerous restrictions on foreign direct investment. By 1976, however, foreign direct investment had been liberalized in virtually all nonfinancial sectors. With the amendment of the Foreign Exchange and Foreign Control Law in December 1980, the automatic approval system—which nonetheless required adminis-

Table 9.2 Post–Tokyo Round (1987) Tariffs by Sector in the Major Industrialized Countries (percent; weighted by 1976 own-country imports)

Sector	ISIC	ALA	ATA	BLX	CND	DEN	FIN	FR	GFR	IRE
Agr., for., & fisheries	(1)	7.5	8.6	4.7	2.2	5.0	11.0	4.6	4.7	5.2
Food, bev., & tobacco	(310)	21.9	20.7	10.1	6.1	13.4	23.8	9.1	11.2	10.8
Textiles	(321)	21.2	15.9	7.2	16.7	8.7	22.5	7.3	7.4	7.8
Wearing apparel	(322)	61.8	36.2	13.4	24.2	13.2	35.5	13.2	13.4	13.2
Leather products	(323)	20.3	7.7	2.5	6.3	1.8	9.3	1.6	3.2	1.8
Footwear	(324)	33.8	23.4	11.4	21.9	11.5	17.4	11.3	11.7	11.9
Wood products	(331)	12.5	3.7	2.4	3.2	3.4	0.4	2.4	2.9	2.5
Furniture & fixtures	(332)	31.2	22.1	5.6	14.3	5.5	5.5	5.6	5.6	5.7
Paper & paper products	(341)	7.7	12.3	6.9	6.7	7.9	4.5	5.5	5.2	8.0
printing & publishing	(342)	1.8	1.5	1.5	1.0	2.8	1.1	2.2	2.1	1.5
Chemicals	(35A)	5.4	4.7	8.0	7.5	8.5	1.8	7.6	8.0	7.6
Petroleum & rel. prod.	(35B)	0.2	4.4	1.5	0.3	3.3	0.1	0.5	1.8	3.8
Rubber products	(355)	11.2	9.9	4.2	6.7	4.4	13.5	3.5	3.8	3.7
Nonmetallic min. prod.	(36A)	11.5	5.9	3.7	6.4	5.0	2.9	4.7	3.6	4.5
Glass & glass products	(362)	18.9	12.9	8.0	7.2	7.5	22.3	7.4	7.9	7.3
Iron & steel	(371)	10.8	5.8	4.6	5.4	5.5	4.2	4.9	4.7	5.9
Nonferrous metals	(372)	4.2	3.3	1.6	3.0	6.6	0.8	2.6	1.9	6.5
Metal products	(381)	23.7	10.4	5.4	8.5	5.5	7.7	5.4	5.5	5.4
Nonelectric machinery	(382)	13.9	6.4	4.3	4.5	4.4	6.1	4.4	4.5	4.3
Electric machinery	(383)	21.6	14.7	7.4	5.8	7.1	6.0	7.7	8.3	7.2
Transport equipment	(384)	21.2	22.1	7.9	1.6	7.2	3.8	7.9	7.7	10.2
Misc. manufacturing	(38A)	12.8	8.7	3.0	5.4	6.1	12.6	5.8	5.6	6.5
All sectors		14.8	11.3	5.4	4.6	6.4	6.2	4.9	5.7	6.6

	ISIC	IT	JPN	NL	NZ	NOR	SWD	SWZ	UK	US
Agri., For., & Fisheries	(1)	6.1	21.8	4.7	3.8	1.5	1.8	5.2	4.5	1.8
Food, bev., & tobacco	(310)	7.7	28.5	10.6	16.2	8.7	3.7	13.3	10.3	4.7
Textiles	(321)	5.6	3.3	8.5	12.3	13.3	10.3	6.6	6.7	9.2
Wearing apparel	(322)	13.2	13.9	13.5	58.5	21.7	14.2	12.4	13.3	22.7
Leather products	(323)	0.7	3.1	3.0	15.3	5.8	4.0	2.1	1.2	4.2
Footwear	(324)	10.4	15.7	11.2	40.7	21.7	13.7	9.0	12.5	8.8
Wood products	(331)	0.8	0.3	2.8	11.4	1.6	0.7	3.2	3.1	1.7
Furniture & fixtures	(332)	5.6	5.1	5.6	38.3	5.1	4.0	9.2	5.6	4.1
Paper & paper products	(341)	2.6	2.9	6.2	20.5	1.9	2.4	4.3	4.9	0.2
Printing & publishing	(342)	1.8	0.1	2.2	1.1	4.3	0.2	0.7	2.1	0.7
Chemicals	(35A)	8.1	4.8	8.1	8.1	6.2	4.8	0.9	7.9	2.4
Petroleum & rel. prod.	(35B)	0.6	2.2	1.0	0.6	0.1	0.0	0.0	1.1	1.4
Rubber products	(355)	2.7	1.1	4.1	9.5	6.6	6.1	1.7	2.7	2.5
Nonmetallic min. prod.	(36A)	2.8	0.5	3.3	12.7	2.4	2.8	2.5	2.4	5.3
Glass & glass products	(362)	7.6	5.1	7.5	13.5	8.0	7.1	3.1	7.9	6.2
Iron & steel	(371)	3.5	2.8	5.6	5.2	1.7	3.7	1.7	4.7	3.6
Nonferrous metals	(372)	1.8	1.1	3.6	4.1	0.9	0.7	2.4	1.7	0.7
Metal products	(381)	5.5	5.2	5.4	26.5	4.4	4.0	2.8	5.6	4.8
Nonelectric machinery	(382)	4.5	4.4	4.3	22.1	5.2	3.5	1.2	4.2	3.3
Electric machinery	(383)	8.0	4.3	7.8	19.6	6.9	4.5	1.6	8.1	4.4
Transport equipment	(384)	8.8	1.5	9.0	26.8	2.2	5.1	6.1	7.2	2.5
Misc. manufacturing	(38A)	5.8	4.6	5.2	18.2	7.4	4.6	1.1	3.0	4.2
All sectors		4.4	6.2	5.7	13.8	4.5	3.9	3.5	4.9	3.3

Source: Calculated by Deardorff and Stern (1986), based on information provided by the Office of the U.S. Trade Representative.

Table 9.3 NTB Coverage by Product Category for the Major Industrial Countries, 1983 (in percentages)

Industrial Country Markets	All products	All, less Fuels	Agriculture	Manufactures	Textiles	Footwear	Iron & Steel	Electrical Machinery	Vehicles	Rest of Manufactures
EEC	22.3	21.1	36.4	18.7	52.0	9.5	52.6	13.4	45.3	10.3
Belgium-Luxembourg	26.0	33.9	55.9	33.6	38.2	12.3	47.4	19.5	54.3	30.6
Denmark	11.7	15.9	28.5	13.2	46.5	13.6	49.9	6.7	35.0	5.4
France	57.1	28.1	37.8	27.4	48.4	6.6	73.9	41.7	42.9	19.4
West Germany	12.4	18.3	22.3	18.5	57.0	9.7	53.5	6.8	52.0	6.6
Greece	13.4	23.2	46.4	20.4	21.8	22.8	54.5	13.5	65.5	8.5
Ireland	13.4	15.0	24.8	13.8	31.7	8.8	23.0	0.5	65.8	6.6
Italy	6.9	14.6	39.9	9.3	37.2	0.2	48.6	7.1	10.2	2.6
Netherlands	25.5	28.0	51.9	17.8	57.3	12.0	35.5	4.0	49.7	10.7
U.K.	14.3	17.5	34.9	14.8	59.6	12.2	42.1	12.7	44.3	6.7
Australia	34.1	24.1	36.1	23.6	30.9	50.0	55.6	48.7	0.7	21.6
Austria	4.9	6.0	41.7	2.4	2.2	0.1	0.0	0.0	2.9	3.0
Finland	34.9	9.2	31.5	6.7	31.0	68.8	43.9	0.0	0.0	0.4
Japan	11.9	16.9	42.9	7.7	11.8	34.1	0.0	0.0	0.0	7.7
Norway	5.7	5.8	24.2	4.1	42.9	5.4	0.1	0.0	0.2	0.4
Switzerland	32.2	23.6	73.4	17.6	57.4	0.0	3.9	28.1	1.1	14.6
U.S.A.	43.0	17.3	24.2	17.1	57.0	11.5	37.7	5.2	34.2	6.1
All industrial country markets	27.1	18.6	36.1	16.1	44.8	12.6	35.4	10.0	30.4	8.8

Source: Adapted from Nogués, Olechowski, and Winters (1985).

trative review—was changed to a prior notification system. Under Article 3 of the OECD Code of Liberalization of Capital Movements (to which Japan adheres), on being notified, the Ministry of Finance and other relevant ministries may recommend against foreign investment in industries necessary for defense and maintenance of social order. In Japan, this has been understood to include industries producing aircraft, weapons, explosives, gunpowder, atomic power, aerospace equipment, narcotics, and vaccines.[8] Under its adherence to the OECD Code, Japan also reserved its right to restrict foreign investment in agriculture, forestry, fisheries, mining, petroleum, and hides. It is also possible that Japan will restrict foreign investment undertaken by a national or company from a country without treaties or reciprocity for Japanese investments.

Both private domestic and foreign investment are completely prohibited in Japanese industries which are treated as government monopolies or are otherwise set aside to be handled by public corporations. Such industries have included water supply, postal services, telecommunication services, tobacco, industrial alcohol, and salt. As part of Japan's administrative reform program during the 1980s, telecommunication services, tobacco, and some parts of postal services have been deregulated and the public corporations and other agencies producing these services have been privatized. Substantial foreign investment in at least some of these industries is expected in the future.[9]

The May 1984 Yen-Dollar Agreement provided for the opening of Japanese financial markets to greater competition.[10] Thus far foreign firms have been permitted to participate in trust banking, securities trading, and offshore banking, as well as in insurance and leasing. These recent changes have resulted in large new investments by foreign financial firms.

Despite the substantial changes that have taken place in Japan's statutory framework and in individual provisions governing foreign investment, many foreign observers question the extent of these changes. For example, as Henderson (1986, 143) has noted: ". . . liberalization there has been, but not to open competitive opportunities where it has made real differences to inward transactions in significant Japanese markets, such as the markets that the Japanese have come to share in the United States."

In Canada, there are some statutory restrictions that apply to foreign ownership of capital in certain industries. According to Price Waterhouse (1983a), a license to operate a broadcasting station or a network of stations can only be granted to a Canadian citizen or to a corporation that is 80 percent owned or controlled by Canadians. There are also limitations on the percentage of shares that nonresidents may hold in Canadian chartered banks and companies engaged in life insurance, sales finance, or trusts. There appear to be comparatively few explicit restrictions on foreign investment in Canada and there are no industries that are specifically closed to private enterprise, including foreign investors. However, it is well known that there was a con-

Table 9.4 Estimated Ad Valorem Equivalents of Nontariff Barriers in the Major Industrialized Countries (in percentages)

Sector	ISIC	ALA	ATA	BLX	CND	DEN	FIN	FR	GFR	IRE
Agr., for., & fisheries	(1)	1.4	7.0	18.4	1.0	9.4	10.4	10.9	3.6	8.2
Food, bev., & tobacco	(310)	9.2	11.4	14.3	4.1	7.3	8.1	8.8	4.5	6.3
Textiles	(321)	3.3	0.1	5.3	6.7	12.3	4.4	12.3	7.9	8.4
Wearing apparel	(322)	16.6	0.1	5.3	21.7	6.5	2.1	4.3	7.0	4.4
Leather products	(323)	9.8	0.0	0.0	0.0	0.0	0.0	0.0	0.0	0.0
Footwear	(342)	13.0	0.0	3.2	5.3	3.5	18.0	1.9	2.5	2.3
Wood products	(331)	0.0	0.0	0.0	0.0	0.0	0.0	0.0	0.0	0.0
Furniture & fixtures	(332)	0.0	0.0	0.0	0.0	0.0	0.0	0.0	0.0	0.0
Paper & paper products	(341)	0.0	0.0	0.0	0.0	0.0	0.0	2.3	0.0	0.0
Printing & publishing	(342)	0.0	0.0	0.0	0.0	0.0	0.0	10.1	0.0	0.0
Chemicals	(35A)	1.7	3.0	0.0	0.0	0.0	0.3	1.5	0.0	0.0
Petroleum & rel. prod.	(35B)	17.5	0.2	9.8	0.0	0.0	16.8	89.2	0.0	0.0
Rubber products	(355)	0.0	0.0	0.0	0.0	0.0	0.0	0.0	0.0	3.5
Nonmetallic min. prod.	(36A)	0.0	0.0	1.1	0.0	0.0	0.5	2.0	0.2	0.0
Glass & glass products	(362)	0.0	0.0	0.0	0.0	0.0	0.0	0.0	0.0	0.0
Iron & steel	(371)	16.7	0.0	14.2	0.0	15.0	13.2	22.2	16.1	6.9
Nonferrous metals	(372)	0.0	0.0	0.0	0.0	0.0	0.0	0.0	0.0	0.0
Metal products	(381)	0.8	0.0	1.9	0.0	0.8	0.7	0.0	0.0	0.0
Nonelectric machinery	(382)	0.0	0.0	0.0	0.0	0.0	0.0	0.0	0.0	0.0
Electric machinery	(383)	7.0	0.0	2.8	1.4	1.0	0.0	10.0	1.0	0.1
Transport equipment	(384)	0.1	0.3	6.2	3.9	4.0	0.0	4.9	5.9	7.5
Misc. manufacturing	(38A)	2.2	0.3	3.1	0.0	0.5	0.0	4.5	0.0	0.0
All sectors		4.0	1.2	5.7	1.9	3.0	5.3	24.4	2.5	2.6

	ISIC	IT	JPN	NL	NZ	NOR	SWD	SWZ	UK	US
Agr., for., & fisheries	(1)	13.2	48.5	17.1	0.4	12.7	3.1	22.8	11.5	0.3
Food, bev., & tobacco	(310)	10.2	27.1	13.3	4.1	15.7	6.3	18.3	8.9	14.5
Textiles	(321)	8.8	5.2	15.1	10.1	11.3	3.2	15.2	9.7	12.4
Wearing apparel	(322)	1.1	2.7	8.0	8.3	12.4	11.4	8.0	9.1	17.8
Leather products	(323)	0.0	0.0	0.0	0.0	0.0	0.0	0.0	0.0	0.0
Footwear	(324)	0.1	6.1	3.1	0.0	1.4	29.1	0.0	3.2	4.3
Wood products	(331)	0.0	0.0	0.0	0.0	0.0	0.0	0.0	0.0	0.0
Furniture & fixtures	(332)	0.0	0.0	0.0	0.0	0.0	0.0	0.0	0.0	0.0
Paper & paper products	(341)	0.0	0.0	0.0	0.0	0.0	0.0	0.0	0.0	0.0
Printing & publishing	(342)	0.0	0.0	0.0	0.0	0.0	0.0	0.0	0.0	22.3
Chemicals	(35A)	3.4	1.1	0.0	1.7	4.5	1.1	4.3	1.7	0.0
Petroleum & rel. prod.	(35B)	0.0	1.3	3.9	6.1	0.9	0.0	16.8	0.0	0.0
Rubber products	(355)	3.3	0.0	1.1	0.0	0.0	0.0	0.0	0.0	0.0
Nonmetallic min. prod.	(36A)	1.0	1.1	1.1	0.8	0.0	0.5	0.0	0.0	0.0
Glass & glass products	(362)	0.0	0.0	0.0	0.0	0.0	0.0	0.0	0.0	0.0
Iron & steel	(371)	14.6	0.0	10.6	0.0	0.0	0.0	1.2	12.6	11.3
Nonferrous metals	(372)	0.0	0.0	0.0	0.0	0.0	0.0	0.0	0.0	0.0
Metal products	(381)	1.4	0.0	1.9	0.8	0.7	0.0	0.2	0.0	0.0
Nonelectric machinery	(382)	1.6	0.0	0.0	0.0	0.0	0.0	0.0	0.0	0.0
Electric machinery	(383)	1.0	0.0	0.6	0.7	0.0	0.0	4.0	1.8	0.2
Transport equipment	(384)	1.2	0.0	5.7	2.4	0.0	0.0	0.1	5.1	3.9
Misc. manufacturing	(38A)	1.0	0.8	0.1	0.4	0.0	0.0	0.1	0.0	0.0
All sectors		4.0	8.2	5.1	2.5	2.2	1.3	6.3	3.3	2.4

Source: Adapted from Deardorff and Stern (1987).

certed effort beginning in the early 1970s to screen new investments by means of the Foreign Investment Review Act (FIRA) and in 1980 to increase Canadian ownership and control of its energy industry. These federal policies have been significantly altered in recent years, although, as will be noted below, there are still some sectors in which foreign ownership and control are subject to restriction. Also, provincial policies may impinge at times on the investment activities of foreign companies.

9.2.2 Evidence on Informal Barriers

In contrast to tariffs and explicit NTBs, there is no unambiguous way to identify informal barriers. What constitutes an informal barrier will be a matter of perception and judgment on the part of firms and governments who believe that their economic interests are being adversely affected by the policies and practices of other countries. Thus, informal barriers can presumably be identified on the basis of complaints by the affected parties. The difficulty of course is to determine if the complaints are valid and how important empirically the economic effects of the alleged informal barriers may be.

In section 303 of the U.S. Trade and Tariff Act of 1984, the Office of the U.S. Trade Representative (USTR) is directed to submit an annual report on significant foreign barriers affecting goods, services, investment, and intellectual property.[11] It is interesting to consider the specific foreign barriers that the USTR identified in the cases of Canada and Japan as of 1986. These are listed in appendix tables A9.2 and A9.3. Note that the tables include such formal barriers as Canada's relatively high tariffs on manufactures and certain relatively high Japanese tariffs and restrictive quotas on agricultural products and raw materials. In interpreting these tables, it is important to note that Canadian tariffs on imports from the United States will be phased out over a ten-year period beginning in 1989 in accordance with the U.S.-Canadian Free Trade Agreement. In the case of Japan, some notable actions to liberalize imports of agricultural products and to increase access of foreign manufactures and services to the Japanese market were introduced after 1986.

As far as the informal barriers in Canada are concerned, they relate especially to federal government policies and procedures involving procurement, freight subsidies, lack of copyright protection for retransmission of broadcast signals, compulsory licensing of pharmaceuticals, the protection of culturally sensitive industries, restrictions on foreign data processing, and encouragement of domestic energy ownership and development. In addition, there are barriers arising from provincial policies and institutions, including provincial liquor boards, procurement, and trucking. It is interesting that provincial resource policies are not listed, especially in light of the 1986 U.S. action to countervail against the alleged subsidy arising from the softwood-lumer stumpage policies of the major lumber-producing provinces.

As for Japan, it has been singled out for many years, especially by U.S. government officials, as the leading example of a nation that maintains an endless variety of informal barriers. The United States has been involved with Japan for some time now in efforts to improve access to the Japanese market. Thus, in several instances recent changes have been made in Japanese policies, and these new policies are now being monitored by the United States with regard to their effectiveness in complying with the GATT codes. This is especially the case for certain items listed under standards, testing, labeling, and certification and government procurement. Nonetheless, there are a variety of other administrative barriers and preferences noted, as in aluminum fabricating, fish products, the lack of protection of intellectual property, bidding on construction projects, and approval of the introduction of new consumer products. Japanese business practices are listed as a barrier in the case of soda ash. Finally, the regulations restricting the establishment of large-scale retail stores call attention to the way in which the organization of Japan's distribution system may serve to reinforce the importance of smaller firms to foster a less efficient system of distribution.

It is of some interest to compare the 1986 USTR list of Japanese barriers with some other recent compilations that have appeared in the literature. Thus, for example, Christelow (1985/86) identifies Japanese restrictive product standards and related inspection and certification procedures, the wholesale and retail distribution systems, and government procurement procedures as the major intangible barriers to imports. Bergsten and Cline (1987, esp. 63–71) include government procurement, regulation, oligopoly behavior, industrial targeting, certain cultural attributes, and the retail distribution system. Rapp (1986) and Balassa (1986) have the most exhaustive list of informal barriers. Between them they include: administrative guidance; customs procedures; standards, testing, and certification requirements; procurement; regulations concerning intellectual property; distribution channels; academic discounts; policies for the defense of depressed industries; and policies for the promotion of high-technology industries. Presumably, many of the informal barriers described by Rapp and Balassa would cover both trade and foreign direct investment, although in several instances their examples appear to be outdated.

Having set forth rather imposing lists of informal barriers for Canada and Japan, it seems natural to inquire about the informal barriers that may exist in the United States. While the USTR (1986, 2) admits that all nations have trade barriers, including the United States, they do not provide a list of the U.S. barriers. But such a list has been compiled by the European Community (1987) using a format similar to the one followed by the USTR. The main U.S. barriers are listed in appendix table A9.4. They include such formal barriers as relatively high tariff rates on selected manufactures, customs fees, differential import taxes, and agricultural import quotas. Informal barriers include procedures for administering certain import quotas and restraints on foreign exporters, implementation of testing and inspection requirements for selected products, some particular procedures involving government procurement, a variety of export and domestic subsidies, government-funded R&D, procedures for approving foreign patents, administration of U.S. trade laws, repair servicing, and state tax preferences and policies.)

While it is not clear whether this list of U.S. barriers covers all of the items of concern to Canadian and Japanese interests, it may nonetheless call attention to the most obvious barriers. This is especially true with respect to the U.S. system of administered protection. We have already noted that there are established procedures in U.S. trade law to enter complaints over such alleged unfair foreign trading practices as dumping, subsidies, and other foreign government policies to limit market access or promote exports. While the procedures for investigating these complaints are on the whole quite explicit, it can be argued that the ease with which an action can be brought may introduce an important element of uncertainty and even harassment of foreign export interests and thus represent an informal barrier. Furthermore, there is evidence that the complaint and investigative process may become politicized, with protectionist measures taken by the U.S. president even though prior investigation may have found little or no evidence to support the complaints of unfair trade practices. Some examples that come to mind here include the U.S. voluntary export restraints on automobiles from Japan, steel from a variety of countries, and the countervailing duty imposed on imports of Canadian softwood lumber. There are indications in the 1988 Omnibus Trade Act that the U.S. position on unfair foreign trading practices has hardened, in which case we can expect to see a continuation and maybe an expansion of U.S. actions against alleged unfair foreign trading practices.)

It might be argued, furthermore, that there are many U.S. government programs and policies that provide special advantages to American firms. Some information is given in appendix table A9.5 on projected expenditures for U.S. industrial support programs for 1984. These involve direct expenditures, the net costs of loans and loan guarantees (i.e., credit expenditures), and a variety of tax expenditures. It is evident that a substantial part of the direct and credit expenditures involves the support of U.S. agriculture and related activities, whereas the manufacturing and services sectors are the prime beneficiaries of tax expenditures. It is important to note that the expenditures listed in appendix table A9.5 include only those programs "with the primary intent of promoting commerce and industry." Thus, according to the Congressional Budget Office (1984b, xii–xiii):

> The tally excludes programs that may have significant industrial effects, but which Congress undertakes for other purposes. Programs excluded have much greater costs than those included. Department of Defense purchases of goods

and services are projected to approach $140 billion. Programs to aid individuals, such as medical and housing subsidies, equal $110 billion. Excluded research and development programs exceed $35 billion. In short, 14 programs that are excluded, but have identifiable commercial effects, total almost $300 billion.[12]

It could also be argued that some regulatory policies have benefitted U.S. firms, although the reduction or removal of regulations in many sectors in recent years have resulted in significant realignments and increased efficiency in these sectors. Finally, as noted above, U.S. antitrust policies and the extraterritorial interpretation of U.S. laws might be considered by some observers as potentially important informal barriers to inward foreign direct investment.

The point of our discussion should be clear by now. It is simply that informal barriers to trade and investment come in a variety of forms, and these barriers may be important in the United States itself, as well as in its two largest trading partners. As mentioned above, it is difficult to assess the validity of the complaints about informal barriers and to determine how countries compare in their reliance on these barriers. Moreover, as McCulloch (1988) has noted, the evidence based on complaints may be seriously biased insofar as no account is taken of the successful and profitable experiences that exporting firms and foreign multinationals have realized in penetrating foreign markets, even in Japan. In any event, it is necessary to analyze the existing informal barriers in an empirical context and it is to this that we now turn.

9.3 Measuring the Effects of Formal and Informal Barriers

In the preceding section, an effort was made to elucidate the main characteristics of formal and informal barriers and to identify the major barriers that exist currently in the United States, Canada, and Japan. The next step is to determine how important these barriers are empirically in each country. This raises a number of difficult conceptual issues that we first discuss.[13] We then review several studies that have attempted to empirically assess the effects of the barriers, and we offer some new evidence of our own as well.

9.3.1 Conceptual Issues

We have made a distinction in our discussion between formal and informal barriers. If one wished to quantify the effects of some formal barrier, it would be best to look at the specific details of the implementation of that barrier. For example, an explicit quota usually permits an announced quantity of imports of a certain type, and an analysis of the quota should begin, therefore, with direct information pertaining to that quantity. There are serious disadvantages to this direct approach in dealing with a variety of formal barriers, and, of course, we are left in the dark with respect to informal barriers.

The direct approach can obviously capture only those barriers that have been explicitly identified. If a country or industry makes use of a particular type of barrier that the investigator does not recognize or include in the analysis, then trade may appear much freer than it actually is. Furthermore, even for those barriers that are included, it is difficult to process the diverse direct information that is available on each barrier in a way that will be comparable across barriers and thus permit them to be aggregated to obtain a total measure of trade interference. An additional point is that if more than one barrier is present in a given industry, it is conceivable that the presence of one reduces the effects of another, so that a separate analysis of each of them may lead to an overstatement of their total effects. Finally, in attempting to evaluate overall levels of protection involving both formal and informal barriers, general equilibrium effects are bound to matter, such as the effects of barriers in one sector on trade in another, and the effects of all together on exchange rates. Thus, even though direct information about barriers is likely to be the most accurate available, it does not provide a good starting point for a general analysis and, in any event, by definition does not apply to informal barriers.

There are in principle two types of general approaches that can bypass some of the difficulties just mentioned, although admittedly introducing new ones. These are *price-impact measures* calculated in terms of tariff equivalents or price relatives, and *quantity-impact measures* based upon econometric estimates of models of trade flows.

Price-impact measures involve calculating the price effects of existing barriers based on observed differentials between domestic prices and import or world prices. Such measures have the advantage of capturing the complex of formal and informal barriers that may impede trade but cannot be measured explicitly. However, it is difficult to interpret price measures without actual information about import demand and supply conditions or an approximation of the equilibrium prices in the absence of the barriers, and whether supply conditions are competitive or monopolistic. The data requirements are also formidable, especially insofar as domestic and imported goods are imperfect substitutes. For example, in cases where imports are differentiated by country of origin, where there is monopolistic competition, or where commodity aggregates reflect a diversity of goods, domestic and foreign price comparisons may be difficult to interpret. It is even conceivable that these comparisons could go in the wrong direction, reflecting lower domestic than world prices even when there are barriers to trade. A final point is that comparisons using observed prices will not capture the effects of such barriers as government procurement or other preferential restrictions that may raise the *shadow* price of imports to some domestic purchasers.

The alternative to looking at price-impact measures of barriers is to consider the quantity impacts involved. It would appear that a quantity measure is preferable to a price measure in that it comes closer to telling us what we really want to know about the effects of barriers: that is, by how much they reduce trade. Conceptually, the objective is to estimate what trade would have been in the absence of existing barriers and compare this to the trade that actually occurs. To accomplish this, we need a satisfactory model of the determinants of trade as well as data covering a sufficient variety of trading situations. The latter is needed in order to identify, or extrapolate to, a situation in which trade is at least approximately free.

What is the most appropriate model of trade to use for empirical purposes? This depends to a considerable extent on precisely what we wish to explain. Where inter-industry trade is at issue, the Heckscher-Ohlin model, with its stress on differences in factor endowments as the primary determinants of trade, is generally seen as most helpful. Alternatively, where the focus is on intra-industry trade, the Helpman-Krugman model (1985), which makes product differentiation and scale economies the central forces determining trade, is a plausible alternative. The Helpman-Krugman model is a development of the last decade, while the theoretical aspects of the Heckscher-Ohlin model have been explored in the literature for many years. In both instances, however, it is only very recently that rigorous and empirical viable frameworks for estimating the determinants of trade have been derived and implemented for either model. These theories, however, are not in conflict, as Helpman and Krugman note (p. 145). That is, the explanation of intra-industry trade in terms of product differentiation, scale economies, and specialization can be entirely consistent with the explanation of inter-industry trade in terms of differences in factor endowments.

In examining this recent empirical work, it is important to call attention to some possibly important qualifications. First, the conceptual procedure of attributing to barriers all departures of trade from what a model's exogenous variables can explain places a large burden on the model that has been used to explain trade. Indeed, the worse is the model of trade flows, the greater will be the estimates of the effects of barriers, suggesting a considerable upward bias in their estimation in given circumstances. While this is a serious objection, it would not appear to apply to comparisons of the effects of barriers across countries unless countries differ among themselves in the extent to which the model is appropriate for explaining their trade.

A second point is that theoretical trade models such as Heckscher-Ohlin and Helpman-Krugman are capable of determining patterns of trade only when a series of highly unrealistic assumptions are made.[14] In their absence, such models can only determine patterns of trade in an average sense and are not adequate to the task of predicting trade exactly for particular industries and countries. Thus, a departure of actual trade from what is predicted by a regression model may only reflect this indeterminacy and not the presence of barriers.

Finally, the approach using trade models can only make comparisons among industries or countries. They cannot tell us how far patterns depart from free trade. For if barriers restrict trade everywhere, that may be embedded in the parameters of the regressions and will not be reflected in the residuals or coefficients of the dummy variables used to represent unusual characteristics. Subject to these qualifications, the approach based on trade models is useful for identifying *relative* levels of nontariff protection. It is in this context that our review and assessment of the empirical studies of trade structure should be placed.

For our purposes here, there are seven sets of noteworthy studies that have attempted a quantitative assessment of whether national trade barriers are distinctive and therefore serve to limit foreign access into the domestic market. The studies include work by Saxonhouse (1983a, 1986), Leamer (1984, 1988), Bergsten and Cline (1987), Balassa (1986), Staiger, Deardorff, and Stern (1985, 1987), Noland (1987), and Lawrence (1987). Each of these studies permits us to look at Japan, the United States, and Canada in a comparative context and to determine whether their barriers are of distinctive importance. Given that these studies differ substantially in the time period examined, countries sampled, level of aggregation, and specification employed, it is useful to discuss the conceptual frameworks and issues addressed in them and their principal conclusions. To set the stage for our discussion, we have summarized in table 9.5 the main characteristics of the aforementioned studies.

As noted previously, the Heckscher-Ohlin and Helpman-Krugman models have provided the basis for most of the studies of interest to us here. It is useful to begin accordingly with some formal analysis that will be helpful in discussing the relevant empirical issues and findings.

Assume that all goods are differentiated by country of origin.[15] Given identical and homotheic preferences, each country will consume identical proportions of each variety of each good. This means that country j's consumption of all the different varieties of good i can be described by:

$$C_{ij} = M_{ij}^+ + C_{ij}^j \qquad (1)$$
$$M_{ij}^+ = S_j(\overline{Q} - Q_{ij}) \qquad (2)$$

and

$$C_{ij}^j = S_j Q_{ij} \qquad (3)$$

where

$C_{ij} \equiv$ consumption of good i by country j

$C_{ij}^j \equiv$ consumption of good i of variety j by country j

$M_{ij}^+ \equiv$ imports of good i by country j

$Q_{ij} \equiv$ production of good i in country j

$\overline{Q}_i \equiv \sum_j Q_{ij} \equiv$ global production of good i

$\Pi_j \equiv \sum_i Q_{ij} \equiv$ GNP of country j

$\overline{\Pi} \equiv \sum_j \Pi_j \equiv$ global GNP

$S_j \equiv \dfrac{\Pi_j}{\overline{\Pi}} \equiv$ share of country j in global GNP

Equations (2) and (3) can be combined to obtain:

$$\frac{M_{ij}^+}{M_{ij}^+ + S_j Q_{ij}} = \frac{S_j(\overline{Q}_i - Q_{ij})}{M_{ij}^+ + S_j Q_{ij}} = \frac{S_j(\overline{Q}_i - Q_{ij})}{S_j(\overline{Q}_i - Q_{ij}) + S_j Q_{ij}}$$

$$= \frac{S_j(\overline{Q}_i - Q_{ij})}{S_j \overline{Q}_i} = 1 - \frac{Q_{ij}}{\overline{Q}_i} \tag{4}$$

Equation (4) states that imports of good i by country j will be equal to the proportion of good i that is produced outside of j. Thus, the less competitive a country is in the production of good i, the more it will import. Alternatively,

$$\frac{M_{ij}^+}{M_{ij}^+ + S_j Q_{ij}} = 1 - \frac{Q_{ij}}{\overline{Q}_i} = 1 - \frac{(1 - S_j)Q_{ij}}{(1 - S_j)\overline{Q}_i}$$

$$= 1 - \frac{X_{ij}^+}{(1 - S_j)\overline{Q}_i} \tag{4'}$$

where $X_{ij}^+ \equiv$ exports of good i by country j.

Imports of good i by country j as a proportion of total use by j will be equal to the proportion of foreign consumption of i that is foreign produced.

Equations (4) and (4') explain import shares by the shares of domestic production in global production or by export shares. Imports (and exports) can also be directly explained by national factor endowments. From (2) and (4'), we have:

$$M_{ij}^+ = S_j(\overline{Q}_i - Q_{ij}) \text{ and} \tag{2}$$

$$X_{ij}^+ = (1 - S_j)Q_{ij}. \tag{5}$$

Table 9.5 Studies of the Quantitative Impact of Trade Barriers

Author(s) of Study	Time Period	Countries in Sample	Level of Aggregation	Dependent Variable	Independent Variable	Model	Findings
Balassa (1986)	1973–83	17	One economy-wide sector, imports disaggregated by type, manufacturing, primary, and by source: developing, industrialized economies	Log Import/GNP; Import/GNP	Log GNP/per capita; log population; primary imports/total imports; transport costs	Stylized version of Chenery (1960)	Significant dummy variables for Japan, U.S.
Bergsten-Cline (1985, 1987)	1974–84	11	One economy-wide sector	Import/GNP	Log GNP, log crude, log oil per capita, log arable land per capita, transport costs, iron reserves, dummy	Stylized version of Heckscher-Ohlin	Insignificant dummy variable for Japan
Lawrence (1987)	1970, 1980, 1983	13	21 manufacturing sectors	Imports/total domestic use	Exports/total OECD use; production/total OECD production; distance	Helpman-Krugman	Generally significant Japanese dummies indicating underimporting of manufactures; some significant U.S. and Canadian dummies indicating overimporting of manufactures
Leamer (1984)	1958, 1975	60	10 sectors	Net trade	Capital, 3 varieties of labor, 4 varieties of land, coal, oil, minerals	Heckscher-Ohlin with factor price equalization	Generally significant Canadian dummies for 1958; two significant dummies each for U.S., Japan and Canada for 1975

Study	Years		Sectors	Trade measure	Factors/variables	Model	Results
Saxonhouse (1983a)	1959, 1962, 1964, 1967, 1969, 1971, 1973	9	109 sectors	Net trade	Capital, 2 varieties of labor, petroleum reserves, iron ore deposits, arable land, distance	Heckscher-Ohlin with factor price equalization normalized for factor quality	17 significant Japanese dummy variables out of 109 possible instances; covers 4.9% of total trade; 11 significant dummy variables for Canada
Saxonhouse (1986)	1964, 1971, 1979	22	109 sectors	Net trade	Capital, 2 varieties of labor, petroleum reserves, iron ore deposits, arable land, distance	Hecksher-Ohlin with factor price equalization normalized for factor quality	61 out of 327 instances Japanese trade outside forecast interval; covers 6.1% of Japanese gross external trade; 39 out of 327 instances for Canada; 30 out of 327 instances for U.S.
Noland (1987)	1980	45	One economy-wide sector	Log imports, log exports, log trade volume	Log GDP, log GDP per capita, factor endowment similarity index, transport costs	Stylized version of Heckscher-Ohlin and Helpman-Krugman	Insignificant dummy variables for U.S., Canada, and Japan
Staiger, Deardorff, and Stern (1985, 1987)	1970s	34	22 traded sectors; 7 nontradables	Employment; net trade; factor content of trade	Capital, 8 categories of labor	Multisector, multicountry computational model	Japanese barriers have greatest impact on its agricultural sector and thus on U.S. agricultural interests

Now let us assume an indirect trade-utility function H, which expresses the maximum level of utility that an open economy can attain as a function of output prices and national factor endowments.[16] The usefulness of the indirect trade-utility function stems from its convenient properties. In particular, net export functions can be derived directly from it by differentiation, using an extension of Roy's Identity.[17] It is easiest to proceed by recognizing that H is made up two components: the GNP function, Π, and an indirect utility function, g. Π and g represent the maximum levels of GNP and utility, respectively, that an economy can attain for a given level of output prices and factor endowments. The forms of Π and g are unknown, but a few familiar restrictions will yield equations that can readily be estimated. If it is assumed that Π is a continuous, nonnegative, homogeneous-of-degree-one GNP function and that the utility function from which g is derived is positive, continuous, nondecreasing, quasi-concave, and homogeneous, then with factor-price equalization, by extension of Roy's Identity, it is required that:

$$W_s = \frac{\partial H}{\partial L_s} \qquad s = 1, 2, \ldots, K \tag{6}$$

and

$$\frac{\partial W_s}{\partial L_s} = \frac{\partial^2 H}{\partial L_s^2} = 0 \qquad s = 1, 2, \ldots, K \tag{7}$$

where

$W_s \equiv$ rental for factor of production s; and
$L_s \equiv$ endowment of factor of production s.

From (2) and (5) and the restrictions on Π and g, we have:

$$S_j = \frac{\sum_j W_{sj} L_{sj}}{\sum_i \overline{Q}_i} \tag{8}$$

and by Hotelling's Lemma from Π we get:[18]

$$Q_{ij} = \sum_s R_{is} L_{sj} \tag{9}$$

where R_{is} is a function of parameters of Π and output prices, all assumed to be constant.

Substituting (8) and (9) into (2), imports and exports of good i in country j will be given by

$$M_{ij}^+ = \sum_{s=1}^{K} B_{is}^+ L_{sj} + \sum_{s=1}^{K} \sum_{r=1}^{K} D_{isr}^+ L_{sj} L_{rj} \qquad i1, \ldots ,N \qquad (10)$$

$$X_{ij}^+ = \sum_{s=1}^{K} R_{is} L_{sj} + \sum_{s=1}^{K} \sum_{r=1}^{K} D_{isr}^+ L_{sj} L_{rj} \qquad i=1, \ldots ,N \qquad (11)$$

where B_{is}^+ and D_{is}^+ are functions of parameters of Π and output prices and will be constant under the assumptions already made. If equation (10) is subtracted from equation (11), we obtain net exports (Z_{ij}):

$$Z_{ij} = (X_{ij}^+ - M_{ij}^+) = \sum_{s=1}^{K} (R_{is} - B_{is}^+)L_{sj} \qquad i=1, \ldots ,N^{19} \qquad (12)$$

By contrast with equations (10) and (11), equation (12) is the traditional Heckscher-Ohlin equation with net exports as a linear function of factor endowments (see Saxonhouse 1983a and Leamer 1984). When we consider just *net* trade, as within the Heckscher-Ohlin framework, the nonlinear terms in equations (10) and (11) cancel out. Since equation (12) can be derived from (10) and (11), which are the basic Helpman-Krugman equations, this should demonstrate the compatibility of these two approaches. That is, the incorporation of scale economies and product differentiation into conventional models of international trade in order to account for *intra*-industry trade in no way invalidates the Heckscher-Ohlin interpretation of *inter*-industry trade.

Note that total imports and total exports will be given by:

$$M_{j}^+ = \sum_{i}^{N} \sum_{s}^{K} B_{is}^+ L_{sj} + \sum_{i}^{N} \sum_{r=1}^{K} \sum_{s=1}^{K} D_{isr}^+ L_{sj} L_{rj}$$
$$i=1,2, \ldots ,N \qquad (13)$$

$$X_{j}^+ = \sum_{i}^{N} \sum_{s}^{K} R_{is} L_{sj} + \sum_{i}^{N} \sum_{r=1}^{K} \sum_{s=1}^{K} D_{isr}^+ L_{sj} L_{rj}$$
$$i=1,2, \ldots ,N \qquad (14)$$

As equations (13) and (14) make clear, unlike Heckscher-Ohlin, the Helpman-Krugman approach allows for explanations of total export volumes and total import volumes.

9.3.2 Trade Structure Studies

Equation (12) provides the basis for the estimation framework used by Leamer (1984) with which he attempts to explain cross-national net trade flows for 1958 and 1975 for sixty countries with ten aggregate sectors, using capital stock, three varieties of labor, four varieties of land, coal production, oil production, and mineral production as explanatory variables representing national factor endowments. His conclusions (p. 187) are worth quoting:

> What emerges from this data analysis is a surprisingly good explanation of the main features of the trade data in terms of a relatively brief list of resource endowments. There are apparent problems with measuring some of the resources, and there is some evidence of non-linearities, but overall, the simple linear model does an excellent job. It explains a large amount of the variability of net exports across countries, and it also identifies sources of comparative advantage that we all "know" are there, thereby increasing the credibility of the results in cases where we do not "know" the sources of comparative advantage.

If Leamer's conclusions are accepted, they suggest that there may be a relatively small role for distinctive sectoral trade policies to play in explaining national trade patterns. National policies promoting or inhibiting sectoral trade may exist and even be important, but may be sufficiently similar across countries such that when allowance is made for differences in factor endowments, their influence is simply incorporated in the parameters of equation (12).[20] Few countries appear to have cross-nationally distinctive sectoral policies. Alternatively, trade policies may differ significantly across countries, but their impact may be felt exclusively in macrolevel, aggregate factor accumulation. Frameworks such as (12) cannot separately distinguish such policy influences from any of the other possible influences on factor accumulations. Thus, (12) is only helpful in identifying sectoral policies. It is at this level, however, that most diplomatic energy is expended, especially in U.S.-Japan relations.

Leamer attempts to examine how equation (12) explains the trade structure for individual countries in his sample by including country dummy variables in each of his ten equations, one country at a time. A statistically significant country dummy thus suggests an extreme value for a country's net trade that cannot be explained by equation (12). Of 1,200 possible significant country dummies, he found only 77 that were actually statistically significant. These include six Canadian dummies, five U.S. dummies, and only one Japanese dummy (1984, 168). The results are summarized in table 9.6. It is important to note that the extreme observations listed in table 9.6 may not necessarily be the result of special government intervention. As Leamer points out, given the strong assumptions made in deriving equation (12) and the crude data used, it is quite possible that errors in specification (e.g., nonlinearities) and errors in measurement may have shaped his findings.[21] Following Bowen, Leamer, and Sveikauskas (1987), it is interesting to consider whether some of the previous assumptions can be relaxed. Thus, suppose that instead of equation (12), we have:

**Table 9.6   Leamer's Unusual Net Trade Observations for Canada, the United States, and
Japan**

1958

Canada exports less forest products than expected
Canada imports less labor-intensive products than expected
Canada imports less capital-intensive products than expected
Canada imports less chemical products than expected

U.S. imports less raw materials than expected

1975

Canada exports less forest products than expected
Canada imports less chemical products than expected

U.S. imports more petroleum than expected
U.S. imports less forest products than expected
U.S. imports less tropical products than expected
U.S. exports more cereals than expected

Japan exports more capital-intensive products than expected

Source: Adapted from Leamer (1984, 168).

$$a_s W_s = \frac{\partial H}{\partial(a_s L_s)} \qquad s = 1, 2, \ldots, K \tag{6'}$$

$$\frac{\partial a_s W_s}{\partial(a_s L_s)} = \frac{\partial^2 H}{\partial(a_s L_s)^2} = 0. \qquad s = 1, 2, \ldots, K \tag{7'}$$

and

$$Z_i = \sum_{s=1}^{K} B'_{is} a_s L_s \qquad 1, \ldots, N \tag{12'}$$

where $a_s \equiv$ quality of factor s and/or measurement error.

The foregoing equations can be interpreted as international trade equalizing factor prices only when factor units are normalized for differences in quality. Thus, for example, observed international differences in the compensation of unskilled labor may be accounted for by differences in labor quality.[22] This is a substantial weakening of the condition that Leamer imposed on his data.[23]

Equation (12') can be estimated for N commodity groups from cross-national data. Formally, the estimation of (12') with a_s differing across countries and unknown is a multivariate, multiplicative errors-in-variable problem. Instrumental variables methods will allow consistent estimates of the B'_{is}. For any given net-trade cross section, a_s will not be identified. In the particular specification adopted in (12'), however, at any given time there are

N cross sections that contain the identical independent variables. This circumstance can be exploited to permit consistent estimation of a_s, which is a measure of factor quality and data quality for each factor endowment for each country. These estimates of a_s can then be used to obtain new, more efficient estimates of B_{is}.[24]

The preceding approach has been used by Saxonhouse (1983a, 1986). For example, equation (12') was estimated with data taken from 23 countries for 109 trade sectors for the years 1964, 1971, and 1979. The factors treated as central to the explanation of changing trade structure include: directly productive capital stock, labor, educational attainment, petroleum reserves, iron ore reserves, arable land, and distance. The inclusion of distance means that transport services are treated symmetrically with other factor endowments. Economies that are close to their major trading partners can be thought of as well endowed with transport services. Those far away from their trading partners are transport-services scarce.

Analogously with Leamer, Saxonhouse has attempted to examine how well estimates of equation (12') explain the trade structure for individual countries by excluding one country at a time from his sample. Using that country's independent variables and the estimates of (12'), a 95 percent ex post forecast interval was constructed and compared with the actual trade structure. Such forecast intervals were constructed for a number of countries in the sample, including Japan, Canada, and the United States. Saxonhouse found that relatively few of the actual Japanese, Canadian, and U.S. trade flows fell outside the ex post forecast interval. That is, in the estimates of 327 net trade equations over three years, there were 61 instances in which Japanese trade flows fell outside the forecast interval. For Canada and the United States, in only 37 and 30 instances, respectively, were observed trade flows outside the forecast interval. These cases are all reported in table 9.7. While extreme Japanese observations were for sectors that averaged 6.1 percent of

Table 9.7 Saxonhouse's Extreme Observations for Japanese, Canadian, and U.S. Trade Flows

Commodity	Years
Japan	
Maize, unmilled	1964, 1971, 1979
Other cereals	1964, 1971, 1979
Bananas and plantain	1964, 1971, 1979
Other fruits and nuts	1964, 1971, 1979
Saw/veneer logs, conifer	1979
Saw/veneer logs, non-conifer	1964, 1971, 1979
Shaped wood	1964, 1979
Pulp and waste paper and cork manufactures	1964, 1971, 1979
Veneer plywood	1971, 1979

Silk	1979
Crude fertilizers	1964, 1979
Leather, pressed fur	1964, 1971, 1979
Plastic materials	1964, 1971
Glass	1964, 1971, 1979
Pearls, precious and semiprecious stones	1964, 1971
Aluminum	1964, 1971, 1979
Zinc	1964, 1971, 1979
Aircraft engines	1971, 1979
Other clothing equipment	1971, 1979
Footwear	1964, 1971, 1979
Medical instruments	1964, 1971, 1979
Photo, cinema supplies	1964, 1971, 1979
Pianos and other musical instruments	1964, 1971, 1979
Fishing, hunting, and sports equipment	1964, 1979

Canada

Fish and preparations	1964, 1971
Saw/veneer logs, conifer	1964, 1971, 1979
Saw/veneer logs, non-conifer	1964, 1971, 1979
Shaped wood	1964, 1971, 1979
Pulp and waste paper	1964, 1971, 1979
Iron ore concentrates	1964, 1979
Leather, pressed fur	1964, 1971
Paper, paperboard, and manufactures	1964, 1971, 1979
Glass	1971, 1979
Nickel	1964, 1971, 1979
Zinc	1964, 1971
Paper mill machinery	1964, 1979
Electric machinery	1964, 1971, 1979
Footwear	1964
Medical instruments	1971
Pianos and other musical instruments	1964, 1979

United States

Wheat	1971, 1979
Maize, unmilled	1964, 1971, 1979
Other cereals	1964, 1971, 1979
Manganese ores	1964, 1971, 1979
Petroleum products	1971, 1979
Plastic materials	1964, 1971, 1979
Rubber manufacturers	1979
Glass	1971, 1979
Lead	1964, 1979
Ball and roller bearings	1964, 1979
Print and binding machinery	1964, 1971, 1979
Clothing	1964, 1971, 1979
Motor vehicle parts	1979

Source: Adapted from Saxonhouse (1986).

its gross external trade, and the U.S. observations were for sectors that averaged 5.5 percent of its gross external trade, the extreme Canadian observations were for sectors that averaged 13.4 percent of external trade.[25]

Inevitably, the proportion of trade in sectors where there is evidence of statistically significant barriers is a downward-biased measure of the overall impact of such barriers, since trade in these sectors is in all likelihood less important than would be the case in the absence of the barriers. With prohibitive barriers, this measure yields the totally paradoxical finding that no trade at all is being diverted. A better approach for summarizing the influence of trade barriers on trade structure is to jointly test for distinctiveness over all sectors for each country. That is, for all 109 sectors taken together, is trade structure significantly different statistically from what might be expected?

In order to test the null hypothesis that the ex post forecast on the extra sample values of Japanese, Canadian, and U.S. trade structure, respectively, do not differ significantly from their historical values, the following test statistic can be utilized:[26]

$$
P = \sum_{i=1}^{109} \{\hat{Z}_{ij} - Z_{ij})/\hat{\sigma}_{\hat{Z}_{ij}}\}^2
\tag{15}
$$

where $\hat{Z}_i \equiv$ forecast of trade flow in the ith sector and $\hat{\sigma} \equiv$ estimated standard error.

Since the calculated values of P for Japan, Canada, and the United States are 92.6, 87.1, and 85.8 for 1964; 97.5, 92.0, and 83.1 for 1971; and 102.1, 98.5, and 96.3 for 1979; and the 5 percent critical value is 109.4, it is apparent that for all three countries, for each of the three sample years, the null hypothesis cannot be rejected.[27] These comprehensive statistical tests therefore reinforce the impression gained from an examination of the sectoral evidence. That is, it does not appear that trade policy has dramatically altered the Japanese, Canadian, or U.S. trade structure.[28]

Lawrence (1987) has argued that empirical work on trade barriers using the Heckscher-Ohlin equations (12) and (12') misses at least one central issue in current policy discussions. As its derivation makes clear, equation (12') is defined for net trade. Yet it is frequently argued that what is distinctive about Japan's trade patterns is its very meager participation in intra-industry trade in manufactures (Sazanami 1981). The issue then is that the structure of Japan's net trade flows might appear normal, even while its gross trade pattern might be highly distinctive.

The focus on net trade flows in explaining inter-industry trade may ignore the possibility that Japanese policy has worked to keep down both imports and exports. From the point of view of the trade policy debate in the United States, however, this may not be a serious omission. The point here is that it is unlikely that, compared to other countries, Japanese policy has unfairly kept imports down in many sectors unless this policy has simultaneously been keeping exports down in precisely the same sectors. From the American side, at least, U.S.-Japanese economic conflict is not about this aspect of Japanese policy. Rather, it is about sectoral trade balances, and it would appear that this aspect of the policy debate is well handled by the Heckscher-Ohlin framework of research.

Equations (4) and (4'), which by having gross imports and gross exports as their dependent variable, allow for intra-industry trade and thus provide the basic framework for Lawrence's (1987) empirical work on cross-national trade structure. However, Lawrence does not use cross-national data on trade structure and production to test the restrictions implied by either (4) or (4'). Rather, he argues that (4) and (4') apply only to a world where distance imposes no cost on trade. In a world where transport costs are nonzero and a determinant of trade flows, Lawrence prefers to estimate the logarithmic version of (4) and (4'):

$$\log \left(\frac{M_{ij}^+}{M_{ij}^+ + Q_{ij}} \right) = U_i + v_i \log \left(\frac{Q_{ij}}{\overline{Q}_i} \right) + y_i \log T_j \qquad (4a)$$

and/or

$$\log \left(\frac{M_{ij}^+}{M_{ij} + Q_{ij}} \right) = U_i^* + v_i^* \log \left(\frac{X_{ij}^+}{(1 - S_j)\overline{Q}_i} \right) + y_i^* \log T_j \qquad (4a')$$

where $T_j \equiv$ transport cost or distance.

Like Leamer, Lawrence examines how well equations (4a) and (4a') explain trade structure for individual countries in his sample by including country dummies in each of twenty-one sectoral equations and a pooled equation for each of the years included, one country at a time. Compared to the other twelve countries included in his sample, the Japanese dummy variable is most often statistically significant and less than zero. That is, imports are a smaller share of domestic consumption than might be expected, given the share of the world market held by Japanese exports or given Japan's share of global production. By contrast, for some years the United States and Canadian dummies are significantly positive, suggesting that the United States and Canada import more than expected. Lawrence's results are summarized in table 9.8.

While Lawrence's findings are in striking contrast with the aforementioned works by both Leamer and Saxonhouse, his findings are not necessar-

Table 9.8 Lawrence's Unusual Gross Import Observations for Canada, the United States, and Japan

Pooled Results	Sectoral Results
	1970
	Production share model (equation 4a)
Canada imports more than expected	Japan imports less than expected of the following products: electrical components, motor vehicles, rubber/plastics, other transportation, stone/clay/glass, ferrous metals, fabricated metals, paper products, wood/furniture
Japan imports less than expected	
	Export share model (equation 4a')
Canada imports more than expected	Japan imported less than expected of the following products: motor vehicles, wood/furniture
Japan imports less than expected	
	1980
	Production share model (equation 4a)
Canada imports more than expected	Japan imports less than expected of the following products: electrical components, electrical machinery, motor vehicles, nonelectrical machinery, rubber/plastic, other transportation, stone/clay/glass, ferrous metals, fabricated metals
United States imports more than expected	
Japan imports less than expected	
	Japan imports more than expected of the following products: nonferrous metals
	Export share model (equation 4a')
Japan imports less than expected	Japan imports less than expected of the following products: electrical machinery, motor vehicles, nonelectrical machinery, rubber/plastic, stone/clay/glass, fabricated metals
	Japan imports more than expected of the following products: nonferrous metals
	1983
	Production share model (equation 4a)
United States imports more than expected	Japan imports less than expected of the following products: electrical components, electrical machinery, motor vehicles, nonelectrical machinery, rubber/plastic, other transportation, fabricated metals, wood/furniture, clothing/shoes
Japan imports less than expected	
	Japan imports more than expected of the following products: nonferrous metals
	Export share model (equation 4a')
Japan imports less than expected	Japan imports less than expected of the following products: electrical components, electrical machinery, motor vehicles, nonelectrical machinery, rubber/plastic, other transportation, fabricated metals, wood/furniture
	Japan imports more than expected from the following products: nonferrous metals

Source: Adapted from Lawrence (1987), tables 8 and 9.

ily inconsistent with these works. It is important to remember that Lawrence is explaining gross trade, while Leamer's and Saxonhouse's dependent variables are net trade. Despite this difference, it is extremely difficult to reconcile Lawrence's conclusion that, in the absence of unusual trade barriers, Japan's manufactured goods trade surplus would have declined by $9.4 billion with either Saxonhouse's (1983a, 1986) results for 1979 (table 9.7) or Leamer's (1984) for 1975 (table 9.6).

Leamer, Saxonhouse, and Lawrence all assume homotheticity in their empirical work. Lawrence's use of production shares and export shares rather than factor endowments as explanatory variables, however, makes homotheticity the driving force of his interpretation of differences in trade structure. Lawrence's empirical work may thus be viewed primarily as a test of this assumption.[29] Unfortunately, Lawrence's test results may be qualified by a number of specification errors.

Quite apart from unresolved issues such as what functional form is appropriate when transport costs are introduced into the Helpman-Krugman model and, indeed, whether it is appropriate to introduce transport costs at all into an export share version of this model, Lawrence's import share, export share, and production share variables are all jointly determined. The issue of simultaneity here is a very real one. In addition to nontrivial estimation bias, there are some important identification issues. While Lawrence is careful in interpreting his results to suggest that there is something distinctive about Japanese trade structure, he does not make it clear why this distinctiveness should be associated with possible Japanese import barriers. For example, in his export share model, there are only three significant Japanese sectoral dummies in 1970, but no less than nine significant sectoral dummies in 1983. Is it really plausible to infer that Japanese protection for manufacturing increased substantially between 1970 and 1983? This is precisely the period when virtually all formal Japanese barriers to the import of manufactured goods were eliminated. If Japanese trade structure did become more distinctive between 1970 and 1983, this can be more properly attributed to increasing foreign barriers against Japanese exports. Japan's import shares of manufactures may well be a better index of Japanese competitiveness than its export shares.

Equations (10) and (11) can be estimated in an effort to reconcile the contrasting approaches of Leamer/Saxonhouse and Lawrence. Like Lawrence, equations (10) and (11) come from the Helpman-Krugman model and, by using gross imports as a dependent variable, they do not net out intra-industry trade. Like Leamer and Saxonhouse, however, simultaneity problems are avoided by using factor endowments as the central explanatory variables. We have estimated equations (10) and (11) for the same 109 trade sectors and the same seven factor endowments as in Saxonhouse (1983a, 1986). In the present case, however, the sample is restricted to a single year

1979, but enlarged to include observations on the fifty-five economies that are listed in table 9.9.[30]

Following the approach taken in Saxonhouse (1983a, 1986) and reported in table 9.7, we have constructed 95 percent ex post forecast intervals based on equations (10) and (11) for Japan, Canada, and the United States, and compared the results with actual trade flows. The results are reported in table 9.10. Of the 109 sectoral gross imports forecast for 1979 for Japan, 24 fell outside the forecast interval. By contrast, 12 sectoral export flows fell outside the forecast interval.[31] For Canada, 21 import flows and 12 export flows were observed outside the forecast interval. And for the United States, 15 import flows and 9 export flows were found outside the forecast interval.[32]

With so many instances of Japanese import flows falling outside the forecast interval, it might appear that the estimation of equations (10) and (11), unlike the estimation of equations (4) and (4'), suggests a distinctive Japanese trade structure. But, when the null hypothesis is tested using equation (15), where the ex post forecast on the extra sample values of Japanese import and export structure do not differ significantly from their historical values, we obtain the same result as before, namely that the null hypothesis cannot be rejected.[33] The finding that Japanese trade structure conforms to international patterns thus appears invariant to whether it is the Helpman-Krugman model or the Heckscher-Ohlin that is being estimated.[34]

9.3.3 Trade Volume Studies

By contrast with the work just discussed, the studies by Bergsten and Cline, Balassa, and Noland listed in table 9.5 examine the impact of barriers on the total volume of trade rather than the structure of trade. Bergsten and Cline (1987) attempt to explain intercountry differences in the ratio of imports to

Table 9.9   Country Sample for a Test of Differentiated Products and Factor Endowments, 1979

Sample				
Argentina	Denmark	India	Morocco	Saudi Arabia
Australia	Dominican Republic	Indonesia	Netherlands	Singapore
Austria	Ecuador	Ireland	New Zealand	Spain
Bangladesh	Egypt	Israel	Nigeria	Sri Lanka
Belgium	Finland	Italy	Norway	Sweden
Brazil	France	Jamaica	Pakistan	Switzerland
Canada	Germany, West	Japan	Panama	Thailand
Chile	Greece	Jordan	Paraguay	Trinidad
Colombia	Honduras	Korea	Peru	Turkey
Costa Rica	Hongkong	Malaysia	Philippines	United Kingdom
Côte d'Ivoire	Iceland	Mexico	Portugal	United States

Table 9.10   Extreme Observations on Japanese, Canadian, and U.S. Trade Flows, 1979

Japan	Canada	United States
	Imports	
Meat and preparations	Dairy products & eggs	Manganese ores
Dairy products & eggs	Fish & preparations	Petroleum products
Tobacco & manufactures	Oil seed, excl. soya beans	Plastic materials
Saw/veneer logs, conifer	Crude & synth. rubber	Rubber manufactures
Saw/veneer logs, non-conifer	Saw/veneer logs, conifer	Silk fabrics, woven
Shaped wood	Saw/veneer logs, non-conifer	Nickel
Rubber manufactures	Shaped wood	Zinc
Cork manufactures	Leather, pressed fur	Ball & roller bearings
Veneer plywood	Rubber manufactures	Print & binding machinery
Glass	Paper, paperboard, &	Motor vehicle parts
Pearls	manufactures	Clothing
All other iron & steel	Silk fabric, woven	Footwear
Silver & platinum	Glass	Optical equipment
Aluminum	Nickel	Photographic equipment
Lead	Zinc	Pianos & other musical
Zinc	Piston engines	instruments
Tin	Paper mill machinery	
Aircraft engines	Print & binding machinery	
Printing & binding machinery	Pump & centrifuges	
Clothing	Electric distrib. machinery	
Footwear	Switch gear	
Optical equipment	Pianos & other musical	
Photographic equipment	equipment	
Fishing, hunting, & sport		
equipment		
	Exports	
Plastic materials	Fish & preparations	Fish & preparations
Rubber manufactures	Shaped wood	Wheat, unmilled
Wool fabrics, woven	Paper, paperboard &	Maize, unmilled
Glass	manufactures	Oil seed, excl. soya beans
Pearls	Nickel	Shaped wood
All other iron & steel	Zinc	All other fertilizers &
Aircraft engines	Paper mill machinery	crude materials
Other clothing equipment	Electric power machines	Coal, coke, & briquette
Print & binding machinery	Electric distrib. machinery	Aircraft engines
Aircraft & parts	Passenger motor vehicles	Aircraft parts
Pumps & centrifuges	Ships and boats	
Photo & cinema supplies	Clothing	
	Fishing, hunting, & sports	
	equipment	

GNP for eleven countries plus the EEC for a pooled cross section from 1974 to 1984. The Bergsten-Cline explanatory variables include: (1) the logarithms of GNP, per capita crude oil production, and per capita arable land; (2) dummy variables for significant iron ore reserves and for Japan; and (3) an index of transportation costs. Of their six explanatory variables, Bergsten and Cline find that only the Japanese dummy is statistically insignificant. From this they conclude (1985, 78):

> The cross-section statistical test confirms the simple scatter diagram: Japan is basically on the line for international norms of imports relative to GNP after taking account of natural resource endowment and transportation costs as well as country size. These results suggest there is nothing special about Japan's import-GNP ratio to attribute to an unusual degree of protection.

While this finding is similar to the conclusions reached by Leamer and Saxonhouse as already noted, the foundation for the Bergsten-Cline equation is by no means obvious. Because Bergsten-Cline use a trade/GNP ratio as their dependent variable, and because most of their explanatory variables enter logarithmically, following the derivation given in the technical appendix to this paper, their equation might be given a translog interpretation as in

$$X^* = \rho + \sum_{s=1}^{K} \delta_{is} \ln L_s \qquad (A4)$$

where $X^* = \dfrac{X}{\pi}$ and

where π is assumed constant.

Unfortunately, such an interpretation of the Bergsten-Cline work requires putting aside the distinction between net and gross trade, and ignoring their entering factor endowments on a per capita basis and their use of GNP as an independent variable.[35]

In contrast to Bergsten-Cline, Balassa (1986) has chosen to explain the logarithm of total imports (and imports from developing countries and industrialized countries, separately) relative to GDP (and total primary imports relative to GDP and total manufactured imports relative to GDP, separately) for a cross section of eighteen industrial countries for 1973–83. He uses as explanatory variables: (1) logarithms of per capita GDP and population; (2) transportation costs and ratio of primary products imports to total imports; and (3) dummy variables for Japan, the EEC, and the European Free Trade Association. Unlike Leamer, Saxonhouse, and Bergsten-Cline, Balassa (p. 8) found his dummy variable for Japan to be negative and highly significant:[36]

> The results show Japan to be an "outlier" among industrial countries, irrespective of whether one considers imports from all sources, from the industrial

countries, or from developing countries. The Japan dummy is significant at the 1 percent level in all the equations and its introduction raises their explanatory power.

Balassa's inspiration for his import equation is based on Chenery (1960), which was an early attempt to provide a general equilibrium rationalization for cross-national work on trade structure. Unfortunately, however, there is no rationale given either by Chenery or by Balassa for why aggregate trade volumes might differ among countries. That is, Chenery (p. 28) moves from a theory of comparative advantage in terms of net imports to a theory of gross imports by simply adding exports to net imports and to his list of independent variables. But even as a framework for studying the determinants of the pattern of net trade, Chenery's approach is a puzzling point of departure for the research that Balassa has undertaken. A reading of Chenery's work shows that he made many arbitrary choices to obtain the import equations that were estimated. These compromises were dictated by lack of data on such variables as capital stock and natural resource endowments and by the limits of economic science at the time that he began what has become thirty years of research on structural change. Even though Balassa presents twenty-eight estimated versions of his import equation, quite apart from the problem of distinguishing between gross and net trade in his analysis, none of Balassa's variants can be derived from a conventional specification of production technology and demand.[37]

Ignoring conceptual problems and issues of specification error, Balassa attributes his distinctive findings to his use of transport costs rather than distance as an explanatory variable.[38] If Balassa's findings were at variance only with studies that use distance as an independent variable, this reasoning would be compelling. However, his findings are at odds not only with studies that use a distance variable (Saxonhouse), but also with studies that use transport costs variables (Bergsten-Cline and Noland) and with studies that use neither distance nor transport costs (Leamer, Saxonhouse).[39] Furthermore, Balassa uses a measure of transport costs which is orders-of-magnitude different from many other estimates.[40] Unfortunately, Balassa's special findings rest critically on the specific construction of his transport cost variable.[41]

Like Lawrence and the work presented in table 9.10, Noland (1987) is guided by Helpman-Krugman in his empirical work. But unlike these other studies, Noland does not attempt a direct test of Helpman-Krugman. Rather, he uses some of the variables suggested by them in an equation that attempts to explain differences in trade volumes. He assumes that the logarithm of trade volume (or total imports or total exports) is a function of: (1) the logarithm of GDP and the logarithm of GDP per capita; (2) a measure of factor endowment similarity; and (3) a measure of transport costs.[42] He estimated this equation for forty-five countries for 1980, and then calculated the "studentized" residuals for each of the countries in his sample. This procedure is equivalent to adding a dummy variable that selects out a single country at a time and calculating its t-statistic.[43] Noland's studentized residuals for Japan, Canada, and the United States were all statistically insignificant, which is consistent with the results obtained by Leamer, Saxonhouse, and Bergsten-Cline already described. It should also be noted that our equations (13) and (14) provide the basis for equations explaining total import and/or total export volumes, which, unlike Noland's equation, can be directly derived from the Helpman-Krugman model. In light of these equations, Noland's analysis and results appear compromised by serious specification error.

The final studies worth noting are by Staiger, Deardorff, and Stern (1985, 1987). Taking the Heckscher-Ohlin model as a point of departure, they have used the Michigan Model of World Production and Trade to calculate the effects of Japanese and American tariffs and NTBs on the factor content of trade and employment in the two countries. For this purpose, as mentioned earlier, they constructed approximations of the ad valorem equivalents of the pre–Tokyo Round NTBs for the United States and Japan. These approximations presumably may reflect formal, and to some extent informal, barriers for the individual sectors. Their computational results suggest that the effects of Japan's NTBs are greater than their tariffs, and that these effects are concentrated especially in the agricultural sector. The effects of NTBs for the United States also appeared to be greater than tariffs, but these effects were spread among a variety of U.S. industries. It is thus especially interesting that if Japanese and American barriers were to be removed, the effects would be primarily to reduce farm employment in Japan and increase it in the United States, while manufacturing employment in the United States is estimated to decline. The results obtained by Staiger et al. are interesting because they suggest that Japan's barriers limiting the importation of agricultural products and food and kindred products may be the dominant forces in its trade policy. This conclusion may be misleading, however, since only Japan and the United States are being compared. As noted earlier, Honma and Hayami (1986) have done a cross-country study of the determinants of agricultural policies and found that Japan does not appear unusual compared to other industrialized countries when differences in national endowments and related characteristics are taken into account.

The Lawrence and Balassa studies notwithstanding, the general conclusion that emerges from our review and assessment of empirical studies of trade structure is that national trade policies do not appear to be an important determinant of trade structure once account is taken of cross-country differences in factor endowments and distance considerations. Thus, while Japan has been singled out for having a relatively low share of manufactures in total imports, as well as a smaller share of manufactured imports from the developing countries in comparison to the United States and other major trading countries,[44] there is no convincing case to be made that the structural characteristics of Japan's trade reflect its distinctive nontariff barriers. This conclusion seems broadly consistent with the evidence on formal and informal barriers that we presented in the preceding section. That is, when we consider the trade coverage of NTBs, Japan does not appear distinctive in comparison to the other major industrialized countries. We also noted that while a litany of informal barriers can be cited in the case of Japan, it is possible to identify a host of such barriers in the United States, Canada, and presumably other industrialized countries as well. There may well be significant protection in a number of sectors in the major trading countries which represent important departures from the ideal of free trade. But the available evidence based on inventories of barriers and econometric estimates of the determinants of trade flows do not enable us to single out individual countries in terms of the impact of their trade policies.[45]

9.3.4   Restrictions on Foreign Direct Investment

In contrast to the empirical research that we have just examined which assessed the barriers to trade for the United States, Japan, and Canada, we know comparatively little about the effects that barriers to foreign direct investment may have. It would appear that there are at present relatively few formal barriers to foreign direct investment in the three countries. With respect to informal barriers, some observers might argue in the case of the United States that certain aspects of national security policies, antitrust policies, securities regulations, and the extraterritorial interpretation of U.S. laws may serve to impede inward direct investment. Canada has maintained administrative procedures for reviewing new foreign direct investment initatives since the 1970s, but these procedures have been considerably relaxed in recent years. It is true, in any event, that Canada has relatively substantial foreign ownership, especially in many of its manufacturing industries.

In Japan, it might appear that historically there was a reluctance to permit foreign direct investment in a variety of Japanese industries, and that there is presently a much smaller degree of foreign ownership as compared with other major industrialized countries. This may well be the case, but it remains to be determined whether Japan is distinctive in terms of its observed pattern of foreign ownership and control as compared to other major industrialized countries, after allowance is made as before for Japan's otherwise distinctive characteristics. The point here is similar to the one made in our preceding discussion concerning the allegations of pervasive trade protectionism by Japan. That is, it remains to be seen whether or not the available empirical evidence would lead one to identify Japan as an outlier in terms of the structure of foreign direct investment.

There is an evident need, therefore, for more research on barriers to foreign direct investment. This is the case not only to learn more about the effects of these barriers, but also to explore the relation between trade barriers and investment barriers. An interesting issue here is whether the Heckscher-Ohlin framework can be used to analyze investment barriers and, if so, what the appropriate empirical specification might be. Alternatively, Helpman and Krugman address in theoretical terms the behavioral determinants of multi-national enterprise activities and the possible impacts on trade that may occur. What is needed then is an effort to parallel our work on trade structure in order to sort out what these different models may contribute in furthering our understanding of cross-country differences in the patterns of foreign direct investment.

9.4   Conclusions and Implications for Research and Policy

We have made an effort in this paper to clarify a number of analytical and empirical issues concerning the nature and consequences of informal barriers to trade and investment with particular reference to the United States, Canada, and Japan. Three main categories of informal barriers were identified: (1) administrative procedures and government regulations and policies; (2) market structure; and (3) political, social, and cultural institutions. While there may be difficulties in distinguishing exactly between formal and informal barriers in given circumstances, there is nonetheless reason to believe that informal barriers exist and may possibly serve to impede international trade and investment in individual sectors and countries.

The issue then is to devise an empirical framework that can be used to determine whether and to what extent informal barriers may in fact distort national trade patterns. We have emphasized the ways in which the Heckscher-Ohlin and Helpman-Krugman models can be adapted for empirical purposes and the results of cross-national studies of trade structure that take into account a variety of national factor endowments as the proximate determinants of trade. Our review of the important studies that have been done in recent years concluded that the Heckscher-Ohlin model does fairly well in explaining cross-national differences in trade structure and that NTBs do not appear to exert a major influence on this structure. This finding does not change even when allowance is made for intra-industry trade within the Helpman-Krugman model. This conclusion is especially important with reference to Japan, for it means that there is not much evidence to support the contention that Japan relies on a variety of informal barriers for the purpose of influencing the structure of its trade. That is, when account is taken of cross-national differences in factor endowments—including capital, labor, and a variety of natural resources—Japan's trade structure does not appear distinctive relative to other major countries.

We were not able to reach any conclusions regarding barriers to foreign direct investment. More research is needed accordingly on the appropriate framework to use in analyzing the structure of foreign direct investment and its interaction with the structure of trade.

Finally, it seems appropriate to ask what policy implications, if any, are suggested by our analysis. Perhaps the main implication is that, in terms of United States–Japan economic relations, it is difficult to build a strong and convincing case that Japan's trade and domestic policies are the root causes of the existing bilateral trade imbalance. The causes of the trade imbalance and the possible solutions should therefore be sought elsewhere, in particular in the macroeconomic structure and determinants of absorption and output in the two countries.

Technical Appendix

If we impose more structure on Π, the GNP function, by approximating it as either Generalized Leontief or translog, we have:

$$\Pi(P,L) = \sum_{i=1}^{N} \sum_{j=1}^{N} \sum_{s=1}^{K} d_{is}\left(\frac{1}{2}P_i^2 + \frac{1}{2}P_j^2\right)^{1/2} L_s +$$
$$\sum_{i=1}^{N} \sum_{s=1}^{K} c_{is} P_i L_s + \sum_{i=1}^{N} \sum_{s=1}^{K} \sum_{r=1}^{N} f_{sr} L_s^{1/2} L_r^{1/2} P_i \tag{A1}$$

where $d_{is} = d_{si}; f_{rs} = f_{sr}; d_{ii} = 0$ for $i = 1,2, \ldots ,N; d_{ss} = 0$ for $s = 1,2, \ldots ,K;$ and $P_i \equiv$ price of good X_i, or

$$\ln \Pi(P,L) = \alpha_o + \sum_{i=1}^{N} \alpha_i \ln P_i + \frac{1}{2}\sum_{i=1}^{N} \sum_{j=1}^{N} \gamma_{ij} \ln P_i \ln P_j +$$
$$\sum_{i=1}^{N} \sum_{s=1}^{K} \delta_{is} \ln P_i \ln L_s + \sum_{s=1}^{K} \beta_s \ln L_s + \tag{A2}$$
$$\frac{1}{2}\sum_{s=1}^{K} \sum_{r=1}^{K} \phi_{sr} \ln L_s \ln L_r$$

where $\sum_{i=1}^{N} \alpha_i = 1; \sum_{i=1}^{N} \delta_{is} = 0$ for $s = 1, \ldots ,K; \sum_{j=1}^{N} \gamma_{ij} = 0$ for $i = 1, \ldots ,$

$,N;\ \sum\limits_{i=1}^{N} \gamma_{ij}$ for $j=1, \ldots ,N;\ \gamma_{ij} = \gamma_{ji};\ \sum\limits_{s=1}^{K} \beta_s = 1;\ \sum\limits_{s=1}^{K} \delta_{is}$ for $i=1, \ldots ,N;$

$\sum\limits_{r=1}^{K} \phi_{sr} = 0$ for $s=1, \ldots ,K;$ and $\sum\limits_{s=1}^{K} \phi_{sr}$ for $r=1, \ldots ,K.$ When (A1) or (A2) is combined with g to form the indirect utility function H', using Roy's Identity and Hotelling's Lemma, we get by differentiation of H':

$$X_i^* = \theta_i + \sum_{s=1}^{K} Q_{is} L_s^* + \sum_{s=1}^{K} \sum_{r=1}^{K} f_{rs} L_s^{*1/2} L_r^{*1/2} \tag{A3}$$

where $Q_{is} \equiv \sum\limits_{j=1}^{N} d_{ij} \left(\frac{1}{2} P_i^2 + \frac{1}{2} P_j^2 \right)^{-1/2} P_i + C_{is}$, and where the starred variables have been normalized by π; and

$$X_i^* = \rho_i + \sum_{s=1}^{K} \delta_{is} \ln L_s \tag{A4}$$

where $\rho_i = \theta_i + \alpha_i + \sum\limits_{j=1}^{N} \gamma_{ij} \ln P_j$

As before, equation (A4) can be adjusted to take account of a quality and measurement error term:[46]

$$X_i^* = \rho_i + \sum_{s=1}^{K} \delta_{is} \ln a_s + \sum_{s=1}^{K} \delta_{is} \ln L_s \tag{A4'}$$

Assuming all consumers have access to goods at the same prices, equations (A3), (A4), and (A4') provide a framework for examining the assumption of factor price equalization. For example, in (A3) or (A4), with factor price equalization, equation (7) implies that:

$$f_{sr} = 0, \ \delta_{is} = 0 \text{ for } s, r, = 1, \ldots ,K \qquad i = 1, \ldots ,N$$

These implications can be tested if equations (A3) or (A4) are estimated.

Table A9.1   Federal and State Regulations Potentially Affecting Foreign Investment in the United States

Sector/Activity	Regulations
1. Air transportation	Foreign acquisitions and provision of certain air services by foreign investors require U.S. government approval. U.S. air carriers must be U.S. citizens.
2. Ocean and coastal shipping	Operators and those seeking government benefits must meet certain U.S. citizenship requirements.
3. Banking	Federally chartered banks must have a majority of U.S. citizens on their boards. Some states restrict foreign-owned banks.
4. Insurance	Some states impose special requirements on foreign-owned insurance operations.
5. Access to classified information	In the absence of an applicable treaty, foreign firms may be unable to obtain the security clearances necessary to perform certain government contracts.
6. Government insurance and loan programs	Overseas investment insurance programs, agricultural emergency loans, and guarantees for electric vehicles are subject to U.S. citizenship requirements.
7. Energy and power production	Foreign investors may generally not receive licenses to own or use nuclear materials and facilities. Leases and licenses for geothermal power, ocean thermal energy conversion facilities, and hydroelectric power facilities require domestic incorporation.
8. Mineral resources	Exploitation of certain federal lands requires domestic incorporation and reciprocity. A few states also restrict the access of foreign investors to mineral resources on state land.
9. Fishing	Foreign flag vessels are subject to certain restrictions. Special government assistance is limited to U.S. citizens.
10. Customhouse brokers	Licenses are limited to U.S. citizens.
11. Ownership of real estate	Publicly owned lands may not be sold to non-U.S. citizens or non-U.S. corporations. Foreign holders of agricultural land must report their ownership. Foreign investors must report their holdings or real property to Internal Revenue Service. About 30 states control ownership of land in some fashion.
12. Radio and television broadcasting	Foreign governments, foreign enterprises, and foreign-controlled domestic corporations may not hold common carrier licenses.
13. Submarine cable service	The Federal Communications Commission can deny licenses to foreigners.
14. Communications Satellite Corporation	Foreigners may own no more than 20 percent of COMSAT.

Source: Adapted from Bale (1983, 45–46).

Table A9.2   USTR Identification of Canadian Barriers, 1986

Barrier	Description
1. Tariffs and other import charges	
a. Tariffs	Despite the reductions in the Tokyo Round, Canadian tariffs on manufactures are among the highest of all industrialized nations.
b. Provincial liquor boards	Certain provincial liquor boards do not carry particular U.S. products, they may charge discriminatory markups, and access to distribution systems may be limited.
c. Canadian Wheat Board (CWB) licensing requirements	The CWB only issues permits for the import of wheat, oats, barley, and related products when the product cannot be found in Canada.
d. Footwear	Canadian footwear quotas were extended on women's and girls' footwear in 1985 at the same time as all other footwear quotas were eliminated.
2. Standards, testing, labeling, certification	
a. Plywood	The plywood standards of the Canadian Standards Association exclude major U.S. plywood species.
3. Government procurement	Where the GATT government procurement code does not apply, federal and provincial government agencies and Crown Corporations favor Canadian-based firms if there is sufficient competition among these firms.
4. Export subsidies	The Western Grain Transportation Act of 1 January 1984 increased the number of products eligible for freight-rate subsidy and designated the U.S. as an eligible export market for subsidized freight rates.
5. Lack of intellectual property protection	
a. Copyright protection	U.S. copyright owners are not compensated for unauthorized cable system retransmission of broadcast signals containing their works.
b. Compulsory pharmaceutical patents licensing	Section 41 of Canada's patent law provides for compulsory licensing of pharmaceutical patents and a nominal 4 percent royalty payment.
6. Services barriers	
a. Border broadcasting	Since 1976, Canadian firms have been denied tax deductions for the cost of advertising in foreign media (mainly TV) when the advertising is directed primarily at Canadians.
b. Restrictions on Canadian advertising in U.S. publications	Nondeductibility of Canadian advertising in U.S. publications, and restrictions on advertising in U.S. publications exported to Canada.
c. Trucking	Some provinces limit market access of U.S. trucking firms.
d. Data processing requirements	Processing and maintenance of Canadian bank operating records must be done in Canada.
e. Discriminatory postal rates	Since 1979, there have been higher second-class postal rates on foreign publications mailed in Canada than on Canadian publications.

Table A9.2   (continued)

Barrier	Description
7. Investment barriers	
a. Unreasonable entry restrictions	The Investment Canada Act of 30 June 1985 permits the government to limit U.S. and other foreign investment. Investments and acquisitions in culturally sensitive areas (both publishing and distribution, film and video, music recordings and print music) are especially subject to review, and certain types of foreign investment in oil and gas are discouraged in order to foster Canadian ownership.
b. Lack of national treatment	Canada maintains limits on granting national treatment to foreign-owned investments in a wide range of activities.
c. Performance requirements	Canada reserves the right to impose domestic performance requirements on foreign investment.

Source: Adapted from USTR (1986, 47–60).

Table A9.3   USTR Identification of Japanese Barriers, 1986

Barrier	Description
1. Tariffs and other import charges	
a. Cigarette and tobacco products	Relatively high tariffs and excise taxes, restricted distribution, and a ban on foreign manufacturing limit U.S. exports to Japan.
b. Wood and paper products	Relatively high tariffs, a restrictive approval system, and discriminatory regulatory procedures limit U.S. sales to Japan.
c. Alcoholic beverages and wine	Japanese tariffs are relatively high, and internal consumption taxes are greater on imports of higher value spirits and wines.
d. Aluminum	Japan has made an effort to develop its aluminum fabricating industry through government financial assistance and other measures.
e. Fresh grapefruit	Japan has a relatively high tariff on imports during its own growing season and a reduced tariff off season.
f. Walnuts	Japan has relatively high tariffs on shelled and unshelled walnuts.
g. Candy and chocolate confectionary	Japan has relatively high tariffs on candy and chocolate confectionary.
2. Quantitative restrictions	
a. Fish products.	Japan's quotas, tariffs, and licensing rules impair the development of Japan's market for U.S. fishery products.
b. Agricultural products	Japan maintains quotas on several agricultural imports, especially beef and citrus products.
c. Leather and leather footwear	Japan maintains a tariff quota system on imports of leather and leather footwear.
3. Standards, testing, labeling, certification[a]	

Table A9.3   (continued)

Barrier	Description
a. Japanese industrial standards (JIS)	The administration of the JIS system is not sufficiently transparent and does not permit effective foreign participation in drafting JIS quality standards.
b. Pharmaceuticals/medical devices	There is ongoing U.S. concern with government involvement in licensing relationships, regulatory and testing issues, and the health insurance reimbursement system.
c. Food additives	Japan's Ministry of Health and Welfare has resisted U.S. processed food manufacturers' interest in approving new food additives.
4. Government procurement[a]	
a. Satellites	Japanese government entities are prohibited from buying U.S.-built satellites.
5. Export subsidies	There is U.S. concern that Japan and other OECD countries are abusing the use of tied aid credits to promote commercial exports.
6. Lack of intellectual property protection	
a. Copyrights	Enforcement of Japan's copyright laws is lax, and there is not full cooperation with U.S. firms to enforce copyright protection.
b. Patents	Japan's patent registration system is especially slow, and its judicial procedures do not adequately protect foreign holders of patents.
c. Trademarks	The trademark registration process is especially slow such that U.S. firms may be deterred in introducing their products to Japan.
7. Services barriers[a]	
a. Construction and engineering	The Japanese system of designated bidding has hindered foreign firms seeking to bid on and obtain contracts, especially for the $8 billion Kansai International Airport project.
b. High cube containers	Regulatory impediments and paperwork requirements have limited the economical use of high cube containers in Japan.
c. Tobacco shipping	U.S. shipping lines are limited in transporting leaf tobacco to Japan.
8. Other barriers[a]	
a. Soda ash	There may be anticompetitive activities by Japanese soda ash companies that discriminate against purchases from U.S. suppliers.
b. Japanese marketing practice restrictions	Japan's "fair competition codes" may inhibit the introduction of new foreign consumer products in Japan.
c. Japanese law on large retail stores	There are restrictions on the establishment of large-scale retail stores that serve to perpetuate the complexity and costliness of the existing distribution system.

[a]Excludes barriers listed by the USTR that are currently being addressed by Japan.
Source: Adapted from USTR (1986, 144–62).

Table A9.4   European Community Identification of U.S. Barriers, 1987

Barrier	Description
1. Tariffs and other import charges	
a. Tariff barriers	Tariffs on selected textiles, chemicals, ceramics, porcelain, knives, cheese, and shoes remain exceptionally high.
b. Customs and other user fees	Fees for processing formal entries of merchandise, arrivals of foreign passengers and commercial vessels, immigration inspection, and harbor maintenance are burdensome to commerce.
c. Superfund taxes	Differential taxes are levied on imported petroleum products and imported chemical derivatives of feedstocks to help finance cleanup of toxic waste sites.
d. Tariff reclassifications	Unilateral changes in U.S. tariff classification of imported products may result in increased duties, but U.S. compensation as specified in the GATT has not been forthcoming.
2. Quantitative restrictions and import surveillance	
a. Agricultural import quotas	U.S. import quotas on selected dairy products, sugar and syrups, articles containing sugar, certain cotton staples, cotton waste and strip, and peanuts are covered by a 1955 GATT waiver, which may not be justifiable.
b. Import licensing for quota measures	Invoice clearance for merchandise shipped subject to quota cannot be obtained until the merchandise has landed and a determination made that the quota has not been filled.
c. Machine tools	Maximum market share levels have been imposed on some exporters in the absence of a formally negotiated restraint arrangement.
d. Beverages and confectionary	Certain imported products were made subject to quotas in connection with a trade complaint lodged by the U.S.
e. Firearms and munitions	Imports of firearms and munitions are prohibited except when authorized by the Secretary of the Treasury to meet certain purposes.
3. Customs barriers	
a. Origin marking for pipes and tubes	Origin marking is required for certain imported, but not for domestic, pipes and fittings.
b. U.S. origin rules for textiles	The EC as such does not qualify in determining the origin of textile products.
4. Standards, testing, labeling, and certification	
a. Telecommunications	EC suppliers of switches and transmission equipment are subject to unusually lengthy and costly approval procedures in attempting to sell in the U.S. market.
b. Federal Aviation Administration (FAA) requirement on spare parts for aircraft	Inspection requirements are being applied without advance notice and retroactively to imports already entered into the U.S.
c. Parma ham	Imports remain prohibited despite a finding that no health hazard exists.

Table A9.4 (continued)

Barrier	Description
5. Public procurement	
a. Buy American policy on machine tools	U.S. procurement of machine tools for defense-related purposes must be from U.S. or Canadian sources.
b. Foreign-built dredges and other vessels	Only U.S. registered vessels can be used in U.S. territorial waters for dredging, towing, salvaging, etc. Vessels engaged in coastal commerce must be built in the U.S.
c. High voltage power equipment	U.S. firms are given a 30% preference for equipment to be supplied to selected entities.
6. Export subsidies	
a. Export enhancement program	The U.S. Department of Agriculture is authorized to use up to $1.5 billion of existing government stocks to subsidize U.S. exports of selected commodities.
b. Targeted export assistance	The Secretary of Agriculture is authorized to provide $110 million annually to offset the adverse effect of foreign subsidies, import quotas, or other unfair trade practices.
c. Corn gluten feed and other cereals substitutes	These products benefit from various direct and indirect subsidies and tax incentives involving the processing of corn.
d. Foreign sales corporation	The tax deferment provided under the previous Domestic International Sales Corporation (DISC) legislation has been converted into definitive tax remission.
e. Public R&D funds	Defense-related R&D expenditures may be directly beneficial to U.S. manufacturers of commercial aircraft.
7. Intellectual property	
a. Section 337 of the Trade Act of 1930	U.S. International Trade Commission investigation of foreign patent validity may impose undue delays and costs and possibly be in violation of the national treatment clause of the GATT.
b. Other issues	The U.S. uses the date of an international patent application in defining the state of the art, and rules out prior inventive activity abroad in granting a U.S. patent.
8. U.S. legislation and practice on countervailing and anti-dumping duties	The U.S. has several legislative ambiguities and questionable practices, including the treatment of upstream subsidies, the definition and calculation of a subsidy or dumping margin, imposition of duties even before imports have occurred, and automatic assessment of duties on the basis of the preliminary finding rather than the final determination.
9. Section 301 of the Trade Act of 1974	The U.S. may introduce unilateral measures against unjustifiable, unreasonable, or discriminatory foreign acts, policies, or practices that burden or restrict U.S. commerce.
10. Exports controls/restrictions on technology transfer	Export controls based on foreign policy considerations may be instituted in a purely discretionary and extraterritorial manner by the United States.
11. Semiconductors agreement	The U.S.-Japan agreement on prices in third-country markets and promises of market access may be prejudicial to the interests of other nations.

Table A9.4   (continued)

Barrier	Description
12. Repair servicing	
a. Foreign repair of U.S. aircraft	The scope of repair and maintenance work performed in foreign repair stations has been severely curtailed.
b. Repairs of ships abroad	The U.S. applies a 50% tariff on most repairs of U.S. ships abroad.
13. Tax barriers	
a. Tax treatment of small passenger aircraft	Purchasers of small aircraft produced in selected states are entitled to special tax benefits under U.S. law.
b. State unitary taxation	Corporate income taxes on foreign-owned companies in certain states may be levied on income earned outside the state's jurisdiction.

Source: Adapted from European Community (1987).

Table A9.5   Projected Expenditures for Industrial Support Programs in the United States, 1984

Category of Expenditures	Amount (billions of $)
Direct expenditures	*$13.6*
Commodity Credit Corporation	6.1
Energy supply R&D	1.8
Economic development	1.4
Agricultural research and services	1.2
Aeronautical research and technology	0.7
Water transportation	0.5
Mining	0.5
Other	1.4
Credit expenditures[a]	8.8
Rural Electrification Administration	4.0
Commodity Credit Corporation	2.1
Agricultural Credit Insurance Fund	0.8
Export-Import Bank	0.9
Small Business Administration	0.6
Other	0.4
Tax expenditures	*b*
Accelerated cost recovery system	18.3
Preferential treatment of capital gains	16.4
Investment tax credit	15.7
Reduced rates on corporate income	6.5
Interest exclusion on state and local bonds	5.0
Expensing of R&D expenditures	2.5
Depletion allowances on fuels	2.1

Table A9.5   (continued)

Safe harbor leasing provisions	1.9
Deferral of income on DISCs	1.2
Expensing of exploration and development costs for fuels	1.2

[a]Represents the net cost, including both interest subsidies and defaults, of loans and loan guarantees, which were projected to total $20.9 billion and $12.7 billion, respectively.
[b]Because of interactions between different tax provisions, the true total may not equal the arithmetic sum of individual tax expenditures. No total is, therefore, given.
Source: Adapted from Congress of the United States, Congressional Budget Office (1984b, x, 25, and 30).

Notes

1. The table is based on the classification used by GATT in compiling and maintaining its inventory of existing NTBs, with the exception that the government category (III) has been expanded somewhat. Inventories of NTBs are also maintained by UNCTAD and the IMF. The UNCTAD classification is based on the apparent intent of the measures and further distinguishes them according to whether they operate through quantitative restraints or through costs and prices. The IMF classification relates chiefly to restrictive exchange rate practices and international financial measures. NTBs are also monitored in such U.S. Government agencies as the Office of the U.S. Trade Representative and Department of Commerce. The various inventories and monitoring systems are generally organized by types of NTBs, country, and sector, and may also contain information on the relevant trade categories and related economic magnitudes.

It should be noted that the nontariff measures in table 9.1 include trade-expanding policies, such as subsidies, in addition to trade-restricting policies. Subsidies might then be understood to be negative NTBs designed to stimulate trade and investment.

2. Thus, the 1986 softwood-lumber case was in effect directed by the United States against British Columbian stumpage fees. While the case was resolved, at least temporarily, on a binational level, the federal and provincial governments in Canada had then to coordinate their respective policies.

3. Actually, in several instances, Japan accelerated its tariff reductions as part of its various market opening initiatives prior to 1987.

4. The tariffs are weighted by 1976 trade, which was the reference period used in the Tokyo Round negotiations. The actual rates in effect presently may differ somewhat from those indicated in table 9.2 insofar as the composition of trade may have changed since 1976. If we were to remove agricultural products, food and kindred products, and petroleum from the weighting process and focus only on industrial products, Japan's weighted-average tariff rate becomes 2.9 percent as compared to 4.3 percent for the United States and 5.2 percent for Canada. For further details, see Deardorff and Stern (1986, 51).

5. According to Nogués, Olechowski, and Winters (1986, 182–84), the NTBs include border measures that are product specific and for which internationally comparable data are available. Five groups are covered: quantitative import restrictions, voluntary export restraints, measures for the enforcement of decreed prices, tariff-type

measures, and monitoring measures. Subsidies are excluded as are the various informal barriers mentioned in our discussion above. Research in progress by Edward Leamer suggests that the NTB coverage indexes reported in table 9.3 may be sensitive to which NTBs are included or excluded and to the trade weights used for purposes of calculation.

6. Some reservations on the use and interpretation of the measures of price effects of NTBs are discussed in Deardorff and Stern (1985, esp. 21). The NTB ad valorem equivalent estimates given in table 9.4 are based on estimates in the literature and have been adjusted according to the NTB coverage indexes reported in table 9.3. For details on the sources utilized and the methodology underlying the estimates, see Deardorff and Stern (1987, app. B).

7. As noted by Bale (1983, 37–38):

> Some of the restrictions can be overcome by simply incorporating (thus establishing U.S. citizenship) in one of the fifty U.S. states. There are few restrictions on the naturalization of foreign enterprises, and this approach generally overcomes barriers in banking, insurance, and mineral leasing operations. Notwithstanding certain restrictions in these sectors, foreign-owned or controlled enterprises have extensive interests in U.S. banking, insurance, and federal on-shore and off-shore mineral properties.

8. Five years of bilateral U.S.-Japan negotiations have led to more transparent testing, certification, and approval procedures for new drugs and vaccines being sold in Japan. This has stimulated renewed foreign direct investment in this industry in Japan.

9. Since the domestic telecommunications market was opened up to private firms on 1 April 1985, a large number of foreign firms have made significant investments. It is widely believed, however, that continuing efforts by the Ministry of Posts and Telecommunication to limit competition in this industry have prevented more foreign investment from taking place.

10. See Frankel (1984).

11. As noted in USTR (1986, 5), the Reagan administration declared in September 1985 its commitment to "free and fair trade" by opening markets and instituting an aggressive attack on unfair foreign trade practices. A Trade Strike Force was established under the direction of the Secretary of Commerce. The actions taken in the first year are listed in USTR (1986, 293–95).

12. These amounts refer presumably to 1984. For information on U.S. programs of support for R&D and innovation and for high-technology industries, see Congressional Budget Office (1984a, 1985). By comparison with American efforts, Japanese government tax expenditures and direct subsidies to promote industries other than agriculture are relatively modest. See Saxonhouse (1983b).

13. This section is based in part on Deardorff and Stern (1985).

14. See the assumptions outlined in Leamer (1984, ch. 1) and Helpman and Krugman (1985, ch. 1).

15. As noted in Saxonhouse (1983a), differentiated products can easily be introduced into the familiar utility function which is positive, continuous, nondecreasing, quasi-concave, and homogeneous. See also Helpman and Krugman (1985, ch. 6).

16. This formulation rests critically on the existence of direct community-utility functions. For conditions under which this might be true, see Samuelson (1956) and Eisenberg (1961). For a more general discussion, see Woodland (1982).

17. For a discussion of Roy's Identity, see Varian (1984, 126).

18. The GNP function π as previousely defined needs to allow for differentiated products and economies of scale. Following Helpman and Krugman, this can be done by including optimal firm scale in π. Provided optimal firm scale is small relative to market size, changes in industry output can be achieved by changes in the number of identical firms. This means at an industry level that there will be constant returns to scale.

19. In the likely case that the number of goods exceeds the number of factors ($N > K$), trade will be indeterminant. In estimating models of this kind, Leamer (1984, 18) suggests that the indeterminacy can be resolved by assuming small international transportation costs that deter and determine trade but are otherwise negligible. Alternatively, Saxonhouse (1983a, 1986) assumes that $N = K$, but that the included and excluded dependent and independent variables have properties such that the exclusion of relevant variables does not bias the parameters that are estimated.

It should be noted that the derivation of equation (11) does not necessarily require that the trade balance be zero or exogenously fixed at all. If securities are incorporated into the indirect trade utility function, then, with trade taking place in securities as well as in goods, it is possible to use the same model to examine the influence of sectoral trade policy on both trade structure and the overall current account on international transactions. See Helpman and Razin (1978).

20. A similar conclusion has been drawn explicitly with reference to agricultural policy in Honma and Hayami (1986).

21. Bowen, Leamer, and Sveikauskas (1987) find that the Heckscher-Ohlin equations linking input requirements, resource supplies, and trade should be rejected in favor of weaker models that allow for measurement errors, technological differences, and/or factor price differences.

22. This line of reasoning was first advanced as a possible explanation for the empirical failures of the simple Heckscher-Ohlin model of Leontief (1956).

23. Note, however, that as long as twenty years ago, Krueger (1968) challenged the traditional viewpoint that factor prices are greatly disparate across countries. As she noted (657–58):

. . . that more than half of the differences between United Nations estimates of per capita income of each of the less developed countries in the sample and the United States is explained by demographic variables alone must surely cast some doubt on the degree of conviction with which the factor-price equalization model is held to be unrealistic.

Also, see Leamer (1984, 28–29).

24. The approach taken here is analogous to the two-step "jack-knife" procedures proposed in Guilkey and Schmidt (1973) and Zellner (1962). To illustrate further, let $a_s = 1 + a'_s$, assuming that $E(a'_s) = 0$. Using instrumental variable techniques in the presence of multiplicative errors allows consistent estimates of the B'_{is}.

Using these estimates, for each economy an $NX1$ vector $[V_i]$ of net trade equation residuals can be formed for each time period. Consistent estimates of the quality and measurement error terms for each time period can then be obtained from:

$$\{[\hat{B}'_{is} L_s]'[\hat{B}'_{is} L_s]\}^{-1} \{[\hat{B}'_{is} L_s]'[V_i]\}.$$

25. We would like to reiterate that the Leamer-Saxonhouse methodology is intended to reflect the presence of both formal and informal barriers to trade rather than informal barriers only. If we had direct information on the quanity-reducing effects of particular formal barriers, we could presumably use such information in the analysis. Unfortunately, such information is not available in comparable and comprehensive form. The industries identified as outliers, therefore, in tables 9.6 and 9.7 are thus presumed to be subject to both formal and informal barriers. Also, as already mentioned, the methodology being used is intended to measure deviations from the norm, once national factor endowments and distance considerations are taken into account. Consequently, we cannot implement the suggestion made by Kreinin in his comment below that we use the information on national barriers presented in appendix tables A9.2–9.4, since thre is no way to determine how distinctive these barriers may be in particular sectors.

In his comment below, Markusen argues that the Leamer-Saxonhouse methodology does not reflect national differences in the level of protection. This is not correct, and indeed the evidence presented in tables 9.6 and 9.7 can be interpreted to the effect that Canada has higher barriers in comparison to the United States.

26. A similar test on the distinctiveness of Japanese trade structure using a different sample is described in Saxonhouse (1987).

27. Markusen wonders in his comment about how sensitive the methodology may be to differences in protection. While this is an interesting question, it was not our purpose to test for different levels of protection. The point rather was to determine whether protection was distinctive for sectors within individual countries. We agree with Markusen that the sectoral focus may be what policymakers and producing interests care the most about, and it seems clear that this is what our results are designed to show, namely, the sectors that are apparently most affected by trade policies. Further, our calculations here of the confidence intervals for the overall results suggest that the confidence intervals for the individual sectors are also fairly small. Additional evidence at the sectoral level that is pertinent is given in Saxonhouse (1987). Another point made by Markusen in his comment is that computable general equilibrium models provide small estimates of the effects of trade barriers and do not provide sectoral details. But what this overlooks is the fact that existing barriers may not be as large as sometimes believed. Also, sectoral detail is in fact what some computational models are designed to yield, the Deardorff and Stern (1986) Michigan Model being a case in point.

28. In his specific comments below, Markusen is critical of the Leamer-Saxonhouse methodology on the grounds that it does not reflect a number of endogenous effects of protection. He notes, for example, that national factor endowments may respond to protection and that these responses will not show up in the empirical analysis. This may be true, but we would note that it is not immediately relevant in

the case of Japan since foreign capital has been of minor importance as a part of Japan's total capital endowment. Markusen also contends that protection may encourage the transfer of technology and permit firms to realize scale economies, with the result that the protection may at some point appear to be redundant. Here again we suggest that Markusen has misconstrued the methodology since, if these effects are important, they should show up as sectoral outliers in the empirical results. We thus do not share Markusen's conclusion that the Leamer-Saxonhouse methodology is open to criticism on the grounds that it does not capture the cumulative effects of protection.

29. Bowen, Leamer, and Sveikauskas (1987), in the course of their investigation of the Heckscher-Ohlin model, find that they cannot reject the hypothesis that cross-national data are consistent with homotheticity. For contrary evidence that supports nonhomotheticity, see Markusen (1986, esp. 1003–4).

30. Since the factor endowment variables in (10) and (11) explain national development, there is no need to limit the sample used here to just the most advanced countries.

31. Unlike the import equations, the gross export equations given by (10) will have many zero observations. This suggests that these equations should be specified as a Tobit model. The estimation method used here is described in Greene (1981).

32. The approaches taken in equations (12) and (12') can be extended in a number of directions. A set of equations that are linear in factor endowments is not the only possible specification for a model explaining trade structure. Thus, suppose that the assumption of factor price equalization is dropped altogether. In the absence of equations (6) and (7) or (6') and (7'), an explicit equation to replace (12) or (12') can only be obtained by imposing more structure on Π, the GNP function. As indicated in the Technical Appendix below, the approximation of (12) as either Generalized Leontief or translog can be shown to yield estimating equations which are nonlinear in factor endowments but otherwise linear in parameters. The Generalized Leontief, translog, and related flexible forms are discussed in Diewert (1974). For other functional forms that might be used, see Gallant (1981). Such a framework is more general than those previously used by Leamer and Saxonhouse and offers the possibility of testing for factor price equalization without actually using factor price data.

33. The calculated values of P for import and export forecasts are 96.3 and 81.5, respectively.

34. In his comment on the original version of this chapter, Kreinin asked whether the Heckscher-Ohlin or the Helpman-Krugman model is the most appropriate model to be used. Our response, after testing both models, is that the Heckscher-Ohlin model appears to be fairly robust in explaining cross-country variations in the structure and volume of trade. Kreinin also stressed the need to take international general equilibrium effects into account in assessing the impacts of trade barriers. We agree with him on this point, but at the same time believe that the reduced-form estimating equation used in the Leamer-Saxonhouse methodology takes these international general equilibrium effects into account.

35. Equation (A4) does not suggest using GNP as an independent variable except perhaps as a proxy for other omitted variables.

36. Balassa (1986, 18) also found a dummy variable for the United States to be negative and significant, but he does not attribute this result to the existence of Amer-

ican barriers to trade. Balassa's methodology and results are reproduced, with further discussion, in Balassa and Noland (1988).

37. Like Bergsten and Cline, Balassa (1986, 73) moves towards a translog specification by replacing his dependent variable by its antilogarithm and finds that his results are not markedly changed by this substitution. Unfortunately, while this is a step in the right direction, it is still insufficient to provide his work with an adequate conceptual foundation. Abstracting from the need to conduct his empirical work on a more disaggregated basis and then aggregate upward in order to explain trade volume rather than net trade, if Balassa's empirical work is to follow from a translog specification of the indirect trade utility function as noted in our Technical Appendix below, his independent variable represented by per capita income also needs to be altered. Once again this is a problem that follows from Balassa being guided too much by Chenery's earlier work. Chenery introduced per capita income into his work as a proxy for physical capital per unit of labor and human capital per unit of labor. Unfortunately, the same translog specification that makes his new dependent variable attractive also suggests his capital variables should not be entered in factor-intensive form.

Further, even if Balassa could enter his capital variables properly, the difficulties in providing a translog indirect-trade-utility-function foundation for his work would not end. In this instance, while he would finally have a conceptual foundation for a net import equation, he would still face difficult problems in interpretation should he find the Japan dummy significant. It is especially noteworthy that Balassa makes no allowance in his empirical work for differences in factor quality across countries. Since factor endowments enter his equations logarithmically, a statistically significant dummy variable would more likely reflect statistically significant differences in the quality of Japanese factors rather than special features of Japan's trade policy. This can be seen from equation (A4') in the Technical Appendix.

38. As he notes (1986, 68):

The next question concerns the introduction of transportation costs in the estimating equation. Using distance for this purpose will not be appropriate since transportation costs are several times lower by sea than by land and decline greatly with distance. In particular, employing a distance variable as a proxy for transportation costs introduces a bias in regard to Japan that cannot use the land route in its international trade and, apart from Australia, has by far the longest average distance from its trading partners among industrial countries.

Thus, the use of the distance variable gives rise to a problem of identification in the case of Japan as to whether the statistical results pertaining to this variable reflect transportation costs or other country characteristics, in particular, trade policies.

39. Reestimating equation (12') in Saxonhouse (1986) without using a distance variable, there were 68 instances in 327 cases where Japanese trade flows fall outside the forecast interval. These accounted for 7.6 percent of Japan's gross external trade.

40. For example, Balassa assumes transport costs, as a proportion of total value of manufactured goods, to be one-sixth of what was found in the well-known work by Lipsey and Weiss (1974).

41. As noted above, Balassa is critical of using distance as an explanatory variable. Contrary to his contention, however, treating distance as a linear term in a trade equation is quite compatible with the assumption that average transport costs decline with distance. Of course, a linear term only assumes that marginal cost is constant. In a semilogarithmic translog trade equation, treating distance symmetrically with other independent variables is entirely compatible with both declining average and marginal costs. This is also true for Balassa's logarithmic formulation. Note Lawrence (1987) adopts Saxonhouse's distance variable in his empirical work.

42. Noland (1987, 7) states that the equation he estimates is formally derived from the Helpman-Krugman model that he presents in his appendix A. A comparison of his appendix A with his estimated equation, however, makes it difficult to see the basis for this claim. See also Balassa and Noland (1988).

43. See Belsley, Kuh, and Welsch (1980, 20).

44. It is interesting to note in this regard that Japan's import shares of manufactures have in fact increased substantially in recent years. See Sazanami's discussion in chapter 3 above for details.

45. A similar conclusion is to be found in Winters (1987). For a Japanese perspective on these issues, see Japan Economic Research Institute (1984).

46. Equation (A3) is not adjusted for a quality and measurement error term because, in the absence of assuming factor price equalization, a_s cannot be identified within the Generalized Leontief framework.

References

Balassa, Bela. 1986. Japan's trade policies. *Weltwirtschaftliches Archiv* Band 122, Heft 4: 745–90.

Balassa, Bela, and Marcus Noland. 1988. *Japan in the world economy.* Washington, D.C.: Institute for International Economics.

Bale, Harvey E., Jr. 1983. The U.S. federal government's policy towards foreign direct investment. In *Regulation of foreign direct investment in Canada and the United States,* eds. Earl H. Fry and Lee H. Radebaugh. Provo, Utah: Brigham Young University.

Bank of Japan. 1979. *Showa go-ju yon-nen-kokusai bukka hikaku.* Tokyo.

———. 1982. *Showa go-ju nana-nen-kokusai bukka hikaku.* Tokyo.

Belsley, David A., Edwin Kuh, and Roy E. Welsch. 1980. *Regression diagnostics.* New York: John Wiley & Sons.

Bergsten, C. Fred, and William R. Cline. 1985. *The United States–Japan economic problem.* Revised Janaury 1987. Washington, D.C.: Institute for International Economics.

Bowen, Harry P., Edward E. Leamer, and Leo Sveikauskas. 1987. Multicountry, multifactor tests of the factor abundance theory. *American Economic Review* 77 (December): 791–809.

Chenery, Hollis B. 1960. Patterns of industrial growth. *American Economic Review* 50 (September): 624–54.

Christelow, Dorothy. 1985/86. Japan's intangible barriers to trade in manufactures. Federal Reserve Bank of New York, *Quarterly Review* 10 (Winter): 11–18.

Congress of the United States, Congressional Budget Office. 1984a. *Federal support for R&D and innovation.* Washington, D.C.: Government Printing Office.

———. 1984b. *Federal support of U.S. business.* Washington, D.C.: Government Printing Office.

———. 1985. *Federal financial support for high-technology industries.* Washington, D.C.: Government Printing Office.

Davidow, Joel. 1984. The implementation of international antitrust principles. In *Emerging standards of international trade and investment: Multinational codes and corporate conduct,* eds. Seymour J. Rubin and Gary Clyde Hufbauer. Totowa, New Jersey: Rowman & Allanheld.

Deardorff, Alan V., and Robert M. Stern. 1985. Methods of measurement of nontariff barriers. United Nations Conference on Trade and Development. UNCTAD/ST/MD/28, United Nations, Geneva.

———. 1986. *The Michigan Model of World Production and Trade: Theory and applications.* Cambridge, Mass.: MIT Press.

———. 1987. A computational analysis of alternative scenarios for multilateral trade liberalization. In process.

Diewert, W. E. 1974. Applications of duality theory. In *Frontiers of quantitative economics,* vol. 2, eds. M. E. Intriligator and D. A. Kendrick. New York: Elsevier.

Eisenberg, E. 1961. Aggregation of utility functions. *Management Science* 7 (July): 337–50.

European Community. 1987. *1987 Report on U.S. trade barriers.* Brussels: European Community.

Frankel, Jeffrey. 1984. *The Yen/Dollar Agreement: Liberalizing Japanese capital markets.* Washington, D.C.: Institute for International Economics.

Gallant, A. Ronald. 1981. On the bias in flexible functional form and an essentially unbiased form: The Fourier flexible form. *Journal of Econometrics* 15 (February): 211–46.

Greene, William H. 1981. On the asymptotic bias of the ordinary least squares estimator of the Tobit model. *Econometrica* 49 (March): 505–11.

Guilkey, D. C., and P. Schmidt. 1973. Estimation of seemingly unrelated regressions with vector autoregressive errors. *Journal of the American Statistical Association* 68 (September): 642–47.

Helpman, Elhanan, and Paul R. Krugman. 1985. *Market structure and foreign trade: Increasing returns, imperfect competition, and the international economy.* Cambridge, Mass.: MIT Press.

Helpman, Elhanan, and Assaf Razin. 1978. Uncertainty and international trade in the presence of stock markets. *Review of Economic Studies* 45 (June): 239–50.

Henderson, Dan F. 1986. Access to the Japanese market: Some aspects of foreign exchange controls and banking law. In *Law and trade policies of the Japanese economy,* eds. Gary R. Saxonhouse and Kozo Yamamura. Seattle: University of Washington Press.

Honma, Masayoshi, and Yujiro Hayami. 1986. Structure of agricultural protection in industrial countries. *Journal of International Economics* 20 (February): 115–30.

Japan Economic Research Institute. 1984. *Analysis of the degree of openness of the Japanese market.* Tokyo, August.

Krueger, Anne O. 1968. Factor endowments and per capita income differences among countries. *Economic Journal* 78 (September): 641–59.

Lawrence, Robert Z. 1987. Does Japan import too little: Closed minds or markets. *Brookings Papers in Economic Actitivy* 2: 517–54.

Leamer, Edward E. 1984. *Sources of international comparative advantages.* Cambridge, Mass.: MIT Press.

———. 1988. Measures of openness. In *Trade policy issues and empirical analysis,* ed. Robert E. Baldwin. Chicago: University of Chicago Press.

Leontief, W. W. 1956. Factor proportions and the structure of American trade: Further theoretical and empirical analysis. *Review of Economics and Statistics* 38 (November): 386–407.

Lipsey, Robert E. and Merle Yahr Weiss. 1974. The structure of ocean transport charges. *Explorations in Economic Research* 1(1): 162–93. Cambridge, Mass.: National Bureau of Economic Research.

McCulloch, Rachel. 1988. United States–Japan Economic Relations. In *Trade policy issues and empirical analysis,* ed. Robert E. Baldwin. Chicago: University of Chicago Press.

Markusen, James R. 1986. Explaining the volume of trade: An eclectic approach. *American Economic Review* 76 (December): 1002–11.

Moroz, Andrew. 1985. Some observations on non-tariff barriers and their use in Canada. In *Canada–United States free trade,* eds. John Whalley and Roderick Hill. Toronto: University of Toronto Press.

Nogués, Julio J., Andrzej Olechowski, and L. Alan Winters. 1985. The extent of non-tariff barriers to imports of industrial countries. World Bank Staff Working Paper 789. Washington, D.C.: World Bank.

———. 1986. The extent of nontariff barriers to industrial countries' imports. *World Bank Economic Review* 1 (September): 181–99.

Noland, Marcus. 1987. An econometric model of the volume of international trade. Washington, D.C.: Institute for International Economics. Typescript.

Price Waterhouse. 1983a. *Doing business in Canada.*

———. 1983b. *Doing business in Japan.*

Rapp, William V. 1986. Japan's invisible barriers to trade. In *Fragile interdependence: Economic issues in U.S.-Japanese trade and investment,* eds. Thomas A. Pugel and Robert G. Hawkins. Lexington: Lexington Books.

Samuelson, Paul A. 1956. Social indifference curves. *Quarterly Journal of Economics* 70 (February): 1–22.

Saxonhouse, Gary R. 1983a. The micro- and macroeconomics of foreign sales to Japan. In *Trade policy for the 1980s,* ed. William R. Cline. Cambridge, Mass.: MIT Press.

———. 1983b. What's all this about Japanese "industrial targeting"? *The World Economy* 6 (September): 253–74.

———. 1986. What's wrong with Japanese trade structure? *Pacific Economic Papers* 137 (July): 1–45.

———. 1987. Comparative advantage and structural change. In *Japan's political economy: The international transformation*, eds. Takashi Inoguchi and Daniel Okimoto. Stanford: Stanford University Press.

Sazanami, Yoko. 1981. Possibilities of expanding intra-industry trade in Japan. *Keio Economic Studies* 18 (2): 27–44.

Staiger, Robert W., Alan V. Deardorff, and Robert M. Stern. 1985. The effects of protection on the factor content of Japanese and American foreign trade. Research seminar in International Economics, The University of Michigan, Discussion Paper no. 159.

———. 1987. The employment effects of Japanese and American protection. In *the new protectionist threat to world welfare*, ed. Dominick Salvatore. Amsterdam: North-Holland.

Stern, Robert M., John H. Jackson, and Bernard M. Hoekman. 1988. *An assessment of the GATT codes on non-tariff measures*. Thames Essay no. 55. Aldershot, New York: Gower for the Trade Policy Research Centre.

United States Trade Representative (USTR), U.S. Office. 1986. *National trade estimate: 1986 Report on foreign trade barriers*. Washington, D.C.: Government Printing Office.

Varian, Hal. 1984. *Microeconomics*. 2d ed. New York: Norton.

Winters, L. Alan. 1987. Patterns of world trade in manufactures: Does trade policy matter? Centre for Economic Policy Research, Discussion Paper no. 160, March.

Woodland, A. D. 1982. *International trade and resource allocation*. Amsterdam: North-Holland.

Zellner, Arnold. 1962. An efficient method for estimating seemingly unrelated regressions and tests for aggregation bias. *Journal of the American Statistical Association* 57 (June): 348–68.

Comment

James R. Markusen

General Remarks

This paper is in large part a survey of previously published work. This of course makes the job of a discussant somewhat difficult unless one wants to get into the task of carefully digesting the mountain of material behind the paper. It is also likely to be a fairly barren mountain for a discussant insofar as it will have been stripped of most things of interest to a discussant (e.g., errors) en route to publication. Because of my theoretical background, I also know few relevant empirical facts or anecdotes that might help me contradict the paper and cast doubt on its principal conclusions. Nevertheless, in true academic tradition I will manage to say a few things, beginning with some general comments.

While they do record some general differences in opinion, the authors tend to accept the conclusion that the evidence does not suggest that Japan has higher informal barriers than the United States or Canada. The work of various authors is studied, but most of the analysis is devoted to the works of Leamer (1984) and Saxonhouse (1983, 1986). Thus, in the spirit of focusing my comments and reducing my workload, I will devote my space to reviewing the work of these authors. While the purposes of the two authors are different, both use the methodology of estimating a linear mapping from a country's endowment vector to its vector of net exports. (Leamer is not interested in estimating the implied level of protection, but rather in testing the hypothesis of a linear mapping.) As Leamer (1984) shows, this mapping is implied by a Heckscher-Ohlin production structure plus (1) commodity and factor-price equalization among countries, (2) identical and homothetic demand structures across countries, and so forth. By Heckscher-Ohlin production structure I mean identical, constant-returns technologies across countries, perfect competition, and diversified production.

Leamer finds that the predicted trade vectors generated by the linear mapping are closely consistent with actual trade vectors for most countries and hence he recommends the Heckscher-Ohlin-plus model as a good approximation of reality. Saxonhouse uses a similar linear model to generate counterfactual trade vectors that are assumed to characterize the world in a free (really free) trade equilibrium. Comparing the counterfactual to the actual trade vectors, Saxonhouse concludes that there is little or no evidence to support the notion that Japan has higher informal barriers to trade.

While I have no expertise with which to criticize these findings from an econometric point of view, they leave me uncomfortable. Note first that the comparison of the actual and counterfactual trade vectors picks up the influence of formal barriers (tariffs, quotas, and VERs), in addition to identifying informal barriers. Thus this procedure should, according to the theory behind the methodology, succeed in identifying what we all know is already there: the influence of the measurable formal trade barrriers.

We know on the basis of extensive study that the trade-weighted Canadian barriers to trade (tariffs and nontariffs) are approximately double those of the United States. Thus, when we look at the residual difference between the actual and predicted trade vectors of the two countries, we should be able to clearly see this influence if the methodology is of any use at all. Yet my impression from this paper is that the Leamer/Saxonhouse methodology does not identify Canada as being more protectionist than the United States in some well defined way. (Again, Leamer is not interested in identifying trade barriers, but rather in testing the factor-proportions model). I think that twice the protection is a large difference and thus the methodology appears not very sensitive. I might add that I doubt that it could be claimed that higher informal protection in the United States offsets higher formal protection in Canada. At least conventional wisdom runs the other way (of course, the validity of conventional wisdom is precisely what we are trying to test).

Following on from this point, it makes me uncomfortable that we cannot do any sensitivity analysis on these estimates. Suppose that we were to triple the protection level in one of the countries as a conceptual experiment. Would the country in question show up as a statistical outlier in the Leamer/ Saxonhouse methodology? We cannot ask that type of question with that methodology and thus we have no way of knowing how sensitive the methodology is. The only thing that I can suggest is to go back to the data, select countries that we know to be highly protectionist, and test whether the methodology reveals them to be statistical outliers. Perhaps this has been done.

I wonder (and I mean wonder, as opposed to think) if there is a parallel between the Leamer/Saxonhouse results and the results that we often get from computable general-equilibrium analysis (CGE). From the latter, we get the result that the effects of trade liberalization will be small (the work of Richard Harris is the exception). In the spirit of my comment in the previous paragraph, we learn that we could probably triple the protection levels among the developed countries without perturbing national outputs very much. Using a computational GE model with scale economies and capital mobility, it was found in Markusen and Wigle (1989) that a tripling of U.S. protection against Canada affects the latter's GNP by less than 2 percent. From the work of Leamer, we learn that the Heckscher-Ohlin model, with all the added assumptions of commodity and factor-price equalization, is a good fit even when we know that average protection levels in the sample are far from zero. Saxonhouse adds that actual trade vectors are close to the fitted trade vectors generated by an ideal, frictionless world à la Heckscher-Ohlin, so we infer that protection is small. It strikes me that we could reach one of two conclusions. First, we could conclude that the actual effects of large changes in protection are quite small. If this is the case, I suppose that we tell policymakers to quit worrying and go home. Second, we could conclude that our models are not very sensitive. This has the usual implication that we call for more research and bigger research grants.

I suggest, before we adopt either alternative, that we take a closer look at our results. In particular, why don't we try doing what we would do if we were businessmen down in the trenches? Why don't we forget about confidence intervals for a moment (if we are Leamer/Saxonhouse types) or aggregate GNP (if we are CGE types) and look at changes in sector output levels and trade flows? These are the data of concern to individual industries and therefore to policymakers and politicians. I know from my own CGE work with Wigle that policy changes that generate a meager 1 percent change in GNP may, at the same time, generate changes in an industry's trade flow on the order of 10 to 30 percent and changes in that industry's output of 3 to 10 percent. If we make the reasonable assumption that exporting in the aggregate industries we examine is concentrated in a minority of the firms in that aggregate, we could infer that the policy change affects those firms on the order of 5 to 15 percent of base output or, in some cases, considerably more. If I were a businessman or labor leader in one of these industries, I would regard these changes as very significant indeed, especially if I produced with sharply decreasing costs. My point is that policy changes which are insignificant from the point of view of aggregate welfare may be highly significant from the point of view of sectoral disruption, sectoral employment, and sectoral profitability.

I wonder if there is a parallel with the Leamer/Saxonhouse work. I would like to know if a deviation in a trade flow of 25 percent can nevertheless be inside the relevant confidence interval. Point estimates are still presumably our best guesses, and thus I would like to see some statistics on precisely how actual volumes of trade differ from their predicted values. Once again, I am rather sure that businessmen would be interested in these best-guess values, to hell with confidence intervals. To return to the discipline of my training again, I also question the interpretation of confidence intervals that are generated by an obviously misspecified and highly aggregated model.

Specific Comments

Consider the following linear mapping

$$\mathbf{X} = [\mathbf{A}]\mathbf{L} \tag{1}$$

where $\mathbf{X}$ is a country's vector of net exports, $[\mathbf{A}]$ is the Rybczynski matrix, and $\mathbf{L}$ is the country's vector of fixed factor endowments. Under the assumptions of identical, constant-returns technologies, perfect competition, diversified production, commodity and factor-price equalization, and identical, homothetic demand, this mapping will be the same for each country. Leamer and Saxonhouse estimate this $[\mathbf{A}]$ matrix across countries and then use it, in combination with the endowment vector, to generate the fitted or predicted net trade vector for each country.

There are many reservations and objections to this procedure, some of which are raised by Saxonhouse and Stern in their paper. I wish to comment on some additional considerations which they do not raise. The general thrust of my comments is that both the elements of the $[\mathbf{A}]$ matrix and the endowment vector are endogenous to the level of protection. With respect to the elements of $[\mathbf{A}]$, I am not referring to their dependence on factor price and thus on the level of protection. This dependence is well understood by the authors and, indeed, that is what they are counting on to reveal the effects of protection. I will refer to the added dependence of [A] on technical knowledge and industry/firm scale and argue that the response of these variables to protection may be to make protection less significant. But first the endogeneity of endowments is considered.

Endogeneity of Factor Endowments
Suppose that a capital-scarce country levies a tariff protecting its capital-intensive import sector. In a Heckscher-Ohlin world of fixed factors, we could recognize this protection by examining the deviation of that country's net export vector from the fitted vector generated by equation (1). Now let capital be perfectly mobile (we could assume the existence of some sector-specific factors to prevent full specialization). Capital will flow into the protected country in response to the higher rate of return generated by the protection (the Stolper-Samuelson effect). While general proofs are difficult, it is easy to construct an example with specific factors where the induced capital flow moves the elements of the [A] matrix back toward their factor-price equalization values. In the extreme (true both in the Heckscher-Ohlin and specific-factors models), factor prices are re-equalized by the factor movement after imports of the good in question are eliminated and equation (1) once again fits exactly. Production of the relevant sector has increased in the importing country and decreased in the exporting country, but the extent of this protection is not identified by the Leamer/Saxonhouse methodology.

Endogeneity of Technology
Suppose that a country initially imports a good X because that country does not possess the technology to produce it domestically. Now, the country levies protection against imports of X. This creates an incentive for a foreign multinational enterprise to transfer the technology to the country or for a domestic firm to develop that technology. If either happens, the protection may eventually become redundant as the country efficiently produces the good itself. When we compare its fitted and actual trade vectors, we find a good match. But once again, the protection has indeed had the very real effect of transferring production from the exporting to the importing country.

It strikes me that this is exactly what Japan has often done according to the (often suspect) conventional wisdom. The home market is reserved for domestic producers via protection until they become competitive in world markets. I have suggested that this phenomenon holds for Canada, in that while protection may have been needed to initiate an industry, this protection may now be redundant in the context of U.S.-Canada free trade. This strong effect due to protection has nothing to do with Heckscher-Ohlin economics and will not show up in the Leamer/Saxonhouse methodology.

Endogeneity of Unit Costs

Another example might be a country that imports X due to an inefficient scale of domestic production. But we know that there may be many equilibria with scale economies (particularly with few fixed factors and without the Armington assumption). Protection of an industry may then allow that industry to capture internal and external scale economies and allow it to lower its costs, possibly to the point where it becomes an efficient exporter. This point was made by Krugman (1984). Ex post to the capture of scale economies, we may find that the net export vector of the country corresponds closely to its fitted value. Nevertheless, protection has had a powerful effect on the output and profitability levels of the industries of the two countries. Baldwin and Krugman (1987) suggest that this is exactly the story of the Japanese semiconductor industry.

Endogeneity of Protection

The final point I would like to raise has been mentioned elsewhere, but not in the present paper under discussion. Present levels of protection in Japan and Canada may indeed be fairly low, but perhaps only on account of continual pressure from the United States. If this is true, then the statement "what is the United States complaining about?" totally misses the point. To preserve the status quo, liberal as it may or may not be, the United States and other countries must continue to complain, threaten, and pressure their trading partners in order to offset protectionist elements in those countries.

Summary

I am not convinced by the general conclusion of this paper that there is little evidence to suggest that Japanese informal trade barriers are significant relative to those of other countries. At the very least, my faith in the general view that Japanese trade barriers have had a tremendous cumulative influence over the past decades in shaping production and distorting world trade is not shaken. As I have noted in the previous section, there are strong arguments to suggest that the relevant mechanisms may work in ways such that their influence is completely missed by the Leamer/Saxonhouse methodology. The final point is one of political economy (strange ground for a theorist). If Japanese (Canadian, U.S.) trade barriers are indeed low, that does not imply that the United States (Canada, Japan) should stop the complaining and the pressure.

Let me conclude by admitting that I have nothing very constructive to offer. The authors may well be correct in their conclusions, but I feel that their evidence does not prove the case. The important problem of measuring informal trade barriers remains elusive.

References

Baldwin, Richard, and Paul R. Krugman. 1987. Market access and competition: A simulation study of 16K random access memories. In *Empirical methods for international trade*, ed. Robert Feenstra. Cambridge, Mass.: MIT Press.

Harris, Richard G., with David Cox. 1980. *Trade, industrial policy and Canadian manufacturing*. Toronto: University of Toronto Press.

Krugman, Paul R. 1984. Import protection as export promotion: International competition in the presence of oligopoly and economies of scale. In *Monopolistic competition in international trade*, ed. Henryk Kierzkowski. London: Oxford University Press.

Leamer, Edward. 1984. *Sources of international comparative advantage*. Cambridge, Mass.: MIT Press.

Markusen, James R., and Randall M. Wigle. 1989. Nash equilibrium tariffs for the U.S. and Canada: The roles of country size, scale economies, and capital mobility. *Journal of Political Economy*, forthcoming.

Saxonhouse, Gary R. 1893. The micro- and macroeconomics of foreign sales to Japan. In *Trade policy for the 1980s*, ed. William R. Cline. Cambridge, Mass.: MIT Press.

―――. 1986. What's wrong with Japanese trade structure? *Pacific Economic Papers* (July).

Comment
Mordechai E. Kreinin

This paper contains a comprehensive and very useful survey of trade barriers employed by the United States, Canada, and Japan, as well as a review of empirical studies estimating their restrictive effects. Particularly illuminating is the section on "conceptual issues" involved in the measurement efforts.

The paper consists of two distinct parts. First there is a listing, accompanied by discussion, of formal and informal trade barriers in the three countries. It is compiled from several sources, such as national governments and international organizations. To that list I might add one anecdotal story about the sale of my *International Economics* textbook in Japan. A professor who teaches in Tokyo wanted (in 1985) to order the fourth edition of the book for his students. He discovered that, because of some collusive arrangement between the bookstore and/or distributor, the book would be priced at a yen equivalent of over $60.00 (double the U.S. price). Attempts by the publisher to change that were to no avail. In 1987, after the sharp rise in the exchange value of the yen, the situation remained unchanged: The fifth edition of the book continued to be priced well above the U.S. price.

In a more serious vein, the lists of barriers presented by the authors are very comprehensive. They include policies that may have direct or indirect bearing on trade flows, such as measures that affect saving behavior and those classified as institutional factors. Since practically everything affects trade, however indirectly, many measures are included. It occurs to me that policies or practices pertaining to the "forced" transfer of technology, or to borrowing, copying, adoption and adaptation of foreign technologies should be high on the list, for they facilitate developments that later affect international trade. The reader gets the impression that the list of barriers is motivated at least in part by the overall trade imbalances, rather than by the inefficiencies created through differential protection accorded to various industries. Yet the trade imbalances are macroeconomic phenomena.

Be that as it may, the lists themselves offer no clue as to how restrictive is the regime: how much imports are excluded, or alternatively, by how much are domestic prices raised above international prices. Although the lists of barriers are useful in and of themselves, for they lay the groundwork for future estimation of their restrictive effects, it is desirable to classify the restrictions in some analytically meaningful way. The following possible classifications come to mind, although others are possible:

1. Whether or not the measure is sensitive to relative price (import/domestic) change, such as exchange rate variations. NTBs may or may not be offset by such changes, and in some sense those that are sensitive may be considered more flexible and less harmful than those that are not. Presumably cultural biases, such as a preference to "buy domestic," could be overcome by a lower price, so that import penetration can occur. The selling country's terms of trade would be lowered by such a bias on the part of consumers in the importing country.

2. An intercountry comparison of the *structure* of protection. During the years when the tariff reigned supreme, its structure (though not its level) was discovered to be similar among the industrial countries, in the sense that the same types of products were heavily or lightly protected by all countries. Is this phenomenon preserved with respect to the NTBs?

3. Classify NTBs by stage of production of the protected commodities, so that some idea of effective protection may be gleaned from the list.

The second part of the paper is related to the first in that it attempts to assess the trade-restrictive effects of the NTBs. But in a very real sense the two parts are unrelated. For the second part summarizes the results of several empirical studies which estimate deviations of the country's trade volume from some measure of an expected level, and declare the deviation to be a result of the protective structure. In doing so, it does not make use of the compiled list of NTBs in any way. At the very least, the NTB list should be used as a check on the statistical results, or the outcome of the empirical investigation should be compared to a priori knowledge of formal restrictions.

In concluding that Japan is not an "outlier" with respect to the influence of its trade policies, it should be stressed that the methodology employed in reaching this conclusion is fraught with difficulties, most of which are recognized by the authors in an excellent section on "conceptual issues." This methodology is based on the Heckscher-Ohlin model (which is designed to explain the pattern and not the volume of trade), but it contains elements of gravity models, where the expected (counterfactual) trade values are based on cross-country comparisons.

What if the structure of protection is similar in all countries, so that the expected value itself is affected by the NTBs? Are there important variables missing from the estimation of expected trade values, such as diversification of the industrial or resource base? Also, is manufacturing trade (with differentiated products) better described by the Helpman-Krugman type model, which does not yet lend itself to empirical estimation, than by the Heckscher-Ohlin model used here? In my view, the results are not yet in on the restrictive effect of informal NTBs.

A final point relates to the need emphasized by the authors to incorporate domestic general equilibrium effects in evaluating the overall level of protection. It might be added that international general equilibrium effects are also important. For example, a (widespread) policy such as the voluntary export restraint (VER) is inherently discriminatory. It can have profound effects on countries other than those directly involved in the negotiated restriction. Thus, it is shown in Dinopoulos and Kreinin (1988) that, in the particular case of the U.S.-Japan VER on automobiles, European producers were induced to raise their prices by more than 25 percent, and that in 1984 the U.S. welfare loss to Europe exceeded its loss to Japan. International general equilibrium effects are important accordingly in other cases of trade restrictions.

Reference

Dinopoulos, Elias, and Mordechai E. Kreinin. 1988. Effects of the U.S.-Japan auto VER on European prices and U.S. welfare. *Review of Economics and Statistics* 70, no. 3 (August): 484–91.

4 MACROECONOMIC ISSUES

10 Liberalization of Financial Markets and the Volatility of Exchange Rates

Dale W. Henderson
William E. Alexander

A Theoretical Analysis

Dale W. Henderson

Introduction

Since the mid-1970s there has been a significant reduction in restrictions on financial transactions in several major industrial countries, including Japan. This reduction in restrictions is often referred to as financial liberalization. During the same period, most measures of exchange rate volatility have increased. One important aspect of financial liberalization has been the substantial relaxation of exchange controls and capital controls. Many argue that this relaxation has contributed to the increase in exchange rate volatility.

My purpose here is to provide a theoretical analysis of the effects of financial liberalization on exchange rate volatility. I use a two-country portfolio balance model. The basic premise is that financial liberalization affects exchange rate volatility by increasing the degree of substitution between assets denominated in different currencies. I analyze the effects of increases in both currency substitution (CS)—substitution between different moneys—and bond substitution (BS)—substitution between bonds denominated in different currencies. The central question is whether increases in CS and BS exaggerate or dampen the exchange rate changes resulting from changes in exogenous variables. I consider changes in three "exogenous" variables: the

Editor's note: This chapter contains the expanded and revised versions of comments by Dale W. Henderson and William E. Alexander on a paper dealing with a theoretical and empirical analysis of exchange rate volatility that was presented at the conference. Because the paper had some conceptual problems that could not be readily resolved, in order to avoid an undue delay in publication it has not been included in this volume.

foreign interest rate, the home money supply, and the expected future exchange rate.

Those familiar with the literature on CS might be somewhat surprised by the results for increases in CS. Girton and Roper (1981) show that increases in CS exaggerate the exchange rate changes resulting from changes in the money growth rate. This result might have led some to expect that increases in CS always increase exchange rate volatility. However, it turns out that increases in CS may either increase or reduce exchange rate volatility depending on which exogenous variable is changing. Increases in CS dampen the exchange rate changes resulting from changes in the foreign interest rate and the home money supply. These results confirm those obtained by Horiuchi (1987) in a portfolio balance model with no valuation effects. Increases in CS exaggerate the exchange rate changes resulting from changes in the expected future exchange rate. Changes in the expected future exchange rate and changes in the money growth rate are similar disturbances, so this result is consistent with the Girton and Roper result.

There are no surprises in the results for increases in BS. Increases in BS increase exchange rate volatility no matter which of the three exogenous variables is changing.

The results obtained here must be interpreted with care. Here financial liberalization is viewed as increases in CS and BS. It is shown that increases in CS may or may not increase exchange rate volatility and that increases in BS definitely increase exchange rate volatility. However, no assessment of the quantitative importance of the effects of increases in CS and BS is provided. The observed increase in exchange rate volatility may be due mainly to increases in the variances of disturbances rather than to increases in CS and BS given the same distributions of disturbances. Furthermore, even if it were determined that the increase in exchange rate volatility is due in large part to increases in CS and BS, it would not be appropriate to conclude that financial liberalization has been undesirable. Any costs of increased exchange rate volatility would have to be weighed against any efficiency gains from financial liberalization.

The Model

This section contains a portfolio balance model of international financial markets. The model is a description of the behavior of private agents in two countries, the home country and the foreign country. In equilibrium, these agents must be satisfied to hold stocks of four financial assets: home money ($\bar{M}$), home (currency) bonds ($\bar{B}$), foreign (currency) bonds ($\bar{F}$), and foreign money ($\bar{N}$). The conditions for equilibrium in the four financial markets are

$$\tilde{M} = [\alpha - \lambda i + \varepsilon - \mu(\bar{E}/E - 1)]\tilde{Y}, \tag{1}$$

$$\tilde{B} = (-\alpha + \lambda i)\tilde{Y} + [\gamma + \beta(i - \overset{*}{i} - \bar{E}/E + 1)]\tilde{W}, \tag{2}$$

$$E\tilde{F} = (-\alpha + \lambda\overset{*}{i})\tilde{Y} + [(1 - \gamma) - \beta(i - \overset{*}{i} - \bar{E}/E + 1)]\tilde{W}, \tag{3}$$

$$E\tilde{N} = [\alpha - \lambda\overset{*}{i} - \varepsilon + \mu(\bar{E}/E - 1)]\tilde{Y}, \tag{4}$$

where E is the exchange rate defined as the home currency price of foreign currency.

Private agents have the same asset preferences no matter which country they live in. Their asset demand functions have familiar properties. There is substitution between home money and home bonds. An increase in the home interest rate (i) causes a shift out of home money into home bonds by λ times the home currency value of world nominal income ($\tilde{Y}$). There is substitution between foreign money and foreign bonds. An increase in the foreign interest rate causes a shift out of foreign money into foreign bonds by $\lambda\tilde{Y}$. There is CS. The money return differential is the expected rate of depreciation of the home currency (s), the ratio (q) of the expected future exchange rate ($\bar{E}$) to the current exchange rate minus one:

$$s = q - 1, \qquad q = \bar{E}/E. \tag{5}$$

An increase in the money return differential causes a shift out of home money into foreign money by $\mu\tilde{Y}$. There is BS. The bond return differential (k) is the home interest rate minus the sum of the foreign interest rate and the expected rate of depreciation of the home currency:

$$k = i - \overset{*}{i} - \bar{E}/E + 1. \tag{6}$$

An increase in the bond return differential causes a shift out of foreign bonds into home bonds by β times the home currency value of world nominal wealth ($\tilde{W}$). For simplicity it is assumed that there is no substitution between the money of one country and the bonds of another.

Two definitions are needed to complete the model:

$$\tilde{Y} = Y + E\overset{*}{Y}, \tag{7}$$

$$\tilde{W} = \tilde{M} + \tilde{B} + E(\tilde{F} + \tilde{N}). \tag{8}$$

World nominal income is the sum of home nominal income (Y) and the exchange rate times foreign nominal income ($\overset{*}{Y}$). It is assumed that Y and $\overset{*}{Y}$ are exogenous. World nominal wealth is equal to the sum of home currency nominal assets and the exchange rate times foreign currency nominal assets.

The sum of private agents' demands for the four assets is identically equal to world wealth which, in turn, is equal to the sum of the supplies of these assets. Therefore, only three of the four financial market equilibrium conditions are independent.

In order to simplify the analysis, I reduce the model to two independent market equilibrium conditions in two endogenous variables, the home interest rate and the exchange rate. I assume that the foreign authorities use open market operations in foreign money and foreign bonds to fix the foreign interest rate. Under this assumption, substituting (7) and (8) into (1) and (2) yields two independent market equilibrium conditions in the home interest rate and the exchange rate.

Consider the effects of an increase in the home interest rate and a depreciation of the home currency on excess demand in each of the markets. An increase in i reduces the excess demand for money and increases the excess demand for home bonds. The effect on the excess demand for home bonds is greater in absolute value because the increase in i causes not only substitution out of home money into home bonds, but also substitution out of foreign bonds into home bonds. A depreciation of the home currency (an increase in E) increases the excess demand for home money for two reasons. First, it reduces the money return differential causing substitution out of foreign money into home money. Second, it raises the home currency value of foreign nominal income, generating a positive money market valuation effect:

$$(\alpha - \lambda i + \varepsilon - \mu s)\overset{*}{Y} = m\overset{*}{Y} > 0. \tag{9}$$

Equation (1) implies that m must be positive. Under the assumptions of this section, a depreciation of the home currency also increases the excess demand for home bonds for two reasons. First, it increases the bond return differential causing substitution out of foreign bonds into home bonds. Second, it raises the home currency value of both foreign nominal income and foreign assets generating a bond market valuation effect that is assumed to be positive:[1]

$$(-\alpha + \lambda i)\overset{*}{Y} + (\gamma + \beta k)(\tilde{F} + \tilde{N}) = a\overset{*}{Y} + b(\tilde{F} + \tilde{N}) > 0. \tag{10}$$

For what follows it is useful to consider the effects of a shift in asset preferences toward home money away from foreign money ($d\varepsilon > 0$). The excess demand for home money causes the home currency to appreciate. Appreciation of the home currency creates an excess supply of home bonds, so the home interest rate rises. Both the appreciation and the interest rate increase work to offset the initial excess demand for home money.

It is also useful to consider the effects of a shift in asset preferences away from home bonds and toward foreign bonds ($d\gamma < 0$). The excess supply of home bonds causes the home interest rate to rise. The rise in the home interest rate creates an excess supply of money, so the home currency depreciates. Both the rise in the home interest rate and the depreciation of the home currency work to offset the initial excess supply of home bonds.

The Effects of Increases in CS and BS

It is now possible to determine how increases in CS and BS change the effects of increases in the foreign interest rate, the home money supply, and the expected future exchange rate on the home interest rate and the exchange rate. An increase in the foreign interest rate has the same effects on i and E as a shift in asset preferences away from home bonds toward foreign bonds and for the same reasons. Thus, i rises, and E rises.

In order to determine how these results are affected by an increase in CS, it is useful to ask what happens to the money return differential (s) because this variable is multiplied by the CS parameter μ. Since E rises, s falls. If there is an increase in CS (a rise in μ), the fall in s that was compatible with money market equilibrium when μ was low now implies an excess demand for money. That is, with higher CS this fall in s has the same effect as a shift in asset preferences toward home money away from foreign money. It was argued above that such a shift causes i to rise and E to fall. Thus, with higher CS an increase in i^* causes a larger rise in i and a smaller rise in E.[2]

In order to determine how the results of an increase in i^* are affected by an increase in BS, it is useful to ask what happens to the bond return differential (k) because this variable is multiplied by the BS parameter β. The rise in i^* tends to reduce k, and the rises in i and E tend to increase it. Under the assumptions of this section, k must fall. The rise in i causes a shift out of home money into home bonds, and the bond market valuation effect of the increase in E is positive. If k were unchanged, the demand for home bonds would increase. The supply of home bonds is fixed. Therefore, k must fall. If there is an increase in BS (a rise in β), the fall in k that was compatible with bond market equilibrium when β was low now implies an excess supply of home bonds. That is, with higher BS this fall in k has the same effect as a shift in asset preferences away from home bonds toward foreign bonds. It was argued above that such a shift causes i to rise and E to rise. Thus, with higher BS an increase in i^* causes larger rises in both i and E.

Now consider the effects of an increase in the home money supply achieved through an expansionary open market operation ($d\tilde{M} = -d\tilde{B} > 0$). The open market operation creates an excess supply of money and an excess demand for bonds that are equal in absolute value. Suppose i falls by enough to reequilibrate the bond market. There is still an excess supply of money. Decreases in i cause shifts out of home bonds into home money, but they also cause shifts out of home bonds into foreign bonds. Therefore, the home currency must depreciate.

How are these effects changed by increases in CS and BS? This question can be answered by using the same method as above. This method involves determining what happens to s and k. Since E rises, s must fall. Therefore, increasing CS is like increasing the demand for money. Increasing CS dampens the fall in i and the rise in E. The fall in i tends to lower k, but the rise in E tends to raise it. Since the increase in E helps to remove the initial excess supply of money, the shift from home bonds into home money caused by the fall in i must be less than the initial excess supply of money which equals the initial excess demand for bonds. The bond market valuation effect of the increase in E is positive. If k were unchanged, there would still be excess demand for bonds, so k must fall. Therefore, increasing BS is like reducing the demand for bonds. Increasing BS dampens the fall in i and exaggerates the rise in E.

Finally, consider the effects of an increase in the expected future exchange rate ($d\bar{E} > 0$). An increase in $\bar{E}$ increases s and reduces k, thereby causing excess supplies of both home money and home bonds. The home currency must depreciate. What happens to i depends upon the relative sizes of the initial excess supplies in the two markets and the relative sizes of the effects of depreciation in the two markets. Suppose E rises by enough to reequilibrate the money market. This rise in E may reequilibrate the bond market, leave excess supply in the bond market, or create excess demand there. If the rise in E reequilibrates the bond market, i remains unchanged. If the rise in E leaves excess supply in the bond market, i rises, and if it creates excess demand, i falls.

The percentage increase in E must be smaller than the percentage increase in $\bar{E}$. First, consider the case in which i remains unchanged. In the money market the only effect of an increase in $\bar{E}$ is to raise s. An increase in E not only lowers s but also raises the demand for money through the money market valuation effect. Therefore, the percentage increase in E required to reequilibrate the money market must be smaller than the percentage increase in $\bar{E}$. Now, consider the case in which i falls. The fall in i helps to remove the initial excess supply of money. Thus, there is a second reason why the percentage increase in E must be less than the percentage increase in $\bar{E}$. Finally, consider the case in which i rises. In the bond market the only effect of an increase in $\bar{E}$ is to reduce k. An increase in E not only raises k but also raises the demand for bonds through the bond market valuation effect. Therefore, even if i remained unchanged, the percentage increase in E required to reequilibrate the bond market would be smaller than the percentage increase in $\bar{E}$. The rise in i helps to remove the initial excess supply of bonds. Thus, there is a second reason why the percentage increase in E must be less than the percentage increase in $\bar{E}$.

As before, discovering what changes are caused by increases in CS and BS involves determining what happens to s and k. It has been established that the percentage increase in E is less than the percentage increase in $\bar{E}$, so s rises. Therefore, increasing CS is like reducing the demand for money. An increase in CS exaggerates the rise in E, exaggerates the movement in i when i falls, and dampens the movement in i when i rises. It can be established that k falls no matter what happens to i. Since s rises, it is obvious that k falls when i remains unchanged or falls. Now consider the case in which i rises. Since both E and i rise, there would be an excess demand for bonds if k rose or remained unchanged, so k must fall in this case as well. Therefore, increasing BS is always like reducing the demand for bonds. An increase in BS exaggerates the rise in E, dampens the movement in i when i falls, and exaggerates the movement in i when i rises.

Appendix

This appendix contains a formal derivation of the results presented in the text and a brief discussion of the implications of relaxing the assumption that the home bond market valuation effect is positive. Substituting (7) and (8) into (1) and (2), totally differentiating the resulting equations, and expressing the results in matrix form yields

$$
\begin{bmatrix} \lambda\tilde{Y} & -(mE\overset{*}{\tilde{Y}} + \mu\tilde{Y}q) \\ \lambda\tilde{Y} + \beta\tilde{W} & aE\overset{*}{\tilde{Y}} + bE(\bar{F} + \tilde{N}) + \beta\tilde{W}q \end{bmatrix} \begin{bmatrix} di \\ de \end{bmatrix} =
$$
$$
\begin{bmatrix} -d\tilde{M} - \mu\tilde{Y}qd\bar{e} + \tilde{Y}d\varepsilon \\ d\tilde{B} + \beta\tilde{W}qd\bar{e} + \beta\tilde{W}d\overset{*}{i} - \tilde{W}d\gamma \end{bmatrix} \tag{A1}
$$

where

$$
de = dE/E, \qquad d\bar{e} = d\bar{E}/\bar{E}. \tag{A2}
$$

In what follows, units are chosen so that the initial value of E is unity.

The results of changing several exogenous variables are reported. In the text it is assumed that the bond market valuation effect is positive $[a\overset{*}{\tilde{Y}} + b(\bar{F} + \tilde{N}) > 0]$. For each exogenous variable the results for this case are reported first. Then there is a brief discussion of other cases.

The determinant of the matrix of coefficients is definitely positive if the bond market valuation effect is positive:

$$
\Delta = \lambda\tilde{Y}[a\overset{*}{\tilde{Y}} + b(\bar{F} + \tilde{N}) + \beta\tilde{W}q] +
$$
$$
(\lambda\tilde{Y} + \beta\tilde{W})(m\overset{*}{\tilde{Y}} + \mu\tilde{Y}q) > 0. \tag{A3}
$$

The determinant may be positive even if the bond market valuation effect is negative. The determinant has been assumed to be positive in the preceding discussion. If it were negative, changes in the exogenous variables would not have their normal effects on the endogenous variables.

The effects of an increase in ε on i and E are

$$di/d\varepsilon = (\tilde{Y}/\Delta)[a\overset{*}{Y} + b(\bar{F} + \tilde{N}) + \beta\tilde{W}q] > 0, \tag{A4}$$

$$de/d\varepsilon = -(\tilde{Y}/\Delta)(\lambda\tilde{Y} + \beta\tilde{W}) < 0. \tag{A5}$$

The interest rate rises as long as the effect of a rise in E on the excess demand for bonds is positive, even if the bond market valuation effect is negative.

The effects of an increase in γ on i and E are

$$di/d\gamma = -(\tilde{W}/\Delta)(m\overset{*}{Y} + \mu\tilde{Y}q) < 0, \tag{A6}$$

$$de/d\gamma = -(\tilde{W}/\Delta)\lambda\tilde{Y} < 0. \tag{A7}$$

The effects of an increase in $\overset{*}{i}$ on i, E, and k are

$$di/d\overset{*}{i} = (1/\Delta)[\beta\tilde{W}(m\overset{*}{Y} + \mu\tilde{Y}q)] > 0, \tag{A8}$$

$$de/d\overset{*}{i} = -(1/q)(ds/d\overset{*}{i}) = (1/\Delta)\lambda\tilde{Y}\beta\tilde{W} > 0, \tag{A9}$$

$$dk/d\overset{*}{i} = -(\lambda\tilde{Y}/\Delta)[a\overset{*}{Y} + b(\bar{F} + \tilde{N}) + m\overset{*}{Y} + \mu\tilde{Y}q] < 0. \tag{A10}$$

Thus, k falls as long as the expression in square brackets is positive, even if the bond market valuation effect is negative.

The effects of an increase in $\tilde{M}$ achieved through an expansionary open market operation ($d\tilde{M} = -d\bar{B} > 0$) on i, E, and k are

$$di/d\tilde{M} = -(1/\Delta)[a\overset{*}{Y} + b(\bar{F} + \tilde{N}) + \tag{A11}$$
$$\beta\tilde{W}q + m\overset{*}{Y} + \mu\tilde{Y}q] < 0,$$

$$de/d\tilde{M} = -(1/q)(ds/d\tilde{M}) = (1/\Delta)\beta\tilde{W} > 0, \tag{A12}$$

$$dk/d\tilde{M} = -(1/\Delta)[a\overset{*}{Y} + b(\bar{F} + \tilde{N}) + m\overset{*}{Y} + \mu\tilde{Y}q] < 0. \tag{A13}$$

The interest rate falls as long as the expression in square brackets in (A11) is positive, even if the bond market valuation effect is negative. This expression is definitely positive if a rise in E has a positive effect on the excess demand for bonds. For a rise in $\tilde{M}$ just as for a rise in $\overset{*}{i}$, k falls as long as the expression in square brackets in (A13) is positive, even though the bond market valuation effect is negative.

The effects of an increase in $\bar{E}$ on i, E, and k are

$$di/d\bar{e} = (1/\Delta)\{- \mu\tilde{Y}q[a\overset{*}{Y} + b(\bar{F} + \bar{N}) + \beta\tilde{W}q] + \quad\quad\quad (A14)$$
$$\beta\tilde{W}q(m\overset{*}{Y} + \mu\tilde{Y}q)\} ?,$$
$$0 < de/d\bar{e} = - (1/q)(ds/d\bar{e}) + 1 = (1/\Delta[\lambda\tilde{Y}\beta\tilde{W}q + \quad\quad\quad (A15)$$
$$\mu\tilde{Y}q(\lambda\tilde{Y} + \beta\tilde{W})] < 1,$$
$$dk/d\bar{e} = (1/\Delta)\{- (\mu + \lambda)\tilde{Y}q[a\overset{*}{Y} + b(\bar{F} + \bar{N})] -$$
$$q\lambda\tilde{Y}m\overset{*}{Y}\} < 0. \quad\quad\quad (A16)$$

Thus, i may rise or fall as long as the sign of the expression in curly brackets in (A14) is ambiguous. The sign of this expression is ambiguous if a rise in E raises excess demand in the bond market, even if the bond market valuation effect is negative. The expression is negative if an increase in E lowers excess demand in the bond market. Also, $de/d\bar{e}$ is less than one, as long as the sum of the terms in Δ not appearing in the square brackets in (A15) is positive, even if the bond market valuation effect is negative. Finally, k falls as long as the expression in curly brackets in (A16) is negative even if the bond market valuation effect is negative.

Notes

1. The bond market valuation effect can be negative because a can be and would be expected to be negative. This valuation effect is definitely positive under a plausible set of assumptions. Suppose that at the initial exchange rate foreign nominal income is a fraction δ of world nominal income and that foreign nominal assets are the same fraction of world wealth. Equation (2) implies that $\tilde{B} = a\tilde{Y} + b\tilde{W} > 0$. Since $E\overset{*}{Y} = \delta\tilde{Y}$ and $E(\bar{F} + \bar{N}) = \delta\tilde{W}$, it follows that $\delta\tilde{B}/E = a\overset{*}{Y} + b(\bar{F} + \bar{N}) > 0$. The implications of relaxing the assumption that the bond market valuation effect is positive are explored briefly in the appendix.

2. The verbal derivation of the effects of increasing CS on $di/d\overset{*}{i}$ and $dE/d\overset{*}{i}$ can be confirmed mathematically by differentiating the expressions for these derivatives in the appendix with respect to μ. Readers who perform this exercise will find that the signs of the results depend on the sign of the expression for $ds/d\overset{*}{i}$ and on the signs of the expressions for $di/d\varepsilon$ and $de/d\varepsilon$ in the appendix. Later verbal derivations of the effects of increases in CS and BS on various derivatives can be confirmed in an analogous way.

References

Girton, Lance, and Don Roper. 1981. Theory and implications of currency substitution. *Journal of Money, Credit and Banking* 13 (February): 12–30.

Horiuchi, Akiyoshi. 1987. Liberalization of financial markets and the volatility of exchange rates: The experience of the Japanese yen since 1980. Paper presented at the Conference on U.S.-Canadian Trade and Investment Relations with Japan, Ann Arbor, Michigan, April.

Some Empirical Considerations
William E. Alexander

Introduction

What explains the relative volatility of exchange rates? Why, for example, is
it the case that by almost every measure the yen/U.S. dollar exchange rate is
more volatile than the Canada/U.S. dollar rate?

There are many possible explanations, but two theoretical possibilities
include the degree of currency substitution (CS), which measures the willingness of asset holders to substitute between domestic and foreign moneys as
the preferred form of transactions balances, and capital mobility (CM), that
is, bond substitution, which measures the willingness to substitute between
domestic- and foreign-currency-denominated interest bearing claims. Girton
and Roper (1981), as well as Horiuchi (1987) and Henderson above, show
that the degree of currency substitution will influence the sensitivity of exchange rates to movements in key exogenous variables, such as domestic and
foreign monetary conditions (as measured by interest rates or money supplies) and exchange rate expectations. Henderson shows that when currency
substitution is present, and depending on the type of shock to which the
exchange rate is subject, volatility can be either increased or decreased.

My purpose here is to summarize empirical evidence on the degree of
CS and CM in Canada. To anticipate my conclusions:

1. Work that has been carried out within the Bank of Canada over the
   last eight years finds statistically significant evidence of currency substitution in Canadian M1 equations. This confirms other work, see for
   example, Miles (1978), Cuddington (1983), and Daniel and Fried
   (1983). However, we have been unable to find evidence that it has
   risen in importance during the 1980s, and we have concluded that the
   economic significance of CS is very small. That is, it adds very little
   predictive power to an M1 equation which includes only domestic variables.
2. Capital mobility, as defined above, is extremely high. Information
   from a variety of sources suggests that, in Canada, for short term assets, it is virtually perfect for periods of time longer than a quarter.
   This suggests that factors other than the degree of asset substitutability
   are more important determinants of (relative) exchange rate volatility.
   I will conclude with some general observations on what these factors
   might be.

The views expressed in this paper are my own, and no responsibility for them should be attributed
to the Bank of Canada or the Economic Council of Canada.

On Currency Substitution

A popular approach to testing for the presence of currency substitution involves specifying a demand for money equation which includes the usual domestic determinants of demand as well as foreign variables, such as a short-term interest rate and a measure of the expected depreciation of the exchange rate. The latter is often measured by the forward foreign exchange rate premium. A statistically significant coefficient on the forward premium is taken as a measure of the elasticity of currency substitution. This approach has tended to yield statistically significant evidence of CS when applied to Canadian data.

An important limitation to this approach is that obtaining a statistically significant coefficient on the expected rate of depreciation is not in itself an unambiguous test of the presence of currency substitution. In the general portfolio model, returns on domestic bonds (defined as the domestic interest rate, i), foreign currency bonds (defined as the foreign interest rate, if, plus the expected rate of depreciation, x) and foreign currency (defined as the expected rate of depreciation, x), will enter the specification of the demand for domestic money balances. Conceptually, the existence of CM can be inferred from the coefficient on $(if + x)$ and the existence of CS from the coefficient on x. However, as noted by Cuddington (1983), the presence of collinearity problems—possibly reflecting nearly perfect covered arbitrage—makes it unlikely that all variables can be included. Therefore, if the variables are included in pairs in the regression, it follows that the presence of either CS or CM would cause the expected rate of depreciation to be statistically significant. Since most of the empirical work that is available has not used all of the rates-of-return variables simultaneously, available evidence on the presence of CS must be interpreted cautiously.

A second limitation of this approach is that it presumes the existence of a stable demand for money. In the case of Canada, this is a particularly strong presumption. Indeed, the Bank of Canada formally abandoned monetary targeting in 1982 because the demand for M1 had become unstable. This instability did not seem to be related to currency substitution, although much effort was expended trying to establish such a link. Instead, the research undertaken within the Bank (see Freedman 1983) indicated that M1 instability was due to endogenous response to record high interest rates, financial innovation in domestic markets resulting from increased competition from small banks, and the diffusion of computer technology. The latter destabilized the demand for money by permitting the spread of cash management packages to small businesses and the introduction of new retail accounts paying interest on minimum daily balances. An implication is that estimates of the elasticity of currency substitution using post-1982 data are highly suspect unless the M1 equations on which they are based can explain the institutionally-driven shifts in money demand. Given these shifts in money demand, estimates of the elasticity of CS tend to be highly sensitive to the choice of estimation sample period.

The foregoing difficulties aside, there remains a question as to the economic significance of CS. In the Bank of Canada research, when CS variables were added to what were apparently stable M1 equations specified to include only domestic variables—but also to reflect important institutional details (e.g., postal strikes) accurately—the coefficients on CS, when significant, were small.[1] Moreover, they added very little to dynamic simulations. This was particularly true over the post-1980 period, when it might be expected that the wide swings in interest and exchange rates might have been conducive to isolating evidence of CS.

Results such as these have led researchers at the Bank to conclude that CS is not economically significant for Canada.

On Capital Mobility

It has long been accepted that Canadian financial markets are closely integrated with U.S. markets, and the degree of capital mobility is extremely high. Boothe et al. (1985) contains a comprehensive survey of the evidence relating to the degree of substitutability between U.S. and Canadian dollar-denominated assets. This study focuses to some extent on models of exchange rate determination, and concludes that the portfolio balance models (which assume imperfect asset substitutability), simply do not work. It is concluded (p. 6) that:

> Overall, perfect capital substitutability cannot be rejected, except in the short run. . . . In particular, changes in the stocks of Canadian or U.S. government bonds and shifts in financial wealth do not appear to affect expected differences in rates of return on Canadian and U.S. dollar instruments. Empirically, the interest rate in Canada is approximately equal to the interest rate in the United States plus the expected rate of depreciation of the Canadian dollar.

On Other Explanations of Volatility

If currency substitution is not the answer, why is the Canadian dollar less volatile than the Japanese yen? One reason is probably the high degree of integration between the U.S. and Canadian economies. As a result of this high degree of integration—something like 65 percent of bilateral trade is accounted for by two hundred multinational corporations, for example—the two economies appear to have a tendency to adjust relatively rapidly to exogenous shocks, and tend to be subject to common shocks, thereby requiring less overshooting of the exchange rate than would otherwise be required.

A more important reason is that central banks may not respond passively to incipient exchange rate fluctuations. Particularly in the period after 1982, the Bank of Canada did give some weight to the rate of depreciation when determining the course of monetary policy (unsterilized intervention).[2] In the face of rising foreign interest rates, for example, the Bank's typical response in the short run was to resist the extent of depreciation by permitting some upward adjustment in domestic interest rates.[3] It is not surprising, therefore, that the Canadian dollar shows limited response to movements in U.S. interest rates.

Conclusion

I would like to conclude with some general comments on capital mobility and exchange rate volatility. As noted in the Bank of International Settlements (BIS) (1986), rising capital mobility has been accompanied (and caused in part) by technological change, which has reduced the costs of distributing information and increased its rate of dissemination on a worldwide basis, heightened global competition among national financial institutions, and reduced transactions costs. Important financial innovations have occurred, involving products and markets that are derivative to exchange rates and foreign exchange markets, such as futures, options, and futures options. The authors of the BIS report speculated that these innovations were themselves contributing to increased volatility. Rising capital mobility has also been accompanied by a rise in foreign exchange trading strategies that are triggered when particular chart-point levels are reached, by news services that distribute news and rumors worldwide virtually instantaneously, and by increased popularity of mechanical program-type trading. Markets are becoming "one-sided" in the sense that so-called expert forecasts are instantaneously available to all the large players, and expectations about future developments are often tightly dispersed around the "expert" opinion. When opinions change, for whatever reason, markets jump. Finally, the period can be characterized as one of extreme policy uncertainty. The consequence has been that exchange rate expectations have not been firmly anchored. Thus, for example, large and rapid changes in the yen/U.S. dollar exchange rate have occurred in response to shifts in expectations. Whether these changes should be attributed exclusively to high capital mobility or to unstable expectations is unclear. I personally believe that developments such as these will go further in explaining relative volatility than will the existence or nonexistence of currency substitution.

Notes

1. A typical result was that a sustained forward premium of 4 percent (historically very large) would lead to a reduction in M1 balances of about 2.5 percent. See Alexander (1981).

2. See Bank of Canada (1985, 8).

3. Ibid.

References

Alexander, W. E. 1981. Influencias del exterior sobre la demanda de dinero en une economia abierto: el caso de Canada. *Monetaria* 4 (Enero-Marzo): 17–38.

Bank of Canada. 1985. *Annual report of the governor 1984.* Ottawa: Bank of Canada.

Bank for International Settlements (BIS). 1986. *Recent innovations in international banking.* Basle: BIS.

Boothe, P., K. Clinton, A. Cote, and D. Longworth. 1985. *International asset substitutability: Theory and evidence for Canada.* Ottawa: Bank of Canada.

Cuddington, John T. 1983. Currency substitution, capital mobility, and money demand. *Journal of International Money and Finance* 2 (August): 111–13.

Daniel, B. C., and H. O. Fried. 1983. Currency substitution, postal strikes, and Canadian money demand. *Canadian Journal of Economics* 16 (November): 612–24.

Freedman, C. 1983. Financial innovation in Canada: Causes and consequences. *American Economic Review* 73 (May): 101–6.

Girton, Lance, and Don Roper. 1981. Theory and implications of currency substitution. *Journal of Money, Credit and Banking* 13 (February): 12–30.

Horiuchi, Akihoshi. 1987. Liberalization of financial markets and the volatility of exchange rates: The experience of the Japanese yen since 1980. Paper presented at the Conference on U.S.-Canadian trade and investment relations with Japan, Ann Arbor, Michigan, April.

Miles, Marc A. 1978. Currency substitution, flexible exchange rates, and monetary independence. *American Economic Review* 68 (June): 428–36.

11 Correcting Global Imbalances: A Simulation Approach

Warwick McKibbin, Nouriel Roubini, and
Jeffrey D. Sachs

11.1 Introduction

During the 1980s, the industrial countries have experienced remarkable
swings in trade balances and exchange rates. As shown in table 11.1, the
U.S. trade deficit relative to GNP widened significantly during the period
1980–86, while Japan's surplus rose considerably. The non-oil developing
countries experienced an equally dramatic change, with their large trade deficits at the end of the 1970s moving to approximate balance by the mid-
1980s. During this period, the real exchange rate of the U.S. dollar moved in
remarkable amplitude, as shown in table 11.2, appreciating in real terms by
about 24 percent between 1980 and 1985 relative to the yen, and then depreciating by 30 percent between 1985 and 1986.

One of the alleged culprits for these large swings is the divergent macroeconomic policies of the United States, Japan, and the other OECD economies, especially in regard to the budget. The differing movements in the
fiscal budgets of the leading countries, as measured by changes in the structural (full-employment) inflation-adjusted budget deficit, can be seen in table
11.3. Between 1979 and 1985, the U.S. structural budget deficit widened by
4.4 percent of potential GNP, while the Japanese deficit was reduced by 3.7
percent of GNP. In the rest of the OECD, Germany also reduced its structural
deficit by 3.3 percent of GNP, while the smaller economies generally had a
small increase in their structural deficits. In the most common interpretation
of the trade imbalances (and one that is largely supported in this paper), the
U.S. fiscal expansion with Japanese and German fiscal contraction raised
U.S. interest rates relative to Japanese and German rates, induced a capital
inflow from Japan and Germany, and caused a dollar appreciation and a worsening of the U.S. trade imbalance.

The views expressed in this paper do not necessarily reflect those of the institutions with which
the authors are affiliated.

379

Table 11.1 Changes in Trade Balances

	Average Trade Balance (% of GNP), 1978–80	Trade Balance (% of GNP), 1985	Change
United States	−1.2	−3.1	−1.9
Japan	1.0	4.2	3.2
Canada	2.3	3.8	1.5
Rest of OECD,[a] including:	−0.6	0.4	1.0
Germany	2.4	4.6	2.2
France	−0.9	−0.9	0.0
United Kingdom	−0.7	−0.5	0.2
10 Smaller countries[b]	−2.2	−0.3	1.9
Non-oil LDC's[c]	−2.2	−0.3	1.9

[a]1982 Weights.
[b]Australia, Austria, Belgium, Denmark, Finland, Greece, Netherlands, Norway, Spain, Sweden.
[c]Percent of U.S. GNP.
Source: IMF, *International Financial Statistics.*

Table 11.2 Real Bilateral Exchange Rate vis-à-vis $U.S. (1978–80 = 100)

	1985	1986	Change 1978–80/1985	Change 1985/1986
Japan	76	106	−24	30
Canada	91	91	−9	0
Rest of OECD, including:	61	77	−39	16
Germany	55	73	−45	18
France	58	76	−42	18
United Kingdom	68	78	−32	10

Notes: The real exchange rate is defined as $P/E*P^u$, where P is the CPI of the country or region, E is in units of currency per dollar, and P^u is the CPI of the United States. A rise in the index signifies a real depreciation of the dollar.
Source: IMF, *International Financial Statistics.*

Table 11.3 Changes in General Government Financial Balances, 1979–85 (percent of GNP)

	Actual Balance	Inflation-Adjusted Structural Balance
United States	−4.3	−4.4
Japan	3.6	3.7
Canada	−3.6	−2.2
Rest of OECD,[a] including:	−1.3	0.5
Germany	1.3	3.3
France	−3.1	0.5
United Kingdom	0.5	1.9
10 Smaller countries[b]	−2.0	−0.8

[a]1982 GDP weights.
[b]Australia, Austria, Belgium, Denmark, Finland, Greece, Netherlands, Norway, Spain, Sweden.
Source: Atkinson and Chouraqui (1985, 6).

The swings in trade balances and exchange rates have led to growing economic tensions among the industrial economies. The most obvious manifestation of these tensions is the rise in protectionist sentiment in the United States, as exemplified by the popularity of the Gephardt Amendment, which is a Congressional proposal calling for U.S. tariff increases against foreign countries that have large bilateral trade surpluses vis-à-vis the United States and are certified by the International Trade Commission to be engaging in unfair trade practices against U.S. goods.[1]

Against this background it is timely to examine the macroeconomic factors that have contributed to the current imbalances in trade and the swings in exchange rates, and to discuss the policy options available to the major industrialized countries to ameliorate the current situation. This paper studies the macroeconomic interdependence among the United States, Canada, Japan, and the rest of the OECD by using a medium-sized dynamic general equilibrium model to measure the macroeconomic linkages in the world economy. This model, which we call the MSG2 model, is a further development of the McKibbin-Sachs Global (MSG) model which has been described elsewhere.[2] The new version, which is still in the developmental stage, extends the earlier model by a more careful treatment of the microeconomic foundations of aggregate supply. Much of the ground covered in this paper is also treated in a companion paper by Sachs and Roubini (1987).

Our plan in this paper is as follows. We introduce the model in section 11.2, and then use it in section 11.3 to examine the international transmission effects of macroeconomic policies and to study the links between divergent trade balances and divergent macroeconomic policies in the United States and Japan.[3] In section 11.4, we discuss some possible reasons for the fall in the dollar after 1985, as well as the prospects for a major improvement in the U.S. trade balance in the next few years.

11.2 The MSG2 Model of the World Economy

The MSG2 is a dynamic general equilibrium model of a six-region world economy, divided into the United States, Japan, Canada, the rest of the OECD countries (denoted ROECD, and constituted mainly by OECD Europe), and non-oil developing countries (LDCs), and OPEC. The model is of moderate size (about three dozen behavioral equations per industrial region).[4] It is distinctive relative to most other global models in that it solves for a full intertemporal equilibrium in which agents have rational expectations of future variables. The model has a mix of Keynesian and classical properties by virtue of a maintained assumption of slow adjustment of nominal wages in the labor markets of the United States, Canada, and the ROECD (Japan is treated somewhat differently, as described below).

The model is solved in a linearized form in order to facilitate policy optimization exercises and especially to use linear-quadratic dynamic game theory and dynamic programming solution techniques.[5] The global stability of the linearized model is confirmed by an analysis of the model's eigenvalues. At this point, the model is parameterized by choosing parameters based on existing econometric research in the literature, rather than by undertaking our own econometric estimation of the model parameters. The procedure of relying on other research estimates for key parameters represents, in our opinion, a healthy division of labor between those who focus on general equilibrium modelling and those who focus on the econometric study of particular aspects of the macroeconomy.

Speaking broadly, the model has several attractive features. First, all stock-flow relationships are carefully observed. Budget deficits cumulate into stocks of public debt; current account deficits cumulate into net foreign investment positions; and physical investment cumulates into the capital stock. Underlying growth of Harrod-neutral productivity plus labor force growth is assumed to be 4 percent per region. Given the long-run properties of the model, the world economy settles down to the 4 percent steady-state growth path following any set of initial disturbances.

A second attractive feature is that the asset markets are efficient in the sense that asset prices are determined by a combination of intertemporal arbitrage conditions and rational expectations. By virtue of the rational expectations assumption and the forward-looking behavior of households and firms, the model can be used to examine the effects of anticipated future policy changes, such as the sequence of future budget deficit cuts called for by the Gramm-Rudman-Hollings legislation in the United States. Indeed, one of the difficulties of using the MSG2 model is that every simulation requires that the "entire" future sequence of anticipated policies be specified. In practice, forty-year paths of policy variables, or endogenous policy rules, must be specified.

A third attractive feature of the model is the specification of the supply side. There are several noteworthy points here. First, factor input decisions are based (with a few exceptions) on intertemporal profit maximization by firms. Labor and intermediate inputs are selected to maximize short-run profits given a stock of capital which is fixed within each period. The capital stock is adjusted according to a "Tobin's q" model of investment, derived along the lines in Hayashi (1983). Tobin's q is the shadow value of capital, and evolves according to a rational expectations forecast of future post-tax profitability.

Another point of interest regarding the supply side is the specification of the wage-price dynamics in each of the industrial regions. Extensive macroeconomic research has demonstrated important differences in the wage-price processes in the United States, Europe, and Japan, and these differences are incorporated in the model. In particular, the United States and Canada are characterized by nominal wage rigidities arising from long-term nominal wage contracts. In Japan, on the contrary, nominal wages are assumed to be renegotiated on an annual, synchronized cycle, with nominal wages selected for the following year to, on average, clear the labor market. In the ROECD, nominal wages are assumed to be more forward looking than in the United States and Canada.

A third feature of the supply side of some interest is the assumption regarding trade prices. Many observers have recently pointed out the fairly significant lag in the pass-through of exchange rate changes into import price changes in the U.S. economy (and probably in the other economies as well, which have been less extensively examined). The appreciation of the dollar during 1981–85 did not bring about an instantaneous and equivalent fall in U.S. import prices, and the recent depreciation of the dollar has not brought about an equivalent rise in prices. To capture part of this effect, we assume that exporters into the U.S. market set their prices in dollars one period in advance, in order to equate the export price with the *expected* home market price in the following period. If the dollar then unexpectedly appreciates, the importers into the U.S. reap an unanticipated windfall, in that the price that they receive in the U.S. market, expressed in local currency at the spot market exchange rate, exceeds the domestic price of output. This divergence will be eliminated, on average, in the following period, when the trade prices are reset. There are, of course, other reasons for the failure of exchange rate movements to pass through into prices, most of which involve imperfect competition in trade (see Dornbusch 1987 or Krugman 1986 for details). We plan to incorporate such imperfect competition features into a later version of the model.

11.3 Simulation Results for Monetary and Fiscal Policies

We now employ the model to try to understand the reasons for the shifts in global trade and financial imbalances in recent years, and to understand better the nature of the international transmission of macroeconomic policies. We begin with standard simulations of the effects of monetary and fiscal policy, and then turn to the policy changes of the period 1980–85.

11.3.1 Fiscal Policy in the United States, Japan, and Canada

Various simulation results for fiscal policies are shown in the next few tables. Before discussing these results, however, it is important to understand the precise experiment that is being undertaken. In line with rational expectations modelling, policy experiments must define an entire future path of policies, and not just a change during the simulation period. In the case of fiscal policy, it is important that tax and spending policies be consistent with the intertemporal budget constraint of the public sector. In particular, starting from any initial stock of public debt, the discounted value of current and future taxes must equal the discounted value of government spending plus the initial value of outstanding public debt.

In our case, a permanent fiscal expansion, as shown in table 11.4, is treated in the following way. The basic experiment is a rise in sustained government spending (later we consider a cut in taxes). Government final expenditure rises permanently by 1 percent of potential GNP. Initially, the tax schedule remains unchanged, with taxes increasing only to the extent that the fiscal expansion raises output and thereby induces an endogenous tax increase (in other words, the cyclically adjusted budget deficit rises by 1 percent of GNP, the full amount of the spending increase). The actual fiscal deficit rises by about 0.85 percent of GNP following the 1 percent of GNP rise in government spending, because of the induced increase in taxes of 0.15 percent of GNP. The deficit is financed entirely by the issuance of public debt, with the money stock held constant.

If the tax schedule were not subsequently altered, the stock of public debt would eventually rise without bound, at an explosive geometric rate. To prevent this, we assume that labor income taxes are increased each year by enough to cover the increasing interest costs on the rising stock of public debt. In this way, the overall deficit remains fairly constant at about 1 percent of GNP following a rise in government spending (it fluctuates slightly due to fluctuations in real economic activity). The primary deficit (government spending net of interest payments, minus total taxes), given as $(G_t - T_t)$, eventually turns to a surplus, as is necessary to prevent an explosive growth in debt. Since the level of debt eventually stabilizes given the way that we have conducted this experiment, while the real economy grows at its potential rate of 4 percent in the long run, the debt to GNP ratio in fact eventually falls to zero after an initial increase following the rise in government spending.

Consider now the effects of a permanent rise in U.S. government spending shown in table 11.4. All variables are expressed as deviations from an initial (1985) baseline. Output is recorded as a percentage deviation from the initial baseline, while consumption, investment, exports, imports, and the trade balance are all reported as deviations from the baseline in percent of potential GNP. Thus, in 1986, private consumption falls relative to the baseline by −0.22 percent of U.S. GNP. Labor input (total manhours in the economy), is measured as a percentage deviation from the baseline. Inflation and interest rates are measured as percentage-point deviations from the baseline. Thus, inflation in the first year of the fiscal expansion falls by 0.04 percentage points, while short-term interest rates increase by 0.86 percentage points. The three real bilateral exchange rates are reported as percent changes from baseline values. Note that a negative value for the exchange rate indicates a real appreciation of the dollar.[6]

Table 11.4   Permanent U.S. Fiscal Expansion (1% GNP)

	Year 1	2	3	4	5
U.S. Economy					
Output (%)	0.37	0.23	0.37	0.34	0.27
Private consumption (%GNP)	−0.22	−0.07	−0.04	−0.05	−0.10
Private investment (%GNP)	0.00	−0.16	−0.07	−0.12	−0.15
Government consumption (%GNP)	1.00	1.00	1.00	1.00	1.00
Exports (%GNP)	−0.18	−0.16	−0.15	−0.15	−0.15
Imports (%GNP)	0.16	0.13	0.14	0.13	0.12
Imports, quant. (%GNP)	0.23	0.37	0.36	0.34	0.33
Trade balance (%GNP)	−0.34	−0.29	−0.29	−0.28	−0.28
Labor demand (%)	0.52	0.32	0.57	0.54	0.48
Inflation (D)	−0.04	−0.26	−0.06	0.03	0.09
Interest rate, short (D)	0.86	0.44	0.54	0.50	0.52
Interest rate, long (D)	0.59	0.53	0.50	0.46	0.44
Tobin's q (%)	−3.15	−2.61	−2.62	−2.68	−2.86
Real exchange rate					
$/ECU (%)	−3.85	−3.15	−2.80	−2.54	−2.42
$/yen (%)	−4.20	−3.58	−3.36	−3.27	−3.32
$/Can (%)	−2.66	−2.23	−2.02	−1.80	−1.67
ROECD Economies					
Output (%)	0.07	−0.07	−0.20	−0.33	−0.44
Private consumption (%GNP)	−0.16	−0.23	−0.30	−0.36	−0.42
Private investment (%GNP)	−0.13	−0.23	−0.23	−0.26	−0.28
Government consumption (%GNP)	0.00	0.00	0.00	0.00	0.00
Trade balance (%GNP)	0.27	0.24	0.22	0.19	0.18
Labor demand (%)	0.25	−0.04	−0.14	−0.25	−0.33
Inflation (D)	0.29	0.14	0.15	0.13	0.13
Interest rate, short (D)	0.41	0.33	0.40	0.42	0.48
Japanese Economy					
Output (%)	0.03	−0.04	−0.10	−0.15	−0.20
Private consumption (%GNP)	−0.20	−0.31	−0.38	−0.41	−0.46
Private investment (%GNP)	−0.14	−0.27	−0.24	−0.25	−0.27
Government consumption (%GNP)	0.00	0.00	0.00	0.00	0.00
Trade balance (%GNP)	0.39	0.38	0.37	0.36	0.36
Labor demand (%)	0.31	−0.00	−0.00	−0.00	−0.00
Inflation (D)	0.28	0.18	0.12	0.07	0.08
Interest rate, short (D)	0.51	0.41	0.51	0.53	0.58
Canadian Economy					
Output (%)	0.18	0.54	0.46	0.28	0.12
Private consumption (%GNP)	−0.10	−0.07	−0.10	−0.17	−0.25
Private investment (%GNP)	−0.11	−0.16	−0.18	−0.23	−0.26
Government consumption (%GNP)	0.00	0.00	0.00	0.00	0.00
Trade balance (%GNP)	0.50	0.48	0.48	0.46	0.43
Labor demand (%)	0.30	0.32	0.31	0.15	0.00
Inflation (D)	−0.12	0.00	0.10	0.14	0.17
Interest rate, short (D)	0.47	0.39	0.46	0.45	0.50

How do the simulation results compare with our expectations from the simple Mundell-Fleming model of policy transmission under flexible exchange rates? According to the standard model, we should expect a bond-financed fiscal expansion, in the presence of perfect substitutability of home and foreign financial assets, to result in a rise in domestic income, an appreciation of the exchange rate, a rise in short- and long-term interest rates, and a worsening of the trade balance. Tobin's q might rise or fall. On the one hand, higher interest rates will tend to depress q, while on the other hand, higher output (and greater profits) will tend to raise q, with the overall effect being ambiguous. We see from table 11.4 that the model behaves in line with these expectations. Output rises, though with a multiplier considerably less than one. The dollar appreciates in real terms by 3.85 percent vis-à-vis the ECU, 4.20 percent vis-à-vis the yen, and 2.66 percent vis-à-vis the Canadian dollar. Short-term interest rates rise by 0.86 percentage points, and long-term rates rise by 0.59 percentage points. The trade balance deteriorates by 0.34 percent of potential GNP in the first year, with the deficit persisting for the next several years. Note that Tobin's q in fact falls, by 3.15 percent. Investment is unchanged in the first year of the fiscal expansion and depressed relative to the baseline in the later years.

Let us next turn to the international transmission effects. Importantly, the Mundell-Fleming model, when extended to allow for endogenous wages and prices, teaches that the international transmission effect of a fiscal expansion is ambiguous. On the one hand, the U.S. expansion raises world interest rates, which tends to depress investment abroad. On the other hand, the expansion causes an appreciation of the dollar, which tends to raise net exports abroad. Europe, Japan, and Canada benefit from a trade boom, but suffer a drop in domestic investment. The net effect on output is theoretically ambiguous, despite a tendency of many commentators to assume that foreign fiscal expansions are necessarily stimulative of the domestic economy.

As described in Bruno and Sachs (1985, ch. 5) and in Oudiz and Sachs (1984), the transmission is more likely to be negative if foreign wages and prices rise rapidly in response to the depreciation of the foreign currencies relative to the dollar. If foreign nominal wages are perfectly fixed, as in the original Mundell-Fleming model, then the U.S. fiscal expansion must raise output abroad. The simple Mundell-Fleming model is probably the source of the misconception that fiscal expansions are always transmitted positively.

As can be seen in table 11.4, only for Canada is there an uninterrupted positive transmission from the United States. For Japan and the rest of the OECD, the transmission is positive in the first year, but then negative in later years. Note that net exports indeed expand everywhere abroad as expected, but that both consumption and investment tend to get crowded out by the U.S. expansion. The negative effect on foreign consumption derives from the adverse effect of the fiscal expansion on the value of foreign Tobin's q. As q

falls abroad, not only does investment decline, but so too does consumption, due to a negative wealth effect. Since Canada is so dependent on U.S. trade, the expansionary trade effects dominate the contractionary effects on consumption and investment. In the ROECD and Japan, however, the negative effects on domestic spending dominate the export stimulus.

Table 11.5 records the dynamic adjustments to a permanent fiscal expansion in Japan. Note that by the assumption of wage setting in Japan, the rise in Japanese employment following the fiscal expansion can last just one period. By the secod period, Japanese wages increase sufficiently to restore exact full employment in the labor market. As in the United States, the Japanese fiscal expansion raises output, depresses Tobin's q at home and abroad, appreciates the yen vis-à-vis the other currencies, and worsens the Japanese trade balance. Indeed, the adverse effect on the trade balance is even larger than in the U.S. as a percent of own GNP, with the trade balance falling by 0.6 percent of GNP.

The Japanese fiscal expansion has a contractionary effect on the other economies after the first year. Inflation rises, and output goes down. It is true that the U.S. trade balance improves, but by a miniscule $2–3 billion (at 1987 potential output levels) for each 1 percent of GNP Japanese fiscal expansion. This improvement in the trade balance is more than crowded out by a drop in investment and consumption. Many observers have stressed the need for a Japanese fiscal expansion to help stabilize world growth, and particularly growth in the United States. Table 11.5 should give them some pause.

Finally, we consider in table 11.6 the effect of a 1 percent fiscal expansion in Canada. One can observe that, as in the U.S. and Japanese cases, the exchange rate appreciates and short-term interest rates increase, but the amount of real appreciation and increase in interest rates are smaller than was true for the United States (table 11.4) or Japan (table 11.5). Given the small size of Canada, with a GNP around one-tenth of the United States, an increase in its fiscal deficit has a much smaller effect on world total savings than does a U.S. fiscal expansion. Therefore, the increase in world real interest rates and fall in q is much smaller in the case of a Canadian fiscal expansion. It follows that investment and private consumption in Canada are not crowded out, but actually rise following the Canadian fiscal shock. Real output growth in Canada, therefore, is larger and sustained for a longer period of time than was true for fiscal expansions in the U.S. and Japan. Similarly, the fiscal expansion in Canada causes a larger trade deficit relative to GNP (-0.70 percent), than was true for the U.S. (-0.34 percent) or Japan (-0.63 percent). At the same time, the real appreciation in Canada (1.8 percent against the U.S. dollar) is smaller than the appreciations following a U.S or Japanese fiscal expansion. The greater degree of openness of the Canadian economy leads to a much greater trade balance effect per 1 percent real appreciation of the exchange rate than in the United States and Japan.

Table 11.5 Permanent Japanese Fiscal Expansion (1% GNP)

	Year 1	2	3	4	5
U.S. Economy					
Output (%)	0.01	−0.02	−0.13	−0.22	−0.29
Private consumption (%GNP)	−0.02	−0.09	−0.16	−0.22	−0.27
Private investment (%GNP)	−0.06	−0.08	−0.12	−0.14	−0.15
Government consumption (%GNP)	0.00	0.00	0.00	0.00	0.00
Trade balance (%GNP)	0.07	0.06	0.06	0.06	0.06
Labor demand (%)	0.01	−0.01	−0.14	−0.22	−0.28
Inflation (D)	0.05	0.15	0.12	0.11	0.09
Interest rate, short (D)	0.01	0.11	0.13	0.19	0.23
Interest rate, long (D)	0.21	0.21	0.21	0.20	0.19
Tobin's q (%)	−0.76	−1.03	−1.22	−1.39	−1.53
Real exchange rate					
$/ECU (%)	0.08	0.03	0.02	−0.02	−0.04
$/yen (%)	3.93	3.56	3.43	3.22	3.03
$/Can (%)	0.07	0.06	0.07	0.05	0.03
ROECD Economies					
Output (%)	0.04	−0.06	−0.13	−0.19	−0.26
Private consumption (%GNP)	−0.07	−0.12	−0.17	−0.22	−0.26
Private investment (%GNP)	−0.06	−0.10	−0.11	−0.13	−0.14
Government consumption (%GNP)	0.00	0.00	0.00	0.00	0.00
Trade balance (%GNP)	0.07	0.07	0.07	0.07	0.07
Labor demand (%)	0.05	−0.06	−0.12	−0.18	−0.23
Inflation (D)	0.13	0.09	0.09	0.09	0.08
Interest rate, short (D)	0.08	0.09	0.15	0.19	0.23
Japanese Economy					
Output (%)	0.38	0.02	−0.00	−0.02	−0.05
Private consumption (%GNP)	0.08	0.03	−0.04	−0.08	−0.13
Private investment (%GNP)	0.06	−0.11	−0.09	−0.09	−0.10
Government consumption (%GNP)	1.00	1.00	1.00	1.00	1.00
Exports (%GNP)	−0.35	−0.53	−0.52	−0.51	−0.49
Imports (%GNP)	0.09	0.07	0.07	0.06	0.06
Imports, quant. (%GNP)	0.42	0.37	0.36	0.34	0.32
Trade balance (%GNP)	−0.63	−0.60	−0.59	−0.57	−0.55
Labor demand (%)	0.24	0.00	0.00	0.00	0.00
Inflation (D)	−0.33	0.09	0.09	0.06	0.05
Interest rate, short (D)	0.38	0.20	0.28	0.32	0.35
Canadian Economy					
Output (%)	0.00	−0.15	−0.24	−0.32	−0.39
Private consumption (%GNP)	−0.07	−0.15	−0.22	−0.29	−0.34
Private investment (%GNP)	−0.06	−0.12	−0.13	−0.14	−0.15
Government consumption (%GNP)	0.00	0.00	0.00	0.00	0.00
Trade balance (%GNP)	0.06	0.07	0.06	0.06	0.06
Labor demand (%)	0.05	−0.11	−0.21	−0.29	−0.36
Inflation (D)	0.17	0.13	0.12	0.11	0.10
Interest rate, short (D)	0.09	0.11	0.15	0.20	0.24

Table 11.6 Permanent Canadian Fiscal Expansion (1% GNP)

	Year 1	2	3	4	5
U.S. Economy					
Output (%)	0.01	0.01	−0.02	−0.03	−0.04
Private consumption (%GNP)	−0.01	−0.02	−0.03	−0.04	−0.04
Private investment (%GNP)	−0.01	−0.01	−0.02	−0.02	−0.03
Government consumption (%GNP)	0.00	0.00	0.00	0.00	0.00
Trade balance (%GNP)	0.03	0.02	0.02	0.02	0.02
Labor demand (%)	0.01	0.01	−0.02	−0.03	−0.03
Inflation (D)	0.00	0.03	0.02	0.01	0.01
Interest rate, short (D)	0.02	0.03	0.03	0.04	0.04
Interest rate, long (D)	0.05	0.05	0.05	0.04	0.04
Tobin's q (%)	−0.20	−0.23	−0.26	−0.29	−0.31
Real exchange rate					
$/ECU (%)	−0.09	−0.09	−0.10	−0.10	−0.10
$/yen (%)	−0.18	−0.18	−0.19	−0.21	−0.23
$/Can (%)	1.76	1.31	1.06	0.94	0.91
ROECD Economies					
Output (%)	0.01	−0.01	−0.02	−0.03	−0.04
Private consumption (%GNP)	−0.02	−0.02	−0.03	−0.04	−0.04
Private investment (%GNP)	−0.01	−0.02	−0.02	−0.02	−0.03
Government consumption (%GNP)	0.00	0.00	0.00	0.00	0.00
Trade balance (%GNP)	0.02	0.02	0.02	0.02	0.02
Labor demand (%)	0.02	−0.00	−0.01	−0.02	−0.03
Inflation (D)	0.02	0.01	0.01	0.01	0.01
Interest rate, short (D)	0.03	0.03	0.03	0.04	0.05
Japanese Economy					
Output (%)	0.01	−0.00	−0.01	−0.01	−0.02
Private consumption (%GNP)	−0.02	−0.03	−0.03	−0.04	−0.04
Private investment (%GNP)	−0.01	−0.02	−0.02	−0.02	−0.03
Government consumption (%GNP)	0.00	0.00	0.00	0.00	0.00
Trade balance (%GNP)	0.03	0.03	0.03	0.03	0.03
Labor demand (%)	0.02	−0.00	−0.00	−0.00	−0.00
Inflation (D)	0.03	0.02	0.01	0.01	0.01
Interest rate, short (D)	0.03	0.03	0.04	0.05	0.05
Canadian Economy					
Output (%)	0.38	0.40	0.54	0.58	0.55
Private consumption (%GNP)	0.13	0.27	0.33	0.33	0.30
Private investment (%GNP)	0.05	0.12	0.09	0.07	0.05
Government consumption (%GNP)	1.00	1.00	1.00	1.00	1.00
Exports (%GNP)	−0.16	−0.38	−0.32	−0.29	−0.28
Imports (%GNP)	0.26	0.32	0.33	0.33	0.31
Imports, quant. (%GNP)	0.64	0.60	0.56	0.53	0.52
Trade balance (%GNP)	−0.70	−0.70	−0.65	−0.61	−0.59
Labor demand (%)	0.11	0.52	0.67	0.70	0.65
Inflation (D)	−0.47	−0.22	−0.10	−0.02	0.03
Interest rate, short (D)	0.15	0.12	0.09	0.08	0.08

One can finally observe that, given the size of Canada, the transmission of its policies to other countries is negligible. As table 11.6 shows, most of these effects are close to zero.

11.3.2   Monetary Policy in the United States, Japan, and Canada

As with fiscal policy, the international transmission of monetary policy to foreign output has a theoretically ambiguous sign. A domestic monetary expansion almost surely raises home output temporarily, but it may raise or lower output abroad, depending on the strength of two competing channels. In one, the monetary expansion tends to depreciate the domestic currency, thus shifting demand away from foreign goods and toward home goods. In the other, the monetary expansion lowers real interest rates and raises Tobin's q abroad as well as at home, and thereby spurs investment and consumption spending. In the simple Mundell-Fleming model with nominal wage rigidity, the (adverse) exchange rate effect dominates, so that foreign output falls when the home country expands the money supply. In more general models, with more flexible wages, the direction of effect can readily be reversed.

Monetary policy also has an ambiguous effect on the domestic trade and current account balances. Higher domestic money improves international competitiveness by depreciating the exchange rate. Assuming that the usual Marshall-Lerner conditions hold (as in MSG2), the exchange rate effect tends to raise output, national savings, and the trade and current account balances. However, the fall in real interest rates and the rise in Tobin's q tend to spur investment demand, thereby worsening the current account and trade balances. Since both savings and investment tend to rise, the effect on the balance of savings minus investment (i.e., the external balance) is theoretically ambiguous.

Let us now examine these issues in the model. Table 11.7 reports the results of a permanent increase in the U.S. nominal money stock of 1 percent. The monetary expansion in the United States causes output to rise by 0.73 percent in the first year, and causes the real exchange rate to depreciate by around 1 percent. U.S. inflation increases by 0.28 percentage points in the first year, and 0.20 percentage points in the second.

Note that there is far more inflation per unit of output increase than was found with the fiscal expansion in table 11.4. A 2.7 percent of GNP increase in G raises U.S. GNP by 1.0 percent in the first year, and lowers inflation by 0.11 percentage points. A 1.37 percent monetary expansion also raises first-period output by 1 percent, but raises inflation by 0.28 percent. The differential effects on inflation of monetary and fiscal policy of course result from their opposite effects on the dollar exchange rate: fiscal policy induces a currency appreciation, which reduces import prices, while monetary policy induces a depreciation, which raises import prices.

Table 11.7 Permanent U.S. Monetary Expansion (1%)

	Year 1	2	3	4	5
	U.S. Economy				
Output (%)	0.73	0.45	0.34	0.24	0.17
Private consumption (%GNP)	0.41	0.33	0.23	0.17	0.12
Private investment (%GNP)	0.31	0.03	0.04	0.02	0.01
Government consumption (%GNP)	0.00	0.00	0.00	0.00	0.00
Exports (%GNP)	0.06	0.05	0.04	0.03	0.02
Imports (%GNP)	0.06	0.03	0.02	0.02	0.01
Imports, quant. (%GNP)	0.05	−0.05	−0.03	−0.02	−0.01
Trade balance (%GNP)	−0.00	0.02	0.01	0.01	0.01
Labor demand (%)	1.00	0.52	0.36	0.22	0.12
Inflation (D)	0.28	0.20	0.15	0.10	0.08
Interest rate, short (D)	−0.00	−0.25	−0.15	−0.12	−0.08
Interest rate, long (D)	−0.04	−0.04	−0.03	−0.02	−0.01
Tobin's q (%)	0.95	0.78	0.47	0.28	0.15
Real exchange rate					
$/ECU (%)	1.01	0.89	0.57	0.37	0.24
$/yen (%)	1.06	0.94	0.64	0.45	0.31
$/Can (%)	1.00	0.83	0.55	0.35	0.21
	ROECD Economies				
Output (%)	0.00	−0.00	0.03	0.04	0.03
Private consumption (%GNP)	0.02	0.04	0.04	0.04	0.02
Private investment (%GNP)	0.01	0.02	0.02	0.01	0.01
Government consumption (%GNP)	0.00	0.00	0.00	0.00	0.00
Exports (%GNP)	0.02	−0.03	−0.01	0.00	0.01
Imports (%GNP)	0.00	0.01	0.01	0.01	0.00
Imports, quant. (%GNP)	0.04	0.04	0.03	0.02	0.01
Trade balance (%GNP)	−0.01	−0.03	−0.01	−0.00	0.01
Labor demand (%)	−0.04	−0.01	0.03	0.03	0.02
Inflation (D)	−0.05	−0.04	0.00	0.01	0.02
Interest rate, short (D)	−0.06	−0.10	−0.07	−0.05	−0.04
	Japanese Economy				
Output (%)	0.03	0.00	0.01	0.01	0.01
Private consumption (%GNP)	0.02	0.05	0.04	0.03	0.03
Private investment (%GNP)	0.01	0.02	0.01	0.01	0.00
Government consumption (%GNP)	0.00	0.00	0.00	0.00	0.00
Exports (%GNP)	0.04	−0.04	−0.02	−0.01	−0.00
Imports (%GNP)	0.00	0.01	0.00	0.00	0.00
Imports, quant. (%GNP)	0.03	0.04	0.02	0.02	0.01
Trade balance (%GNP)	−0.02	−0.05	−0.03	−0.02	−0.01
Labor demand (%)	−0.04	0.00	0.00	0.00	0.00
Inflation (D)	−0.04	−0.05	0.02	0.02	0.01
Interest rate, short (D)	−0.07	−0.09	−0.07	−0.05	−0.03

Remarkably, there is almost no effect of the dollar expansion on the U.S. trade balance, or on output and the trade balances in the other regions. *This is a striking and seemingly robust result of this model: monetary policy can be pursued by each region independently, without spillovers on the trade balance or level of economic activity in other regions.* The reason for the absence of spillovers has already been noted. Monetary expansion in the United States depreciates the dollar, which tends to reduce aggregate demand abroad, but it also lowers real interest rates abroad (and raises Tobin's q), thereby spurring aggregate demand. Moreover, while the dollar depreciation spurs U.S. exports, the fall in U.S. real interest rates spurs U.S. spending and U.S. imports, keeping the trade balance almost exactly unchanged.

As can be seen from tables 11.8 and 11.9, the results on U.S. monetary policy also apply to .a Japanese and Canadian monetary expansion. Once again, the monetary expansion raises output, depreciates the currency, lowers real interest rates, and has little effect on the trade balance or the rest of the world. Because of the rapid labor market clearing in the case of Japan, the domestic effects of the monetary expansion on the real economy are dissipated by the second period. According to these results, the United States stands to benefit little from an easier monetary policy in Japan (or in the ROECD). One can also observe that, following a monetary expansion, the initial pass-through effect of a devaluation on domestic inflation is the greatest for Canada (with a rise in inflation of 0.40 percent) and the smallest for the U.S. (0.28 percent), and in between the two for Japan (0.34 percent). Again, the greater degree of openness of the Canadian economy relative to the United States and Japan accounts for this result.[7]

11.3.3   Divergent Fiscal Policies and the Recent Trade Imbalances

We are now ready to ask whether the model can help us to understand the sources of the trade and international financial patterns noted at the beginning of the paper: the large U.S. trade deficits and Japanese trade surpluses, the sharp appreciation of the dollar during 1981–85, the rise in real interest rates, and the subsequent sharp fall in the dollar beginning in 1985 and accelerating in 1986. In this section we consider the period 1980–85, when the dollar appreciated strongly, while in the next section of the paper, we take up the period since 1985, during which time the dollar has declined sharply in value relative to the yen and the European currencies. Importantly, this division also marks off two policy phases in the United States and Japan. During the first period, the U.S. fiscal deficit widened significantly, while in Japan there was a steady reduction in the structural deficit. In the second period, the U.S. deficit is projected to decline, while the Japanese deficit is expected to stabilize, or even increase slightly.

Table 11.8   Permanent Japanese Monetary Expansion (1%)

	Year 1	2	3	4	5
U.S. Economy					
Output (%)	0.00	−0.00	0.01	0.01	0.01
Private consumption (%GNP)	−0.00	0.01	0.01	0.01	0.01
Private investment (%GNP)	0.00	0.00	0.01	0.00	0.00
Government consumption (%GNP)	0.00	0.00	0.00	0.00	0.00
Exports (%GNP)	0.00	−0.00	0.00	0.00	0.00
Imports (%GNP)	0.00	0.00	0.00	0.00	0.00
Imports, quant. (%GNP)	0.00	0.01	0.00	0.00	0.00
Trade balance (%GNP)	0.00	−0.00	−0.00	0.00	0.00
Labor demand (%)	0.00	−0.00	0.02	0.01	0.01
Inflation (D)	−0.00	−0.02	0.00	0.00	0.00
Interest rate, short (D)	0.00	−0.02	−0.00	−0.01	−0.00
Interest rate, long (D)	−0.00	−0.00	−0.00	−0.00	−0.00
Tobin's q (%)	0.02	0.04	0.02	0.02	0.01
Real exchange rate					
$/ECU (%)	0.01	0.01	0.01	0.02	0.02
$/yen (%)	−0.71	−0.45	−0.07	−0.05	−0.05
$/Can (%)	−0.01	−0.00	−0.00	0.01	0.01
ROECD Economies					
Output (%)	−0.00	0.00	0.01	0.00	−0.00
Private consumption (%GNP)	0.01	0.01	0.01	0.01	0.00
Private investment (%GNP)	0.00	0.01	0.00	−0.00	−0.00
Government consumption (%GNP)	0.00	0.00	0.00	0.00	0.00
Exports (%GNP)	0.01	−0.00	0.00	−0.00	−0.00
Imports (%GNP)	0.00	0.00	0.00	0.00	0.00
Imports, quant. (%GNP)	0.02	0.01	0.00	0.00	0.00
Trade balance (%GNP)	0.01	−0.00	−0.00	−0.00	−0.00
Labor demand (%)	−0.00	0.00	0.01	−0.00	−0.01
Inflation (D)	−0.02	−0.01	0.01	0.01	0.00
Interest rate, short (D)	−0.00	−0.01	−0.01	−0.01	−0.00
Japanese Economy					
Output (%)	0.83	0.08	0.03	0.03	0.03
Private consumption (%GNP)	0.44	0.14	0.02	0.02	0.01
Private investment (%GNP)	0.33	−0.17	−0.00	0.00	0.00
Government consumption (%GNP)	0.00	0.00	0.00	0.00	0.00
Exports (%GNP)	0.07	0.07	0.01	0.01	0.01
Imports (%GNP)	0.08	0.00	0.00	0.00	0.00
Imports, quant. (%GNP)	0.02	−0.04	−0.00	−0.00	−0.00
Trade balance (%GNP)	0.02	0.07	0.01	0.01	0.01
Labor demand (%)	1.16	0.00	0.00	0.00	0.00
Inflation (D)	0.34	0.48	0.14	0.01	0.00
Interest rate, short (D)	0.23	−0.24	−0.01	−0.01	−0.01

Table 11.9 Permanent Canadian Monetary Expansion (1%)

	Year 1	2	3	4	5
U.S. Economy					
Output (%)	0.00	−0.00	0.01	0.01	0.01
Private consumption (%GNP)	−0.00	0.01	0.01	0.01	0.01
Private investment (%GNP)	0.00	0.00	0.01	0.00	0.00
Government consumption (%GNP)	0.00	0.00	0.00	0.00	0.00
Trade balance (%GNP)	0.00	−0.00	−0.00	−0.00	0.00
Labor demand (%)	0.00	−0.01	0.01	0.01	0.01
Inflation (D)	0.00	−0.02	−0.00	−0.00	0.00
Interest rate, short (D)	0.00	−0.01	−0.01	−0.01	−0.01
Interest rate, long (D)	−0.00	−0.00	−0.00	−0.00	−0.00
Tobin's q (%)	0.02	0.04	0.03	0.03	0.02
Real exchange rate					
$/ECU (%)	0.01	0.01	0.01	0.02	0.02
$/yen (%)	0.02	0.02	0.02	0.03	0.02
$/Can (%)	−0.76	−0.64	−0.37	−0.21	−0.10
ROECD Economies					
Output (%)	0.00	−0.00	0.00	0.00	0.00
Private consumption (%GNP)	0.00	0.01	0.01	0.01	0.00
Private investment (%GNP)	0.00	0.00	0.00	0.00	0.00
Government consumption (%GNP)	0.00	0.00	0.00	0.00	0.00
Trade balance (%GNP)	0.00	−0.00	−0.00	−0.00	−0.00
Labor demand (%)	0.00	−0.00	0.00	0.00	0.00
Inflation (D)	−0.01	−0.01	0.00	0.00	0.00
Interest rate, short (D)	0.00	−0.01	−0.01	−0.01	−0.01
Japanese Economy					
Output (%)	−0.00	−0.00	0.00	0.00	0.00
Private consumption (%GNP)	0.00	0.00	0.00	0.00	0.00
Private investment (%GNP)	0.00	0.00	0.00	0.00	0.00
Government consumption (%GNP)	0.00	0.00	0.00	0.00	0.00
Trade balance (%GNP)	0.00	−0.00	−0.00	−0.00	−0.00
Labor demand (%)	−0.00	0.00	0.00	0.00	0.00
Inflation (D)	−0.00	−0.00	0.00	0.00	0.00
Interest rate, short (D)	−0.00	−0.01	−0.00	−0.00	−0.00
Canadian Economy					
Output (%)	0.71	0.48	0.29	0.17	0.09
Private consumption (%GNP)	0.38	0.26	0.16	0.10	0.06
Private investment (%GNP)	0.30	−0.03	−0.01	−0.01	−0.01
Government consumption (%GNP)	0.00	0.00	0.00	0.00	0.00
Exports (%GNP)	0.06	0.18	0.11	0.06	0.03
Imports (%GNP)	0.20	0.07	0.05	0.03	0.01
Imports, quant. (%GNP)	0.04	−0.07	−0.03	−0.02	−0.01
Trade balance (%GNP)	−0.01	0.11	0.06	0.04	0.02
Labor demand (%)	1.16	0.56	0.33	0.16	0.06
Inflation (D)	0.40	0.22	0.15	0.09	0.06
Interest rate, short (D)	0.13	−0.08	−0.04	−0.03	−0.02

It is beyond the reach of this paper to investigate the year-to-year move-ments in trade balances and exchange rates, since that would require an in-tensive investigation of the precise timing of macroeconomic policies in the various OECD economies. We propose instead to ask whether the overall changes in fiscal policies between 1980 and 1985 in the various OECD econ-omies can explain the overall shift in trade balances and exchange rates. Our focus is on *the United States and Japan,* as we have neglected a detailed modelling of important changes in the Canadian economy in addition to fiscal policy.

The "policy package" that we investigate is as follows:

A rise in the U.S. structural deficit of approximately 4.4 percent of U.S. GNP;

A reduction in the Japanese structural budget deficit of approximately 3.4 percent of GNP;

An increase in the structural deficit in Canada of approximately 2.2 percent of GNP, and an increase in the structural budget surplus in the ROECD of approximately 0.5 percent of GNP;

An *exogenous* reduction in the net flow of new borrowing (i.e., the current account deficit) of the LDCs in the magnitude of 1.4 percent of U.S. GNP;[8] and

An assumed offset of monetary policy in the OECD countries to main-tain an unchanged level of employment (we thereby abstract from short-run cyclical swings of the trade balance).

The combined effect of these changes (as a deviation from a baseline) is shown in table 11.10, where we see that indeed the dollar appreciates sharply and the U.S. trade balance worsens significantly as a percent of GNP. In table 11.11, we compare the predicted effects on the trade balance, dollar exchange rate, and the short-term real interest rate with the actual effects observed in comparing the years 1978–80 with the year 1985. In table 11.12, we appor-tion the overall predicted shift in the U.S. trade balance and real bilateral exchange rates to the various underlying disturbances. Not surprisingly, the largest factor in explaining the U.S. and Japanese trade balance changes is the fiscal policy in the own country. Cross-country effects play a far smaller role in the evolution of each country's trade imbalances.

There are several puzzles not explained by the simulation model. Most importantly, while the model tracks the appreciation of the dollar vis-à-vis the yen during the period, it fails to track the larger appreciation of the dollar vis-à-vis the ROECD currencies. We fear that part of the problem here is one of aggregation. The ROECD is a varied mix of countries with a quite varied mix of policies during this period. At the center of the ROECD we have West Germany, which pursued highly contractionary fiscal policies (see table 11.2)

Table 11.10   1981–85 Global Scenario with Money Stabilizing Employment

	1981	1982	1983	1984	1985
U.S. Economy					
Output (%)	−0.00	0.07	0.08	0.05	0.01
Private consumption (%GNP)	1.50	2.89	3.38	3.66	3.59
Private investment (%GNP)	0.27	0.08	−0.04	−0.14	−0.17
Government consumption (%GNP)	0.00	0.00	0.00	0.00	0.00
Exports (%GNP)	−0.91	−0.96	−1.08	−1.15	−1.13
Imports (%GNP)	0.55	0.61	0.69	0.73	0.71
Imports, quant. (%GNP)	0.86	1.93	2.19	2.33	2.27
Trade balance (%GNP)	−1.46	−1.57	−1.77	−1.88	−1.84
Labor demand (%)	0.05	0.05	0.05	0.04	0.03
Inflation (D)	−0.75	−2.19	−2.52	−2.68	−2.56
Interest rate, short (D)	−2.45	−3.98	−3.09	−1.50	−1.50
Interest rate, long (D)	−0.83	−0.64	−0.37	−0.17	−0.09
Tobin's *q* (%)	−0.49	−1.10	−3.16	−4.49	−4.49
Real exchange rate					
$/ECU (%)	−14.52	−15.65	−17.60	−18.63	−18.11
$/yen (%)	−20.98	−23.74	−27.40	−29.63	−28.96
$/Can (%)	−5.94	−5.75	−6.44	−6.60	−6.40
ROECD Economies					
Output (%)	−0.42	−0.11	−0.17	−0.22	−0.26
Private consumption (%GNP)	−0.45	−0.69	−0.85	−0.94	−0.89
Private investment (%GNP)	−0.24	−0.24	−0.25	−0.24	−0.23
Government consumption (%GNP)	0.00	0.00	0.00	0.00	0.00
Exports (%GNP)	−0.32	0.18	0.22	0.23	0.16
Imports (%GNP)	−0.10	−0.12	−0.15	−0.16	−0.15
Imports, quant. (%GNP)	−0.59	−0.63	−0.70	−0.73	−0.70
Trade balance (%GNP)	0.14	0.30	0.37	0.39	0.31
Labor demand (%)	−0.01	−0.01	−0.01	−0.00	−0.00
Inflation (D)	0.56	0.73	0.96	1.10	1.13
Interest rate, short (D)	0.64	1.30	1.63	1.71	1.63
Japanese Economy					
Output (%)	−1.09	−0.16	−0.28	−0.37	−0.43
Private consumption (%GNP)	−1.58	−2.15	−2.47	−2.34	−2.30
Private investment (%GNP)	−0.62	−0.49	−0.44	−0.36	−0.33
Government consumption (%GNP)	−0.50	−1.00	−1.50	−2.20	−2.20
Exports (%GNP)	0.38	2.00	2.38	2.61	2.52
Imports (%GNP)	−0.20	−0.27	−0.33	−0.36	−0.36
Imports, quant. (%GNP)	−1.22	−1.48	−1.75	−1.92	−1.89
Trade balance (%GNP)	1.62	2.27	2.71	2.97	2.88
Labor demand (%)	−0.07	−0.00	−0.00	−0.00	−0.00
Inflation (D)	1.13	0.01	0.03	0.05	0.04
Interest rate, short (D)	1.47	2.01	1.72	0.48	0.44

Table 11.11   Actual and Predicted Changes in Trade Balances and Real Exchange Rates (1985 compared with average of 1978–80)

	Actual	Predicted
Trade Balance Change (percent of GDP)		
U.S.	1.9	1.8
Japan	3.2	2.8
Rest of OECD	1.0	0.3
Real Exchange Rate Change of the U.S. relative to:		
Japan	24.0	28.0
Rest of OECD	41.0	18.0

Source: "Actual" from tables 11.1 and 11.3; "Predicted" from 1985 data in table 11.10.

and thus the Deutsche mark should be expected to have a large real depreciation relative to the dollar, as in fact occurred. On the other hand, most of the little OECD countries included in ROECD pursued mildly expansionary fiscal policies, and thus should not have experienced as large a real depreciation in their currencies relative to the dollar, as in fact occurred. The dollar rate vis-à-vis the currencies of the overall ROECD, however, seems to behave more in line with what would be predicted from German fiscal policy, rather than overall ROECD policy. This might be explained by the fact that many non-German ROECD countries peg their currencies to the Deutsche mark, and by the fact that much of the non-German ROECD has relatively closed capital markets (in which case a fiscal expansion leads to a depreciation).

11.4   The Decline of the Dollar and U.S. Trade Prospects

Since 1985, there have been some significant changes in the economic outlook, as well as large swings in exchange rates. Most importantly, the dollar has depreciated significantly, reversing much of its real appreciation since 1980 relative to the other currencies of the OECD. On the policy front, there has been a brightening of prospects for a significant improvement in the U.S. fiscal situation. Those prospects are reflected in the legislative commitment in the Gramm-Rudman-Hollings (GRH) law to a balanced budget by 1992. While the precise targets of GRH are unlikely to be reached, most observers feel that significant reductions in the budget deficit will be achieved.

In this section, we investigate three questions. First, how much, by itself, would GRH contribute to a reduction in the U.S. trade deficit, and what has been its likely role in the depreciation of the dollar? Second, what other factors in addition to GRH may have contributed to the fall of the dollar? And third, are the recent shifts in budget prospects and the fall in the dollar, taken together, sufficient to restore trade balance to the U.S. economy in the coming few years?

We will raise at least six possible interpretations of the recent decline

Table 11.12 Decomposition of Changes in Trade Balances and Exchange Rates

| | | Fiscal Policies in: | | | Sum of Effects of: | |
Effect on:	Total Predicted Effect	U.S.	Japan	ROECD + Canada	Cutoff in LDC Lending	Offsetting Monetary Policy
U.S. trade balance	−1.84	−1.01	−0.23	−0.03	−0.40	−0.17
Japan trade balance	2.88	1.36	1.91	−0.06	−0.61	0.28
U.S.-Japan real exchange rate	28.9	11.8	10.6	−0.03	−0.11	6.64

of the dollar. Each of these possibilities has been the focus of some attention in the recent policy debates. The first interpretation is that the decline has come from a shift in macroeconomic policies (mainly a move to tighter budgets and easier money in the United States), both current and *anticipated*. The second possibility is that private demand in the United States has declined (i.e., private saving rates have risen or private investment rates have fallen) with an offset of easier money and a depreciating dollar. A third interpretation is that the decline in the dollar represents the bursting of a speculative bubble that had built up during the period of dollar appreciation. A fourth possibility is that private portfolio holders have begun to demand a larger risk premium for holding dollar assets, following a saturation of private portfolios with dollar claims in recent years (if this fourth interpretation is correct, the shift in the required risk premium must have been unanticipated to account for the fact that the dollar first rose sharply, then fell). A fifth interpretation is that monetary policy, both current and anticipated, has become more expansionary in the United States than abroad. The sixth possibility, of course, is that the market simply has it all wrong now, with the recent depreciation representing a new speculative bubble against the dollar, which will have to be reversed by dollar appreciation later.

Let us turn first to the possibility that the decline is a result of a shift in expectations regarding U.S. budget deficits. Suppose that the public's expectations shifted in 1986 from an anticipation of continuing U.S. budget deficits on the order of 5 percent of GNP, to a sequence of falling budget deficits along the lines of the GRH law. Would such a shift (amounting to a drop in expected budget deficits of 5 percent of GNP by 1992) be enough to account for the drop in the dollar? In table 11.13, we simulate this shift in fiscal policy under the maintained assumption that the Federal Reserve Board accommodates the fiscal contraction with easier monetary policy, as necessary, in order to stabilize employment.

The results are interesting for several reasons. First, the dollar depreciates, as expected, but only by about 8 percent in real terms on impact (relative to the yen). Thus, the shift in budget expectations (the actual magnitude of which is almost surely exaggerated by the experiment carried out in table 11.13) is insufficient to account for the extent of the depreciation of the dollar. It is evident that the shift to GRH causes the long-term interest rate to fall by more than 1.6 percentage points on impact, though the short-term nominal rate rises. Inflation increases modestly after the first year because of the dollar depreciation. The U.S. is forced to give up part of the low-inflation dividend that it enjoyed during the period of dollar appreciation, a point that was discussed at length in Sachs (1985).

Note that according to the results of table 11.13, GRH by itself is unlikely to lead to an elimination of the U.S. trade deficits by the early 1990s. With a complete elimination of the budget deficit by 1992, the improvement

Table 11.13   Gramm-Rudman-Hollings with Money Stabilizing Employment in the U.S.

	1986	1987	1988	1989	1990
U.S. Economy					
Output (%)	−0.06	−0.05	0.05	0.19	0.39
Private consumption (%GNP)	−0.72	−1.18	−1.13	−1.04	−0.83
Private investment (%GNP)	0.04	0.33	0.61	0.84	1.05
Government consumption (%GNP)	0.00	−0.65	−1.35	−1.80	−2.25
Exports (%GNP)	0.28	0.43	0.60	0.71	0.82
Imports (%GNP)	−0.21	−0.30	−0.38	−0.42	−0.44
Imports, quant. (%GNP)	−0.34	−1.03	−1.32	−1.48	−1.60
Trade balance (%GNP)	0.50	0.73	0.98	1.13	1.26
Labor demand (%)	−0.05	−0.05	−0.04	−0.04	−0.04
Inflation (D)	0.29	1.14	1.40	1.43	1.35
Interest rate, short (D)	4.12	4.11	2.39	1.36	−0.18
Interest rate, long (D)	−1.62	−1.92	−2.21	−2.36	−2.44
Tobin's q (%)	2.68	6.49	10.75	13.96	16.82
Real exchange rate					
$/ECU (%)	6.62	9.14	11.49	12.58	13.33
$/yen (%)	8.16	10.98	14.05	16.15	17.98
$/Can (%)	3.52	5.95	8.59	9.91	10.69
Money supply	−2.52	−2.02	0.23	2.25	4.58
ROECD Economies					
Output (%)	0.28	0.34	0.90	1.62	2.37
Private consumption (%GNP)	0.28	0.66	1.19	1.75	2.33
Private investment (%GNP)	0.59	0.76	1.05	1.29	1.49
Government consumption (%GNP)	0.00	0.00	0.00	0.00	0.00
Exports (%GNP)	−0.18	−0.50	−0.59	−0.57	−0.52
Imports (%GNP)	0.11	0.18	0.28	0.37	0.46
Imports, quant. (%GNP)	0.41	0.58	0.75	0.85	0.93
Trade balance (%GNP)	−0.45	−0.68	−0.86	−0.94	−0.98
Labor demand (%)	0.16	0.26	0.77	1.42	2.07
Inflation (D)	−0.32	−0.80	−1.05	−1.12	−1.14
Interest rate, short (D)	0.27	−0.49	−1.16	−1.81	−2.47
Japanese Economy					
Output (%)	0.35	0.17	0.39	0.63	0.88
Private consumption (%GNP)	0.50	1.00	1.47	1.87	2.26
Private investment (%GNP)	0.71	0.92	1.08	1.21	1.32
Government consumption (%GNP)	0.00	0.00	0.00	0.00	0.00
Exports (%GNP)	−0.37	−1.09	−1.31	−1.46	−1.57
Imports (%GNP)	0.09	0.14	0.19	0.24	0.28
Imports, quant. (%GNP)	0.49	0.66	0.84	0.99	1.13
Trade balance (%GNP)	−0.86	−1.23	−1.51	−1.70	−1.85
Labor demand (%)	−0.07	0.00	0.00	0.00	0.00
Inflation (D)	−0.47	−0.86	−0.83	−0.76	−0.72
Interest rate, short (D)	−0.12	−0.97	−1.75	−2.42	−3.02

in the trade balance (at full employment) is in the order of 1.3 percent of GNP, leaving a trade deficit on the order of 2 to 2.5 percent of potential GNP ($80–100 billion in 1987). Why is it that a complete elimination of the U.S. budget deficit would be insufficient to restore trade balance at full employment? There are three main reasons. First, even before the buildup of the U.S. fiscal deficit after 1980, the U.S. was running a trade deficit on the order of 1 to 1.5 percent of GNP. Second, part of the shift in the trade balance was due to the cutoff in LDC financing, which looks unlikely to be reversed in the near term. And third, about 0.2 percent of GNP of the trade deficit resulted from the contraction of Japanese fiscal policies, another shift which is unlikely to be reversed entirely (if at all).

Clearly the GRH legislation and the attendant shift in public expectations over U.S. fiscal policy do not take us very far in explaining the collapse of the dollar. Let us therefore turn to the other factors mentioned earlier that may also have contributed to the dollar depreciation. For convenience, we study these other factors in a "normalized" form, by asking the following question:

Suppose that factor "x" changes in 1986 in an amount sufficient to cause a *10 percent real depreciation* of the dollar vis-à-vis the yen. What would be the accompanying economic implications of such a shift in "x"?

The six hypotheses are described by the data in table 11.14. For each possible cause of the dollar decline, we show the effects on the U.S. trade balance, interest rates, employment, consumption, and investment in the United States. This exercise is helpful in two ways. First, it can aid us in identifying the most likely culprits in the dollar depreciation by identifying the kinds of economic adjustments that should be expected to accompany each of the various shocks. Second, it can help in identifying the implications of the alternative hypotheses for the longer-run evolution of the U.S. trade deficits.

Referring to table 11.14, we now discuss each of the alternatives in turn. The first case is the one already considered: a fiscal contraction balanced by monetary expansion. The effects of such a change are a fall in long-term interest rates and an improvement of the trade balance by 0.72 percent of GNP for each 10 percent depreciation of the dollar (in 1987, $30 billion for each 10 percent depreciation). As public consumption falls, both private consumption and private investment rise with this policy shift. Note that if the 10 percent depreciation came from an anticipated change in the policy mix, the initial effect on the trade balance would be smaller than 0.72 percent of GNP.

The second possibility is an autonomous decline in private spending, rather than public spending. This is modelled as an autonomous rise in the private saving rate sufficient to cause a 10 percent real depreciation of the dollar (a fall in private investment produces similar results). The effects on

Table 11.14 Effects of Alternative Policies Leading to a 10% Real Depreciation of the Dollar Relative to the Yen

			Effect on:			
			Absorption (percent of GDP):			
Type of Shock	Trade Balance (percent of GDP)	U.S. Long-Term Interest Rate	C	I	G	Total
1. Policy mix	0.72	−1.47	0.86	0.34	−2.08	−0.88
2. Rise in private savings	0.72	−1.46	−1.23	0.35	0.00	−0.88
3. Collapse of a bubble	0.79	0.24	−1.14	−0.40	0.00	−1.54
4. Risk premium	0.74	1.85	−0.39	−0.52	0.00	−1.91
5. Money expansion	−0.03	−0.42	3.90	2.96	0.00	6.86
6. New bubble	0.75	0.93	−0.39	−0.54	0.00	−0.93

Notes: In all cases, the $U.S.-yen real exchange rate depreciates by 10 percent in 1986. Subsequent movements in the exchange rate are determined endogenously. The table records the first-period effects of the various shocks.

1. *Policy mix:* U.S. fiscal contraction (2.08% GNP) with money stabilizing employment in the U.S. 2. *Rise in private savings:* Exogenous permanent fall in private consumption (2.11% GNP) in the U.S. with money stabilizing employment. 3. *Collapse of a bubble:* Exchange rate bubble on the U.S. dollar starting in 1983 and bursting in 1986 (with 10% depreciation in 1986). Money stabilizing employment in the U.S. 4. *Risk premium:* Emergence of a permanent risk premium on the dollar (2.97% per annum) with money stabilizing employment. 5. *Money expansion:* Permanent one-shot rise of U.S. money (9.5%) starting in 1986. 6. *New bubble:* Beginning of a new exchange rate bubble against the U.S. dollar starting in 1986 and bursting in 1989, with money stabilizing employment.

interest rates and the trade balance are almost identical to the case of a cut in government spending. The only real difference with the first case lies in the difference in composition of the presumed shift in spending (private consumption now falls instead of rising as in case 1).

The third possibility for explaining the fall of the dollar is a collapse of a speculative bubble. This is modelled as a speculative bubble beginning in 1984 and collapsing in 1986, with a 10 percent real depreciation occurring in 1986 as a result of a bubble collapse. It is assumed in the simulation that the Fed accommodates the speculative bubble in order to maintain employment at the full employment level in all years. The result of the bubble collapse is a rise in interest rates in 1986 (relative to the years 1984–85), and an improvement in the trade balance of 0.79 percent of GNP. As the bubble collapses, both private consumption and private investment fall relative to their pre-collapse levels, while public consumption remains unchanged. Thus, in comparing the bubble with the first two interpretations, the trade balance effects are *virtually identical,* though the effects on interest rates and the patterns of spending are very different among the three cases.

The fourth interpretation of the falling dollar is a rising risk premium on dollar assets. In this case, U.S. interest rates rise and the dollar depreciates, as investors attempt to shift out of dollars and into assets of other currencies. We assume, as in cases 1 through 3, that the Fed accommodates the shock in order to maintain full employment. The result (when scaled to produce a 10 percent real depreciation) is an improvement in the trade balance of 0.74 percent of GNP, almost identical to the first three cases. Now, as in case 3, interest rates rise, and private consumption and investment decline.

A fifth possible cause of the falling dollar is a monetary expansion by the Fed. As shown in table 11.14, the monetary expansion is a permanent one-shot increase in the U.S. money supply (alternative cases of anticipated increases in money could also be considered). Here, unlike the other cases, *the trade balance hardly improves, since the real depreciation occurs in the context of rising output and rising imports.* Also, unlike cases 1–4, the depreciation brought about by monetary expansion does not persist in real terms, since the rise in U.S. inflation after 1986 leads to a reversal of the real depreciation.

The final possibility that we examine is the start of a new bubble. In this interpretation, the dollar has simply overshot its true "fundamental" level, perhaps because of the U.S. government's seeming attempts to talk the dollar lower in 1985–87. We assume that the bubble bursts in the fourth year (1989), at which point the dollar appreciates and returns to its fundamental level. As in cases 1–4, the Fed is assumed to accommodate this shift in order to stabilize employment. The result is a temporary rise in interest rates and a temporary improvement in the trade balance, until the collapse of the bubble. The rise in interest rates due to the bubble crowds out investment and consumption, and thus produces the decline in absorption needed to generate an improvement in the trade balance.

Before turning to the evidence for and against these various interpretations, it is useful to summarize our findings. Most importantly, except for case 5 (the depreciation induced by a monetary expansion), the real depreciation of the dollar leads to a significant, and nearly identical, improvement in the trade balance, of 0.72–0.79 percent of GNP per 10 percent depreciation of the dollar.[9] This is a happy finding: to a large extent it is not necessary to understand exactly the source of the dollar decline in order to quantify the effects on the trade balance, assuming that the decline is not merely due to expansionary monetary policy (in which case the depreciation is reversed in future years), and that the real decline can be regarded as permanent. The main differences among the various cases lie in their implications for the patterns of spending in the U.S. economy and in their effects on interest rates, rather than in the overall implications for the trade balance.

The actual real depreciation of the dollar by early 1987 relative to the average for 1985 is on the order of 25 percent vis-à-vis a weighted average of OECD currencies. Using the rule of thumb that each 10 percent depreciation leads to a trade balance improvement of 0.75 percent of GNP, we would predict an improvement in the U.S. trade deficit on the order of 1.9 percent of GNP, or about one-half of the current deficit. This conclusion must be modified to the extent that the dollar has declined because of monetary expansion (in which case the U.S. trade balance will not improve by much), or because of a speculative bubble against the dollar (in which case, any improvement in the trade balance is likely to be reversed when the bubble bursts).

Of course there is no reason to choose a single explanation for the dollar depreciation. No doubt, a confluence of events ushered in the depreciation since 1985. The prospective shift in the U.S. policy mix is certainly one factor that has played a role. There is also evidence for some of the other interpretations. Without going into great detail, we can adduce the following points.

First, in addition to the prospective turnaround in fiscal policy, there is an apparent decline in private spending as well, with the rate of fixed investment expenditure declining relative to GNP in 1986 (and early 1987), despite declining real interest rates. Thus, the private investment rate (as a proportion of GNP) has been as follows:

1984	1985	1986	1987:1
17.5	16.5	16.3	16.2

Part of this decline might reflect the rise in effective marginal tax rates on new investments that are part of the 1986 tax reform act. Another part might reflect an autonomous shift in "animal spirits." In either case, the result should be a depreciation of the dollar, and an improvement in the trade balance.

There is relatively little evidence that a rising risk premium on the dollar has been a major factor in the depreciation, at least until early 1987. This is because the depreciation has occurred in the context of a falling long-term interest rate differential vis-à-vis Japan, Germany, and the other main OECD economies, rather than in the context of a rising interest rate differential, as would be predicted by a rising risk premium. The evolution of the long-term interest rate differential on U.S. and Japanese government bonds since 1984 has been as follows:

	1984	1985	1986
U.S.	12.48	10.97	8.56
Japan	6.81	6.34	5.23
U.S.-Japan difference	5.67	4.63	3.33

There is, on the other hand, considerable evidence that differential monetary policies, rather than portfolio shocks, *have* played an important role. U.S. monetary policy, as measured by the growth in M1, has been considerably more expansionary than monetary policy in Germany and Japan. Consider the following year-over-year rates of increase of M1 in the three countries:

	1984	1985	1986:1	1986:2	1986:3	1986:4
U.S.	5.7	12.1	11.6	12.9	13.4	16.6
Japan	6.8	3.0	1.6	8.3	6.1	10.4
Germany	5.9	6.6	9.7	11.4	10.8	8.1

The monetary interpretation is bolstered by the fact that the U.S. economy is accelerating in 1987, while the German and Japanese economies seem to be decelerating. Thus, monetary policy may be doing more than merely offsetting demand shocks coming from other parts of the economy.

Of course, *to the extent that it is simply relatively fast monetary expansion that is behind much of the fall of the dollar, the ultimate result will not be an improvement of the U.S. trade balance* but rather a rise in U.S. prices, and an eventual reversal of the real depreciation. The big trick for the Federal Reserve Board is to accommodate demand shifts without independently overheating the economy by overexpansionary monetary policy. The Fed must not "target" the trade balance with monetary policy, since a monetary expansion by itself can do nothing to improve the trade balance. Monetary ease is helpful only to the extent that it accompanies another source of decline in spending in the economy (whether a shift in G, C, I, or a rise in the risk premium on dollar-denominated assets).

11.5 Conclusions

The MSG2 model provides a useful research vehicle for investigating the nature of international macroeconomic interdependence. In this paper, we have used the model for three purposes. First, we have examined the international transmission of macroeconomic policies among the major regions of the OECD. While interdependence is certainly evident in the model, the extent and nature of interdependence is somewhat different from that which is typically assumed. A fiscal expansion raises output and worsens the trade balance of the initiating country, but does little to stimulate growth abroad. A monetary expansion also raises output, but with little effect on the trade balance. As with fiscal policy, a monetary expansion has little effect on foreign output.

The model demonstrates that divergent fiscal policies can largely explain the rise of U.S. trade deficits and Japanese trade surpluses since 1980. The model predicts that fiscal swings of the observed magnitude should have caused the dollar to appreciate in real terms between 1980 and 1985 by about 28 percent vis-à-vis the yen, compared with the actual appreciation of 24 percent. The model does less well in accounting for the dollar–ROECD currencies exchange rate.

The success of the model for the period 1980–85 is, however, somewhat of an embarrassment for the period after 1985. For if the model explains why the dollar was strong in the early period, can it also explain the subsequent weakness of the dollar? Several possible explanations of the post-1985 recent weakness of the dollar are proposed. A pleasing result of investigating these alternatives is that the effects of the depreciation on the U.S. trade balance are largely independent of the cause of the depreciation, except in the case of a depreciation brought about by expansionary U.S. monetary policy (in which case little trade balance improvement should be expected). The actual reasons for the decline in the dollar after 1985 are no doubt diverse, but casual empiricism points to a combination of three main factors: the anticipated shift to tighter fiscal policy; a decline in private investment demand in the United States (perhaps linked to the 1986 tax reform act); and relatively expansionary U.S. monetary policies. Given this package of causes and the magnitude of the dollar decline that has been observed, it is likely that there will be some improvement in the U.S. trade deficit, but not enough to restore trade balance by the early 1990s.

Appendix: Six-Region World Model

This appendix provides a more detailed description of the analytical structure of the MSG model.[10] Since the structural equations for the four industrialized regions are very similar, only the equations for the United States will be described in detail, while those for the other regions will be discussed only when different from the U.S. equations.

Each of the regions in the model produces a good which is an imperfect substitute in the production and spending decisions of the other regions. Each industrialized region produces one final good which is used for investment and consumption purposes in that region and in all of the other regions. LDC and OPEC each produce one good which is a primary input in the production processes of the industrial regions. Demands for the outputs of LDC and OPEC are therefore derived demands for the production inputs. The United States, Europe, and Canada are also each assumed to produce an exogenous amount of domestic oil, which is a perfect substitute for imports from OPEC.

In the model version in this paper, only the four industrial country regions are fully modelled with an internal macroeconomic structure. In LDC and OPEC, only the foreign trade and external financial aspects are modelled (we are now upgrading the model to include an internal macroeconomic structure for LDC). Note that in referring to variables of the various regions, we will use the following notation: U.S. (U); ROECD (R); Japan (J); Canada (C); OPEC (O); and LDC (L). The currency of the ROECD will be termed *ECU,* though in fact the countries included in the ROECD and in the actual ECU are not exactly the same. All quantities are defined as deviations from potential output that is growing at the exogenous rate α.

Households

Let us consider first the demand side of the model. Total private consumption spending is written as a function of labor income net of labor taxes (τ_L is the labor income tax rate), earnings from domestic oil production, and total nominal financial wealth $P*F$, as in:

$$P^{cU} \, C^U = \beta_{28} \, P^U \, F^U + \beta_{31} \, [W^U L^U \, (1 - \tau_1) - TAX^U + P^O \, OIL^U]$$

This equation is certainly the most problematic of the model. The equation is an ad hoc compromise between alternative conceptions of aggregate consumption, in line with the empirical evidence that consumption is partly determined along life-cycle lines, with some intertemporal consumption smoothing, and partly along simpler Keynesian lines (perhaps because of liquidity-constrained households). Thus, we specify that spending is a fixed proportion of current net-of-tax labor income (with no consumption smoothing of the labor income flow), as in standard Keynesian models, and a fixed proportion of wealth, as in standard life-cycle models with infinite-lived individuals. We are presently experimenting with other specifications of the consumption function.

Once $P^{c}*C$ is determined, it is divided into purchases of the domestic good (C^{dU} and imported final goods (C^{mU}). The division of $P^{c}*C$ is made to maximize an instantaneous utility function of CES form:

$$U^{U} = \log \left[\beta_2 \left(C^{dU}\right)^{\beta_3} + (1 - \beta_2) \left(C^{mU}\right)^{\beta_3} \right]^{(1/\beta_3)}$$

$$\sigma_1^{U} = \frac{1}{1 - \beta_3}.$$

Consumption of imported goods is in turn a CES function of the imports of goods from the ROECD (C_R^{U}), Japan (C_J^{U}) and Canada (C_C^{U}):

$$C^{mU} = \left[\beta_4 \left(C_R^{U}\right)^{\beta_5} + \beta_1 \left(C_J^{U}\right)^{\beta_5} + (1 - \beta_1 - \beta_4) \left(C_C^{U}\right)^{\beta_5} \right]^{(1/\beta_5)}$$

$$\alpha_2^{U} = \frac{1}{1 - \beta_5}$$

The result is demands for home goods and imported goods of the form:

$$C^{dU} = C^{U} \frac{P^{cU}}{P^{U}} \left[\frac{1}{1 + \Omega_1\beta_6} \right] \qquad \beta_6 = \left[\frac{1 - \beta_2}{\beta_2} \right]^{\sigma_1^{U}}$$

$$C^{mU} = C^{U} \frac{P^{cU}}{P^{mU}} \left[\frac{\Omega_1\beta_6}{1 + \Omega_1\beta_6} \right]$$

with:

$$\Omega_1 = \left[\frac{P^{mU}}{P^{U}} \right]^{(1 - \sigma_1^{U})}$$

and:

$$C_R^{U} = C^{mU} \frac{P^{mU}}{E^{R}P^{R}} \left[\frac{1}{1 + \beta_7\Omega_2 + \beta_{27}\Omega_3} \right]$$

$$C_J^U = C^{mU} \frac{P^{mU}}{E^J P^J} \left[\frac{\beta_7 \Omega_2}{1 + \beta_7 \Omega_2 + \beta_{27} \Omega_3} \right]$$

$$C_C^U = C^{mU} \frac{P^{mU}}{E^C P^C} \left[\frac{\beta_{27} \Omega_3}{1 + \beta_7 \Omega_2 + \beta_{27} \Omega_3} \right]$$

where:

$$\beta_7 = \left[\frac{\beta_1}{\beta_4} \right]^{\sigma_2^U} \; ; \; \beta_{27} = \left[\frac{1 - \beta_1 - \beta_4}{\beta_4} \right]^{\sigma_2^U}$$

$$\Omega_2 = \left[\frac{E^J P^J}{E^R P^R} \right]^{(1 - \sigma_2^U)} \; ; \; \Omega_3 = \left[\frac{E^C P^C}{E^R P^r} \right]^{(1 - \sigma_2^U)}$$

The CES price indexes corresponding to these CES utility functions and goods demands are then:

$$P^{cU} = \left[\beta_2^{\sigma_1^U} P^{U(1 - \sigma_1^U)} + \left(1 - \beta_2 \right)^{\sigma_1^U} P^{mU(1 - \sigma_1^U)} \right]^{1/(1 - \sigma_1^U)}$$

$$\text{or } P^{cU} = P^{U\beta_2} P^{mU(1 - \beta_2)} \text{ if } \sigma_1^U = 1$$

$$P^{mU} = \left[\beta_4^{\sigma_2^U} \left(E^R P^R \right)^{(1 - \sigma_2^U)} + \beta_1^{\sigma_2^U} \left(E^J P^J \right)^{(1 - \sigma_2^U)} \right.$$
$$\left. + (1 - \beta_1 - \beta_4)^{\sigma_2^U} \left(E^C P^C \right)^{(1 - \sigma_2^U)} \right]^{(\sigma_2^U - 1)}$$

$$\text{or } P^{mU} = \left(E^R P^R \right)^{\beta_4} \left(E^J P^J \right)^{\beta_1} \left(E^C P^C \right)^{(1 - \beta_1 - \beta_4)} \text{ if } \sigma_2^U = 1$$

The price of imports is derived as follows. U.S. imports from ROECD, Canada, and Japan are invoiced in dollars, according to an equation which makes the invoice price in period $t+1$ equal to the (rationally) expected dollar price of the output of country i in period $t+1$:

$$\left(p_w^i \right)_{t+1} = {}_t p_{t+1}^i + {}_t e_{t+1}^i$$

where $_tx_{t+1}$ signifies the period t rational expectations of variable X at time $t+1$. This equation holds that the (log) price in period $t+1$ of a U.S. import from country i is determined in period t, as the sum of the (log) expected exchange rate and the (log) price of output in country i in period $t+1$. On average, the import price will equal the U.S. dollar price of output in country i. However, if the actual exchange rate of the dollar in period $t+1$ turns out to be stronger (weaker) than expected, the import price in the U.S. market will be higher (lower) than the price of country i output converted at the actual exchange rate.

The United States is in fact the only major market in which import prices are invoiced in the *importer's* currency. In most other markets, the imports are invoiced in the exporter's currency, so that exchange rate changes of the importing country are quickly passed through into import prices. Thus, for all exports of final goods by country i to country k other than the United States, ($k = R, J, C$), the price of imports in country k is given by the contemporaneous P^i multiplied by E^k, the contemporaneous exchange rate between the dollar and currency k.

We also assume that the government divides spending G among the final goods in the same proportion as does the private sector (this assumption is for convenience only and can easily be altered), so that:

$$G_i^U / G^U = C_i^U / C^U \quad \text{for } i = C, R, J$$

Firms

The cornerstone of aggregate supply in the model is a representative firm which maximizes income by producing a single output Q at price P, subject to a two-input production function (for simplicity, potential growth is ignored in the equations that follow, even though a constant underlying potential growth rate of 4 percent is included in the model). Thus, the aggregate gross output equation is given as a Cobb-Douglas function of labor (L), capital (K) and primary imported inputs (N):

$$Q^U = \beta_{19} \left(L^U\right)^{\beta_8} \left(K^U\right)^{\beta_9} \left(N^U\right)^{\beta_{10}}$$

Gross output Q is produced with value added V and primary inputs N. In turn, V is produced with capital K and labor L, while N is produced with the imports from OPEC (net of domestic oil production) N_O and the LDCs N_L according to a CES function:

$$N^U = \left[\beta_{12}\left(N_O^U\right)^{\beta_{13}} + (1-\beta_{12})\left(N_L^U\right)^{\beta_{13}} \right]^{(1/\beta_{13})} \qquad \sigma_4^U = \frac{1}{1 - \beta_{13}}$$

The capital stock changes according to the rate of fixed capital formation J^U and the rate of geometric depreciation δ:

$$K_{t+1}^U = (J_t^U + (1-\delta) K_t^U) / (1 + \alpha)$$

J is itself a composite good, produced with a Cobb-Douglas technology that has as inputs the domestic goods and the final goods of Canada, Europe, and Japan:

$$J^U = J_U^{U^{\beta_{16}}} \left(J^J\right)^{\beta_{17}} \left(J^R\right)^{\beta_{18}} \left(J^C\right)^{(1-\beta_{16}-\beta_{17}-\beta_{18})}$$

Then the price of J^U is simply a weighted average of the prices of the home goods P (P^U for the U.S.) and the dollar import prices of goods from the other OECD regions:

$$P^{JU} = P^{U^{\beta_{16}}} \left(E^J P^J\right)^{\beta_{17}} \left(E^R P^R\right)^{\beta_{18}} \left(E^C P^C\right)^{(1-\beta_{16}-\beta_{17}-\beta_{18})}$$

Import demands for investment goods from each region are then derived as:

$$J_R^U = \beta_{18} J^U / \Lambda^R$$
$$J_J^U = \beta_{17} J^U / \Lambda^J$$
$$J_C^U = (1 - \beta_{16} - \beta_{17} - \beta_{18}) J^U / \Lambda^C$$

As is customary in modern models of investment, it is assumed that the investment process is subject to rising marginal costs of installation, with total nominal investment expenditures P^J*I equal to the value of direct purchases of investment P^J*J, plus the per unit costs of installation. These per unit costs, in turn, are assumed to be a linear function of the rate of investment J/K, so that adjustment costs are $P^J*J \left[(\beta_{15}/2)(J/K)\right]$. Total investment expenditure is therefore:

$$P^{JU} I^U = P^{JU} J^U [1 + (\beta_{15}/2) J^U / K^U]$$

The goal of the firm is to choose inputs of L, N, and J to maximize intertemporal net-of-tax profits. In fact, the firm faces a stochastic problem, a point which is ignored in the derivation of the firm's behavior (in other words, the firm is assumed to hold its estimates of future variables with subjective certainty). The firm's deterministic problem, formally stated, is:

$$\max \sum_{\tau=t}^{\infty} (1+R_\tau)^{-1} [Q^U - (W^U/P^U) L^U$$
$$- (P^{nU}/P^U) N^U - (P^{JU}/P^U) I^U]$$

where $(1+R_\tau)^{-1}$ is a discount factor equal to:

$$\prod_{i=t}^{\tau} (1 + r_i)^{-1} (1 + \alpha)$$

and r_i is the period i short-term real interest rate and α is the real growth factor.

The solution to the firm's problem is well known (see Bruno and Sachs 1985, as an example). There are three key points. First, inputs of L and N are purchased up to the level where marginal productivities of these factors equal their factor prices. This leads to equations for the derived demand for L and N of the form:

$$L^U = \beta_8 \left[\frac{P^U Q^U}{W^U} \right]$$

$$N^U = \beta_{10} \left[\frac{P^U Q^U}{P^{nU}} \right]$$

$$N_O^U = \left[\beta_{12} \frac{P^{nU} N^U}{P^O} \right]^{\sigma_4^U} - OIL^U$$

$$N_L^U = \left[(1 - \beta_{12}) \frac{P^{nU} N^u}{P^L} \right]^{\sigma_4^U}$$

where OIL^U is the domestic production of oil.

The price index for imported inputs is then:

$$P^{nU} = \left[\beta_{12}{}^{\sigma_4^U} \left(P^O\right)^{(1-\sigma_4^U)} + (1 - \beta_{12})^{\sigma_4^U} \left(P^L\right)^{(1-\sigma_4^U)} \right]^{1/(1-\sigma_4^U)}$$

or $P^{nU} = (P^O)^{\beta_{12}} (P^L)^{(1-\beta_{12})}$ if $\sigma_4^U = 1$

Gross fixed capital formation can be written in terms of Tobin's "marginal" q, in the following manner:

$$J^U = \beta_{29} \left[(q^U - 1)/ \beta_{15}\right] K^U$$

Third, the equation of motion of q (the shadow value of investment) is given by:

$$q_{t+1}^U = (1 + r_t^U + \beta_{14})q_t^U - \frac{\partial Q^U}{\partial K^U}(1 - \tau_2) - \frac{P^{JU}}{P^U}(0.5\beta_{15}) \left(J_t^U/K_t^U\right)^2$$

where the marginal product of capital is:

$$\frac{\partial Q^U}{\partial K^U} = \beta_9 \left[\frac{Q^U}{K^U} \right]$$

Then, q equals the discounted value of future profits, with q given by:

$$q^U / P^{JU} = \sum_{\tau=t}^{\infty} (1 + R_\tau)^{-1} \left(\frac{\partial Q^U}{\partial K^U} + \Phi_k^U \right)$$

Here Φ_k^U is the marginal product of capital in reducing adjustment costs in investment.

In the specific application in the model, the gross output production function is taken to be a two-level CES function in V and N, with V a Cobb-Douglas function of L and K, and N a CES function of oil and non-oil primary inputs. The investment function derived above is also modified, for empirical realism, by writing J as a function not only of q, but also of the level of flow capital income at time t and the change in the level of gross output along standard investment accelerator lines. The modified investment equation is of the form:

$$J^U = \beta_{29} (q^U - 1) \frac{1}{\beta_{15}} K^U + (1 - \beta_{29}) \left\{ Q^U - W^U L^U / P^U - P^{nU} / P^n \right\} +$$
$$\beta_{32} (Q_t - Q_{t-1})$$

For the primary goods of OPEC and the LDCs, there is a single uniform world price of goods which applies in all markets at all times (i.e., the law of one price holds). Letting P^O be the *dollar* price of OPEC goods, we assume that P^O is a variable markup over a basket of OECD goods, so that:

$$P^O = \left(P^U\right)^{\gamma_1} \left(P^R E^R\right)^{\gamma_2} \left(P^J E^J\right)^{\gamma_3} \left(P^C E^C\right)^{\gamma_4} \left(P^L\right)^{(1 - \gamma_1 - \gamma_2 - \gamma_3 - \gamma_4)}$$
$$\left(C_O^U + C_O^R + C_O^O + C_O^J + C_O^C\right)^{\gamma_5}$$

Note that E^i is in units of dollars per unit of currency i. The pricing function is linear homogenous and increasing in the prices of the OECD goods. The bracketed function makes the OPEC markup an increasing function of the total demand for OPEC exports to the other regions. A similar equation governs the price of LDC commodities:

$$P^L = \left(P^U\right)^{\mu_1} \left(P^R E^R\right)^{\mu_2} \left(P^J E^J\right)^{\mu_3} \left(P^C E^C\right)^{\mu_{s4}} \left(P^O\right)^{(1 - \mu_1 - \mu_2 - \mu_3 - \mu_4)}$$
$$\left(C_L^U + C_L^R + C_L^O + C_L^J + C_L^C\right)^{\mu_5}$$

The supply side of the U.S. block of the model is completed with the wage equation, which makes the nominal wage change a function of past consumer price (p^c) changes, rationally expected future price changes, and the level of unemployment in the economy, according to a standard Phillips curve mechanism:

$$w_{t+1}^U = w_t^U + \beta_{25} \left(_t p_{t+1}^{cU} - p_t^{cU}\right) +$$
$$(1 - \beta_{25})(p_t^{cU} - p_{t-1}^{cU}) + .1(L_t^U - L^f)$$

where $w = \log W$; $p^c = \log P^c$; and where L^f represents the inelastically supplied full-employment stock of labor. The parameter β_{25} determines how much weight is given to backward-looking versus forward-looking price expectations.

As already noted, we allow for differences in the wage dynamics of the different regions. In Japan, we specify that wages are set one period ahead at their expected *market clearing* levels. Thus, let $(_tw_{t+1})^f$ be the wage expected to clear the labor market at time $t+1$, in the sense that $_tL_{t+1} = L^f$. Then:

$$w^J_{t+1} = (_tw^J_{t+1})^f$$

Asset Markets and Balance of Payments

The rest of the model can be now be stated. Prices in the United States (and the other OECD regions) are fully flexible within each period, so that demand for U.S. output (domestic demand plus export demand) equals output supply. Money demand equations are specified for each OECD region in a standard Goldfeld-type transactions demand equation:

$$m^U - p^U = \sigma_6 Q^U - \sigma_7 i^U$$

where $m^U = \log M^U$, and $p^U = \log P^U$.

Asset markets are assumed to be perfectly integrated across the OECD regions. Expected returns of loans denominated in the currencies of the various regions are equalized period to period, according to the following interest arbitrage relations:

$$i^i_t = i^j_t + _t(e^i_j)_{t+1} - e^i_{jt}$$

Thus, we do not allow for risk premia on the assets of alternative currencies. We choose the assumption of perfect capital mobility and zero risk premia in light of the failure of the empirical exchange rate literature to demonstrate the existence of stable risk premia across international currencies.

For the United States, Canada, Japan, ROECD, and OPEC, the current account is determined under the assumption that domestic agents have free unrationed access to international borrowing and lending at the international interest rate. It is assumed for simplicity that all international borrowing and lending take place in dollar-denominated assets. The U.S. trade balance and current account are then defined as:

$$TB^U = C^R_U + C^J_U + C^L_U + C^O_U + C^C_U + I^R_U + I^J_U + I^C_U -$$
$$\Lambda^R(C^U_R + I^U_R) - \Lambda^J(C^U_J + I^U_J) - \Lambda^C(C^U_C + I^U_C) - \Lambda^O N^U_O -$$
$$\Lambda^L N^U_L$$
$$CA^U = TB^U + r^U(A^U_L - A^P_U - A^R_U - A^J_U - A^C_U)$$

where A^i_j is a claim by country i against country j and where the real exchange rates of the U.S. dollar are defined as:

$$\Lambda^R = P^R E^R / P^U$$
$$\Lambda^J = P^J E^J / P^U$$
$$\Lambda^C = P^C E^C / P^U$$
$$\Lambda^L = P^L / P^U$$
$$\Lambda^O = P^O / P^U$$

Real GNP is defined as gross output minus the input of primary goods plus domestic oil income and interest payments on net foreign assets:

$$Y^U = Q^U - \frac{P^{nU}}{P^U} N^U + \frac{P^O}{P^U} OIL^U + r^U (B^U + A_L^U - A_U^R - A_U^J - A_U^O - A_U^C)$$

Real financial wealth is the sum of public debt, net foreign assets, value of the equity, and real money balances:

$$F^U = B^U + A_L^U - A_U^R - A_U^O - A_U^J - A_U^C + q^U K^U + (M^U / P^U)$$

The expectations hypothesis on the relation between short- and long-term interest rates is described by:

$$r_t^U = R_t^U - \left({}_t R_{t+1}^U - R_t^U \right) / R_t^U$$

and the nominal interest rate is equal to the sum of the real interest rate and the inflation rate:

$$i_t^U = r_t^U + \Pi_t^U$$
$$\Pi_t^U = \left(P_{t+1}^U - P_t^U \right) / P_t^U$$
$$\Pi_t^{cU} = \left(P_{t+1}^{cU} - P_t^{cU} \right) / P_t^{cU}$$

Government Sector

A final set of equations for the United States represents the behavior of the government sector. The public sector deficit is equal to government expenditures plus interest payment on the public debt minus taxes:

$$DEF^U = G^U + r^U B^U - T^U$$

Taxes are the sum of an autonomous component, labor income taxes and corporate taxes:

$$T^U = TAX^U + \tau_1 \frac{W^U L^U}{P^U} + \tau_2 \left(Q^U - \frac{W^U L^U}{P^U} - \frac{P^{nu} N^U}{P^U} \right)$$

and autonomous taxes are equal to interest on debt and an exogenous lump-sum component:

$$TAX^U = r^U B^U + TAXE^U$$

Public debt grows according to the following accumulation equation:

$$B^U_{t+1} = (B^U_t + DEF^U_t) / (1 + \alpha)$$

LDC Equations

The LDC bloc imports final goods from the OECD countries and oil from OPEC. The value of total LDC imports is divided between expenditures on U.S., ROECD, Japanese, Canadian, and OPEC goods on the basis of constant expenditure shares (μ's) (i.e., Cobb-Douglas utility) so that:

$$C^L_U = \mu_1 \left(C^L_U + \Lambda^R C^L_R + \Lambda^O C^L_O + \Lambda^J C^L_J + \Lambda^C C^L_C \right)$$

$$C^L_R = \mu_2 \left(C^L_U + \Lambda^R C^L_R + \Lambda^O C^L_O + \Lambda^J C^L_J + \Lambda^C C^L_C \right) / \Lambda^R$$

$$C^L_J = \mu_3 \left(C^L_U + \Lambda^R C^L_R + \Lambda^O C^L_O + \Lambda^J C^L_J + \Lambda^C C^L_C \right) / \Lambda^J$$

$$C^L_C = \mu_4 \left(C^L_U + \Lambda^R C^L_R + \Lambda^O C^L_O + \Lambda^J C^L_J + \Lambda^C C^L_C \right) / \Lambda^C$$

$$C^L_O = (1 - \mu_1 - \mu_2 - \mu_3 - \mu_4) \left(C^L_U + \Lambda^R C^L_R + \right.$$
$$\left. \Lambda^O C^L_O + \Lambda^J C^L_J + \Lambda^C C^L_c \right) / \Lambda^O$$

and the LDC trade balance is therefore defined as:

$$TB^L = \Lambda^L \left(C^U_L + C^R_L + C^O_L + C^J_L + C^C_L \right) - C_L U -$$
$$\Lambda^R C^L_R - \Lambda^O C^L_O - \Lambda^J C^L_J - \Lambda^C C^L_C$$

For the LDCs, in distinction, the scale of borrowing is set *exogenously* under the assumption that the amount of loans available to the LDCs is rationed by country-risk considerations.

$$CA_t^L = \overline{CA}$$

The LDC external debt is then defined as:

$$DEBT = A_L^U + A_L^R \Lambda^R + A_L^O + A_L^J \Lambda^J + A_L^C \Lambda^C$$

and the equations of motions of the components of the LDC debt (A_j^i's) are then:

$$A_{Lt+1}^i \Lambda_t^i = \mu_j \left[\left(A_{Lt+1}^U + A_{Lt+1}^R \Lambda_t^R + A_{Lt+1}^O + A_{Lt+1}^J \Lambda_t^J + A_{Lt+1}^C \Lambda_t^C \right) \right.$$
$$\left. - \left(A_{Lt}^U + A_{Lt}^R \Lambda_t^R + A_{Lt}^O + A_{Jt}^J \Lambda_t^J + A_{Lt}^C \Lambda_t^C \right)(1-\alpha) \right] + A_{Lt}^i \Lambda_t^i (1-\alpha)$$

with $i = R, O, J, C$ and $j = 8, 9, 10, 11$ and:

$$A_{Lt+1}^U = -CA_t^L - \left[\left(A_{Lt+1}^J \Lambda_t^J + A_{Lt+1}^C \Lambda_t^C + A_{Lt+1}^R \Lambda_t^R + A_{Lt+1}^O \right) \right] +$$
$$\left(A_{Lt}^U + A_{Jt}^J \Lambda_t^J + A_{Lt}^C \Lambda_t^C + A_{Lt}^R \Lambda_t^R + A_{Lt}^O \right)(1 - \alpha)$$

Here the μ_j coefficients represent the share of the LDC current account financing undertaken by each region.

OPEC Equations

The import demand equations for the OPEC area are similar to the LDC ones:

$$C_U^O = \gamma_1 \left(C_U^O + \Lambda^R C_R^O + \Lambda^L C_L^O + \Lambda^J C_J^O + \Lambda^C C_C^O \right)$$

$$C_R^O = \gamma_2 \left(C_U^O + \Lambda^R C_R^O + \Lambda^L C_L^O + \Lambda^J C_J^O + \Lambda^C C_C^O \right) / \Lambda^R$$

$$C_J^O = \gamma_3 \left(C_U^O + \Lambda^R C_R^O + \Lambda^L C_L^O + \Lambda^J C_J^O + \Lambda^C C_C^O \right) / \Lambda^J$$

$$C_C^O = \gamma_4 \left(C_U^O + \Lambda^R C_R^O + \Lambda^L C_L^O + \Lambda^J C_J^O + \Lambda^C C_C^O \right) / \Lambda^C$$

$$C_L^O = (1 - \gamma_1 - \gamma_2 - \gamma_3 - \gamma_4) \left(C_U^O + \Lambda^R C_R^O + \right.$$
$$\left. \Lambda^L C_L^O + \Lambda^J C_J^O + \Lambda^C C_C^O \right) / \Lambda^L$$

OPEC total wealth is the sum of the assets held by the region against the rest of the world:

$$H^O = A_U^O + A_R^O + A_L^O + A_J^O \Lambda^J$$

The trade balance and current account of the OPEC area are defined as:

$$TB^O = \Lambda^O \left(C_O^U + C_O^R + C_O^L + C_O^J + C_O^C \right) - C_U^O - \Lambda^R C_R^O - \Lambda^L C_L^O - \Lambda^J C_J^O - \Lambda^C C_C^O$$

and:

$$CA_t^O = \gamma_5 \left[\gamma_6 \left(C_{Ot}^U + C_{Ot}^R + C_{Ot}^L + C_{Ot}^J + C_{Ot}^C \right) \left(P_t^O / P_t^U \right) - H_{t-1}^O \right] + \alpha H_{t-1}^O$$

The accumulation equations for OPEC foreign assets are:

$$A_{Ut+1}^O = CA_t^O - \left(A_{Rt+1}^O \Lambda_t^R + A_{Lt+1}^O + A_{Jt+1}^O \Lambda_t^J + A_{Ct+1}^O \Lambda_t^C \right) + \left(A_U^O + A_{Rt}^O \Lambda_t^R + A_{Lt}^O + A_{Jt}^O \Lambda_t^J + A_{Ct}^O \Lambda_t^C \right)$$

$$A_{it+1}^O \Lambda_t^i = \gamma_j \left[A_{Ut+1}^O + A_{Rt+1}^O \Lambda_t^R + A_{Lt+1}^O + A_{Jt+1}^O \Lambda_t^J + A_{Ct+1}^O \Lambda_t^C \right) - \left(A_{Ut}^O + A_{Rt}^O \Lambda_t^R + A_{Lt}^O + A_{Jt}^O \Lambda_t^O + A_{Ct}^O \Lambda_t^C \right) (1 - \alpha) \right] + A_{it}^O \Lambda_t^i (1 - \alpha)$$

with $i = R, J, C$ and $j = 7, 8, 9$. Here the γ_j coefficients represent the share of the OPEC current account surpluses invested in the assets of each region.

The model is parameterized using estimates of behavioral and technological parameters from the econometric literature. Thus, elasticities of demand for home and foreign goods, the elasticities of demand for money balances, the factor shares in the production function, etc., are taken from other studies. The only real calibration that takes place using actual data is in the trade bloc, where the free parameters of the utility function are selected to reproduce the patterns of trade among the various industrial regions as of

1986. Thus, by choice of utility function parameters, the baseline of the model exactly reproduces the direction of trade among the various regions in the first half of 1986. Choosing 1986 as the basis for linearization is of course a bit problematic for simulations of the 1981–86 period, but we chose to use the 1986 base to give a better picture here of the *current* policy multipliers.

Variable Definitions

A_i^j real claims by country j against country i

B real government debt

B_i^j real concessional claims by country j against country i

C real consumption of goods

C^d real consumption of domestic goods

C^m real consumption of imported goods

C_j^i consumption by country i of country j good

CA current account balance

$DEBT$ LDC debt

DEF real budget deficit

E nominal exchange rate ($/ECU)

F real financial wealth

G real government expenditure on goods

H real human wealth

$HOPEC$ net asset position of OPEC

i short nominal interest rate

I nominal investment expenditure inclusive of adjustment costs

I_j^i demand for country j good for investment in country j

J gross fixed capital formation

K capital stock

L demand for labor

M nominal money supply

N basket of intermediate inputs used in production

N_j^i import of country j good used as intermediate input in i

P price of domestic goods

P^m price of imported goods

P^c price of a basket of imported and domestic goods

P^I price of investment goods

P^n price of intermediate goods

Π product price inflation

Π^c consumer price inflation

Q real gross output

q Tobin's q

R long real interest rate

      r short real interest rate
      T total nominal tax receipts
    TAX lump sum tax on households
   $TAXE$ exogenous tax
     TB trade balance
      v short real concessional interest rate on LDC debt
     W nominal wage
     α growth rate of population plus labor-augmenting technical change
     τ_1 tax rate on household income
     τ_2 tax rate on corporate profits
     σ_1 elasticity of substitution between domestic and imported goods
     σ_3 elasticity of substitution between capital and labor
    Λ^R real exchange rate (relative price of ROECD goods)
    Λ^J real exchange rate (relative price of Japanese goods)
    Λ^L real exchange rate (relative price of LDC goods)
    Λ^O real exchange rate (relative price of OPEC goods)

Parameters

$\alpha = 0.040$

US.

$\beta1 = 0.332$	$\beta12 = 0.202$	$\beta23 = 0.089$
$\beta2 = 0.931$	$\beta13 = 0.000$	$\beta24 = 0.000$
$\beta3 = 0.000$	$\beta14 = 0.083$	$\beta25 = 0.250$
$\beta4 = 0.355$	$\beta15 = 8.000$	$\beta26 = 0.000$
$\beta5 = 0.471$	$\beta16 = 0.933$	$\beta27 = 0.785$
$\beta6 = 0.074$	$\beta17 = 0.022$	$\beta28 = 0.050$
$\beta7 = 0.881$	$\beta18 = 0.025$	$\beta29 = 0.200$
$\beta8 = 0.706$	$\beta19 = 1.429$	$\beta30 = 0.000$
$\beta9 = 0.263$	$\beta20 = 1.000$	$\beta31 = 0.850$
$\beta10 = 0.031$	$\beta21 = 0.000$	$\beta32 = 0.250$
$\beta11 = -9.000$	$\beta22 = 1.000$	
$\tau1 = 0.350$	$\tau2 = 0.000$	$\tau3 = 0.000$
$\sigma1 = 1.000$	$\sigma4 = 1.000$	$\sigma7 = 0.600$
$\sigma2 = 1.891$	$\sigma5 = 1.000$	$\theta = 0.080$
$\sigma3 = 0.100$	$\sigma6 = 1.000$	

ROECD

$\beta1 = 0.354$	$\beta12 = 0.318$	$\beta23 = 0.070$
$\beta2 = 0.936$	$\beta13 = 0.000$	$\beta24 = 0.000$
$\beta3 = 0.000$	$\beta14 = 0.077$	$\beta25 = 0.500$
$\beta4 = 0.463$	$\beta15 = 8.000$	$\beta26 = 0.000$
$\beta5 = 0.285$	$\beta16 = 0.934$	$\beta27 = 0.274$
$\beta6 = 0.069$	$\beta17 = 0.023$	$\beta28 = 0.050$
$\beta7 = 0.688$	$\beta18 = 0.034$	$\beta29 = 0.200$

β8 = 0.697   β19 = 1.506   β30 = 0.000
β9 = 0.251   β20 = 1.000   β31 = 0.850
β10 = 0.052   β21 = 0.000   β32 = 0.250
β11 = −9.000   β22 = 1.000
τ1 = 0.350   τ2 = 0.000   τ3 = 0.000
σ1 = 1.000   σ4 = 1.000   σ7 = 0.600
σ2 = 1.399   σ5 = 1.000   θ   = 0.080
σ3 = 0.100   σ6 = 1.000

Japan

β1 = 0.473   β12 = 0.546   β23 = 0.031
β2 = 0.950   β13 = 0.000   β24 = 0.000
β3 = 0.000   β14 = 0.095   β25 = 0.500
β4 = 0.423   β15 = 8.000   β26 = 0.000
β5 = 0.146   β16 = 0.950   β27 = 0.195
β6 = 0.052   β17 = 0.023   β28 = 0.050
β7 = 1.139   β18 = 0.027   β29 = 0.200
β8 = 0.652   β19 = 1.558   β30 = 0.000
β9 = 0.292   β20 = 1.000   β31 = 0.850
β10 = 0.055   β21 = 0.000   β32 = 0.250
β11 = −9.000   β22 = 1.000
τ1 = 0.350   τ2 = 0.000   τ3 = 0.000
σ1 = 1.000   σ4 = 1.000   σ7 = 0.600
σ2 = 1.171   σ5 = 1.000   θ   = 0.080
σ3 = 0.100   σ6 = 1.000

Canada

β1 = 0.303   β12 = 0.229   β23 = 0.008
β2 = 0.760   β13 = 0.000   β24 = 0.000
β3 = 0.000   β14 = 0.055   β25 = 0.500
β4 = 0.324   β15 = 8.000   β26 = 0.000
β5 = 0.912   β16 = 0.644   β27 = 4.800
β6 = 0.316   β17 = 0.273   β28 = 0.050
β7 = 0.461   β18 = 0.057   β29 = 0.200
β8 = 0.776   β19 = 1.329   β30 = 0.000
β9 = 0.203   β20 = 1.000   β31 = 0.850
β10 = 0.022   β21 = 0.000   β32 = 0.250
β11 = −9.000   β22 = 1.000
τ1 = 0.350   τ2 = 0.000   τ3 = 0.000
σ1 = 1.000   σ4 = 1.000   σ7 = 0.600
σ2 = 11.410   σ5 = 1.000   θ   = 0.080
σ3 = 0.100   σ6 = 1.000

Notes

1. As of May 1987, the Gephardt Amendment was included in the Omnibus Trade Bill approved by the U.S. House of Representatives. The trade legislation has since come under consideration by a joint conference of the U.S. Senate and House of Representatives. The president has stated that he will veto a trade bill that includes the Gephardt Amendment in its current form.

2. A detailed description of the new version of the model is available in McKibbin and Sachs (1988a). Previous versions are presented in McKibbin and Sachs (1988b) and Ishii, McKibbin, and Sachs (1986).

3. See Sachs and Roubini (1987) for further details on the material in sections 11.2 and 11.3.

4. A more detailed description of the equations and structure of the model is given in the appendix below.

5. In general, quantity variables are linearized around their levels relative to potential GNP, while for price variables, the linearization is in log levels.

6. Specifically, the bilateral real exchange rate of the U.S. and country i is $P^i E^i / P^U$ where:

P^i is the price of the good produced in country i in country i currency;

E^i is the nominal exchange rate of the dollar relative to the currency of country i (dollars per units of foreign currency); and

P^U is the dollar price of the good produced in the U.S.

7. The assumption made in the model about the dollar pricing by foreign exporters to the U.S. markets also helps to account for the smaller first period pass-through effect to prices of a U.S. dollar devaluation.

8. See Sachs and Roubini (1987, table 11) for a simulation analysis of an exogenous decline in lending to the LDCs. In the period under investigation, the current account balance of the market-borrowing LDCs was as follows (in billions of dollars; percent of U.S. GNP in parentheses): 1978, -33.2 (-1.5); 1979, -49.7 (-2.0); 1980, -74.4 (-2.8); and 1985, 28.7 ($+0.7$). The average deficit during 1978–80 was 2.1 percent of U.S. GNP, so that the shift from 1978–80 to 1985 was on the order of 1.4 percent of U.S. GNP.

9. In the exercises, the improvement is immediate, though in practice, depending on the mix of actual versus anticipated shocks and depending on various adjustment lags, the trade balance improvements might arise over several years.

10. This appendix draws on and expands upon the description of the model in Sachs and Roubini (1987).

References

Atkinson, Paul, and Jean-Claude Chouraqui. 1985. The origins of high real interest rates. *OECD Economic Studies* Autumn: 7–56.

Bruno, Michael, and Jeffrey D. Sachs. 1985. *Economics of worldwide stagflation.* Cambridge, Mass.: Harvard University Press.

Dornbusch, Rudiger. 1987. Exchange rates and prices. *American Economic Review* 77 (March): 93–106.

Hayashi, Fumio. 1983. Tobin's marginal q and average q: A neoclassical interpretation. *Econometrica* 50:213–23.

Ishii, Naoko, Warwick McKibbin, and Jeffrey D. Sachs. 1986. The economic policy mix, policy cooperation and protectionism: Some aspects of macroeconomic interdependence among the United States, Japan, and other OECD countries. *Journal of Policy Modelling* 7:533–72.

Krugman, Paul. 1986. Pricing to market when exchange rates change. National Bureau of Economic Research Working Paper no. 1927. Cambridge, Mass.: NBER.

McKibbin, Warwick, and Jeffrey D. Sachs. 1988a. An introduction to the MSG2 model. Mimeo, Harvard University.

———. 1988b. Coordination of monetary and fiscal policies in the industrial economies. In *International aspects of fiscal policy,* ed. Jacob A. Frenkel. Chicago: University of Chicago Press.

Oudiz, Gilles, and Jeffrey D. Sachs. 1984. Macroeconomic policy coordination among the industrial economies. *Brookings Papers on Economic Activity* 1:1–64.

Sachs, Jeffrey D. 1985. The dollar and the policy mix: 1985. *Brookings Papers on Economic Activity* 1:117–85.

Sachs, Jeffrey D., and Nouriel Roubini. 1987. Sources of macroeconomic imbalances in the world economy: A simulation approach. Presented at the conference "Toward a World of Economic Stability: Optimal Monetary Framework and Policy," Tokyo, Japan, June.

Comment

Edwin M. Truman

The academic-turned-central-banker who reads papers such as that by McKibbin, Roubini, and Sachs (MRS) hopes to learn something useful about the causes of international imbalances in the 1980s and the prospects for correcting them. That person necessarily applies a more pragmatic test to the results of such papers than would the academic because of a closer proximity to the real world in the sense that the questions asked are: Is this a plausibly accurate representation of a familiar phenomenon? What lies behind a particular result? What makes me willing to believe the conclusions?

I cannot avoid this perspective. I like the paper, and the results are worthy of consideration, but I believe the authors are too glib in claiming useful policy insights. They assume a largely hypothetical, but internally consistent, structure of the world economy. The hypothetical world is simulated and various inferences are drawn from the results. However, before one takes the analysis too seriously one has to decide what one thinks about an approach that is based upon a simulation model that relies on assumed coefficients. On the one hand, the model (MSG2) is theoretically elegant, but by taking coefficients "off the shelf" the researchers release themselves from a critical constraint; their model does not have to be consistent with the underlying data. The methodological issue is whether a simulation model of this type can be useful in conducting what are essentially hypothesis tests. Even if the model fits the facts, we have no way to judge whether it is the only model that can do so. For example, a property of the MRS model is the "rule of thumb" that each 10 percent depreciation of the dollar leads to an improvement in the U.S. trade balance of 0.75 percent of GNP, but how "confident" can one be in those results?

Moreover, when one buys into the MRS results, one buys into their framework which they describe as solving "for a full intertemporal equilibrium in which agents have rational expectations of future variables." Such a framework has a certain appeal, but as applied it necessarily influences the results in ways that are not consistent with the real world observations. For example, the simulation of the 1981–85 period in effect starts from "equilibrium" in 1980. As such, it fails to recognize that the policies and problems of the 1980s are in large part the legacy of the problems and policy failures of the 1970s. Any analysis that does not connect the international imbalances of the 1980s with the domestic instabilities of the 1970s is fundamentally incomplete. To compound this shortcoming, the simulation presented to "explain" the appreciation of the dollar during 1981–85 by divergent fiscal policies within the OECD group of countries assumes, contrary to fact, that monetary policy held unemployment unchanged. As a consequence of these defects, the simulation fails to take account of the protracted deflationary process that prevailed in these years as evidenced by the sustained declines in the prices of petroleum and other commodities.

The staff at the Federal Reserve draws upon its Multi-Country Model (MCM) to examine these kinds of issues. The MCM differs from the MSG2 in three important respects: (1) the MCM is not solved with forward-looking expectations; (2) the parameters in the MCM are estimated and not imposed; and (3) the MCM is more highly disaggregated. I believe it is useful to compare the MCM's results with the MSG2 results, not because they are necessarily closer to the truth, but because they are different and, I would submit, equally plausible as a basis for policy advice. As a consequence, I would be inclined to caution policymakers against relying heavily on some of the rather dogmatic conclusions found in MRS.

In the MCM, the effects of a U.S. fiscal expansion are larger and more persistent than in MSG2, both at home and abroad. Moreover, in the MCM the effects of a U.S. fiscal expansion on real GNPs abroad are generally positive, not negative, contrary to the MSG2 result that shows positive effects only for Canada. The MSG2 result is a consequence of the MRS parameterization of their model. One might expect for a result as crucial as this that MRS would spend more time justifying their parameterization, especially in an area where the signs of effects are ambiguous as MRS acknowledge. As it is presented, their result and their policy conclusions have limited credibility.

In the MCM, the effects on the United States of a Japanese fiscal expansion are small and relatively transient, but they are an order of magnitude larger than in the MSG2. I would also note that the MSG2 apparently produces a rather large impact of a fiscal expansion on Japanese trade with developing countries, and it is a bit mysterious why this does not feed back to improve the external accounts of the United States and Canada.

MCM simulations do not confirm the MSG2 result that the spillover effects of monetary policy are trivial; this is especially true for U.S. monetary policy (see Edison and Tryon, 1986, for details). This is an example of where MRS link their simulation results with a few stylized facts and come up with a rather strong conclusion, "The Fed must not 'target' the trade balance with monetary policy, since a money expansion by itself can do nothing to improve the trade balance." The simulation result is a so-called "robust result" that monetary policy in each region can be pursued independently without spillover effects on the trade balance and level of economic activity of the region.

This results has two aspects. The first aspect is that the direct effect of the dollar's depreciation on the U.S. trade balance as a consequence of a U.S. monetary expansion is offset by the expansionary effects of lower interest rates on U.S. domestic demand and by an eventual rise in inflation. This result is not shared by the MCM. Moreover, one wonders why MRS focus on the trade balance rather than the current account balance. Indeed, one shortcoming of the MSG2 model is that it has an incomplete capital account abstracting from direct investment stocks and flows. Consequently, it fails to pick up in the current account the important positive effect (for the United States) of depreciation on inflows of direct investment income.

The second aspect of the simulation is that while a U.S. monetary expansion depreciates the dollar, which tends to reduce aggregate demand abroad, it also reduces real interest rates abroad which tends to stimulate aggregate demand. On the one hand, this aspect appears to contradict the first—that the U.S. trade balance does not improve. On the other hand, it is a knife-edge conclusion, and it is difficult to imagine in what sense it should be regarded as robust.

Finally, in their policy analysis, MRS put forward a simplistic characterization of U.S. monetary policy. They present data on growth rates for M1 and conclude that U.S. policy was relatively expansionary in 1986, while ignoring the well-known fact that dollar interest rates declined in that year and the interest elasticity of U.S. M1 has increased markedly in recent years relative to that abroad.

I have already noted my uneasiness about the MRS treatment of monetary policy and commodity prices in the simulation of the period 1981–85. My final comment on the MRS paper involves the simulation for the period up to 1992 under the influence of Gramm-Rudman-Hollings (GRH). The specification of this simulation seems a bit odd. If I understand the structure of the model, it is assumed in effect that the long-run government budget constraint holds, and private agents know this fact. Therefore, I wonder what it means to simulate GRH by itself, especially when agents must have assumed all along that something like GRH would occur.

In conclusion, I regret to say that the MRS paper does not provide much guidance on how to protect ourselves from international imbalances in the future. The authors would have a more useful and responsible product if they spent a bit more time digging into the reasons for their results and less time preaching about policy.

Reference

Edison, Hali, and Ralph Tryon. 1986. An empirical analysis of policy coordination in the United States, Japan, and Europe. Board of Governors of the Federal Reserve System, International Finance Discussion Paper no. 286, July.

Comment
Koichi Hamada

This paper begins by pointing out large swings in trade balances and exchange rates in the industrial countries. These swings are, as the authors observe, often attributed to the divergent macroeconomic policies of the United States, Japan, and other industrial countries, in particular, divergent fiscal policies. This paper introduces a new version of the McKibbin-Sachs Global (MSG) model and attempts to determine by way of simulation if this conventional view is right.

Their results can be briefly summarized as follows. Sustained fiscal expansion by increasing expenditures of the United States, Japan, or Canada increases domestic income and deteriorates the trade balance. The positive transmission effect through depreciation of foreign currencies can be partly or more than fully offset by rising world interest rates. In their simulation, this transmission effect is generally positive for Canada. For Japan and the rest of the OECD countries, however, it starts out being positive in the first year and becomes negative in later years. The Japanese fiscal expansion raises output, appreciates the yen, and worsens the trade balance. After the first year, it has a negative effect on the other economies through investment reduction due to the increase in Tobin's q. Because of the openness of Canada, its fiscal expansion deteriorates its own trade balance much more than that of other countries. On the other hand, fiscal expansion in Canada has a negligible effect on other countries because the scale of the Canadian economy is small.

A permanent increase in the money stock generally results in increased domestic output, depreciation of the currency, lower interest rates, and relatively little effect on the trade balance. The interdependencies between monetary policies are weak, and monetary policy can be pursued by each country (or region) almost independently.

Then the authors try to regenerate the actual course of events from 1980 to 1985 by a certain combination of macroeconomic policies. The model succeeds in tracing the appreciation of the dollar vis-à-vis the yen, but fails to trace the larger appreciation of the dollar vis-à-vis the rest of the OECD countries. Among various factors that might have been important for the depreciation of the dollar, they include the effect of the Gramm-Rudman-Hollings law through expectations of future fiscal balance and U.S. monetary expansion. But the last factor does not improve the U.S. trade balance.

This paper gives us vivid illustrations of movements of various macroeconomic variables based on simulation exercises under alternative assumptions in the MSG model. Most of the results are interesting and insightful. Economic theory seldom provides us with quantitative statements on the magnitude of changes as a result of comparative statics or dynamics. It often gives us qualitative statements on the direction of changes, although unfortunately it sometimes leaves us with ambiguous answers, even with regard to the direction. Simulation exercises, if they are properly done as in this paper, may thus provide us with information on the magnitude as well as the direction of changes. The reader may then feel satisfied to find that his economic intuition accords with the simulation results, in particular that while fiscal policy has a spillover effect on other regions, monetary policy can be quite independently pursued by each region.

Nonetheless, simulation exercises can be frustrating to the reader since precise details of the process of simulation may not be evident. Thus, I feel as if I were looking at an iceberg of which nine-tenths of its volume is under the sea. I will point out accordingly some of the crucial features of the MSG model and the simulation exercises, and, at the same time, offer a number of caveats to the reader who may wish to base policy decisions on these exercises.

First, the MSG model is not a model that is estimated by the authors. They made their policy simulation much easier by choosing parameters based on econometric research, because in most model building it is difficult to directly obtain estimates of parameters that are of reasonable sign and magnitude. Indeed, their short cut enabled them to do many useful exercises, but it remains a question whether this procedure reflects a "healthy" division of labor. Is it not possible that the authors may choose the parameter values that are convenient to describe the economic cosmos they initially have in mind?

In particular, the model incorporating rational expectations requires a certain combination of stable roots and unstable roots. Is it not possible that some arbitrariness enters into the choice of parameters?

Second, one good feature of the MSG model is that it takes into account the forward-looking behavior of economic agents. Thus, expected changes in future economic variables affect the economic behavior as do observed changes. At the same time, this feature makes the simulation a delicate procedure. The expected changes in future policy paths imply that those changes are announced as well as believed, and that the economic agents take them into consideration. Therefore, simulation exercises should not be confused with temporary changes in policy or the announcement of future policy changes about which the public is not completely convinced.

Closely related to this feature is the problem of how to handle bubbles or bursting of bubbles. But there may be innumerable ways to define bubbles, because there are innumerable numbers of paths that satisfy the Euler conditions for the adjacent time periods, but do not satisfy the transversality condition. Here, again, arbitrariness is involved in executing the simulation.

Third, perhaps most importantly, there seems to be a lot of arbitrariness in the dynamic formulation. As the authors themselves recognize, consumption behavior is not full maximization over time, but is dynamically linked by the wealth variable. One of the most controversial questions with regard to fiscal policy is whether or not households project into the future the impact of changing taxes in relation to the intertemporal government budget constraint. This question is not answered rigorously in the present version of the MSG model. Similarly, the lag of one period in export price setting is an interesting one, but, at the same time, I wonder why the length of lags coincides with the length of period (presumably one year) used in this model.

Fourth, this paper treats both fiscal and monetary policy as independent policy instruments. However, in actual situations in some countries during the sample period, monetary policy may have involved some feedback rule and the public may have believed the particular rule. The experiments in this paper thus do not necessarily answer the policy questions in such situations. I also wonder why the authors have not conducted any experiments on the effect of real exogenous shocks. Volatile movements in exchange rates may be the result of such real disturbances during the period as the strength of the monopoly power of OPEC and people's conception about it, and sustained current account changes may reflect such real factors as the difference in rates of time preference and difference in the structure of relative prices.

Finally, in this kind of simulation, the scale of the country or region matters significantly. As MRS point out, the economic scale of Canada is about one-tenth of that of the U.S. economy. The scale of the Japanese economy grew from one-third to more than a half of the scale of the U.S. economy, primarily because of the appreciation of the yen and also because of the fast economic growth of Japan. In any case, the same ratio of economic variables to GNP implies quite different absolute magnitudes. Therefore, the policy package representing a given ratio of fiscal (or monetary) variables to GNP would affect the rest of the world quite differently depending on whether this package is implemented by, for example, the United States or Canada. This point should be noted clearly because we often hear the statement that a 1 percent of GNP increase in fiscal policy would affect the Japanese trade account (relative to GNP) much more than that of the United States.

In summary, the experiments conducted in this paper are carefully planned and convey many interesting economic messages concerning the interdependence of national economic policies from a global perspective. Most of the results from these experiments are gratifying. But for the various reasons described above, their predictions and policy prescriptions should be taken with a grain of salt. One has to ask before any policy decisions whether or not a certain result is obtained from ad hoc assumptions explicitly or implicitly embedded in the construction of the experiment.

Sponsoring Organizations

The Institute of Public Policy Studies provides professional training at the graduate level at The University of Michigan for individuals who wish to pursue a career in the field of domestic and international public policy. The Institute was founded originally in 1914 as the Institute of Public Administration. It was reorganized in 1968, and the curriculum was redesigned along interdisciplinary lines, with a strong emphasis on the teaching of analytical skills and quantitative methods. The Institute faculty all have joint appointments in academic departments at the University, and several of those involved have had extensive experience as staff members and consultants in a variety of government and nonprofit organizations. Besides its teaching program, the Institute includes a number of research and conference activities. The present conference was sponsored in part by the Institute's Program for Research on International Trade Policy. This research program is directed by Robert M. Stern and funded mainly by a continuing grant from the Ford Foundation.

The Department of Economics at The University of Michigan has for many years maintained a strong interest in training specialists and doing research on the Japanese economy. With funding from foundations and corporations in both the United States and Japan, special fellowships for Japanese-language training and summer internships in Japanese government agencies are offered to selected graduate students in economics. An active program of research on the structure and operation of the Japanese economy and U.S.-Japanese economic relations is also ongoing. These activities are conducted as part of the Japan Economy Program under the direction of Gary R. Saxonhouse.

The Centre for the Study of International Economic Relations (CSIER) was established in association with the Department of Economics at the University of Western Ontario in 1980, with support from the University's Second Century Fund, and serves to stimulate and facilitate research, graduate training, and a visiting scholars program in international trade and economic development. Recently, CSIER has been awarded grants from the Donner Canadian Foundation, Ford Foundation, and Sloan Foundation. The Donner award facilitates CSIER research on Canadian trade policy. The Ford grant is for a three-year study of the role of developing countries in multilateral negotiations and brings together researchers from eleven countries for scholarly exchanges. The Sloan award, which is shared by CSIER and the Department of Economics at Western Ontario, provides graduate student funding and supports a workshop program in international trade. The activities of CSIER are under the direction of John Whalley.

Participants

William E. Alexander
International Division
Bank of Canada

David Aschauer
Department of Economics
The University of Michigan

Alan J. Auerbach
Department of Economics
University of Pennsylvania

Robert E. Baldwin
Department of Economics
University of Wisconsin

David Beardsell
Ministere du Commerce Exterieur et
du Developpement Technologique
Gouvernement du Quebec

Brian Bethune
Economics Department
Bank of Montreal

Ronald Blum
UAW Research Department
Detroit, Michigan

Drusilla K. Brown
Department of Economics
Tufts University

Colin A. Carter
Department of Agricultural Economics
University of California, Davis

Marshall Casse
Planning and Economic Analysis Staff
U.S. State Department

Daniel Citrin
International Monetary Fund

Donald J. Daly
Faculty of Administrative Studies
York University, Toronto

Alan V. Deardorff
Department of Economics and Institute
of Public Policy Studies
The University of Michigan

Elias Dinopoulos
Department of Economics
Michigan State University

John T. Eby
Corporate Strategy Staff
Ford Motor Company

William Ehrlich
Pacific Trade Development Division
External Affairs, Ottawa

Mitsuhiro Fukao
Monetary and Fiscal Policy Division
OECD

Robert Gayner
Business Fund for Canadian Studies in
the United States, Ottawa

Earl L. Grinols
Department of Economics
University of Illinois

Koichi Hamada
Department of Economics ·
Yale University

Richard G. Harris
Department of Economics
Queen's University, Kingston

Erland Heginbotham
U.S. International Trade Commission

William Helkie
Division of International Finance
Board of Governors of the Federal Reserve System

John F. Helliwell
Department of Economics
University of British Columbia

Dale W. Henderson
Department of Economics
Georgetown University

Paul W. Holtgreive
Department of Economics
Wayne State University

Masayoshi Honma
Department of Economics
Otaru University of Commerce

Akiyoshi Horiuchi
Department of Economics
Tokyo University

Hiromitsu Ishi
Department of Economics
Hitotsubashi University

Motoshige Itoh
Department of Economics
Tokyo University

Mordechai E. Kreinin
Department of Economics
Michigan State University

David Laidler
Department of Economics
University of Western Ontario

Robert Z. Lawrence
Brookings Institution

Allen J. Lenz
Office of Trade and Investment Analysis
U.S. Department of Commerce

Helene C. McCarren
Institute of Public Policy Studies
The University of Michigan

Paul W. McCracken
Graduate School of Business Administration
The University of Michigan

Warwick McKibbin
Reserve Bank of Australia

Ronald I. McKinnon
Department of Economics
Stanford University

James R. Markusen
Department of Economics
University of Western Ontario

Keith Maskus
Planning and Economic Analysis Staff
U.S. Department of State

Steven Matusz
Department of Economics
Michigan State University

G. Mustafa Mohatarem
General Motors Corp.
Detroit, Michigan

William G. Moller, Jr.
Graduate School of Business Adminis-
tration
The University of Michigan

Toshio Nakamura
Japan External Trade Organization
(JETRO)
Chicago, Illinois

Marcus Noland
Institute for International Economics
Washington, D.C.

Saburo Okita
Institute for Domestic and Interna-
tional Policy Studies
Tokyo

Masahiro Okuno-Fujiwara
Department of Economics
Tokyo University

Machiko Osawa
Department of Economics
The University of Michigan, Dearborn

Arvind Panagariya
Department of Economics
University of Maryland

Stephen Parker
Congressional Budget Office

Hugh T. Patrick
Center on Japanese Economics and
Business
Columbia University School of Busi-
ness

James Reitzes
Federal Reserve Bank of New York

Paul Robertson
External Affairs, Ottawa

Nouriel Roubini
Department of Economics
Yale University

Jeffrey D. Sachs
Department of Economics
Harvard University

Marc P. Santucci
Michigan Department of Commerce

Gary R. Saxonhouse
Department of Economics
The University of Michigan

Yoko Sazanami
Department of Economics
Keio University

Andrew Schmitz
Department of Agricultural Economics
University of Saskatchewan

Nancy E. Schwartz
U.S. Department of Agriculture

Brian Shea
U.S. Department of Labor

Philip Smith
Department of Social Services
Michigan State University

Robert M. Stern
Department of Economics and Institute
of Public Policy Studies
The University of Michigan

Sally Stevens
Department of Economics
St. Lawrence University

John W. Suomela
U.S. International Trade Commission

Akihisa Tamaki
Ministry of International Trade and Industry

Gary R. Teske
Office of Trade and Investment Analysis
U.S. Department of Commerce

Marie Thursby
Department of Economics
The University of Michigan

Michael J. Trebilcock
Faculty of Law
University of Toronto

Irene Trela
University of Western Ontario
Department of Economics

Edwin M. Truman
International Division
Board of Governors of the Federal Reserve System

John Whalley
Centre for the Study of International
Economic Relations (CSIER)
University of Western Ontario

Randy Wigle
Department of Economics
University of Western Ontario

Bernard M. Wolf
Department of Economics
Glendon College, York University

Ronald J. Wonnacott
Department of Economics
University of Western Ontario

Kozo Yamamoto
Minister's Secretariat
Ministry of Finance, Tokyo

Helen Youngelson
Department of Economics
Portland State University

Yuji Yui
Department of Economics
Seijo University

Name Index

Subject Index